Quantum Darwinism and Friends

Quantum Darwinism and Friends

Editors

Sebastian Deffner
Raymond Laflamme
Juan Pablo Paz
Michael Zwolak

MDPI • Basel • Beijing • Wuhan • Barcelona • Belgrade • Manchester • Tokyo • Cluj • Tianjin

Editors

Sebastian Deffner
University of Maryland, Baltimore County
USA

Raymond Laflamme
University of Waterloo
Canada

Juan Pablo Paz
Universidad de Buenos Aires
Argentina

Michael Zwolak
National Institute of Standards and Technology
USA

Editorial Office
MDPI
St. Alban-Anlage 66
4052 Basel, Switzerland

This is a reprint of articles from the Special Issue published online in the open access journal *Entropy* (ISSN 1099-4300) (available at: https://www.mdpi.com/journal/entropy/special_issues/quantum_darwinism).

For citation purposes, cite each article independently as indicated on the article page online and as indicated below:

LastName, A.A.; LastName, B.B.; LastName, C.C. Article Title. *Journal Name* **Year**, *Volume Number*, Page Range.

ISBN 978-3-0365-6249-0 (Hbk)
ISBN 978-3-0365-6250-6 (PDF)

Cover image courtesy of Michael Zwolak

© 2023 by the authors. Articles in this book are Open Access and distributed under the Creative Commons Attribution (CC BY) license, which allows users to download, copy and build upon published articles, as long as the author and publisher are properly credited, which ensures maximum dissemination and a wider impact of our publications.

The book as a whole is distributed by MDPI under the terms and conditions of the Creative Commons license CC BY-NC-ND.

Contents

Preface to "Quantum Darwinism and Friends" vii

Wojciech Hubert Zurek
Quantum Theory of the Classical: Einselection, Envariance, Quantum Darwinism and Extantons
Reprinted from: *Entropy* **2022**, *24*, 1520, doi:10.3390/e24111520 1

Barış Çakmak, Özgür E. Müstecaplıoğlu, Mauro Paternostro, Bassano Vacchini and Steve Campbell
Quantum Darwinism in a Composite System: Objectivity versus Classicality
Reprinted from: *Entropy* **2021**, *23*, 995, doi:10.3390/e23080995 101

Aurélien Drezet
Justifying Born's Rule $P_\alpha = |\Psi_\alpha|^2$ Using Deterministic Chaos, Decoherence, and the de Broglie–Bohm Quantum Theory
Reprinted from: *Entropy* **2021**, *23*, 1371, doi:10.3390/e23111371 115

Nicolás Mirkin and Diego A. Wisniacki
Many-Body Localization and the Emergence of Quantum Darwinism
Reprinted from: *Entropy* **2021**, *23*, 1377, doi:10.3390/e23111377 139

Akram Touil and Sebastian Deffner
Environment-Assisted Shortcuts to Adiabaticity
Reprinted from: *Entropy* **2021**, *23*, 1479, doi:10.3390/e23111479 153

Thao P. Le, Andreas Winter and Gerardo Adesso
Thermality versus Objectivity: Can They Peacefully Coexist?
Reprinted from: *Entropy* **2021**, *23*, 1506, doi:10.3390/e23111506 167

Luis Pedro García-Pintos and Adolfo del Campo
Limits to Perception by Quantum Monitoring with Finite Efficiency
Reprinted from: *Entropy* **2021**, *23*, 1527, doi:10.3390/e23111527 187

Shuangshuang Fu and Shunlong Luo
Quantifying Decoherence via Increases in Classicality
Reprinted from: *Entropy* **2021**, *23*, 1594, doi:10.3390/e23121594 201

Jin-Fu Chen, Tian Qiu and Hai-Tao Quan
Quantum–Classical Correspondence Principle for Heat Distribution in Quantum Brownian Motion
Reprinted from: *Entropy* **2021**, *23*, 1602, doi:10.3390/e23121602 223

Abraham G. Kofman and Gershon Kurizki
Does Decoherence Select the Pointer Basis of a Quantum Meter?
Reprinted from: *Entropy* **2022**, *24*, 106, doi:10.3390/e24010106 247

William F. Braasch, Jr. and William K. Wootters
A Classical Formulation of Quantum Theory?
Reprinted from: *Entropy* **2022**, *24*, 137, doi:10.3390/e24010137 257

Alexia Auffèves and Philippe Grangier
Revisiting Born's Rule through Uhlhorn's and Gleason's Theorems
Reprinted from: *Entropy* **2022**, *24*, 199, doi:10.3390/e24020199 277

Harold Ollivier
Emergence of Objectivity for Quantum Many-Body Systems
Reprinted from: *Entropy* **2022**, 24, 277, doi:10.3390/e24020277 283

Andreas Albrecht
Equilibration and "Thermalization" in the Adapted Caldeira–Leggett Model
Reprinted from: *Entropy* **2022**, 24, 316, doi:10.3390/e24030316 297

Piotr Mironowicz, Paweł Horodecki and Ryszard Horodecki
Non-Perfect Propagation of Information to a Noisy Environment with Self-Evolution
Reprinted from: *Entropy* **2022**, 24, 467, doi:10.3390/e24040467 321

Andrew Smith, Kanupriya Sinha and Christopher Jarzynski
Quantum Coherences and Classical Inhomogeneities as Equivalent Thermodynamics Resources
Reprinted from: *Entropy* **2022**, 24, 474, doi:10.3390/e24040474 341

Michael Zwolak
Amplification, Inference, and the Manifestation of Objective Classical Information
Reprinted from: *Entropy* **2022**, 24, 781, doi:10.3390/e24060781 363

Preface to "Quantum Darwinism and Friends"

Wojciech Hubert Zurek has made seminal contributions to several areas of theoretical physics. This includes decoherence, where he had the key insight that physical environments superselect certain "pointer" states, and the foundations of quantum and classical information (e.g., the no-cloning theorem and quantum discord). His work on the dynamics of non-equilibrium phase transitions led to the Kibble–Zurek mechanism. Quantum Darwinism—the subject of this volume—is a culmination of advances that started with decoherence. It accounts for the emergence of objective classical reality in our quantum universe.

Wojciech Zurek earned his MSc in Krakow, in his native Poland, and his PhD at the University of Texas at Austin, where he remained until 1981 as a postdoctoral fellow of John Archibald Wheeler. In 1981, Zurek joined the group of Kip Thorne at Caltech as a Tolman Fellow and arrived at Los Alamos in 1984 as an Oppenheimer Fellow. He rose to the position of group leader of the Theoretical Astrophysics Group in 1991. In 1996, Zurek was named Laboratory Fellow of the Theory Division.

In his long career, Wojciech Zurek has won many honors and awards. A non-comprehensive list includes the Phi Beta Kappa Visiting Lecturer (2004), the Alexander von Humboldt Prize (2005), the Marian Smoluchowski Medal (2009), the Albert Einstein Professorship (awarded in 2010 by the Ulm University), the Order of Polonia Restituta (2012), and the Los Alamos Medal (2014).

How many of us have heard, or maybe even made, the statement that "quantum mechanics is weird"? As human beings that evolved at classical energy and lengths scales, we are so used to the fact that things look "classical" that the actual workings of our quantum Universe constantly have us in awe, confuse us, and sometimes even appall us.

Take, for instance, the frequently maltreated cat. If any two of us look at the same cat, we will both conclude that we are looking at a cat. Well, actually, we conclude that we both "perceive" a cat, and we will agree about its state of well-being. From a fundamental point of view, the question has to be: why? The answer originates in the fact that any fraction of photons that we intercept with our eyes carries the same, classical information about the lovely beast. The more formal analysis of the emergence of this classical objectivity is known as Quantum Darwinism, as it relies on Darwinian fitness of certain states—their ability to not just survive immersion in the environment, but create, multiple "offspring" of the information about themselves in the photon (and other) environments, where they can be accessed by observers such as us.

Quantum Darwinism shows how the perception of objective classical reality arises via selective amplification and the spreading of information in our fundamentally quantum universe. Quantum Darwinism goes beyond decoherence, as it recognizes that the many copies of the system's pointer states are imprinted on the environment: agents acquire data indirectly, by intercepting environment fragments (rather than directly measuring systems of interest). The data disseminated through the environment provide us with shared information about stable, effectively classical pointer states. Humans rely primarily on the photon environment, eavesdropping on "objects of interest" by intercepting tiny fractions of photons that contributed to decoherence.

In essence, Zurek has taught us nothing short of understanding why our world looks classical, despite the fact that our Universe is quantum to the core. This special issue collected a wide range of recent contributions motivated and inspired by Zurek's work all leveraging in one way or another the power of quantum correlations and their ephemeral nature.

Sebastian Deffner, Raymond Laflamme, Juan Pablo Paz, and Michael Zwolak
Editors

Review

Quantum Theory of the Classical: Einselection, Envariance, Quantum Darwinism and Extantons

Wojciech Hubert Zurek

Theory Division, Mail Stop B213, LANL, Los Alamos, NM 87545, USA

Citation: Zurek, W.H. Quantum Theory of the Classical: Einselection, Envariance, Quantum Darwinism and Extantons. *Entropy* **2022**, *24*, 1520. https://doi.org/10.3390/e24111520

Academic Editor: Ronnie Kosloff

Received: 6 December 2021
Accepted: 21 March 2022
Published: 24 October 2022

Publisher's Note: MDPI stays neutral with regard to jurisdictional claims in published maps and institutional affiliations.

Copyright: © 2022 by the authors. Licensee MDPI, Basel, Switzerland. This article is an open access article distributed under the terms and conditions of the Creative Commons Attribution (CC BY) license (https:// creativecommons.org/licenses/by/ 4.0/).

Abstract: Core quantum postulates including the superposition principle and the unitarity of evolutions are natural and strikingly simple. I show that—when supplemented with a limited version of predictability (captured in the textbook accounts by the repeatability postulate)—these core postulates can account for all the symptoms of classicality. In particular, both objective classical reality and elusive information about reality arise, via quantum Darwinism, from the quantum substrate. This approach shares with the Relative State Interpretation of Everett the view that collapse of the wavepacket reflects perception of the state of the rest of the Universe *relative* to the state of observer's records. However, our "let quantum be quantum" approach poses questions absent in Bohr's Copenhagen Interpretation that relied on the preexisting classical domain. Thus, one is now forced to seek preferred, predictable, hence effectively classical but ultimately quantum states that allow observers keep reliable records. Without such *(i) preferred basis* relative states are simply "too relative", and the ensuing *basis ambiguity* makes it difficult to identify events (e.g., measurement outcomes). Moreover, universal validity of quantum theory raises the issue of *(ii) the origin of Born's rule*, $p_k = |\psi_k|^2$, relating probabilities and amplitudes (that is simply postulated in textbooks). Last not least, even preferred pointer states (defined by *einselection*—*en*vironment—*in*duced super*selection*)— are still quantum. Therefore, unlike classical states that exist objectively, quantum states of an individual system cannot be found out by an initially ignorant observer through direct measurement without being disrupted. So, to complete the 'quantum theory of the classical' one must identify *(iii) quantum origin of objective existence* and explain how the information about objectively existing states can appear to be essentially inconsequential for them (as it does for states in Newtonian physics) and yet matter in other settings (e.g., thermodynamics). I show how the mathematical structure of quantum theory supplemented by the only uncontroversial measurement postulate (that demands immediate repeatability—hence, predictability) leads to preferred states. These *(i) pointer states* correspond to measurement outcomes. Their stability is a prerequisite for objective existence of effectively classical states and for events such as quantum jumps. Events at hand, one can now enquire about their probability—the probability of a pointer state (or of a measurement record). I show that the symmetry of entangled states—*(ii) entanglement*—*assisted invariance* or *envariance*—implies Born's rule. Envariance also accounts for the loss of phase coherence between pointer states. Thus, decoherence can be traced to symmetries of entanglement and understood without its usual tool—reduced density matrices. A simple and manifestly noncircular derivation of $p_k = |\psi_k|^2$ follows. Monitoring of the system by its environment in course of decoherence typically leaves behind multiple copies of its pointer states in the environment. Only pointer states can survive decoherence and can spawn such plentiful information-theoretic progeny. This *(iii) quantum Darwinism* allows observers to use *environment as a witness*—to find out pointer states indirectly, leaving systems of interest untouched. Quantum Darwinism shows how epistemic and ontic (coexisting in *epiontic* quantum state) separate into robust objective existence of pointer states and detached information about them, giving rise to *extantons*—composite objects with system of interest in the core and multiple records of its pointer states in the halo comprising of environment subsystems (e.g., photons) which disseminates that information throughout the Universe.

Keywords: decoherence; einselection; quantum jumps; Born's rule; envariance; quantum Darwinism; quantum-classical transition; existential interpretation; extantons

Contents

1 **Introduction**   3
    1.1 Core Quantum Postulates   3
    1.2 Quantum States, Information, and Existence   5
    1.3 Interpreting Relative States Interpretation   7
    1.4 Preview   9

2 **Quantum Jumps and Einselection from Information Flows and Predictability**   10
    2.1 Repeatability and the Quantum Origin of Quantum Jumps   11
    2.2 Mixed States of the "Target"   13
    2.3 Predictability Killed the (Schrödinger's) Cat   15
    2.4 Records and Branches: Degenerate "Control"   15
       2.4.1 Repeatability and Actionable Information   17
    2.5 Pointer Basis, Information Transfer, and Decoherence   19
    2.6 Irreversibility of Perceived Events, or "Don't Blame the 2nd Law—Wavepacket Collapse Is Your Own Fault!"   21
       2.6.1 Classical Measurement Can Be Reversed Even when Record of the Outcome is Kept   21
       2.6.2 Quantum Measurement Can't Be Reversed when the Record of the Outcome is Kept   22
    2.7 Summary: Events, Irreversibility, and Perceptions   23

3 **Born's Rule from the Symmetries of Entanglement**   24
    3.1 Envariance   26
    3.2 Decoherence as a Result of Envariance   27
    3.3 Swaps, Counterswaps, and Equiprobability   28
    3.4 Born's Rule from Envariance   31
       3.4.1 Additivity of Probabilities from Envariance   33
       3.4.2 Algebra of Records as the Boolean Algebra of Events   35
    3.5 Inverting Born's Rule: Why Is the Amplitude a Square Root of the Frequency of Occurrence?   36
    3.6 Relative Frequencies from Relative States   39
    3.7 Envariance—An Overview   41
       3.7.1 Implications and the Scope of Envariance: Why Entanglement? Why Schmidt States?   41
       3.7.2 Towards the Experimental Verification of Envariance   43

4 **Quantum Darwinism**   45
    4.1 Mutual Information, Redundancy, and Discord   48
       4.1.1 Mutual Information   48
       4.1.2 Quantum Discord   50
       4.1.3 Evidence and Its Redundancy   52
       4.1.4 Mutual Information, Pure Decoherence, and Branching States   54
       4.1.5 Surplus Decoherence and Redundant Decoherence   56
       4.1.6 Information Gained by Pure and Mixed Environments   57
       4.1.7 Environment as a Communication Channel   58
       4.1.8 Quantum Darwinism and Amplification Channels   59
    4.2 Quantum Darwinism in Action   59
       4.2.1 C-Nots and Qubits   60
       4.2.2 Central Spin Decohered by Noninteracting Spins   61
       4.2.3 Quantum Darwinism in a Hazy Environment   64

		4.2.4	Quantum Darwinism and Pointer States	65
		4.2.5	Redundancy vs. Relaxation in the Central Spin Model	68
		4.2.6	Quantum Darwinism in Quantum Brownian Motion	71
		4.2.7	Huge Redundancy in Scattered Photons	74
	4.3	Experimental Tests of Quantum Darwinism		78
	4.4	Summary: Environment as an Amplification Channel		80
5	Quantum Darwinism and Objective Existence: Photohalos and Extantons			82
	5.1	Anatomy of an Extanton		82
		5.1.1	Extantons and "The Classical"	83
		5.1.2	Photohalos, Photoextantons, and Information Detached from Existence	84
		5.1.3	Photohalos and the Quantum Origins of Irreversibility	85
	5.2	Quantum Darwinism and the Existential Interpretation		85
	5.3	From Quantum Core Postulates to Objective Classical Reality		86
	5.4	Extantons and the Existential Interpretation		87
	5.5	Decoherence and Information Processing		88
	5.6	Quantum Darwinism and "Life as We Know It"		89
	5.7	Bohr, Everett, and Wheeler		90
	5.8	Closing Remarks		92

References 94

1. Introduction

Quantum mechanics is often regarded as an essentially probabilistic theory, where the random collapses of the wavepacket with probabilities governed by the rule conjectured by Max Born (1926) [1] play a central role. Yet, evolution dictated by the Schrödinger Equation is deterministic. This clash of quantum determinism of the unitary evolutions of the fundamental quantum theory with the quantum randomness of its phenomenological practice is at the heart of the interpretational controversies.

The aim of this review is to assess the progress made in the wake of the earlier developments (including in particular theory decoherence and einselection) since the beginning of this millennium. This includes the realization that selection of preferred states—einselection of the pointer states usually justified using decoherence—is a consequence of the tension between the linearity of quantum theory and the nonlinearity of copying processes involved in the acquisition of information. Derivation of Born's rule based on the symmetries of entangled quantum states shores up and simplifies foundations of quantum theory.

Quantum Darwinism will be discussed especially carefully, but nevertheless with significant omissions that are inevitable in reviewing a rapidly evolving field. In such a case one is faced with a "moving target"—the most recent developments are inevitably either left out or treated only in the superficial manner (since assessing their impact on the future development of the field is difficult).

We will also reconsider the status of the quantum measurement problem [2]. I shall claim that perception of the objective classical reality is accounted for by the developments mentioned briefly above and discussed in more detail below.

We shall start by reviewing the assumptions—postulates of quantum theory—and by selecting from their textbook version core postulates that are consistent and can be used to address the issues usually dealt with via measurement axioms that are also included in the textbook presentations but are inconsistent with the quantum core. More detailed preview of the content of this review can be found at the end of this introductory section.

1.1. Core Quantum Postulates

The difficulty of reconciling quantum determinism with quantum randomness is reflected in the postulates that provide textbook summary of quantum mechanics (see, e.g., Dirac, 1958) [3]. We list them starting with four uncontroversial core postulates, cornerstones of the *quantum theory of the classical* we shall develop. Two are very familiar:

(i) *The state of a quantum system is represented by a vector in its Hilbert space* $\mathcal{H}_S$.
(ii) *Evolutions are unitary (i.e., generated by the Schrödinger Equation).*

They imply, respectively, the *quantum superposition principle* and the *unitarity of evolutions*, and we shall often refer to them by citing their physical consequences. They provide an almost complete summary of the formal structure of the theory.

One more postulate should be added to (i) and (ii) to complete the mathematics of quantum mechanics:

(o) *Quantum state of a composite system is a vector in a tensor product of the Hilbert spaces of its subsystems.*

Postulate (o) (von Neumann, 1932 [4]; Nielsen and Chuang, 2000 [5]) is often omitted from textbooks as obvious. However, composite systems are essential, as in absence of subsystems Schrödinger Equation provides a *deterministic* description of the evolution of an indivisible Universe, and the measurement problem disappears [6,7]. In absence of at least a measured system and a measuring apparatus questions about the outcomes cannot be even posed. We shall need at least one more ingredient—an environment—to address them.

The measurement problem arises because a quantum state of a collection of systems can evolve from a Cartesian product (where definite state of the whole implies definite states of each subsystem) into an entangled state represented by tensor product: State of the whole is still definite and pure, but states of the subsystems are indefinite. By contrast, in classical settings completely known (pure) composite states are always represented by Cartesian products of pure states—state of each subsystem is also perfectly known.

Postulates (o)–(ii) provide a complete summary of the *mathematics* of quantum theory. They contain no premonition of either collapse or probabilities. Using them and the obvious additional ingredients (initial states and Hamiltonians) one can justify and carry out every quantum calculation. However, in order to relate quantum theory to experiments one needs to establish a correspondence between abstract state vectors in $\mathcal{H}_S$ and experiments. This task starts with the *repeatability postulate*:

(iii) *Immediate repetition of a measurement yields the same outcome.*

Postulate (iii) is idealized—it is hard to perform such non-demolition measurements, but in principle it can be done. Yet—as a fundamental postulate—it is also indispensable. The very concept of a "state" embodies predictability that requires axiom (iii): The role of states is to allow for predictions, and the most basic prediction is that a state is what it is known to be. Repeatability postulate asserts that confirmation of this prediction is in principle possible.

Postulate (iii) is also uncontroversial: Repeatability is taken for granted in the classical setting where it follows from the assumption that one can find out an unknown state without perturbing it. This classical version is a much stronger assumption than the repeatability postulated above in (iii). It is responsible for the familiar "objective reality" of the classical world: It detaches existence of classical states from what is known about them.

Quantum measurement problem arises because—by contrast—unknown quantum states are re-prepared by the attempts to find out what they are. So, quantum repeatability postulate (iii) signals a significant weakening of the role states play in our quantum Universe: Repeatability guarantees only that the existence of a *known* quantum state can be confirmed, but it no longer implies their objective existence: Unlike classical states, unknown quantum state cannot be simply found out independently by many initially ignorant observers through direct measurements.

This quantum intertwining of the epistemic and ontic function of a state is the central quantum feature regarded as a key interpretational problem. One of our goals is to understand how (as a consequence of quantum Darwinism) one can recover objective existence—states that survive discovery by an initially ignorant observer, so others can confirm their identity.

We will show that the essence of the remaining textbook postulates can be deduced from the above quantum core that includes the mathematical postulates (o)–(ii) and the repeatability postulate (iii) that begins to deal with the experimental consequences of quantum theory such as information transfers, including the measurements.

1.2. Quantum States, Information, and Existence

So far, we have outlined a consistent set of core quantum postulates, (o)–(iii). They will serve as a basis for the derivation of the emergence of classical behavior in a quantum Universe. In this subsection, we consider textbook axioms (iv) and (v) that are at odds with the quantum core. The whole (o)–(v) list is, of course, given by textbooks. The inconsistency is usually "resolved" through some version of Bohr's strategy. That is, textbooks assume that quantum theory can be applied only to a part of the Universe. The rest of the Universe—including observers and measuring devices—must be classical, or at the very least out of quantum jurisdiction. Our aim will be to show that the classical domain need not be postulated, and that the measurement process (the focus of axioms (iv) and (v)) can be accounted for by using the quantum core postulates (o)–(iii).

In contrast to classical physics (where an unknown preexisting state can be found out by an initially ignorant observer) the very next textbook axiom explicitly limits predictive attributes of quantum states:

(iv) *Measurement outcome is an eigenstate of the Hermitian operator corresponding to the measured observable.*

Thus, in general, a measurement will return something else than the preexisting state of the system. Repeatability postulate (iii) is in a sense an exception to this quantum undermining of the predictive role of states. Axiom (iv) can be usefully subdivided into:

(iva) *Allowed measurement outcomes correspond to the eigenstates of a Hermitian operator.*

(ivb) *Only one outcome is seen in each run.*

This splitting may seem pedantic, but it is useful. Textbooks often separate our (iv) into such two axioms.

We emphasize that already (iva) limits predictive attributes of quantum states: When the Hermitian operator representing the measured observable does not have, as one of its eigenstates, the preexisting state of the system, the outcome cannot be predicted with certainty even when the preexisting state is perfectly known (pure).

Nevertheless, repeatability means that when the same measurement is immediately repeated on the very same system, the outcome will be the same. This is, operationally, the essence of the collapse: The preexisting pure state will give an unpredictable result that can be, however, confirmed and reconfirmed by re-measurement of the outcome. What you saw you will get, again and again. Therefore, as soon as (iva) can be accounted for (which we shall do in Section 2), then—in combination with the repeatability of (iii)—the symptoms of the "wavepacket collapse" postulated by (ivb) can be also recovered.

Collapse axiom is the first truly controversial item in the textbook list. In its literal form it is inconsistent with the first two postulates: Starting from a general state $|\psi_S\rangle$ in a Hilbert space of the system (postulate (i)), an initial state $|A_0\rangle$ of the apparatus $\mathcal{A}$, and assuming unitary evolution (postulate (ii)) one is led to a superposition of outcomes;

$$|\psi_S\rangle|A_0\rangle = (\sum_k a_k|s_k\rangle)|A_0\rangle \Rightarrow \sum_k a_k|s_k\rangle|A_k\rangle, \tag{1.1}$$

which is in apparent contradiction with (iv).

The impossibility to account—starting with the core quantum postulates (o)–(iii)—for the literal collapse to a single state postulated by (ivb) was appreciated since Bohr (1928) [8] and von Neumann (1932) [4]. It was—and often still is—regarded as an indication of the insolubility of the measurement problem. It is straightforward to extend such insolubility demonstrations to various more realistic situations, e.g., by allowing the state of the apparatus to be initially mixed. As long as the superposition and unitarity postulates (i) and (ii) hold, one is forced to admit that the quantum state of $\mathcal{AS}$ after they interacted contains a superposition of many alternative outcomes rather than just one of them as the literal reading of the collapse axiom (and our immediate experience) suggest (see Figure 1).

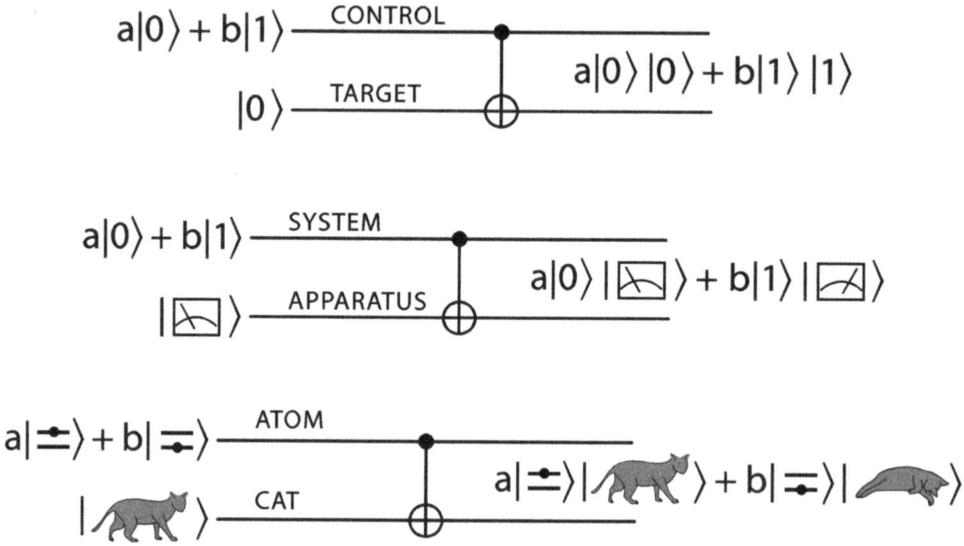

Figure 1. Controlled-not, measurement, and Schrödinger's cat: We expect this figure to be self-explanatory. It is included primarily to establish the nomenclature (i.e., "control" and "target"), to illustrate Equation (1.1), and to emphasize the parallels be between the three situations illustrated above.

Given this clash between the mathematical structure of the theory and the expectation of the literal collapse (that captures the subjective impressions of what happens in the real-world measurements), one is tempted to accept—following Bohr—primacy of our immediate experience and blame the inconsistency of (iv) with the core of quantum formalism (superposition principle and unitarity, (i) and (ii)) on the nature of the apparatus: Copenhagen Interpretation regards apparatus, observer, and, generally, macroscopic objects as *ab initio* classical. They do not abide by the quantum principle of superposition—their evolutions need not be unitary. Therefore, according to Copenhagen Interpretation, the unitarity postulate (ii) does not apply to measurements, and the literal collapse can happen on the border between quantum and classical.

Uneasy coexistence of the quantum and the classical postulated by Bohr is a challenge to the unification instinct of physicists. Yet, it has proven surprisingly durable.

At the heart of many approaches to the measurement problem is the desire to reduce the relation between existence and information about what exists to what could have been taken for granted in a world where the fundamental theory was Newtonian physics. There, classical systems had real states that existed independently of what was known about them. They could be found out by measurements. Many initially ignorant observers could measure the same system without perturbing it. Their records would agree, reflecting reality of the underlying state and confirming its objective existence.

Immunity of classical states to measurements suggested that, in classical settings, the information was unphysical. Information was a mere immaterial shadow of real physical states. It was irrelevant for physics.

This dismissive view of information run into problems already when Newtonian classical physics confronted classical thermodynamics. Clash of these two classical theories led to Maxwell's demon, and is implicated in the origins of the arrow of time.

The specter of information was haunting classical physics since XIX century. The seemingly unphysical shadowy record state was beginning to play a role reserved for the "real" state.

Attempts to solve measurement problem often follow the strategy where the underlying state of the quantum system somehow becomes classical. Even decoherence can be, in a sense, regarded as a completely quantum version of such a strategy, with the effective classicality arising in the world that is fundamentally quantum. Other proposals assert supremacy of existence over information and suggest modifications of quantum evolution equations (e.g., abandoning unitarity) as discussed by Weinberg (2012) [9].

It is conceivable that, one day, we may find discrepancies of quantum theory with experiments. However, evidence to date supports view that our Universe is quantum to the core, and we have to reconcile superposition principle, unitarity and their consequences—illustrated, e.g., by the violation of Bell's inequality—with our perceptions. Nonlocality of quantum states and other experimental manifestations of quantumness are here to stay.

The strategy adopted by the program discussed in this review is to start with the core quantum postulates (o)–(iii). They have the simplicity that rivals postulates of special relativity. Given this "let quantum be quantum" starting point we shall show how (and to what extent) both attributes of the familiar classical world—objective existence and information about it—emerge from the epiontic quantum substrate.

1.3. Interpreting Relative States Interpretation

The alternative to Bohr's Copenhagen Interpretation and a new approach to the measurement problem was proposed by Hugh Everett III, student of John Archibald Wheeler, over half a century ago (Everett, 1957 [10,11]; Wheeler, 1957 [12]; DeWitt and Graham, 1973 [13]). The basic idea was to abandon the literal view of collapse and recognize that a measurement (including the appearance of the collapse) is already implicit in Equation (1.1). One just needs to include an observer in the wavefunction, and consistently interpret the consequences of this step.

The obvious problem raised by (ivb)—"Why don't I, the observer, perceive such splitting, but register just one outcome at a time?"—is then answered by asserting that while the right-hand side of Equation (1.1) contains all the possible outcomes, the observer who recorded outcome #17 will (from then on) perceive "branch #17" that is consistent with the outcome reflected in his records. In other words, when the global state of the Universe is $|Y\rangle$, and my state is $|\mathcal{I}_{17}\rangle$, for me the state of the rest of the Universe collapses to $|\gamma_{17}\rangle \sim \langle \mathcal{I}_{17}|Y\rangle$. Since this is the only state I (actually, $|\mathcal{I}_{17}\rangle$!) am aware of, following the correlation, I should renormalize the state vector $|\gamma_{17}\rangle$ of the rest of the Universe to reflect my certainty about my branch—this is now my only Universe[1].

---

[1] Much confusion and a heated ongoing debate has been sparked by the question of what happens to observers $|\mathcal{I}_1\rangle...|\mathcal{I}_{16}\rangle$ and $|\mathcal{I}_{18}\rangle...|\mathcal{I}_\infty\rangle$. If the quantum state of the whole Universe were classical—in the sense that we could attribute to it real existence—there would indeed be Many Worlds, each inhabited by a different $|\mathcal{I}_n\rangle$ (see, e.g., DeWitt, 1970 [14]; 1971 [15]; DeWitt and Graham, 1973 [13]; Deutsch, 1985 [16]; 1997 [17]; Saunders et al., 2010 [18]; Wallace, 2012 [19]). However, the elusive status of states in quantum theory—they can be confirmed (repeatability), but not found out—suggests a less radical possibility. After all, a patch in classical phase space also represents a state. When this patch collapses into a point upon measurement, it does not mean that there are other observers who from now on live in Universes with different outcomes, and have a memory consistent with these outcomes. The key difference between these two attitudes is in the extent to which a state is thought to be epistemic (as is a patch in phase space, representing ignorance of the observer) or ontic (as is the phase space point, that can be not only confirmed, but found out by others, even when observers are ignorant of its location beforehand). Only a classical—ontic—view of the state would make Many Worlds view (with all the branches equally real) inevitable. Quantum theory does not impose it, so in this sense Many Worlds Interpretation (in contrast to the Relative State view) is just "too classical" as it asserts objective existence of a quantum state of the Universe as a whole. I have no stake in this debate, but I shall comment on these matters in due course, after discussion of quantum Darwinism and the quantum origins of objective existence.

This "let quantum be quantum" view of the collapse is supported by the repeatability postulate (iii); upon immediate re-measurement, the same state will be found. Everett's assertion: "The discontinuous jump into an eigenstate is thus only a relative proposition, dependent on the mode of decomposition of the total wave function into the superposition, and relative to a particularly chosen apparatus-coordinate value...". is consistent with the core quantum postulates: In the superposition of Equation (1.1) record state $|A_{17}\rangle$ can indeed imply detection of the corresponding state of the system, $|s_{17}\rangle$.

Two questions immediately arise. The first one concerns the part (iva) of the collapse postulate: What constrains the set of outcomes—the preferred states of the apparatus or the observer. By the principle of superposition (postulate (i)) the state of the system or of the apparatus after the measurement can be written in infinitely many ways, each corresponding to one of the unitarily equivalent bases in the Hilbert space of the pointer of an apparatus (or a memory cell of an observer);

$$\sum_k a_k |s_k\rangle |A_k\rangle = \sum_k a'_k |s'_k\rangle |A'_k\rangle = \sum_k a''_k |s''_k\rangle |A''_k\rangle = ... \quad (1.2)$$

This *basis ambiguity* is not limited to the pointers of measuring devices or cats, which for Schrödinger (1935) [20] play a role of the apparatus (see Figure 1). One can show that also very large systems (such as satellites of planets) can evolve into very nonclassical superpositions on surprisingly short timescales [21–23]. In reality, this does not seem to happen. So, there is something that (in spite of the egalitarian superposition principle enshrined in (i)) picks out certain preferred quantum states, and makes them effectively classical while banishing their superpositions.

Postulate (iva) anticipates this need for preferred states—destinations for quantum jumps: Before there is a collapse (as in (ivb)), a set of preferred states (one of which is selected by the collapse) must be somehow chosen. Indeed, discontinuity of quantum jumps Everett emphasizes in the quote above would be impossible without some underlying discontinuity in the set of the possible choices. Yet, there is nothing in Everett's writings that would provide a criterion for such preferred outcomes states, and nothing to even hint that he was aware of this question. We shall show how such discontinuities arise in the framework defined by the core quantum postulates (o)–(iii).

The second question concerns probabilities: How likely it is that—after I, the observer, measure $\mathcal{S}$—I will become $|\mathcal{I}_{17}\rangle$? Everett was very aware of its significance.

The preferred basis problem was settled by the *pointer basis* that is singled out by the environment—induced superselection (*einselection*), a consequence of decoherence (Zurek, 1981; 1982 [24,25]).

As emphasized by Dieter Zeh (1970) [26], apparatus, observers, and other macroscopic objects are immersed in their environments. The problem of preferred basis was not pointed out at that time, perhaps because this issue is never pointed out by Everett which motivated Zeh's paper. Indeed, it appears Everettians, (e.g. DeWitt, [14,15]) did not fully appreciate its importance until the advent of the pointer basis.

Decoherence leads to monitoring of the system by its environment, described by analogy with Equation (1.1). When this monitoring is focused on a specific observable of the system, its eigenstates form a *pointer basis*: They entangle least with the environment (and, therefore, are least perturbed by it). This resolves basis ambiguity. Pointer basis and einselection [24,25] were developed and are discussed elsewhere [6,7,24,25,27–33]. However, their original derivation comes at a price that would have been unacceptable to Everett: Theory of decoherence, as it is usually practiced, employs reduced density matrices. Their physical significance derives from averaging (Landau, 1927 [34]; Nielsen and Chuang, 2000 [5]; Zurek 2003 [35]) and is thus based on probabilities that follow from Born's rule:

(v) *Probability p_k of finding an outcome $|s_k\rangle$ in a measurement of a quantum system that was previously prepared in the state $|\psi\rangle$ is given by $|\langle s_k|\psi\rangle|^2$.*

Born's rule (1926) [1] completes standard textbook discussions of the foundations of quantum theory. In contrast to the wavepacket collapse of axiom (iv), axiom (v) is not in obvious contradiction with the core postulates (o)–(iii), so one can adopt the view that Born's rule is a part of the axiomatics of quantum theory. One can then use core postulates (o)–(iii) plus Born's rule to justify preferred basis and explain the symptoms of collapse through decoherence and einselection. This is the usual practice of decoherence (Zurek, 1991 [27]; 1998 [36]; 2003 [7]; Paz and Zurek, 2001 [28]; Joos et al., 2003 [29]; Schlosshauer, 2005 [31]; 2006 [37]; 2007 [32]; 2019 [33]). It relies, however, on the statistical interpretation of the reduced density matrices that depends on accepting Born's rule.

Nevertheless, (as Everett argued) axiom (v) is inconsistent with the spirit of the "let quantum be quantum" approach. Therefore, one might guess, he would not have been satisfied with the usual approach to decoherence and its consequences. Indeed, Everett attempted to derive Born's rule from the other quantum postulates. We shall follow his lead, although not his strategy which—as is now known—was flawed (DeWitt, 1971 [15]; Kent, 1990 [38]; Squires, 1990 [39]).

1.4. Preview

Our first goal is to shore up quantum foundations—to understand the emergence of stable classical states from the quantum substrate, and to deduce the origin of the rules governing randomness at the quantum-classical border. To this end, in the next two sections we shall derive collapse axiom (iva) and Born's rule (v) from the core postulates (o)–(iii). We shall then, in Section 4, account for the "objective existence" of pointer states. This succession of results provides a wholly quantum account of the emergence of classical reality.

We start with a derivation of the preferred set of *pointer states*—(iva), the business end of the collapse postulate. We will show that the nature of the information transfer—nature of the coupling to the measuring device—determines this preferred set, and that any set of orthogonal states will do. We will also see how these states are (ein)selected by the dynamics of the process of information acquisition, thus following the spirit of Bohr's approach which emphasized the ability to communicate the results of measurements. Orthogonality of outcomes implies that repeatedly measurable quantum observable must be Hermitian. We shall then compare this approach (obtained without resorting to reduced density matrices or any other appeals to Born's rule) with a decoherence-based approach to pointer states and the usual view of einselection.

Pointer states—terminal states for quantum jumps—are determined by the dynamics of information transfer. They define the outcomes independently of the instantaneous reduced density matrix of the system and of its initial state. Fixed outcomes define events, and call for the derivation of probabilities. In Section 3 we also take a fresh and very fundamental look at decoherence: It arises—along with Born's rule—from the symmetries of entangled quantum states.

Given Born's rule and preferred pointer states one is still faced with a problem. Quantum states are fragile. An initially ignorant observer cannot find out an unknown quantum state without endangering its existence: Collapse postulate means that selection of what to measure implies a set of outcomes. Therefore, only a lucky guess of an observable could let the observer find out an unknown state without repreparing it. The criterion for pointer states implied by postulates (o)–(iii) turns out to be equivalent to their stability under decoherence, and still leaves one with the same difficulty: How to find out an effectively classical but ultimately quantum pointer state and leave it intact?

The answer turns out to be surprisingly simple: Continuous monitoring of $\mathcal{S}$ by its environment results in redundant records of its pointer states in $\mathcal{E}$. Thus, observers can find out the state of the system indirectly, from small fragments of the same $\mathcal{E}$ that caused decoherence. Recent and still ongoing studies discussed in Section 4 show how this replication selects the "fittest" states that can survive monitoring, and yields copious qmemes[2], their information-theoretic offspring: Quantum Darwinism favors pointer observables at the expense of their complements. Objectivity of the preferred states is quantified by their redundancy—by the number of copies of the state of the system deposited in $\mathcal{E}$. Stability in spite of the interaction with the environment is clearly a prerequisite for large redundancy. Pointer states do best in this information—theoretic "survival of the fittest".

The classical world we perceive consists predominantly of macroscopic objects. Bohr decreed their states were classical "by fiat", so that information about them could be acquired without perturbing them, thus restoring classical independence of existence from information. We recognize instead that quantum theory is universal. States of macroscopic objects become effectively classical (as Bohr wanted), but as a consequence of decoherence and einselection. Objects are immersed in the decohering environment consisting of subsystems (such as photons). Superpositions of pointer states are unstable, quickly turning into their mixtures. Thus, predictably evolving quantum states of macroscopic objects are restricted to stable, effectively classical pointer states einselected by decoherence. In the course of decoherence fragments of the environment that monitors them become inscribed with the data about their pointer states.

Extanton is a composite entity with the object of interest in its core embedded in the information-laden halo, part of the environment that monitors its pointer states. Information about them is heralded by the fragments of the environment, and disseminated throughout the Universe. Fragments of the halo intercepted by observers inform about the state of its core. Extanton combines the source of information (extanton core) with the means of its transmission (halo, often consisting of photons).

John Bell (1975 [40]; 1987 [41]) imagined "beables" (as in "to be or not to be"). In contrast to observables, beables were supposed to be robust, much like states of macroscopic objects in the classical domain posited by Bohr. They would exist, and (in contrast to quantum states), their states would be immune to observation.

Extantons are quantum, but fulfill these desiderata. Environment determines pointer states through einselection. Pointer states of extanton cores persist (hence, exist) and the environment broadcasts information about them. That information reaches observers, revealing the pointer state of the macroscopic system at the extanton core without the need for direct measurement (hence, without disrupting the state preselected by the decoherence).

We are immersed in such extaton halos, inundated with the information about pointer states in their cores. This is how the classical world we perceive emerges from within our quantum Universe.

As we shall see, several steps based on interdependent insights are needed to account for quantum jumps, for the appearance of the collapse, for preferred pointer states, for the probabilities and Born's rule, and, finally, for the consensus, the essence of objective reality—for the emergence of 'the classical' from within a quantum Universe. It is important to take these steps in the right order, so that each step is based only on what is already established. This is our aim, and this order has determined the structure of this paper: The next three sections describe three crucial steps. Nevertheless, each section can be read separately: Preceding sections are important to provide the right setting, but are generally not essential as a background. An overview of the resulting quantum theory of the classical is presented and the interpretational implications are discussed in Section 5.2.

2. Quantum Jumps and Einselection from Information Flows and Predictability

This section shows how the core quantum postulates (o)–(iii) lead to the discreteness we regard as characteristic of the quantum world. In textbooks this discreteness is introduced via the collapse axiom (iva) designating the eigenstates of the measured observable as the only possible outcomes. Here, we show that discontinuous quantum jumps between

---

[2] This term is a quantum version of the familiar *meme*, that according to Wikipedia, stands for "...an image ... that is copied (often with slight variations) and spread rapidly".

a restricted set of orthogonal states turn out to be a consequence of symmetry breaking that resolves the tension between the unitarity of quantum evolutions and repeatability. We shall also see how preferred Hermitian observables defined by the resulting orthogonal basis are related to the familiar pointer states.

Unitary evolution of a general initial state of a system $\mathcal{S}$ interacting with an apparatus $\mathcal{A}$ leads—as illustrated by Equation (1.1)—to an entangled state of $\mathcal{SA}$. Thus, there is no single outcome—no literal collapse—and an apparent contradiction with our immediate experience. It may seem that the measurement problem cannot be addressed unless unitarity is somehow circumvented (e.g., along the *ad hoc* lines of the Copenhagen Interpretation).

We start with the same assumptions and follow similar steps, but arrive at a different conclusion. This is because instead of demanding a single outcome we shall only require that the result of the measurement can be confirmed (by a re-measurement), or communicated (by making a copy of the record). In either case, copying some state (of the system or of the apparatus) is essential. As "perception" and "consciousness" presumably depend on copying and other such information processing tasks (as they undoubtedly do) then the necessity to deal with the Universe "one branch at a time" can produce symptoms of collapse while bypassing the need for it to be "literal".

Amplification—the ability to make copies, qmemes of the original—is the essence of the repeatability postulate (iii). It calls for nonlinearity (one needs to replicate the original state, or at least its salient features) that would appear to be in conflict with the unitarity (hence, linearity) demanded by postulate (ii).

As we shall see, copying is possible for orthogonal subsets of states of the original. Each such subset is determined by the measurement device—by the unitary evolution that implements copying. When, beforehand, the system is not in one of such copying eigenstates, its state is not preserved. This shows (Zurek, 2007 [42]; 2013 [43]) why one cannot find out an unknown quantum state. Most importantly, we reach this conclusion (where the role of the copying device parallels function of the classical apparatus in Bohr's Copenhagen Interpretation) without calling on the collapse axiom (iv) or on Born's rule, axiom (v).

2.1. Repeatability and the Quantum Origin of Quantum Jumps

Consider a quantum system $\mathcal{S}$ interacting with another quantum system $\mathcal{E}$ (which can be an apparatus, or—as the present notation suggests—an environment). Let us suppose (in accord with the repeatability postulate (iii)) that there are states of $\mathcal{S}$ that remain unperturbed by this operation, e.g., that this interaction implements a measurement—like information transfer from $\mathcal{S}$ to $\mathcal{E}$:

$$|s_k\rangle|\varepsilon_0\rangle \implies |s_k\rangle|\varepsilon_k\rangle. \tag{2.1}$$

We now establish:

Theorem 1. *The set of the unperturbed states $\{|s_k\rangle\}$ of the "control"—of the system $\mathcal{S}$ that is being measured or decohered—must be orthogonal.*

Proof. From the linearity implied by the unitarity of (ii) and Equation (2.1) we get, for an arbitrary initial state $|\psi_\mathcal{S}\rangle$ in $\mathcal{H}_\mathcal{S}$ (allowed by the superposition principle, postulate (i));

$$|\psi_\mathcal{S}\rangle|\varepsilon_0\rangle = \left(\sum_k \alpha_k |s_k\rangle\right)|\varepsilon_0\rangle \Rightarrow \sum_k \alpha_k |s_k\rangle|\varepsilon_k\rangle = |\Psi_{\mathcal{SE}}\rangle. \tag{2.2}$$

But, again by (ii), the norm must be preserved,

$$\left|\sum_k \alpha_k |s_k\rangle\right|^2 = \left|\sum_k \alpha_k |s_k\rangle|\varepsilon_k\rangle\right|^2,$$

so that elementary algebra leads to:

$$Re \sum_{j,k} \alpha_j^* \alpha_k \langle s_j|s_k\rangle = Re \sum_{j,k} \alpha_j^* \alpha_k \langle s_j|s_k\rangle \langle \varepsilon_j|\varepsilon_k\rangle. \qquad (2.3)$$

This must hold for every $|\psi_\mathcal{S}\rangle$ in $\mathcal{H}_\mathcal{S}$—for any set of complex $\{\alpha_k\}$. Thus, for any two states in the set $\{|s_k\rangle\}$:

$$\langle s_j|s_k\rangle(1 - \langle \varepsilon_j|\varepsilon_k\rangle) = 0. \qquad (2.4)$$

This equality immediately implies that $\{|s_k\rangle\}$ must be orthogonal if they are to leave any imprint—deposit any information—in $\mathcal{E}$ while remaining intact: It can be satisfied only when $\langle s_j|s_k\rangle = \delta_{jk}$, unless $\langle \varepsilon_j|\varepsilon_k\rangle = 1$—that is, unless the information transfer has failed, as $|\varepsilon_j\rangle = |\varepsilon_k\rangle$—the states of $\mathcal{E}$ bear no imprint of the states of $\mathcal{S}$. □

Equation (2.4) establishes postulate (iva)—the orthogonality of the outcome states (i.e., of the "originals" of the copying eigenstates). As we have noted, (iva) is the essence, the "business end" of the collapse axiom (iv). When the outcome states are orthogonal, any value of $\langle \varepsilon_j|\varepsilon_k\rangle$ is admitted, including $\langle \varepsilon_j|\varepsilon_k\rangle = 0$, which corresponds to a perfect record.

Note that—as long as the state, Equation (2.1) is a direct product before and after the measurement—this conclusion holds for an arbitrary initial state of $\mathcal{E}$, since Equation (2.4) demands orthogonality whenever there is any transfer of information from $\mathcal{S}$ to $\mathcal{E}$—that is, whenever $\langle \varepsilon_j|\varepsilon_k\rangle \neq 1$. It is of course possible that there are subsets of orthogonal states that cannot be distinguished by the environment. We shall consider such degeneracy shortly.

The limitation of copying to distinguishable (orthogonal) outcome states is then a direct consequence of the uncontroversial core postulates (o)–(iii). It can be seen as a resolution of the tension between linearity of quantum theory (superpositions and unitarity of (i) and (ii)) and nonlinearity of the process of proliferation of information—of amplification. This nonlinearity is especially obvious in cloning, as cloning in effect demands "two of the same". The main difference is that in cloning copies must be perfect. Therefore, scalar products must be the same, $\varsigma_{j,k} = \langle \varepsilon_j|\varepsilon_k\rangle = \langle s_j|s_k\rangle$. Consequently, in cloning we have a special case of Equation (2.4): $\varsigma_{j,k}(1 - \varsigma_{j,k}) = 0$. Clearly, there are only two possible solutions; $\varsigma_{j,k} = 0$ (which implies orthogonality), or the trivial $\varsigma_{j,k} = 1$.

Indeed, we can deduce orthogonality of states that remain unperturbed while leaving small but distinct imprints in $\mathcal{E}$ directly from the no-cloning theorem [44–46]) that limits copying allowing it for orthogonal sets of states (thus precluding use of entangled quantum states for superluminal communication): As the states of $\mathcal{S}$ remain unperturbed by assumption, arbitrarily many imperfect copies can be made. However, each extra imperfect copy brings the collective state of all copies correlated with, say, $|s_j\rangle$, closer to orthogonality with the collective state of all of the copies correlated with any other state $|s_k\rangle$. Therefore, one could distinguish $|s_j\rangle$ from $|s_k\rangle$ by a measurement on a collection of sufficiently many copies, and use that information to produce their "clones". As a consequence, also imperfect copying (any value of $\langle \varepsilon_j|\varepsilon_k\rangle$ except 1) that preserves the "original" is prohibited.

We now have a useful definition of an *event*. Wheeler [47]—following Bohr—insisted that "No phenomenon is a phenomenon until it is a measured (recorded) phenomenon". Our contribution is to supply—using information transfer and the dynamics of copying—an operational definition of a "recorded phenomenon". We have just demonstrated that the ability to record events repeatedly associates them with a set of orthogonal states. This in turn implies discreteness, and the inevitability of jolts, quantum jumps that force the system to choose one of the items on the discrete menu of final (outcome) states.

Events that get recorded repeatedly precipitate quantum jumps. They emerge—as a consequence of the discreteness we have just deduced—from within the quantum measurement setting (as discussed, e.g., by von Neumann, 1932 [4]) where both the state of the measured system and of the apparatus are initially pure, and the final state (while entangled) is also pure. The defining characteristic of an event is a transition from before the measurement (from the old state of the system that was known, but it was not known what will happen when the new measurement is made) to when the outcome of the new measurement can be confirmed by repeated re-measurements.

Appearance of events in a pure state case prompts the question about their probabilities. If we were to proceed logically we would suspend discussion of how the core postulates (o)–(iii) imply the essence of axiom (iv), derive Born's rule, and only then come back and consider how quantum jumps—the essence of the collapse—emerge in the mixed state case using the relation between pure states and reduced density matrices, the usual tools of decoherence. This course of argument would require a detour before we can come back and complete the discussion that we have already started.

We shall avoid this, but we shall also avoid using probabilities and Born's rule, as in [35,48]. Some readers may nevertheless prefer to take that detour on their own, "jump" to Section 3, and return to the discussion below after they are convinced that Born's rule emerges from the symmetries of entanglement in the pure state case. While the reasoning below does not depend on probabilities computed using $p_k = |\psi_k|^2$, it employs ideas (such as purification) and mathematical tools (such as trace) that are suggested by decoherence and useful in the "Church of Larger Hilbert Space" approach to mixtures.

We also note that our tasks differ depending on whether mixed states of the control or mixed states of the target (see Figure 1) are the focus of attention. We start below with the simpler case—a target (e.g., an environment) that is in the mixed state. In that case generalization from pure states to mixtures is relatively straightforward, as the challenge is primarily technical [42,49].

Generalization of our discussion to the case when the control—the source of information—is allowed to be in a mixed state must take into account an additional complication: The state of control can change, and yet result in the same copy—a quantum meme or a *qmeme*—of the essential information. This degeneracy is important in considering readout of information from a macroscopic apparatus pointer or any other macroscopic device that is supposed to keep reliable records [43]. Obviously, the detailed microscopic state of such a device is of little consequence—the information of interest is what gets copied. It resides in the corresponding (likely macroscopic) degrees of freedom (e.g., of an apparatus pointer). Many microscopic states may (and usually will) represent the same information. Therefore, degeneracy—the fact that many microstates represent the same record and will result in the same copy of that record—must be considered along with the possibility of mixed states of the control. We shall return to this case of mixed and degenerate control later in this section.

2.2. Mixed States of the "Target"

Equations (2.1)–(2.4) are based on idealizations that include purity of the initial state of $\mathcal{E}$. Regardless of whether $\mathcal{E}$ designates an environment or an apparatus, this is unlikely to be a good assumption. However, this assumption is also easily bypassed: An unknown state of $\mathcal{E}$ can be represented as a pure state of an enlarged system. This is the purification (aka "Church of Larger Hilbert Space") strategy: Instead of a density matrix $\rho_\mathcal{E} = \sum_i p_i |\varepsilon_i\rangle\langle\varepsilon_i|$ of a mixed state one can deal with a pure entangled state of $\mathcal{E}$ and $\mathcal{E}'$ defined in $\mathcal{H}_\mathcal{E} \otimes \mathcal{H}_{\mathcal{E}'}$:

$$|\varepsilon\varepsilon'\rangle = \sum_i \sqrt{p_i} |\varepsilon_i\rangle |\varepsilon_i'\rangle, \tag{2.5a}$$

so that;

$$\rho_\mathcal{E} = \sum_i p_i |\varepsilon_i\rangle\langle\varepsilon_i| = \mathrm{Tr}_{\mathcal{E}'} |\varepsilon\varepsilon'\rangle\langle\varepsilon\varepsilon'|. \tag{2.5b}$$

Therefore, when the initial state of $\mathcal{E}$ is mixed, there is always a pure state in an enlarged Hilbert space. Instead of (2.1) we can then write $|s_k\rangle|\varepsilon_0\varepsilon'\rangle \Rightarrow |s_k\rangle|\varepsilon_k\varepsilon'\rangle$ in obvious notation, and all of the steps that lead to Equations (2.3)–(2.4) can be repeated, so that:

$$\langle s_j|s_k\rangle(1 - \langle\varepsilon_j\varepsilon'|\varepsilon_k\varepsilon'\rangle) = 0 \tag{2.6}$$

and forcing one to the same conclusions as Equation (2.4).

Purification relates pure states and density matrices by treating $\rho_\mathcal{E} = \sum_i p_i |\varepsilon_i\rangle\langle\varepsilon_i|$ as a result of a trace. The connection of $\rho_\mathcal{E}$ with $|\varepsilon\varepsilon'\rangle = \sum_i \sqrt{p_i}|\varepsilon_i\rangle|\varepsilon_i'\rangle$ does involve tracing. However, there is no need to regard weights p_i as probabilities. They are just coefficients that relate a state of the whole $|\varepsilon\varepsilon'\rangle$ and of its part $\rho_\mathcal{E}$ by a mathematical operation—a trace. Thus, $\rho_\mathcal{E}$ is a mathematical object that represents a reduction of a pure state that exists in the larger Hilbert space, but does not yet—in absence of Born's rule—merit statistical interpretation.

Indeed, there is no need to even mention $\rho_\mathcal{E}$. All of the above discussion can be carried out right from the start with a pure state in a larger Hilbert space. It suffices to assume only that *some* such pure state in the enlarged Hilbert space exists and that lack of purity of $\mathcal{E}$ is a result of its entanglement with the rest of the Universe. This does not rely on Born's rule, but it does assert that ignorance that is reflected in a mixed local state (here, of $\mathcal{E}$) can be regarded as a consequence of entanglement. This assertion is established in the next section, so—as we have already noted—readers can break the order of the presentation, consult the derivation of Born's rule in the next section, and return here afterwards.

There is also an alternative way to proceed that leads to the same conclusions but does not require purification. Instead, we assume at the outset that we can represent states as density matrices. Unitary evolution preserves scalar products, i.e., Hilbert-Schmidt norm of density operators defined by $\mathrm{Tr}\rho\rho'$. Therefore, one is led to:

$$\mathrm{Tr}|s_j\rangle\langle s_j|\rho_\mathcal{E}|s_k\rangle\langle s_k|\rho_\mathcal{E} = \mathrm{Tr}|s_j\rangle\langle s_j|\rho_{\mathcal{E}|j}|s_k\rangle\langle s_k|\rho_{\mathcal{E}|k},$$

where $\rho_{\mathcal{E}|j}$ and $\rho_{\mathcal{E}|k}$ are mixed states of $\mathcal{E}$ affected by the two states of $\mathcal{S}$ that are unperturbed by copying. This in turn yields;

$$|\langle s_j|s_k\rangle|^2 (\mathrm{Tr}\rho_\mathcal{E}^2 - \mathrm{Tr}\rho_{\mathcal{E}|j}\rho_{\mathcal{E}|k}) = 0, \tag{2.7}$$

which can be satisfied only in the same two cases as before: Either $\langle s_j|s_k\rangle = 0$, or $\mathrm{Tr}\rho_\mathcal{E}^2 = \mathrm{Tr}\rho_{\mathcal{E}|j}\rho_{\mathcal{E}|k}$ which implies (by Schwarz inequality) that $\rho_{\mathcal{E}|j} = \rho_{\mathcal{E}|k}$ (i.e., there can be no record of nonorthogonal states of $\mathcal{S}$).

This conclusion can be reached even more directly: Obviously, $\rho_{\mathcal{E}|j}$ and $\rho_{\mathcal{E}|k}$ have the same eigenvalues p_m as $\rho_\mathcal{E} = \sum_m p_m |\varepsilon_m\rangle\langle\varepsilon_m|$ from which they have unitarily evolved. Consequently, they could differ from each other only in their eigenstates that could contain record of the state of $\mathcal{S}$, e.g.,: $\rho_{\mathcal{E}|k} = \sum_m p_m |\varepsilon_{m|k}\rangle\langle\varepsilon_{m|k}|$. However, $\mathrm{Tr}\rho_{\mathcal{E}|j}\rho_{\mathcal{E}|k} = \sum_m p_m^2 |\langle\varepsilon_{m|j}|\varepsilon_{m|k}\rangle|^2$, coincides with $\mathrm{Tr}\rho_\mathcal{E}^2$ iff $|\langle\varepsilon_{m|j}|\varepsilon_{m|k}\rangle|^2 = 1$ whenever $p_m \neq 0$. It follows that $\rho_{\mathcal{E}|j} = \rho_{\mathcal{E}|k}$. Therefore, unless $\langle s_j|s_k\rangle = 0$, states $|s_j\rangle$ and $|s_k\rangle$ cannot leave any imprint that distinguishes them—cannot deposit any record—in $\mathcal{E}$.

In other words, in case of mixed target we can establish our key result using only pure states in an enlarged Hilbert space (purification), or only density matrices. The only reason one might want to invoke Born's rule is to provide a physically (rather than only mathematically) motivated bridge between these two representations of "impure" states of $\mathcal{E}$. Such a bridge is obviously useful, but it is not essential in arriving at the desired conclusions we reach in this section.

The economy of our assumptions stands in stark contrast with the uncompromising nature of our conclusions: Predictability—the demand that information transfer preserves the state of the system (embodied in postulate (iii))—was, along with the superposition principle (i) and unitarity of quantum evolutions (ii)—key to our derivation of the discreteness of states that can be repeatedly accessed. Discrete terminal states are behind the inevitability of quantum jumps.

We shall see in Section 4 that existence of stable terminal points allows for amplification and for the resulting preponderance of records about the states in which the system persist—in spite of the coupling to the environment—for long time periods. These sojourns of predictable evolution can be occasionally interrupted by a jump into another stable terminal state caused by perturbations that do not commute with the pointer observables monitored by the environment.

2.3. Predictability Killed the (Schrödinger's) Cat

There are several ways to describe our conclusions so far. To restate the obvious, we have established that repeatedly accessible outcome states must be orthogonal. This is the interpretation—independent part of axiom (iv)—all of it except for the literal collapse. The core quantum postulates alone make it impossible to find out preexisting quantum states.

This is enough for the relative state account of quantum jumps—collapse axiom (iv) is not necessary for that. So, a cat suspended between life and death [20] cannot be seen in the records it leaves in the monitoring environment. Repeated records of only one of these two options will be available because only the two stable states (unperturbed by copying) allow for repeatability (postulate (iii))—for predictability (hence the above title).

Another way of stating our conclusion is to note that a set of orthogonal states defines a Hermitian operator when supplemented with real eigenvalues. The above discussion is then a derivation of the Hermitian nature of observables. It justifies the focus on Hermitian operators often invoked in textbook version of measurement axioms [3].

We note that "strict repeatability" (that is, assertion that states $\{|s_k\rangle\}$ cannot change at all in the course of a measurement) is not needed: They can evolve providing that their scalar products remain unaffected. That is,

$$\sum_{j,k} \alpha_j^* \alpha_k \langle s_j | s_k \rangle = \sum_{j,k} \alpha_j^* \alpha_k \langle \tilde{s}_j | \tilde{s}_k \rangle \langle \varepsilon_j | \varepsilon_k \rangle \tag{2.8}$$

leads to the same conclusions as Equation (2.2) as long as $\langle s_j | s_k \rangle = \langle \tilde{s}_j | \tilde{s}_k \rangle$. Thus, when $|\tilde{s}_j\rangle$ and $|\tilde{s}_k\rangle$ are related with their progenitors by a transformation that preserves scalar product (as would, e.g., any reversible evolution) the proof of orthogonality goes through unimpeded. Both unitary and antiunitary transformations are in this class. Other similar generalizations are also possible [50,51].

We can also consider situations when this is not the case—$\langle s_j | s_k \rangle \neq \langle \tilde{s}_j | \tilde{s}_k \rangle$. An extreme example of this arises when the state of the measured system retains no memory of what it was before (e.g., $|s_j\rangle \Rightarrow |0\rangle$, $|s_k\rangle \Rightarrow |0\rangle$). For example, photons are usually absorbed by detectors, and coherent states (that are not orthogonal) play the role of the outcomes. Then the apparatus can (and, indeed, by unitarity, has to) "inherit" the distinguishability—the information—previously residing in the system. In that case the need for orthogonality of $|s_j\rangle$ and $|s_k\rangle$ disappears. Of course such measurements do not fulfill postulate (iii)—they are not repeatable.

We emphasize that Born's rule was not used above. The values of the scalar product that played a role in the proofs are $\langle s_j | s_k \rangle = 0$ or $\langle s_j | s_k \rangle = 1$, and the key distinction was between the zero and non-zero value of $\langle s_j | s_k \rangle$. Both "0" and "1" correspond to certainty. For instance, when we have asserted immediately below Equation (2.4) that $\langle \varepsilon_j | \varepsilon_k \rangle = 1$, this implies that these two states of $\mathcal{E}$ are certainly identical. We have therefore derived probability for a very special case already. We shall relying on this special case—certainty—in the derivation of probabilities in Section 3.

2.4. Records and Branches: Degenerate "Control"

Our discussion so far is based on one key assumption—repeatability of measurement outcomes—which we have usually simplified to mean "nondemolition measurements", i.e., repeatable accessibility of the same "original" state of the measured system. However, as we have already noted, for microscopic systems this is at best an exception. On the other hand, repeatability is essential for an apparatus $\mathcal{A}$, at the level of measurement *records*. Pointer of an apparatus can be read out many times, and everyone should agree on where does it point—on what is the record. Indeed, this repeatable accessibility is a property of not just apparatus pointers, but a defining property of states that comprise "objective classical reality". So, while the repeatability postulate (iii) at the level of quantum systems is an idealization of a theorist (e.g., Dirac, [3]), persistence of records stored in $\mathcal{A}$ as well as of effectively classical states of macroscopic quantum systems we encounter in our everyday experience is an essential fact of life and, therefore, a key desideratum of a successful theory of objective classical reality. Here, we extend our discussion of repeatability to account for it using our core quantum postulates.

We start by noting that one is almost never interested in the state of the apparatus as a whole: Finding out pure states of an object with Avogadro's number of atoms (and, hence, with Hilbert space dimension of the order of $10^{10^{23}}$) is impractical and unnecessary. Obviously, there are many microstates of the apparatus that correspond to the same memory state and yield the same readout. We have to modify our above "nondemolition" approach to allow for perturbations of the microscopic states and to account for this degeneracy. Once we have done this, we shall also find it easier to deal with mixed states of $\mathcal{A}$ that, for any macroscopic system, are certainly typical.

Consider two pure states $|v_1\rangle$ and $|v_2\rangle$ that represent the same record "v". We take this to mean that observers or other memory devices $\mathcal{M}, \mathcal{M}', \ldots$ will register the same state after interacting with $\mathcal{A}$ in either $|v_1\rangle$ or $|v_2\rangle$:

$$|v_1\rangle|\mu\rangle|\mu'\rangle\ldots \Rightarrow |\tilde{v}_1\rangle|\mu_v\rangle|\mu'\rangle\ldots \Rightarrow |\tilde{\tilde{v}}_1\rangle|\mu_v\rangle|\mu'_v\rangle,$$
$$|v_2\rangle|\mu\rangle|\mu'\rangle\ldots \Rightarrow |\tilde{v}_2\rangle|\mu_v\rangle|\mu'\rangle\ldots \Rightarrow |\tilde{\tilde{v}}_2\rangle|\mu_v\rangle|\mu'_v\rangle. \quad (2.9v)$$

Note that evolution of the "original" is allowed (e.g., $|v_1\rangle \Rightarrow |\tilde{v}_1\rangle \Rightarrow |\tilde{\tilde{v}}_1\rangle$). as long as it does not affect the repeatability of what is read out by $\mathcal{M}, \mathcal{M}', \ldots$.

It is straightforward to see that any superposition or any mixed state of $|v_1\rangle$ and $|v_2\rangle$ will also register the same way—as $|\mu_v\rangle$—in the memory $\mathcal{M}$. Registration of a different outcome—different readout w—by memory $\mathcal{M}$ can be represented as:

$$|w_1\rangle|\mu\rangle|\mu'\rangle\ldots \Rightarrow |\tilde{w}_1\rangle|\mu_w\rangle|\mu'\rangle\ldots \Rightarrow |\tilde{\tilde{w}}_1\rangle|\mu_w\rangle|\mu'_w\rangle,$$
$$|w_2\rangle|\mu\rangle|\mu'\rangle\ldots \Rightarrow |\tilde{w}_2\rangle|\mu_w\rangle|\mu'\rangle\ldots \Rightarrow |\tilde{\tilde{w}}_2\rangle|\mu_w\rangle|\mu'_w\rangle. \quad (2.9w)$$

Again, there are many microstates—$|w_1\rangle, |w_2\rangle$, etc.—that yield the same readout $|\mu_w\rangle$.

The above account offers a model of what happens when an apparatus $\mathcal{A}$ is consulted by many observers that can be represented by distinct $\mathcal{M}$'s. They can perturb the microstate but leave the record intact.

We can now repeat the pure state reasoning from above, assuming that the "control"—which was before the measured system, and may now be the apparatus $\mathcal{A}$—is in a pure state. We are led to an analogue of Equation (2.4) that can be satisfied in two different ways: Either the memory devices register the same readout regardless of the underlying microscopic state of the system, as in:

$$\forall_{k,l} \ \langle v_k|v_l\rangle = \langle \tilde{v}_k|\tilde{v}_l\rangle\langle \mu_v|\mu_v\rangle, \quad (2.10)$$

(so that $\langle \mu_v|\mu_v\rangle = 1$, in which case scalar products between the underlying states of $\mathcal{A}$ can take any value), or the readouts can differ,

$$\forall_{k,l} \ \langle v_k|w_l\rangle = \langle \tilde{v}_k|\tilde{w}_l\rangle\langle \mu_v|\mu_w\rangle, \quad (2.11)$$

and $\langle v_k|w_l\rangle$ have to be orthogonal when they lead to distinct records in $\mathcal{M}, \mathcal{M}', \ldots$.

The relation between the states of the control defined by the readout—by the imprints they leave on the state on the "target" $\mathcal{M}$—is reflexive, symmetric and transitive. Hence, it defines equivalence classes: States that leave imprint "v" form a class $\mathcal{V}$ distinct from states in $\mathcal{W}$ that imprint "w". Record states in $\mathcal{V}$ ($\mathcal{W}$, etc.) should retain class membership under the evolutions generated by readouts (otherwise they cannot be repeatedly consulted and keep the record). It is natural to represent such equivalence classes of states with orthogonal subspaces in the Hilbert space $\mathcal{H}_\mathcal{A}$. It is also possible to define probabilities as measures on such equivalence classes and regard them as (macroscopic or coarse-grained) "events" (see e.g., Gnedenko, 1968, [52]).

Generalization to when the apparatus is in a mixed state can be carried out using purification strategy as before (this time purifying the "control" $\mathcal{A}$) or by using preservation of the Hilbert-Schmidt product. Thus, unitary evolutions;

$$\rho_{\mathcal{V}}^{\mathcal{A}}|\mu\rangle\langle\mu| \Longrightarrow \tilde{\rho}_{\mathcal{V}}^{\mathcal{A}}|\mu_v\rangle\langle\mu_v|, \qquad (2.12v)$$

$$\rho_{\mathcal{W}}^{\mathcal{A}}|\mu\rangle\langle\mu| \Longrightarrow \tilde{\rho}_{\mathcal{W}}^{\mathcal{A}}|\mu_w\rangle\langle\mu_w|, \qquad (2.12w)$$

where $\rho_{\mathcal{V}}^{\mathcal{A}}$ ($\rho_{\mathcal{W}}^{\mathcal{A}}$, etc.) is any density matrix with support restricted to only $\mathcal{V}$ ($\mathcal{W}$, etc.) imply equality:

$$\mathrm{Tr}\rho_{\mathcal{V}}^{\mathcal{A}}\rho_{\mathcal{W}}^{\mathcal{A}}|\langle\mu|\mu\rangle|^2 = \mathrm{Tr}\tilde{\rho}_{\mathcal{V}}^{\mathcal{A}}\tilde{\rho}_{\mathcal{W}}^{\mathcal{A}}|\langle\mu_v|\mu_w\rangle|^2. \qquad (2.13)$$

This is an analogue of the derivation of Equations (2.4)–(2.7) when the mixed state of the control is represented by a density matrix. As before, we conclude that $\mathrm{Tr}\rho_{\mathcal{V}}^{\mathcal{A}}\rho_{\mathcal{W}}^{\mathcal{A}} = 0$ unless $|\langle\mu_v|\mu_w\rangle|^2 = 1$.

In contrast to Equation (2.6) (where "control" $\mathcal{S}$ was pure, but the state of the "target" $\mathcal{E}$ was mixed) now the target is the memory $\mathcal{M}$, and its state starts and remains pure. This shifting of "mixedness" from the target (as in Equation (2.7)) to the control may seem somewhat arbitrary, but—in the present setting—it is well justified. The motivation before was the process of decoherence or measurement, and the focus of attention was the system $\mathcal{S}$. Now, the motivation is the readout of the state of the apparatus pointer by observers (but information flow in decoherence and in quantum Darwinism we discuss in Section 4 can be treated in the same manner).

2.4.1. Repeatability and Actionable Information

Previously we have modeled the acquisition of information about a system by a (possibly macroscopic) apparatus or by the environment in the course of decoherence. In either case "target" could be expected to be in a mixed state but the "control" was pure. Now we are dealing with an apparatus acting as a macroscopic control. Its microscopic state is in general mixed, and can be influenced by the readout, but we still expect it to retain the record (e.g., of a measurement outcome). This is possible because of degeneracy—many microscopic states represent the same record.[3]

This record should be repeatedly accessible and unambiguous. Before, in the discussion following Equations (2.1)–(2.4), repeatability was assured by insisting that the state of the system—of the control—should remain unchanged during the readout. Now, we can no longer count on the preservation of the *state* of the original to establish repeatability. Instead, we demand—as a criterion for repeatable accessibility—that; (i) the copies should contain the same information, and; (ii) that information should suffice to distinguish record $\mathcal{V}$ from $\mathcal{W}$.

Above, we have seen how this demand can be implemented when the states of the memories $\mathcal{M}, \mathcal{M}'$, etc. are pure. Relaxing the assumption of pure memory states is possible. One can also allow for decoherence caused by the environment $\mathcal{E}$. Thus, consider sequence of copying operations that, along with decoherence, lead to:

$$\rho_{\mathcal{V}}^{\mathcal{A}}\rho_0^{\mathcal{M}}\rho_0^{\mathcal{M}'}...\rho_0^{\mathcal{E}} \Longrightarrow \rho_{\mathcal{V}}^{\mathcal{A}\mathcal{M}\mathcal{M}'...\mathcal{E}}, \qquad (2.14v)$$

$$\rho_{\mathcal{W}}^{\mathcal{A}}\rho_0^{\mathcal{M}}\rho_0^{\mathcal{M}'}...\rho_0^{\mathcal{E}} \Longrightarrow \rho_{\mathcal{W}}^{\mathcal{A}\mathcal{M}\mathcal{M}'...\mathcal{E}}. \qquad (2.14w)$$

Note that we allow the apparatus $\mathcal{A}$ that contains the original record, various memories, as well as $\mathcal{E}$ to remain correlated. Such a general final state suggests an obvious question: How can we test whether, say, memory $\mathcal{M}$ has indeed acquired a copy of the record in $\mathcal{A}$ that offers (at least partial) distinguishability of $\mathcal{V}$ from $\mathcal{W}$?

To address this question we propose an operational criterion: The information contained in each of the memories should be *actionable*—it should allow one to alter the state

---

[3] Schrödinger cat comes to mind, with many microscopic states consistent with "alive" or "dead".

of a test system $\mathcal{T}$. Thus, copy in $\mathcal{M}$ will be certified as "actionable" when there is a conditional unitary transformation $U(\mathcal{T}|\mathcal{M})$ that alters the state of the test system so that:

$$\rho_\mathcal{V}^{\mathcal{AMM'}\ldots\mathcal{E}} \otimes \rho_0^\mathcal{T} \stackrel{U(\mathcal{T}|\mathcal{M})}{\Longrightarrow} \tilde{\rho}_\mathcal{V}^{\mathcal{AMM'}\ldots\mathcal{E}} \otimes \rho_\mathcal{V}^\mathcal{T}, \qquad (2.15v)$$

$$\rho_\mathcal{W}^{\mathcal{AMM'}\ldots\mathcal{E}} \otimes \rho_0^\mathcal{T} \stackrel{U(\mathcal{T}|\mathcal{M})}{\Longrightarrow} \tilde{\rho}_\mathcal{W}^{\mathcal{AMM'}\ldots\mathcal{E}} \otimes \rho_\mathcal{W}^\mathcal{T}. \qquad (2.15w)$$

The test of actionability will be successful—the information in $\mathcal{M}$ will be declared actionable—when there exists an initial state $\rho_0^\mathcal{T}$ of the test system such that:

$$\mathrm{Tr}(\rho_0^\mathcal{T})^2 > \mathrm{Tr}\rho_\mathcal{V}^\mathcal{T}\rho_\mathcal{W}^\mathcal{T}. \qquad (2.16a)$$

Preservation of Schmidt–Hilbert norm under unitary evolutions implies that—unless $\rho_\mathcal{V}^{\mathcal{AMM'}\ldots\mathcal{E}}$ and $\rho_\mathcal{W}^{\mathcal{AMM'}\ldots\mathcal{E}}$ are orthogonal to begin with—the overlap between the two "branches" should increase to compensate for the decrease of overlap in the test system states, Equation (2.16a), so that;

$$\mathrm{Tr}\rho_\mathcal{V}^{\mathcal{AMM'}\ldots\mathcal{E}}\rho_\mathcal{W}^{\mathcal{AMM'}\ldots\mathcal{E}} < \mathrm{Tr}\tilde{\rho}_\mathcal{V}^{\mathcal{AMM'}\ldots\mathcal{E}}\tilde{\rho}_\mathcal{W}^{\mathcal{AMM'}\ldots\mathcal{E}}. \qquad (2.16b)$$

Moreover, as we have assumed that in $\mathcal{M}, \mathcal{M}'\ldots\mathcal{M}^{(k)}\ldots$ there are many copies of the original record in $\mathcal{A}$, this test of actionability can be repeated. However, the overlap of the density matrices of $\mathcal{AMM'}\ldots\mathcal{E}$ on the RHS above cannot increase indefinitely as a result of such multiple iterations of actionability tests, as it is bounded from above by unity. Consequently, we conclude via this *reductio ad absurdum* reasoning that the ability to make multiple copies implies $\mathrm{Tr}\rho_\mathcal{V}^{\mathcal{AMM'}\ldots\mathcal{E}}\rho_\mathcal{W}^{\mathcal{AMM'}\ldots\mathcal{E}} = 0$. Therefore,

$$\mathrm{Tr}\rho_\mathcal{V}^\mathcal{A}\rho_\mathcal{W}^\mathcal{A} = 0 \qquad (2.17)$$

is needed to allow for repeatable copying of the original record (or, more generally, the features distinguishing $\mathcal{V}$ from $\mathcal{W}$ of the original macroscopic state) in $\mathcal{A}$.

We have assumed above that there is no preexisting correlation between the test system and the rest, $\mathcal{AMM'}\ldots\mathcal{M}^{(k)}\ldots\mathcal{E}$. We could have actually assumed a pure state of $\mathcal{T}$: When there is a $U(\mathcal{T}|\mathcal{M})$ that alters a mixed state of $\mathcal{T}$, there will certainly be a pure state of $\mathcal{T}$ that can be altered.

We also note that (as before) the whole argument can be recast in the language of the "Church of Larger Hilbert Space" [43]. That is, one can carry it out without any appeals to Born's rule. There is an interesting subtlety in such treatments: The actionable information we have tested for above is local—it resides in a specific $\mathcal{M}^{(k)}$. This need not be always the case: Actionable information may be nonlocal—it may reside in correlations between systems. Such an example is discussed in [43]. The locus of actionable information is assured by the selection of the conditional evolution operator $U(\mathcal{T}|\mathcal{M}^{(k)})$ that—above—couples only specific $\mathcal{M}^{(k)}$ to $\mathcal{T}$.

We conclude that only orthogonal projectors (above, of $\mathcal{A}$) can act as "originals" for unlimited numbers of copies. Of course, many of the outcome states of quantum system $\mathcal{S}$ inferred from the measurement records in $\mathcal{A}$ are not orthogonal. Measurements that result in such outcomes are not repeatable: State of $\mathcal{S}$ is perturbed, but its record in $\mathcal{A}$ is repeatedly accessible, so there is no contradiction. Repeatability of the records is therefore possible even when the recorded states of $\mathcal{S}$ at the roots of the corresponding branches are not orthogonal. Positive operator valued measures (POVM's, that is generalized measurements with outcomes that do not represent orthogonal states of the measured system, see [5]) arise naturally in this setting [43].

The reasoning behind the conclusions of this subsection parallels the pure states case, Equations (2.1)–(2.4), but the mathematics and, above all, the physical motivation, differ. Before we were dealing with the abstract postulate of repeatability that is found in Dirac [3] and other textbooks, but this idealized version is almost never implemented in the laboratory practice in measurements of microscopic quantum systems. In spite of its idealizations, the abstract Dirac version of repeatability of measurements should not be dismissed too easily: Being able to confirm that a state is what it is known to be is essential to justify the very idea of a state in general, and of a quantum state in particular. The role of the state is, after all, to enable predictions, and the simplest prediction (captured by repeatability, no matter how difficult nondemolition measurements are to implement in practice) is that existence of a state can be confirmed. Indeed, this is how quantum states can give rise to "existence" we have become accustomed to in our quantum Universe.

In a classical Universe repeatability is taken for granted, as an unknown classical state can be found out without endangering its existence. Repeatability in a quantum setting allows one to use fragile quantum states as building blocks of classical reality, as we shall see in more detail in Section 4.

In practice predictability and even repeatability are encountered not in the measured microscopic quantum system $\mathcal{S}$ but, rather, in the memory of the measuring apparatus $\mathcal{A}$, and, indeed, in the states of macroscopic systems. Apparatus pointer can be, after all, repeatedly consulted, as can be any effectively classical state. Moreover, our perception of the collapse arises not from the direct evidence of the behavior of some microscopic quantum $\mathcal{S}$, but, rather, from the records of its state inscribed in the memory of a macroscopic (albeit still quantum) $\mathcal{A}$.

We have seen that the same condition of repeatability that led to orthogonality (and, hence, discreteness) in the set of possible outcomes in the pure case of $\mathcal{S}$ enforces orthogonality of the subspaces of $\mathcal{A}$ (even when the microscopic state of $\mathcal{A}$ is allowed to change). Thus, while Equations (2.1)–(2.4) account for quantum jumps in the idealized case of quantum postulates (Dirac, 1958) [3], this subsection shows that discrete quantum jumps can occur as a result of orthogonality of the whole subspaces of the Hilbert space $\mathcal{H}_\mathcal{A}$ corresponding to repeatedly accessible records—to macroscopic pointer subspaces of the measuring device.

2.5. Pointer Basis, Information Transfer, and Decoherence

We are now equipped with a set of measurement outcomes or, to put it in a way that ties in with the study of probabilities we shall embark on in Section 3, with a set of possible *events*. Our derivation above did not appeal to decoherence, but decoherence yields einselection (which is, after all, due to the information transfer to the environment). We will now see that einselection based on repeatability and einselection based on decoherence are in effect two views of the same phenomenon.

Popular accounts of decoherence and its role in the emergence of 'the classical' often start from the observation that when a quantum system $\mathcal{S}$ interacts with some environment $\mathcal{E}$ "phase relations in $\mathcal{S}$ are lost". This is, at best, incomplete if not misleading, as it begs the more fundamental question: "Phases between *what*?". This in turn leads directly to the main issue addressed by einselection: "*What is the preferred basis*?". This key question is often muddled in the "folklore" accounts of decoherence.

The crux of the matter—the reason why interaction with the environment can impose classicality—is precisely the emergence of the preferred states. The basic criterion that selects preferred pointer states was discovered when the analogy between the role of the environment in decoherence and the role of the apparatus in a nondemolition measurement was recognized: What matters is that there are interactions that transfer information and yet leave some states of the system unaffected [24].

The criterion for selecting such preferred states is persistence of correlation between two systems (e.g., system $\mathcal{S}$ and apparatus $\mathcal{A}$). For the preferred pointer states this correlation should persist in spite of immersion of $\mathcal{A}$ in the environment. It is obvious that states (of, e.g., $\mathcal{A}$) that are best at retaining correlations (with, e.g., $\mathcal{S}$) also retain identity—i.e., correlation with me, the observer—and resist entanglement with the environment.

Our discussion above confirms that the simple idea of preserving a state while transferring the information about it—also the central idea of einselection—is powerful, and can be analyzed using minimal purely quantum ingredients—core postulates (o)–(iii). It leads to breaking of the unitary symmetry and singles out preferred states of the apparatus pointer (supplied in textbooks by axiom (iv)) without any need to invoke physical (statistical) view of the reduced density matrices (which is central to the decoherence approach to collapse).

This is important, as partial trace (understood as an averaging procedure) and reduced density matrices (understood as probability distributions) employed in decoherence theory rely on Born's rule (which endows them with physical significance). Our goal in the next section will be to arrive at Born's rule, axiom (v)—to relate state vectors and probabilities. Obtaining preferred basis and deducing events without invoking density matrices and trace—without relying on Born's rule—is essential if we are to avoid circularity in its derivation.

To compare derivation of the preferred states in decoherence with their emergence from symmetry breaking imposed by axioms (o)–(iii) we return to Equation (2.2). We also temporarily suspend prohibition on the use of partial trace to compute reduced density matrix of the system:

$$\rho_S = \sum_{j,k} \alpha_j \alpha_k^* \langle \varepsilon_k | \varepsilon_j \rangle | s_j \rangle \langle s_k | = Tr_\mathcal{E} |\Psi_{\mathcal{E}S}\rangle\langle\Psi_{\mathcal{E}S}|. \quad (2.18)$$

Above we have expressed ρ_S in the pointer basis defined by its resilience in spite of the monitoring by $\mathcal{E}$ and not in the Schmidt basis. Therefore, until decoherence in that basis is complete, and the environment acquires perfect records of pointer states;

$$\langle \varepsilon_j | \varepsilon_k \rangle = \delta_{jk}, \quad (2.19)$$

the eigenstates of ρ_S do not coincide with the pointer states selected for their resilience in spite of the immersion in $\mathcal{E}$.

Resilience—quantified by the ability to retain correlations in spite of the environment, and, hence, by persistence, as in Equations (2.4) and (2.7)—is the essence of the original definition of pointer states and einselection [24,25]. Such pointer states will be in general different from the instantaneous Schmidt states of $\mathcal{S}$—the eigenstates of ρ_S. They will coincide with the Schmidt states of

$$|\Psi_{\mathcal{E}S}\rangle = \sum_k a_k |s_k\rangle |\varepsilon_k\rangle \quad (2.20)$$

only when $\{|\varepsilon_k\rangle\}$—their records in $\mathcal{E}$—become orthogonal. We did not need orthogonality of $\{|\varepsilon_k\rangle\}$ to prove orthogonality of pointer states earlier in this section. It will be, however, useful in the next section, as it assures additivity of probabilities of the pointer states.

For pure states this discussion of additivity can be carried out in a setting that is explicitly free of any reference to density matrices or trace, and relies only on correlations (Zurek, 2005) [48]. Born's rule would be needed to establish the connection between them and to endow reduced density matrix with physical (statistical) interpretation, but—as we have seen—orthogonality of outcomes central for the definition of events can be established without Born's rule.

So, a piece of decoherence "folklore"—responsible for statements such as "decoherence causes reduced density matrix to be diagonal"—is at best imprecise, and often incorrect. The error is mathematical and obvious: ρ_S is Hermitian, so it is always diagonalized by the Schmidt states of $\mathcal{S}$. In addition, what we want in pointer states is preservation of their identity.

Still, "folklore" often assigns classicality to the eigenstates of ρ_S, and that would make them candidate to the status of events. This was even occasionally endorsed by some of the practitioners of decoherence (Zeh, 1990; [53]; 2007 [54]; Albrecht, 1992 [55], but see Albrecht et al., 2021 [56,57]) and taken for granted by others (see, e.g., [58]). However, by and large it is no longer regarded as viable [31,32,36]: The eigenstates of ρ_S are not stable. They depend on the time and on the initial state of $\mathcal{S}$, which disqualifies them as events in the sense needed to develop probability theory, and do not fit the bill as "elements of classical reality". There are also situations where the eigenstates of ρ_S can be (in contrast to pointer states that are local whenever the coupling with the environment is local) very nonlocal [59–61].

Nonlocality of pointer states need not necessarily be a problem. The role of decoherence is to predict what happens—what states are "pointer" given the physical context (including Hamiltonians, the nature of the environment, etc.). Thus, testing it in situations when its predictions clash with our classical intuition is of interest (see, e.g., Poyatos, Cirac, and Zoller, 1996 [62]). The problem with the eigenstates of ρ_S is—primarily—their dependence on the initial state of the system. This is eliminated by the predictability sieve ([6,28,63]) and the repeatability-based approach (see also Refs. [42,43,49]).

As is often the case with folk wisdom, a grain of truth is nevertheless reflected in such oversimplified "proverbs": When the environment acquires perfect knowledge of the states it monitors without perturbing them, and $\langle \varepsilon_j | \varepsilon_k \rangle = \delta_{jk}$, pointer states "become Schmidt", and end up on the diagonal of ρ_S. Effective decoherence favors such alignment of Schmidt states with the pointer states. Given that decoherence is—at least in the macroscopic domain—very fast, this can happen essentially instantaneously.

Still, this coincidence should not be used to attempt a redefinition of pointer states as instantaneous eigenstates of ρ_S—instantaneous Schmidt states. As we have already seen, and as will become even clearer in the rest of this paper, it is essential to distinguish the process that fixes preferred pointer states (that is, dynamics of the information transfer that results in the measurement as well as decoherence, but does not depend on the initial state of the system) from the reasoning that assigns probabilities to these outcomes. These probabilities are determined by the initial state.

2.6. Irreversibility of Perceived Events, or "Don't Blame the 2nd Law—Wavepacket Collapse Is Your Own Fault!"

Irreversibility has been blamed for the collapse of the wavepacket since at least von Neumann (1932) [4]. The causes of irreversibility invoked in this context have typically classical analogues that go back to Boltzmann and the loss of information implicated in the Second Law (Zeh, 2007) [54].

Discrete quantum jumps occur as a consequence of the collapse. They are uniquely quantum, and a central conundrum of quantum physics. They reset the evolution relevant for the future of the observer putting it onto a course consistent with the measurement outcome (and prima facie at odds with the unitarity of quantum evolutions).

We have just seen how the discreteness of quantum jumps follows from the quantum core postulates. We now point out that—in addition to the "usual suspects" traditionally blamed for irreversibility—there is a uniquely quantum reason why events associated with quantum jumps are fundamentally irreversible. It is distinct from the information loss associated with the dynamics that is responsible for the Second Law.

This uniquely quantum source of irreversibility is a result of the information *gain* (rather than its loss). It is noteworthy that quantum physics provides a uniquely quantum key that solves the distinctly quantum conundrum of the wavepacket collapse.

We shall see below that information about the measurement outcome does not preclude reversal of the classical measurement, but makes it impossible to undo evolution that leads to a quantum measurement whenever a superposition of the potential outcomes—hence, the wavepacket collapse—is involved.

2.6.1. Classical Measurement Can Be Reversed Even when Record of the Outcome is Kept

Let us first examine a measurement carried out by a classical agent/apparatus **A** on a classical system **S**. The state s of **S** (e.g., location of **S** in phase space) is measured by a classical **A** that starts in the "ready to measure" state A_0:

$$sA_0 \xRightarrow{\mathcal{E}_{SA}} sA_s. \qquad (2.21a)$$

The question we address is whether the combined state of **SA** can be restored to the pre-measurement sA_0 even after the information about the outcome is retained somewhere—e.g., in the memory device **D**.

The dynamics $\mathfrak{E}_{SA}$ responsible for the measurement is assumed to be reversible and, in Equation (2.21a), it is classical. Therefore, classical measurement can be undone simply by implementing $\mathfrak{E}_{SA}^{-1}$. An example of $\mathfrak{E}_{SA}^{-1}$ is (Loschmidt inspired) instantaneous reversal of velocities.

Our main point is that the reversal;

$$sA_s \xRightarrow{\mathfrak{E}_{SA}^{-1}} sA_0. \qquad (2.21a')$$

can be accomplished even after the measurement outcome is copied onto the memory device **D**;

$$sA_s D_0 \xRightarrow{\mathfrak{E}_{AD}} sA_s D_s, \qquad (2.22a)$$

so that the pre-measurement state of **S** is recorded elsewhere (here, in **D**). Above, $\mathfrak{E}_{AD}$ plays the same role as $\mathfrak{E}_{SA}$ in Equation (2.21a). That is, the states of **S** and **A** separately, or the combined state **SA** will not reveal any evidence of irreversibility. After the reversal;

$$sA_s D_s \xRightarrow{\mathfrak{E}_{SA}^{-1}} sA_0 D_s, \qquad (2.23a)$$

the state of **SA** is identical to the pre-measurement state, even though the recording device still has the copy of the outcome. Starting with a partly known state of the system does not change this conclusion [23].

2.6.2. Quantum Measurement Can't Be Reversed when the Record of the Outcome is Kept

Consider now a measurement of a quantum system $\mathcal{S}$ by a quantum $\mathcal{A}$:

$$\left(\sum_s \alpha_s |s\rangle\right) |A_0\rangle \xRightarrow{\mathfrak{U}_{\mathcal{SA}}} \sum_s \alpha_s |s\rangle |A_s\rangle. \qquad (2.21b)$$

The evolution operator $\mathfrak{U}_{\mathcal{SA}}$ is unitary (for example, $\mathfrak{U}_{\mathcal{SA}} = \sum_{s,k} |s\rangle\langle s| |A_{k+s}\rangle\langle A_k|$ with orthogonal $\{|s\rangle\}, \{|A_k\rangle\}$ would do the job). Therefore, evolution that leads to a measurement is in principle reversible. Reversal implemented by $\mathfrak{U}_{\mathcal{SA}}^\dagger$ will restore the pre-measurement state of $\mathcal{SA}$:

$$\sum_s \alpha_s |s\rangle |A_s\rangle \xRightarrow{\mathfrak{U}_{\mathcal{SA}}^\dagger} \left(\sum_s \alpha_s |s\rangle\right) |A_0\rangle. \qquad (2.21b')$$

Let us, however, assume that the measurement outcome is copied before the reversal is attempted:

$$\left(\sum_s \alpha_s |s\rangle |A_s\rangle\right) |D_0\rangle \xRightarrow{\mathfrak{U}_{AD}} \sum_s \alpha_s |s\rangle |A_s\rangle |D_s\rangle. \qquad (2.22b)$$

Here $\mathfrak{U}_{AD}$ plays the same role and can have the same structure as $\mathfrak{U}_{\mathcal{SA}}$.

Note that unitary evolutions above implement *repeatable* measurement/copying on the states $\{|s\rangle\}, \{|A_s\rangle\}$ of the system and of the apparatus, respectively. That is, these states of $\mathcal{S}$ and $\mathcal{A}$ remain untouched by the measurement and copying processes. As we have seen, such repeatability implies that the outcome states $\{|s\rangle\}$ as well as the record states $\{|A_s\rangle\}$ are orthogonal.

When the information about the outcome is copied, the pre-measurement state $(\sum_s \alpha_s |s\rangle) |A_0\rangle$ of $\mathcal{SA}$ pair cannot be restored by $\mathfrak{U}_{\mathcal{SA}}^\dagger$. That is:

$$\mathfrak{U}_{\mathcal{SA}}^\dagger \left(\sum_s \alpha_s |s\rangle |A_s\rangle |D_s\rangle\right) = |A_0\rangle \left(\sum_s \alpha_s |s\rangle |D_s\rangle\right). \qquad (2.23b)$$

The apparatus is restored to the pre-measurement $|A_0\rangle$, but the system remains entangled with the memory device. On its own, its state is represented by the mixture:

$$\varrho^{\mathcal{S}} = \sum_s w_{ss} |s\rangle\langle s|,$$

where $w_{ss} = |\alpha_s|^2$. Reversing quantum measurement of a state that corresponds to a superposition of the potential outcomes is possible only providing the memory of the outcome is no longer preserved anywhere else in the Universe. Moreover, that means that the information transfer has to be "undone"—scrambling the record makes it inaccessible, but does not get rid of the evidence of the outcome.

We have now demonstrated the difference between the ability to reverse quantum and classical measurement. Information flows do not matter for classical, Newtonian dynamics. However, when information about a quantum measurement outcome is communicated—copied and retained by any other system—the evolution that led to that measurement cannot be reversed.

Quantum irreversibility can result from the information gain rather than just its loss—rather than just an increase of the (von Neumann) entropy. Recording of the outcome of the measurement resets, in effect, initial conditions within the observer's (branch of) the Universe, resulting in an irreversible, uniquely quantum "wavepacket collapse". Thus, from the point of view of the measurer, information retention about an outcome of a quantum measurement implies irreversibility. Quantum states are epiontic.

2.7. Summary: Events, Irreversibility, and Perceptions

What the observer knows is inseparable from what the observer is: the physical state of the agent's memory represents the information about the Universe. The reliability of this information depends on the stability of its correlation with external observables. In this very immediate sense, decoherence brings about the apparent collapse of the wavepacket: after a decoherence time scale, only the einselected memory states will exist and retain useful correlations [27,36,64,65]. The observer described by some specific einselected state (including a configuration of memory bits) will be able to access ("recall") only that state.

Collapse is a consequence of einselection and of the one-to-one correspondence between the physical state of the observer's memory and of the information encoded in it. Memory is simultaneously a description of the recorded information and part of an identity tag, defining the observer as a physical system. It is as inconsistent to imagine an observer perceiving something other than what is implied by the stable (einselected) records as it is impossible to imagine the same person with a different DNA. Both cases involve information encoded in a state of a system inextricably linked with the physical identity of an individual.

Distinct memory/identity states of the observer (which are also his states of knowledge) cannot be superposed. This censorship is strictly enforced by decoherence and the resulting einselection. Distinct memory states label and inhabit different branches of Everett's many-worlds universe. The persistence of correlations between the records (data in possession of the observers) and the recorded states of macroscopic systems is all that is needed to recover objective classical reality. In this manner, the distinction between ontology and epistemology—between what is and what is known to be—is dissolved. There can be *no information without representation* [66].Quantum states are *epiontic*.

The discreteness underlying "collapse of the wavepacket" has a well-defined origin—it resolves the conflict between the linearity of the unitary quantum evolutions and the nonlinearity associated with the amplification of information in measurements but also in the monitoring by the environment—in decoherence. Any process that involves (even modest) amplification—that leads to copies, qmemes of an "original state" (which, in view of the demand of repeatability, should survive the copying)—demands orthogonality.

Copying (as any other quantum evolution) is unitary, so it will not result in collapse. However, perception of the collapse will arise as a consequence of the irreversibility induced by the information transfer we have just discussed. This purely quantum irreversibility provides a mechanism for collapse of the wavepacket that was not available (and not needed) in the classical setting—a mechanism that is fundamental, and uniquely quantum. The old question about the origins of irreversibility acquires a new quantum aspect especially apparent in the context of quantum measurements: Thus, while in the classical setting measuring of an evolving state of the system need not alter its evolution, in the quantum setting measurement derails evolution and redirects it onto the track consistent with the record made by the observer. One might say that a measurement re-sets the initial condition of the evolving quantum system [23].

Thus, while the irreversible wavepacket collapse was sometimes blamed on the consciousness of the observer (von Neumann, 1932 [4]; London and Bauer, 1939 [67]; Wigner, 1961 [68]), we have identified a purely physical cause of the collapse: Observer retaining information about the outcome precludes the reversal.

In the next section, we derive Born's rule. We build on einselection, but in a way ([7,35,48]) that does not rely on axioms (iv) or (v). In particular, the use of reduced density matrices we allowed temporarily shall be prohibited. We shall be able to use them again only after Born's rule has been derived.

From the point of view of axiom (v) and the rest of this paper the most important conclusion of the present section is that *repeatability requires distinguishability*. In a quantum setting of Hilbert spaces and unitarity of evolutions—postulates (i) and (ii)—this means that *repeatability begets orthogonality*. to assure repeatability—ability to reconfirm what is known—one must focus on mutually exclusive events represented by orthogonal states.

We end this section with a simple purely quantum definition of events in hand: Record made in the measurement resets initial conditions relevant for the subsequent evolution of the branch of the universal state vector tagged by that record. We now take up the question: What is the probability of a particular record—specific new initial condition—given the preexisting superposition of the possible outcome states.

3. Born's Rule from the Symmetries of Entanglement

The first widely accepted definition of probability was codified by Laplace (1820) [69]: When there are N possible distinct outcomes and the observer is ignorant of what will happen, all alternatives appear equally likely. Probability observer should then assign to any one outcome is $1/N$. Laplace justified this *principle of equal likelihood* using *invariance* encapsulated in his 'principle of indifference': Player ignorant of the face value of cards (Figure 2a) will be *indifferent* when they are swapped before he gets the card on top, even when one and only one of the cards is favorable (e.g., a spade he needs to win).

Laplace's invariance under swaps captures *subjective* symmetry: Equal likelihood is a statement about observers 'state of mind' (or, at best, his records), and *not* a measurable property of the real physical state of the system (which is, after all, altered by swaps; see Figure 2b). In the classical setting probabilities defined in this manner are therefore ultimately unphysical. Moreover, indifference, likelihood, and probability are all ill-defined attempts to quantify ignorance. Expressing one undefined concept in terms of another is not a definition.

It is therefore no surprise that equal likelihood is no longer regarded as a sufficient foundation for classical probability, and several other attempts are vying for primacy [70]. Among them, relative frequency approach has perhaps the largest following, although it needs infinite (hence, fictitious) ensembles (von Mises, 1939) [71], and, thus, it is doubtful if it addresses the issue of "subjectivity".[4] Nevertheless, popularity of relative frequency approach made it an obvious starting point in the attempts to derive Born's rule, especially in the relative states context where "branches" of the universal state vector can be counted. However, attempts to date (Everett [10,11]; DeWitt [14,15]; Graham [72]; Geroch [73]) have been found lacking. This is because counting of many world branches does not suffice.

---

[4] After all, there are no infinite ensembles in our Universe, so the ones used to compute relative frequencies are abstract imaginary ensembles defined by *subjective* extrapolation from an assessment based on finite data sets.

"Maverick" branches that have frequencies of events very different from those predicted by Born's rule are also a part of the universal state vector. Relative frequencies alone do not imply that an observer is unlikely to be found on such a branch. To get rid of them one would have to assign to them—without physical justification—vanishing probabilities related to their small amplitudes. This amplitude-probability connection goes beyond the relative frequency approach, in effect requiring—in addition to frequencies—another measure of probability. Papers mentioned above introduce it *ad hoc*. This is consistent with Born's rule, but deriving it on this basis is circular (Stein [74]; Kent [38]; Joos [75]; Weinberg [76]). Indeed, formal attempts based on the "frequency operator" lead to mathematical inconsistencies (Squires [39]).

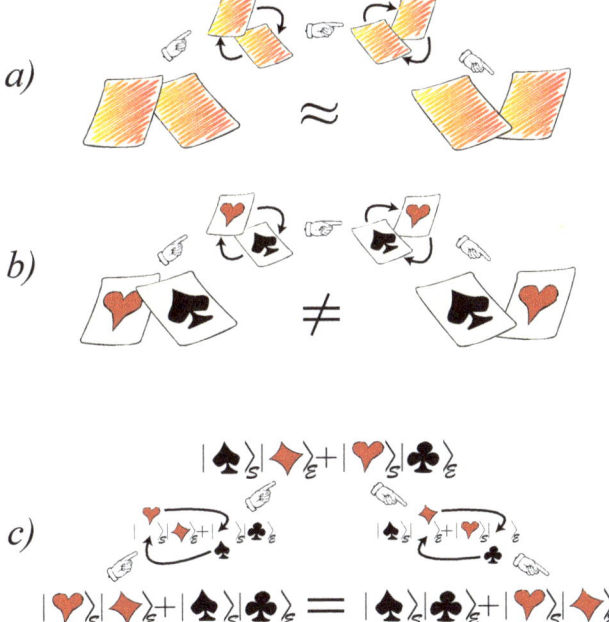

Figure 2. Probabilities and symmetry: (**a**) Laplace (1820) [69] appealed to subjective invariance (associated with 'indifference' based on observer's ignorance of the real physical state) to define probability via *principle of equal likelihood*: When ignorance means observer is indifferent to swapping (e.g., of cards), alternative events should be considered equiprobable. So, for the cards above, subjective probability $p_\spadesuit = \frac{1}{2}$ would be inferred by an observer who does not know their face value, but knows that one (and only one) of the two cards is a spade. (**b**) Nevertheless, the real physical state of the system is independent from what is known about it. Moreover, the order of the cards is altered by the swap—it is not 'indifferent'—illustrating subjective nature of Laplace's approach. Subjectivity of equal likelihood probabilities poses foundational problems for, e.g., statistical physics. This led to an alternative definition employing relative frequency—an objective property (albeit of a fictitious—and, hence, subjective—infinite ensemble). (**c**) Quantum theory allows for an objective definition of probabilities based on *a perfectly known state* of a composite system and on the symmetries of entanglement [7,35,48,77,78]. When two systems ($\mathcal{S}$ and $\mathcal{E}$) are maximally entangled (i.e., Schmidt coefficients differ only by phases, as in the Bell state above), a swap $|\spadesuit\rangle\langle\heartsuit| + |\heartsuit\rangle\langle\spadesuit|$ in $\mathcal{S}$ can be undone by 'counterswap' $|\clubsuit\rangle\langle\diamondsuit| + |\diamondsuit\rangle\langle\clubsuit|$ in $\mathcal{E}$. Certainty about entangled state of the whole in combination with the symmetry between $|\spadesuit\rangle$ and $|\heartsuit\rangle$—certainty that $p_\spadesuit = p_\heartsuit$—means that $p_\spadesuit = p_\heartsuit = \frac{1}{2}$. Equiprobability follows from the objective symmetry of entanglement. This *entanglement*-assisted in*variance* (envariance) also establishes decoherence of Schmidt states, allowing for additivity of probabilities of the effectively classical pointer states. Probabilities derived through envariance quantify indeterminacy of the state of $\mathcal{S}$ alone given the global entangled state of $\mathcal{SE}$.

The problem can be "made to disappear"—coefficients of maverick branches become vanishingly small (along with coefficients of *all* branches)—in the limit of *infinite* and fictitious (and, hence, subjectively assigned) ensembles (Hartle, 1968 [79]; Farhi, Goldstone, and Guttman, 1989 [80]). Such infinite ensembles—one might argue—are always required by the frequentist approach in the classical case, but this is a poor excuse (see Kent, 1990) [38]. As noted above, infinite ensembles are unphysical, subjective, and a weak spot of relative frequencies approach also in a classical setting. Moreover, in quantum mechanics infinite ensembles may pose problems that have to do with the structure of infinite Hilbert spaces (Poulin, 2005 [81]; Caves and Shack, 2005 [82]). It is debatable whether these mathematical problems are fatal, but it is also difficult to disagree with Kent (1990) [38] and Squires (1990) [39] that the need to go to a limit of infinite ensembles to define probability in a finite Universe disqualifies use of relative frequencies in the relative states setting.

The other way of dealing with this issue is to modify physics so that branches with small enough amplitude simply do not count (Geroch, 1984 [73]; Buniy, Hsu, and Zee, 2006 [83]). At least until experimental evidence for the required modifications of quantum theory is found one can regard such attempts primarily as illustration of the seriousness of the problem of the origin of Born's rule.

Kolmogorov's approach—probability as a measure (see, e.g., Gnedenko, 1968 [52])—bypasses the question we aim to address: How to relate probabilities to (quantum) states. It only shows that any sensible assignment (non-negative numbers that for a mutually exclusive and exhaustive set of events sum up to 1) will do. Moreover, Kolmogorov assumes additivity of probabilities while quantum theory insists—via superposition principle—on the additivity of state vectors. These two additivity requirements are at odds, as double slit experiment famously demonstrates.

Gleason's theorem (Gleason, 1957) [84] implements Kolmogorov's axiomatic approach to probability by looking for an additive measure on Hilbert spaces. It leads to Born's rule, but provides no physical insight into why the result should be regarded as probability. Clearly, it has not settled the issue: Rather, it is often cited [38,72,79,80] as a motivation to seek a physically transparent derivation of Born's rule.

We shall now demonstrate how quantum entanglement leads to probabilities based on a symmetry, but—in contrast to subjective equal likelihood based on ignorance—on an *objective* symmetry of *known* quantum states.

3.1. Envariance

A pure entangled state of a system $\mathcal{S}$ and of another system (which we call "an environment $\mathcal{E}$", anticipating connections with decoherence) can be always written as:

$$|\psi_{\mathcal{SE}}\rangle = \sum_{k=1}^{N} a_k |s_k\rangle |\varepsilon_k\rangle . \tag{3.1}$$

Here a_k are complex amplitudes while $\{|s_k\rangle\}$ and $\{|\varepsilon_k\rangle\}$ are orthonormal states in the Hilbert spaces $\mathcal{H}_\mathcal{S}$ and $\mathcal{H}_\mathcal{E}$. This *Schmidt decomposition* of a pure entangled $|\psi_{\mathcal{SE}}\rangle$ is a consequence of a theorem of linear algebra that predates quantum theory.

Schmidt decomposition demonstrates that any pure entangled bipartite state is a superposition of *perfectly correlated outcomes* of judiciously chosen measurements on each subsystem: Detecting $|s_k\rangle$ on $\mathcal{S}$ implies, with certainty, outcome $|\varepsilon_k\rangle$ for $\mathcal{E}$, and *vice versa*.

Even readers unfamiliar with Equation (3.1) have likely relied on its consequences: Schmidt basis $\{|s_k\rangle\}$ appears on the diagonal of the reduced density matrix $\rho_\mathcal{S} = Tr_\mathcal{E} |\psi_{\mathcal{SE}}\rangle \langle \psi_{\mathcal{SE}}|$. (We have used this fact "in reverse" in the preceding section to "purify" mixed states.) But tracing is tantamount to averaging over states of the traced-out systems with weights given by the squares of their amplitudes. Therefore, physical interpretation of the resulting reduced density matrix (which is central in the usual treatments of decoherence) presumes Born's rule we aim to derive (see [5] for discussion of how Born's rule is used to justify physical significance of reduced density matrices). Consequently, we shall avoid employing tools of decoherence or relying on the statistical interpretation of ρ_S in this section as this could introduce circularity. Instead, we derive Born's rule from the symmetries of $|\psi_{S\mathcal{E}}\rangle$.

Symmetries reflect invariance. Rotation of a circle by an arbitrary angle, or of a square by multiples of $\pi/2$ are familiar examples. Entangled quantum states exhibit a new kind of symmetry—*entanglement-assisted invariance* or *envariance*: When a state $|\psi_{S\mathcal{E}}\rangle$ of a pair $S, \mathcal{E}$ can be transformed by $U_S = u_S \otimes \mathbf{1}_\mathcal{E}$ acting solely on S,

$$U_S|\psi_{S\mathcal{E}}\rangle = (u_S \otimes \mathbf{1}_\mathcal{E})|\psi_{S\mathcal{E}}\rangle = |\eta_{S\mathcal{E}}\rangle, \qquad (3.2)$$

but the effect of U_S can be undone by acting solely on $\mathcal{E}$ with an appropriately chosen $U_\mathcal{E} = \mathbf{1}_S \otimes u_\mathcal{E}$:

$$U_\mathcal{E}|\eta_{S\mathcal{E}}\rangle = (\mathbf{1}_S \otimes u_\mathcal{E})|\eta_{S\mathcal{E}}\rangle = |\psi_{S\mathcal{E}}\rangle, \qquad (3.3)$$

then $|\psi_{S\mathcal{E}}\rangle$ is called *envariant* under U_S [7,35].

Envariance can be seen on any entangled $|\psi_{S\mathcal{E}}\rangle$. Any unitary operation diagonal in Schmidt basis $\{|s_k\rangle\}$:

$$u_S = \sum_{k=1}^{N} \exp(i\phi_k)|s_k\rangle\langle s_k|, \qquad (3.4a)$$

is envariant: It can be undone by a *countertransformation*

$$u_\mathcal{E} = \sum_{k=1}^{N} \exp(-i\phi_k)|\varepsilon_k\rangle\langle\varepsilon_k|, \qquad (3.4b)$$

acting solely on the environment.

In contrast to familiar symmetries (when a transformation has no effect on a state of an object) envariance is an *assisted symmetry*: The global state of $S\mathcal{E}$ is transformed by U_S, but it can be restored by acting on $\mathcal{E}$, physically distinct (e.g., spatially separated) from S. When the global state of $S\mathcal{E}$ is envariant under some U_S, the local state of S alone must be obviously invariant under it. There are analogies between envariance and gauge symmetries, with $\mathcal{E}$ assuming the role of a gauge field.

Entangled states might seem an unusual starting point for the study of probabilities. After all, the textbook statement of Born's rule deals with pure states of individual systems. Nevertheless, already in Schrödinger's famous "cat" paper [20] the discussion of entangled quantum states leads to the realization that "Best possible knowledge of the whole does not necessarily lead to the same for its parts...", as well as "The whole is in a definite state, the parts taken individually are not". Our aim is to recast such essentially negative qualitative statements (which can be read as a realization of the limitations imposed by the tensor structure of quantum states on their predictive powers) into a derivation of Born's rule, the quantitative tool used for predictions.

Entanglement is also the essence of decoherence responsible for the emergence of "the classical" in a quantum Universe. It is therefore natural to investigate symmetries of entangled quantum states, and explore their implication for how much can be known about parts when the whole is entangled. In addition, as we shall see below, envariance allows one to reassess the role of the environment and sheds new light on the origin of decoherence.

3.2. Decoherence as a Result of Envariance

Envariance of entangled states leads to our first conclusion: Phases of Schmidt coefficients are envariant under local (Schmidt) unitaries, Equations (3.4). Therefore, when a composite system is in an entangled state $|\psi_{S\mathcal{E}}\rangle$, the state of S (or $\mathcal{E}$) alone is *invariant under the change of phases* of a_k. In other words, the *state* of S (understood as a set of all measurable properties of S alone) cannot depend on phases of Schmidt coefficients: It can depend only on their absolute values and on the outcome states—on the set of pairs $\{|a_k|, |s_k\rangle\}$. In particular (as we demonstrate below) probabilities cannot depend on these phases.

We have just seen that the loss of phase coherence between Schmidt states—decoherence is a consequence of envariance: Decoherence is, after all, a selective loss of relevance of phases for the state of $\mathcal{S}$. We stumbled here on its essence while exploring an unfamiliar territory, without the usual backdrop of dynamics and without employing trace and reduced density matrices.

However, decoherence viewed from the vantage point of envariance may look unfamiliar. What other landmarks of decoherence can we find without using trace and reduced density matrices (which rely on Born's rule, something we do not yet have)? The answer is—all the essential ones [42,48,49]. We have already seen in Section 2 that pointer states (states that retain correlations, are predictable, and, hence, good candidates for classical domain) are singled out directly by repeatability—by the nature of information transfers. So, we already have a set of preferred pointer states and we have seen that when they are aligned with Schmidt basis, phases between them lose relevance for $\mathcal{S}$ alone. Indeed, models of decoherence ([7,24,25,27–29,32,33]) predict that after a brief (decoherence time) interlude Schmidt basis will typically settle down to coincide with pointer states determined through other criteria (such as predictability in spite of the coupling to the environment). There are exceptions that we have already mentioned in the previous section. They tend to arise when decoherence is incomplete, and/or when the reduced density matrix (that is diagonalized by Schmidt states) is so close to maximally mixed (i.e., some of its eigenvalues are nearly degenerate) that any complete set of states (including pointer states selected for their predictability) can express it while leaving it in a nearly diagonal form (see, e.g., [85]).

This encounter with decoherence on the way to Born's rule is good omen: Quantum phases must be rendered irrelevant for the additivity of probabilities to replace additivity of complex amplitudes. Of course, one could postulate additivity of probabilities by fiat. This was done by Gleason (1957) [84], but such an assumption is at odds with the overarching additivity principle of quantum mechanics—with the principle of superposition (as is illustrated by the double slit experiment). So, if we set out to understand emergence of the classical domain from the quantum substrate defined by axioms (o)–(iii), additivity of probabilities should be derived (as it is done in Laplace's approach, see Gnedenko, 1968 [52]) rather than imposed as an axiom (as it happens in Kolmogorov's measure—theoretic approach, and in Gleason's theorem).

Assuming decoherence to get $p_k = |\psi_k|^2$ (Zurek, 1998 [36]; Deutsch, 1999 [86]; Wallace, 2003 [87]) would mean, at best, starting half way, and raises concerns of circularity [7,32, 35,48,88–90] as the physical significance of the reduced density matrix—standard tool in the usual treatment of decoherence—is justified using Born's rule. By contrast, envariant derivation, if successful, can be fundamental, independent of the usual tools of decoherence: It can justify, starting from the basic quantum postulates, the use of the trace and physical significance of reduced density matrices in the study of the quantum-classical transition.

As perceptive analysis by Drezet (2021) [91] shows, envariance has been recently adopted (Wallace, 2010; 2012) [19,92] even in the (modified) decision theory approach that initially dealt with states of a single system, and, therefore, encountered difficulties with circularity of the argument by invoking decoherence before establishing Born's rule ([35,48, 89,90]). We noted this problem already and will discuss it briefly below, in Section 3.7.

3.3. Swaps, Counterswaps, and Equiprobability

Envariance of pure states is purely quantum: Classical state of a composite classical system is given by a Cartesian (rather than tensor) product of its constituents. Therefore, to completely know a state of a composite classical system one must know a state of each subsystem. It follows that when one part of a classical composite system is affected by a transformation—a classical analogue of a swap $U_\mathcal{S}$—state of the whole cannot be restored by acting on some other part. Hence, *pure classical states are never envariant*.

However, a mixed state (of, say, two coins) can mimic envariance: When we only know that a dime and a nickel are 'same side up', we can 'undo' the effect of the flip of a dime by flipping a nickel. This classical analogue depends on partial ignorance: To emulate envariance, we cannot know individual states of the two coins—just the fact that they are the same side up—just their correlation.

In quantum physics, tensor structure of states for composite systems means that 'pure correlation' is possible. We shall now prove that a maximally entangled "even" state with equal absolute values of Schmidt coefficients:

$$|\bar{\psi}_{\mathcal{SE}}\rangle \propto \sum_{k=1}^{N} e^{-i\phi_k}|s_k\rangle|\varepsilon_k\rangle \tag{3.5}$$

implies equal probabilities for any orthonormal set of states $|s_k\rangle$ of $\mathcal{S}$ and any corresponding set of $|\varepsilon_k\rangle$ of $\mathcal{E}$.

Such an *even* state is envariant under a *swap* operation

$$u_{\mathcal{S}}(k \rightleftharpoons l) = |s_k\rangle\langle s_l| + |s_l\rangle\langle s_k|. \tag{3.6a}$$

A swap is a quantum version of the operation that exchanges two cards (Figure 2). It is a unitary that permutes states $|s_k\rangle$ and $|s_l\rangle$ of the system. A swap $|\text{Heads}\rangle\langle\text{Tails}| + |\text{Tails}\rangle\langle\text{Heads}|$ would flip a coin.

A swap on $\mathcal{S}$ is envariant when $|a_k| = |a_l|$ because $u_{\mathcal{S}}(k \rightleftharpoons l)$ can be undone by a *counterswap* on $\mathcal{E}$;

$$u_{\mathcal{E}}(k \rightleftharpoons l) = e^{i(\phi_k - \phi_l)}|\varepsilon_l\rangle\langle\varepsilon_k| + e^{-i(\phi_k - \phi_l)}|\varepsilon_k\rangle\langle\varepsilon_l|, \tag{3.6b}$$

as is seen in Figure 2c.

We want to *prove* that probabilities of envariantly swappable outcome states must be equal. But let us proceed with caution: Invariance under a swap is not enough—probability could depend on some other 'intrinsic' property of the state. For instance, in a superposition $|g\rangle + |e\rangle$, the ground and excited state can be invariantly swapped, as $|g\rangle + |e\rangle = |e\rangle + |g\rangle$, but *energies* of $|g\rangle$ and $|e\rangle$ are different. Why should probability—like energy—not depend on some intrinsic property[5] of the state?

Envariance can be used to prove that this cannot happen—that probabilities of envariantly swappable states are indeed equal. To this end we first define what is meant by "the state" and "the system" more carefully. Quantum role of these concepts is elucidated by three "Facts"—three definitions that recognize what is known about systems and their (mixed) states, but phrase it in a way that does not appeal to the Born-rule dependent tools and concepts (e.g., reduced density matrices):

Fact 1: Unitary transformations must act on a system to alter its state. That is, when an operator does not act on the Hilbert space $\mathcal{H}_{\mathcal{S}}$ of $\mathcal{S}$, (e.g., when it has a form $... \otimes \mathbf{1}_{\mathcal{S}} \otimes ...$) the state of $\mathcal{S}$ does not change.

Fact 2: The state of the system $\mathcal{S}$ is all that is needed (and all that is available) to predict measurement results, including probabilities of outcomes.

Fact 3: The state of a larger composite system that includes $\mathcal{S}$ as a subsystem is all that is needed (and all that is available) to determine the state of $\mathcal{S}$.

Note that the states defined this way need not be pure. In addition, note that Facts—while 'naturally quantum'—are not in conflict with the role of states in classical physics.

Facts are a consequence of quantum theory. They are not, in any sense, additional assumptions. Rather, they clarify operational meanings of concepts (such as "a state") that will play key role in the derivation of Born's rule: Facts are the attributes that any sensible notion of a "state" (and, in particular, a "mixed state") should possess. They also help

---

[5] In a sense, hidden variable theories (such as the Bohm—de Broglie approach) use a strategy of "tagging" an element of the total superposition in this manner. Therefore, hidden variable theories can violate assumptions of our derivation, as they allow physical properties of a state that determine measurement outcomes to depend on more than just the state vector.

distinguish purely quantum view based on the core quantum postulates from, e.g., hidden variable theory (where, for example, Fact 2 would not hold).

We can now *prove*:

Theorem 2. *When Schmidt coefficients satisfy* $|a_k| = |a_l|$ *in an even state* $|\bar{\psi}_{S\mathcal{E}}\rangle \propto \sum_{k=1}^{N} e^{-i\phi_k}|s_k\rangle|\varepsilon_k\rangle$ *Equation (3.5), the local state of* S *is invariant under a swap* $u_S(k \rightleftharpoons l) = |s_k\rangle\langle s_l| + |s_l\rangle\langle s_k|$.

Proof. Swap changes partners in the Schmidt decomposition (and, therefore, alters the global state). However, when the coefficients of the swapped outcomes differ only by a phase, a swap can be undone (without acting on S) by a corresponding counterswap, Equation (3.6b), in $\mathcal{E}$. As the global state of $S\mathcal{E}$ is restored, it follows (from Fact 3) that the local state of S must have been also restored. However, (by Fact 1) the state of S could not have been affected by a counterswap acting only on $\mathcal{E}$. So, (by Fact 2) the state of S must be left intact by a swap, in S, of Schmidt states that have the same absolute values of Schmidt coefficients. □

We conclude that envariance of a pure global state of $S\mathcal{E}$ under swaps implies invariance of the corresponding local state of S. We could now follow Laplace, appeal to subjective indifference, apply equal likelihood, and "declare victory"—claim that subjective probabilities must be equal. However, as we have just seen with the example of the superposition $|g\rangle + |e\rangle$ of the eigenstates of energy, invariance of a local state under a swap implies only that the property associated with the swapped states (i.e., energies or probabilities) gets swapped when the states are swapped. Without an appeal to subjective ignorance this does not yet establish that the properties of interest (probabilities or energies) must be equal.

Entanglement (via envariance) allows us to get rid of such subjectivity altogether. The simplest way to prove the desired equality of probabilities is based on perfect correlation between the Schmidt states of S and $\mathcal{E}$. These relative Schmidt states in, e.g., Equations (3.1) or (3.5) are orthonormal, and $|s_k\rangle$ are correlated with $|\varepsilon_k\rangle$ one-to-one. This implies the same probability for each member of every such Schmidt pair. Moreover (and for the very same reason—perfect correlation) after a swap on S probabilities of swapped states must be the same as probabilities of their two new partners in $\mathcal{E}$. That is, after a swap $u_S(k \rightleftharpoons l) = |s_k\rangle\langle s_l| + |s_l\rangle\langle s_k|$ probability of $|s_k\rangle$ must be the same as probability $|\varepsilon_l\rangle$, and probability of $|s_l\rangle$ must be the same as that of $|\varepsilon_k\rangle$.

We now focus on an even state, Equation (3.5). It is envariant under all local unitaries (and, hence, under all swaps). Thus (by Fact 1) the state of $\mathcal{E}$ (and, by Fact 2, probabilities it implies) are not affected by swaps in S. So, *swapping Schmidt states of S exchanges their probabilities, and when the state is even it also keeps them the same!* This can be true only when the probabilities of envariantly swappable states are equal.

We can now state our conclusion:

Corollary 1. *When all N coefficients in the Schmidt decomposition have the same absolute values (as in the even states of Equation (3.5)), probability of each Schmidt state must be the same, and, therefore, by normalization, it is* $p_k = 1/N$.

Readers may regard this as obvious, but (as recognized by Barnum (2003) [93], Schlosshauer and Fine (2005) [94], Drezet (2021) [91] and others) this is the key to Born's rule. Equation (3.5) is envariant under swaps. This symmetry allowed us to extract physical consequences from quantum mathematics with a very minimal set of ingredients at hand. In the language of the Kolmogorov measure-theoretic axioms we have now established that—when the entangled state is even, Equation (3.5)—positive numbers (the 'measures' of probability for events corresponding to individual Schmidt states) must be equal.

Still, this may seem like a lot of work to arrive at something seemingly obvious: The case of unequal coefficients is our next goal. However—as we will see—it can be reduced to the equal coefficient case we have just settled. The symmetry of entanglement inherent in the equal coefficients case provides the crucial link between the quantum state vectors and the experimental consequences. Simple algebra along with the special case of probability—certainty—will lead us directly to Born's rule[6].

We emphasize that in contrast to many other approaches to both classical and quantum probability, our envariant derivation is based not on a subjective assessment of an observer, but on an objective, experimentally verifiable symmetry of entangled states. Observer is forced to conclude that probabilities of local outcomes are equal not because of subjective ignorance, but because of certainty about something else: Certainty about the symmetries of the global state of the composite system implies—via symmetries of entanglement encapsulated in envariance—that local Schmidt states are equiprobable[7].

Envariant probability is also a probability of an individual event—there is no need for an ensemble of many events, so that relative frequency of "favorable" events can be used to define probability. Rather, we are decomposing the future possibilities into equiprobable alternatives, and deducing probability from the ratio of the number of favorable alternatives to the total. Above, just one favorable out of N equiprobable alternatives leads to $p_k = 1/N$ for even states. We now extend this approach to general states.

3.4. Born's Rule from Envariance

To illustrate general "finegraining" strategy of reducing cases with unequal coefficients to the previously described equal coefficient case (see (Zurek, 1998) [36] for its density matrix version) we start with an example involving a two-dimensional Hilbert space of the system spanned by states $\{|0\rangle, |2\rangle\}$ and (at least) a three-dimensional Hilbert space of the environment:

$$|\psi_{S\mathcal{E}}\rangle = \sqrt{\frac{2}{3}}|0\rangle_S|+\rangle_\mathcal{E} + \sqrt{\frac{1}{3}}|2\rangle_S|2\rangle_\mathcal{E}. \qquad (3.7a)$$

System is represented by the leftmost kets, and $|+\rangle_\mathcal{E} = (|0\rangle_\mathcal{E} + |1\rangle_\mathcal{E})/\sqrt{2}$ exists in (at least a two-dimensional) subspace of $\mathcal{E}$ that is orthogonal to the state $|2\rangle_\mathcal{E}$, so that $\langle 0|1\rangle_\mathcal{E} = \langle 0|2\rangle_\mathcal{E} = \langle 1|2\rangle_\mathcal{E} = \langle +|2\rangle_\mathcal{E} = 0$. We already know we can ignore phases in view of their irrelevance for states of subsystems, so we omitted them above. From now on we shall also drop the overall normalization, as the probabilities will only depend on the relative values of the coefficients associated with the alternatives.

To reduce this case to an even state we extend "uneven" $|\psi_{S\mathcal{E}}\rangle$ above to a state $|\bar{\Psi}_{S\mathcal{E}\mathcal{C}}\rangle$ with equal coefficients by letting $\mathcal{E}$ act on an ancilla $\mathcal{C}$. (By Fact 1, since $\mathcal{S}$ is not acted upon, probabilities we shall infer for it cannot change.) Transformation into an even state can be accomplished by a generalization of controlled-not acting between $\mathcal{E}$ (control) and $\mathcal{C}$ (target), so that (in an obvious notation):

$$|k\rangle|0'\rangle \Rightarrow |k\rangle|k'\rangle,$$

---

[6] There is an amusing corollary to the above corollary: One can now *prove* that states appearing in the Schmidt decomposition with vanishing coefficients (that is, states with $a_k = 0 = a$) have vanishing probability, $p_k = p = 0$: Consider a part of the sum representing Schmidt decomposition given by $a(|0\rangle|0\rangle + |1\rangle|1\rangle + |2\rangle|2\rangle)$, where the first ket corresponds to $\mathcal{S}$ and the second to $\mathcal{E}$. Let us now carry out a c-not on the first two terms: $|0\rangle|0\rangle + |1\rangle|1\rangle \Rightarrow |0\rangle|0\rangle + |1\rangle|0\rangle = (|0\rangle + |1\rangle)|0\rangle = \sqrt{2}|+\rangle|0\rangle$. Note that $|+\rangle$ is normalized, and the initial sequence is transformed as $a(|0\rangle|0\rangle + |1\rangle|1\rangle + |2\rangle|2\rangle) \Rightarrow \sqrt{2}a|+\rangle|0\rangle + a|2\rangle|2\rangle$ (that is, it has one less term). However, as $a = 0$, $\sqrt{2}a = a = 0$. Therefore, $a(|0\rangle|0\rangle + |1\rangle|1\rangle + |2\rangle|2\rangle) = a(|+\rangle|0\rangle + |2\rangle|2\rangle)$. The operations we have employed could not have changed the probability assigned to this part of the Schmidt decomposition. Yet, there are now only two rather than three terms with equal coefficients (hence, equal probability) in that sum. More generally, there will be $n - 1$ rather than n terms when analogous operations involve a sum with n vanishing coefficients. So the probability p of any state with zero amplitude would have to satisfy $np = (n - 1)p$ (i.e., $3p = 2p$ in our example). This equality holds only when $p = 0$. (Note that this argument would obviously fail—as it should—when $a \neq 0$ in $a|0\rangle|0\rangle + a|1\rangle|1\rangle + a|2\rangle|2\rangle$.)

[7] We leave it to the reader to find out why this strategy proves the equality of probabilities, but fails to establish equality of energies in an "even" entangled state such as $|e\rangle|e\rangle + |g\rangle|g\rangle$.

leading to:

$$(\sqrt{2}|0\rangle|+\rangle + |2\rangle|2\rangle)|0'\rangle \Longrightarrow \sqrt{2}|0\rangle\frac{|0\rangle|0'\rangle + |1\rangle|1'\rangle}{\sqrt{2}} + |2\rangle|2\rangle|2'\rangle = |\Psi_{SC\mathcal{E}}\rangle. \quad (3.8a)$$

Above, and from now on we skip subscripts: State of S will be always listed first, and state of C will be primed. The cancellation of $\sqrt{2}$ makes it obvious that this is an equal coefficient ("even") state:

$$|\Psi_{SC\mathcal{E}}\rangle \propto |0,0'\rangle|0\rangle + |0,1'\rangle|1\rangle + |2,2'\rangle|2\rangle. \quad (3.9a)$$

Note that we have now combined state of S and C and (in the next step) we shall swap states of SC together.

Clearly, for joint states $|0,0'\rangle, |0,1'\rangle$, and $|2,2'\rangle$ of SC this is a Schmidt decomposition of $(SC)\mathcal{E}$. The three orthonormal product states have coefficients with the same absolute value. Therefore, they can be envariantly swapped. It follows that the probabilities of these Schmidt states—$|0\rangle|0'\rangle, |0\rangle|1'\rangle$, and $|2\rangle|2'\rangle$—are all equal, so by normalization they are $\frac{1}{3}$. Moreover, and for the same envariant reason, the probability of state $|2\rangle$ of the system is $\frac{1}{3}$. As $|0\rangle$ and $|2\rangle$ are the only two outcome states for S; it also follows that probability of $|0\rangle$ must be $\frac{2}{3}$. Consequently:

$$p_0 = \frac{2}{3}; \quad p_2 = \frac{1}{3}. \quad (3.10a)$$

This is Born's rule! Probabilities are proportional to the squares of the amplitudes from $|\psi_{S\mathcal{E}}\rangle$, Equation (3.7a).

Note that above we have avoided assuming additivity of probabilities: $p_0 = \frac{2}{3}$ not because it is a sum of two fine-grained alternatives each with probability $\frac{1}{3}$, but rather because there are only two (mutually exclusive and exhaustive) alternatives for S; $|0\rangle$ and $|2\rangle$, and it was separately established that $p_2 = \frac{1}{3}$. So, by normalization, $p_0 = 1 - \frac{1}{3}$.

Bypassing appeal to additivity of probabilities is essential in interpreting theory with another principle of additivity—quantum superposition principle—which trumps additivity of probabilities or at least classical intuitive ideas about what should be additive (e.g., in the double slit experiment). Here, this conflict is averted: Probabilities of Schmidt states can be added because of the loss of phase coherence that follows directly from envariance, as we have established earlier, and as was discussed in (Zurek, 2005) [48]. We return to this point in the additivity Lemma below.

Consider now a more general case of arbitrary coefficients. For simplicity we focus on entangled state with just two non-zero Schmidt coefficients:

$$|\psi_{S\mathcal{E}}\rangle = \alpha|0\rangle|\varepsilon_0\rangle + \beta|1\rangle|\varepsilon_1\rangle, \quad (3.7b)$$

and assume $\alpha = \sqrt{\frac{\mu}{\mu+\nu}}$; $\beta = \sqrt{\frac{\nu}{\mu+\nu}}$, with integer μ, ν.

As before, the strategy is to convert a general entangled state into an even state, and then to apply envariance under swaps. To implement it, we assume $\mathcal{E}$ has sufficient dimensionality[8] to allow decomposition of $|\varepsilon_0\rangle$ and $|\varepsilon_1\rangle$ in a different orthonormal basis $\{|e_k\rangle\}$:

$$|\varepsilon_0\rangle = \sum_{k=1}^{\mu}|e_k\rangle/\sqrt{\mu}; \quad |\varepsilon_1\rangle = \sum_{k=\mu+1}^{\mu+\nu}|e_k\rangle/\sqrt{\nu}.$$

---

[8] This assumption is not essential. One could instead use two ancillas C' and C'' with sufficient dimensionality and a c-not like gate to obtain a fine-grained state $\propto \sum_{k=1}^{\mu}|0,c'_k\rangle|e_k,c''_k\rangle + \sum_{k=\mu+1}^{\mu+\nu}|1,c'_k\rangle|e_k,c''_k\rangle$ that allows for envariant swaps and leads to identical conclusions, but with a more cumbersome notation.

Envariance we need is associated with counterswaps of $\mathcal{E}$ that undo swaps of the joint state of the composite system $\mathcal{SC}$. To exhibit it, we let ancilla $\mathcal{C}$ interact with $\mathcal{E}$ as before, e.g., by employing $\mathcal{E}$ as a control to carry out a 'controlled-not - like' operation;

$$|e_k\rangle|c_0\rangle \rightarrow |e_k\rangle|c_k\rangle,$$

where $|c_0\rangle$ is the initial state of $\mathcal{C}$ in some suitable orthonormal basis $\{|c_k\rangle\}$. Thus;

$$|\Psi_{\mathcal{SCE}}\rangle \propto \sqrt{\mu}|0\rangle \sum_{k=1}^{\mu} \frac{|c_k\rangle|e_k\rangle}{\sqrt{\mu}} + \sqrt{\nu}|1\rangle \sum_{k=\mu+1}^{\mu+\nu} \frac{|c_k\rangle|e_k\rangle}{\sqrt{\nu}}. \quad (3.8b)$$

Such $\mathcal{CE}$ interaction can happen far from $\mathcal{S}$, so by Fact 1 it cannot influence probabilities in $\mathcal{S}$. $|\Psi_{\mathcal{SCE}}\rangle$ is envariant under swaps of states $|s, c_k\rangle$ (where s stands for 0 or 1, as needed) in the composite system $\mathcal{SC}$. This is even more apparent after the obvious cancellations;

$$|\Psi_{\mathcal{SCE}}\rangle \propto \sum_{k=1}^{\mu} |0, c_k\rangle|e_k\rangle + \sum_{k=\mu+1}^{\mu+\nu} |1, c_k\rangle|e_k\rangle. \quad (3.9b)$$

Hence, $p_{0,k} = p_{1,k} = \frac{1}{\mu+\nu}$. Therefore, it follows that the probabilities of $|0\rangle$ and $|1\rangle$ are:

$$p_0 = \frac{\mu}{\mu+\nu} = |\alpha|^2; \quad p_1 = \frac{\nu}{\mu+\nu} = |\beta|^2. \quad (3.10b)$$

Born's rule thus emerges here from the most quantum aspects of the theory—entanglement and envariance.

In contrast with other approaches, probabilities in our envariant derivation are a consequence of complementarity, of the incompatibility of the purity of the entangled state of the whole with the purity of the states of parts. Born's rule appears in a completely quantum setting, without any *a priori* imposition of symptoms of classicality that would violate the spirit of quantum theory.

Envariant derivation (in contrast to Gleason's successful but unphysical proof and in contrast to unsuccessful "frequentist" attempts in the Everettian "Many-Worlds" setting) does not require additivity as an assumption: The strategy that bypasses appeal to additivity used in the simple case of Equation (3.10a) can be generalized (for details see below and Zurek, 2005 [48]). The assumption of additivity is not needed. In a quantum setting this is an important advance. Additivity of probabilities is a consequence of the envariance of phases of Schmidt coefficients that leads to decoherence. The case of more than two outcomes is straightforward, as is extension by continuity to incommensurate probabilities.

3.4.1. Additivity of Probabilities from Envariance

Kolmogorov's axiomatic formulation of the probability theory (see Gnedenko, 1968 [52]) as well as the proof of Born's rule due to Gleason (1957) [84] *assume* additivity of probabilities. This assumption is motivated by the assertion that probability is a *measure*. On the other hand, in the standard approach of Laplace (1820) [69] additivity can be established starting from the definition of probability of a composite event as a fraction of the favorable equiprobable events to the total (see discussion in Gnedenko, 1968 [52]). The key ingredient that makes this derivation of additivity possible is equiprobability

We have already established—using *objective* symmetries (in contrast to Laplace, who had to rely on the subjective 'state of mind')—that envariantly swappable events are equiprobable. We can now follow Laplace's strategy and use equiprobability along with decoherence already justified directly by envariance (see Section 3.2) to prove additivity. This is important, as additivity of probabilities should not be automatically and uncritically adopted in the quantum setting. After all, quantum theory is based on the principle of superposition, our core postulate (i): The principle of superposition asserts supremacy of the additivity of state vectors which is *prima facie* incompatible with additivity of probabilities, as is illustrated by the double slit experiment.

Phases between the record (pointer) states (or, more generally, between any set of Schmidt states) do not influence the outcome of any local measurement that can be carried out on the apparatus (or on decohered records in the memory of the observer). This independence of the local state from the global phases in the Schmidt decomposition invalidates the principle of superposition when the system of interest (or the pointer of the apparatus, or the memory of the observer) are 'open', entangled with their environments. Therefore, we can now *establish* (rather than postulate) the probability of a composite event:

Lemma 1. *Probability of a composite (coarse-grained) event consisting of a subset*

$$\kappa \equiv \{k_1 \vee k_2 \vee \cdots \vee k_{n_\kappa}\} \qquad (3.11)$$

of n_κ of the total N envariantly swappable mutually exclusive exhaustive fine-grained events associated with records corresponding to pointer states of the global state;

$$|\Psi_{\mathcal{SAE}}\rangle = \sum_{k=1}^{N} e^{i\phi_k}|s_k\rangle|A_k\rangle|\varepsilon_k\rangle = \sum_{k=1}^{N} e^{i\phi_k}|s_k, A_k(s_k)\rangle|\varepsilon_k\rangle,$$

is given by:

$$p(\kappa) = \frac{n_\kappa}{N}. \qquad (3.12)$$

To prove additivity of probabilities using envariance we consider the state:

$$|Y_{\bar{\mathcal{A}}\mathcal{A}\mathcal{S}\mathcal{E}}\rangle \propto \sum_{\kappa} |A_\kappa^\in\rangle \sum_{k\in\kappa} |A_k\rangle|s_k\rangle|\varepsilon_k\rangle \qquad (3.13)$$

representing both the fine-grained and coarse-grained records. The coarse-graining is implemented by the apparatus $\bar{\mathcal{A}}$ with pointer states $|A_\kappa^\in\rangle$.

We first note that the form of $|Y_{\bar{\mathcal{A}}\mathcal{A}\mathcal{S}\mathcal{E}}\rangle$ justifies assigning zero probability to $|s_j\rangle$'s that do not appear—i.e., appear with zero amplitude—in the initial state of the system. Quite simply, there is no state of the observer with a record of such zero-amplitude Schmidt states of the system in $|Y_{\bar{\mathcal{A}}\mathcal{A}\mathcal{S}\mathcal{E}}\rangle$, Equation (3.13).

To establish this Lemma we exploit basic implications of envariance: When there are total N envariantly swappable outcome states, and they exhaust all of the possible outcomes, each should be assigned probability of $1/N$. We also note that when coarse-grained events are defined via $|A_\kappa^\in\rangle$ as unions of fine-grained events, the conditional probability of the coarse grained event is:

$$p(\kappa|k) = 1 \quad k \in \kappa, \qquad (3.14a)$$

$$p(\kappa|k) = 0 \quad k \notin \kappa. \qquad (3.14b)$$

To demonstrate the above Lemma we need one more property—the fact that when an event $\mathcal{U}$ that is certain ($p(\mathcal{U}) = 1$) can be decomposed into two mutually exclusive events,

$$\mathcal{U} = \kappa \vee \kappa^\perp, \qquad (3.15)$$

their probabilities must add to unity:

$$p(\mathcal{U}) = p(\kappa \vee \kappa^\perp) = p(\kappa) + p(\kappa^\perp) = 1. \qquad (3.16)$$

This assumption introduces (in a very limited setting) additivity. It is equivalent to the statement that "something will certainly happen". Note that this very limited version of additivity holds in quantum setting (i.e., it is not challenged by the double slit experiment, and, more generally, by the superposition principle, providing that the events are indeed mutually exclusive).

Proof. Proof of the Lemma starts with the observation that probability of any composite event κ of the form of Equation (3.11) can be obtained recursively—by subtracting, one by one, probabilities of all the fine-grained events that belong to $\kappa^\perp$, and exploiting the consequences of the implication, Equation (3.14)–(3.16). Thus, as a first step, we have:

$$p(\{k_1 \vee k_2 \vee \cdots \vee k_{n_\kappa} \vee \cdots \vee k_{N-1}\}) + p(k_N) = 1.$$

Moreover, for all fine-grained events $p(k) = \frac{1}{N}$. Hence;

$$p(\{k_1 \vee k_2 \vee \cdots \vee k_{n_\kappa} \vee \cdots \vee k_{N-1}\}) = 1 - \frac{1}{N}.$$

Furthermore (and this is the next recursive step) the conditional probability of the event $\{k_1 \vee k_2 \vee \cdots \vee k_{n_\kappa} \vee \cdots \vee k_{N-2}\}$ given the event $\{k_1 \vee k_2 \vee \cdots \vee k_{n_\kappa} \vee \cdots \vee k_{N-1}\}$ is:

$$p(\{k_1 \vee k_2 \vee \cdots \vee k_{N-2}\}|\{k_1 \vee k_2 \vee \cdots \vee k_{N-1}\}) = 1 - \frac{1}{N-1},$$

and so the unconditional probability must be:

$$p(\{k_1 \vee k_2 \vee \cdots \vee k_{n_\kappa} \vee \cdots \vee k_{N-2}\}|\mathcal{U}) = (1 - \frac{1}{N})(1 - \frac{1}{N-1}).$$

Repeating this procedure untill only the desired composite event κ remains we have:

$$p(\{k_1 \vee k_2 \vee \cdots \vee k_{n_\kappa}\}) = (1 - \frac{1}{N}) \ldots (1 - \frac{1}{N - (N - n_\kappa - 1)}). \tag{3.17}$$

After some elementary algebra we finally recover:

$$p(\{k_1 \vee k_2 \vee \cdots \vee k_{n_\kappa}\}) = \frac{n_\kappa}{N}.$$

Hence, Equation (3.12) holds. □

Corollary 2. *Probability of mutually compatible exclusive events $\kappa, \lambda, \mu, \ldots$ that can be decomposed into unions of envariantly swappable elementary events are additive:*

$$p(\kappa \vee \lambda \vee \mu \vee \ldots) = p(\kappa) + p(\lambda) + p(\mu) + \ldots \tag{3.18}$$

Note that in establishing additivity Lemma we have only considered situations that can be reduced to certainty or impossibility (that is, cases corresponding to the absolute value of the scalar product equal to 1 and 0). This is in keeping with our strategy of deriving probability and, in particular, of arriving at Born's rule from certainty and symmetries.

3.4.2. Algebra of Records as the Boolean Algebra of Events

Algebra of events (see, e.g., Gnedenko, 1968 [52]) can be then defined by simply identifying events with records inscribed in the coarse-grained pointer states such as $|A_\kappa^\in\rangle$ in Equation (3.13) of the apparatus $\bar{\mathcal{A}}$. Logical product of any two coarse-grained events κ, λ corresponds to the product of the projection operators that act on the memory Hilbert space—on the corresponding records:

$$\kappa \wedge \lambda \stackrel{\text{def}}{=} P_\kappa P_\lambda = P_{\kappa \wedge \lambda}. \tag{3.19a}$$

Logical sum is represented by a projection onto the union of the Hilbert subspaces:

$$\kappa \vee \lambda \stackrel{\text{def}}{=} P_\kappa + P_\lambda - P_\kappa P_\lambda = P_{\kappa \vee \lambda}. \tag{3.19b}$$

Last not least, a complement of the event κ corresponds to:

$$\kappa^\perp \stackrel{\text{def}}{=} P_\mathcal{U} - P_\kappa = P_{\kappa^\perp} . \qquad (3.19c)$$

With this set of definitions it is now fairly straightforward to show:

Theorem 3. *Events corresponding to the records stored in the memory pointer states define a Boolean algebra.*

Proof. To show that the algebra of records is Boolean we need to show that coarse—grained events satisfy any of the (several equivalent, see, e.g., Sikorski, 1964 [95]) sets of axioms that define Boolean algebras:

(a) Commutativity:
$$P_{\kappa \vee \lambda} = P_{\lambda \vee \kappa}; \quad P_{\kappa \wedge \lambda} = P_{\lambda \wedge \kappa} . \qquad (3.20a, a')$$

(b) Associativity:
$$P_{(\kappa \vee \lambda) \vee \mu} = P_{\lambda \vee (\kappa \vee \mu)}; \quad P_{(\kappa \wedge \lambda) \wedge \mu} = P_{\lambda \wedge (\kappa \wedge \mu)} . \qquad (3.20b, b')$$

(c) Absorptivity:
$$P_{\kappa \vee (\lambda) \wedge \lambda} = P_\kappa; \quad P_{\kappa \vee (\lambda \wedge \kappa)} = P_\kappa . \qquad (3.20c, c')$$

(d) Distributivity:
$$P_{\kappa \vee (\lambda \wedge \mu)} = P_{(\kappa \vee \lambda) \wedge (\kappa \vee \mu)}; \quad P_{\kappa \wedge (\lambda \vee \mu)} = P_{(\kappa \wedge \lambda) \vee (\kappa \wedge \mu)} . \qquad (3.20d, d')$$

(e) Orthocompletness:
$$P_{\kappa \vee (\lambda \wedge \lambda^\perp)} = P_\kappa; \quad P_{\kappa \wedge (\lambda \vee \lambda^\perp)} = P_\kappa . \qquad (3.20e, e')$$

Proofs of (a)–(e) are straightforward manipulations of projection operators. We leave them as an exercise to the interested reader. As an example we give the proof of distributivity: $P_{\kappa \wedge (\lambda \vee \mu)} = P_\kappa (P_\lambda + P_\mu - P_\lambda P_\mu) = P_\kappa P_\lambda + P_\kappa P_\mu - (P_\kappa)^2 P_\lambda P_\mu = P_{\kappa \wedge \lambda} + P_{\kappa \wedge \mu} - P_{\kappa \wedge \lambda} P_{\kappa \wedge \mu} = P_{(\kappa \wedge \lambda) \vee (\kappa \wedge \mu)}$. The other distributivity axiom is demonstrated equally easily. □

These record projectors commute because records are associated with the orthonormal pointer basis of the memory of the observer or of the apparatus: It is impossible to consult memory cell in any other basis, so the problems with distributivity pointed out by Birkhoff and von Neumann simply do not arise—when records are kept in orthonormal pointer states, there is no need for 'quantum logic'.

Theorem 3 entitles one to think of the outcomes of measurements—of the records kept in various pointer states—in classical terms. Projectors corresponding to pointer subspaces define overlapping but compatible volumes inside the memory Hilbert space. Algebra of such composite events (defined as coarse grained records) is indeed Boolean. The danger of the loss of additivity (which in quantum systems is intimately tied to the principle of superposition) has been averted: Distributive law of classical logic holds.

3.5. Inverting Born's Rule: Why Is the Amplitude a Square Root of the Frequency of Occurrence?

The strategy we have pursued above to derive Born's rule for unequal coefficients was to consider two different splits, $\mathcal{SE}|\mathcal{C}$ and $\mathcal{SC}|\mathcal{E}$ of the same composite tripartite system $\mathcal{SEC}$. In the beginning we had a bipartite state of $\mathcal{SE}$ with unequal coefficients, Equations (3.7). We have finegrained it into an equal coefficient envariantly swappable state by introducing an additional system $\mathcal{C}$, which entangled with $\mathcal{SE}$ in such a way that the resulting state of $\mathcal{SEC}$ was even, Equations (3.9). In that even state the finegrained probabilities were provably equal. One could then count the number of contributions that included the two alternatives of interest—states $|0\rangle$ and $|1\rangle$ of $\mathcal{S}$. Unequal probabilities were proportional to the number of equiprobable fine-grained contributions in the resulting even states, Equations (3.9).

This reasoning can be reversed: We shall now use the strategy of moving the line dividing the two subsystems of interest in a tripartite composite system to show that the amplitudes must be proportional to the square roots of the frequencies of occurrence of the corresponding events.

We consider the probability of getting a count of m 1's in a measurement by an apparatus $\mathcal{A}$ on an ensemble of identically prepared two-state systems:

$$|\check{\psi}_\mathcal{S}\rangle = \bigotimes_{k=1}^{M} (\alpha|0\rangle + \beta|1\rangle)_k.$$

In course of the (pre-)measurement memory cells of $\mathcal{A}$ entangle with $\mathcal{S}$, so, in obvious notation, the resulting state is a product of M identical copies:

$$|\Psi_{\mathcal{S}\mathcal{A}}\rangle = \bigotimes_{k=1}^{M} (\alpha|0\rangle|a_0\rangle + \beta|1\rangle|a_1\rangle)_k = \bigotimes_{k=1}^{M} |\Psi_{\mathcal{S}\mathcal{A}}\rangle_k. \quad (3.21a)$$

We shall work with the case of $\alpha = \beta$ to avoid cumbersome notation. With these simplifications the state vector $|\Psi_{\mathcal{S}\mathcal{A}}\rangle_k = (|0\rangle|a_0\rangle + 1\rangle|a_1\rangle)_k$ is envariant under a swap $(|0\rangle\langle 1| + |1\rangle\langle 0|)_k$ acting on k's member of the ensemble, as such a swap can be undone by a counterswap $(|a_0\rangle\langle a_1| + |a_1\rangle\langle a_0|)_k$ acting on $\mathcal{A}$. This envariance must also hold when the state vector is expanded into a sum:

$$|\Psi_{\mathcal{S}\mathcal{A}}\rangle \propto \sum_{m=0}^{M} |\tilde{s}_m\rangle. \quad (3.21b)$$

In this expression, each unnormalized vector $|\tilde{s}_m\rangle$ represents all sequences of outcomes and records that have resulted in m detections of "1", that is;

$|\tilde{s}_0\rangle = |00...0\rangle|A_{00...0}\rangle$
$|\tilde{s}_1\rangle = |10...0\rangle|A_{10...0}\rangle + |01...0\rangle|A_{01...0}\rangle + ... + |00...1\rangle|A_{00...1}\rangle$
.....
$|\tilde{s}_m\rangle = |11...10...0\rangle|A_{11...10...0}\rangle + ... + |00...01...1\rangle|A_{00...01...1}\rangle$
.....
$|\tilde{s}_M\rangle = |11...1\rangle|A_{11...1}\rangle.$ (3.22)

The memory state of $\mathcal{A}$ contains record of all the outcomes—it is the product of memory states of individual cells, e.g., $|A_{10...0}\rangle = |a_1\rangle_1|a_0\rangle_2...|a_0\rangle_M$. All the sequences of the outcomes and the corresponding sequences of the records are orthonormal. Therefore, the sum of the sequences of outcome states and corresponding record states—Equation (3.21b) expressed in terms of Equation (3.22)—constitutes a Schmidt decomposition of $|\Psi_{\mathcal{S}\mathcal{A}}\rangle$.

The number of distinct outcome sequence states in $|\tilde{s}_m\rangle$ is $\frac{M!}{m!(M-m)!} = \binom{M}{m}$. Every outcome sequence state is equiprobable since it can be envariantly swapped with any other outcome sequence state. Therefore, the probability of detecting m 1's must be proportional to $\binom{M}{m}$, the number of equiprobable records with m detections of 1.[9] Moreover, as we have set $\alpha = \beta$, the relative normalization of every such sequence is the same. Consequently, every permutation of the outcomes—every specific sequence of 0's and 1's, regardless of the number of 1's—has a probability of 2^{-M}. This includes "maverick" states with the unlikely total counts such as $|\tilde{s}_0\rangle$ and $|\tilde{s}_M\rangle$.

---

[9] For instance, $|00...0\rangle$ in $|\tilde{s}_0\rangle$ can be swapped with $|10...0\rangle$ in $|\tilde{s}_1\rangle$. The pre-swap $|\Psi_{\mathcal{S}\mathcal{A}}\rangle$ can be restored by counterswap of the corresponding $|A_{00...0}\rangle$ with $|A_{10...0}\rangle$.

We now relate probability of a specific count of m 1's to the amplitude of the corresponding state. We prepare to address this question by adding a quantum system that counts 1's and enters their number in the *register* $\mathcal{R}$. The result is an entangled state of $\mathcal{S}$, $\mathcal{A}$, and $\mathcal{R}$:

$$|\check{Y}_{\mathcal{SAR}}\rangle \propto \sum_{m=0}^{M} |\tilde{s}_m\rangle |m\rangle_{\mathcal{R}}. \tag{3.23a}$$

Above, $|m\rangle_{\mathcal{R}}$ are the orthogonal states of $\mathcal{R}$ with distinct total counts.

We shall now use envariance of $|\check{Y}_{\mathcal{SAR}}\rangle$ to relate probability of a specific count m to the amplitude of the corresponding state $|m\rangle_{\mathcal{R}}$. To this end we first normalize states $|\tilde{s}_m\rangle$: Without normalization, amplitudes we are trying to deduce would have no meaning.

Normalizing states of $\mathcal{SA}$ is not difficult: Every individual sequence of 0's and 1's that corresponds to a possible records has the same norm, and the number of sequences that yield total count of m 1's determines the norm of $|\tilde{s}_m\rangle$;

$$\langle \tilde{s}_m | \tilde{s}_m \rangle \propto \binom{M}{m}.$$

This is a first step in a purely *mathematical* operation that converts $|\tilde{s}_m\rangle$ into the corresponding normalized state $|s_m\rangle$ that can be later legally used to implement the Schmidt decomposition.

It is now easy to see that states;

$$|s_m\rangle = \binom{M}{m}^{-\frac{1}{2}} |\tilde{s}_m\rangle, \tag{3.24}$$

have the same normalization. The state of the whole ensemble is then:

$$|\check{Y}_{\mathcal{SAR}}\rangle \propto \sum_{m=0}^{M} \binom{M}{m}^{\frac{1}{2}} |s_m\rangle |m\rangle_{\mathcal{R}} = \sum_{m=0}^{M} \gamma_m |s_m\rangle |m\rangle_{\mathcal{R}}. \tag{3.23b}$$

This is also a Schmidt decomposition, as $|s_m\rangle$ and $|m\rangle_{\mathcal{R}}$ are orthonormal. Given our previous discussion we already know that the probability p_m of any specific count m is given by the fraction of such sequences. That is:

$$p_m = 2^{-M} \binom{M}{m}.$$

This follows from counting of the number of envariant (and, hence, equiprobable) permutations of 0's and 1's contributing to $|s_m\rangle$ and, hence, corresponding to $|m\rangle_{\mathcal{R}}$.

Indeed, Equation (3.23b) is a coarse-grained version of Equations (3.22) and (3.23a). So, the above expression for $|\check{Y}_{\mathcal{SAR}}\rangle$ shows that the amplitude γ_m of $|m\rangle_{\mathcal{R}}$—of the state of the register that holds the count of m 1's—is proportional to the square root of the number of equiprobable sequences that lead to that count;

$$|\gamma_m| \propto \sqrt{\binom{M}{m}} = \sqrt{\frac{M!}{m!(M-m)!}}, \tag{3.25a}$$

or;

$$|\gamma_m| = \sqrt{p_m}. \tag{3.25b}$$

Equation (3.25) is the main result of our discussion. We have now deduced that absolute values $|\gamma_m|$ of the Schmidt coefficients are proportional to the *square roots* of relative frequencies—to the square roots of the cardinalities of subsets of 2^M equiprobable sequences that yield such 'total count = m'' of composite events. In a sense, our calculation "inverts" the derivation of Born's rule we have presented before.

As in the earlier derivation of Born's rule, the key was to express the same tripartite global state $|\check{Y}_{\mathcal{SAR}}\rangle$ as two different Schmidt decompositions. Thus,

$$
\begin{aligned}
|\check{Y}_{\mathcal{S}|\mathcal{AR}}\rangle \propto \ & |00...0\rangle(|A_{00...0}\rangle|0\rangle_{\mathcal{R}}) \\
& + |10...0\rangle(|A_{10...0}\rangle|1\rangle_{\mathcal{R}}) + |01...0\rangle(|A_{01...0}\rangle|1\rangle_{\mathcal{R}}) + \\
& \ldots + |00...1\rangle(|A_{00...1}\rangle|1\rangle_{\mathcal{R}}) \\
& \ldots \\
& + |11...1100...00\rangle(|A_{11...1100...00}\rangle|m\rangle_{\mathcal{R}}) + \\
& \ldots + |00...0011...11\rangle(|A_{00...0011...11}\rangle|m\rangle_{\mathcal{R}}) \\
& \ldots \\
& + |11...1\rangle(|A_{11...1}\rangle|M\rangle_{\mathcal{R}}),
\end{aligned}
\qquad (3.26a)
$$

for the split $\mathcal{S}|\mathcal{AR}$ of the whole into two subsystems, and;

$$
|\check{Y}_{\mathcal{SA}|\mathcal{R}}\rangle \propto \sum_{m=0}^{M} \sqrt{\binom{M}{m}} |s_m\rangle |m\rangle_{\mathcal{R}} = \sum_{m=0}^{M} \gamma_m |s_m\rangle |m\rangle_{\mathcal{R}}, \qquad (3.26b)
$$

for the alternative $\mathcal{SA}|\mathcal{R}$.

The location of the border between the two parts of the whole $\mathcal{SAR}$ is the key difference. It redefines "events of interest". The top $|\check{Y}_{\mathcal{S}|\mathcal{AR}}\rangle$ treats binary sequences of outcomes as "events of interest", and, by envariance, assigns equal probabilities 2^{-M} to each outcome sequence state. By contrast, in $|\check{Y}_{\mathcal{SA}|\mathcal{R}}\rangle$ the total count m is an "event of interest", but now its probability can be deduced from $|\check{Y}_{\mathcal{S}|\mathcal{AR}}\rangle$, as both Schmidt decompositions represent the same state—the same physical situation. This implies (a converse of) Born's rule: Amplitude of a state $|m\rangle_{\mathcal{R}}$ of the register $\mathcal{R}$ is proportional to the square root of the number of sequences of counts that yield m.

Generalization to when $\alpha \neq \beta$ is conceptually simple (although notationally cumbersome). Global state after the requisite adjustment of the relative normalizations is:

$$
|\check{Y}_{\mathcal{SAR}}\rangle \propto \sum_{m=0}^{M} \binom{M}{m}^{\frac{1}{2}} \alpha^{M-m} \beta^{m} |s_m\rangle |m\rangle_{\mathcal{R}} = \sum_{m=0}^{M} \Gamma_m |s_m\rangle |m\rangle_{\mathcal{R}}.
$$

Coefficients Γ_m that multiply $|s_m\rangle|m\rangle_{\mathcal{R}}$ combine on equal footing preexisting amplitudes α and β of $|0\rangle$ and $|1\rangle$ from the initial state, $|\tilde{\psi}_{\mathcal{S}}\rangle = \bigotimes_{k=1}^{M}(\alpha|0\rangle + \beta|1\rangle)_k$ with the square roots of Newton's symbols that arise from counting—with the numbers of the corresponding outcome sequences. Once the state representing the whole ensemble is written as $\sum_{m=0}^{M} \Gamma_m |s_m\rangle|m\rangle_{\mathcal{R}}$, the origin of the coefficients Γ_m (or γ_m before) is irrelevant: Observer presented with a state $\sum_{m=0}^{M} \Gamma_m |s_m\rangle|m\rangle_{\mathcal{R}}$ and asked to assess probabilities of outcomes $|s_m\rangle|m\rangle_{\mathcal{R}}$ has no reason to delve into combinatorial origins of Γ_m. For a measurement with outcome states $|s_m\rangle|m\rangle_{\mathcal{R}}$ the origin of the amplitudes Γ_m that multiply them do not matter. Their absolute values, however, do matter: Observer could implement envariant derivation "from scratch", starting with whatever coefficients are there in the initial state, and finegraining (as before, Equations (3.8)), to deduce probabilities of various outcomes.

3.6. Relative Frequencies from Relative States

We shall now use envariance to deduce relative frequencies from amplitudes. In view of the discussion immediately above the relation between amplitudes and frequencies is already apparent, so this may seem superfluous, but we shall sketch it anyway "for the sake of completeness", and also because it provides a different—experimentally motivated, one could say—point of view of the alternatives. A much more complete derivation of relative frequencies from envariance is also available in Ref. [48].

We emphasize that we do not need relative frequencies to define probabilities: Probabilities are already in place. They are "single shot", defined not by counting the number of "favorable events" (as in the relative frequency approach), but, rather, by first establishing equiprobability of a certain class of events, and then by counting the number of equiprobable favorable possibilities. Therefore, the calculation immediately below is, in a sense, only a consistency check.

Consider M distinguishable $\mathcal{SCE}$ triplets, each already in the fine-grained state;

$$|\Psi_{\mathcal{SCE}}^{(\ell)}\rangle = \Big(\sum_{k=1}^{\mu} |0,c_k\rangle|e_k\rangle + \sum_{k=\mu+1}^{\mu+\nu} |1,c_k\rangle|e_k\rangle\Big)^{(\ell)},$$

of Equation (3.9). The state of the whole ensemble is then given by their product;

$$|\hat{\Omega}_{\mathcal{SCE}}^{M}\rangle = \bigotimes_{\ell=1}^{M} |\Psi_{\mathcal{SCE}}^{(\ell)}\rangle = \bigotimes_{\ell=1}^{M} \Big(\sum_{k=1}^{\mu} |0,c_k\rangle|e_k\rangle + \sum_{k=\mu+1}^{\mu+\nu} |1,c_k\rangle|e_k\rangle\Big)^{(\ell)}. \quad (3.27)$$

As in the derivation of the inverse of Born's rule, we can now carry out the product and obtain a sum that will contain $(\mu + \nu)^M$ (instead of just 2^M) terms. As in Equation (3.26a), these terms can be now sorted according to the number of 0's and 1's they contain. We could even attach a register $\mathcal{R}$, and repeat all the steps we have taken above. We shall bypass these intermediate calculations that are conceptually straightforward but notationally cumbersome. What matters in the end is how many equiprobable terms contain, say, m 1's. The answer is clearly, $\binom{M}{m}\mu^{M-m}\nu^{m}$. Therefore, the probability of detecting m 1's in M trials is given by:

$$p_M(m) = \binom{M}{m}\frac{\mu^{M-m}\nu^m}{(\mu+\nu)^M} = \binom{M}{m}|\alpha|^{2(M-m)}|\beta|^{2m}. \quad (3.28)$$

We now assume M is large, not because envariant derivation requires this—we have already obtained Born's rule for individual events, $M = 1$—but because the relative frequency approach needs it (von Mises, 1939 [71]; Gnedenko, 1968 [52]). In that limit binomial can be approximated by a Gaussian:

$$p_M(m) \simeq \frac{\exp-\frac{1}{2}\Big(\frac{m-|\beta|^2 M}{\sqrt{M}|\alpha\beta|}\Big)^2}{\sqrt{2\pi M}|\alpha\beta|}. \quad (3.29)$$

The average number of 1's is, according to Equation (3.29), $\langle m \rangle = |\beta|^2 M$, as expected, establishing a link between relative frequency of events in a large number of trials and Born's rule. This connection between quantum states and relative frequencies does not rest either on circular and *ad hoc* assumptions that relate size of the coefficients in the global state to probabilities (e.g., by asserting that probability corresponding to a small enough amplitude is 0 (Geroch 1984) [73]), or modifications of quantum theory (Weissman, 1999 [96]; Buniy, Hsu, and Zee, 2006 [83]), or on the unphysical infinite limit (Hartle, 1968 [79]; Farhi, Goldstone, and Guttmann, 1989 [80]). Such steps have left past frequentist approaches to Born's rule (including also these of Everett, DeWitt, and Graham) open to criticism (Stein, 1984 [74]; Kent, 1990 [38]; Squires, 1990 [39]; Joos, 2000 [75]; Auletta, 2000 [97]).

Note that we avoid the problem of two independent measures of probability (number of branches *and* size of the coefficients) that derailed previous relative state attempts. We simply count the number of *envariantly swappable* (and hence *provably equiprobable*) sequences of potential events. This settles the issue of "maverick universes"—atypical branches with numbers of e.g., 0's very different from the average $\langle n \rangle$. They are there (as they should be) but they are very improbable. This is established through a physically motivated envariance under swaps. So, maverick branches did not have to be removed either "by assumption" (DeWitt, 1970 [14]; 1971 [15]; Graham, 1973 [72]; Geroch, 1984 [73]) or by an equally unphysical $M = \infty$. Maverick branches are there, but pose no threat to our envariant derivation.

3.7. Envariance—An Overview

Envariance settles a major outstanding quantum foundational problem: The origin of probabilities. Born's rule can be now established on a basis of a solid and simple physical reasoning, and without assuming additivity of probabilities (in contrast to Gleason, 1957 [84]). We have derived $p_k = |\psi_k|^2$ without relying on the tools of decoherence.

There were other attempts to apply Laplacean strategy of invariance under permutations to prove "indifference". This author (Zurek, 1998) [36] noted that all of the possibilities listed on a diagonal of a unit density matrix (e.g., $\sim |0\rangle\langle 0| + |1\rangle\langle 1|$) must be equiprobable, as it is invariant under swaps. This equiprobability—based approach was then extended to the case of unequal coefficients by finegraining, and leads to Born's rule.

However, a reduced density matrix is not the right starting point for the derivation: A pure state, prepared by the observer in the preceding measurement, is. In addition, to get from such a pure state to a mixed (reduced) density matrix one must "trace"—average over, e.g., the environment. Born's rule is involved in averaging, which leads to a concern that such a derivation may be circular [7,35,48,88].

One could attempt to deal with a pure state of a single system instead. Deutsch (1999) [86] and his followers (Wallace, 2003 [87]; Saunders, 2004 [98]) pursued this approach in terms of decision theory. The key was again invariance under permutations. It is indeed there for certain pure states (e.g., $|0\rangle + |1\rangle$) but it disappears when the relative phase is involved. That is, $|0\rangle + |1\rangle$ equals the post-swap $|1\rangle + |0\rangle$, but $|0\rangle + e^{i\phi}|1\rangle \neq |1\rangle + e^{i\phi}|0\rangle$, and the difference is *not* the overall phase. Indeed, $|0\rangle + i|1\rangle$ is *orthogonal* to $i|0\rangle + |1\rangle$, so there is no invariance under swaps, and the argument that the swap does not matter because the pre-swap state is in the end recovered is simply wrong. In isolated systems this problem cannot be avoided. (Envariance of course deals with it very naturally, as the phase of Schmidt coefficients is envariant—see Equations (3.1)–(3.4).)

The other problem with decision theory approaches put forward to date is selection of events one of which will happen upon measurement—the choice of the preferred states. These two problems must be settled, either through appeal to decoherence (as in Zurek, 1998 [36], and in Wallace, 2003 [87]), or by ignoring phases essentially *ad hoc* (Deutsch, 1999) [86], which then makes readers suspect that some "Copenhagen" assumptions are involved. (Indeed, Barnum et al. (2000) [99] criticized Deutsch (1999) [86] by interpreting his approach in the "Copenhagen spirit".) In addition, decoherence—invoked by Wallace, 2003 [87]—employs reduced density matrices, hence, Born's rule. So, as noted by many, it should be "off limits" in its derivation [32,35,48,89,90].

In more recent papers, advocates of the decision theory approach adopt a strategy (Wallace 2007 [100]; 2010 [92]; 2012 [19]) that in effect relies on envariance. This affinity of the updated decision-theoretic approach with envariant derivation of Born's rule has been noticed and analyzed [91].

Envariant derivation of Born's rule we have presented is an extension of the swap strategy in (Zurek, 1998) [36]. However, instead of tracing out the environment, we have incorporated it in the discussion (albeit in the role similar to a gauge field).

Envariance leads to Born's rule, but also to new appreciation of decoherence. Pointer states can be inferred directly from the dynamics of information transfers as was shown in Section 2 (see also Ref. [48]) and, indeed, in the original definition of pointer states [24]. Not everyone is comfortable with envariance (see, e.g., Herbut, 2007 [101], for a selection of views on envariance). This is understandable—interpretation of quantum theory was always rife with controversies.

3.7.1. Implications and the Scope of Envariance: Why Entanglement? Why Schmidt States?

Envariance is firmly rooted in quantum physics. It is based on the symmetries of entanglement. One may be nevertheless concerned about the scope of envariant approach: $p_k = |\psi_k|^2$ for Schmidt states, but how about measurements with other outcomes? The obvious starting point for the derivation of probabilities is not an entangled state of $\mathcal{S}$ and

$\mathcal{E}$, but a pure state of $\mathcal{S}$. In addition, such a state can be expressed in *any* basis that spans $\mathcal{H}_\mathcal{S}$. So, why entanglement? And why Schmidt states?

Envariance of Schmidt coefficient phases is closely tied to the einselection of pointer states: After decoherence has set in, pointer states diagonalize reduced density matrices nearly as well as the Schmidt states (which diagonalize them exactly). Residual misalignment is not going to be a major problem. At most, it might cause minor violations of the laws obeyed by the classical probability for events defined by the pointer states.

Such violations are intriguing, and perhaps even detectable, but unlikely to matter in the macroscopic setting we usually deal with. To see why, we revisit pointer states—Schmidt states (or einselection—envariance) link in the setting of measurements: Observer $\mathcal{O}$ uses an (ultimately quantum) apparatus $\mathcal{A}$, initially in a known state $|A_0\rangle$, to entangle with $\mathcal{S}$, which then decoheres as $\mathcal{A}$ is immersed in $\mathcal{E}$ (Zurek, 1991 [27], 2003 [7]; Joos et al., 2003 [29]; Schlosshauer, 2005 [31]; 2007 [32]). This sequence of interactions leads to:

$$|\psi_\mathcal{S}\rangle|A_0\rangle|\varepsilon_0\rangle \Rightarrow \left(\sum_k a_k|s_k\rangle|A_k\rangle\right)|\varepsilon_0\rangle \Rightarrow \sum_k a_k|s_k\rangle|A_k\rangle|\varepsilon_k\rangle.$$

In a properly constructed apparatus pointer states $|A_k\rangle$ are unperturbed by $\mathcal{E}$ while $|\varepsilon_k\rangle$ become orthonormal on a decoherence timescale. So in the end we have a Schmidt decomposition of $\mathcal{SA}$ (treated as a single entity) and $\mathcal{E}$.

Apparatus is built to measure a specific observable $\sigma_\mathcal{S} = \sum_k \varsigma_k |s_k\rangle\langle s_k|$. Suppose $\mathcal{O}$ knows that $\mathcal{S}$ starts in $|\psi_\mathcal{S}\rangle = \sum_k a_k|s_k\rangle$. The choice of $\mathcal{A}$ (of Hamiltonians, etc.) commits observer to a definite set of potential outcomes: Probabilities will refer to $\{|A_k\rangle\}$, or, equivalently, to $\{|A_k s_k\rangle\}$ in the Schmidt decomposition.

To answer questions we started with (Why entanglement, Why Schmidt states?), entanglement is a result of interactions that cause measurement and decoherence, and only pointer states *of the apparatus* (e.g., states that are near the diagonal, and can play the role of Schmidt states to a very good approximation after decoherence) can be outcomes.

This emphasis on the role of the apparatus in deciding what happens parallels Bohr's view captured by "No phenomenon is a phenomenon until it is a recorded phenomenon" (Wheeler, 1983) [47]. In our case $\mathcal{A}$ is quantum and symptoms of classicality—e.g., einselection as well as the loss of phase coherence between pointer states—arise as a result of entanglement with $\mathcal{E}$.

Envariant approach applies even when $|s_k\rangle$ are not orthogonal: Orthogonality of the record states of the apparatus is assured by their distinguishability. This is because (as noted in Section 2) events agents have direct access to are records in $\mathcal{A}$ (rather than states of $\mathcal{S}$). Indeed, as we shall discuss in the next section, we access records in the measuring devices indirectly, by intercepting small fragments of, e.g., photon environment that has helped decohere them and has einselected distinct states of the apparatus pointer. States of $\mathcal{A}$ that can leave multiple imprints on the environment (so that we can find out measurement outcomes from the tiny fraction of $\mathcal{E}$) must be distinguishable (hence, orthogonal).

Other simplifying assumptions we invoked can be also relaxed [48]. For example, when $\mathcal{E}$ is initially mixed (as will be generally the case), one can 'purify' it by adding extra $\mathcal{E}'$ in the usual manner (see Section 2). Given that we already have a derivation of Born's rule for pure states, the use of the purification strategy (when it is justified by the physical context) does not require apologies, and does not introduce circularity. Indeed, it is tempting to claim that all probabilities in physics *can* be interpreted envariantly.

Probabilities described by Born's rule quantify ignorance of the observer $\mathcal{O}$ *before* he or she finds out the measurement outcome. Therefore, envariant probabilities admit ignorance interpretation—$\mathcal{O}$ is ignorant of the *future* outcome (rather than of an unknown *pre-existing* real state, as was the case classically). Of course, once $\mathcal{O}$'s memory becomes correlated with $\mathcal{A}$, its state registers what $\mathcal{O}$ has perceived (say, $|o_7\rangle$ that registers $|A_7\rangle$). Re-checking of the apparatus will confirm it. Moreover, when many systems are prepared in the same initial state, frequencies of the outcomes will accord with Born's rule.

Envariant approach uses incompatibility between observables of the whole and its parts. It has been now adopted and discussed by others (Barnum, 2003 [93]; Schlosshauer and Fine, 2005 [94]; Schlosshauer, 2005 [31]; 2006 [37]; 2007 [32]; 2019 [33]; Paris, 2005 [102]; Jordan, 2006 [103]; Steane, 2007 [104]; Bub and Pitovsky, 2007 [105]; Horodecki et al., 2009 [106]; Blaylock, 2010 [107]; Seidewitz, 2011 [108]; Hsu, 2012 [109]; Sebens and Carroll, 2018 [110]; Drezet, 2021 [91]).

In retrospect, it seems surprising that envariace was not noticed earlier and used to derive probability or to provide insights into decoherence and einselection: Entangling interactions are key to measurements and decoherence, so entanglement symmetries would seem relevant. However, entanglement was viewed as a paradox, as something that needs to be explained, and not used in an explanation. This attitude is, fortunately, changing.

3.7.2. Towards the Experimental Verification of Envariance

Purifications, use of ancillas, fine-graining, and other steps in the derivation need not be carried out in the laboratory each time probabilities are computed using the state vector: Once established, Born's rule is a *law*. It follows from the tensor product and the geometry of the Hilbert spaces for composite quantum systems. We used assumptions about $\mathcal{C}, \mathcal{E}$, etc., to demonstrate $p_k = |\psi_k|^2$, but this rule must be obeyed even when no one is there to immediately verify compliance. So, even when there is no ancilla $\mathcal{C}$ at hand, or when $\mathcal{E}$ is initially mixed or too small for fine-graining, one could (at some later time, using purification, extra environments and ancillas) verify that bookkeeping implicit in assigning probabilities to $|\psi_\mathcal{S}\rangle$ or pre-entangled $|\psi_{\mathcal{SE}}\rangle$ abides by the symmetries of entanglement.

The obvious next question is how to verify envariance directly. Testing whether the global state is recovered following a swap and a counterswap using tools that favor dealing locally with individual systems is the essence of the experimental difficulties. The few tests of envariance carried out to date approach these challenges differently. The first (and, to date, most precise) test uses pairs of entangled photons to perform the requisite transformations (Vermeyden et al., 2015) [111]. The final global state is acquired by measurements on the individual photons, and characterized using quantum tomography.

Envariance was indeed confirmed with impressive accuracy. Aware of the dangers of circularity Vermeyden et al. used Bhattacharyya coefficient to analyze the experimental data. They have also tested (and constrained) the theory of Son (2014) [112] which allows for powers other than the standard square, $p_k = |\psi_k|^2$, in the relation between probability and amplitude. Entangled quantum states were found to be (99.66 ± 0.04)% envariant as measured using the quantum fidelity, and (99.963 ± 0.005)% as measured using a modified Bhattacharyya coefficient. According to the authors, the systematic deviations are due to the less-than-maximal entanglement in their photon pairs.

The experiment of Harris et al. (2016) [113] verified envariance by showing that pure quantum states consisting of two maximally entangled degrees of freedom are left unaltered by the action of successive 'swapping' operations, each of which is carried out on a different (entangled) degree of freedom. Moreover, it tested and confirmed the perfect correlation used in the derivation of Born's rule. That is, it showed that Schmidt partners—states that belong to different Hilbert spaces but are linked to one another via tensor product in a Schmidt decomposition—are detected together upon measurement. Bhattacharyya coefficients were again used in testing and the accuracies of well over 99% were attained.

The advent of quantum computers has allowed theorists to act as experimenters. A pioneering example is the test of envariance using 5 qubits of IBM's Quantum Experience carried out by Deffner (2016) [114]. In addition to testing envariance on entangled pairs, he has also investigated larger GHZ-like states with up to five entangled qubits. The accuracy to which envariance holds decreased with the increasing number of qubits from ∼95% for pairs to ∼75% for quintuples. Final measurement was again done on individual spins. Clearly, quantum computers are at this point no match for serious laboratory experiments, but as they improve, even small quantum devices may be useful as tests of fundamental physics.

While present day quantum computers are imperfect, the progress is, of recent, relatively rapid. It seems therefore likely that much more accurate implementations of strategies that test this fundamental symmetry as well as more advanced tests (needed to verify "fine-graining" in the case of unequal absolute values of the coefficients) should be within reach soon. A possible circuit that can be used to verify envariance is illustrated in Figure 3A.

A. 'Quantum Agent' Circuit Test of Envariance.

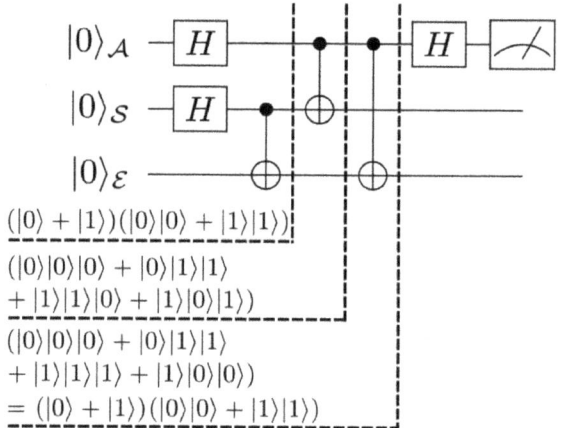

B. Hong-Ou-Mandel Experimental Test of Envariance.

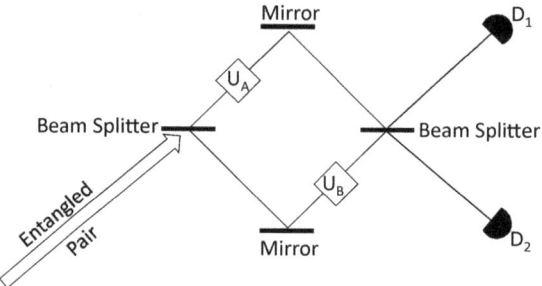

Figure 3. Testing envariance: A. "Quantum agent" circuit test of envariance: Hadamard gates put agent $\mathcal{A}$ and the system $\mathcal{S}$ in a superposition, and the leftmost c-not creates an entangled $\mathcal{SE}$ state. The next c-not performs a superposition of a swap on $\mathcal{S}$ (when $\mathcal{A}$ is in the state $|1\rangle$) or does nothing (when $\mathcal{A}$ is in $|0\rangle$). After the second c-not the $\mathcal{SE}$ pair is in a superposition of swapped an untouched, and state of $\mathcal{A}$ is mixed. However, after the last gate performs a conditional counterswap on $\mathcal{E}$, the entangled state of $\mathcal{SE}$ should be restored, and the state of $\mathcal{A}$ should disentangle from $\mathcal{SE}$ and become pure again. B. Testing envariance with an entangled photon pair and a Hong-Ou-Mandel [115] interferometer. The initial state is $|0\rangle|1\rangle - |1\rangle|0\rangle$. As photons in the two arms of the interferometer are distinguishable (have "opposite" polarizations) they should not emerge together at the end of the interferometer. As a result, detectors should click in coincidence. However, after a swap $U_A = |0\rangle\langle 1| + |1\rangle\langle 0|$ on one of the photons changes the state into $|0\rangle|0\rangle - |1\rangle|1\rangle$, both photons should emerge at the same output. This will suppress coincidence clicks of the two detectors. This swap can be of course undone by a counterswap $U_B = |0\rangle\langle 1| + |1\rangle\langle 0|$ on the second photon, restoring the initial state, and restoring coincidences between the two detectors. Partial rotations of polarization and phase shifts can probe envariance for more general transformations.

In the meantime, it may be useful to consider other experimental settings and other designs that require laboratory tests but that allow one to verify that (in the wake of a swap and a counterswap) nothing happens that the global state is restored. A possible design of such a test that employs Hong-Ou-Mandel (HOM) interferometry (Hong, Ou, and Mandel, 1987 [115]; Milonni and Eberley, 2010 [116]) is shown in Figure 3B.

4. Quantum Darwinism

Objective existence in classical physics was an attribute of the state of a system. An unknown classical state could be measured and found out by many, and yet retain its identity—remain unchanged—even when observers were initially ignorant of what it is.

In contrast to classical states, quantum states are fragile—they cannot be, in general, found out without getting perturbed by the measurement. Objective existence in a quantum world emerges—we shall see—as a consequence of correlations between a system and its environment. It is not (as in classical physics) "sole responsibility" of the system.

Quantum states can, in effect, exist objectively—retain their identity and result in compatible records of independent measurements by many observers—providing observers measure only observables that commute with the preexisting state of the system. In the aftermath of decoherence, this means restriction to its pointer observable. In that case, observers will agree about the outcomes—their measurements will not invalidate one another and will not be erased by decoherence. Therefore, a consensus about the state based on independent measurements—the essence of objectivity—can be established. Such a consensus is the only operational requirement for the "objective existence of classical reality" in our quantum Universe. However, why should observers measure only pointer observables?

Quantum Darwinism provides a simple and natural explanation of this restriction, and, hence, of objective existence—bulwark of classicality—for the einselected states. Quantum Darwinism recognizes that the information we acquire about the Universe comes to us indirectly, through the evidence systems of interest deposited in their environments, and that the only states capable of depositing multiple copies—many quantum memes or qmemes—are the einselected pointer states. Observers access directly only the record made in a fraction of the environment—an imprint of the original state of $\mathcal{S}$ on a fragment $\mathcal{F}$ of $\mathcal{E}$. There are usually multiple copies of that original (e.g., of this text) that are disseminated throughout $\mathcal{E}$ (e.g., by the photon environment—by the light scattered by a printed page or emitted by a computer screen). Observers can find out states of various systems indirectly and agree about their findings because correlations of $\mathcal{S}$ with $\mathcal{E}$ (which we quantify below using mutual information) allow $\mathcal{E}$ to be a *witness* to the pointer state of the system.

In this section we define mutual information, and use it to characterize the information that can be gained about $\mathcal{S}$ from $\mathcal{E}$. Objectivity arises because of redundancy—the same information can be obtained independently by many observers from many fragments of $\mathcal{E}$. So, in a sense, objectivity of an observable is quantified by the redundancy of its records—the number of its copies—in $\mathcal{E}$.

The multiplicity of records of the pointer observable of $\mathcal{S}$ in $\mathcal{E}$ accounts for all the symptoms of the "wavepacket collapse" that are accessible via localized measurements of the environment: Observers who have detected a fragment of $\mathcal{E}$ that bears an imprint of the pointer observable of the system will—in the future—encounter only states of the rest of the environment fragments that convey message consistent with the pointer state they have initially seen, and will be able to communicate only with others who have recorded the same pointer state (and are therefore on the same "branch"). Moreover, an observer who decides to verify the state of $\mathcal{S}$ (either by measuring it directly, or by intercepting additional fragments of $\mathcal{E}$) will obtain data which confirm that $\mathcal{S}$ is in a pointer state that was revealed by the initial measurement on the fragment $\mathcal{E}$ that was measured first.

The system itself is untouched—it is not measured directly. Observers acquire their information indirectly, from the qmemes in the environment that has "measured" the system while decohering it. What we find out about our quantum Universe as a consequence of decoherence (that restricts stable states of macroscopic systems to the einselected pointer states) and of quantum Darwinism (selective proliferation of the information about these pointer states). What we see looks classical—it is our familiar classical world: Environment communicates information about pointer states that were selected by decoherence.

We perceive our reality as classical because we are immersed in the information bearing halos of macroscopic systems—because our world consists of extantons, composite entities that combine the source of information (the pointer observable of the macroscopic object that resides in the extanton core) with the means of its delivery (information-bearing halo of, e.g., photons). We only pay attention to the message (the state of the extanton core) and take for granted—ignore—its means of delivery (extanton halo laden with data about the pointer state of the core).

Fragility of individual quantum states is no longer a problem. Observers will generally destroy the evidence (e.g., absorb photons in their retina) while acquiring information. However, there are now many copies of the same information—all imprinted with the data about the underlying state of the system. Therefore, even though evidence of the state of the system may be in part erased, consensus about it will emerge in the end, even as observers measure different fragments of the environment in ways that obliterate carriers of that information.

Last not least, even when observers do not know what are the pointer states of the system, the environment does, and will let them know: Consensus between the evidence carried by different fragments of $\mathcal{E}$ emerges as these measurements contain redundant information only about the pointer states[10].

Quantum Darwinism can be developed starting from the same assumptions as decohrence theory. Nevertheless, results of the two previous sections are essential when one aims to arrive at a consistent and comprehensive *quantum theory of the classical*. Derivation of the pointer states via repeatability in Section 2 allows us to anticipate preferred states capable of leaving multiple records in $\mathcal{E}$ with minimal assumptions that tie directly to the narrative of quantum Darwinism. Only states that are monitored by $\mathcal{E}$ without getting perturbed can survive long enough to deposit copious qmemes, their information—theoretic progeny, in the environment: The no-cloning theorem is not an obstacle when "cloning" involves not an unknown quantum state, but an einselected observable. The copies are then messages with the information about the pointer states. The environment becomes an *amplification channel*—a quantum communication channel that carries multiple qmemes of the classical information about the 'events' corresponding to the pointer states of $\mathcal{S}$.

The inevitable price of the amplification of the preferred observable is the destruction of the information about the complementary observables and about the initial superposition of the pointer states of $\mathcal{S}$. A single copy of that state is diluted in all of $\mathcal{E}$, so quantum information can be obtained only through global measurements that are inaccessible to local observers. Thus, a quantum environment can transmit only classical information about the pointer observable of $\mathcal{S}$. Or, more precisely, the ability to spawn and disseminate qmemes endows pointer states with all the prerogatives of objective classical existence. Such preferred observable is "fittest" in the Darwinian sense—the original pointer state

---

[10] It has been remarked (Healey, 2012) [117] that, in the quantum Darwinist approach to objective existence "One is reminded of Wittgenstein's remark in his *Philosophical Investigations*: *As if someone were to buy several copies of the morning paper to assure himself that what it said was true*". The difference with Wittgenstein's reader of classical newspapers is, of course, that an observer in a quantum Universe does not get a newspaper with a robust, objectively existing content. What an observer will get out of a single copy of the hypothetical quantum newspaper (or a fragment of $\mathcal{E}$) is a combination of what was imprinted on it (by the system) and quantum randomness—by Born's rule and by how the state of that $\mathcal{F}$ collapses when "read" (measured). Therefore, in general, different copies of the same "quantum paper" will "collapse" into distinct messages (because the state of the copy will "collapse" when measured, and also because different observables may be used to read them), even when the underlying state of each copy was the same. Objective reality emerges—the news about the state of the system can be ascertained—only from the consensus between many copies that reveal the "true" state of the $\mathcal{S}$. It can be confirmed by additional measurements (on the environment or even directly on the system). That information will also agree with what other observers have found out about $\mathcal{S}$. In practice, we do not need to search for such consensus between different choices of observables: Our eyes have evolved to measure photons that are imprinted with and can only reveal localized states of systems.

has survived evolutionary pressures of its environment and has spawned copious qmemes, information - theoretic offspring, advertising its objective existence.

To make these ideas rigorous we shall calculate the number of copies of S in $\mathcal{E}$. To do that we will compute entropies of S, $\mathcal{E}$, and various fragments $\mathcal{F}$ of $\mathcal{E}$ (see Figure 4) using reduced density matrices and relevant probabilities. It is therefore fortunate that, in Section 3, we have already derived Born's rule from the symmetries of entanglement. This gives us the right to employ the usual tools of decoherence—trace and reduced density matrices interpreted as statistical entities—to compute entropy.

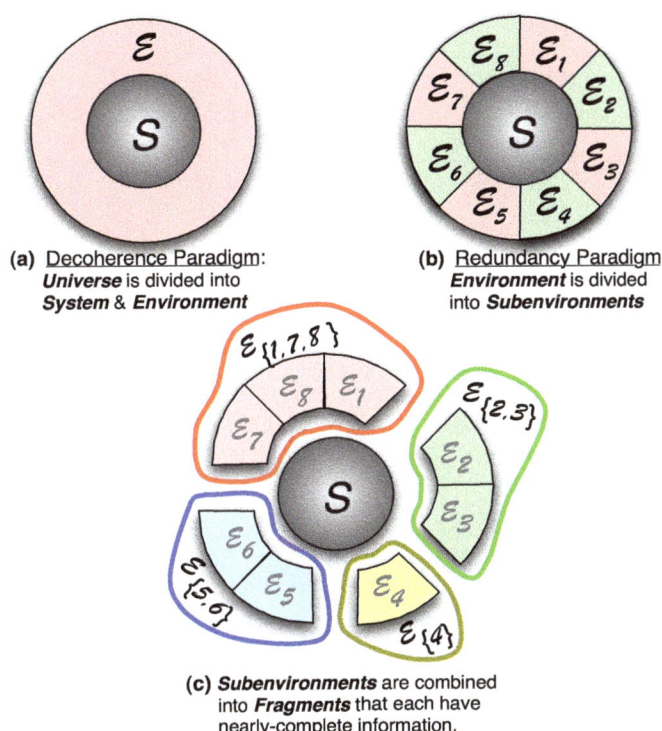

Figure 4. Quantum Darwinism and the structure of the environment. The decoherence paradigm distinguishes between a system (S) and its environment ($\mathcal{E}$) as in (**a**), but makes no further recognition of the structure of $\mathcal{E}$; it could as well be monolithic. In the environment-as-a-witness paradigm, we recognize subdivision of $\mathcal{E}$ into subenvironments—its natural subsystems, as in (**b**). The only essential requirement for a subsystem is that it should be individually accessible to measurements; observables corresponding to different subenvironments commute. To obtain information about the system S from its environment $\mathcal{E}$ one can then carry out measurements of *fragments* $\mathcal{F}$ of the environment—non-overlapping collections of its subsystems. Sufficiently large fragments of the environment that has monitored (and, therefore, decohered) S can often provide enough information to infer the state of S, by combining subenvironments as in (**c**). There are then many copies of the information about S in $\mathcal{E}$, which implies that information about the "fittest" observables that survived monitoring by $\mathcal{E}$ has proliferated throughout $\mathcal{E}$, leaving multiple qmemes, their (quantum) informational offspring. This proliferation of the information about the fittest (pointer) states defines quantum Darwinism. Multiple copies allow many observers to find out the state of S: Environment becomes a reliable witness with redundant copies of information about preferred observables, which accounts for the objective existence of preferred pointer states.

4.1. Mutual Information, Redundancy, and Discord

Quantities that play key role in quantum Darwinism are often expressed in terms of the von Neumann entropy:

$$H(\rho) = -Tr\rho \lg \rho ,\qquad(4.1)$$

The density matrix ρ can describe the state of just one, or of a collection (ensemble) of many quantum systems.

As was done (since at least Laplace) classically, probabilities underlying quantum von Neumann entropy can be regarded as a measure of ignorance[11]. However, the density matrix ρ provides more than just its eigenvalues. It is an operator—it has eigenstates. One may be tempted to add that ρ also determines what one is ignorant of: This is generally not the case. Observer can be interested in an observable whose eigenstates do not diagonalize ρ. Indeed, as Section 2 demonstrated, even the einselected pointer states do not always diagonalize ρ_S. Thus, states that are predictable (because of their stability) and therefore useful may not coincide with instantaneous eigenstates of the reduced density matrix.

What is the ignorance of someone interested in an observable with states $\{|\pi_k\rangle\}$ that differ from the eigenstates of ρ? The corresponding entropy is then the Shannon entropy given by:

$$H(p_k) = -\sum_k p_k \lg p_k ,\qquad(4.2)$$

where probabilities of $\{|\pi_k\rangle\}$ are:

$$p_k = Tr\langle \pi_k|\rho|\pi_k\rangle .\qquad(4.3a)$$

As noted above, $\{|\pi_k\rangle\}$ may be pointer states (indeed, we shall adopt this notation for the pointer states in this section). They will be (almost) as good in diagonalizing the reduced density matrix of the system as its eigenstates after decoherence. As was noted in Section 3, it is only then that one can associate the usual interpretation of probabilities with pointer states. Otherwise additivity of probabilities may be in danger, as consistent histories approach (Griffiths, 1984 [118]; 2002 [119]; Gell-Mann and Hartle, 1990 [120], 1993 [121]; Omnès 1992 [122]; Griffiths and Omnès, 1999 [123]) makes especially clear.

Note that above—in Equations (4.1) and (4.2)—we have used the same H to denote both von Neumann and Shannon entropy. Sometimes different letters (e.g., S and H) are used for this purpose. We will not do that because, to begin with, S is used to denote the system. Moreover, immediately below we shall consider entropies that are in a sense partly von Neumann and partly Shannon. Last not least, throughout most of this section our focus will be on von Neumann entropy and on the corresponding mutual information.

4.1.1. Mutual Information

Mutual information will help us find out how much a fragment of the environment knows about the system, and what does it know. It is the difference between entropy of two systems treated separately and jointly:

$$I(\mathcal{S}:\mathcal{A}) = H(\mathcal{S}) + H(\mathcal{A}) - H(\mathcal{S},\mathcal{A}) .\qquad(4.4)$$

Mutual information $I(\mathcal{S}:\mathcal{A})$ quantifies of how much $\mathcal{S}$ and $\mathcal{A}$ know about one another.

---

[11] We are not "backtracking" here—probabilities in the quantum theory are based on objective quantum symmetry—envariance: Even in the case when global state of $\mathcal{SE}$ is pure, von Neumann entropy of $\mathcal{S}$ quantifies ignorance associated with the probabilities of the eigenstates of its reduced density matrix. The difference between the quantum case and the classical "Laplacean" approach is clear: Subjective assessment of likelihood can be, in quantum setting, replaced by the objective symmetries of the global state.

For classical systems the above definition of $I(\mathcal{S}:\mathcal{A})$ is equivalent to the definition of mutual information that employs conditional entropy (e.g., $H(\mathcal{S}|\mathcal{A})$). Conditional entropy quantifies the ignorance about $\mathcal{S}$ left after the state of $\mathcal{A}$ is found out:

$$H(\mathcal{S},\mathcal{A}) = H(\mathcal{A}) + H(\mathcal{S}|\mathcal{A}) \,. \tag{4.5a}$$

A similar formula reverses the roles of the two parties:

$$H(\mathcal{S},\mathcal{A}) = H(\mathcal{S}) + H(\mathcal{A}|\mathcal{S}) \,. \tag{4.5b}$$

In classical settings, when states can be characterized by probability distributions, one can simply substitute either of the Equations (4.5) for $H(\mathcal{S},\mathcal{A})$ in Equation (4.4) and obtain an equivalent expression for mutual information. In quantum physics "knowing" is not as innocent—it requires performing a measurement that in general alters the joint density matrix into an outcome—dependent *conditional density matrix* describing the state of the system given the measurement outcome—e.g., given the state $|A_k\rangle$ of the apparatus $\mathcal{A}$:

$$\rho_{\mathcal{S}|A_k\rangle} = \langle A_k|\rho_{\mathcal{S}\mathcal{A}}|A_k\rangle/p_k \,. \tag{4.6}$$

Above, in accord with Equation (4.3a),

$$p_k = \mathrm{Tr}\langle A_k|\rho_{\mathcal{S}\mathcal{A}}|A_k\rangle \,. \tag{4.3b}$$

Given the outcome $|A_k\rangle$ the conditional entropy is:

$$H(\mathcal{S}|A_k\rangle) = -\mathrm{Tr}\rho_{\mathcal{S}|A_k\rangle} \lg \rho_{\mathcal{S}|A_k\rangle} \,, \tag{4.7}$$

which leads to the average conditional entropy:

$$H(\mathcal{S}|\{|A_k\rangle\}) = \sum_k p_k H(\mathcal{S}|A_k\rangle) \,. \tag{4.8}$$

This much information about $\mathcal{S}$ one expects will be still missing after a measurement of an observable with the eigenstates $\{|A_k\rangle\}$ on $\mathcal{A}$. Note that, as in the discussion of probabilities and envariance, this estimate of the expected missing information is relevant for a "bystander"—someone who knows what was measured, but does not yet know the result. (Observer who knows the outcome would use Equation (4.7) instead). An average over all the outcomes, Equation (4.8), gives the expected remaining ignorance about $\mathcal{S}$ as long as one does not know the outcome.

Once the observer perceives the outcome, the relevant state of $\mathcal{S}$ (and the corresponding relevant entropy) will be given by Equations (4.6) and (4.7). This is the infamous "collapse"—the range of possibilities is reduced to a single actuality. We note that even for a bystander—observer's friend who knows that the measurement has already happened, but who has not yet found out the outcome[12] the joint state of $\mathcal{SA}$ is usually affected, as the reconstituted density matrix $\sum_k p_k |A_k\rangle\langle A_k|\rho_{\mathcal{S}|A_k\rangle}$ differs in general from the pre-measurement $\rho_{\mathcal{S}\mathcal{A}}$. In particular, the entropy of the reconstituted mixed state is usually larger than the entropy of the pre-measurement $\rho_{\mathcal{S}\mathcal{A}}$.

This increase of entropy is characteristically quantum. It was pointed out already by von Neumann (1932) [4]. Decoherence explains it as an inevitable consequence of the correlations with the environment $\mathcal{E}$ that "monitors" $\mathcal{A}$. From the point of view of the bystander, correlations of $\mathcal{A}$ with the environment or with the observer have a similar effect—they can invalidate some of the information the bystander had about $\mathcal{SA}$, and hence increase entropy.

---

[12] That is, for whom the possibilities have not yet collapsed to a single actuality, but who knows the apparatus $\mathcal{A}$ has already passed on the information to someone else (via a measurement) or to the environment (as a consequence of decoherence).

The entropy in Equation (4.8) can be viewed as a half von Neumann—half Shannon: It involves (quantum) conditional density matrices as well as (effectively classical) probabilities of outcomes. Given $\rho_{\mathcal{SA}}$, one can also address a more specific question, e.g., how much information about a specific observable of $\mathcal{S}$ (characterized by its eigenstates $\{|s_j\rangle\}$) will be still missing after a specific observable with the eigenstates $\{|A_k\rangle\}$ of $\mathcal{A}$ is measured. This can be answered by using $\rho_{\mathcal{SA}}$ to compute the joint probability distribution:

$$p(s_j, A_k) = \langle s_j, A_k | \rho_{\mathcal{SA}} | s_j, A_k \rangle . \tag{4.9}$$

These joint probabilities are in effect classical. They can be used to calculate Shannon joint entropy for any two observables (one in $\mathcal{S}$, the other in $\mathcal{A}$), as well as entropy of each of these observables separately, and to obtain the corresponding (Shannon) mutual information:

$$I(\{|s_j\rangle\} : \{|A_k\rangle\}) = H(\{|s_j\rangle\}) + H(\{|A_k\rangle\}) - H(\{|s_j\rangle\}, \{|A_k\rangle\}) . \tag{4.10}$$

We shall find uses for all of these variants of mutual information. The von Neumann entropy based $I(\mathcal{S} : \mathcal{A})$, Equation (4.4), answers the question "how much the systems know about each other", while the Shannon version immediately above quantifies mutual information between two specific observables. Shannon version is (by definition) basis dependent. It is straightforward to see that, for the same underlying joint density matrix:

$$I(\mathcal{S} : \mathcal{A}) \geq I(\{|s_j\rangle\} : \{|A_k\rangle\}) . \tag{4.11}$$

Equality is attained only for a special choice of the two measured observables, and only when the eigenstates of $\rho_{\mathcal{SA}}$ are direct products $|s_k\rangle|A_k\rangle$ of the orthogonal sets of states $\{|s_k\rangle\}$ and $\{|A_k\rangle\}$ of $\mathcal{S}$ and $\mathcal{A}$. In that case correlations between $\mathcal{S}$ and $\mathcal{A}$ can be regarded as completely classical.

With the help of Equation (4.8) one can define "half way" (Shannon—von Neumann) mutual informations that presume a specific measurement on one of the two systems (e.g., $\mathcal{A}$), but make no such commitment for the other one. For instance,

$$J(\mathcal{S} : \{|A_k\rangle\}) = H(\mathcal{S}) - H(\mathcal{S}|\{|A_k\rangle\}) \tag{4.12a}$$

would be one way to express mutual information defined "asymmetrically" in this way. A corresponding formula;

$$J(\mathcal{A} : \{|s_k\rangle\}) = H(\mathcal{A}) - H(\mathcal{A}|\{|s_k\rangle\}) \tag{4.12b}$$

is relevant when $\mathcal{S}$ is measured in the basis $\{|s_k\rangle\}$.

4.1.2. Quantum Discord

Quantum discord is the difference between the mutual information defined using symmetric von Neumann formula, Equation (4.4), and one of the half-way Shannon—von Neumann versions [124–126]. For example:

$$\mathcal{D}(\mathcal{S}; \{|A_k\rangle\}) = I(\mathcal{S} : \mathcal{A}) - J(\mathcal{S} : \{|A_k\rangle\}) . \tag{4.13a}$$

Discord is a measure of how much information about the two systems is inaccessible locally—how much of the globally accessible mutual information is lost when one attempts to find out the state of $\mathcal{SA}$ starting with a local measurement on $\mathcal{A}$ with outcomes $\{|A_k\rangle\}$.

Discord is asymmetric and basis-dependent, as information gain about $\mathcal{S}$ depends on what gets measured on $\mathcal{A}$. The least discord (corresponding to optimal $\{|A_k\rangle\}$):

$$\mathcal{D}(\mathcal{S}; \mathcal{A}) = \min_{\{|A_k\rangle\}} \{\mathcal{D}(\mathcal{S}; \{|A_k\rangle\})\} = 0 \tag{4.13b}$$

disappears iff $\rho_{\mathcal{SA}}$ commutes with $A = \sum_k \alpha_k |A_k\rangle\langle A_k|$:

$$[\rho_{\mathcal{SA}}, A] = 0. \qquad (4.14a)$$

When that happens, quantum correlation is classically accessible from $\mathcal{A}$. This can be assured iff;

$$[\rho_{\mathcal{SA}}, \rho_{\mathcal{A}}] = 0. \qquad (4.14b)$$

Decoherence of $\mathcal{A}$ that einselects preferred pointer basis $\{|A_k\rangle\}$ will evolve $\rho_{\mathcal{SA}}$ to where Equations (4.14) are satisfied to a good approximation [126].

When the composite system is classical, so that its state can be found out without disturbing it and can be—prior to measurements—characterized by a probability distribution that is independent of the measuring process, the symmetric I (defined using joint entropy, Equation (4.4)) and the asymmetric J (defined using conditional entropy, Equation (4.12)) coincide. The proof (see, e.g., Cover and Thomas, 1991) [127] relies on Bayes' rule relating conditional and joint probabilities. Thus, non-vanishing discord signifies breakdown of Bayes' rule in quantum physics.

We emphasize that the asymmetric "half way" (Shannon—von Neumann) mutual information J is indeed asymmetric—it depends on whether measurements are carried out on $\mathcal{A}$ or $\mathcal{S}$. In the classical case asymmetric-looking definition of J results, courtesy of Bayes' rule, in a symmetric mutual information, as $J(\mathcal{S}:\mathcal{A}) = I(\mathcal{S}:\mathcal{A}) = J(\mathcal{A}:\mathcal{S})$. In the classical case $J(\mathcal{S}:\mathcal{A}) = J(\mathcal{A}:\mathcal{S})$, so this does not matter, but in the quantum case, in general, $J(\mathcal{S}:\mathcal{A}) \neq J(\mathcal{A}:\mathcal{S})$.)

As a consequence of asymmetry between the system that is measured and its partner whose state is inferred indirectly, based on the outcome of that measurement, it is possible to have correlations that are classically accessible only "from one end" [128]. For instance:

$$\rho_{\mathcal{SA}} = \frac{1}{2}(|\uparrow\rangle\langle\uparrow| |A_\uparrow\rangle\langle A_\uparrow| + |\nearrow\rangle\langle\nearrow| |A_\nearrow\rangle\langle A_\nearrow|)$$

will be classically accessible through a measurement on $\mathcal{A}$ with orthogonal record states $\{|A_\uparrow\rangle, |A_\nearrow\rangle\}$ (i.e., when $\langle A_\uparrow | A_\nearrow\rangle = 0$), but classically inaccessible to any measurement on $\mathcal{S}$ when $\langle \uparrow | \nearrow \rangle \neq 0$. Indeed, the original motivation for introducing discord was the observation that decoherence of the apparatus makes the correlations accessible from $\mathcal{A}$ [124].

Minimization used in Equation (4.13b) raises the obvious question: Could one do better if one used positive operator valued measures (POVM's) rather than Hermitian observables with orthogonal eigenstates? The answer is, unsurprisingly, "Yes". In the case of POVM's $\{\pi_k\}$ the asymmetric mutual information coincides with the familiar Holevo quantity χ (Holevo, 1973 [129]) :

$$\chi(\rho_\mathcal{A}) = \max_{\{\pi_k\}}\left(H(\rho_\mathcal{A}) - \sum_k p_k H(\mathcal{A}|\pi_k)\right), \qquad (4.12c)$$

so that the minimum discord can be now expressed as:

$$\mathcal{D}(\mathcal{S};\mathcal{A}) = I(\mathcal{S}:\mathcal{A}) - \chi(\rho_\mathcal{A}). \qquad (4.13c)$$

Holevo quantity bounds the capacity of quantum channels to carry classical information. This role of Holevo χ fits naturally into the discussion of quantum Darwinism where fragments $\mathcal{F}$ of the environment play a role of quantum channels transmitting information about $\mathcal{S}$ that is being decohered by $\mathcal{E}$. In particular, Zwolak and Zurek (2013) [130] point out that χ and $\mathcal{D}$—classical and quantum information transmitted by this channel—are complementary, while Touil et al., (2022) [131] show that the Holevo bound is a reasonable estimate of the information about $\mathcal{S}$ that can be accessed by optimal measurement of $\mathcal{F}$.

Quantum discord has become an active area of research following indications that the "quantumness" it defines may play a fundamental role in operation of quantum thermodynamic demons ([128], also Brodutch and Terno, 2010 [132]), in defining completely positive maps (Rodrígues-Rosario et al., 2008) [133], and, especially, in quantum information processing (Datta, Shaji, and Caves, 2008) [134] as well as quantum communication (Piani, Horodecki and Horodecki, 2008 [135]; Luo and Sun, 2010 [136]; Gu et al., 2012 [137]; Dakic et al., 2012 [138]). Our brief introduction to discord is clearly incomplete (see, however, Modi et al., 2012 [139] and Bera et al., 2018 [140] for reviews), but it will suffice for our purpose.

Questions we shall analyze using mutual information and discord will concern (i) redundancy of information (e.g., how many copies of the record does the environment have about $\mathcal{S}$), and; (ii) what is this information about (that is, what observables of the system are recorded in the environment with large redundancy).

Objectivity appears as a consequence of large redundancy. In the limit of large redundancy the precise value of redundancy has as little physical significance as the precise number of atoms on thermodynamic properties of a large system. So, it will be often enough to show that redundancy is large (rather than to calculate exactly what it is). Discord will turn out to be a measure of the unattainable quantum information that cannot be extracted by local measurements from the fragments of the environment.

One might be concerned that having different measures—different mutual informations could be a problem, as this could lead to contradictory answers, but in practice this never becomes a serious issue for two related reasons: There is usually a well-defined pointer observable that obviously minimizes discord, so various possible definitions of mutual information tend to agree where it matters. Moreover, the effect we are investigating—quantum Darwinism—is not subtle: We shall see thet there are usually many copies of pointer states of $\mathcal{S}$ in $\mathcal{E}$, so (as is discussed by Touil et al. (2022) [131] and Zwolak (2022) [141]) the discrepancy between redundancies computed using different methodologies—differences between the numbers of copies defined through different measures—is irrelevant.

4.1.3. Evidence and Its Redundancy

We study a quantum system $\mathcal{S}$ interacting with a composite quantum environment $\mathcal{E} = \mathcal{E}_1 \otimes \mathcal{E}_2 \otimes \cdots \otimes \mathcal{E}_\mathcal{N}$. The question we consider concerns the information one can obtain about $\mathcal{S}$ from a fragment $\mathcal{F}$ of the environment $\mathcal{E}$ consisting of several of its subsystems (see Figure 4). To be more specific, we partition $\mathcal{E}$ into non-overlapping fragments. Redundancy of the record is then defined as the number of disjoint fragments each of which can supply sufficiently complete information (i.e., all but the *information deficit* $\delta < 1$) about $\mathcal{S}$;

$$I(\mathcal{S} : \mathcal{F}_\delta) \geq (1-\delta)H_\mathcal{S} \ . \tag{4.15}$$

Small information deficit, $\delta \ll 1$, implies that nearly all the classically available information can be obtained from $\mathcal{F}_\delta$. This will not always be the case, and $\delta \ll 1$ is not a condition for the effectively classical behavior or even for an agreement between different observers[13].

We now define redundancy as the number of fragments that can independently supply almost all—all but δ—of the missing information $H_\mathcal{S}$ about the system:

$$R_\delta = \frac{1}{f_\delta} \ . \tag{4.16}$$

Definition of redundancy can be illustrated using partial information plots that show the dependence of the mutual information on the size of the intercepted fraction of the

---

[13] In some situations—e.g., where the information about a text is concerned—this demand certainly justified, and $\delta \ll 1$ assures distinguishability of the letters. However, there are situations (e.g., astronomical observations) where accessing larger fraction of the relevant environment (e.g., using telescope to collect more light emitted by Andromeda Nebula) provides more information, and this alone is a conclusive evidence that δ is not always small. Observers generally recognize that, in such situations, disagreements between what they infer about the object of their indirect observations may be a result of the incompleteness of their data (see also Girolami et al., 2022 [142] for discussion of this issue).

environment: Redundancy is the length of the plateau of $I(S:\mathcal{F})$ measured in the units set by the support of the initial, rising, portion of the graph—the part starting at $I(S:\mathcal{F}) = 0$ and ending when $I(S:\mathcal{F}_\delta) = (1-\delta)H_S$ (see Figure 5). Thus, to estimate redundancy we will need to determine how much information about S can one get from a typical fragment $\mathcal{F}$ that contains a fraction;

$$f_\delta = \frac{\#\mathcal{F}_\delta}{\#\mathcal{E}} = \frac{number\ of\ subsystems\ in\ \mathcal{F}_\delta}{number\ of\ subsystems\ in\ \mathcal{E}}$$

of $\mathcal{E}$. For this we need the dependence of the mutual information $I(S,\mathcal{F})$ on $f = \#\mathcal{F}/\#\mathcal{E}$.

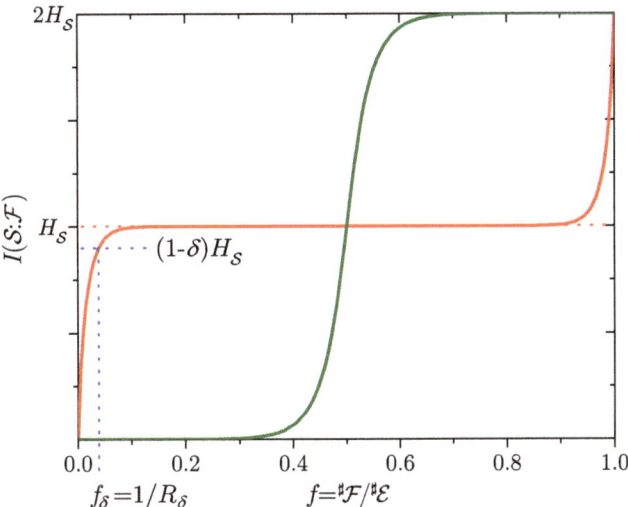

Figure 5. Partial Information Plot (PIP) and redundancy R_δ of the information about a system S stored in its environment $\mathcal{E}$. When global state of $S\mathcal{E}$ is pure, mutual information that can be attributed to a typical fraction f of the environment is antisymmetric around $f = \frac{1}{2}$ and monotonic in f. For pure states picked out at random from the combined Hilbert space $\mathcal{H}_{S\mathcal{E}}$, there is very little mutual information between S and a typical fragment $\mathcal{F}$ smaller than about half of $\mathcal{E}$. However, once threshold fraction $\frac{1}{2}$ is attained, nearly all information is in principle at hand. Thus, such random states (green line above) exhibit only small redundancy. (Strictly speaking redundancy is 2: The environment can be split into two halves, each supplying H_S of information.) By contrast, states of $S\mathcal{E}$ created by decoherence (where the environment $\mathcal{E}$ monitors preferred observables of S) allow one to gain almost all (all but δ) of the information about S accessible through local measurements from a small fraction $f_\delta = 1/R_\delta$ of $\mathcal{E}$. The corresponding PIP (red line above) quickly asymptotes to H_S—the entropy of the system S (either preexisting or caused by decoherence)—which is all of the information about S available from measurements on either $\mathcal{E}$ of S. (More information about $S\mathcal{E}$ can be ascertained only through global measurements on S and a fragment $\mathcal{F}$ corresponding to more than half—indeed, nearly all—of $\mathcal{E}$). H_S is therefore the *classically accessible information*. As $(1-\delta)H_S$ of information can be obtained from a fraction $f_\delta = 1/R_\delta$ of $\mathcal{E}$, there are R_δ such fragments in $\mathcal{E}$, and R_δ is the *redundancy* of the information about S. Large redundancy implies objectivity: The state of the system can be found out independently and indirectly (from fragments of $\mathcal{E}$) by many observers, who will agree about it. In contrast to direct measurements, S will not be perturbed. Thus, *quantum Darwinism accounts for the emergence of objective existence*.

Examples of partial information plots (or "PIPs") of the von Neumann mutual information for a pure composite system consisting of S and $\mathcal{E}$ are shown in Figure 5. The first observation is that these plots are asymmetric around $f = \frac{1}{2}$. This can be demonstrated[14] using elementary properties of the von Neumann mutual information and assuming; (i) $\mathcal{F}$ is typical, and; (ii) the whole of $\mathcal{SE}$ pure [143].

There is a striking difference between the character of PIPs for random pure states in the whole joint Hilbert space $\mathcal{H}_{\mathcal{SE}} = \mathcal{H}_\mathcal{S} \otimes \mathcal{H}_\mathcal{E}$ and states resulting from decoherence—like evolution: For a random state very little information obtains from fragments with $f < \frac{1}{2}$. By contrast, for PIPs that result from decoherence already a small fragment $\mathcal{F}$ of $\mathcal{E}$ ($f \ll 1$) will often supply nearly all the information that can be obtained from less than almost all $\mathcal{SE}$.

The character of such decoherence—generated PIPs suggest dividing information into (i) easily accessible *classical information* $H_\mathcal{S}$ that can be inferred (up to the information deficit δ) from local measurements—from any sufficiently large fragment $\mathcal{F}_\delta$ that is still small compared to half of $\mathcal{E}$, and (ii) *quantum information* that is locally inaccessible, but is present, at least in principle, in the global observables of the whole $\mathcal{SE}$.

This shape of PIPs is a result of einselection: When there is a preferred observable in $\mathcal{S}$ that is monitored but not perturbed by the environment, the information about it is recorded over and over again by different subsystems of $\mathcal{E}$. A combined state of $\mathcal{S}$ and $\mathcal{E}$ resulting from decoherence will have a *branching* structure;

$$|\Psi_{\mathcal{SE}}\rangle = \sum_k e^{i\phi_k} \sqrt{p_k} |\pi_k\rangle \left|\varepsilon_k^{(1)}\right\rangle \left|\varepsilon_k^{(2)}\right\rangle \ldots \left|\varepsilon_k^{(l)}\right\rangle \ldots \quad (4.17)$$

with the pointer states of the system $|\pi_k\rangle$ at the base of each branch. Subsystems of $\mathcal{E}$ are correlated with these pointer states, but, individually, will often contain only poor (far from distinguishable) records of $|\pi_k\rangle$. Nevertheless, even when records contained in individual subsystems are insufficient—$\langle \varepsilon_j^{(l)} | \varepsilon_k^{(l)} \rangle$ is nowhere near δ_{jk}—sufficiently long fragments $\mathcal{F}$ of branches labelled by distinct pointer states $|\pi_k\rangle$ will be approximately orthogonal. As a result, nearly all of the easily accessible classical information can be often recovered from small fragments—a fraction of the environment.

4.1.4. Mutual Information, Pure Decoherence, and Branching States

In quantum Darwinism, fragment $\mathcal{F}$ plays a role of an apparatus or of a communication channel designed to access the same pointer observable that can survive intact in spite of the immersion of $\mathcal{S}$ in $\mathcal{E}$. Decoherence singles out preferred observables of $\mathcal{S}$. They are determined by the dynamics of decoherence, so—in presence of fixed interaction Hamiltonians—they remain unchanged even as more and more copies of the information about the system are deposited in $\mathcal{E}$. This is fortunate, as calculating mutual information is in general difficult. However, when decoherence is the only significant process—when we are dealing with *pure decoherence* that results in perfect branching states—calculations simplify [131,141,144–146]).

Pure decoherence is defined by the system-environment Hamiltonian that commutes with $\{|\pi_k\rangle\}$, pointer states of $\mathcal{S}$, and does not directly correlate subsystems $\mathcal{E}_l$ of the environment:

$$H_{\mathcal{SE}} = \sum_k \sum_l \varsigma_{kl} |\pi_k\rangle\langle\pi_k| \hat{\gamma}_{\mathcal{E}_l}. \quad (4.18a)$$

---

[14] For a pure $\mathcal{SE}$, the joint entropy of $\mathcal{SF}$ must be the same as the entropy of $\mathcal{E}_{/\mathcal{F}}$—the rest of the closed pure $\mathcal{SE}$ (where $\mathcal{E}_{/\mathcal{F}}$ is the remainder of the environment—$\mathcal{E}$ less $\mathcal{F}$). Consequently, mutual information is given by;

$$I(\mathcal{S} : \mathcal{F}) = H_\mathcal{S} + H_\mathcal{F} - H_{\mathcal{S},\mathcal{F}} = H_\mathcal{S} + [H_\mathcal{F} - H_{\mathcal{E}_{/\mathcal{F}}}].$$

When we assume that the fragments of the environment are typical, the entropies in the term in the square brackets are a function of the fraction of the environment contained in the fragment $\mathcal{F}$, so that $H_\mathcal{F} - H_{\mathcal{E}_{/\mathcal{F}}} = H(f) - H(1-f)$, which established the antisymmetry illustrated in Figure 5.

Above, Hermitian operators $\hat{\gamma}_{\mathcal{E}_l}$ act on individual subsystems of $\mathcal{E}$. The resulting evolution operator $U_{\mathcal{SE}}(t)$ factors:

$$U_{\mathcal{SE}}(t) = e^{-iH_{\mathcal{SE}}t/\hbar} = U_{\mathcal{SF}}(t)U_{\mathcal{SE}/\mathcal{F}}(t). \quad (4.18b)$$

This independence of the evolution of a fragment of the environment $\mathcal{F}$ from its remainder $\mathcal{E}/\mathcal{F}$ will greatly simplify our calculations. Addition of a self-Hamiltonian $H_{\mathcal{S}}$ that commutes with $H_{\mathcal{SE}}$ would not affect our discussion. Similarly, one could add self-Hamiltonians of the environment subsystems. As long as $U_{\mathcal{SE}}(t)$ factors as above, our conclusions will be valid.

We now consider evolution of $\rho_{\mathcal{SF}}$ starting from an initially uncorrelated state;

$$\rho_{\mathcal{SE}}(0) = \rho_{\mathcal{S}}(0)\rho_{\mathcal{E}1}(0)\rho_{\mathcal{E}2}(0)...$$

Given our assumptions that include pure decoherence, the evolved state is given by;

$$\rho_{\mathcal{SF}}(t) = U_{\mathcal{SF}}(t)\rho_{\mathcal{S}d\mathcal{E}/\mathcal{F}}(t)\rho_{\mathcal{F}}(0)U_{\mathcal{SF}}(t)^\dagger \quad (4.19)$$

where;

$$\rho_{\mathcal{S}d\mathcal{E}/\mathcal{F}}(t) = \text{Tr}_{\mathcal{E}/\mathcal{F}} U_{\mathcal{SE}/\mathcal{F}}(t)\rho_{\mathcal{S}}(0)\rho_{\mathcal{E}/\mathcal{F}}(0) U_{\mathcal{SE}/\mathcal{F}}(t)^\dagger$$

represents the state of $\mathcal{S}$ decohered by $\mathcal{E}/\mathcal{F}$, the remainder of the environment. The structure of Equation (4.19) implies that the joint entropy of the system $\mathcal{S}$ and the environment fragment $\mathcal{F}$ is given by:

$$H_{\mathcal{SF}}(t) = H_{\mathcal{S}d\mathcal{E}/\mathcal{F}}(t) + H_{\mathcal{F}}(0).$$

This identity is valid for branching states, Equation (4.17), resulting from pure decoherence. It allows us to write (Zurek, 2007 [49]; Zwolak, Quan, and Zurek, 2009 [144]; 2010 [145]):

$$I(\mathcal{S}:\mathcal{F}) = \overbrace{(H_{\mathcal{F}} - H_{\mathcal{F}}(0))}^{\text{local/classical}} + \overbrace{(H_{\mathcal{S}} - H_{\mathcal{S}d\mathcal{E}/\mathcal{F}})}^{\text{global/quantum}}. \quad (4.20)$$

The mutual information is given by the sum of two contributions, which (as indicated above) can often be regarded as, respectively, classical and quantum.

The first contribution, $H_{\mathcal{F}} - H_{\mathcal{F}}(0)$, is the increase of the entropy of the fragment $\mathcal{F}$. In our case of pure decoherence it is all due to the correlation with $\mathcal{S}$—due to the information $\mathcal{F}$ acquires about $\mathcal{S}$. This information about $\mathcal{S}$ can be accessed indirectly, by measuring $\mathcal{F}$, and is available locally (hence, it is within reach of local observers). In the PIP representing decoherence in Figure 5 increase of $H_{\mathcal{F}}$ is responsible for the rapid rise of $I(\mathcal{S}:\mathcal{F})$ that starts at $f=0$ and for its leveling off at the classical plateau at $H_{\mathcal{S}}$ that can happen already at $f \ll 1$. This information about $\mathcal{S}$ is easily accessible because it has been widely disseminated—many independent fragments of $\mathcal{E}$ share it.

The second term, $H_{\mathcal{S}} - H_{\mathcal{S}d\mathcal{E}/\mathcal{F}}$, turns out (Zwolak, Quan, and Zurek, 2010) [145] to be the discord in the pointer basis of $\mathcal{S}$. It is usually negligible when $f < 1$, but can become significant when $f \to 1$ ($\mathcal{F} \to \mathcal{E}$). Consequently, it represents information that can be obtained only via global measurements—measurements that involve nearly all $\mathcal{SE}$. When decoherence by the environment $\mathcal{E}$ is solely responsible for $H_{\mathcal{S}}$, one can rewrite $H_{\mathcal{S}} - H_{\mathcal{S}d\mathcal{E}/\mathcal{F}}$ as $H_{\mathcal{S}d\mathcal{E}} - H_{\mathcal{S}d\mathcal{E}/\mathcal{F}}$—as the difference between the decoherence caused by all of $\mathcal{E}$ and its remainder, $\mathcal{E}/\mathcal{F}$. As long as the remainder $\mathcal{E}/\mathcal{F}$ keeps $\mathcal{S}$ decohered, $H_{\mathcal{S}} - H_{\mathcal{S}d\mathcal{E}/\mathcal{F}} = 0$. Only when, with the increase of f, $\mathcal{E}/\mathcal{F}$ becomes too small to effectively decohere $\mathcal{S}$, $H_{\mathcal{S}d\mathcal{E}/\mathcal{F}}$ begins to be substantially less that $H_{\mathcal{S}}$, and eventually disappears. In that limit of a vanishing remainder $H_{\mathcal{S}} - H_{\mathcal{S}d\mathcal{E}/\mathcal{F}} \to H_{\mathcal{S}}$, and $I(\mathcal{S}:\mathcal{F})$ approaches $2H_{\mathcal{S}}$ for $f \to 1$.

To sum up, the initial climb of $I(\mathcal{S}:\mathcal{F})$ to the classical plateau at $H_{\mathcal{S}}$ is due to $H_{\mathcal{F}} - H_{\mathcal{F}}(0)$. The final climb from that classical plateau to the quantum peak $I(\mathcal{S}:\mathcal{F}) = 2H_{\mathcal{S}}$ happens when the remainder of the environment $\mathcal{E}/\mathcal{F}$ is not enough to keep $\mathcal{S}$ decohered, so that $H_{\mathcal{S}d\mathcal{E}/\mathcal{F}}$ falls below $H_{\mathcal{S}}$. This quantum value of $I(\mathcal{S}:\mathcal{F}) = 2H_{\mathcal{S}}$ can be reached at $f = 1$, and only when $\mathcal{SE}$, as a whole, is pure (so that $H_{\mathcal{SE}} = 0$, and $H_{\mathcal{S}} = H_{\mathcal{E}}$). This additional quantum information can be revealed only by measurements that have global entangled states of $\mathcal{SE}$ as outcomes.

In addition to the need for global measurements there is another reason that suggests that $H_{\mathcal{S}} - H_{\mathcal{S}d\mathcal{E}_{/\mathcal{F}}}$ represents quantum information. It is best illustrated by contrasting the behavior of $H_{\mathcal{S}} - H_{\mathcal{S}d\mathcal{E}_{/\mathcal{F}}}$ for $f \to 1$ when the system starts in a mixture of pointer states (so that its entropy is $H_{\mathcal{S}}$ already before it couples to $\mathcal{E}$, and cannot increase any more due to decoherence by $\mathcal{E}$) with the alternative—when $\mathcal{S}$ starts in a corresponding pure "Schrödinger cat" state (so its entropy is due to decoherence by $\mathcal{E}$, $H_{\mathcal{S}} = H_{\mathcal{S}d\mathcal{E}}$).

In the case of initially pure $\mathcal{E}$ and mixed $\mathcal{S}$ the entropy $H_{\mathcal{S}d\mathcal{E}_{/\mathcal{F}}}$ remains unchanged—the system was pre-decohered—and $I(\mathcal{S} : \mathcal{F})$ levels off at the classical plateau even as $f \to 1$—it can never exceed $H_{\mathcal{S}}$. However, when $\mathcal{S}$ is initially pure, $H_{\mathcal{S}d\mathcal{E}_{/\mathcal{F}}}$ disappears as $\mathcal{F} \to \mathcal{E}$ and $\mathcal{E}_{/\mathcal{F}}$ becomes too small to be an effective decoherer. In that case the additional information that can be in principle recovered from $\mathcal{SE}$ concerns phases between the pointer states (or, to put it differently, observables complementary to the pointer observable).

In the "opposite" case—when $\mathcal{E}$ is initially mixed but $\mathcal{S}$ is initially pure—the first term in Equation (4.20) vanishes, and $H_{\mathcal{F}}(0)$ is already as large as $H_{\mathcal{F}}$ can get, so that classical plateau disappears—the mutual information remains negligible until f is nearly 1. However, even now $H_{\mathcal{S}} - H_{\mathcal{S}d\mathcal{E}_{/\mathcal{F}}}$ eventually attains $H_{\mathcal{S}} = H_{\mathcal{S}d\mathcal{E}}$, as $H_{\mathcal{S}d\mathcal{E}_{/\mathcal{F}}}$ vanishes when $\mathcal{E}_{/\mathcal{F}}$ shrinks with $\mathcal{F} \to \mathcal{E}$. So, at the end of the PIP there is still a quantum peak, but now it rises not above the classical plateau at $I(\mathcal{S} : \mathcal{F}) = H_{\mathcal{S}}$, but, rather from the "sea level", $I(\mathcal{S} : \mathcal{F}) = 0$, so that at $f = 1$ mutual information reaches the peak value of only $H_{\mathcal{S}}$.

4.1.5. Surplus Decoherence and Redundant Decoherence

In realistic situations, observers can intercept only a fraction of the environment. Thus, $f < 1$ (indeed, usually $f \ll 1$). It is therefore often natural to assume that the remainder of the environment suffices to keep $\mathcal{S}$ decohered. This implies that $\rho_{\mathcal{SF}}$ has eigenstates that are products of pointer states of $\mathcal{S}$ with some states of $\mathcal{F}$ (and not, e.g., entangled states of $\mathcal{SF}$; indeed, in this case $\rho_{\mathcal{SF}}$ has vanishing discord—it is classically accessible from $\mathcal{S}$). This will be true providing that there is *surplus decoherence*, so that one does not need all of $\mathcal{E}$ to keep $\mathcal{S}$ decohered—the remainder $\mathcal{E}_{/\mathcal{F}}$ of the environment is enough.

The essence of surplus decoherence is easily traced (and closely tied) to the branching structure of the states of $\mathcal{SE}$ we have already recognized as a consequence of branching states, Equation (4.17), and of pure decoherence, Equation (4.18). Surplus decoherence implies that states of $\mathcal{E}_{/\mathcal{F}}$, the remainder of $\mathcal{E}$, are nearly orthogonal (so they can constitute nearly perfect records of pointer states of $\mathcal{S}$). This guarantees that the same states that are selected by decoherence and diagonalize decohered $\rho_{\mathcal{S}}$ also help diagonalize $\rho_{\mathcal{SF}}$ (i.e., $[\rho_{\mathcal{S}}, \rho_{\mathcal{SF}}] = 0$, Equation (4.14)—the joint state $\rho_{\mathcal{SF}}$ is classically accessible from $\mathcal{S}$, and its discord disappears in the pointer basis). This assumption breaks down when the states of the remainder $\mathcal{E}_{/\mathcal{F}}$ correlated with the pointer states are no longer orthogonal, so that the eigenstates of $\rho_{\mathcal{SF}}$ are entangled or discordant states of $\mathcal{SF}$, and $[\rho_{\mathcal{S}}, \rho_{\mathcal{SF}}] \neq 0$. For an initially pure $\mathcal{SE}$ this will always eventually happen as $f \to 1$, providing that $\mathcal{S}$ started in a superposition of pointer states.

Quantum Darwinism recognizes that situations when there are many copies of $\mathcal{S}$ inscribed in $\mathcal{E}$ are commonplace in our Universe. A single accurate copy in the environment suffices to decohere $\mathcal{S}$. Thus, when there are many copies, one can expect not just "surplus decoherence" but a situation when $\mathcal{S}$ is decohered "many times over". This situation (which often turns out to be generic in our Universe) defines *redundant decoherence*.

Redundant decoherence may sound like an oxymoron—once coherence is lost from $\mathcal{S}$, one might say, there is no way to decohere $\mathcal{S}$ even more. Indeed, redundant decoherence will have no additional effect on $\mathcal{S}$; $\rho_{\mathcal{S}}$ will remain diagonal in the pointer basis, and $H_{\mathcal{S}}$ will no longer increase. However, it will turn out to be useful (e.g., in discussions of irreversibility) to appeal to the redundancy of decoherence R_{δ_D}. Redundancy of decoherence is defined—by analogy with the redundancy of information about $\mathcal{S}$ in $\mathcal{E}$, Equations (4.15) and (4.16)—by enquiring what typical fraction f_{δ_D} of the environment suffices to decohere the system to the extent given by the *decoherence deficit* δ_D:

$$H_{\mathcal{S}d\mathcal{F}_{\delta_D}} = (1 - \delta_D)H_{\mathcal{S}} = (1 - \delta_D)H_{\mathcal{S}d\mathcal{E}}. \quad (4.21)$$

A very small fragment of $\mathcal{E}$, $f_{\delta_D} \ll 1$, will often suffice. The redundancy of decoherence is then defined by:

$$R_{\delta_D} = \frac{1}{\delta_D}, \quad (4.22)$$

and is at least as large (and can be much larger) than the previously defined redundancy of information about $\mathcal{S}$:

$$R_{\delta_D} \geq R_\delta. \quad (4.23)$$

The equality, $R_{\delta_D} = R_\delta$, can be attained only when the environment is initially pure and its subsystems do not interact (so that all of the entropy in its fragments is due to the information it acquires about $\mathcal{S}$). Mixed environment with interacting subsystems can still decohere $\mathcal{S}$ very effectively, but it is generally more difficult to retrieve information about $\mathcal{S}$, so in this case one can have $R_{\delta_D} > R_\delta$ (or even $R_{\delta_D} \gg R_\delta$).

4.1.6. Information Gained by Pure and Mixed Environments

Further simplifications of Equation (4.20) are often possible. Thus, when the environment is initially pure, we get:

$$I(\mathcal{S} : \mathcal{F}) = H_{\mathcal{F}} + \left(H_{\mathcal{S}} - H_{\mathcal{S}d\mathcal{E}_{/\mathcal{F}}}\right).$$

Moreover, when $H_{\mathcal{S}} = H_{\mathcal{S}d\mathcal{E}_{/\mathcal{F}}}$ (due to surplus decoherence):

$$I(\mathcal{S} : \mathcal{F}) = H_{\mathcal{F}} \quad (4.24a)$$

follows. This simple expression for mutual information is valid for pure decoherence in an initially pure environment for f starting at 0 until $\mathcal{F}$ gets to be so large that the decoherence by the (shrinking) remainder $\mathcal{E}_{/\mathcal{F}}$ of the environment is no longer effective and $H_{\mathcal{S}} \neq H_{\mathcal{S}d\mathcal{E}_{/\mathcal{F}}}$.

The opposite case of a completely mixed $\mathcal{E}$ yields:

$$I(\mathcal{S} : \mathcal{F}) = \left(H_{\mathcal{S}} - H_{\mathcal{S}d\mathcal{E}_{/\mathcal{F}}}\right). \quad (4.25)$$

When $\mathcal{S}$ is initially pre-decohered in the pointer basis this implies $I(\mathcal{S} : \mathcal{F}) = 0$. However—and this may seem surprising—for an initially pure $\mathcal{S}$ mutual information will still rise as $f \to 1$, but now (with completely mixed $\mathcal{E}$)—it will reach only $H_{\mathcal{S}}$ (and not $2H_{\mathcal{S}}$ as was the case for pure $\mathcal{S}\mathcal{E}$). This means that quantum phase information is still "out there", and, at least in principle could be recovered (see Ref. [147]), in spite of the completely mixed $\mathcal{E}$.

One might be surprised that completely mixed environments can be effective decoherers. After all, decoherence is caused by the environment "finding out" about the system, and in a completely mixed environment there does not seem to be any place left to accommodate the data. The right way of thinking about this relies on the "Church of Larger Hilbert Space" view of the mixtures, and is very much in tune with the envariant derivation of probabilities and Born's rule in the preceding section. Mixed environment can be regarded as one half of an entangled pair (so that probabilities are due to the symmetries of entangled state involving $\mathcal{E}$ and its purifying "doppelganger" $\mathcal{E}'$ we have explored using Schmidt decomposition in the envariant derivation of Born's rule). That entangled pair will acquire information about $\mathcal{S}$. Thus, even when the environment $\mathcal{E}$ is completely mixed, it will decohere the system as if it was entangled with and "purified" by $\mathcal{E}'$.

The last case (that will be relevant for some of the examples we are about to consider) assumes initially pure $\mathcal{S}$ and $\mathcal{E}$, as well as redundant (or at least surplus) decoherence. In that case:

$$I(\mathcal{S}:\mathcal{F}) = H_\mathcal{F} = H_{\mathcal{S}d\mathcal{F}}. \quad (4.24b)$$

This last equality follows from the Schmidt decomposition of $\mathcal{SE}$ with $\mathcal{F}$ and $\mathcal{SE}_{/\mathcal{F}}$ as subsystems. Under pure decoherence the reduced density matrix $\rho_\mathcal{F}$ does not depend on whether the system is coupled to the remainder of the environment, $\mathcal{E}_{/\mathcal{F}}$. Thus, $\rho_\mathcal{F}$ would be the same if it evolved only in contact with isolated $\mathcal{S}$. However, in that case the system would be decohered only by $\mathcal{F}$, and $H_\mathcal{F} = H_\mathcal{S}$ (by Schmidt decomposition), which establishes $H_\mathcal{F} = H_{\mathcal{S}d\mathcal{F}}$.

This last equality allows one to use standard tools of decoherence to compute $H_\mathcal{F}$. Equality $I(\mathcal{S}:\mathcal{F}) = H_{\mathcal{S}d\mathcal{F}}$ follows from Equation (4.20) under the assumption of surplus decoherence, $H_\mathcal{S} - H_{\mathcal{S}d\mathcal{E}_{/\mathcal{F}}} \approx 0$.

4.1.7. Environment as a Communication Channel

We conclude this section by noting that (with the few simplifications that were already justified) the way in which the information about $\mathcal{S}$ is transmitted by the fragment $\mathcal{F}$ of $\mathcal{E}$ is analogous to the transfer of the (classical) information about the pointer states through a quantum channel. The joint state of $\mathcal{SF}$ has the form:

$$\rho_{\mathcal{SF}} = Tr_{\mathcal{E}_{/\mathcal{F}}} \rho_{\mathcal{SE}} \simeq \sum_k p_k |\pi_k\rangle\langle\pi_k| \rho_{\mathcal{F}_k}. \quad (4.26)$$

Effectively classical pointer states $|\pi_k\rangle\langle\pi_k|$ are encoded in the quantum states $\rho_{\mathcal{F}_k}$ of the channel $\mathcal{F}$. The theorem (due to Holevo, 1973 [129] and Schumacher, 1995 [148]) shows that the capacity of a quantum channel to carry classical information is bounded from above by:

$$\chi(\mathcal{F}:\{\pi_k\}) = H_\mathcal{F} - \sum_k p_k H(\mathcal{F}|\pi_k). \quad (4.27a)$$

When $\pi_k = |\pi_k\rangle\langle\pi_k|$ are orthogonal projectors, χ coincides with the asymmetric mutual information $J(\mathcal{F}|\{|\pi_k\rangle\})$, Equation (4.12). Generalization to where π_k are POVM's is possible. Quantum discord can be then bounded from below by:

$$\mathcal{D}(\mathcal{F}:\{\pi_k\}) = I(\mathcal{F}:\mathcal{S}) - \chi(\mathcal{F}:\{\pi_k\}). \quad (4.27b)$$

Discord is the mutual information that cannot be communicated classically.

One can rewrite the definition of quantum discord as:

$$I(\mathcal{F}:\mathcal{S}) = J(\mathcal{F}:\{\pi_k\}) + \mathcal{D}(\mathcal{F}:\{\pi_k\}). \quad (4.27c)$$

This conservation law (Zwolak and Zurek, 2013) [130] provides a new view of complementarity: The left hand side is fixed and basis—independent, while both terms on the right hand side depend on $\{\pi_k\}$. The first term represents information about the observable ς that can be gained by the measurements on $\mathcal{F}$. This information is maximized for the pointer observable Π. Information inscribed in $\mathcal{F}$ about any other observable ς will be less. One can show [130] that the information about ς that can be obtained from $\mathcal{F}$ is:

$$\chi(\varsigma:\mathcal{F}) = H(\varsigma) - H(\varsigma|\Pi). \quad (4.28)$$

Above, $H(\varsigma|\Pi)$ is the conditional entropy, the information about ς still missing when Π is known. For instance, observables complementary to Π cannot be found out from $\mathcal{F}$.

We can now understand why only the pointer observable (and, possibly, observables closely aligned with it) can be found out by intercepting a fraction of the environment.

Redundant imprinting of an observable ς is possible only when there is a fragment $\mathcal{F}$ that is large enough so that the information about ς can be extracted from it:

$$\chi(\varsigma:\mathcal{F}) \geq (1-\delta)H(\varsigma). \quad (4.29a)$$

Using the earlier expression for $\chi(\varsigma:\mathcal{F})$ one obtains an inequality $H(\varsigma|\Pi) \leq \delta H(\varsigma)$. In other words, redundant information about observables that are so poorly correlated with the pointer observable that the conditional entropy satisfies the inequality:

$$H(\varsigma|\Pi) > \delta H(\varsigma), \quad (4.29b)$$

cannot be obtained from the environment fragments [48,130,149]. We shall return to this subject below.

4.1.8. Quantum Darwinism and Amplification Channels

The usual focus of the communication theory is to optimize the channel capacity. Thus, in quantum communication theory one would consider messages (such as our π_k above) sent with the probabilities p_k, one at a time. Capacity is defined in the limit of many uses of the channel. That is, in this setting one would be dealing with an ensemble described by a density matrix of the form:

$$\varrho_{\mathcal{SF}}^{\mathcal{N}} = \left(\sum_k p_k |\pi_k\rangle\langle\pi_k| \rho_{\mathcal{F}_k}\right)^{\otimes \mathcal{N}}. \quad (4.30a)$$

The theorems are established in the limit of $\mathcal{N} \to \infty$.

By contrast, in quantum Darwinism we are dealing with a state that can be approximately expressed as:

$$\rho_{\mathcal{SF}} \simeq \sum_k p_k |\pi_k\rangle\langle\pi_k| \bigotimes_l^{R_\delta} \rho_{\mathcal{F}_k}^{(l)}. \quad (4.30b)$$

That is, the same message $|\pi_k\rangle\langle\pi_k|$ is inscribed over and over, $\sim R_\delta$ times, in the environment as a whole. This is how its multiple copies can reach many observers.

This is also why an observer who consults one fragment of $\mathcal{E}$ and infers the state of the system from it will get data consistent with the first finding from the consecutive fragments. In view of this structure of the states of the environment the nomenclature "amplification channel" is well justified: Shared quantum information becomes effectively classical, since quantum discord cannot be shared (Streltsov and Zurek, 2013) [150]. Quantum Darwinism implements amplification that provides means of such sharing, shedding new light on the ubiquity of amplification in the transition from quantum to classical.

We shall now illustrate these insights in models of quantum Darwinism. We shall also investigate situations where some or even all of the simplifying assumptions employed above break down. We also note that the above discussion focused on the mutual information defined via von Neumann entropy, and thus, that it prepared us to answer the question about the amount of information that was deposited in, and can be extracted from $\mathcal{F}$. This largely bypasses the question: What is this information about? One can anticipate that the answer is "pointer states". We have already produced evidence of this. We shall confirm and quantify it (by enquiring how much information one can extract from $\mathcal{F}$ about other observables) while discussing quantum Darwinism in specific models.

4.2. Quantum Darwinism in Action

Dissemination of information throughout the environment has not been analyzed until recently. Given the complexity of this process, it is no surprise that the number of results to date is still rather modest, but they have already led to new insights into the nature of the quantum-to-classical transition. The models discussed here show that; (i) *dynamics responsible for decoherence is capable of imprinting multiple copies of the information* about the system in the environment. Whether that environment can serve as a useful witness depends on the memory space it has available to store this information, and whether the information is stored unscrambled and unperturbed and is accessible to observers.

Quantum Darwinism will always lead to decoherence, but the reverse is not true: There are situations where the environment cannot store any information about $\mathcal{S}$ (e.g., because $\mathcal{E}$ is completely mixed to begin with) or where the information it stores becomes scrambled by the dynamics (so that it is effectively inaccessible to local observers).

So, redundancy of records that is so central to quantum Darwinism is not necessarily implied by decoherence. Moreover; (ii) *redundancy can keep on increasing long after decoherence has completely decohered the system*: Copies of the einselected pointer observable can continue to be added—imprinted on $\mathcal{E}$. As we have already noted, redundancy of decoherence is at least as large as R_δ, and can be much larger: It is possible to have hugely redundant decoherence while R_δ remains negligible. However, typically, both redundancies will continue to increase as the system and the environment continue to interact.

Last not least; (iii) *only the einselected pointer states can be redundantly recorded in $\mathcal{E}$*. While multiple copies of the information about the preferred pointer observable are disseminated throughout $\mathcal{E}$, only one copy of the complementary information is (at best) shared by all the subsystems of the environment, making it effectively inaccessible.

Using imperfect analogies with classical devices, one can say that the information flow from $\mathcal{S}$ to $\mathcal{E}$ acts as an amplifier for the pointer observable, and, simultaneously, as a shredder for the complementary observables, dispersing slivers of a single copy of the phase information in the correlations with many subsystems of the environment. All of these fragments would have to be brought together and coherently reassembled to recover preexisting state of $\mathcal{S}$. By contrast, many copies of the information about the pointer observable are readily available from the fragments of $\mathcal{E}$.

In addition to these general characteristics of quantum Darwinism we shall see that realistic models—e.g., photon scattering—can lead to huge redundancies, and that environment that is partially mixed can still serve as an effective communication channel, allowing many observers independent access to the information about the preferred observable of the system.

4.2.1. C-Nots and Qubits

The simplest model of quantum Darwinism is a rather contrived arrangement of many (N) target qubits that constitute subsystems of the environment interacting via a *controlled not* ("c-not") with a single control qubit $\mathcal{S}$. As time goes on, consecutive target qubits become imprinted with the state of the control $\mathcal{S}$:

$$(a|0\rangle + b|1\rangle) \otimes |0_{\varepsilon_1}\rangle \otimes |0_{\varepsilon_2}\rangle \cdots \otimes |0_{\varepsilon_N}\rangle \Longrightarrow$$
$$\Longrightarrow (a|0\rangle \otimes |0_{\varepsilon_1}\rangle + b|1\rangle \otimes |1_{\varepsilon_1}\rangle) \otimes |0_{\varepsilon_2}\rangle \cdots \otimes |0_{\varepsilon_N}\rangle \Longrightarrow$$
$$\Longrightarrow a|0\rangle \otimes |0_{\varepsilon_1}\rangle \otimes \cdots \otimes |0_{\varepsilon_N}\rangle + b|1\rangle \otimes |1_{\varepsilon_1}\rangle \cdots \otimes |1_{\varepsilon_N}\rangle.$$

It is evident that this pure decoherence dynamics is creating branching states with multiple records of the logical (as well as pointer) states $\{|0\rangle, |1\rangle\}$ of the system in the environment. Mutual entropy between $\mathcal{S}$ and a subsystem $\mathcal{E}_k$ can be easily computed. As the k'th c-not is carried out, $I(\mathcal{S} : \mathcal{E}_k)$ increases from 0 to:

$$I(\mathcal{S} : \mathcal{E}_k) = H_\mathcal{S} + H_{\mathcal{E}_k} - H_{\mathcal{S}, \mathcal{E}_k} = -|a|^2 \lg |a|^2 - |b|^2 \lg |b|^2 \ .$$

Thus, each $\mathcal{E}_k$ is a sufficiently large fragment of $\mathcal{E}$ to supply complete information about the pointer observable of $\mathcal{S}$.

The very first c-not causes complete decoherence of $\mathcal{S}$ in its pointer basis $\{|0\rangle, |1\rangle\}$. This illustrates points (i)–(iii) above—the relation between the (surplus and redundant) decoherence and quantum Darwinism, the continued increase of redundancy well after coherence between pointer states is lost, and the special role of the pointer observable.

As each environment qubit is a perfect copy of the pointer states of $\mathcal{S}$, redundancy R in this simple example is eventually given by the number of fragments that have complete information about $\mathcal{S}$—that is, in this case, by the number of environment qubits, $R = N$. There is no need to define redundancy in a more sophisticated manner, using δ, when each environment subsystem contains perfect copy of the pointer state: It will arise only in the more realistic cases when the analogues of c-not's are imperfect. We also note that decoherence is redundant, as each environment qubit suffices to decohere the system, so the redundancy of decoherence is also given by N.

Partial information plots in our example would be trivial: $I(\mathcal{S} : \mathcal{F})$ jumps from 0 to the "classical" value given by $H_{\mathcal{S}} = -|a|^2 \lg |a|^2 - |b|^2 \lg |b|^2$ at $f = 1/N$, continues along the plateau at that level until $f = 1 - 1/N$, and eventually jumps up again to the quantum peak at twice the level of the classical plateau as the last qubit is included: The whole $\mathcal{S}\mathcal{E}$ is still in a pure state, so when $\mathcal{F} = \mathcal{E}$, $H_{\mathcal{S},\mathcal{F}} = H_{\mathcal{S},\mathcal{E}} = 0$. However, this much information exists only in global entangled states, and is therefore accessible only through global measurements.

Preferred pointer basis of the control $\mathcal{S}$ is of course its logical basis $\{|0\rangle, |1\rangle\}$. These pointer states are selected by the "construction" of c-not's. They remain untouched by copying into consecutive environment subsystems $\mathcal{E}_k$. After decoherence takes place;

$$I(\mathcal{S} : \mathcal{F}) = J(\{|0\rangle, |1\rangle\} : \mathcal{F})$$

for any fragment of the environment when there is at least one subsystems of $\mathcal{E}$ correlated with $\mathcal{S}$ left outside of $\mathcal{F}$, which suffices to decohere $\mathcal{S}$. When this is the case, minimum quantum discord disappears:

$$\mathcal{D}(\mathcal{F} : \mathcal{S}) = I(\mathcal{S} : \mathcal{F}) - J(\{|0\rangle, |1\rangle\} : \mathcal{F}) = 0,$$

and one can ascribe probabilities to correlated states of $\mathcal{S}$ and $\mathcal{F}$ in the pointer basis of $\mathcal{S}$ that are singled out by the c-not "dynamics". Discord would reappear only if all of $\mathcal{E}$ got included, as then $I(\mathcal{S} : \mathcal{F}) = 2H_{\mathcal{S}}$, twice the information of the classical plateau of the PIP. Thus, all of $\mathcal{E}$ is needed to detect coherence in $\mathcal{S}$: When a single environment qubit is missing, it is impossible to tell if the initial state was a superposition or a mixture of $|0\rangle$ and $|1\rangle$ of $\mathcal{S}$.

As soon as decoherence sets in, $H_{\mathcal{S}} = H_{\mathcal{S},\mathcal{F}}$ for any fragment $\mathcal{F}$ that leaves enough of the rest of the environment $\mathcal{E}_{/\mathcal{F}}$ to einselect pointer states in $\mathcal{S}$. Consequently;

$$I(\mathcal{S} : \mathcal{F}) = H_{\mathcal{F}},$$

and $H_{\mathcal{F}} = H_{\mathcal{S}d\mathcal{F}}$, illustrating Equations (4.20) and (4.24).

4.2.2. Central Spin Decohered by Noninteracting Spins

A generalization of a model with c-not gates and qubits is a model with a central spin system interacting with the environment of many other spins. In effect, perfect c-not's discussed above become imperfect when a collection of spins interacts with the central spin system via Ising Hamiltonian:

$$\mathbf{H} = \sigma^z \sum_i d_i \sigma_i^z. \qquad (4.31a)$$

Above σ^z and σ_i^z act on the spins of the system and on the subsystems of the environment.

Several different versions of such models were studied as examples of quantum Darwinism ([131,143–146,149,151–157]). In this section, we focus on the steady state situation when the evolution results, at long times, in a PIP that is largely time-independent.

Hamiltonian of Equation (4.31a) provides an example of pure decoherence. It can imprint many copies of the preferred observable σ^z onto the environment. Given the example of c-not's and qubits, this is no surprise.

Copies of the pointer states of $\mathcal{S}$ are, of course, no longer perfect: A single subsystem of the environment is typically no longer perfectly correlated with the system. It is therefore usually impossible for a single subsystem of $\mathcal{E}$ to supply all the information about $\mathcal{S}$. Nevertheless, when the environment is sufficiently large, asymptotic form of $I(\mathcal{S} : \mathcal{F})$ has—as a function of the size of the fragment $\mathcal{F}$—the same character we have already encountered with c-not's: A steep rise (where in accord with Equations (4.20) and (4.24), every bit of information stored in $\mathcal{F}$ reveals new information about $\mathcal{S}$) followed by a plateau (where the information only confirms what is already known). This is clearly seen in Figure 6A: Only when the environment is too small to convincingly decohere the system, PIPs do not have a plateau.

In a central spin model with a large, initially pure and receptive environment (so that there is a pronounced classical plateau) and for a small information deficit δ, mutual information of a fragment $\mathcal{F}$ with $\sharp\mathcal{F}$ finite-dimensional subsystems is approximately [152]:

$$I(\mathcal{S} : \mathcal{F}) = H_{\mathcal{S}} - \frac{1}{2}(e^{H_{\mathcal{S}}} - 1)(d_{\mathcal{E}}^{-\sharp\mathcal{F}} - d_{\mathcal{E}}^{-(\sharp\mathcal{E}-\sharp\mathcal{F})}) \,. \qquad (4.32)$$

Above, $d_{\mathcal{E}}$ is the size of the Hilbert space of the effective memory of a single environment subsystem (e.g., $d_{\mathcal{E}} = 2$ for a spin $\frac{1}{2}$ that can use all its memory to store information about $\mathcal{S}$). This is a good approximation only as $I(\mathcal{S} : \mathcal{F})$ is close to the plateau: For f near 0 or near 1 mutual information is approximately linear in f, see Figure 6B, although actual dependence on f turns out to be more complicated in exactly solvable models (see, e.g., Touil et al., 2022) [131].

When $\delta \ll 1$ and $f < \frac{1}{2}$, we can use Equation (4.32) to estimate redundancy. To this end we retain dominant terms and set $I(\mathcal{S} : \mathcal{F}) = (1 - \delta)H_{\mathcal{S}}$ to get:

$$(1-\delta)H_{\mathcal{S}} \approx H_{\mathcal{S}} - \frac{1}{2}(e^{H_{\mathcal{S}}} - 1)d_{\mathcal{E}}^{-\sharp\mathcal{F}_{\delta}}.$$

A simple formula for $\sharp\mathcal{F}_{\delta}$, the number of subsystems that reduce information deficit to δ follows when $H_{\mathcal{S}} \gg 1$;

$$\sharp\mathcal{F}_{\delta} \approx \log_{d_{\mathcal{E}}} \frac{e^{H_{\mathcal{S}}} - 1}{2\delta H_{\mathcal{S}}} \approx \frac{H_{\mathcal{S}} - \ln 2\delta H_{\mathcal{S}}}{\ln d_{\mathcal{E}}} \approx \frac{H_{\mathcal{S}}}{\ln d_{\mathcal{E}}} \,. \qquad (4.33a)$$

This last approximate answer shows that in the central spin model redundancy is close to what one might guess: It is given by the number of environment fragments that have enough subsystems—$H_{\mathcal{S}}/\ln d_{\mathcal{E}}$—to store information about $\mathcal{S}$. In other words, there are approximately;

$$R_{\delta} = \frac{\sharp\mathcal{E}}{\sharp\mathcal{F}_{\delta}} \approx \frac{\sharp\mathcal{E} \ln d_{\mathcal{E}}}{H_{\mathcal{S}}} \qquad (4.33b)$$

fragments of $\mathcal{E}$ that "know" the state of the system. Note that the information deficit δ does not appear in this approximate answer: We have dropped the subdominant $\ln \delta$ in Equation (4.33a).

In the discussion above $\ln d_{\mathcal{E}}$ enters as a measure of the memory capacity of a subsystem of $\mathcal{E}$. This and the universality of re-scaling in Figure 6B suggest a conjecture: The environment will fill in the space available to store information with qmems of $\mathcal{S}$.

We conclude that, when only a part of the Hilbert space of the environment subsystem is available to record the state of the system $\mathcal{S}$, one should be able to use just this "accessible memory" of the subsystem instead of its maximal information storage capacity $h_m = \ln d_{\mathcal{E}}$ in the estimates of redundancy. We shall now corroborate this conjecture.

A. Partial Information Plots: Qutrits and Qubits

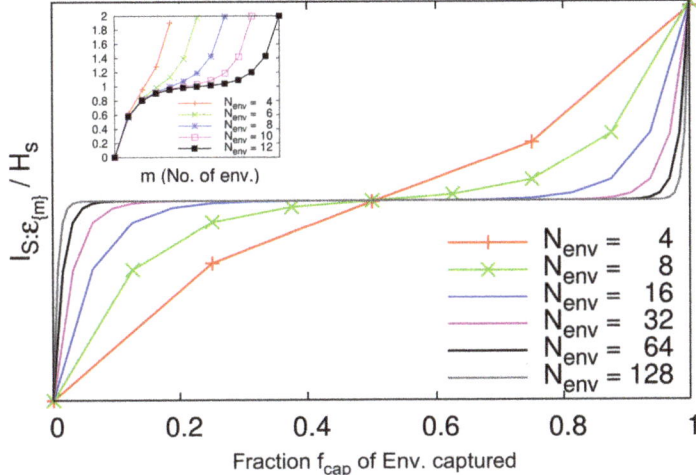

B. Universal Rise of a Partial Information Plot.

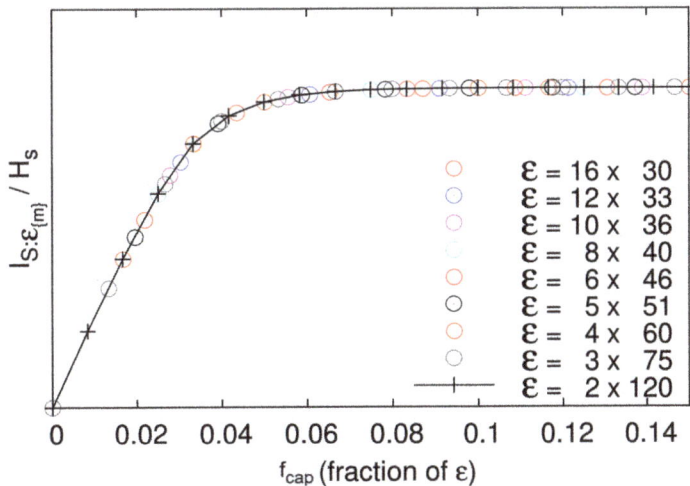

Figure 6. (**A**). **Partial information plots for pure decoherence:** (**A**) A qutrit coupled to $N = 4\ldots 128$ qutrit environment plotted against the fraction $f = {}^{\#}\mathcal{F}/{}^{\#}\mathcal{E}$ (see Blume-Kohout and Zurek, 2006 [152], for details). As the number of the environment subsystems increases, redundancy grows, which is reflected by the increasingly steep slope of the initial part of the plot. The inset [152] depicts rescaled mutual information of a qubit plotted against the number m of the environment qubits (rather than their fraction). Elongation of the plateau leads to the increase of redundancy: R_δ is the length of the PIP measured in units defined by the size (e.g., in the number of environment subsystems needed m_δ, see Figure 5) of the part of the PIP that corresponds to $I(\mathcal{S} : \mathcal{F})$ rising from 0 to $(1 - \delta)H_{\mathcal{S}}$. (**B**). Universal rise of partial information plots of a qutrit coupled to nine different environments with different *subsystem size* $d_\mathcal{E}$ and cardinality ${}^{\#}\mathcal{E}$, but with nearly identical total information capacity plotted as a function of their fractional information capacity.

4.2.3. Quantum Darwinism in a Hazy Environment.

Inaccessibility of the memory of $\mathcal{E}$ can have different causes [144,145,153,158]. The most obvious one is the possibility that the environment starts in a partly mixed state, so that some of its Hilbert space is already "taken up" by the information that is of no interest to observers[15]. It is then tempting to use the available memory of the environmental subsystem, given by the maximal information storage capacity h_m less h, the preexisting entropy, instead of its maximal memory $h_m = \ln d_\mathcal{E}$ in Equation (4.33b). When this substitution is made, the estimated redundancy is:

$$R_\delta^h \approx \frac{\sharp \mathcal{E}}{\sharp \mathcal{F}_\delta} \approx \sharp \mathcal{E} \frac{(h_m - h)}{H_\mathcal{S}}, \qquad (4.33c)$$

or;

$$R_\delta^h \approx \left(1 - \frac{h}{h_m}\right) R_\delta. \qquad (4.33d)$$

That is, redundancy in a partly mixed environment, R_δ^h, decreases compared to the redundancy in the pure environment R_δ in proportion to the memory that is still available to accept the information about the system.

In the manageable case of a single qubit system, $H_\mathcal{S} = \ln 2$, the substitution of $h_m - h$ for $\ln d_\mathcal{E}$ works [145], although the expression we have used above for, e.g., R_δ has to be modified, as the derivation of Equation (4.33a) assumes $H_\mathcal{S} \gg 1$. A rather large environment (hundreds of qubits, with symmetries of the initial state and of the interaction Hamiltonian exploited to keep the size of the memory down) was used to explore a range of values of h. This was necessary because the principal effect of a mixed environment is to lower the slope of the initial part of PIP's by $(1 - h/h_m)$, so now it takes more subsystems of $\mathcal{E}$ to get to the "plateau".

The results for a central spin $\frac{1}{2}$ in the environment of spin $\frac{1}{2}$ subsystems confirmed that the redundancy decreased by approximately $1 - h/h_m$ (Zwolak, Quan, and Zurek, 2010) [145]. This change in R_δ^h was due to the change in the slope of the early part of PIP. Equation (33c,d) became a more accurate approximation when the environment was more mixed, i.e., when h was, to begin with, closer to h_m. Of course, when $h = h_m$, no information about $\mathcal{S}$ can be recovered from the environment, as $H_\mathcal{F}(t)$ cannot increase when it starts at a maximum. Nevertheless, as already noted, mixed environments are still very effective in decohering the system. Thus, even as the classical contribution $H_\mathcal{F}(t) - H_\mathcal{F}(0) = 0$, disappears, the quantum contribution, $H_\mathcal{S} - H_{\mathcal{S}d\mathcal{E}/\mathcal{F}}$, to $I(\mathcal{S}:\mathcal{F})$ remains similar to the case when $\mathcal{E}$ was initially pure.

As we have seen before with c-not's and qubits, the system decoheres as soon as a single copy of its state is imprinted with a reasonable accuracy in $\mathcal{E}$, and—when the environment is initially pure—a few imperfect imprints establish the initial rising part of the PIP. However, as new subsystems of $\mathcal{E}$ become correlated with $\mathcal{S}$, the size of the plateau increases and its elongation (when plotted as a function of $\sharp \mathcal{F}$) occurs without any real change to the early part of the PIP (see inset in Figure 6A). Thus, the number of copies of the information $\mathcal{E}$ has about $\mathcal{S}$ can grow long after the system was decohered. This increase of the number of copies leads to the corresponding increase of the redundancy of decoherence. Moreover, redundancy of decoherence R_{δ_D} exceeds the redundancy of the information available to the observers R_δ, as even mixed environments retain their undiminished ability to decohere.

---

[15] A related question arises in the situation when—in addition to the "quantum system of interest"—there are many other systems "of no interest" that can imprint information on the common environment. There is therefore a danger that the information of interest would be diluted with irrelevant bits, suppressing the redundancy responsible for objectivity. Zwolak and Zurek (2017) [155] show that mixing of the relevant and irrelevant bits of information makes little difference to the redundancy of the information of interest.

4.2.4. Quantum Darwinism and Pointer States

What information is redundantly acquired by $\mathcal{E}$ and can be recovered by observers from its fragments? In systems with discrete observables such as spins one can prove that it concerns pointer states of the system. The proof was first given in the idealized case of perfect environmental records, and then extended to the case of imperfect records (Ollivier, Poulin, and Zurek, 2004 [149]; 2005 [151]).

A natural way to characterize such correlations is to use the mutual information between an observable σ of $\mathcal{S}$ and a measurement $\mathfrak{e}$ on $\mathcal{E}$: Shannon mutual information $I(\sigma : \mathfrak{e})$ measures the ability to predict the outcome of measurement of σ on $\mathcal{S}$ after a measurement $\mathfrak{e}$. For a given density matrix of $\mathcal{S} \otimes \mathcal{E}$, the measurements results are characterized by a joint probability distribution

$$p(\sigma_i, \mathfrak{e}_j) = \text{Tr}\{(\sigma_i \otimes \mathfrak{e}_j)\rho^{\mathcal{SE}}\},$$

where σ_i and $\mathfrak{e}_j$ are the spectral projectors of observables σ and $\mathfrak{e}$. By definition, the mutual information is the difference between the initially missing information about σ and the remaining uncertainty about it when $\mathfrak{e}$ is known. Shannon mutual information is defined using Shannon entropies of subsystems (e.g., $H(\sigma) = -\sum_i p(\sigma_i) \log p(\sigma_i)$) and the joint entropy $H(\sigma, \mathfrak{e}) = -\sum_{i,j} p(\sigma_i, \mathfrak{e}_j) \log p(\sigma_i, \mathfrak{e}_j)$:

$$I(\sigma : \mathfrak{e}) = H(\sigma) + H(\mathfrak{e}) - H(\sigma, \mathfrak{e}).$$

The information about observable σ of $\mathcal{S}$ that can be optimally extracted from ν environmental subsystems is

$$\mathcal{I}_\nu(\sigma) = \max_{\{\mathfrak{e} \in \mathfrak{M}_\nu\}} I(\sigma : \mathfrak{e})$$

where $\mathfrak{M}_\nu$ is the set of all measurements on those ν subsystems. In general, $\mathcal{I}_\nu(\sigma)$ will depend on which particular ν subsystems are considered. For simplicity, we will assume that any *typical* ν environmental subsystems yield roughly the same information. This may appear to be a strong assumption, but relaxing it does not affect our conclusions. By setting $\nu = {}^\sharp\mathcal{E} = N$ to the total number of subsystems of $\mathcal{E}$, we get the information content of the entire environment. The condition;

$$\mathcal{I}_N(\sigma) \approx H(\sigma)$$

expresses the *completeness* prerequisite for objectivity: All (or nearly all) missing information about σ of $\mathcal{S}$ must be in principle obtainable from all of $\mathcal{E}$.

As a consequence of the basis ambiguity, information about many observables σ can be deduced by a suitable (generally, global) measurement on the entire environment [24,25]. Therefore, completeness, while a prerequisite for objectivity, is not a very selective criterion (see Figure 7a for evidence). To claim objectivity, it is not sufficient to have a complete imprint of the candidate property of $\mathcal{S}$ in the environment. There must be many copies of this imprint that can be accessed independently by many observers: *information must be redundant*.

To quantify redundancy, we count the number of copies of the information about σ present in $\mathcal{E}$:

$$R_\delta(\sigma) = {}^\sharp\mathcal{E}/\nu_\delta(\sigma) = N/\nu_\delta(\sigma).$$

Above $\nu_\delta(\sigma)$ is the smallest number of typical environmental subsystems that contain almost all the information about σ (i.e., $\mathcal{I}_\nu(\sigma) \geq (1 - \delta)\mathcal{I}_N(\sigma)$).

The key question now is: What is the structure of the set $\mathfrak{D}$ of observables that are **completely,** $I_N(\sigma) \approx H(\sigma)$, and **redundantly,** $R_\delta(\sigma) \gg 1$ with $\delta \ll 1$, imprinted on the environment? The answer is provided by the theorem:

Theorem 4. *The set $\mathfrak{O}$ is characterized by a unique observable Π, called by definition the* **maximally refined observable**, *as the information $\mathcal{I}_\nu(\sigma)$ about any observable σ in $\mathfrak{O}$ obtainable from a fraction of $\mathcal{E}$ is equivalent to the information about σ that can be extracted from its correlations with the maximally refined observable Π:*

$$\mathcal{I}_\nu(\sigma) = I(\sigma : \Pi) \tag{4.34}$$

for $\nu_\delta(\Pi) \leq m \ll N$.

Proof. Let $\sigma^{(1)}$ and $\sigma^{(2)}$ be two observables in $\mathfrak{O}$ for $\delta = 0$. Since $\sigma^{(1)}$ and $\sigma^{(2)}$ can be inferred from two disjoint fragments of $\mathcal{E}$, they must commute. Similarly, let $\mathfrak{e}^{(1)}$ (resp. $\mathfrak{e}^{(2)}$) be a measurement acting on a fragment of $\mathcal{E}$ that reveals all the information about $\sigma^{(1)}$ (resp. $\sigma^{(2)}$) while causing minimum disturbance to $\rho^{\mathcal{SE}}$. Then, $\mathfrak{e}^{(1)}$ and $\mathfrak{e}^{(2)}$ commute, and can thus be measured *simultaneously*. This combined measurement gives complete information about $\sigma^{(1)}$ and $\sigma^{(2)}$. Hence, for any pair of observables in $\mathfrak{O}$, it is possible to find a more refined observable which is also in $\mathfrak{O}$. The maximally refined observable Π is then obtained by pairing successively all the observables in $\mathfrak{O}$. By construction Π satisfies equality $\mathcal{I}_\nu(\sigma) = I(\sigma : \Pi)$ for any σ in $\mathfrak{O}$. □

Theorem 4 can be extended to nearly perfect records for assumptions satisfied by usual models of decoherence (Ollivier, Poulin, and Zurek, 2005 [151]). The proof is based on the recognition that only the already familiar pointer observable can have a redundant and robust imprint on $\mathcal{E}$. This Theorem can be understood as *a consequence of the ability of the pointer states to persist while immersed in the environment*. This resilience allows the information about the pointer observables to proliferate, very much in the spirit of the "survival of the fittest".

Note that the above Theorem does not guarantee the existence of a *non trivial* observable Π: when the system does not properly correlate with $\mathcal{E}$, the set $\mathfrak{O}$ will only contain the identity operator.

Two important consequences of this theorem follow: (*i*) An observer who probes only a fraction of the environment is able to find out the state of the system as if he measured Π on $\mathcal{S}$; (*ii*) Information about any other observable ς of $\mathcal{S}$ will be inevitably limited by the available correlations existing between ς and Π. In essence, our theorem proves the uniqueness of redundant information, and therefore the selectivity of its proliferation.

We can illustrate this preeminence of the pointer observable in our simple model: a single central spin $\frac{1}{2}$ interacting with a collection of N such spins, Equation (4.31a). As seen in Figure 7a environment as a whole contains information about any observable of $\mathcal{S}$. Preferred role of the pointer observable becomes apparent only when one seeks observables that are recorded *redundantly* in $\mathcal{E}$. Figure 7b shows that only the pointer observable $\Pi = \sigma_z$ (and observables that are nearly co-diagonal with it) are recorded redundantly, illustrating the theorem quoted above. The "ridge of redundancy" is strikingly sharp.

Further confirmation and extension of the theorem quoted above is the relation (derived under the assumption of surplus decoherence; Zwolak and Zurek, 2013 [130]) between the available information (characterized by the Holevo quantity χ, measure of the capacity of the quantum information channel for classical information) about an arbitrary observable ς and the pointer observable Π of the system, see Equation (28), and its consequences, Equations (29a) and (b).

Comparison of Figure 7a,b also shows that redundancy of σ_z increases long after the environment as a whole is strongly entangled with $\mathcal{S}$. This is seen in a steady rise of the redundancy R_δ with the action. Thus, as anticipated, redundancy can continue to increase long after the system has decohered.

The origin of the consensus between different observers is the central lesson that follows from our considerations. In everyday situations, observers have no choice in the observables of systems of interest they will measure. This is because they rely on the "second hand" information they obtain from the same environment that is responsible for decoherence. In addition, the environment that selects a certain pointer observable will record redundantly only the information about that observable.

Information about complementary observables is in principle still "out there", but one would have to intercept essentially all of the environment (to be more precise, all but its $1 - \frac{1}{R_{\delta_D}} \geq 1 - \frac{1}{R_\delta}$ fraction) and measure it in the right way (that is, using an observable with entangled eigenstates) to have any hope of acquiring that information. By contrast, to find out about the pointer observables, a small fraction of the environment $\sim \frac{1}{R_\delta}$ is enough.

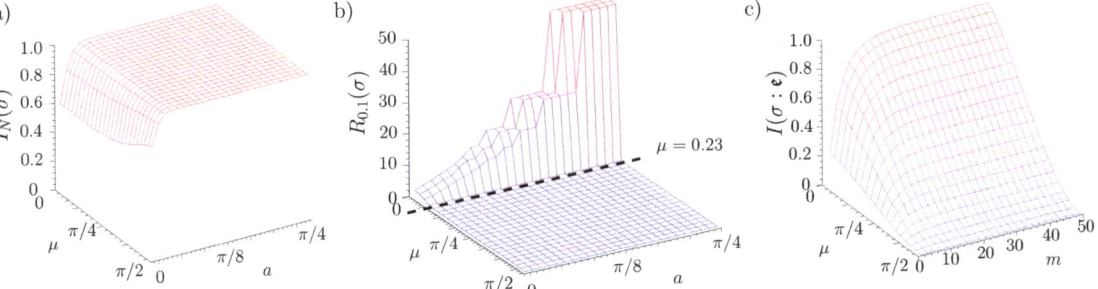

Figure 7. **Selection of the preferred observable in Quantum Darwinism in a simple model of decoherence** (Ollivier, Poulin, and Zurek, 2004 [149]). The system $\mathcal{S}$, a spin-$\frac{1}{2}$ particle, interacts with $N = 50$ qubits of $\mathcal{E}$ through the Hamiltonian $\mathbf{H} = \sigma^z \sum_k g_k \sigma_k^z$ for a time t. The initial state of $\mathcal{S} \otimes \mathcal{E}$ is $\frac{1}{\sqrt{2}}(|0\rangle + |1\rangle) \otimes |0\rangle_{\mathcal{E}_1} \otimes \ldots \otimes |0\rangle_{\mathcal{E}_N}$. Couplings are selected randomly with uniform distribution in the interval (0,1]. All the plotted quantities are a function of the system's observable $\sigma(\mu) = \cos(\mu)\sigma^z + \sin(\mu)\sigma^x$, where μ is the angle between its eigenstates and the pointer states of $\mathcal{S}$—here the eigenstates of σ^z. (**a**) Information acquired by the optimal measurement on the whole environment, $\hat{I}_N(\sigma)$, as a function of the inferred observable $\sigma(\mu)$ and the average interaction action $\langle g_k t \rangle = a$. Nearly all information about every observable of $\mathcal{S}$ is accessible in the *whole* environment for any observables $\sigma(\mu)$ except when the action a is very small (so that $\mathcal{E}$ does not know much about $\mathcal{S}$). Thus, complete imprinting of an observable of $\mathcal{S}$ in $\mathcal{E}$ is not sufficient to claim objectivity. (**b**) Redundancy of the information about the system as a function of the inferred observable $\sigma(\mu)$ and the average action $\langle g_k t \rangle = a$. It is measured by $R_{\delta=0.1}(\sigma)$, which counts the number of times 90% of the total information can be "read off" independently by measuring distinct fragments of the environment. For all values of the action $\langle g_k t \rangle = a$, redundant imprinting is sharply peaked around the pointer observable. Redundancy is a very selective criterion. The number of copies of relevant information is high only for the observables $\sigma(\mu)$ falling inside the theoretical bound (see Equation (4.29)) indicated by the dashed line. (**c**) Information about $\sigma(\mu)$ extracted by an observer restricted to local random measurements on m environmental subsystems. The interaction action $a_k = g_k t$ is randomly chosen in $[0, \pi/4]$ for each k. Because of redundancy, pointer states—and only pointer states—can be found out through this far-from-optimal measurement strategy. Information about any other observable $\sigma(\mu)$ is restricted by the theorem discussed in this subsection (see also Refs. [130,149,151]) to be equal to the information about it revealed by the pointer observable $\Pi = \sigma^z$.

As we shall see, redundancies for, e.g., the photon environment are astronomical. It is therefore no surprise that we rely on the information that can be obtained with little effort from a small fraction of $\mathcal{E}$. In addition, it is also no surprise that the complementary information is inaccessible. Therefore (and as is established through a sequence of results in Girolami et al., 2022 [142] the evidence of quantumness is unavailable from the fragments of $\mathcal{E}$. Moreover, observers that find out about their Universe in this way will agree about the outcomes. This is how objective classical reality emerges from a quantum substrate in our quantum Universe.

4.2.5. Redundancy vs. Relaxation in the Central Spin Model

We have seen defining characteristics of quantum Darwinism in the central spin model. Thus; (i) decoherence begets redundancy which; (ii) can continue to increase long after decoherence saturated entropy of the system at H_S. Moreover, (iii) both decoherence and quantum Darwinism single out the same pointer observable. There are multiple copies of the pointer observable in the environment, and only the information about the pointer states is amplified by the decoherence process. This happens at the expense of the information about the complementary observables (i.e., information about the phases between the pointer states).

Our model is illustrated in Figure 8. It differs from the central spin models we have investigated as now the spins of the environment interact and can exchange information. The effect of the interactions between the environmental subsystems on partial information plots and on the redundancy is seen in Figure 9. The coupling of the central spin to the environmental spins is stronger than their couplings to each other. As a result, partial information plots quickly assume the form characteristic of quantum Darwinism caused by pure decoherence, and redundancy rises to values of the order of the size of the environment.

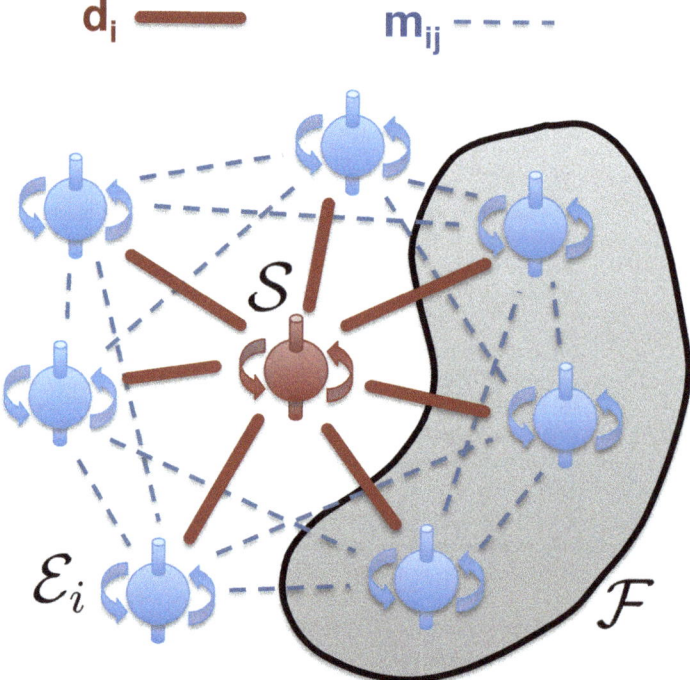

Figure 8. Central spin model with interacting environment subsystems. Decoherence is no longer pure: An environment of 16 spins $\mathcal{E}_i$ coupled to a single system qubit $\mathcal{S}$ with Hamiltonian given by Equation (4.31b) is the basis of the results presented in this subsection and in Figure 9. As before, fragment $\mathcal{F}$ is a subset of the whole environment $\mathcal{E}$. The couplings d_i and m_{ij} were selected from normal distributions with zero mean and standard deviations $\sigma_d = 0.1$ and $\sigma_m = 0.001$. Crucially, the interactions between $\mathcal{S}$ and the $\mathcal{E}_i$ are much stronger than those within $\mathcal{E}$. That is, $\sigma_d \gg \sigma_m$, so that information acquisition by the individual subsystems of the environment happens faster that the exchange of information between them. As a consequence, pure decoherence is initially a reasonable approximation. Eventually, however, interactions between the spins of the environment scramble the information so that fragments of $\mathcal{E}$ composed of individual spins reveal almost nothing about $\mathcal{S}$.

Initially, pure decoherence is a reasonable approximation. However, as time goes on, correlations between spins of the environment gradually build up. Interactions between the spins of $\mathcal{E}$ mean that the state of a fragment of the environment begins to entangle with—begins to acquire information about—the rest of the environment. As a consequence, the information individual spins had about the system becomes delocalized as it is shared with the rest of $\mathcal{E}$. The structure of the states of $\mathcal{SE}$ is no longer branching—it is no longer possible to represent them by Equation (4.17). More general entangled states of the Hilbert space of $\mathcal{SE}$ are explored. Eventually, interactions may take the systems closer to equilibrium (although we do not expect complete equilibration in our model—the central spin decoheres, but its pointer states remain unaffected by the environment). Consequently, over time, PIPs are expected to change character from the steep rise followed by a long plateau characteristic of pure decoherence (red graph in Figure 5) to the approximate step function shape (green graph in Figure 5) that is characteristic of a collection of spins in equilibrium (see Page, 1993 [159]).

All of the models investigated so far were "pure decoherence"—subsystems of the environment interacted only with the system $\mathcal{S}$ via an interaction that left the pointer basis untouched. This assured validity of Equation (4.20), so that the information gained by the environment about the pointer states of $\mathcal{S}$ remained localized, available from the fragments of the environment.

The idealization of pure decoherence is often well-motivated. Photon environment, for example, consists of subsystems (photons) that interact with various systems of interest but do not interact with one another. There are, however, other environments—such as air—that contribute to or even dominate decoherence, but consist of interacting subsystems (air molecules). Thus, while the pointer basis is still untouched by decoherence, information about it will no longer be preserved in the individual subsystems of the environment—it will become delocalized, and, hence, impossible to extract from the local fragments of the environment consisting of its natural subsystems.

To investigate what happens when subsystems of $\mathcal{E}$ interact and exchange information we relax the assumption of pure decoherence and consider a model that adds to the central spin model of Equation (4.31a) interactions between the environmental spins:

$$\mathbf{H} = \sigma^z \sum_i d_i \sigma_i^z + \sum_{j,k} m_{jk} \sigma_j^z \sigma_k^z. \qquad (4.31b)$$

As a consequence, the information about the system of interest is still present in the correlations with the environment, but it will gradually become encrypted in non-local states of $\mathcal{E}$ that are inaccessible to local observers—i.e., that do not provide information about $\mathcal{S}$ via measurements that access small ($f < \frac{1}{2}$) fragments of $\mathcal{E}$ consisting of its subsystems.

The timescale over which pure decoherence is a good approximation depends on the strength of the couplings. In our case, the coupling between the system and the spins of the environment is significantly stronger than the couplings between the spins of $\mathcal{E}$. As a result, states of $\mathcal{SE}$ acquire initially an approximately branching structure and have PIP's that allow significant redundancy to develop. However, over time, interactions within $\mathcal{E}$ take the system closer to equilibrium, and PIPs change. More detailed discussion of this can be found in the caption of Figure 9, and, especially, in Riedel, Zurek, and Zwolak, 2012 [153].

Our simple model with weakly interacting environment subsystems illustrates why environments where the subsystems (photons) are in effect non-interacting are used by observers to gather information rather than environments (such as air) that may be more effective in causing decoherence but scramble information acquired in the process because their subsystems (air molecules) interact with each other.

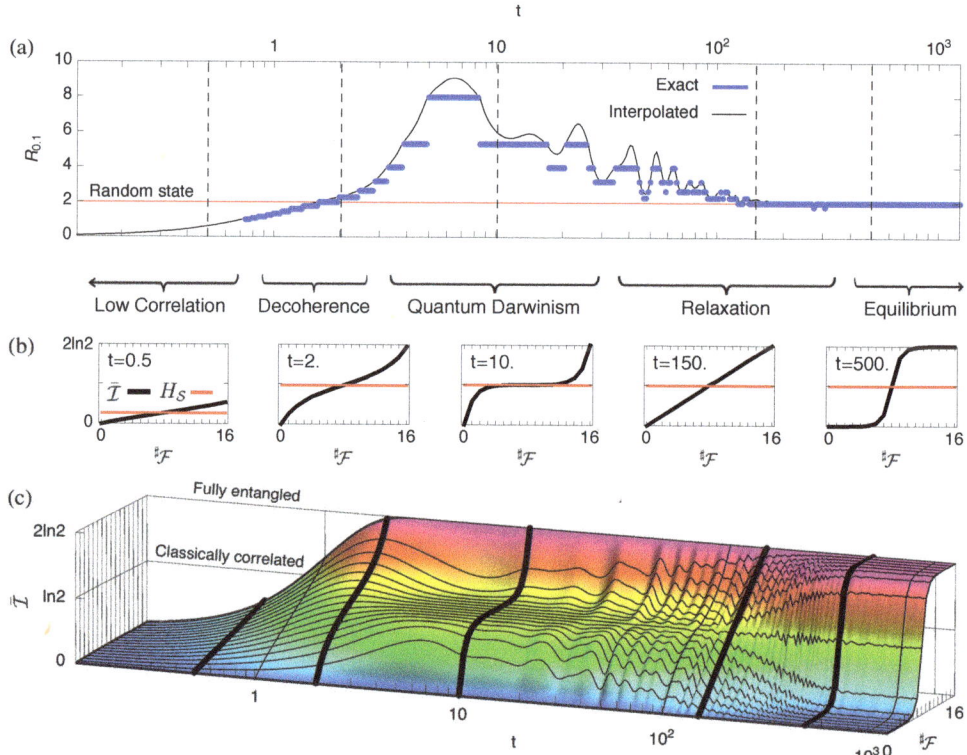

Figure 9. Rise and fall of redundancy in the spin universe of Figure 8 (see Riedel, Zurek, and Zwolak, 2012 [153]). (a) The redundancy R_δ is the number of fragments of $\mathcal{E}$ that provide (here, up to a fractional deficit $\delta = 0.1$) information about the system. The exact redundancy is supplemented with an estimate based on the interpolated value of $I(\mathcal{S} : \mathcal{F}_f)$. The vertical dashed lines mark five instants. (b) The mutual information $I(\mathcal{S} : \mathcal{F}_f)$ versus fragment size $^\#\mathcal{F}$, and the entropy $H_\mathcal{S}$ of the system at five instants corresponding to different qualitative behavior. (c) The mutual information $I(\mathcal{S} : \mathcal{F}_f)$ versus fragment size $^\#\mathcal{F}$ and time t. Thick black lines mark five instants. *Low correlation* ($t = 0.5$) for small times means $\mathcal{E}$ "knows" very little about $\mathcal{S}$. Each spin added to $\mathcal{F}$ reveals a bit more about $\mathcal{S}$, resulting in the linear dependence $I(\mathcal{S} : \mathcal{F}_f)$ on f. *Decoherence* ($t = 2$) sets in near $\tau_d \equiv (\sqrt{N}\sigma_d)^{-1} = 2.5$. By then the density matrix of $\mathcal{S}$ approaches a mixture of the two pointer states $|\uparrow\rangle$ and $|\downarrow\rangle$ singled out by the interaction and the state is approximately branching. Mutual information is still nearly linear in $^\#\mathcal{F}$ and $R_\delta \sim O(1)$. Mixing within $\mathcal{E}$ can be neglected as $t \ll \sigma_m^{-1} = 1000$. *Quantum Darwinism* ($t = 10$) is characterized by $I(\mathcal{S} : \mathcal{F}_f)$ that rises to the plateau; the first few spins reveal nearly all classical information: Additional spins just confirm it. The quantum information (above the plateau) is still present in the global state but accessible only via an unrealistic global measurement of almost all of $\mathcal{SE}$. After $t \sim \sigma_d^{-1} = 10$, few spins suffice to determine the state of $\mathcal{S}$ no matter how large N is, so $R_\delta \sim N$. In the absence of the couplings m_{ij} this (approximately pure decoherence) would persist. (For some environments, such as photons, this is indeed the case.) *Relaxation* ($t = 150$) occurs near $t \sim \tau_m \equiv (\sqrt{N}\sigma_m)^{-1} = 250$. Mixing within the environment entangles any given spin's information about $\mathcal{S}$ with the rest of $\mathcal{E}$, reducing usefulness of the fragments. The mutual information plateau is destroyed, so redundancy plummets. *Equilibrium* ($t = 500$) is reached for $t \sim \sigma_m^{-1} = 1000$, when the actions associated with interaction between spin pairs in the environment reach order unity. The state ceases to be branching. The mutual information plot takes the form of random states in the combined Hilbert space of $\mathcal{SE}$. An observer can learn virtually nothing about the system unless almost half the environment is accessed.

4.2.6. Quantum Darwinism in Quantum Brownian Motion

Evolution of a single harmonic oscillator (the system) coupled through its coordinate with a collection of many harmonic oscillators (the environment) is a well known exactly solvable model (Feynman and Vernon, 1963 [160]; Dekker, 1977 [161]; Caldeira and Leggett, 1983 [162]; Unruh and Zurek, 1989 [163]; Hu, Paz, and Zhang, 1992 [164], Paz, Habib, and Zurek, 1993 [165]; Tegmark and Wheeler, 2001 [166]; Bacciagaluppi, 2004 [167]).

This is not a pure decoherence model. While the environment oscillators do not interact, the self-Hamiltonian of $\mathcal{S}$ does not commute with the interaction Hamiltonian. Therefore, when the oscillations are underdamped preferred states selected by their predictability are Gaussian minimum uncertainty wavepackets (Zurek, Habib, and Paz, 1993 [63]; Tegmark and Shapiro, 1994 [168]; Gallis, 1996 [169]). This is in contrast to spin models (including the model we have just discussed) where exact and orthogonal pointer states can be often identified. So, while decoherence in this model is well understood, quantum Darwinism—where the focus is not on $\mathcal{S}$, but on its relation to a fragment $\mathcal{F}$ of $\mathcal{E}$—presents novel challenges.

Here, we summarize results (Blume-Kohout and Zurek, 2008 [170]; Paz and Roncaglia, 2009 [171]) obtained under the assumption that fragments of the environment are "typical" subsets of its oscillators—that is, subsets of oscillators with the same spectral density as the whole $\mathcal{E}$.

The QBM Hamiltonian:

$$\mathbf{H} = H_\mathcal{S} + \frac{1}{2}\sum_\omega \left(\frac{q_\omega^2}{m_\omega} + m_\omega \omega^2 y_\omega^2\right) + x_\mathcal{S}\sum_\omega C_\omega y_\omega$$

describes a collection of the environment oscillators coupled to the harmonic oscillator system with:

$$H_\mathcal{S} = (\frac{p_\mathcal{S}^2}{m_\mathcal{S}} + m_\mathcal{S}\Omega_0^2 x_\mathcal{S}^2)/2,$$

and the environmental coordinates y_ω and q_ω describe a single band (oscillator) $\mathcal{E}_\omega$. As usual, the bath is defined by its spectral density, $I(\omega) = \sum_n \delta(\omega - \omega_n)\frac{C_n^2}{2m_n\omega_n}$, that quantifies the coupling between $\mathcal{S}$ and each band of $\mathcal{E}$. An *ohmic* bath with a sharp cutoff Λ: $I(\omega) = \frac{2m_\mathcal{S}\gamma_0}{\pi}\omega$ for $\omega \in [0\ldots\Lambda]$ was adopted: A sharp cutoff (rather than the usual smooth rolloff) simplifies numerics. Each coupling is a differential element, $dC_\omega^2 = \frac{4m_\mathcal{S}m_\omega\gamma_0}{\pi}\omega^2 d\omega$ for $\omega \in [0\ldots\Lambda]$. For numerics, whole range of frequencies $[0\ldots\Lambda]$ was discretized by dividing it into into discrete bands of width $\Delta\omega$, which approximates the exact model well up to a time $\tau_{rec} \sim \frac{2\pi}{\Delta\omega}$.

The system was initialized in a squeezed coherent state, and $\mathcal{E}$ in its ground state. QBM's linear dynamics preserve the Gaussian nature of the state, which can be described by its mean and variance:

$$\vec{z} = \begin{pmatrix} \langle x \rangle \\ \langle p \rangle \end{pmatrix}; \Delta = \begin{pmatrix} \Delta x^2 & \Delta xp \\ \Delta xp & \Delta p^2 \end{pmatrix}.$$

Its entropy is a function of $a^2 = \left(\frac{\hbar}{2}\right)^{-2}\det(\Delta)$, its squared symplectic area. Thus;

$$H(a) = \frac{1}{2}((a+1)\ln(a+1) - (a-1)\ln(a-1)) - \ln 2 \approx \ln\left(\frac{e}{2}a\right), \quad (4.35)$$

where e is Euler's constant, and the approximation is excellent for $a > 2$. For multi-mode states, numerics yield $H(\rho)$ exactly as a sum over Δ's symplectic eigenvalues (Serafini et al., 2004) [172]. The theory proposed in Ref. [170] approximates a collection of oscillators as a single mode with a single a^2.

Mutual information illustrated in partial information plots (Figure 10) shows that $I(\mathcal{S} : \mathcal{F})$—the information about $\mathcal{S}$ stored in $\mathcal{F}$—rises rapidly as the fraction of the environment f included in $\mathcal{F}$ increases from zero, then flattens for larger fragments. Most—all but ~ 1 nat—

of $H_\mathcal{S}$ is recorded redundantly in $\mathcal{E}$. When $\mathcal{S}$ is macroscopic, this *non-redundant information* is dwarfed by the total amount of information available from even small fractions of $\mathcal{E}$.

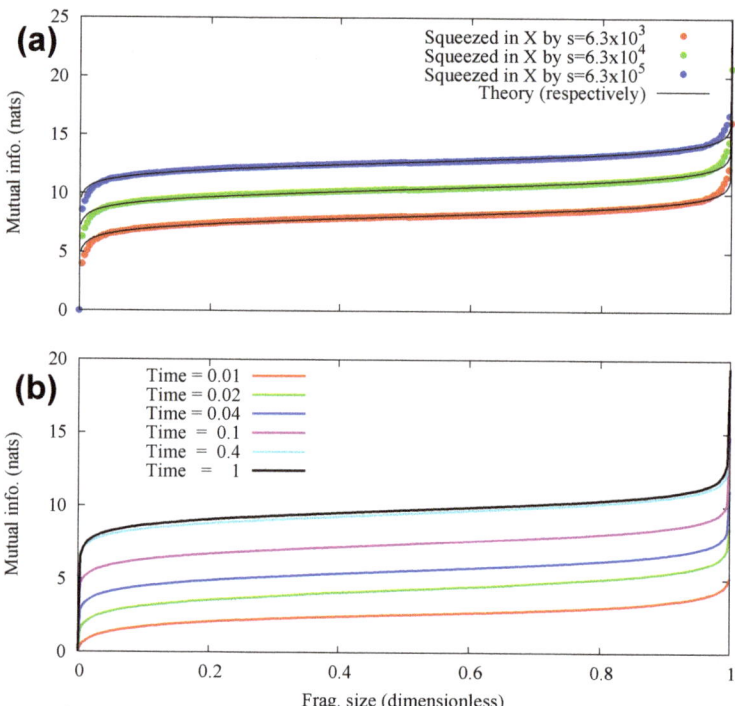

Figure 10. Partial information plots for quantum Darwinism in quantum Brownian motion (see Blume-Kohout and Zurek, 2008 [170]). The system $\mathcal{S}$ was initialized in an x-squeezed state, which decoheres as it evolves into a superposition of localized states. Plot (**a**) shows PIPs for three fully-decohered ($t = 4$) states with different squeezing. Small fragments of $\mathcal{E}$ provide most of the information about $\mathcal{S}$. Squeezing changes the amount of *redundant* information without changing the PIP's shape. The numerics agree with the simple theory, Equation (4.36), discussed in Ref. [170]. Plot (**b**) tracks one state as decoherence progresses. PIPs' shape is invariant; time only changes the redundancy of information.

Calculations simplify in the macroscopic limit where the mass of the system is large compared to masses of the environment oscillators. This regime (of obvious interest to the quantum–classical transition) allows for analytic treatment based on the Born-Oppenheimer approximation: Massive system follows its classical trajectory, largely unaffected by $\mathcal{E}$. The environment will, however, decohere a system that starts in a superposition of such trajectories. In the process, $\mathcal{E}$ that starts in the vacuum will become imprinted with the information about the location of $\mathcal{S}$.

The basic observation is that the area of the $1 - \sigma$ contours in phase space determines entropy. As a result of decoherence, the squared symplectic area corresponding to the state of the system will increase by $\delta a_\mathcal{S}^2$. This is caused by the entanglement with the environment, so the entropies and symplectic areas of environment fragments increase as well. When $\mathcal{F}$ contains a randomly selected fraction f of $\mathcal{E}$, $\rho_\mathcal{F}$'s squared area is $a_\mathcal{F}^2 = 1 + f \delta a_\mathcal{S}^2$, and that of $\rho_{\mathcal{SF}}$ is $a_{\mathcal{SF}}^2 = 1 + (1-f) \delta a_\mathcal{S}^2$. Applying Equation (4.35) (where $\delta a_\mathcal{S}^2 \gg 1$) yields:

$$I(\mathcal{S} : \mathcal{F}) \approx H_\mathcal{S} + \frac{1}{2} \ln\left(\frac{f}{1-f}\right). \tag{4.36}$$

This "universal" $I(S : \mathcal{F})$ (Blume-Kohout and Zurek, 2008 [170]; Roncaglia and Paz, 2009 [171]) is valid for significantly delocalized initial states of S (which implies large H_S). It is a good approximation everywhere except very near $f = 0$ and $f = 1$ (where it would predict singular behavior). It has a classical plateau at H_S which rises as decoherence increases entropy of the system.

In contrast to PIP's we have seen before (e.g., in the central spin model), adding more oscillators to the environment does not simply extend the plateau: The shape of $I(S : \mathcal{F})$ is only a function of f and so it is invariant under enlargement of $\mathcal{E}$. This is because the couplings of individual environment oscillators are adjusted so that the damping constant of the system oscillator remains the same. Therefore, increasing the number of oscillators in the environment does not really increase the number of the copies of the state of the system in $\mathcal{E}$—in a sense it only improves the accuracy with which the environment with a continuum distribution of frequencies (e.g., a field) is modeled using discrete means.

When the above equation for $I(S : \mathcal{F})$ is solved for f_δ one arrives at the estimate for the redundancy:

$$R_\delta \approx e^{2\delta H_S} \approx s^{2\delta}. \tag{4.37}$$

The last equality above follows because an s-squeezed state decoheres to a mixed state with $H_S \approx \ln s$. This simple last formula for R_δ holds where it matters—after decoherence but before relaxation begins to force the system to spiral down towards its ground state.

As trajectories decay, plateau flattens compared to what Equation (4.36) would predict. This will initially increase redundancy R_δ above the values attained after decoherence (see Figure 11). Eventually, as the whole $S\mathcal{E}$ equilibrates, the system will spiral down to occupy a mixture of low-lying number eigenstates, and R_δ will decrease.

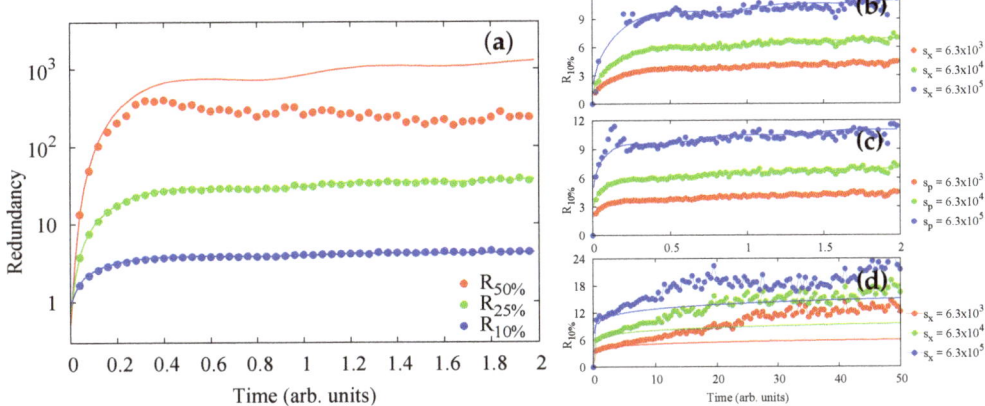

Figure 11. **Delocalized states of a decohering oscillator redundantly recorded by the environment** (Blume-Kohout and Zurek, 2008 [170]). Plot (**a**) shows redundancy R_δ vs. time for three information deficits δ, when the initial state of the system is a Gaussian squeezed in x by $s_x = 6.3 \times 10^3$. Plots (**b**–**d**) show $R_{10\%}$—redundancy of 90% of the available information—vs. initial squeezing (s_x or s_p). Dots denote numerics; lines—theory. S has mass $m_S = 1000$, $\omega_S = 4$. $\mathcal{E}$ comprises oscillators with $\omega \in [0\ldots 16]$ and mass $m = 1$. The frictional coefficient is $\gamma = \frac{1}{40}$. Redundancy develops with decoherence: p-squeezed states [plot (**c**)] decohere almost instantly, while x-squeezed states [plot (**b**)] decohere as a $\frac{\pi}{2}$ rotation transforms them into p-squeezed states. Redundancy persists thereafter [plot (**d**)]; dissipation intrudes by $t \sim O(\gamma^{-1})$, causing $R_{10\%}$ to rise above simple theory. Redundancy increases *exponentially*—as $R_\delta \approx s^{2\delta}$—with the information deficit [plot (**a**)]. So, while $R_\delta \sim 10$ may seem modest, $\delta = 0.1$ implies *very* precise knowledge (resolution of around 3 ground-state widths) of S. This is half an order of magnitude better than a recent results for measuring a micromechanical oscillator (see e.g. Ref. [173]). At $\delta \sim 0.5$—resolving $\sim \sqrt{s}$ different locations within the wavepacket—redundancy reaches $R_{50\%} \gtrsim 10^3$ (maximum numerical resolution of Ref. [170]).

Quantum Brownian motion model confirms that decoherence leads to quantum Darwinism. However, details of quantum Darwinism in QBM setting are different from what we have becomes accustomed to in the models involving discrete Hilbert spaces of $\mathcal{S}$ and of subsystems of $\mathcal{E}$. Partial information plots with the shape that is independent of the size of $\mathcal{E}$ and a scaling of redundancy with the information deficit δ that is not logarithmic as before are clear manifestations of such differences.

Buildup of redundancy still takes longer than the initial destruction of quantum coherence. Nevertheless, various time-dependent processes (such as the increase of redundancy caused by dissipation) remain to be investigated in detail. Moreover, localized states favored by einselection are redundantly recorded by $\mathcal{E}$. So, quantum Darwinism in QBM confirms many of the features of decoherence we have anticipated earlier. On the other hand, we have found an interesting tradeoff between redundancy and information deficit δ, Equation (4.37). It suggests that, in situations where QBM is applicable, objectivity (as measured by redundancy) may come at the price of accuracy.

We also note that surplus decoherence we have described before can be found in the case of QBM. This follows, in effect, from the fact that $a_{\mathcal{S}\mathcal{F}}^2 = 1 + (1-f)\delta a_{\mathcal{S}}^2$ approaches $a_{\mathcal{S}}^2 = 1 + \delta a_{\mathcal{S}}^2$ for small f. Consequently, it is evident that $H_\mathcal{S} - H_{\mathcal{S},\mathcal{E}_{/\mathcal{F}}} \approx 0$, and the mutual information $I(\mathcal{S}:\mathcal{F})$ is given by $H_\mathcal{F}$. This is not obvious from the simple scale-invariant Equation (4.37) above.

To sum up, we note that while broadly defined tenets of quantum Darwinism—multiple records of $\mathcal{S}$ in $\mathcal{E}$, buildup of redundancy to large values, etc.—are satisfied in QBM, there are also interesting differences. Thus, QBM—in contrast to the spin models—does not have an obvious version in which decoherence is pure (as there is no perfect pointer observable that commutes with the whole Hamiltonian of $\mathcal{SE}$). However, when the mass of $\mathcal{S}$ is large and the initial state is delocalized in position, at least early on pure decoherence is a good (Born-Oppenheimer—like) approximation.

Eventually the collection of oscillators begins to relax, and the information about the system flows from their individual states to correlations between them. This is because, even though the oscillators of the environment do not directly interact with each other, they do interact indirectly via the system oscillator: There is no perfect pointer observable for our harmonic oscillator $\mathcal{S}$. The obvious consequence of this is the damping suffered by $\mathcal{S}$. Less obvious is its role in coupling of the environment oscillators: Even though they do not interact directly (as did spins of the environment in Equation (4.31b)), they exchange information about one another indirectly, via $\mathcal{S}$, which in time creates entanglements that make it more difficult to extract information about $\mathcal{S}$ from the fragments of $\mathcal{E}$ defined by collections of the (original) oscillators.

4.2.7. Huge Redundancy in Scattered Photons

The two decoherence models discussed above—central spin model and quantum Brownian motion—are the two standard workhorses of decoherence. They were the early focus of quantum Darwinism primarily because one could analyze them using many of the tools developed to study decoherence. We have thus seen quantum Darwinism in action, and we have already confirmed in these idealized models that the expectations about the shape of partial information plots resulting from decoherence and about the buildup of redundancy are satisfied—with variations—in both cases. This is reassuring. However, while redundancies appeared in both cases, they were modest ($R_\delta \sim 10$), in part as a result of the limited size of the environment. Moreover, neither model is an accurate representation of how we find out about our world.

In our Universe vast majority of data acquired by human observers comes via the photon environment. A fraction f, usually corresponding to a very small fragment $\mathcal{F}_f$ of the photon environment scattered or emitted by the "system of interest" is intercepted by our eyes. This is how we find out about what we have grown accustomed to regard as "objective classical reality".

It is fair to expect that the photon environment should have significant redundancies—we use up only a tiny fraction of photon evidence, and others who look at the same systems generally agree about their states. To investigate quantum Darwinism in (photon) scattering processes we turn to the model of decoherence discussed by Joos and Zeh (1985) [174] that was since updated (Gallis and Fleming, 1990 [175]; Hornberger and Sipe, 2003 [176]; Dodd and Halliwell, 2003 [177]; Halliwell, 2007 [178]) and applied by others, for example to calculate decoherence in the fullerene experiments (Hornberger et al., 2003 [179]; Hackermüller et al., 2004 [180]). The book by Schlosshauer (2007) [32] provides a good overview.

In contrast to Joos and Zeh (1985) [174] who focused on decoherence caused by the isotropic black-body radiation we are interested in the information content of the scattered photons. We shall therefore primarily consider a distant point source that illuminates an object—a dielectric sphere of radius r—that is initially in a non-local superposition (see Figure 12), although we shall also discuss the isotropic case as a counterpoint. We shall assume thermal distribution of energies (and, hence, wavelengths) of the incoming radiation and (at least in the results we shall focus on below) we will assume that photons come as a plane wave from a single direction (which approximates illumination by a distant localized light source such as the Sun or a light bulb). Generalizations to other models of illumination have been considered by Riedel and Zurek, 2011 [158].

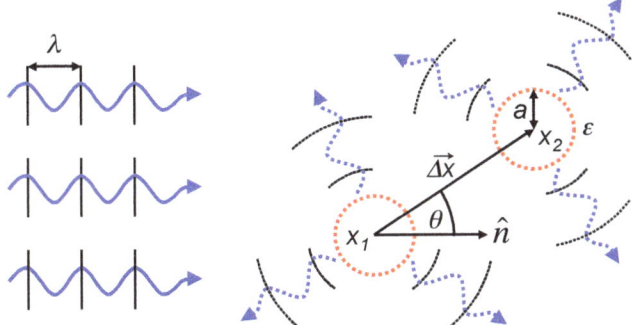

Figure 12. Scattering photons from a dielectric sphere 'Schrödinger's cat' (Riedel and Zurek, 2010; 2011 [158,181]). This is a realistic case of quantum Darwinism: Scattered photons carry multiple copies of the information about the location of $\mathcal{S}$: A dielectric sphere of radius r and permittivity ϵ is initially in a superposition with separation $\Delta x = |x_1 - x_2|$. This object—our systems $\mathcal{S}$—scatters plane-wave radiation with thermally distributed photons of wavelength λ propagating in a direction $\hat{n}$ that makes an angle θ with the vector $\vec{\Delta x}$.

The scattering process is responsible for the decoherence of $\mathcal{S}$ and for the imprinting of information about the location of the scatterer $\mathcal{S}$ in the photon environment. As the initial state of $\mathcal{S}$ we take a nonlocal "Schrödinger cat" superposition of two locations:

$$|\psi_\mathcal{S}(\vec{x})\rangle = (|\vec{x}_1\rangle + |\vec{x}_2\rangle)/\sqrt{2} \, .$$

We ignore the self-Hamiltonian of the sphere so that its pointer states are localized in space. One can justify this approximation by pointing to the large mass of the sphere. Large mass also enables our other approximation—we shall ignore the momentum imparted to the sphere by the photons. Note that—under these assumptions—scattering of photons from $\mathcal{S}$ results in pure decoherence.

Scattering takes the initial pure state density matrix $\rho_\mathcal{S}^0 = |\psi_\mathcal{S}(\vec{x})\rangle\langle\psi_\mathcal{S}(\vec{x})|$ into a mixture with the off-diagonal terms:

$$|\langle\vec{x}_1|\rho_\mathcal{S}|\vec{x}_2\rangle|^2 = \gamma^N |\langle\vec{x}_1|\rho_\mathcal{S}^0|\vec{x}_2\rangle|^2 = \Gamma|\langle\vec{x}_1|\rho_\mathcal{S}^0|\vec{x}_2\rangle|^2 \, .$$

Above, γ is the decoherence factor corresponding to scattering by a single photon. It is given by:
$$\gamma = |\text{Tr}(S_{\vec{x}_1}\rho_S^0 S_{\vec{x}_2}^\dagger)|^2, \quad (4.38)$$
where $S_{\vec{x}_i}$ is the scattering matrix acting on the photon when the dielectric sphere S is located at $\vec{x}_i$. Scattering by N photons results in the decoherence factor $\Gamma = \gamma^N$. The entropy of the decohered system turns out to be:
$$H_S = \ln 2 - \sum_{n=1}^{\infty} \frac{\Gamma^n}{2n(2n-1)} = \ln 2 - \sqrt{\Gamma}\,\text{arctanh}\,\sqrt{\Gamma} - \ln\sqrt{1-\Gamma}. \quad (4.39)$$

To compute the decoherence factor Γ we use the classical cross section of a dielectric sphere in the dipole approximation (where the wavelength of photons is much larger than the size of the sphere and the photons are not sufficiently energetic to individually resolve the superposition). Under these assumptions the decoherence factor Γ due to blackbody radiation can be obtained explicitly, and has a form $\Gamma = \exp(-t/\tau_D)$ where τ_D is the decoherence time. Its inverse, the decoherence *rate*, is given by:
$$\frac{1}{\tau_D} = C_\Gamma(3 + 11\cos^2\theta)\frac{I\tilde{a}^6 \Delta x^2 k_B^5 T^5}{c^6 \hbar^6}, \quad (4.40)$$
where $C_\Gamma = 161{,}280\,\zeta(9)/\pi^3 \approx 5210$ is a numerical constant, I is the *irradiance* (that is, radiative power per unit area) while $\tilde{a} \equiv r[(\epsilon-1)/(\epsilon-2)]^{1/3}$ is the effective radius of the sphere that takes into account its permittivity ϵ, and θ is the angle between the direction of incoming plane wave $\hat{n}$ and $\vec{\Delta x}$ (see Figure 12).

The decoherence rate does not increase for arbitrarily large Δx with the square of the separation, as Equation (4.40) would indicate. Rather, this expression is only valid in the $\Delta x \ll \lambda$ limit we are considering here. For $\Delta x \gg \lambda$, the decoherence rate saturates [175]:
$$\frac{1}{\tilde{\tau}_D} = \tilde{C}_\Gamma \frac{I\tilde{a}^6 k_B^3 T^3}{c^4 \hbar^4}, \quad (4.41)$$
with $\tilde{C}_\Gamma = 57{,}600\,\zeta(7)/\pi^3 \approx 1873$. In the intermediate region, where $\Delta x \sim \lambda$, decoherence time τ_D has a complicated dependence on both Δx and θ. The results discussed here are valid for *all* Δx providing that the correct τ_D is used.

To obtain the mutual information we use the (pure decoherence) identity $I(S:\mathcal{F}) = (H_\mathcal{F} - H_\mathcal{F}(0)) + (H_S - H_{S d\mathcal{E}/\mathcal{F}})$, Equation (4.20). The result is:
$$I(S:\mathcal{F}_f) = \ln 2 + \sum_{n=1}^{\infty} \frac{\Gamma^{(1-f)n} - \Gamma^{fn} - \Gamma^n}{2n(2n-1)}. \quad (4.42)$$

Figure 13 shows the plot of this mutual information as a function of the fraction of the environment f for several times. For large t (small Γ) the sum is dominated by the lowest power of Γ. Thus, for $f < \frac{1}{2}$ we have:
$$I(S:\mathcal{F}_f) = \ln 2 - \frac{1}{2}\Gamma^f. \quad (4.43)$$

This allows us to estimate redundancy for $\delta < 0.5$ as;
$$R_\delta \approx \frac{1}{\ln(2\delta \ln 2)}\frac{t}{\tau_D}. \quad (4.44)$$

As in the case with the central spin (but not with the quantum Brownian motion) redundancy depends only weakly—logarithmically—on the information deficit δ.

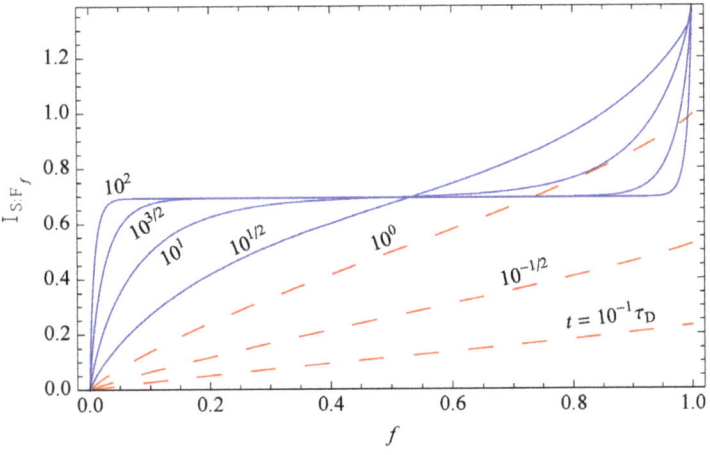

(a) Point-source illumination

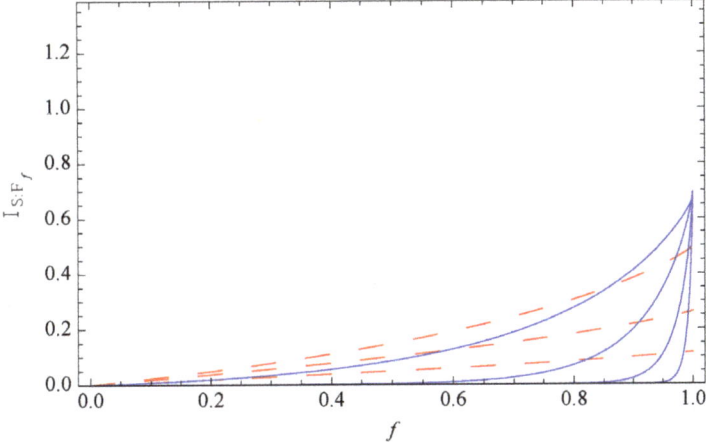

(b) Isotropic illumination

Figure 13. Quantum Darwinism in a photon environment—the origin of the photohalo (Riedel, and Zurek, 2010; 2011 [158,181]). The quantum mutual information $I(\mathcal{S} : \mathcal{F}_f)$ vs. fragment size f at different elapsed times for an object illuminated by a point-source black-body radiation, and by an isotropic black-body radiation. (**a**) **For point-source illumination** individual curves are labeled by the time t in units of the characteristic time τ_D, Equation (4.40). For $t \leq \tau_D$ (red dashed lines), the information about the system available in the environment is low. The linearity in f means each piece of the environment contains new, independent information. For $t > \tau_D$ (blue solid lines), the shape of the partial information plot indicates redundancy; the first few fragments of the environment give a lot of information, while the additional fragments only confirm what is already known. Such a photohalo contains many copies—multiple qmemes—of the record of the location of $\mathcal{S}$. The remaining quantum information (i.e., mutual information above the plateau) is highly encrypted in the global state, in the sense that it can only be accessed by capturing almost all of $\mathcal{E}$ and measuring $\mathcal{SE}$ in the right way. (**b**) **For isotropic illumination** the same time-slicing is used as in (**a**) but there is greatly decreased mutual information because the directional photon states are "full" and cannot store more information about the state of the object.

What is even more important, redundancy continues to increase linearly with time at a rate given by the inverse of the decoherence time τ_D. This is different than in either central spin or quantum Brownian motion models. This difference is due to the nature of these models: There the subsystems of the environment continued to interact with the decohered system, so that the information they acquired about $\mathcal{S}$ sloshed back and forth between $\mathcal{S}$ and correlations with $\mathcal{E}$. As a result, a steady state was reached, and redundancy saturated at modest values. In the case of photons the transfer of information is unidirectional—they scatter and go off to infinity (or fall into the eye of the observer). Even a tiny speck of dust can decohere quickly in a photon environment at very modest cosmic microwave background temperatures as was noted by Joos and Zeh, 1985 [174].

Redundancy of illuminated objects can quickly become enormous [158,181]. For instance, a 1µm speck of dust in a superposition of $\Delta x \sim$ 1µm on the surface of Earth illuminated by sunlight ($T = 5250°$K) would produce $R_\delta \sim 10^8$ records of its state—its location—in just 1 microsecond. As a consequence, huge redundancies that grow linearly with time are inevitable.

By contrast with the case of the point source (or, more generally, with the case where illumination comes from more than one direction (Riedel, and Zurek, 2011) [158]), isotropic illumination by black body radiation (Figure 13b) does not result in the buildup of redundancy. This is understandable, as a maximum entropy of blackbody radiation that fills in all the space near the system has no more room to store the information about the location of $\mathcal{S}$—its initial entropy $H_\mathcal{F}(0)$ is already at a maximum. As a result, $H_\mathcal{F} - H_\mathcal{F}(0) = 0$, and the classical, locally accessible contribution to mutual information disappears. This is in spite of the fact that quantum decoherence caused by blackbody radiation is very effective.

Rapid increase and large values of redundancy signify objectivity—many ($\sim 10^8$ observers after only 1 microsecond!) could in principle obtain the same information and will agree about the state of the systems. Thus, quantum Darwinism resulting from the photon environment is very effective, and accounts for the emergence of the "objective classical reality" in our quantum Universe.

The flip side of the huge redundancies is irreversibility—the difficulty of undoing redundant decoherence. Restoring the state of our (modest) ersatz Schrödinger cat to the preexisting superposition would require control and manipulation all of the fragments of the environment. In our example this means $\sim 10^{14}$ fragments that, after just one second, independently "know" the location of $\mathcal{S}$. Recovery of phase coherence—reversal of decoherence—requires intercepting all of $\mathcal{E}$, including the very last fraction that has a record of $\mathcal{S}$ and that corresponds to the "quantum rise" (at $f \to 1$) in the plots of the mutual information. Moreover, such manipulations of $\mathcal{ES}$ would involve global observables.

Measurement is *de facto* irreversible not just because observer in possession of the record of its outcome cannot reverse evolution that led to the wavepacket collapse (as discussed in Section 2), and not because "observers choose to ignore the environment", but because they cannot get hold of and control all of $\sim 10^{14}$ (or more) fragments of $\mathcal{E}$ with the record of the outcome—and that would be a precondition for the attempted reversal. This is especially obvious with photons: As soon as a minute fraction ($\sim 10^{-14}$ of the photons that scattered) escape within a second the irreversible "reduction of the state vector" is a *fait accompli*. Moreover, escaped photons are gone for good—reversibility of the dynamics of this process is trumped by relativistic causality.

4.3. Experimental Tests of Quantum Darwinism

Experimental study of quantum Darwinism faces the problem familiar already from the tests of decoherence: Both decoherence and quantum Darwinism are so efficient that in everyday life their consequences are taken for granted and even in the laboratory it is difficult to find situations where the effect of the environment can be adjusted at will and quantified.

In the study of decoherence this problem was bypassed by using carefully tuned microsystems with controllable coupling to the environment (Brune et al., 1996 [182]; Hackermüller et al., 2004 [180]; Haroche and Raimond, 2006 [183]). Similar strategy was adopted in the experimental studies of quantum Darwinism, although the branching states that contain information about $\mathcal{S}$ imprinted on $\mathcal{E}$ have to contend with decoherence of the composite $\mathcal{SE}$ coupled to the more distant degrees of freedom (that cause additional decoherence of $\mathcal{SE}$ as a whole): As $\mathcal{E}$ with the record of the pointer states of $\mathcal{S}$ grows, the differences between the growing branches seeded by the pointer states increase, and become more susceptible to decoherence.

The strategy of finding mesoscopic systems where the process that is key to quantum Darwinism—proliferation of multiple copies of information about $\mathcal{S}$—can be controlled and studied has nevertheless led to several experiments. Thus, the groups of Mauro Paternostro (Ciampini et al., 2018) [184] and Jian-Wei Pan (2019) [185] carried out what amounts to logical gates to imprint information about a system initiated in a superposition of pointer states on a collection of photons. The goal was confirmation of the key idea—that a small fraction of $\mathcal{E}$ suffices to gain almost all information about $\mathcal{S}$, and that enlarging that fraction confirms what was already found out. Results are consistent with this expectation. Similar strategy (and similarly positive results) was obtained in an emulation of quantum Darwinism on an IBM 5-qubit quantum computer (Chisholm et al., 2021) [186].

The group of Fedor Jelezko (Unden et al., 2019) [187] used nitrogen vacancy (NV) center as a system, relying on its natural interaction with four surrounding C^{13} nuclei in the diamond, as illustrated in Figure 14. The density matrix of $\mathcal{SE}$ was reconstructed using quantum tomography. The resulting partial information plots demonstrate that the gain of information upon the measurement of the first fragment of $\mathcal{E}$ is largest. As anticipated, information gains from the additional fragments are show diminishing returns.

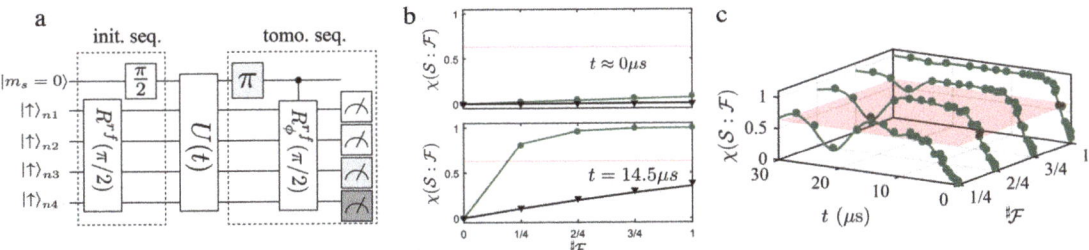

Figure 14. The emergence of redundancy for an NV center decohered by its environment (after Unden et al., 2019 [187]). (a) The measurement protocol starts with the initialization sequence and follows with a free decoherence-inducing evolution, U, for a duration of t. After initial polarization, two $\frac{\pi}{2}$-pulses transform the state into a product of $|+\rangle$ states which then evolve under the direct HF interaction between the NV center (the system $\mathcal{S}$) and nuclear spins (the environment $\mathcal{E}$). The tomography sequence follows. (b) Holevo information versus fraction size for a few different times. For small times, there are no correlations between $\mathcal{S}$ and $\mathcal{E}$. However, as decoherence proceeds, information is transferred into $\mathcal{E}$ resulting in formation of a *classical plateau*. The plateau signifies the appearance of redundant information. When the data is not normalized to the initial degree of polarization (black), only the initial rise of information is seen. (c) Holevo information, $\chi(\mathcal{S}:\mathcal{F})$, versus the environment fragment size $^{\sharp}\mathcal{F}$ and free evolution time t. For small $^{\sharp}\mathcal{F}$ one can see the initial rise in information with time followed by oscillations. This is due to information flowing into the fragment of the environment and then back into the system (i.e., environment spins will first gain information and then transfer it back to $\mathcal{S}$). For larger fractions, however, one sees just a rise and a plateau with time. This is due to different interaction strengths with the environment spins, which favors one way information flow. The solid curves in (b,c) show the result of simulations with and without imperfect initial polarization. The dynamics in simulation are governed by the actual Hamiltonian. The semi-transparent red lines in (b) and the plane in (c) indicate an information deficit of $1/e$, i.e., $I = (1 - 1/e)H_{\mathcal{S}}$. Errors are smaller than the data points. (See Unden et al., 2019 [187], for further details.)

The results of all of these experiments are consistent with what was expected, with one exception: If $\mathcal{SE}$ as a whole was isolated from the other environments, there should have been a corresponding "uptick" in mutual information as $^\sharp\mathcal{F} \to {}^\sharp\mathcal{E}$. There was no convincing evidence of that signature of the overall purity. This is hardly surprising: As noted earlier, in addition to deliberate decoherence resulting in quantum Darwinism, the system-environment composite interacts with other degrees of freedom. Phase coherence between the branches corresponding to the amplified pointer states of $\mathcal{SE}$ is then suppressed by that spurious decoherence.

4.4. Summary: Environment as an Amplification Channel

Decoherence has made it clear that quantum states are far more fragile than their classical counterparts. A state that is stable (and, therefore, can aspire to classicality) is selected—einselected—with the environment having decisive say in the matter. However, even this dramatic change of view (that limits usefulness of the idealization of "isolated systems"—mainstay of classical physics—in explaining how our quantum Universe works) turns out to underestimate the role of the environment.

Quantum Darwinism demonstrates that preferred states are not only selected for their stability (ability to survive the "hostile environment") but are communicated by the very same environment that also serves as a communication channel. Therefore, the environment acts both as a censor (for some states) and as an advertising agent that disseminates many copies of the information about the pointer states while suppressing complementary information about their superpositions.

Regarding the environment as a communication channel is more than a figure of speech: A quantum communication channel can be regarded (see, e.g., Wilde, 2013 [188]; Preskill, 2020 [189]) as a correlated state of an input and an output. Quantum channel used to transmit classical information can be represented by a state:

$$\rho_{S\mathcal{F}} = Tr_{\mathcal{E}/\mathcal{F}} \rho_{S\mathcal{E}} \simeq \sum_k p_k |\pi_k\rangle\langle\pi_k| \rho_{\mathcal{F}_k},$$

where $|\pi_k\rangle$ are effectively classical (i.e., orthogonal) input states—messages that are to be communicated. They are encoded in the output density matrices $\rho_{\mathcal{F}_k}$ that are the records of $|\pi_k\rangle$, and that are to be eventually measured. This was our Equation (4.26).

In the idealized situation when both $\mathcal{S}$ and $\mathcal{E}$ start pure, the initial state of the whole is also pure:

$$\rho_{S\mathcal{E}} = |\Psi_{S\mathcal{E}}\rangle\langle\Psi_{S\mathcal{E}}|$$

where (see Equation (4.17));

$$|\Psi_{S\mathcal{E}}\rangle = \sum_k e^{i\phi_k} \sqrt{p_k} |\pi_k\rangle \left|\varepsilon_k^{(1)}\right\rangle \left|\varepsilon_k^{(2)}\right\rangle \dots \left|\varepsilon_k^{(l)}\right\rangle \dots$$

Tracing over a part of the environment yields a state of the form of $\rho_{S\mathcal{F}}$ above, where $\rho_{\mathcal{F}_k}$ represent states of the fragments correlated with the effectively classical pointer states $|\pi_k\rangle$. Moreover, "roots" of the branches $|\pi_k\rangle\langle\pi_k|$ that appear in $\rho_{S\mathcal{F}}$ are largely independent of what part of the environment is traced over for most of the range of the possible sizes of the the $\mathcal{E}/\mathcal{F}$: This is an excellent approximation for $f_\delta < f < 1 - f_\delta$, that is, all along the plateau of the partial information plots. Thus, the same preferred branches of $\mathcal{SF}$ are singled out regardless of what part of the environment is detected, and what part is out of reach at least as long as $\mathcal{E}/\mathcal{F}$ suffices to decohere the rest.

This transformaton of the communicated message from quantum to classical is implied by one more feature of $\rho_{S\mathcal{E}}$ that can be (see Equation (4.30)) approximated as:

$$\rho_{S\mathcal{E}} \simeq \sum_k p_k |\pi_k\rangle\langle\pi_k| \bigotimes_l^{R_\delta} \rho_{\mathcal{F}_k}^{(l)},$$

when the off-diagonal terms of $\rho_{S\mathcal{E}}$ (obviously still present in $|\Psi_{S\mathcal{E}}\rangle\langle\Psi_{S\mathcal{E}}|$) are out of reach, as would be the case for an observer who cannot acquire all of $S\mathcal{E}$ and measure it in the correct basis. Thus, Equation (4.30) (reproduced above) provides a justification of the existence of branches with many (R_δ) copies of the same message, suggesting a natural extrapolation "by induction" of the objective existence of the "root" $|\pi_k\rangle$ of the branch[16].

Independence of the communicated message from $\mathcal{E}_{/\mathcal{F}}$, the remainder of the environment that is traced over, is key: All the fragments of the environment know about the same observable of the system. Thus, omitting some part of the environment is perfectly justified—up to the information of the order of the information deficit δ it does not alter what is known about the system of interest.

Indeed, it is usually an excellent approximation to assert that, if we were to look at a macroscopic S—if we intercepted even a very small fraction of $\mathcal{E}$, $f \ll f_\delta$, just a few of the photons that bounced off of S—the information we would get would be consistent with S occupying a single as yet unknown pointer state. Our "looking" is usually insufficient to identify such a single state, but if we continued with more precise measurements, we would eventually conclude based on all the data gathered from $\mathcal{E}$ (and confirmed by direct measurement of S, if desired) that whatever pure state we inferred from the incomplete partial information was in the end gradually revealed by the data gathered along the way.

In other words, in many situations our acquisition of information will correspond to the initial rising part of the partial information plot. Our confidence about the existence of a definite state at the end of the information acquisition process is based on cases when the plateau is reached, or even simply on the fact that the additional, higher resolution information is consistent with the information acquired earlier.

The step from the epistemic ("I have evidence of $|\pi_{17}\rangle$".) to ontic ("The system is in the state $|\pi_{17}\rangle$".) is then an extrapolation justified by the nature of $\rho_{S\mathcal{E}}$: Observers who detected evidence consistent with $|\pi_{17}\rangle$ will continue to detect data consistent with $|\pi_{17}\rangle$ when they intercept additional fragments of $\mathcal{E}$. So, while the other branches may be in principle present, observers will perceive only data consistent with the branch to which they got attached by the very first measurement. Other observers that have independently "looked at" S will agree.[17]

Objective existence of classical reality turns out to be an enormously simplifying, exceedingly accurate, and, therefore, very useful approximation. Thus, when agents' success depends on acting in response to perceived "objective reality", they can do that with confidence based on the indirect data obtained from $\mathcal{E}$.

There is a sense in which our strategy explores and vindicates the artificial division of the Universe between quantum and classical introduced by Heisenberg—what John Bell (1990) [193] called a "shifty split"—in measurements. "Shifty" in the description of the "split" was not meant to be a compliment. The split happened somewhere along the von Neumann chain that connected the quantum system with the observer. It divided a quantum part of the chain (where superpositions were allowed) from the classical part (where a single actuality existed). What quantum Darwinism shows is that "shifty" can be regarded as a statement of invariance, and, thus, upgraded from a statement of contempt to a recognition of a symmetry.

Decoherence introduced the environment into the picture of quantum measurement. The original von Neumann's chain has fanned out: Parts of the chain separate from the links that connect S via the apparatus $\mathcal{A}$ with the observer, and go sideways, into $\mathcal{E}$. They disseminate the same information—R_δ copies of it—as the chain connecting S with the observer splits into sub-chains. Indeed, there may be—and often are—other observers benefiting from the information communicated by these sub-chains.

---

[16] More formal arguments that justify regarding fragments of the environment as channels that deliver preselected information about the pointer states have been put forward by Brandão, Piani, and Horodecki (2015) [190] and by Qi and Ranard (2021) [191]; see also Knott et al. (2018) [192].

[17] That is, observer who records "17" will only encounter others whose records are consistent with "branch 17".

Quantum Darwinism recognizes and quantifies this fanning out of the von Neumann chain. Shifty split could be placed anywhere along the plateau of the partial information plot. The information about $\mathcal{S}$ that can be extracted from the chain is invariant under the shift of that split. In addition, every branch of the chain is firmly attached to the effectively classical pointer state singled out by decoherence.

5. Quantum Darwinism and Objective Existence: Photohalos and Extantons

We reviewed research aimed at understanding how the classical world we perceive emerges from the counterintuitive laws of quantum mechanics. It is time to take stock. Do we now understand why we perceive our undeniably quantum Universe as classical?

Quantum Darwinism holds the key to this last question. Deducing discreteness that sets the stage for the wavepacket collapse from repeatability and unitarity reveals quantum origin of quantum jumps, defines "events", and justifies the emphasis on the Hermitian nature of observables, but this is a derivation of one of the *quantum* textbook axioms. The origin of Born's rule in the symmetries of entanglement matters in interpreting *quantum* probabilities, but—as important as axiom (v) is for experimental predictions—its derivation from the core quantum postulates (o)–(iii) does not directly account for the familiar everyday reality.

Quantum Darwinism, by contrast, explains why our world appears classical, and why XIX century physics (physics still relevant for our everyday routine) seemed at the time like the whole story. It shows how the information is channeled from the "objects of interest" to us, observers, leading to consensus about what exists—to the idealization of objective classical reality.

Our everyday world comprises "systems of interest" endowed with the rest mass—the focus of XIX century physics—and environments that often play the role of communication channels. The quantumness of the massive "systems of interest" is suppressed by decoherence that is continually uploading qmemes of their states into the environments that broadcast that information. Thus, every object of interest is ensconced in an expanding halo of qmemes—information-carrying fragments of $\mathcal{E}$. We perceive our world by intercepting fragments of these information-laden halos. We extract data about the systems of interest but tend to ignore the role of the halos—the means of its transmission—in the emergence of the familiar classical reality.

5.1. Anatomy of an Extanton

The combination of the macroscopic, massive core with the information-bearing halo defines an *extanton* (as in "extant"). Extantons are responsible for how we perceive our Universe. The tandem—the macroscopic decohered system along with its information-laden halo—fulfills Bell's desideratum for "beables" (Bell, 1975) [40][18]. As long as an observer relies on the halo of photons (or, possibly, other decohering environments) for the information about $\mathcal{S}$, only the pointer states of the extanton core can be found out.

Extantons exist as beables should: The state of the environment is of course perturbed by agent's measurements (e.g., photons are absorbed by our eyes). However, redundancy means that this does not alter the information about the core still available from the rest of the halo in many redundant ($R_\delta \gg 1$) copies.

The essence of the extanton—the only attribute classical physics cares about—is the state of its core. Information about it is available in multiple copies, and, hence, virtually unaffected by the perturbations of the halo. Indeed, as the environment continues to monitor $\mathcal{S}$, qmemes of its pointer state in $\mathcal{E}$ multiply, and the halo continues to expand while the pointer states stay put (or evolve as a classical system would).

Extantons are not "elementary", but neither are atoms of even elementary particles such as protons or mesons (which are made out of quarks), not to mention planets or stars.

---

[18] We should not presume that Bell (who held strong opinions on interpretational questions [41]) would have approved of extantons as model for 'entities that be'—"beables". We shall therefore call the composite entity consisting of the macroscopic object enveloped in and heralded by its information-carrying halo an extanton.

Yet protons, mesons, atoms, molecules, planets, stars, etc., are all useful in representing and accounting for various phenomena in our Universe.

Extantons account for the classical world of our everyday experience. Quantum Darwinism explains how they come about. We can reduce extantons to their constituents, but—as other higher-level entities such as composite elementary particles, atoms, molecules, viruses, stars—extantons enable an approximate, but simple and useful description of the classical realm, of the familiar world emerging from within the quantum substrate.

Part of that simplification that led to the Newtonian view of the world is our habit of ignoring halos, carriers of the information, and focusing on the extanton cores. These cores are the "objects of interest". Many are subject to Newtonian dynamics. It was convenient to ignore the means by which the information about the cores is delivered, and just focus on the physics of the cores.

Inseparable bond of the core with the halo is responsible for what we perceive. However, conditioned by Newtonian physics we tend to ignore the presence and the role of the halos, and just use the data they deliver to find out about the cores. In the end, only these cores count as elements of our everyday reality. Yet, it is the halos that bear responsibility for the suppression of quantum superpositions and for our perception of the familiar—robust and objective—classical world.

The difficulty with the quantum-classical correspondence arises when the role of the halo is overlooked and the extanton core is treated as if it were isolated, and, therefore, subject to unitary evolution. Core is indeed quantum (as is everything else in our Universe) but it is by no means isolated. Therefore, one cannot expect the core of an extanton to follow a unitary quantum evolution. Nevertheless, whenever Newtonian dynamics is a good approximation)its classical evolution can be approximately reversible.

5.1.1. Extantons and "The Classical"

No one has ever worried about interpretation of classical physics. This is because classical states were thought to be real—to exist independently of what was known about them. There was no need to be concerned about the effect of information acquisition. Even though measurement could perturb a system, that perturbation could always be made as small as required.

The main reason for the interpretational discomfort with quantum theory is our faith in the underlying objective reality. It is based on our everyday experience that leads us to believe the world we inhabit exists independently of the information we (or other agents) have.

We owe this confidence in objective classical reality to the fact that we are immersed in the extanton halos and inundated with the information about their cores. As a result of this overload with "free" data we have grown up believing that we can examine systems and determine their states without perturbing them—classical measurement would just update the record (change the state of the apparatus or of the observer's memory) without 'backreaction'. In the classical setting information about a system is obtained, but its state or its evolution is untouched.

One might call this a *myth of immaculate perception*. It asserts a unidirectional information flow (hence, flow of influence, from the measured system to the observer) that reveals the state of the system but leaves it unaffected. This seems to defy the spirit of Newton's principle that action elicits reaction.

Quantum Darwinism accounts for the origin of this myth. All macroscopic objects telegraph their pointer states via their decohering environments. They are enveloped by information halos—by the environment with multiple records of their decoherence-resistant states. Our everyday world does not consist of isolated systems. Rather it is defined by the extantons consisting of a macroscopic object enveloped in and heralded by its halo, imprinted on the environment.

There is a great variety of extantons. They all consist of the core and the halo that "knows" the state of the core, and may be persuaded to share that information with observers. Planets are extanton cores and so are the grains of photographic emulsion. Any object one can see is likely an extanton core, its state communicated to us by photons—by its photohalo. Some extantons (like planets) follow approximately reversible dynamics. Others (like grains of photographic emulsion or Brownian particles) are heavily damped or embedded in an immobilizing medium competing with the photohalo in monitoring of the core (and, hence, in decohering it). Every apparatus pointer is an extanton core.

Observers intercept fractions of the halo to gain information about the core. Direct measurement of the core is in principle also possible, but only measurements of the pointer observable would lead to predictable results: Other outcomes—superpositions of pointer states—are quickly invalidated by decoherence. Thus, except for laboratory settings (where decoherence can be kept at bay by a near-perfect isolation) the only observables with predictive value are the pointer observables readily available from the halo.

Photohalo is the main channel through which observers find out the state of the core. The information available from the photohalo is usually limited to the data that are in effect macroscopic (therefore, easily imprinted on the halo, such as the location of the dielectric sphere discussed earlier).

5.1.2. Photohalos, Photoextantons, and Information Detached from Existence

Photons play a preeminent role as information carriers. Every object we know is bathed in a radiation environment. Each is surrounded by an information halo, its photons disseminating qmemes with the speed of light. We eavesdrop on these photohalos, intercepting small fractions that nevertheless reveal the state of the core.

Photoextantons are the family of extantons that advertise the state of their core via their photohalos. One can consider extantons where photohalo is the only relevant environment. There are at least two good reasons for this. To begin with, our eyesight is responsible for most of the information we obtain, so it is of interest to consider photoextantons. Perhaps more importantly, there is a sense in which photoextantons come close to the ideal—one might say Platonic ideal—of the separation of existence and information detached from existence.

Information (in the form of the photohalo) has—apart from the dramatic consequences of decoherence—only a negligible effect on the evolution of the cores. Photohalo detaches from the core and runs off seemingly without any dynamical consequences while the core can evolve in approximate accord with Newton's laws. Questions such as "Does the moon exist when no one's looking?" are motivated by the illusion that one can apply quantum theory to the isolated cores of extantons and recover classical reality.

Quantum states are *epiontic*. Quantum physics has eliminated separation of existence and information. Nevertheless, extanton structure restores this separation (with suitable caveats): The core exists (it persists in a pointer state). And the information about it is continually detached and propagates as the photohalo.

Everyday practice of quantum theory has inherited from classical physics the habit of dealing with isolated systems. Yet, we can never encounter isolated macroscopic extanton cores. Trying to understand cores of extantons as if they were isolated is the cause of the "measurement problem". Decoherence and einselection were the first steps towards its resolution, towards the understanding why our Universe looks classical to us. Quantum Darwinism provides the complete answer, and extantons are its embodiment.

Properties of systems that reside in the extanton cores and give rise to the qmemes in $\mathcal{E}$ are untouched by the measurements on the halo, yet they reveal the state of the core. This is guaranteed by the theorems we have already discussed that also imply (depending on specific assumptions) uniqueness or near uniqueness of the states that can be repeatedly imprinted on the halo, and, therefore, deduced from the environment fragments: The optimal strategy for the agent is to find out what the halo redundantly advertises—that is, pointer states of the extanton core—and then use that information to deduce other observables of interest.

5.1.3. Photohalos and the Quantum Origins of Irreversibility

Information in classical, Newtonian physics was immaterial—it was about physics, but it was not a part of physics. Its acquisition did not influence states or the *reversible* dynamics of classical systems. Trajectories in phase space were unaffected by the information transfer. In particular, classical dynamics involved in the measurement process could be reversed even when the outcome of the measurement was recorded. By contrast (and as we have seen in Section 2) copying of a quantum measurement outcome precludes its reversal.

How could an effectively classical realm of our fundamentally quantum Universe follow so respectfully laws that are at odds with the epiontic nature of quantum states? What detaches information about the states from these states so that they can follow classical reversible dynamics, oblivious to what is known about them?

Platonic ideal of the separation of existence and the detached information about what exists would be fulfilled if the information in the photohalo would have no effect on the energy or momentum of the core, but would still decohere it efficiently enough to assure effective classicality of its state. Photohalos exert no (easily) noticeable influence on trajectories of the pointer states of the core. However, cores can interact indirectly with other cores (e.g., via gravitational forces) or scatter elastically (billiard balls) or inelastically. Consequences of such interactions on the motion or the state of the core or on its properties (e.g., merger of the cores in inelastic scattering) will be reflected in the photohalo.

When core is sufficiently massive, emission or scattering of photons has negligible effect on its momentum (although photohalo will still decohere its quantum state very efficiently). How heavy the core should be to make such an approximation accurate depends on the energy of the emitted or scattered photons. Planets are clearly sufficiently massive, and so are billiard balls or even dust grains [21,23,174]. Depending on detailed criteria, one might even classify fullerenes decohered by radiation they emit [180] as photoextantons.

Irreversibility associated with the wavepacket collapse is a natural consequence of the photohalo. As soon as a minute fraction of the photohalo escapes, the 'reduction of the state vector' becomes irreversible, since the escaped photons are gone for good, And, as we have seen in Section 2 (and unlike in the classical realm) presence of even a single record of the measurement outcome—of the pointer state—anywhere in the Universe precludes reversal of the evolution that would bring back superpositions. Thus, the "in principle" reversibility of the equations responsible for inscribing, e.g., 10^{14} copies of the location of the dielectric sphere on the sunlight per second we have discussed earlier is trumped by relativistic causality: Reversal becomes impossible in principle as soon as even one such copy runs off to infinity with the speed of light, never to be turned back[19].

The information about the classical states (of the cores) becomes detached: Separation of the states of the cores from the information about them is how extantons account for the emergence of the objective classical reality. This mechanism is also the uniquely quantum origin of irreversibility in our Universe.

Photohalo may not be the only environment. However, in our Universe interactions depend on distances. Therefore, localized pointer states imprinted on the photohalo are left intact also by the other environments that may be contributing to decoherence but—like air—are not as useful as witnesses.

5.2. Quantum Darwinism and the Existential Interpretation

States in classical physics were "real": Their *objective existence* was established operationally—they could be found out by an initially ignorant observer without getting perturbed in the measurement process. Hence, they existed independently of what was known about them.

---

[19] One can deduce Boltzmann's H-theorem and the Kolmogorov-Sinai entropy increase rate by appealing to such considerations (Zurek and Paz, 1994 [66]; 1995 [21]; Zurek, 1998 [23]), but this subject as well as envariant origin of thermodynamics that emerges along with Born's rule due to the coupling of systems to their environments (Deffner and Zurek, 2016 [194]; Zurek, 2018 [195]) are beyond the scope of this review.

Information was, by contrast, "not real". This was suggested by the immunity of classical states to measurements, and by the fact that, in Newtonian dynamics, information about an evolving system was of no consequence for its evolution. Information was what the observer knew subjectively, a mere shadow of the real state, irrelevant for physics.

This dismissive view of information ran into problems when the classical Universe of Newton confronted thermodynamics. Clash of these two paradigms led to Maxwell's demon, and is echoed in the discussions of the origins of the arrow of time.

The specter of information was and still is haunting physics. The seemingly unphysical record state was beginning to play a role reserved for the real state!

Quantum states are epiontic. They combine information and existence and (like photons or electrons that can be wave-like or particle-like) they can reveal one or the other aspect of their nature depending on circumstances.

We have just seen how, in the quantum setting, in extantons, existence and information about existence intertwine. The state known to observers is defined and made objective by what is known about it—by the information observers can access. "It from bit" comes to mind (Wheeler, 1990) [196].

The main new ingredient is the dramatic upgrade of the role of the environment. It has information—multiple records of S—and is willing to reveal it. It acquires information about the system while causing decoherence and einselection, but—and this is the upgrade—it acts as a communication channel.

In classical Newtonian settings information might have been dismissed as unphysical as it had no significance for dynamics. But *information is physical* (Landauer, 1991) [197]. Moreover, *there is no information without representation*—information must reside somewhere (e.g., in the photohalos). And the presence and availability of such evidence (objective because there are plenty of records of the pointer state) has its legal consequences.

The role of $\mathcal{E}$ in quantum Darwinism is not that of an innocent bystander, who simply reports what has happened. Rather, the environment is an accomplice in the "crime" of selecting and transforming fragile epiontic quantum states into robust, objectively existing classical states. Objective existence has its price: Environment—induced decoherence invalidates quantum principle of superposition, leading to einselection—to censoring the Hilbert space. Information transfer associated with decoherence selects preferred pointer states, and banishes their superpositions.

Moreover, testimony offered by the environment is biased—it depends on how (through what observable) $\mathcal{E}$ monitors S. Fragments of the environment—qmemes carried by the extanton halo—can reveal information only about the very same pointer states $\mathcal{E}$ has helped einselect.

Operational criterion for objective existence is the ability to find out a state without disturbing it. According to this operational definition, pointer states exist in more or less the same way their classical counterparts did: They can be found out without getting perturbed by anyone who examines one of the multiple copies of the record of S "on display" in the environment.

5.3. From Quantum Core Postulates to Objective Classical Reality

In search for the relation between quantum formalism and the real world we have weaved together several ideas that are very quantum to arrive at the *existential interpretation*. Its essence is the operational definition of objective existence of physical states: *To exist, a state must, at the very least, persist or evolve predictably in spite of the immersion of the system in its environment.* Predictability is the key to einselection, but persistence is only a necessary condition.

Objective existence requires more: It should be possible to find out a state without perturbing it—without threatening its existence. When that last desideratum is met, many observers will be able to reach consensus, a well—motivated practical criterion of objective existence.

Let us briefly recapitulate how objective existence arises in the quantum setting: We started with axioms (i) and (ii) that sum up mathematics of quantum theory: They impose the quantum principle of superposition, and demand unitarity, but make no connection with the "real world". Addition of predictability (via the repeatability postulate (iii), the only uncontroversial measurement axiom), and recognition that our Universe consists of systems (axiom (o)) leads to *preferred pointer states*. This is a new insight into the quantum origin of quantum discreteness. Predictability is the "root cause" of the wavepacket collapse and quantum jumps. It also justifies Hermitian nature of quantum observables and explains breaking of the unitary symmetry, the crux of the collapse axiom (iv).

Our next task was to understand *the origin of probabilities and Born's rule*, axiom (v). We have done this without appealing to decoherence (as this would have courted circularity in the derivation). Nevertheless, decoherence—inspired view is reflected in the envariant approach: To assign probabilities to pointer states we first had to show how to get decoherence without using tools of decoherence such as reduced density matrices and demonstrate that relative phases between outcomes do not matter.

Envariance provides the answer, but—strictly speaking—only for Schmidt states. We take this to mean that usual rules of the probability calculus will strictly hold for pointer states only after their superposition has been thoroughly decohered. Pointer states—Schmidt states coincidence is expected to be very good indeed: Probabilities one has in mind ultimately refer to pointer states of measuring or recording devices. These are usually macroscopic, so their interaction with the environment will quickly align Schmidt basis with pointer states. Born's rule (with all the consequences for the frequencies of events) follows.

Probabilities derived from envariance are objective: They reflect an objective—and experimentally testable—symmetry of the global state (usually involving the measured system $\mathcal{S}$, the apparatus $\mathcal{A}$, and its environment $\mathcal{E}$). Before interacting with $\mathcal{A}$ or its $\mathcal{E}$ observer does not know the outcome, but will know the set of pointer states—the menu of possibilities. This ignorance reflects objective symmetries of the global state of $\mathcal{SAE}$ that lead to Born's rule.

Last question was the origin of *objective existence* in the quantum world: How can we find states of systems we encounter in our everyday experience without redefining them by our measurements?

We started by noting that in contrast to fragile arbitrary superpositions in the Hilbert space of the system, pointer states are robust.

Crucially, in the real world observers find out pointer states by letting natural selection take its course: Pointer states are the "robust species", adapted to their environments. They survive intact through such "environmental monitoring". More importantly, multiple records about $\mathcal{S}$ are deposited in $\mathcal{E}$. They record pointer states, which are the "fittest"—they can survive the process of copying and so the information about them can multiply.

There is an extent to which "it had to be so": In order to make one more copy one needs to preserve the original. However, there is a more subtle part of this relation between decoherence, einselection, and quantum Darwinism. Hamiltonians of interaction that allow for copying of certain observables necessarily leave them unperturbed. This conspiracy was noticed early: It is the basis of the commutation criterion for pointer observables (Zurek, 1981; 1982) [24,25]: When $\mathbf{H}_{\mathcal{SE}}$ is a function of some observable Λ of the system, it will also necessarily commute with it, $[\mathbf{H}_{\mathcal{SE}}, \Lambda] = 0$.

5.4. Extantons and the Existential Interpretation

Existential interpretation of quantum theory assigns "relatively objective existence" [6,7,36,198]—key to effective classicality—to widely broadcast quantum states. Objective existence is relative to the redundant records about what persists and (in that sense) exists—evidence of the pointer states imprinted on the environment.

Existential interpretation is obviously consistent with the relative states interpretation: Redundancy of the records disseminated throughout the environment suggests a natural definition of branches that are classical in the sense that an observer can find out a branch with indirect measurements and stay on it, rather than "cut off the branch he is sitting on" with a direct measurement. This is more than einselection, and much more than decoherence, although the key ingredient—environment—is still key, and the key criterion is "survival of the fittest"— immunity of the pointer states to monitoring by $\mathcal{E}$ reflected also in the predictability sieve.

The role of $\mathcal{E}$ is, however, upgraded from a passive "quantum information dump" to a communication channel. Information deposited in $\mathcal{E}$ in the process of decoherence is not lost. Rather, it is stored there, in multiple copies, often—but not always—for all to see. The emphasis on information theoretic significance of quantum states cuts both ways: Environment—as—a—witness paradigm supplies operational definition of objective existence, and shows why and how pointer states can be found out without getting disrupted. However, it also shows that objective existence is not an intrinsic attribute of quantum states, but that it arises along with—and as a result of—information transfer from $\mathcal{S}$ to $\mathcal{E}$.

Extantons combine the source of information (extanton core) with the means of its transmission (halo, often consisting of photons). Extanton is an extant composite entity with the object of interest in its core that is decohering and imprinting qmemes on the information-laden halo, part of the environment that pointer states of the core. Information about them is disseminated by the halos throughout the Universe.

Photohalos are especially efficient in such "advertising". Fragments of the halo intercepted by the observers inform them about the state of its core. Extanton cores persist as classical states would—independent of what is known about them. While they are not fundamental, they are fundamentally important for our perception of the quantum Universe we inhabit as a classical world. Extantons fulfill John Bell's desiderata for "beables".

5.5. Decoherence and Information Processing

Decoherence affects record keeping and information processing hardware (and, hence, information retention and processing abilities) of observers. Therefore, it is relevant for our consciousness, as agents' consciousness presumably reflects states and processes of their neural networks. As was already noted some time ago by Tegmark (2000) [65], individual neurons decohere on a timescale very short compared to, e.g., the "clock time" on which the human brain operates or other relevant timescales. Moreover, even if somehow one could initiate our information processing hardware in a superposition of its pointer states (which would open up a possibility of being conscious of superpositions), it would decohere almost instantly. The same argument applies to the present day classical computers. Thus, even if information that is explicitly quantum (that is, involves superpositions or entanglement) was inscribed in computer memory, it would decohere and (at best) become classical. (More likely, it would become random nonsense.)

It is a separate and intriguing question whether a robot equipped with a quantum computer could "do better" and perceive quantumness we are bound to miss. We note, however, that the relevance of this question for the subject at hand—i.e., why does our quantum Universe appear to us as a classical world devoid of quantum weirdness—is at best marginal. After all, as already noted, rapid decoherence in the neural networks of our brains precludes quantum information processing.

Moreover, if such a robot relied (as we do) on the fragments of the environment for the information about the system of interest, it could access only the same information we can access. This information is redundant—hence, classical (see Girolami et al., 2022 [142])—and quantum information processing capabilities would not help; only pointer states can be accessed through this communication channel.

Existential interpretation—as defined originally (e.g., Zurek, 1993 [6])—relied primarily on decoherence. Decoherence of systems immersed in their environments leads to einselection: Only preferred pointer states of a system are stable, so only they can persist. Moreover, when both systems of interest and means of perception and information storage are subject to decoherence, only the correlations of the pointer states of the measured systems with the corresponding pointer states of agent's memory that store the outcomes are stable—only such einselected correlations can persist.

Decoherence, one might say, "strikes twice": It selects preferred states of the systems, thus defining what can persist, hence, exist. It also limits correlations that can persist, so that the observer's memory or the apparatus pointer will only preserve correlations with the einselected states of the measured system when they are recorded in the einselected memory states.

This is really the already familiar discussion of the quantum measurement problem with one additional twist: Not just the apparatus, but also the systems of everyday interest to observers are subject of decoherence. Thus, the post-measurement correlations (when investigated using discord) must now be "classical-classical" using terminology of Piani, Horodecki, Horodecki, 2008 [135], while in quantum measurements only the apparatus side was guaranteed to be einselected (hence, certifiably classical).

5.6. Quantum Darwinism and "Life as We Know It"

Quantum Darwinism has a Darwinian name, but how Darwinian is it really? This is a vague question about nomenclature, and we shall pass it by. A related and more pointed question is: Does quantum Darwinism have any significance for the evolution of living organisms and for their survival? There are then two even more focused questions one can pose: Are the processes of imprinting information and passing it on (that are central to quantum Darwinism) relevant for natural evolution? Moreover, do living organisms take advantage of the proliferation of information about pointer states?

We note at the outset that natural selection and Darwinian evolution require multiple redundant records (e.g., as DNA). Redundant records imply (as we have seen already in Section 2) preferred set of states—preferred einselected classical basis. Therefore, natural selection and Darwinian evolution take place within a classical post-decoherence realm.

Darwinian evolution depends on the (nearly perfect) preservation of information and its propagation. DNA is disseminated by various means, but DNA molecules are thoroughly decohered carriers of information about an even more decohered parent organism.

The goals and the nature of natural evolution are somewhat different but the transfer of actionable information (see Section 2, Ref. [43]) is the essence of both the "original" and quantum Darwinism. Quantumness in a DNA "blueprint" is long gone, suppressed by decoherence, but the correlation between the pointer state and individual fragment $\mathcal{F}$ of $\mathcal{E}$ is also classical (as quantum discord is suppressed by surplus decoherence).

The key difference with quantum Darwinism appears to be the presence of the feedback in Darwinian evolution: It depends on the ability of the DNA to reproduce a copy of their progenitor so it can in turn produce more DNA. Evolutionary success therefore is judged not by redundancy in amplifying information in a single episode but through multiple generations of the organisms and their DNA memes. Iteration through multiple generations allows for variation and for natural selection. Fitness is still evaluated based on the ability to amplify, but in an iterative process.

The copies of DNA are imperfect—there are mutations. They are not deliberate—error correction guards against them–but they still happen. That imperfection in combination with the feedback is what allows for gradual change of the DNA and for the adaptation of the organisms driven by the natural selection and survival of the fittest.

By contrast, amplification and dissemination of quantum information appear to be enough to attain the goal of quantum Darwinism: They suffice to account for the emergence of objective classical reality. The ultimate fate of qmeme carriers such as photons is—at first sight—unimportant, and so, one might think, is the fate of the information: Once the state of the system or an event are made "objective", they are an element of reality, and that is it.

Or is it? After all, following their detection photons (and other carriers of information accessible through other senses that also deliver data about the Universe) are no longer needed. Nevertheless, there is the next generation of records—in the apparatus, in the retina, or in the brain of the observer. Such information repositories inherit the memes—the essence of the information detected by the senses.

That leads to further consequences: Agents (living organisms) react to data. Their actions (hence, the state of the part of the Universe affected by them) depend on what they have perceived. In the evolutionary context such actions are taken to optimize their chances of survival. Hence, evolutionary success in the original Darwinian sense depends on the ability to acquire and process information about extantons that is obtained through quantum Darwinian processes that starts with decoherence and proliferation of qmemes.

Redundancy facilitates accessibility and explains the objective nature of events, and, hence, emergence of the objective classical reality. Consequences of such events influence multiple generations of their records and have implications for their recipients: After all, actions taken by the living organisms are based on perceptions—on what was recorded. Knowledge of events that take place is essential for survival. This is feedback. It does not necessarily require conscious decisions (e.g., sunflowers following the sun are taking advantage of such feedback), but it allows, and indeed, calls for, adaptation. Feedback is also what allows for learning from experience. Thus, while natural selection and Darwinism can be analyzed without any reference to quantum goings on, it does involve steps that depend on decoherence and proliferation of information.

Seeing Is Believing

Our senses did not evolve to test and verify quantum theory. Rather, they evolved through natural selection where survival of the fittest played a decisive role. When there is nothing to be gained from prediction, there is no evolutionary reason for perception. Only classical states that pass through the predictability sieve and deposit redundant easily accessible records in their environment are robust and easy to access.

Quantum Darwinian requirement of redundancy appears to be built into our senses, and, in particular, into our eyesight: The wiring of the nerves that pass on the signals from the rods in the eye—cells that detect light when illumination is marginal, and that appear sensitive to individual photons (Nam et al., 2014) [199]—tends to dismiss cases when fewer than ~7 neighboring rods fire simultaneously (Rieke and Baylor, 1998) [200]. Thus, while there is evidence that even individual photons can be (occasionally and unreliably) detected by humans (Tinsley et al., 2016) [201], redundancy (more than one photon) is needed to pass the signal onto the brain.

This makes evolutionary sense—rods can misfire, so such built-in veto threshold suppresses false alarms. Frogs and toads have apparently lower veto thresholds, possibly because they are cold-blooded, so they may not need to contend with as much noise, as thermal excitation of rods appears to be the main source of "false positives".

Quantum Darwinism relies on repeatability. As observers perceive outcomes of measurements indirectly—e.g., by looking at the pointer of the apparatus or at the photographic plate that was used in a double-slit experiment—they will depend, for their perceptions, on redundant copies of photons that are scattered from (or absorbed by) the apparatus pointer or the blackened grains of photographic emulsion. Thus, repeatability is not just a convenient assumption of a theorist: This hallmark of quantum Darwinism is built into our senses. And—as we have seen in Section 2—the discreteness of the possible measurement outcomes—possible perceptions —follows from the distinguishability of the preferred states that can be redundantly recorded in the environment [42,43].

What we are conscious of is then based on redundant evidence. Quantum Darwinist update to the existential interpretation is to demand that states exist providing that one can acquire redundant evidence about them indirectly, from the environment. This of course presumes stability in spite of decoherence (so there is no conflict with the existential interpretation that was originally formulated primarily on the basis of decoherence [6,36]) but the threshold for the state to objectively exist is nevertheless raised.

5.7. Bohr, Everett, and Wheeler

This paper has largely avoided issues of interpretation, focusing instead on consequences of quantum theory that are "interpretation independent", but may constrain interpretational options. We have been led by quantum formalism to our conclusions, but they are largely beyond interpretational disputes. Our "existential interpretation" is in that sense not an interpretation—it simply points out the consequences of quantum formalism and some additional rudimentary assumptions. It recognizes that quantum states are epiontic: Like photons or electrons that can act as waves or particles, quantum states can exhibit epistemic or ontic side of their nature, depending on circumstances. In contrast to Bohr (who regarded them as purely epistemic) of Everett (who thought the universal state vector was ontic) they can perform either as robust elements of reality or as information carriers. These two roles are complementary: both are essential for extantons.

It is nevertheless useful to see how the two best known interpretations of quantum theory—Bohr's "Copenhagen Interpretation" (CI) and Everett's "Relative State Interpretation" (RSI) fit within the constraints that we have derived above by acknowledging the paramount role of the environment. To anticipate the conclusion, we quote John Archibald Wheeler (1957) [12], who—comparing CI with RSI—wrote: "*(1) The conceptual scheme of "relative state" quantum mechanics is completely different from the conceptual scheme of the conventional "external observation" form of quantum mechanics and (2) The conclusions from the new treatment correspond completely in familiar cases to the conclusions from the usual analysis*".

Bohr insisted on preexistence of the classical domain of the Universe to render outcomes of quantum measurements firm and objective. Quantum Darwinism accomplishes that goal: Decoherence takes away quantumness of the system, but a system that is not quantum need not be immediately classical: Objective nature of events and, above all, of extantons arises as a result of redundancy. Consensus about what happened and what exists is reached only in presence of large redundancy. Large redundancy yields a very good approximation of "the classical", like finite many-body systems that have a critical point marking a phase transition which is, strictly speaking, precisely defined only in the infinite size limit. Indeed, Quantum Darwinism might be regarded as a purely quantum implementation of the "irreversible act of amplification" that was such an important element of CI.

Physical significance of a quantum state in CI was purely epistemic (Bohr, 1928 [8]; Peres, 1993 [202]; Fuchs and Peres, 2000 [203]; Fuchs and Schack, 2013 [204]): Quantum states were only carriers of information—they correlated outcomes of measurements. Only the classical part of the Universe existed in the sense we are used to.

In the account we have given here there are really several different sorts of states. There are pure states—vectors in the Hilbert space. However, there are also objectively unknown states defined by the "Facts 1–3" of Section 3. They describe a subsystem and derive from the pure state of the whole using envariance, the symmetries of entanglement. And there are states defined through the spectral decomposition of a quantum operator. Last not least, there are decoherence-resistant pointer states that retain correlations and allow for prediction based on indirect measurements, as they are best known to and widely advertised by the environment.

In contrast to CI that split the Universe into only two domains—quantum and classical—we have seen that classicality is a matter of degree, and a matter of a criterion. For example, objectivity (which is in a sense the strongest criterion) is attained only in the limit of large redundancy. It is clear why this is a good approximation in the case of macroscopic systems. However, it is also clear that there are intermediate stages on the way from quantum to classical, and that a system can be no longer quantum but be still far away from classical objective existence.

There are two key ideas in Everett's writings. The first one is to let quantum theory dictate its own interpretation. We took this "let quantum be quantum" point very seriously. The second message (that often dominates in popular accounts) is the Many Worlds mythology. In contrast "let quantum be quantum" it is less clear what it means, so—in the opinion of this author—there is less reason to take it at face value.

It is encouraging for the relative states point of view that the long - standing problem of the origin of probabilities has an elegant solution that is very much "relative state" in the spirit. We have relied on symmetries of entangled states. This allowed us to derive objective probabilities for individual events. We note that this is the first such *objective* derivation of probabilities not just in the quantum setting, but also in the history of the concept of probability.

Envariant derivation of Born's rule is based on entanglement (which is at the heart of the relative states approach). We have not followed either proposals that appeal directly to invariant measures on the Hilbert space [10,11], or attempts to derive Born's rule from frequencies by counting many worlds branches (Everett, 1957 [11]; DeWitt, 1970 [14], 1971 [15]; Graham 1973 [72], Geroch, 1984 [73]): As noted by DeWitt (1971) [15] and Kent (1990) [38], Everett's appeal to invariance of Hilbert space measures makes no contact with physics, and makes less physical sense than the mathematically rigorous proof of Gleason (1957) [84]. In addition, frequentist derivations are circular—in addition to counting branches they implicitly use Born's rule to dismiss "maverick universes".

5.8. Closing Remarks

The emergence of the classical world from within our quantum Universe is a difficult problem. The traditional (and still occasionally encountered) expectation—that it will be somehow resolved by a single new idea—did not pan out. Rather, several interdependent new insights were needed to account for quantum jumps, for the appearance of the collapse, for the preferred pointer states, for probabilities, and for the perception of the objective reality—for all the familiar ingredients of 'the classical'.

Our strategy was to avoid purely interpretational issues and to focus instead on technical questions. They can often be answered in a definitive manner. In this way, we have gained new insights into selection of preferred pointer states that go beyond decoherence, found out how probabilities arise from entanglement, and discovered how objectivity follows from redundancy.

All of that fits well with the relative states point of view and with a similar although less Everettian approach of e.g. Rovelli [205]. There are also questions that are related to the technical developments we have discussed but are, at present, less definite—less technical—in nature. We signal some of them here.

The first point concerns the nature of quantum states, and its implications for the interpretation. One might regard states as purely epistemic (as did Bohr) or attribute to them "existence". Technical results described above suggest that truth lies somewhere between these two extremes, and these two aspects are complementary in the sense of Bohr. It is therefore doubtful whether one is forced to attribute "reality" to all of the branches of the universal state vector. Indeed, such a view combines a very quantum idea of a state in the Hilbert space with a very classical literal ontic interpretation of that concept.

These two views of the universal state vector are incompatible. As we have emphasized, an unknown quantum state cannot be found out. It can acquire objective existence only by "advertising itself" in the environment[20]. This is obviously impossible for the universal state vector as the Universe has no environment.

The insistence on the absolute existence of the universal state vector as an indispensable prerequisite in interpreting quantum theory brings to mind the insistence on the absolute time and space. They seemed indispensable since Newton, yet both became relative and observer-dependent in special relativity. The absolute universal state vector may be—like the Newtonian absolute space and time, or for that matter, like isolated systems of classical physics—an idealization that is untenable in the quantum realm.

As noted in Section 2.6, observations reset the state of the Universe—they re-adjust initial conditions relevant for the future of the observer who has the record of their outcome.

---

[20] The theorem of Pusey, Barrett, and Rudolph (2012) [206] offers an interesting perspective on the existence of quantum states. An intriguing observation by Frauchiger and Renner (2018) [207] raises the "Wigner Friend" question of whether it is possible to employ quantum theory to model complex systems that include agents who are themselves described using quantum theory. The concerns raised in that paper are allayed in presence of a decohering environment [208,209].

The rest of the state vector becomes unreachable. Thus, the relative state reading of Everett rests on a safer foundation than the "Many Worlds" alternative, which is—as Wheeler (1957) [12] pointed out—compatible with the consequences of Bohr's views. There is nothing in the relative state interpretation that would elevate all the branches—especially the ones that "did not happen" to the observer—to the same ontological status as the one that is consistent with the observer's perceptions.

Objective existence can be acquired (via quantum Darwinism) only by a relatively small fraction of all degrees of freedom within the quantum Universe: The rest is needed to "keep records". Extantons (with a classical core and a vast information carrying halo) are a good illustration. Clearly, there is only a limited (if large) memory space available for this at any time. This limitation on the total memory available means that not all quantum states that exist or quantum events that happen now "really happen" in the sense of the existential interpretation: Only a small fraction of what occurs will be still available from the records in the future. So the finite memory capacity of the Universe implies indefiniteness of the present and impermanence of the past.

To sum it up, one can extend John Wheeler's dictum "the past exists only insofar as it is recorded in the present". This is one of the topics that could have been discussed in this review, but was not. Fortunately, Ref. [210] provides an introduction to the quantum Darwinian view of the emergence of objective past in our Universe.

Consensus can be reached about objective histories, a more selective set than histories that are just consistent. This may help settle the so-called class selection problem—that is, selecting candidates for physically relevant histories from among the set of all consistent histories—which is one of the central unresolved issues of the consistent histories interpretation of quantum physics (see Griffiths, 1984 [118]; 2002 [119]; Gell-Mann and Hartle, 1990 [120]; 1993 [121]; 2012 [211]; Omnès, 1992 [122]; Griffiths and Omnès, 1999 [123]; Halliwell, 1999 [212] for a selection of points of view on this subject).

As long as we are discussing subjects that are related, but beyond the scope of this review, we should mention the so-called "strong quantum Darwinism" and "spectrum broadcast structures". They share with quantum Darwinism the main idea—that the objectively existing states are reproduced in many copies and can be independently accessed without a disturbance. They differ in the details of its implementation (e.g., by invoking different measures of what and how much the environment fragments know about the system). Fortunately, there are papers by Horodecki, Korbicz, and Horodecki (2015) [213], Le and Olaya-Castro (2018; 2020) [214,215], and there is a recent review by Korbicz (2021) [216]. These references discuss 'strong quantum Darwinism" and "spectrum broadcast structures" and provide useful entries into the relevant literature.

Some of the quantum information theoretic tools used to implement criteria for objective existence have also been 'beyond the scope'. In particular, quantum Chernoff bound has been successfully used in models [146], and we expect it to be useful in the future. Fortunately, a recent paper by Zwolak (2022) [141] discusses how quantum Chernoff bound can be used to analyze quantum Darwinism (e.g., in the c-maybe model [131]).

These results confirm that there is no need for a unique best quantum information-theoretic tool to study quantum Darwinism. We have already seen that Shannon and von Neumann mutual entropy, and various half-way quantities including Holevo χ (as well as Chernoff bound) lead to useful estimates of redundancy.

In presence of sufficiently large redundancy the precise number of records in the environment does not matter: As long as redundancy is large, emergence of the consensus—hence, objective classical reality—will be confirmed by perceptions of observers.

All of our conclusions followed from the core quantum postulates (o)–(iii) and the insight that quantum states are epiontic. These two aspects of their nature are complementary (like the wave and particle traits of photons and electrons). They both play a role in the emergence of objective classical reality with information and existence seemingly separated – the state of affairs we are accustomed to in our everyday experience.

In the field known for divergent views and lively discussions it is too early to expect consensus on which of the mysteries of the quantum-classical correspondence have been explained, but deducing inevitability of the discreteness and of quantum jumps, a simple and physically transparent derivation of Born's rule, and—above all—accounting for the emergence of objective existence from the fragile quantum states mark a significant progress. Moreover, there are no obvious obstacles in pursuing the program outlined here to provide an even fuller account of the interrelation of the epistemic and ontic aspects of quantum states, or to incorporate evolving quantum states—thus exploring emergence of objective histories—within the framework of quantum Darwinism.

Funding: This research was supported by DoE under the LDRD program at Los Alamos, and, in part, by the John Templeton Foundation as well as by FQXi, including most recently the Foundational Questions Institute's 'Consciousness in the Physical World' program, administered in partnership with the Fetzer Franklin Fund.

Acknowledgments: I would like to thank Scott Aaronson, Dorit Aharonov, Andreas Albrecht, Robert Alicki, Andrew Arrasmith, Alain Aspect, Alexia Auffeves, Howard Barnum, Charles Bennett, Robin Blume-Kohout, Adan Cabello, Adolfo del Campo, Carlton Caves, Lukasz Cincio, Patrick Coles, Fernando Cucchietti, Diego Dalvit, Bogdan Damski, Luiz Davidovich, Sebastian Deffner, Jacek Dziarmaga, Christopher Fuchs, Bartlomiej Gardas, Murray Gell-Mann, Davide Girolami, Terrence Goldman, Philippe Grangier, Jonathan Halliwell, Serge Haroche, James Hartle, Theodor Hänsch, Ryszard Horodecki, Pawel Horodecki, Michal Horodecki, Karol Horodecki, Bei-Lok Hu, Christopher Jarzynski, Fedor Jelezko, Emmanuel Knill, Chris Monroe, Raymond Laflamme, Seth Lloyd, Shunlong Luo, Eric Lutz, Harold Ollivier, Don Page, Juan Pablo Paz, Roger Penrose, David Poulin, Hai-Tao Quan, Jean-Michel Raimond, Marek Rams, Jess Riedel, Carlo Rovelli, Avadh Saxena, Wolfgang Schleich, Maximilian Schlosshauer, Mark Srednicki, Leonard Susskind, Maximilian Tegmark, Akram Touil, William Unruh, Lev Vaidman, Yoshihisa Yamamoto, Bin Yan, David Wallace, Christoph Wetterich, David Wineland, William Wootters, Jakub Zakrzewski, Anton Zeilinger, Michael Zwolak, Marek Żukowski and Karol Życzkowski for stimulating discussion. Special thanks go to Sebastian Deffner, Jess Riedel, and Akram Touil who offered helpful comments and invaluable assistance in preparing this review.

Conflicts of Interest: The author declares no conflict of interest.

References

1. Born, M. Quantum mechanics of collision processes. *Zeits. Phys.* **1926**, *37*, 863; English translation in Wheeler and Zurek, 1983 [2]. [CrossRef]
2. Wheeler, J.A.; Zurek, W.H.; Eds. *Quantum Theory and Measurement*; Princeton University Press: Princeton, NJ, USA, 1983.
3. Dirac, P.A.M. *Quantum Mechanics*; Clarendon Press: Oxford, UK, 1958.
4. von Neumann, J. *Mathematical Foundations of Quantum Theory*; Translated from German original by R. T. Beyer; Princeton University Press: Princeton, NJ, USA, 1932.
5. Nielsen, M.A.; Chuang, I.L. *Quantum Computation and Quantum Information*; Cambridge University Press: Cambridge, UK, 2000.
6. Zurek, W.H. Preferred states, predictability, classicality and the environment-induced decoherence. *Progr. Theor. Phys.* **1993**, *89*, 281. [CrossRef]
7. Zurek, W.H. Decoherence, einselection, and the quantum origins of the classical. *Rev. Mod. Phys.* **2003**, *75*, 715. [CrossRef]
8. Bohr, N. The quantum postulate and the recent development of atomic theory. *Nature* **1928**, *121*, 580. [CrossRef]
9. Weinberg, S.W. Collapse of the State Vector. *Phys. Rev. A* **2012**, *85*, 062116. [CrossRef]
10. Everett, H., III. "Relative state" formulation of quantum mechanics. *Rev. Mod. Phys.* **1957**, *29*, 454. [CrossRef]
11. Everett, H., III. Quantum Mechanics by the Method of the Universal Wave Function. PhD Dissertation, Princeton University, Princeton, NJ, USA, 1957, reprinted in DeWitt and Graham, 1973, [13].
12. Wheeler, J.A. Assessment of Everett's "Relative States" Formulation of Quantum Theory. *Rev. Mod. Phys.* **1957**, *29*, 463. [CrossRef]
13. DeWitt, B.S.; Graham, N.; Eds. *The Many—Worlds Interpretation of Quantum Mechanics*; Princeton University Press: Princeton, NJ, USA, 1973.
14. DeWitt, B.S. Quantum mechanics and reality. *Phys. Today* **1970**, *23*, 30. [CrossRef]
15. DeWitt, B.S. *Foundations of Quantum Mechanics*; d'Espagnat, B., Ed.; Academic Press: New York, NY, USA, 1971; reprinted in DeWitt and Graham, 1973, [13].
16. Deutsch, D. Quantum theory as a universal physical theory. *Int. J. Theory Phys.* **1985**, *24*, 1. [CrossRef]
17. Deutsch, D. *The Fabric of Reality*; Penguin: New York, NY, USA, 1997.

18. Saunders, S.J.; Barrett, A.; Kent, A.; Wallace, D. *Many Worlds?: Everett, Quantum Theory, and Reality*; Oxford University Press: Oxford, UK, 2010.
19. Wallace, D. *The Emergent Multiverse: Quantum Theory According to the Everett Interpretation*; Oxford University Press: Oxford, UK, 2012.
20. Schrödinger, E. *Naturwissenschaften* **1935**, *23*, 807–812, 823–828, 844–849. English translation in Wheeler and Zurek, 1983 [2]. [CrossRef]
21. Zurek, W.H.; Paz, J.-P. Quantum chaos: A decoherent definition. *Physica D* **1995**, *83*, 300–308. [CrossRef]
22. Zurek, W.H.; Paz, J.-P. Zurek and Paz Reply. *Phys. Rev. Lett.* **1995**, *75*, 351351. [CrossRef]
23. Zurek, W.H. Quantum reversibility is relative, or does a quantum measurement reset initial conditions? *Phil. Trans. R. Soc. Lond. Ser. A* **2018**, *376*, 20170315. [CrossRef]
24. Zurek, W.H. Pointer basis of quantum apparatus: Into what mixture does the wave packet collapse? *Phys. Rev. D* **1981**, *24*, 1516. [CrossRef]
25. Zurek, W.H. Environment-induced superselection rules. *Phys. Rev. D* **1982**, *26*, 1862. [CrossRef]
26. Zeh, H.D. On the interpretation of measurement in quantum theory. *Found. Phys.* **1970**, *1*, 69. [CrossRef]
27. Zurek, W.H. From quantum to classical. *Phys. Today* **1991**, *44*, 36; see also an 'update', quant-ph/0306072. [CrossRef]
28. Paz, J.-P.; Zurek, W.H. *Coherent Atomic Matter Waves, Les Houches Lectures*; Kaiser, R., Westbrook, C., David, F., Eds.; Springer: Berlin, Germany, 2001; p. 533.
29. Joos, E.; Zeh, H.D.; Kiefer, C.; Giulini, D.; Kupsch, J.; Stamatescu, I.-O. *Decoherence and the Appearancs of a Classical World in Quantum Theory*; Springer: Berlin, Germany, 2003.
30. Breuer, H.P.; Petruccione, F. *The Theory of Open Quantum Systems*; Oxford University Press: Oxford, UK, 2002.
31. Schlosshauer, M. Decoherence, the measurement problem, and interpretations of quantum mechanics. *Rev. Mod. Phys.* **2005**, *76*, 1267. [CrossRef]
32. Schlosshauer, M. *Decoherence and the Quantum-to-Classical Transition*; Springer: Berlin, Germany, 2007.
33. Schlosshauer, M. Quantum decoherence. *Phys. Rep.* **2019**, *831*, 1–57. [CrossRef]
34. Landau, L.D. The damping problem in quantum mechanics. *Z. Phys.* **1927**, *45*, 430–441. [CrossRef]
35. Zurek, W.H. Environment-assisted invariance, entanglement, and probabilities in quantum physics. *Phys. Rev. Lett.* **2003**, *90*, 120404. [CrossRef]
36. Zurek, W.H. Decoherence, einselection and the existential interpretation (the rough guide). *Phil. Trans. R. Soc. Lond. Ser. A* **1998**, *356*, 1793. [CrossRef]
37. Schlosshauer, M. Experimental motivation and empirical consistency in minimal no-collapse quantum mechanics. *Ann. Phys. (N.Y.)* **2006**, *321*, 112. [CrossRef]
38. Kent, A. Against many-worlds interpretations. *Int. J. Mod. Phys.* **1990**, *A5*, 1745. [CrossRef]
39. Squires, E.J. On an alleged "proof" of the quantum probability law. *Phys. Lett.* **1990**, *A145*, 67. [CrossRef]
40. Bell, J.S. The theory of local beables, Ref. TH. 2053-CERN, **1975**, reprinted in Bell, 1987 [41]).
41. Bell, J.S. *Speakable and Unspeakable in Quantum Mechanics*; Cambridge University Press: Cambridge, UK, 1987.
42. Zurek, W.H. Quantum origin of quantum jumps: Breaking of unitary symmetry induced by information transfer and the transition from quantum to classical. *Phys. Rev. A* **2007**, *76*, 052110. [CrossRef]
43. Zurek, W.H. Actionable Information, Repeatability, Quantum Jumps, and the Wavepacket Collapse. *Phys. Rev. A* **2013**, *87*, 052111. [CrossRef]
44. Wootters, W.K.; Zurek, W.H. A single quantum cannot be cloned. *Nature* **1982**, *299*, 802. [CrossRef]
45. Dieks, D. Communication by EPR devices. *Phys. Lett.* **1982**, *92A*, 271. [CrossRef]
46. Yuen, H.P. Amplification of quantum states and noiseless photon amplifiers. *Phys. Lett.* **1986**, *113A*, 405. [CrossRef]
47. Wheeler, J.A. Law without law. In *Quantum Theory and Measurement*, Wheeler, J.A.; Zurek, W.H.; Eds.; Princeton University Press: Princeton, NJ, USA, 1983. pp. 182–213, [2].
48. Zurek, W.H. Probabilities from entanglement, Born's rule $p_k = |\psi_k|^2$ from envariance. *Phys. Rev. A* **2005**, *71*, 052105. [CrossRef]
49. Zurek, W.H. Relative States and the Environment: Einselection, Envariance, Quantum Darwinism, and the Existential Interpretation. *arXiv* **2007**, arXiv:0707.2832.
50. Luo, S. From quantum no-cloning to wave-packet collapse. *Phys. Lett. A* **2010**, *374*, 1350–1353. [CrossRef]
51. Zander, C.; Plastino, A.R. Fidelity measure and conservation of information in general probabilistic theories. *Europhys. Lett.* **2009**, *86*, 18004. [CrossRef]
52. Gnedenko, B.V. *The Theory of Probability*; Chelsea: New York, NY, USA, 1968.
53. Zeh, H.D. Quantum Measurements and Entropy. In *Complexity, Entropy, and the Physics of Information*; Zurek, W.H., Ed.; Addison Wesley: Redwood City, NC, USA, 1990, p. 405.
54. Zeh, H.D. *The Physical Basis of the Direction of Time*; Springer: Berlin, Germany, 2007.
55. Albrecht, A., Investigating decoherence in a simple system, *Phys. Rev. D* **1992**, *46*, 5504. [CrossRef]
56. Albrecht, A.; Baunach, R.; Arrasmith, A. Einselection, Equilibrium and Cosmology. *arXiv* **2021**, arXiv:2105.14017.
57. Albrecht, A.; Baunach, R.; Arrasmith, A. Adapted Caldeira-Leggett Model. *arXiv* **2021**, arXiv:2105.14040.
58. Bousso, R.; Susskind, L. Multiverse interpretation of quantum mechanics. *Phys. Rev. D* **2012**, *85*, 045007. [CrossRef]

59. Bacciagaluppi, G. Delocalized Properties in the Modal Interpretation of a Continuous Model of Decoherence. *Found. Phys.* **2000**, *30*, 1431–1444.:1026453817453. [CrossRef]
60. Page, D.N. Quantum Uncertainties in the Schmidt Basis Given by Decoherence. *arXiv* **2011** arXiv:1108.2709.
61. Page, D.N. Does Decoherence Make Observations Classical? *arXiv* **2021**, arXiv:2108.13428.
62. Poyatos, J.F.; Cirac, J.I.; Zoller, P. Quantum Reservoir Engineering with Laser Cooled Trapped Ions. *Phys. Rev. Lett.* **1996**, *77*, 4728–4731. [CrossRef]
63. Zurek, W.H.; Habib, S.; Paz, J.-P. Coherent states via decoherence. *Phys. Rev. Lett.* **1993**, *70*, 1187. [CrossRef]
64. Zurek, W.H. Decoherence, chaos, quantum-classical correspondence, and the algorithmic arrow of time. *Phys. Scr.* **1998**, *T76*, 186. [CrossRef]
65. Tegmark, M. Importance of quantum decoherence in brain processes. *Phys. Rev. E* **2000**, *61*, 4194. [CrossRef]
66. Zurek, W.H.; Paz, J.-P. Decoherence, Chaos, and the Second Law. *Phys. Rev. Lett.* **1994**, *72*, 2508–2511. [CrossRef]
67. London, F.; Bauer, E. *La Théorie de l'Observation en Méchanique Quantique*; Hermann: Paris, France, 1939. English translation in Wheeler and Zurek, 1983 [2].
68. Wigner, E.P. *The Scientist Speculates*; Good, I.J., Ed.; Heinemann: London, UK, 1961; pp. 171–183.
69. Laplace, P.S. *A Philosophical Essay on Probabilities*; English translation of the French original by F. W. Truscott and F. L. Emory; Dover: New York, NY, USA, 1820.
70. Fine, T.L. *Theories of Probability: An Examination of Foundations*; Academic Press: New York, NY, USA, 1973.
71. von Mises, R. *Probability, Statistics, and Truth*; McMillan: New York, NY, USA, 1939.
72. Graham, N. The Measurement of Relative Frequency. In *The Many—Worlds Interpretation of Quantum Mechanics*; DeWitt, B.S., Graham, N., Eds.; Princeton University Press: Princeton, NJ, USA, 1973; pp. 229–253.
73. Geroch, R. The Everett interpretation. *Noûs* **1984**, *18*, 617. [CrossRef]
74. Stein, H. The Everett interpretation of quantum mechanics: Many worlds or none? *Noûs* **1984**, *18*, 635. [CrossRef]
75. Joos, E.; Blanchard, P.; Giulini, D.; Joos, E.; Kiefer, C.; Stamatescu, I.-O. *Decoherence: Theoretical, Experimental, and Conceptual Problems*; Springer: Berlin, Germany, 2000; pp. 1–17.
76. Weinberg, S.W. *Quantum Theory*; Cambridge University Press: Cambridge, UK, 2013.
77. Zurek, W.H. Entanglement Symmetry, Amplitudes, and Probabilities: Inverting Born's Rule. *Phys. Rev. Lett.* **2011**, *106*, 250402. [CrossRef]
78. Zurek, W.H., Quantum Darwinism, classical reality, and the randomness of quantum jumps, *Physics Today* **2014**, *67* (10) 44. [CrossRef]
79. Hartle, J.B. Quantum mechanics of individual systems. *Am. J. Phys.* **1968**, *36*, 704–712. [CrossRef]
80. Farhi, E.; Goldstone, J.; Gutmann, S. How probability arises in quantum mechanics. *Ann. Phys.* **1989**, *192*, 368–382. [CrossRef]
81. Poulin, D. Macroscopic observables. *Phys. Rev. A* **2005**, *71*, 22102. [CrossRef]
82. Caves, C.M.; Schack, R. Properties of the frequency operator do not imply the quantum probability postulate. *Ann. Phys.* **2005**, *315*, 123. [CrossRef]
83. Buniy, R.V.; Hsu, S.D.H.; Zee, A. Discrete Hilbert Space, the Born Rule, and Quantum Gravity. *Phys. Lett.* **2006**, *B640*, 219. [CrossRef]
84. Gleason, A.M. Measures on the closed subspaces of a Hilbert space. *J. Math. Mech.* **1957**, *6*, 885–893. [CrossRef]
85. Dalvit, D.A.R.; Dziarmaga, J.; Zurek, W.H. Predictability sieve, pointer states, and the classicality of quantum trajectories. *Phys. Rev. A* **2005**, *72*, 062101. [CrossRef]
86. Deutsch, D. Quantum theory of probability and decisions. *Proc. R. Soc. Lond. Ser. A* **1999**, *455* 3129. [CrossRef]
87. Wallace, D. Everettian rationality: defending Deutsch's approach to probability in the Everett interpretation. *Stud. Hist. Phil. Mod. Phys.* **2003**, *34*, 415-439. [CrossRef]
88. Zeh, H.D. *New Developments on Fundamental Problems in Quantum Mechanics*; Ferrero, M., van der Merwe, A., Eds.; Kluwer: Dordrecht, The Netherlands, 1997.
89. Baker, D.J. The Born rule and its interpretation. *Stud. Hist. Phil. Mod. Phys.* **2007**, *38*, 153. [CrossRef]
90. Forrester, A. Decision theory and information propagation in quantum physics. *Stud. Hist. Phil. Mod. Phys.* **2007**, *38*, 815–831. [CrossRef]
91. Drezet, A. Making sense of Born's rule $p_\alpha = ||\Psi_\alpha||^2$ with the many-minds interpretation. *Quantum Stud. Math. Found.* **2021**, *8*, 315. [CrossRef]
92. Wallace, D. How to prove Born's rule? In *Many Worlds?: Everett, Quantum Theory, and Reality*; Saunders, S.J.; Barrett, A.; Kent, A.; Wallace, D. Eds.; Oxford University Press: Oxford, UK, 2010, [18].
93. Barnum, H. No-signalling-based version of Zurek's derivation of quantum probabilities: A note on "Environment-assisted invariance, entanglement, and probabilities in quantum physics. *arXiv* **2003**, arXiv:0312150.
94. Schlosshauer, M.; Fine, A. On Zurek's derivation of the Born rule. *Found. Phys.* **2005**, *35*, 197. [CrossRef]
95. Sikorski, R. *Boolean Logic*; Springer: Berlin, Germany, 1964.
96. Weissman, M.B. Emergent measure-dependent probabilities from modified quantum dynamics without state-vector reduction. *Found. Phys. Lett.* **1999**, *12*, 407. [CrossRef]
97. Auletta, G. *Foundations and Interpretation of Quantum Theory*; World Scientific: Singapore, 2000.
98. Saunders, S. Derivation of the Born rule from operational assumptions. *Proc. R. Soc. Lond. Ser. A* **2004**, *460*, 1 [CrossRef]

99. Barnum, H.; Caves, C.M.; Finkelstein, J.; Fuchs, C.A.R. Quantum probability from decision theory? *Proc. R. Soc. Lond.* **2000**, *A456*, 1175. [CrossRef]
100. Wallace, D. Quantum probability from subjective likelihood: improving on Deutsch's proof of the probability rule. *Stud. Hist. Phil. Mod. Phys.* **2007**, *38*, 311–332. [CrossRef]
101. Herbut, F. Quantum probability law from 'environment-assisted invariance' in terms of pure-state twin unitaries. *J. Phys.* **2007**, *A40*, 5949.
102. Paris, M.G.A. Unitary local invariance. *Int. J. Quantum. Inform.* **2005**, *3*, 655. [CrossRef]
103. Jordan, T.F. Assumptions that imply quantum dynamics is linear. *Phys. Rev. A* **2006**, *73*, 022101. [CrossRef]
104. Steane, A.M. Context, spacetime loops and the interpretation of quantum mechanics. *J. Phys.* **2007**, *A40*, 3223. [CrossRef]
105. Bub, J.; Pitovsky, I. Two dogmas about quantum mechanics. *arXiv* **2007**, arXiv:0712.4258.
106. Horodecki, R.; Horodecki, P.; Horodecki, M.; Horodecki, K. Quantum entanglement. *Rev. Mod. Phys.* **2009**, *81*, 865. [CrossRef]
107. Blaylock, G. The EPR paradox, Bell's inequality, and the question of locality. *Am. J. Phys.* **2010**, *78*, 111. [CrossRef]
108. Seidewitz, E. Consistent histories of systems and measurements in spacetime. *Found. Phys.* **2011**, *41*, 1163. [CrossRef]
109. Hsu, S.D.H. On the origin of probability in quantum mechanics. *Mod. Phys. Lett.* **2012**, *27*, 1230014. [CrossRef]
110. Sebens, C.T.; Carroll, S.M. Self-locating Uncertainty and the Origin of Probability in Everettian Quantum Mechanics. *British J. Phil. Sci.* **2018**, *69*, 24–75. [CrossRef]
111. Vermeyden, L.; Ma, X.; Lavoie, J.; Bonsma, M.; Sinha, U.; Laflamme, R.; Resch, K. Experimental test of environment-assisted invariance. *Phys. Rev. A* **2015**, *91*, 012120. [CrossRef]
112. Son, W. Consistent theory for causal non-locality beyond the Born's rule. *J. Korean Phys. Soc.* **2014**, *64*, 499–503. [CrossRef]
113. Harris, J.; Bouchard, F.; Santamato, E.; Zurek, W.H.; Boyd, R.W.; Karimi, E. Quantum probabilities from quantum entanglement: experimentally unpacking the Born rule. *N. J. Phys.* **2016**, *18*, 053013. [CrossRef]
114. Deffner, S. Demonstration of entanglement assisted invariance on IBM's quantum experience. *Heliyon* **2016**, *3*, e00444. [CrossRef] [PubMed]
115. Hong, C.K.; Ou, Z.Y.; Mandel, L. Measurement of subpicosecond time intervals between two photons by interference. *Phys. Rev. Lett.* **1987**, *59*, 2044–2046. [CrossRef] [PubMed]
116. Milonni, P.W.; Eberley, J.H. *Laser Physics*; Wiley: New York, NY, USA, 2010.
117. Healey, R. Observation and Quantum Objectivity. *Philos. Sci.* **2012**, *80*, 434–53. [CrossRef]
118. Griffiths, R.B. Consistent Histories and the Interpretation of Quantum Mechanics. *J. Stat. Phys.* **1984**, *36*, 219. [CrossRef]
119. Griffiths, R.B. *Consistent Quantum Theory*; Cambridge University Press: Cambridge, UK, 2002.
120. Gell-Mann, M.; Hartle, J.B. Quantum Mechanics in the Light of Quantum Cosmology. In *Complexity, Entropy, and the Physics of Information*; SFI Studies in the Sciences of Complexity; Zurek, W.H., Ed.; Addison Wesley: Reading, MA, USA, 1990; Volume VIII.
121. Gell-Mann, M.; Hartle, J.B. Classical Equations for Quantum Systems. *Phys. Rev. D* **1993**, *47*, 334. [CrossRef]
122. Omnès, R. Consistent interpretations of quantum mechanics. *Rev. Mod. Phys.* **1992**, *64*, 339–382. [CrossRef]
123. Griffiths, R.B.; Omnès, R. Consistent Histories and Quantum Measurements. *Phys. Today* **1999**, *52*, 26–31. [CrossRef]
124. Zurek, W.H. Einselection and Decoherence from an Information Theory Perspective. *Ann. Phys. (Leipzig)* **2000**, *9*, 855. [CrossRef]
125. Henderson, L.; Vedral, V. Classical, quantum and total correlations. *J. Phys.* **2001**, *A34*, 6899. [CrossRef]
126. Ollivier, H.; Zurek, W.H. Quantum Discord: A Measure of the Quantumness of Correlations. *Phys. Rev. Lett.* **2001**, *88*, 017901. [CrossRef] [PubMed]
127. Cover, T.M.; Thomas, J.A. *Elements of Information Theory*; Wiley: New York, NY, USA, 1991.
128. Zurek, W.H. Quantum discord and Maxwell's demons. *Phys. Rev. A* **2003**, *67*, 012320. [CrossRef]
129. Holevo, A.S. Bounds for the quantity of information transmitted by a quantum communication channel. *Probl. Pereda. Inf.* **1973**, *9*, 3.
130. Zwolak, M.; Zurek, W.H. Complementarity of quantum discord and classically accessible information. *Sci. Rep.* **2013**, *3*, 1729. [CrossRef]
131. Touil, A.; Yan, B.; Girolami, D.; Deffner, S.; Zurek, W.H. Eavesdropping on the decohering environment: quantum Darwinism, amplification, and the origin of objective classical reality. *Phys. Rev. Lett.* **2022**, *128*, 010401 [CrossRef]
132. Brodutch, A.; Terno, D.R. Quantum discord under two-side projective measurements. *Phys. Rev. A* **2010**, *81*, 062103 [CrossRef]
133. Rodrígues-Rosario, C.A.; Modi, K.; Kuah, A.-M.; Shaji, A.; Sudarshan, E.C.G. Completely positive maps and classical correlations. *J. Phys. A Math. Theor.* **2008**, *41*, 205301. [CrossRef]
134. Datta, A.; Shaji, A.; Caves, C.M. Quantum Discord and the Power of One Qubit. *Phys. Rev. Lett.* **2008**, *100*, 050502. [CrossRef]
135. Piani, M.; Horodecki, P.; Horodecki, R. No-Local-Broadcasting Theorem for Multipartite Quantum Correlations. *Phys. Rev. Lett.* **2008**, *100*, 090502. [CrossRef]
136. Luo, S.; Sun, W. Decomposition of bipartite states with applications to quantum no-broadcasting theorems. *Phys. Rev. A* **2010**, *82*, 012338. [CrossRef]
137. Gu, M.; Chrzanowski, H.M.; Assad, S.M.; Symul, T.; Modi, K.; Ralph, T.C.; Vedral, V.; Lam, P.K. Observing the operational significance of discord consumption. *Nat. Phys.* **2012**, *8*, 671–675. [CrossRef]
138. Dakic, B.; Lipp, Y.O.; Ma, X.; Ringbauer, M.; Kropatschek, S.; Barz, S.; Paterek, T.; Vedral, V.; Zeilinger, A.; Brukner, C.; et al. Quantum discord as resource for remote state preparation. *Nat. Phys.* **2012**, *8*, 666–670. [CrossRef]

139. Modi, K.; Brodutch, A.; Cable, H.; Paterek, T.; Vedral, V. The classical-quantum boundary for correlations: Discord and related measures. *Rev. Mod. Phys.* **2012**, *84*, 1655. [CrossRef]
140. Bera, A.; Das, T.; Sadhukhan, D.; Roy, S.S.; De, A.S.; Sen, U. Quantum discord and its allies: A review of recent progress. *Rep. Prog. Phys.* **2018**, *81*, 024001. [CrossRef] [PubMed]
141. Zwolak, M. Amplification, Inference, and the Manifestation of Objective Classical Information *Entropy* **2022**, *24*, 781. [CrossRef] [PubMed]
142. Girolami, D.; Touil, A.; Yan, B.; Deffner, S.; Zurek, W.H. Redundantly Amplified Information Suppresses Quantum Correlations in Many-Body Systems. *Phys. Rev. Lett.* **2022**, *129*, 010401. [CrossRef]
143. Blume-Kohout, R.; Zurek, W.H. A Simple Example of "Quantum Darwinism": Redundant Information Storage in Many-Spin Environments. *Found. Phys.* **2005**, *35*, 1857. [CrossRef]
144. Zwolak, M.; Quan, H.-T.; Zurek, W.H. Quantum Darwinism in a hazy environment. *Phys. Rev. Lett.* **2009**, *103*, 110402. [CrossRef]
145. Zwolak, M.; Quan, H.-T.; Zurek, W.H. Redundant imprinting of information in nonideal environments: Objective reality via a noisy channel. *Phys. Rev. A* **2010**, *81*, 062110. [CrossRef]
146. Zwolak, M.; Riedel, C.J.; Zurek, W.H. Amplification, redundancy, and quantum Chernoff information. *Phys. Rev. Lett.* **2014**, *112*, 140406. [CrossRef]
147. Gregoratti, M.; Werner, R.F. Quantum lost and found. *J. Modern Opt.* **2003**, *50*, 915–933. [CrossRef]
148. Schumacher, B. Quantum coding. *Phys. Rev. A* **1995**, *51*, 2738–2747. [CrossRef] [PubMed]
149. Ollivier, H.; Poulin, D.; Zurek, W.H. Objective Properties from Subjective Quantum States: Environment as a Witness. *Phys. Rev. Lett.* **2004**, *93*, 220401. [CrossRef]
150. Streltsov, A.; Zurek, W.H. Quantum discord cannot be shared. *Phys. Rev. Lett.* **2013**, *111*, 040401. [CrossRef] [PubMed]
151. Ollivier, H.; Poulin, D.; Zurek, W.H. Environment as a witness: Selective proliferation of information and emergence of objectivity in a quantum universe. *Phys. Rev. A* **2005**, *72*, 423113. [CrossRef]
152. Blume-Kohout, R.; Zurek, W.H. Quantum Darwinism: Entanglement, branches, and the emergent classicality of redundantly stored quantum information. *Phys. Rev. A* **2006**, *73*, 062310. [CrossRef]
153. Riedel, C.J.; Zurek, W.H.; Zwolak, M. The Rise and Fall of Redundancy in Decoherence and Quantum Darwinism. *New J. Phys.* **2012**, *14*, 083010. [CrossRef]
154. Zwolak, M.; Riedel, C.J.; Zurek, W.H. Amplification, decoherence and the acquisition of information by spin environments. *Sci Rep.* **2016**, *6*, 25277. [CrossRef]
155. Zwolak, M.; Zurek, W.H. Redundancy of einselected information in quantum Darwinism: The irrelevance of irrelevant environment bits. *Phys. Rev. A* **2017**, *95*, 030101(R). [CrossRef]
156. Mirkin, N.; Wisniacki, D.A. Many-Body Localization and the Emergence of Quantum Darwinism. *Entropy* **2021**, *23*, 1377. [CrossRef]
157. Çakmak, B.; Müstecaplıoğlu, Ö.E.; Paternostro, M.; Vacchini, B.; Campbell, S. Quantum Darwinism in a Composite System: Objectivity versus Classicality. *Entropy* **2021**, *23*, 995. [CrossRef] [PubMed]
158. Riedel, C.J.; Zurek, W.H. Redundant information from thermal illumination: quantum Darwinism in scattered photons. *New J. Phys.* **2011**, *13*, 073038. [CrossRef]
159. Page, D.N. Average entropy of a subsystem. *Phys. Rev. Lett.* **1993**, *71*, 1291–1294. [CrossRef] [PubMed]
160. Feynman, R.P.; Vernon, R.L. The Theory of a General Quantum System Interacting with a Linear Dissipative System. *Ann. Phys. (N. Y.)* **1963**, *192*, 368.
161. Dekker, H. Quantization of the linearly damped harmonic oscillator. *Phys. Rev.* **1977**, *A16*, 2126. [CrossRef]
162. Caldeira, A.O.; Leggett, A.J. Path integral approach to quantum Brownian motion. *Phys. A* **1983**, *121*, 587. [CrossRef]
163. Unruh, W.G.; Zurek, W.H. Reduction of a wave packet in quantum Brownian motion. *Phys. Rev. D* **1989**, *40*, 1071. [CrossRef]
164. Hu, B.L.; Paz, J.P.; Zhang, Y. Quantum Brownian motion in a general environment: Exact master equation with nonlocal dissipation and colored noise. *Phys. Rev. D* **1992**, *45*, 2843. [CrossRef]
165. Paz, J.P.; Habib, S.W.; Zurek, H. Reduction of the wave packet: Preferred observable and decoherence time scale. *Phys. Rev. D* **1993**, *47*, 488–501. [CrossRef]
166. Tegmark, M.; Wheeler, J.A. 100 years of quantum mysteries. *Sci. Am.* **2001**, *284*, 68–75. [CrossRef]
167. Bacciagaluppi, G. *The Stanford Encyclopedia of Philosophy*; Zalta, E.N., Ed.; 2004. Available online: http://plato.stanford.edu/entries/qm-decoherence (accessed on 8 May 2021).
168. Tegmark, M.; Shapiro, H.S. Decoherence produces coherent states: An explicit proof for harmonic chains. *Phys. Rev. E* **1994**, *50*, 2538. [CrossRef] [PubMed]
169. Gallis, M.R. Emergence of classicality via decoherence described by Lindblad operators. *Phys. Rev. A* **1996**, *53*, 655. [CrossRef] [PubMed]
170. Blume-Kohout, R.; Zurek, W.H. Quantum Darwinism in Quantum Brownian Motion . *Phys. Rev. Lett.* **2008**, *101*, 240405. [CrossRef] [PubMed]
171. Paz, J.P.; Roncaglia, A.J. Redundancy of classical and quantum correlations during decoherence. *Phys. Rev. A* **2009**, *80*, 042111. [CrossRef]
172. Serafini, A.; de Siena, S.; Illuminati, F.; Paris, M.G.A. Minimum decoherence cat-like states in Gaussian noisy channels. *J. Opt. B Quant. Semiclass. Opt.* **2004**, *6*, S591. [CrossRef]

173. LaHaye, M.; Buu, O.; Camarota, B.; Schwab, K. Approaching the quantum limit of a nanomechanical resonator. *Science* **2004**, *304*, 74. [CrossRef]
174. Joos, E.; Zeh, H.D. The emergence of classical properties through interaction with the environment. *Z. Phys.* **1985**, *B59*, 223 [CrossRef]
175. Gallis, M.R.; Fleming, G.N. Environmental and spontaneous localization. *Phys. Rev. A* **1990**, *42*, 38–48. [CrossRef]
176. Hornberger, K.; Sipe, J.E. Collisional decoherence reexamined. *Phys. Rev. A* **2003**, *68*, 012105. [CrossRef]
177. Dodd, P.J.; Halliwell, J.J. Decoherence and records for the case of a scattering environment. *Phys. Rev. D* **2003**, *67* 105018. [CrossRef]
178. Halliwell, J.J. Two derivations of the master equation of quantum Brownian motion. *J. Phys. A* **2007**, *40*, 3067–3080. [CrossRef]
179. Hornberger, K.; Uttenthaler, S.; Brezger, B.; Hackermüller, L.; Arndt, M.; Zeilinger, A. Collisional decoherence observed in matter wave interferometry. *Phys. Rev. Lett.* **2003**, *90*, 160401. [CrossRef] [PubMed]
180. Hackermüller, L.; Hornberger, K.; Brezger, B.; Zeilinger, A.; Arndt, M. Decoherence of matter waves by thermal emission of radiation. *Nature* **2004**, *427*, 711–714. [CrossRef] [PubMed]
181. Riedel, C.J.; Zurek, W.H. Quantum Darwinism in an Everyday Environment: Huge Redundancy in Scattered Photons. *Phys. Rev. Lett.* **2010**, *105*, 020404. [CrossRef] [PubMed]
182. Brune, M.; Hagley, E.; Dreyer, J.; Maître, X.; Wunderlich, C.; Raimond, J.-M.; Haroche, S. Observing the Progressive Decoherence of the "Meter" in a Quantum Measurement. *Phys. Rev. Lett.* **1996**, *77*, 4887–4890. [CrossRef]
183. Haroche, S.; Raimond, J.-M. *Exploring the Quantum: Atoms, Cavities, and Photons*; Oxford University Press: Oxford, UK, 2006.
184. Ciampini, M.A.; Pinna, G.; Mataloni, P.; Paternostro, M. Experimental signature of quantum Darwinism in photonic cluster states. *Phys. Rev. A* **2018**, *98*, 020101. [CrossRef]
185. Chen, M.-C.; Zhong, H.-S.; Li, Y.; Wu, D.; Wang, X.-L.; Li, L.; Liu, N.-L.; Lu, C.-Y.; Pan, J.-W. Emergence of Classical Objectivity of Quantum Darwinism in a Photonic Quantum Simulator. *Sci. Bull.* **2019**, *64*, 580–585. [CrossRef]
186. Chisholm, D.A.; García-Pérez, M.A.C.; Rossi, S.; Maniscalco, M. G. Palma, Witnessing Objectivity on a Quantum Computer. *arXiv* **2021**, arXiv:2110.06243.
187. Unden, T.K.; Louzon, D.; Zwolak, M.; Zurek, W.H.; Jelezko, F. *Phys. Rev. Lett.* Revealing the emergence of classicality using nitrogen-vacancy centers. **2019**, *123*, 140402. [CrossRef]
188. Wilde, M.M. *From Classical to Quantum Shannon Theory*; Cambridge University Press: Cambridge, UK, 2013.
189. Preskill, J. 2020. Available online: http://theory.caltech.edu/~preskill/ph219/ph219_2020-21.html (accessed on 8 May 2021).
190. Brandão, F.G.S.L.; Piani, M.; Horodecki, P. Generic emergence of classical features in quantum Darwinism. *Nat. Commun.* **2015**, *6*, 7908. [CrossRef]
191. Qi, X.-L.; Ranard, D. Emergent classicality in general multipartite states and channels. *Quantum* **2021**, *5*, 555. [CrossRef]
192. Knott, P.A.; Tufarelli, T.; Piani, M.; Adesso, G. Generic emergence of objectivity of observables in infinite dimensions. *Phys. Rev. Lett.* **2018**, *121*, 160401. [CrossRef] [PubMed]
193. Bell, J.S. Against 'measurement'. *Phys. World* **1990**, *3*, 33–40. [CrossRef]
194. Deffner, S.; Zurek, W.H. Foundations of statistical mechanics from symmetries of entanglement. *New J. Phys.* **2016**, *18*, 063013. [CrossRef]
195. Zurek, W.H. Eliminating Ensembles from Equilibrium Statistical Physics: Maxwell's Demon, Szilard's Engine, and Thermodynamics via Entanglement. *Phys. Rep.* **2018**, *755*, 1–21. [CrossRef]
196. Wheeler, J.A. Information, Physics, Quantum: The Search for Links. In *Complexity, Entropy, and the Physics of Information*; Zurek, W.H., Ed.; Addison Wesley: Redwood City, NC, USA, 1990.
197. Landauer, R. Information is Physical. *Phys. Today* **1991**, *44*, 23. [CrossRef]
198. Zurek, W.H. Quantum theory of the classical: quantum jumps, Born's Rule and objective classical reality via quantum Darwinism. *Phil. Trans. R. Soc. Lond. Ser. A* **2018**, *376*, 20180107. [CrossRef]
199. Phan, N.M.; Cheng, M.F.; Bessarab, D.A.; Krivitsky, L.A. Interaction of Fixed Number of Photons with Retinal Rod Cells. *Phys. Rev. Lett.* **2014**, *112*, 213601. [CrossRef]
200. Rieke, F.; Baylor, D.A. Single-photon detection by rod cells of the retina. *Rev. Mod. Phys.* **1998**, *70*, 1027. [CrossRef]
201. Tinsley, J.N.; Molodtsov, M.I.; Prevedel, R.; Wartmann, D.; Espigulé-Pons, J.; Lauwers, M.; Vaziri, A. Direct detection of a single photon by humans. *Nat. Commun.* **2016**, *7*, 12172 [CrossRef]
202. Peres, A. *Quantum Theory: Concepts and Methods*; Kluwer: Dordrecht, The Netherlands, 1993.
203. Fuchs, C.A.; Peres, A. Quantum theory needs no 'interpretation'. *Phys. Today* **2000**, *53*, 70–71. [CrossRef]
204. Fuchs, C.A.; Schack, R. Quantum-Bayesian coherence. *Rev. Mod. Phys.* **2013**, *85*, 1693–1715. [CrossRef]
205. Rovelli, C. Relational Quantum Mechanics. *Int. J. of Theor. Phys.* **1996**, *35*, 1637. [CrossRef]
206. Pusey, M.F.; Barrett, J.; Rudolph, T. On the reality of the quantum state. *Nat. Phys.* **2012**, *8* , 475–478. [CrossRef]
207. Frauchiger, D.; Renner, R. Quantum theory cannot consistently describe the use of itself. *Nat. Comm.* **2018**, *9*, 3711. [CrossRef] [PubMed]
208. Relaño, A. Decoherence framework for Wigner's friend experiments. *Phys. Rev. A* **2020** *101*, 032107. [CrossRef]
209. Żukowski; M.; Markiewicz, M., Physics and Metaphysics of Wigner's Friends: Even performed pre-measurements have no results. *Phys. Rev. Lett.* **2021**, *126*, 130402. [CrossRef]

210. Riedel, C.J.; Zurek, W.H.; Zwolak, M. Objective past of a quantum universe: Redundant records of consistent histories. *Phys. Rev. A* **2016**, *93*, 032126. [CrossRef]
211. Gell-Mann, M.; Hartle, J.B. Decoherent Histories Quantum Mechanics with One 'Real' Fine-Grained History. *Phys. Rev. A* **2012**, *85*, 062120. [CrossRef]
212. Halliwell, J.J. Somewhere in the Universe: Where is the Information Stored When Histories Decohere? *Phys. Rev. D* **1999**, *60*, 105031. [CrossRef]
213. Horodecki, R.; Korbicz, J.K.; Horodecki, P. Quantum origins of objectivity. *Phys. Rev. A* **2015**, *91*, 032122. [CrossRef]
214. Le, T.P.; Olaya-Castro, A. Witnessing non-objectivity in the framework of strong quantum Darwinism. *Quantum Sci. Technol.* **2020**, *5*, 045012. [CrossRef]
215. Le, T.P.; Olaya-Castro, A. Objectivity (or lack thereof): Comparison between predictions of quantum Darwinism and spectrum broadcast structure. *Phys. Rev. A* **2018**, *98*, 032103. [CrossRef]
216. Korbicz, J.K. Roads to objectivity: Quantum Darwinism, Spectrum Broadcast Structures, and Strong quantum Darwinism—A review. *Quantum* **2021**, *5*, 571 [CrossRef]

Article

Quantum Darwinism in a Composite System: Objectivity versus Classicality

Barış Çakmak [1,*], Özgür E. Müstecaplıoğlu [2], Mauro Paternostro [3], Bassano Vacchini [4,5] and Steve Campbell [6,7,*]

1. College of Engineering and Natural Sciences, Bahçeşehir University, Beşiktaş, Istanbul 34353, Turkey
2. Department of Physics, Koç University, Sarıyer, Istanbul 34450, Turkey; omustecap@ku.edu.tr
3. Centre for Theoretical Atomic, Molecular and Optical Physics, School of Mathematics and Physics, Queen's University Belfast, Belfast BT7 1NN, UK; m.paternostro@qub.ac.uk
4. Dipartimento di Fisica "Aldo Pontremoli", Università degli Studi di Milano, via Celoria 16, 20133 Milan, Italy; bassano.vacchini@mi.infn.it
5. Istituto Nazionale di Fisica Nucleare, Sezione di Milano, via Celoria 16, 20133 Milan, Italy
6. School of Physics, University College Dublin, Belfield, Dublin 4, Ireland
7. Centre for Quantum Engineering, Science, and Technology, University College Dublin, Belfield, Dublin 4, Ireland
* Correspondence: baris.cakmak@eng.bau.edu.tr (B.Ç.); steve.campbell@ucd.ie (S.C.)

Abstract: We investigate the implications of quantum Darwinism in a composite quantum system with interacting constituents exhibiting a decoherence-free subspace. We consider a two-qubit system coupled to an N-qubit environment via a dephasing interaction. For excitation preserving interactions between the system qubits, an analytical expression for the dynamics is obtained. It demonstrates that part of the system Hilbert space redundantly proliferates its information to the environment, while the remaining subspace is decoupled and preserves clear non-classical signatures. For measurements performed on the system, we establish that a non-zero quantum discord is shared between the composite system and the environment, thus violating the conditions of strong Darwinism. However, due to the asymmetry of quantum discord, the information shared with the environment is completely classical for measurements performed on the environment. Our results imply a dichotomy between objectivity and classicality that emerges when considering composite systems.

Keywords: quantum Darwinism; decoherence; open quantum systems

1. Introduction

The theory of open quantum systems provides frameworks to describe how an environment destroys quantum superpositions. The environment is an active player in the loss of quantumness and emergence of classicality. In particular, quantum Darwinism [1–3] and spectrum broadcast structures [4,5] establish mathematically rigorous approaches to quantitatively assess the mechanisms by which classically objective, accessible states emerge. The former employs an entropic approach, where classical objectivity follows from the redundant encoding of copies of the system's pointer states (preferred basis states immune to spoiling by system–environment coupling) across fragments of the environment. Objectivity becomes possible only if the information content of the system is redundantly encoded throughout the environment, such that the mutual information shared between the system and arbitrary fractions of the environment is the same and equal to the system entropy. Quantitatively, this implies that the mutual information, given as

$$\mathcal{I}(\rho_{S:\mathcal{E}_f}) = S(\rho_S) + S(\rho_{\mathcal{E}_f}) - S(\rho_{S:\mathcal{E}_f}), \quad (1)$$

where $S(\rho) = -\text{tr}[\rho \log \rho]$ is the von Neumann entropy, takes the value $\mathcal{I}(\rho_{S:\mathcal{E}_f}) = S(\rho_S)$ independently of the size of the environmental fraction $\mathcal{E}_f$ for $f < 1$, and attains the maximum value of $2S(\rho_S)$ only when one has access to the whole environment, i.e., $f = 1$.

Spectrum broadcast structures approach the problem by rather examining the geometric structure of the state, establishing strict requirements that it must fulfill. Nevertheless, both employ the same notion of objectivity as defined in Ref. [6]:

"A system state is objective if it is (1) simultaneously accessible to many observers (2) who can all determine the state independently without perturbing it and (3) all arrive at the same result [3,4,7]."

Recently, the close relationship between quantum Darwinism and spectrum broadcasting structures was established, demonstrating that the latter follows when more stringent conditions, giving rise to the so-called strong quantum Darwinism, are imposed on the former [6,8–10].

Establishing whether a given state can be viewed as classically objective has proven to be a difficult task. While any measurement is objective for a classical system, for two or more observers to agree on their measurement results in the quantum case, the basis that they measure must form orthogonal vector sets [11]. Recent studies have shown that the emergence of a redundancy plateau in the mutual information, the characteristic signal of quantum Darwinism, may not imply classical objectivity [4,8,12]. Several critical analyses of quantum Darwinism have demonstrated that, while a generic feature of quantum dynamics [13], it is nevertheless sensitive to seemingly small changes in the microscopic description [14,15], and non-Markovian effects can suppress the emergence of the phenomenon, although the relation between non-Markovianity and quantum Darwinism is yet to be fully understood [16–21]. Going beyond the single system particle, the proliferation of system information in spin registers interacting with spin [22] and boson [23] environments have shown to present different characteristics. In addition, while not necessary for decoherence, system–environment entanglement is required for objectivity as defined by quantum Darwinism [24]. Experimental tests of this framework in platforms consisting of photonic systems [25–27] and nitrogen-vacancy centers [28] have recently been reported.

This work presents a detailed analysis of redundant information encoding, classical objectivity, and quantum Darwinism for a composite system. We consider two interacting qubits that are coupled to a dephasing environment, as shown in Figure 1. We show that clear Darwinistic signatures are present when the mutual interaction between the two systems is excitation preserving. However, while the composite system establishes precisely the strong correlations necessary for the redundant proliferation of the relevant information, (in this case the system's total spin), the system establishes a decoherence-free subspace for the dynamics, which is blind to the environmental effects and allows the system to maintain highly non-classical features. We carefully assess whether the redundant information is classical or not by studying the asymmetric quantum discord [29], and demonstrating that the classicality of the mutual information is relative to the observer's perspective on measuring the system or the environment. For measurements on the system, the state has a significant non-zero quantum discord. Therefore, it violates the conditions set out for objectivity, according to the strong quantum Darwinism criteria [6]. On the other hand, for measurements on the environment side, which are arguably more in the original spirit of quantum Darwinism, the accessible information is completely classical. Our results suggest that the conditions for the objectivity of a system state, as shared by many observers, have to be distinguished from its classicality, understood as the absence of quantum correlations, for the case in which the system has a composite structure. This point turns out to be particularly subtle, as the lack of classicality may not be perceived by an external observer, due to the asymmetry of quantum discord.

The remainder of the manuscript is organized as follows. In Section 2, we introduce details of the composite system model in which we investigate quantum Darwinism. We continue with the behavior of coherences and correlations among the constituents of our model throughout the dynamics, and discuss them in relation to the emergence of Darwinism and objectivity in Section 3. In Section 4, we put forward some considerations on the relation between the phenomenology observed in the case here at hand and the formalism of strong quantum Darwinism, pointing at the asymmetry of quantum discord and its implications for the ascertaining of classicality. In Section 5, we draw our conclusions.

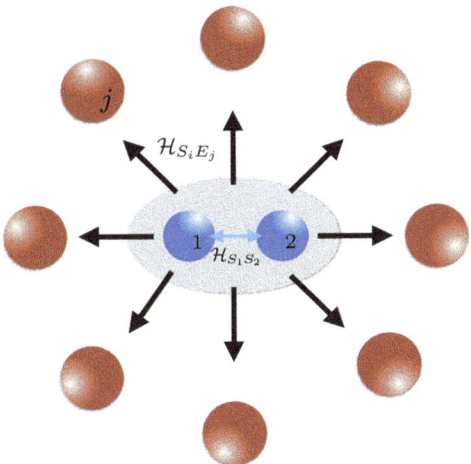

Figure 1. Schematics of the considered model. A composite system that is made up of two interacting qubits, which are also coupled to a fragmented environment. For a excitation preserving interaction between the system qubits, i.e., $J_x = J_y$ in Equation (2) and pure dephasing interaction between the system qubits and the environment, the interaction Hamiltonians commute, leading to Equation (4).

2. Composite System Model

We begin by introducing the dynamical model that we consider throughout the paper. Our focus is on exploring how signatures of redundant encoding and objectivity manifest when the system itself is a complex entity with internal interactions among its components. To this end, our system consists of two qubits, S_1 and S_2, interacting via the following:

$$\mathcal{H}_{S_1 S_2} = \sum_{j=x,y,z} J_j \sigma_{S_1}^j \otimes \sigma_{S_2}^j. \qquad (2)$$

The composite system interacts with a bath of spins $\{E_k\}$ via a pure dephasing interaction $\mathcal{H}_{S_i E_k} = J_{SE} \sigma_{S_i}^z \otimes \sigma_{E_k}^z$ with $i = 1, 2$ and $k = 1, 2, \ldots, N$. A single interaction between any two qubits in the model is realized by the application of the unitary operator $U = e^{-i\mathcal{H}t}$ to the state of the system, where $\mathcal{H} = \mathcal{H}_{S_1 S_2}$ ($\mathcal{H} = \mathcal{H}_{S_i E_k}$) for the interactions between S_1-S_2 (S_i-E_k). We set the initial state of the system and environmental qubits to be a factorized state of the following form:

$$|\Psi_0\rangle = |\phi\rangle_{S_1} \otimes |\phi\rangle_{S_2} \bigotimes_{k=1}^{N} |\Phi\rangle_k, \qquad (3)$$

where $|\phi\rangle_{S_j} = \cos\theta_j |0\rangle_{S_j} + \sin\theta_j |1\rangle_{S_j}$ ($j = 1,2$), and $|\Phi\rangle_k = |+\rangle_k = (|0\rangle_k + |1\rangle_k)/\sqrt{2}$, with $\{|0\rangle, |1\rangle\}$ being the eigenvectors of σ^z for any of the subsystems involved.

In order to make the model analytically tractable, we enforce the number of interactions with the environment to be uniformly distributed, i.e., both system qubits interact with each environmental qubit in an identical manner, cf. Figure 1. This condition is important since, as demonstrated in Ref. [15], allowing for a bias in the interactions between the system and particular environmental constituents results in a deviation from a Darwinistic behavior that would otherwise be present in the model. Furthermore, by taking the interaction between the system qubits as excitation preserving (i.e., for $J_x = J_y = J$) the system–system and combined system–environment interaction Hamiltonians commute, i.e., $[\mathcal{H}_{S_1S_2}, (\mathcal{H}_{S_1E_k} + \mathcal{H}_{S_2E_k})] = 0$. This implies that the ordering of interactions does not matter. Note that when this condition does not hold, the dynamics can still be well simulated by the collisional approach [15,30–32]; however, as discussed in Ref. [15], other system–environment interaction terms often lead to a loss in redundant encoding. This simplification allows us to work with the continuous-time t, always measured in inverse units of the coupling strength J, rather than employing the sequential collisional approach of Ref. [15]. This leads to an analytical expression for the dynamics of the whole S-E state after time t, which we write as follows:

$$\begin{aligned}|\Psi\rangle &= e^{-iNJ_zt}\alpha|00\rangle_{S_1S_2}\bigotimes_{k=1}^{N}\frac{1}{\sqrt{2}}\left(e^{-i2J_{SE}t}|0\rangle_k + e^{i2J_{SE}t}|1\rangle_k\right) \\ &+ e^{iNJ_zt}[\beta\cos(Jt) - i\gamma\sin(Jt)]|01\rangle_{S_1S_2}\bigotimes_{k=1}^{N}\frac{1}{\sqrt{2}}(|0\rangle_k + |1\rangle_k) \\ &+ e^{iNJ_zt}[\gamma\cos(Jt) - i\beta\sin(Jt)]|10\rangle_{S_1S_2}\bigotimes_{k=1}^{N}\frac{1}{\sqrt{2}}(|0\rangle_k + |1\rangle_k) \\ &+ e^{-iNJ_zt}\delta|11\rangle_{S_1S_2}\bigotimes_{k=1}^{N}\frac{1}{\sqrt{2}}\left(e^{i2J_{SE}t}|0\rangle_k + e^{-i2J_{SE}t}|1\rangle_k\right)\end{aligned} \quad (4)$$

with $\alpha = \cos\theta_1\cos\theta_2$, $\beta = \cos\theta_1\sin\theta_2$, $\gamma = \sin\theta_1\cos\theta_2$, $\delta = \sin\theta_1\sin\theta_2$. Immediately we see some tell-tale signatures of Darwinism appearing: $|00\rangle$ and $|11\rangle$ states imprint the same type of phase on the environmental qubits as shown in Ref. [15]. We see that in the single excitation subspace of S, while the mutual interaction only exchanges populations, the environmental qubits are not affected. In what follows, we demonstrate that these features conspire to complicate the decision on whether a classically objective state has been achieved or not: the state in Equation (4) exhibits clear signatures of redundant encoding in the environment while allowing the system to maintain highly non-classical features within a subspace that the environment is, in effect, "blind" to.

3. Quantum Darwinism and Objectivity

Quantitatively, quantum Darwinism is signaled by a plateau in the mutual information shared between the system and a fraction of the environment at the entropy of the system's state plotted against the fraction size. This behavior is indicative of a redundant encoding of the system information throughout the environment such that, regardless of what fragment of the environment is queried, an observer only ever has access to the same information. While there can be a "minimum fragment" size necessary to reach the redundancy plateau [3], we focus on the extreme case where it is sufficient to query a single environmental qubit in order to obtain all the accessible information. This amounts to tracking the mutual information $\mathcal{I}(\rho_{S_1S_2:E_k})$ between the composite two-qubit system and a single environmental qubit together with the entropy of the former $S(\rho_{S_1S_2})$, such that $\mathcal{I}(\rho_{S_1S_2:E_k}) = S(\rho_{S_1S_2})$ indicates we are witnessing a classically objective state, according to quantum Darwinism. Unless stated otherwise, we fix the mutual interaction between the qubits to be $H_{S_1S_2} = J(\sigma_x\otimes\sigma_x + \sigma_y\otimes\sigma_y)$ and the system–environment coupling is $J_{SE} = 0.1J$ to consider conditions of weak system–environment coupling. The system qubits are assumed to be initially prepared in identical states with $\theta_1 = \theta_2 = \pi/6$. This choice is only dictated by the convenience of the illustration of our results and, aside from some minor quantitative differences, qualitatively similar results hold for any choice or combination of J and J_z, including non-interacting system qubits, i.e., $J = J_z = 0$, and also for different initial system states. Finally, we note that, as we assume uniform coupling to all environmental units, it is immaterial which is chosen in the evaluation of $\mathcal{I}(\rho_{S_1S_2:E_k})$.

Figure 2a shows the mutual information, $\mathcal{I}(\rho_{S_1S_2:E_k})$ and the composite system entropy $S(\rho_{S_1S_2:E_k})$ for environments consisting of $N = 6$ (solid) and $N = 250$ qubits (dashed). We immediately see that only at $t = \pi/4$ do we find $\mathcal{I}(\rho_{S_1S_2:E_k}) = S(\rho_{S_1S_2})$. For $N = 250$, the system entropy quickly saturates to a maximum value, which is dependent on the chosen initial states, and remains so for most of the dynamics with the notable exception of $t = \pi/4$, where it rapidly drops. A qualitatively identical behavior is exhibited by the coherence present in the two-qubit system state, $C = \sum_{i \neq j} |\rho_{S_1 S_2}^{i,j}|$, shown in Figure 2b. While each system qubit quickly becomes diagonal, remarkably, the composite system maintains a minimum value of coherence, indicating that it retains some genuine non-classicality, with the magnitude of the coherence being dependent on the particular choice of initial states for the systems.

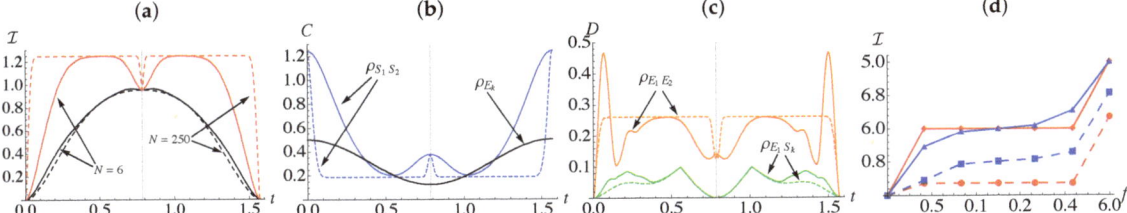

Figure 2. Both system qubits are prepared in a symmetric initial state with $\theta_{S_1} = \theta_{S_2} = \pi/6$ with the interaction parameters $J_{SE} = 1$, $J = 10$, and we consider environments of size $N = 6$ (solid curves) and $N = 250$ (dashed curves). (**a**) Dynamics of mutual information between the composite system and a single environmental qubit, $\mathcal{I}(\rho_{S_1 S_2 : E_k})$, (darker, black) and the entropy of the composite system, $S(\rho_{S_1 S_2})$ (lighter, red). (**b**) Coherence present in the composite system state, $|\rho_{S_1 S_2}^{1,2}|$ (lighter, blue) and coherences in the state of a single environmental qubit $|\rho_{E_k}^{1,2}|$ (darker, black). (**c**) Quantum discord shared between the two system qubits, $D^{\rightarrow}(\rho_{S_1 S_2})$ (lighter, orange) and quantum discord between one of the system qubits and a single environmental constituent $D^{\rightarrow}(\rho_{S_1 E_k})$ (darker, green). In panels (**a**–**c**) the faint vertical line at $t = \pi/4$ denotes the time at which we have $\mathcal{I}(\rho_{S_1 S_2 : E_k}) = S(\rho_{S_1 S_2})$, i.e., the emergence of Darwinism. (**d**) $\mathcal{I}(\rho_{S_1 S_2 : \mathcal{E}_f})/S(\rho_{S_1 S_2})$ vs. the size of the environment fraction f (upper, solid) and $\mathcal{I}(\rho_{S_1 : \mathcal{E}_f})//S(\rho_{S_1})$ (lower, dashed) at two instants of time, $t = \pi/4$ where perfect redundant encoding is observed (lighter, red) and $t = \pi/4 - 0.1$ (darker, blue).

The mutual information shared between the system qubits and an environment, shown in Figure 2a (darker, black curves), varies more gradually and is inversely related with the behavior of the environmental qubit's coherence, $|\rho_{E_k}^{1,2}|$, shown in Figure 2b (darker, black curve). The point at which $\mathcal{I}(\rho_{S_1 S_2 : E_k}) = S(\rho_{S_1 S_2})$ corresponds to the minimum in the environment coherence establishing that in order for signatures of objectivity to emerge a mutual dephasing is necessary [15]. Nevertheless, Figure 2b is remarkable, as it indicates that we do not require all constituents to become fully classical, i.e., the coherence does not necessarily vanish. In Figure 2d, the solid lines show the mutual information between the composite system and fractions of the environment at $t = \pi/4$ and $t = (\pi/4 - 0.1)$ for a $N = 6$ qubit environment. When $t = (\pi/4 - 0.1)$, there are no clear indications of Darwinistic behavior, while at $t = \pi/4$, we clearly observe the characteristic plateau, indicating that the system information is redundantly encoded into the environmental degrees of freedom. From these results, we see that the presence of a redundancy plateau does not necessarily imply a complete loss of all non-classicality within a complex composite system.

We can examine these features more quantitatively by directly computing the reduced and the total states of the system for $t = \pi/4$. The density matrix for $S_1 S_2$ is X-shaped, which in turn enforces the reduced states to be diagonal as follows:

$$\rho_{S_1 S_2} = \begin{pmatrix} \alpha^2 & 0 & 0 & \alpha\delta \\ 0 & \beta^2 & \beta\gamma & 0 \\ 0 & \beta\gamma & \gamma^2 & 0 \\ \alpha\delta & 0 & 0 & \delta^2 \end{pmatrix},$$

$$\rho_{S_1} = \begin{pmatrix} \alpha^2 + \beta^2 & 0 \\ 0 & \gamma^2 + \delta^2 \end{pmatrix}, \quad \rho_{S_2} = \begin{pmatrix} \alpha^2 + \gamma^2 & 0 \\ 0 & \beta^2 + \delta^2 \end{pmatrix}.$$

Therefore, the non-zero coherence we see in Figure 2 when the Darwinistic plateau emerges can be analytically determined to be $\sum_{i>j} |\rho_{S_1 S_2}^{i,j}| = |\alpha\delta| + |\beta\gamma|$. The coherence contained in a single environmental qubit $|\rho_{E_k}^{1,2}|$ is dependent on the initial states of the system qubits but independent with regards to the overall size of the environment, N. In particular, when $t = \pi/4$, we find $|\rho_{E_k}^{1,2}| = (\beta^2 + \gamma^2 - \alpha^2 - \delta^2)/2$, indicating that the environmental qubits themselves will fully decohere only when either θ_1 or $\theta_2 = \pi/4$, while for all other values of initial states some non-classicality remains within the environmental constituents.

Since the composite system maintains non-zero coherence, even when a redundancy plateau is observed, it is relevant to examine any non-classical correlations present in the overall state, cfr. Figure 2c, where we show the quantum discord [33,34] between two system qubits $D^{\rightarrow}(\rho_{S_1 S_2})$ and quantum discord between one of the system particles and a single environment $D^{\rightarrow}(\rho_{S_1 E_k})$. Mathematically, quantum discord between two parties is defined as [33,34]

$$D^{\rightarrow}(\rho_{AB}) = I(\rho_{AB}) - J^{\rightarrow}(\rho_{AB}). \tag{5}$$

Here, $J^{\rightarrow}(\rho^{AB}) = S(\rho^B) - \min_{\{\Pi_k^A\}} \sum_k p_k S(\rho_k^B)$ is called the Holevo information, where $\{\Pi_k^A\}$ represents the set of all possible measurement operators that can be performed on subsystem A, and $\rho_k^B = (\Pi_k^A \otimes \mathbb{I}) \rho^{AB} (\Pi_k^A \otimes \mathbb{I})/p_k$ are the post-measurement states of B after obtaining the outcome k with probability $p_k = \text{tr}[(\Pi_k^A \otimes \mathbb{I}) \rho^{AB}]$. In other words, $J^{\rightarrow}(\rho_{AB})$ measures the amount of information that one can obtain about subsystem B by performing measurements on subsystem A. The non-zero coherence present in the $S_1 S_2$ state mean that there are genuine quantum correlations in the form of the discord shared between the system qubits and, despite exhibiting a sharp decrease near the point where the characteristic plateau emerges, they remain non-zero throughout the dynamics. Thus, it is natural to question whether we can consider the state as truly objective when the relevant system information has clearly proliferated into the environment. Examining the correlations established between a given system qubit and one environmental constituent, $D^{\rightarrow}(\rho_{S_1 E_k})$, we find the quantum discord vanishes when the redundancy plateau is observed, implying that, at least at the level of a single system constituent, only classical information is accessible. We thus have a situation in which, due to the presence of a decoherence-free subspace to which the environmental degrees of freedom is blind, the overall composite system maintains non-classical features, and therefore, is arguably not objective, despite the redundant encoding and proliferation of the system information. Such a situation is reminiscent of settings where solely focusing on the mutual information can provide a false flag for classical objectivity [8]. Therefore, in the following section, we turn our attention to tighter conditions for objectivity given by strong quantum Darwinism [6,8], or equivalently spectrum broadcast structures [4,5].

Before moving on, we believe it is also meaningful to explore whether Darwinistic signatures are exhibited when considering how much information the environment can access about the individual system constituents, i.e., whether in addition to checking $\mathcal{I}(\rho_{S_1 S_2 : \mathcal{E}_f}) = S(\rho_{S_1 S_2})$ for various fragment sizes, we also test whether $\mathcal{I}(\rho_{S_i : \mathcal{E}_f}) = S(\rho_{S_i})$. We note, however, already that the latter quantity is upper bounded by the former, i.e., $\mathcal{I}(\rho_{S_1 S_2 : \mathcal{E}_f}) \geq \mathcal{I}(\rho_{S_1 : \mathcal{E}_f})$ for all $\mathcal{E}_f$ and at all times since discarding a system never increases the mutual information, due to the strong subadditivity of von Neumann entropy [35].

Figure 2d shows $\mathcal{I}(\rho_{S_1 S_2 : \mathcal{E}_f})$ (solid) and $\mathcal{I}(\rho_{S_1 : \mathcal{E}_f})$ (dashed) against the fraction size of the environment f for $t = \pi/4$ (red) and $t = (\pi/4 - 0.1)$ (blue). Focusing on $t = \pi/4$, it is clear that the composite system exhibits the characteristic redundancy plateau with the mutual information exactly equaling the composite system entropy. While we observe a similar plateau for the mutual information between a reduced system state and environment fractions, in this case, it is below the entropy of the considered system particle. Therefore, the redundantly encoded information regarding the single system qubit does not contain the full information about the qubit itself, and this is due to the fact that some of the information—specifically, that which is tied up in the non-classical correlations shared between the two system qubits—is not classically accessible to the environment.

The discrepancy between $\mathcal{I}(\rho_{S_1 S_2 : \mathcal{E}_f})$ and $\mathcal{I}(\rho_{S_1 : \mathcal{E}_f})$, which is related to the gap between the two curves in Figure 2d, can be quantitatively determined by directly computing their difference $\Delta \mathcal{I} = \mathcal{I}(\rho_{S_1 S_2 : \mathcal{E}_f}) - \mathcal{I}(\rho_{S_1 : \mathcal{E}_f})$ and finding the following (see Appendix A):

$$\Delta \mathcal{I} = \mathcal{I}(\rho_{S_2 : \mathcal{E}}) - \mathcal{I}(\rho_{S_2 : \overline{\mathcal{E}}_f}), \tag{6}$$

where $\overline{\mathcal{E}}_f$ is the complement of $\mathcal{E}_f$. Note that this result is completely independent of the nature of the dynamics and valid for arbitrary fractions at any given instant, only relying on the assumption of a pure initial state. Furthermore, another useful insight regarding this mutual information gap can be provided by exploiting the Koashi–Winter relation [36], which helps us to bound the discrepancy as follows:

$$0 \leq \Delta \mathcal{I} \leq S(\rho_{S_1 S_2}) + D^{\leftarrow}(\rho_{S_1 S_2 : \mathcal{E}_f}). \tag{7}$$

Considering the fraction to be the whole environment, i.e., $\overline{\mathcal{E}}_f$ is an empty set, the expressions above reduce to the following simple form $\Delta \mathcal{I} = \mathcal{I}(\rho_{S_2 : \mathcal{E}})$, which corresponds to the gap at the end of the curves. Equations (6) and (7) demonstrate that the non-classical correlations present in the composite system prevent the environment from gaining complete and unambiguous information regarding the state of an individual subsystem (see Appendix A for more details).

4. Strong Quantum Darwinism

The previous section demonstrates that, despite observing the signature plateau for redundant encoding, the constituents of the model still carry certain signatures of quantumness, namely non-zero coherences and discord of the composite system state. This naturally leads us to question of whether one can argue that the system state is truly classically objective or not. While it is clear that there is a proliferation and redundant encoding of system information within the environment, the fact that the system itself persists in displaying non-classical features implies that there might be a subtle distinction between the proliferation of relevant system information and genuine classical objectivity of a quantum state, with the former being a necessary but not sufficient requirement for the latter. Such a critical analysis of the conditions for classical objectivity is formalized within the framework of spectrum broadcast structures and strong quantum Darwinism [4,8,12]. In particular, the *strong Darwinism* condition [6,9] amounts to determining whether or not the mutual information shared between the system and an environment fraction is purely composed of classical information as quantified by the Holevo information. Equivalently, this condition can be stated as whether or not the system has a vanishing discord with that environment fraction. While stated originally based on measurements performed *solely on the system*, this condition was shown to be a necessary and sufficient condition for classical objectivity [6]. However, it is known that quantum discord is an asymmetric quantity, dependent on precisely which subsystem is measured and, therefore, allows for curious situations where non-classical correlations can be shared in one direction but not the other, so-called quantum-classical states. Therefore, even though the framework of strong Darwinism established in Ref. [6] is well motivated, we argue that, while objectivity is a property based on information that can be accessed by measurements on the *environment only*, classicality is a more subtle issue, and due to the asymmetry of quantum discord, a system state, though assessed as classically objective from the environment or a fraction of it, can retain quantum correlations [37].

The calculation of quantum discord is involved, even for two-qubit states [29]; in fact, it can be shown to be a NP-complete problem [38]. However, for our purposes, it suffices simply to check whether or not there exists discord without computing its numerical value. Thus, we focus on the correlation properties shared between the composite system and a single environment, taking into account the asymmetric nature of the discord. We employ a nullity condition, which provides a necessary and sufficient condition to witness whether the state, $\rho_{S_1S_2:E_k}$, has zero discord [39–41]. An arbitrary state ρ_{AB} has a vanishing quantum discord with measurements on A or B if and only if one can find an orthonormal basis $\{|n\rangle\}$ or $\{|m\rangle\}$ in the Hilbert space of A or B, such that the total state can be written in a block-diagonal form in this basis. Mathematically, it is possible to express this condition as follows:

$$D^{\rightarrow}(\rho_{A:B}) = 0 \iff \rho_{AB} = \sum_n p_n |n\rangle\langle n| \otimes \rho_n^B, \tag{8}$$

$$D^{\leftarrow}(\rho_{A:B}) = 0 \iff \rho_{AB} = \sum_m q_m \rho_m^A \otimes |m\rangle\langle m|. \tag{9}$$

Note that in our case, we make the identification $A \rightarrow S_1S_2$ and $B \rightarrow E_1$. In Appendix B, we explicitly calculate a necessary and sufficient condition for the nullity of quantum discord introduced in [40,41], separately considering both cases of measurements performed on the system and the environment side. When the mutual information plateau is observed while $D^{\rightarrow}(\rho_{S_1S_2:E_1})$ is non-zero, for measurements performed in the environmental qubit, the discord $D^{\leftarrow}(\rho_{S_1S_2:E_1})$ vanishes. Thus, we have a quantum–classical state implying that, as far as measurements are only performed on the environment, all the accessible information is completely classical in nature. As already discussed, this result implies an important subtlety regarding the connection between quantum Darwinism and the emergence of objectivity or classicality in composite quantum systems. While, locally, both system qubits are completely decohered, the composite state of the system is still coherent and shares some non-classical correlations with the environment. It is, thus, non-classical from the perspective of the system. However, from the perspective of the environment, the system is both objective, as the accessible information about the composite system is redundantly encoded throughout its degrees of freedom, and classical in that quantum discord for the measurement performed on the environment is equal to zero.

5. Conclusions

We have examined the emergence of quantum Darwinism for a composite system consisting of two qubits interacting with a N-partite bath. For an excitation-preserving interaction between the system qubits, we established that the system information is faithfully, redundantly encoded throughout the environment; therefore, we see the emergence of clear Darwinistic signatures. Nevertheless, a decoherence-free subspace permits the system to create and maintain significant non-classical features in the form of quantum discord. Employing the framework of strong quantum Darwinism, which insists that in addition to a mutual information plateau, the discord between the system and an environment fragment must vanish, we have shown that whether or not this state is interpreted as objective and classical depends on how the discord is evaluated. Following the framework of Ref. [6], for measurements on the system, the sizable non-zero coherence present in the decoherence-free subspace implies that this state is definitively not objective. However, as quantum Darwinism posits that classicality and objectivity are dictated by what information can be learned by measuring the environment, and due to the asymmetric nature of the quantum discord when measurements are made on the environment, we find that the discord is vanishing and therefore conclude a classically objective state. To better understand this point, we demonstrated that redundant encoding at the level of the composite system does not imply the same for the individual constituents. Specifically, when non-classical correlations are established between the system qubits, there is still a redundant proliferation of *some* of the system information into the environment; however, the correlations between the two system qubits prevent all of the system's information from being redundantly shared with the environment.

Author Contributions: All authors contributed equally to this work. All authors have read and agreed to the published version of the manuscript.

Funding: S.C. gratefully acknowledges the Science Foundation Ireland Starting Investigator Research Grant "SpeedDemon" (No. 18/SIRG/5508) for financial support. B.Ç. is supported by the BAGEP Award of the Science Academy and by The Research Fund of Bahçeşehir University (BAUBAP) under project No. BAP.2019.02.03. B.V. and acknowledges the UniMi Transition Grant H2020. M.P. is supported by the H2020-FETOPEN-2018-2020 project TEQ (grant No. 766900), the DfE-SFI Investigator Programme (grant 15/IA/2864), the Royal Society Wolfson Research Fellowship (RSWF\R3\183013), the Leverhulme Trust Research Project Grant (grant No. RGP-2018-266), and the U.K. EPSRC (grant No. EP/T028106/1).

Institutional Review Board Statement: Not Applicable.

Informed Consent Statement: Not Applicable.

Data Availability Statement: Not Applicable.

Conflicts of Interest: The authors declare no conflict of interest.

Appendix A. Derivations of Equations (6) and (7)

Appendix A.1. Direct Approach

Using the definition of mutual information, one has $\mathcal{I}(\rho_{S_1 S_2 : \mathcal{E}_f}) = S(\rho_{S_1 S_2}) + S(\rho_{\mathcal{E}_f}) - S(\rho_{S_1 S_2 \mathcal{E}_f})$ and $\mathcal{I}(\rho_{S_1 : \mathcal{E}_f}) = S(\rho_{S_1}) + S(\rho_{\mathcal{E}_f}) - S(\rho_{S_1 \mathcal{E}_f})$, from which $\Delta \mathcal{I} = \mathcal{I}(\rho_{S_1 S_2 : \mathcal{E}_f}) - \mathcal{I}(\rho_{S_1 : \mathcal{E}_f})$ can be calculated as the following:

$$\Delta \mathcal{I} = \left[S(\rho_{S_1 \mathcal{E}_f}) - S(\rho_{S_1}) \right] - \left[S(\rho_{S_1 S_2 \mathcal{E}_f}) - S(\rho_{S_1 S_2}) \right] \quad (A1)$$
$$= \left[S(\rho_{S_2 \overline{\mathcal{E}}_f}) - S(\rho_{\overline{\mathcal{E}}_f}) \right] - \left[S(\rho_{S_2 \mathcal{E}}) - S(\rho_{\mathcal{E}}) \right].$$

In passing to the second line, we assume that the total $S_1 S_2 \mathcal{E}$ system starts from a pure state and $\overline{\mathcal{E}}_f$ denotes the part of the environment that is not included in the fraction $\mathcal{E}_f$, i.e., $\overline{\mathcal{E}}_f$ is the complement of $\mathcal{E}_f$. We continue by adding and subtracting $S(\rho_{S_2})$ to the right hand side of the above equation and rearranging to obtain the following:

$$\Delta \mathcal{I} = \left[S(\rho_{S_2}) + S(\rho_{\mathcal{E}}) - S(\rho_{S_2 \mathcal{E}}) \right] - \left[S(\rho_{S_2}) + S(\rho_{\overline{\mathcal{E}}_f}) - S(\rho_{S_2 \overline{\mathcal{E}}_f}) \right] \quad (A2)$$
$$\Delta \mathcal{I} = \mathcal{I}(\rho_{S_2 : \mathcal{E}}) - \mathcal{I}(\rho_{S_2 : \overline{\mathcal{E}}_f}).$$

We note that this result is completely independent of the nature of the dynamics and valid for arbitrary fractions at any given instant. Considering the fraction to be the whole environment, i.e., $\overline{\mathcal{E}}_f$ is an empty set, the second term in the above equation vanishes and reduces to the following simple form:

$$\Delta \mathcal{I} = \mathcal{I}(\rho_{S_2 : \mathcal{E}}), \quad (A3)$$

which corresponds to the gap at the end of the curves.

Appendix A.2. Koashi–Winter Relation

Given an arbitrary tripartite quantum system ρ_{ABC}, the Koashi–Winter (KW) relation [36] states the following inequality:

$$E_f(\rho_{AB}) \leq S(\rho_A) - J^{\leftarrow}(\rho_{AC}), \quad (A4)$$

with equality attained if ρ_{ABC} is pure and $E_f(\cdot)$ denotes the entanglement of formation. Here, we will try to exploit this inequality to present bounds on the mutual information shared between the different fractions of the system and environment.

In addition to our usual assumption of a pure $S_1 S_2 \mathcal{E}$ state, we also introduce a pure auxiliary unit $\mathcal{A}$ that serves only as a mathematical tool to ensure that our set up fits within the framework of the KW relation. Identifying $A \to S_1 S_2$, $B \to \mathcal{A}$ and $C \to \mathcal{E}_f$, and noting that by definition $E_f(\rho_{S_1 S_2 \mathcal{A}}) = 0$, we have the following:

$$J^{\leftarrow}(\rho_{S_1S_2:\mathcal{E}_f}) \leq S(\rho_{S_1S_2}) \tag{A5}$$
$$\mathcal{I}(\rho_{S_1S_2:\mathcal{E}_f}) \leq S(\rho_{S_1S_2}) + D^{\leftarrow}(\rho_{S_1S_2:\mathcal{E}_f})$$

which provides an upper bound on the information that we can obtain on the total system by probing a fraction of the environment.

We now use the KW relation to bound the mutual information between a single system qubit and fractions of the environment. To that end, we shift our labeling to $A \to S_1$, $B \to S_2$ and $C \to \mathcal{E}_f$ again with the assumption that S_1, S_2 and the whole environment $\mathcal{E}$ is in a pure state. The KW relation gives the following:

$$E_f(\rho_{S_1S_2}) \leq S(\rho_{S_1}) - J^{\leftarrow}(\rho_{S_1\mathcal{E}_f}). \tag{A6}$$

Adding $\mathcal{I}(\rho_{S_1:\mathcal{E}_f})$ to both sides we get

$$E_f(\rho_{S_1S_2}) + \mathcal{I}(\rho_{S_1:\mathcal{E}_f}) \leq S(\rho_{S_1}) + D^{\leftarrow}(\rho_{S_1\mathcal{E}_f}) \tag{A7}$$
$$\mathcal{I}(\rho_{S_1:\mathcal{E}_f}) \leq S(\rho_{S_1}) + D^{\leftarrow}(\rho_{S_1\mathcal{E}_f}) - E_f(\rho_{S_1S_2}).$$

Comparing Equations (A5) and (A7) can help us to understand the discrepancy between the mutual information curves presented in Figure 2d. Naturally, we have both $\mathcal{I}(\rho_{S_1S_2:\mathcal{E}_f})$ and $\mathcal{I}(\rho_{S_1:\mathcal{E}_f})$ greater than zero, and moreover, we know that discarding a subsystem never increases the mutual information, thus $\mathcal{I}(\rho_{S_1S_2:\mathcal{E}_f}) \geq \mathcal{I}(\rho_{S_1:\mathcal{E}_f})$. Together, this allows us to restrict the gap between the curves as the following:

$$0 \leq \Delta \mathcal{I} \leq S(\rho_{S_1S_2}) + D^{\leftarrow}(\rho_{S_1S_2:\mathcal{E}_f}). \tag{A8}$$

Finally, let us also specifically look at the gap at the end of the curves in Figure 2d, i.e., $\mathcal{E}_f = \mathcal{E}$, where we can use the equality in the KW relations given in Equations (A5) and (A7), and obtain a more precise expression. A pure $S_1 S_2 \mathcal{E}$ state implies that $\mathcal{I}(\rho_{S_1S_2:\mathcal{E}}) = 2S(\rho_{S_1S_2})$, and we have the following:

$$\Delta \mathcal{I} = 2S(\rho_{S_1S_2}) - S(\rho_{S_1}) - D^{\leftarrow}(\rho_{S_1\mathcal{E}}) + E_f(\rho_{S_1S_2}) \tag{A9}$$
$$= 2S(\rho_{S_1S_2}) - S(\rho_{S_1}) - S(\rho_\mathcal{E}) + S(\rho_{S_1\mathcal{E}})$$
$$= S(\rho_{S_2}) + S(\rho_\mathcal{E}) - S(\rho_{S_2\mathcal{E}})$$
$$= \mathcal{I}(\rho_{S_2:\mathcal{E}}).$$

In passing from the first to the second line we resort to the basic definition of $\mathcal{I}(\rho_{S_1:\mathcal{E}})$. Note that this is exactly the same result we obtain in Equation (A3) using the direct approach.

Appendix B. Testing the Strong Quantum Darwinism Criteria

We would like to assess whether the mutual information between the system particles and a single environment state $\mathcal{I}(\rho_{S_1S_2:E_1})$ is purely classical. To that end, we need to check whether the state $\rho_{S_1S_2E_1}$ has a vanishing quantum discord or not, for which we have two options to consider: measurements performed on the system or environment side. The former is the condition of *strong Darwinism* introduced in [6] and the latter is an alternative constraint recently put forward in Ref. [37].

Here, we present the explicit calculation of the nullity condition for quantum discord introduced in [40,41] considering both measurement scenarios mentioned in the paragraph above. An arbitrary state ρ_{AB} has a vanishing quantum discord with measurements on A or B if and only if one can find an orthonormal basis $\{|n\rangle\}$ or $\{|m\rangle\}$ in the Hilbert space of A or B such that the total state can be written in block-diagonal form in this basis. Mathematically, it is possible express this condition as follows:

$$D^{\rightarrow}(\rho_{A:B}) = 0 \iff \rho_{AB} = \sum_n p_n |n\rangle\langle n| \otimes \rho_n^B, \tag{A10}$$

$$D^{\leftarrow}(\rho_{A:B}) = 0 \iff \rho_{AB} = \sum_m q_m \rho_m^A \otimes |m\rangle\langle m|. \tag{A11}$$

Note that in our case, we make the identification $A \to S_1 S_2$ and $B \to E_1$.

Let us start with checking the former condition. We pick an arbitrary orthogonal basis in the Hilbert space of the environmental qubit as $\{|e_i\rangle\}$ and express the state at hand as follows:

$$\rho_{S_1 S_2 E_1} = \sum_{i,j} \rho_{ij}^{S_1 S_2} \otimes |e_i^E\rangle\langle e_j^E|, \tag{A12}$$

In order for the state in Equation (A12) to be written as the one given in Equation (A11), all $\rho_{ij}^{S_1 S_2}$'s must be simultaneously diagonalizable and, if it exists, the basis in which they are diagonal is then $\{|n\rangle\}$. It was shown in [40,41] that mathematically, this implies the following: $D^{\rightarrow}(\rho_{S_1 S_2 : E_1}) = 0$ if and only if one has $\left[\rho_{ij}^{S_1 S_2}, \rho_{i'j'}^{S_1 S_2}\right] = 0$. Similarly, this condition can be stated as $\rho_{ij}^{S_1 S_2}$'s must be normal matrices such that $\left[\rho_{ij}^{S_1 S_2}, \left(\rho_{ij}^{S_1 S_2}\right)^{\dagger}\right] = 0$, and also commute with each other [40,41].

Using our analytics, we can write the general form of $\rho_{S_1 S_2 E_1}$ at the instant we observe Darwinism, i.e., $J_{SE} t = \pi/4$, as follows:

$$\rho_{S_1 S_2 E_1} = \left(\begin{array}{cccc|cccc} a & -a & 0 & 0 & 0 & 0 & b & -b \\ -a & a & 0 & 0 & 0 & 0 & -b & b \\ 0 & 0 & c & c & d & d & 0 & 0 \\ 0 & 0 & c & c & d & d & 0 & 0 \\ \hline 0 & 0 & d^* & d^* & e & e & 0 & 0 \\ 0 & 0 & d^* & d^* & e & e & 0 & 0 \\ b^* & -b^* & 0 & 0 & 0 & 0 & f & -f \\ -b^* & b^* & 0 & 0 & 0 & 0 & -f & f \end{array}\right), \tag{A13}$$

where $a = \alpha^2/2$, $b = (-1)^N \alpha \delta/2$, $c = \left[\beta^2 \cos^2\left(\frac{J\pi}{2}\right) + \gamma^2 \sin^2\left(\frac{J\pi}{2}\right)\right]/2$, $d = [2\beta\gamma + i(\beta - \gamma)(\beta + \gamma)\sin(J\pi)]/4$, $e = \left[\gamma^2 \cos^2\left(\frac{J\pi}{2}\right) + \beta^2 \sin^2\left(\frac{J\pi}{2}\right)\right]/2$ and $f = \delta^2/2$. Recall that parameters $\alpha = \cos\theta_1 \cos\theta_2$, $\beta = \cos\theta_1 \sin\theta_2$, $\gamma = \sin\theta_1 \cos\theta_2$, $\delta = \sin\theta_1 \sin\theta_2$ are dependent on the initial states of the system qubits. The dimensions of our the system particles and the environmental qubit are $d_{S_1 S_2} = 4$ and $d_{E_1} = 2$, respectively, which means that the set $\{|e_i\rangle\}$ is composed of two elements and we have 4 $\rho_{ij}^{S_1 S_2}$ matrices that are 4×4 in size. Horizontal and vertical lines dividing the density matrix in Equation (A13) in fact denote these 4 matrices. Explicitly, we have the following:

$$\rho_{S_1 S_2}^{11} = \begin{pmatrix} a & -a & 0 & 0 \\ -a & a & 0 & 0 \\ 0 & 0 & c & c \\ 0 & 0 & c & c \end{pmatrix}, \quad \rho_{S_1 S_2}^{12} = \begin{pmatrix} 0 & 0 & b & -b \\ 0 & 0 & -b & b \\ d & d & 0 & 0 \\ d & d & 0 & 0 \end{pmatrix},$$

$$\rho_{S_1 S_2}^{21} = \begin{pmatrix} 0 & 0 & d^* & d^* \\ 0 & 0 & d^* & d^* \\ b^* & -b^* & 0 & 0 \\ -b^* & b^* & 0 & 0 \end{pmatrix}, \quad \rho_{S_1 S_2}^{22} = \begin{pmatrix} e & e & 0 & 0 \\ e & e & 0 & 0 \\ 0 & 0 & f & -f \\ 0 & 0 & -f & f \end{pmatrix}.$$

The diagonal matrices are clearly normal matrices, i.e., they satisfy $\left[\rho_{S_1 S_2}^{ii}, \left(\rho_{S_1 S_2}^{ii}\right)^{\dagger}\right] = 0$. However, the off-diagonal ones are not normal in general. In fact, using the parameters we use in our simulations (setting S_1-S_2 interaction $J = 10$), they do not commute independently of the initial state of the system. As a result, it is not possible to write $\rho_{S_1 S_2 E_1}$ in the form given in Equation (A11), and thus $D^{\rightarrow}(\rho_{S_1S_2:E_1}) > 0$ implying that the condition for strong Darwinism, as defined in [6], is not satisfied.

Considering the alternative approach of checking the condition of vanishing discord with measurements on the environment side, $D^{\leftarrow}(\rho_{S_1S_2:E_1}) > 0$, similar to the previous case, we start by expressing our total state in an arbitrary orthogonal basis in the Hilbert space of the system qubits $\{s_k\}$ as the following:

$$\rho_{S_1S_2E_1} = \sum_{k,l} \left|s_k^S\right\rangle\left\langle s_l^S\right| \otimes \rho_{E_1}^{kl}. \tag{A14}$$

Recalling that $d_{S_1S_2} = 4$, it is possible to identify the set $\{s_k\}$ consists of four elements and we have 16 $\rho_{E_1}^{kl}$ matrices which are 2×2 in size, denoted by the horizontal and the vertical lines below:

$$\rho_{S_1S_2E_1} = \begin{pmatrix} a & -a & 0 & 0 & 0 & 0 & b & -b \\ -a & a & 0 & 0 & 0 & 0 & -b & b \\ 0 & 0 & c & c & d & d & 0 & 0 \\ 0 & 0 & c & c & d & d & 0 & 0 \\ 0 & 0 & d^* & d^* & e & e & 0 & 0 \\ 0 & 0 & d^* & d^* & e & e & 0 & 0 \\ b^* & -b^* & 0 & 0 & 0 & 0 & f & -f \\ -b^* & b^* & 0 & 0 & 0 & 0 & -f & f \end{pmatrix}, \tag{A15}$$

Following [40,41] again, checking the nullity condition amounts to checking whether the commutators satisfy the condition $\left[\rho_{E_1}^{kl}, \rho_{E_1}^{k'l'}\right] = 0$. It is possible to show that these commutators indeed vanish, which implies that from the point of view put forward in Ref. [37], all mutual information we have between the system qubits and environment fractions at the instant we observe the plateau is classical, and therefore objective.

References

1. Ollivier, H.; Poulin, D.; Zurek, W.H. Objective Properties from Subjective Quantum States: Environment as a Witness. *Phys. Rev. Lett.* **2004**, *93*, 220401. [CrossRef] [PubMed]
2. Blume-Kohout, R.; Zurek, W.H. Quantum Darwinism: Entanglement, branches, and the emergent classicality of redundantly stored quantum information. *Phys. Rev. A* **2006**, *73*, 062310. [CrossRef]
3. Zurek, W.H. Quantum Darwinism. *Nat. Phys.* **2009**, *5*, 181. [CrossRef]
4. Horodecki, R.; Korbicz, J.K.; Horodecki, P. Quantum origins of objectivity. *Phys. Rev. A* **2015**, *91*, 032122, [CrossRef]
5. Korbicz, J.K.; Horodecki, P.; Horodecki, R. Objectivity in a Noisy Photonic Environment through Quantum State Information Broadcasting. *Phys. Rev. Lett.* **2014**, *112*, 120402. [CrossRef] [PubMed]
6. Le, T.P.; Olaya-Castro, A. Strong Quantum Darwinism and Strong Independence are Equivalent to Spectrum Broadcast Structure. *Phys. Rev. Lett.* **2019**, *122*, 010403. [CrossRef]
7. Balaneskovica, N.; Mendler, M. Dissipation, dephasing and quantum Darwinism in qubit systems with random unitary interactions. *Eur. Phys. J. D* **2016**, *70*, 177. [CrossRef]
8. Le, T.P.; Olaya-Castro, A. Objectivity (or lack thereof): Comparison between predictions of quantum Darwinism and spectrum broadcast structure. *Phys. Rev. A* **2018**, *98*, 032103. [CrossRef]
9. Le, T.P.; Olaya-Castro, A. Witnessing non-objectivity in the framework of strong quantum Darwinism. *Quantum Sci. Technol.* **2020**, *5*, 045012. [CrossRef]
10. Korbicz, J.K. Roads to objectivity: Quantum Darwinism, Spectrum Broadcast Structures, and Strong quantum Darwinism. *arXiv* **2020**, arXiv:2007.04276.
11. Li, S.W.; Cai, C.Y.; Liu, X.F.; Sun, C.P. Objectivity in Quantum Measurement. *Found. Phys.* **2018**, *48*, 654. [CrossRef]
12. Pleasance, G.; Garraway, B.M. Application of quantum Darwinism to a structured environment. *Phys. Rev. A* **2017**, *96*, 062105. [CrossRef]
13. Brandão, F.G.S.L.; Piani, M.; Horodecki, P. Quantum Darwinism: Entanglement, branches, and the emergent classicality of redundantly stored quantum information. *Nat. Commun.* **2015**, *6*, 7908. [CrossRef] [PubMed]
14. Ryan, E.; Paternostro, M.; Campbell, S. Quantum Darwinism in a structured spin environment. *arXiv* **2020**, arXiv:2011.13385.
15. Campbell, S.; Çakmak, B.; Müstecaplıoğlu, Ö.E.; Paternostro, M.; Vacchini, B. Collisional unfolding of quantum Darwinism. *Phys. Rev. A* **2019**, *99*, 042103. [CrossRef]
16. Oliveira, S.M.; de Paula, A.L.; Drumond, R.C. Quantum Darwinism and non-Markovianity in a model of quantum harmonic oscillators. *Phys. Rev. A* **2019**, *100*, 052110. [CrossRef]

17. Giorgi, G.L.; Galve, F.; Zambrini, R. Quantum Darwinism and non-Markovian dissipative dynamics from quantum phases of the spin-1/2 XX model. *Phys. Rev. A* **2015**, *92*, 022105. [CrossRef]
18. Galve, F.; Zambrini, R.; Maniscalco, S. Non-Markovianity hinders Quantum Darwinism. *Sci. Rep.* **2016**, *6*, 19607. [CrossRef] [PubMed]
19. Milazzo, N.; Lorenzo, S.; Paternostro, M.; Palma, G.M. Role of information backflow in the emergence of quantum Darwinism. *Phys. Rev. A* **2019**, *100*, 012101. [CrossRef]
20. Lorenzo, S.; Paternostro, M.; Palma, G.M. Reading a Qubit Quantum State with a Quantum Meter: Time Unfolding of Quantum Darwinism and Quantum Information Flux. *Open Syst. Inf. Dyn.* **2019**, *26*, 1950023. [CrossRef]
21. Lampo, A.; Tuziemski, J.; Lewenstein, M.; Korbicz, J.K. Objectivity in the non-Markovian spin-boson model. *Phys. Rev. A* **2017**, *96*, 012120. [CrossRef]
22. Mironowicz, P.; Należyty, P.; Horodecki, P.; Korbicz, J.K. System information propagation for composite structures. *Phys. Rev. A* **2018**, *98*, 022124. [CrossRef]
23. Tuziemski, J.; Lampo, A.; Lewenstein, M.; Korbicz, J.K. Reexamination of the decoherence of spin registers. *Phys. Rev. A* **2019**, *99*, 022122. [CrossRef]
24. García-Pérez, G.; Chisholm, D.A.; Rossi, M.A.C.; Palma, G.M.; Maniscalco, S. Decoherence without entanglement and quantum Darwinism. *Phys. Rev. Res.* **2020**, *2*, 012061. [CrossRef]
25. Ciampini, M.A.; Pinna, G.; Mataloni, P.; Paternostro, M. Experimental signature of quantum Darwinism in photonic cluster states. *Phys. Rev. A* **2018**, *98*, 020101. [CrossRef]
26. Ciampini, M.A.; Pinna, G.; Paternostro, M.; Mataloni, P. Experimental Quantum Darwinism simulator using photonic cluster states. In *Quantum Information and Measurement (QIM) V: Quantum Technologies*; Optical Society of America: Washington, DC, USA, 2019; p. S2D.6. [CrossRef]
27. Chen, M.C.; Zhong, H.S.; Li, Y.; Wu, D.; Wang, X.L.; Li, L.; Liu, N.L.; Lu, C.Y.; Pan, J.W. Emergence of classical objectivity of quantum Darwinism in a photonic quantum simulator. *Sci. Bull.* **2019**, *64*, 580–585. [CrossRef]
28. Unden, T.K.; Louzon, D.; Zwolak, M.; Zurek, W.H.; Jelezko, F. Revealing the Emergence of Classicality Using Nitrogen-Vacancy Centers. *Phys. Rev. Lett.* **2019**, *123*, 140402. [CrossRef]
29. Modi, K.; Brodutch, A.; Cable, H.; Paterek, T.; Vedral, V. The classical-quantum boundary for correlations: Discord and related measures. *Rev. Mod. Phys.* **2012**, *84*, 1655–1707. [CrossRef]
30. Campbell, S.; Vacchini, B. Collision models in open system dynamics: A versatile tool for deeper insights? *EPL* **2021**, *133*, 60001. [CrossRef]
31. Ciccarello, F.; Lorenzo, S.; Giovannetti, V.; Palma, G.M. Quantum collision models: Open system dynamics from repeated Interactions. *arXiv* **2021**, arXiv:2106.11974.
32. Ciccarello, F. Collision models in quantum optics. *Quant. Meas. Quant. Metrol.* **2017**, *4*, 53. [CrossRef]
33. Ollivier, H.; Zurek, W.H. Quantum Discord: A Measure of the Quantumness of Correlations. *Phys. Rev. Lett.* **2001**, *88*, 017901. [CrossRef]
34. Henderson, L.; Vedral, V. Classical, quantum and total correlations. *J. Phys. A Math. Gen.* **2001**, *34*, 6899–6905. [CrossRef]
35. Nielsen, M.; Chuang, I. *Quantum Computation and Quantum Information*; Cambridge University Press: Cambridge, UK, 2000.
36. Koashi, M.; Winter, A. Monogamy of quantum entanglement and other correlations. *Phys. Rev. A* **2004**, *69*, 022309. [CrossRef]
37. Touil, A.; Yan, B.; Girolami, D.; Deffner, S.; Zurek, W.H. Eavesdropping on the Decohering Environment: Quantum Darwinism, Amplification, and the Origin of Objective Classical Reality. *arXiv* **2021**, arXiv:2107.00035.
38. Huang, Y. Computing quantum discord is NP-complete. *New J. Phys.* **2014**, *16*, 033027. [CrossRef]
39. Ferraro, A.; Aolita, L.; Cavalcanti, D.; Cucchietti, F.M.; Acín, A. Almost all quantum states have nonclassical correlations. *Phys. Rev. A* **2010**, *81*, 052318. [CrossRef]
40. Huang, J.H.; Wang, L.; Zhu, S.Y. A new criterion for zero quantum discord. *New J. Phys.* **2011**, *13*, 063045. [CrossRef]
41. Bylicka, B.; Chruściński, D. Circulant States with Vanishing Quantum Discord. *Open Syst. Inf. Dyn.* **2012**, *19*, 1250006. [CrossRef]

Article

Justifying Born's Rule $P_\alpha = |\Psi_\alpha|^2$ Using Deterministic Chaos, Decoherence, and the de Broglie–Bohm Quantum Theory

Aurélien Drezet

Institut NEEL, CNRS and Université Grenoble Alpes, F-38000 Grenoble, France; aurelien.drezet@neel.cnrs.fr

Abstract: In this work, we derive Born's rule from the pilot-wave theory of de Broglie and Bohm. Based on a toy model involving a particle coupled to an environment made of "qubits" (i.e., Bohmian pointers), we show that entanglement together with deterministic chaos leads to a fast relaxation from any statistical distribution $\rho(x)$ of finding a particle at point x to the Born probability law $|\Psi(x)|^2$. Our model is discussed in the context of Boltzmann's kinetic theory, and we demonstrate a kind of H theorem for the relaxation to the quantum equilibrium regime.

Keywords: quantum probability; pilot-wave mechanics; entanglement; deterministic chaos

1. Introduction and Motivations

The work of Wojciech H. Zurek is universally recognized for its central importance in the field of quantum foundations; in particular, concerning decoherence and the understanding of the elusive border between the quantum and classical realms [1]. Zurek emphasized the role of pointer states and environment-induced superselection rules (einselections). In recent years, part of his work has gone beyond mere decoherence and averaging focused on quantum Darwinism and envariance. The main goal of quantum Darwinism is to emphasize the role of multiple copies of information records contained in the local quantum environment. Envariance aims is to justify the existence and form of quantum probabilities; i.e., deriving Born's rule from specific quantum symmetries based on entanglement [2]. In recent important reviews of his work, Zurek stressed the importance of some of these concepts for discussing the measurement problem in relation with various interpretations of quantum mechanics [3,4]. Recent works showed, for instance, the importance of such envariance to the establishment of Born's rule in the many-world and many-mind contexts [5,6]. While in his presentations, Zurek generally advocated a neutral position perhaps located between the Copenhagen and Everett interpretations, we believe his work on entanglement and decoherence could have a positive impact on other interpretations, such as the de Broglie–Bohm theory. We know that Zurek has always been careful concerning Bohmian mechanics (see for example his remarks in [7] p. 209) perhaps because of the strong ontological price one has to pay in order to assume a nonlocal quantum potential and surrealistic trajectories (present even if we include decoherence [3,8]). Moreover, the aim of this work is to discuss the pivotal role that quantum entanglement with an environment of "Bohmian pointers" could play in order to justify Born's rule in the context of such a Bohmian interpretation. The goal is thus to suggest interesting and positive implications that decoherence could have on ontologies different from Everettian or consistent histories approaches. In this work, we were strongly inspired and motivated by the success of envariance for justifying quantum probabilities. Moreover, as mentioned above, Zurek's envariance emphasizing the role of entanglement is more "interpretation independent". Therefore, for comparison, we also include in the conclusion a short summary of Zurek's proof for the Born rule and compare the result with ours.

The de Broglie–Bohm quantum theory (BBQT) introduced by de Broglie in 1927 [9–11] and further discussed by Bohm in 1952 [12,13], is now generally accepted as a satisfactory interpretation of quantum mechanics, at least for problems dealing with non-relativistic systems [14–16]. Within this regime, BBQT is a clean, deterministic formulation of quantum mechanics preserving the classical concepts of point-like particles moving continuously in space-time. This formulation is said to be empirically equivalent to the orthodox description axiomatized by the Copenhagen school, meaning that BBQT is able to justify and reproduce the probabilistic predictions made by the standard quantum measurement theory. More specifically, this implies recovering the famous Born rule, which connects the probability

$$P_\alpha = |\Psi_\alpha|^2 \tag{1}$$

of observing an outcome α (associated with the quantum observable $\hat{A}$) to the amplitude Ψ_α in the quantum state expansion $|\Psi\rangle = \sum_\alpha \Psi_\alpha |\alpha\rangle$ (i.e., $|\alpha\rangle$ is an eigenstate of $\hat{A}$ for the observable eigenvalue α).

This issue has been a recurrent subject of controversies since the early formulation of BBQT (see for example Pauli's objection in [17,18]). It mainly arises because BBQT is a deterministic mechanics and therefore, like for classical statistical mechanics, probabilities in BBQT can only be introduced in relation with ignorance and uncertainty regarding the initial conditions of the particle motions. Moreover, after more than one and a half centuries of developments since the times of Maxwell and Boltzmann, it is well recognized that the physical and rigorous mathematical foundation of statistical mechanics is still debatable [19]. BBQT, which in some sense generalizes and extends Newtonian mechanics, clearly inherits these difficulties, constituting strong obstacles for defining a clean basis of its statistical formulation. This fact strongly contrasts with standard quantum mechanics, for which randomness has been axiomatized as genuine and inevitable from the beginning.

Over the years, several responses have been proposed by different proponents of BBQT to justify Born's rule (for recent reviews, see [20–22]). Here, we would like to focus on the oldest approach, which goes back to the work of David Bohm on deterministic and molecular chaos. Indeed, in 1951–1952, Bohm already emphasized the fundamental role of the disorder and chaotic motion of particles for justifying Born's rule [12,13]. In his early work, Bohm stressed that the complexity of the de Broglie–Bohm dynamics during interaction processes, such as quantum measurements, should drive the system to quantum equilibrium. In other words, during interactions with an environment such as a measurement apparatus, any initial probability distribution $\rho(X) \neq |\Psi(X)|^2$ for N particles in the configuration space (here $X = [\mathbf{x}_1,...,\mathbf{x}_M] \in \mathbb{R}^{3M}$ is a vector in the N-particles configuration space) should evolve in time to reach the quantum equilibrium limit $\rho(X) \to |\Psi(X)|^2$ corresponding to Born's rule. In this approach, the relaxation process would be induced by both the high sensitivity to changes in the initial conditions of the particle motions (one typical signature of deterministic chaos) and by the molecular thermal chaos resulting from the macroscopic nature of the interacting environment (i.e., with $\sim 10^{23}$ degrees of freedom). Furthermore, in this strategy, Born's rule $\rho(X) = |\Psi(X)|^2$ should appear as an attractor similar to the microcanonical and canonical ensemble in thermodynamics. In 1953, Bohm developed an example model [23] (see [24] for a recent investigation of this idea) where a quantum system randomly submitted to several collisions with external particles constituting a bath was driven to quantum equilibrium $\rho(X) = |\Psi(X)|^2$. In particular, during his analysis, Bohm sketched a quantum version of the famous Boltzmann H-theorem to prove the irreversible tendency to reach Born's rule (for other clues that Bohm was already strongly fascinated by deterministic chaos in the 1950s, see [25] and the original 1951 manuscript written by Bohm in 1951 [26] and rediscovered recently).

However, in later works, especially in the work conducted with Vigier [27] and then subsequently Hiley [14], Bohm modified the original de Broglie–Bohm dynamics by introducing stochastic and fluctuating elements associated with a subquantum medium forcing the relaxation towards quantum equilibrium $\rho(X) \to |\Psi(X)|^2$. In this context, we mention that very important works have been done in recent years concerning "Stochastic Bohmian mechanics" based on the Schrödinger–Langevin framework, the Kostin equation and involving nonlinearities [28–30]. While this second semi-stochastic approach was motivated by general philosophical considerations [31], proponents of BBQT have felt divided concerning the need for such a modification of the original framework. In particular, starting in the 1990s, Valentini has developed an approach assuming the strict validity of BBQT as an underlying deterministic framework and introduced mixing and coarse-graining à la Tolman–Gibbs in the configuration space in order to derive a Bohmian "subquantum" version of the H-theorem [32,33]. However, we stress that the Tolman–Gibbs derivation [34] and therefore Valentini's deduction can be criticized on many grounds (see for example [21] for a discussion). For instance, Prigogine already pointed out that the Tolman–Gibbs "proof" is a priori time-symmetric and cannot therefore be used to derive a relaxation. Furthermore, what the theorems show is that if we define a coarse-grained entropy $S[\bar{\rho}]_t$, we have necessarily (i.e., from the concavity of the entropy function) $S[\bar{\rho}]_t \geq S[\rho]_t = S[\rho]_{t=0} \equiv S[\bar{\rho}]_{t=0}$ (the second equality $S[\rho]_t = S[\rho]_{t=0}$ comes from unitarity and Liouville's theorem, and the third one $S[\rho]_{t=0} \equiv S[\bar{\rho}]_{t=0}$ is an initial condition where the fine-grained and coarse-grained distributions are identical). However, this result cannot be used to directly prove the relation $S[\bar{\rho}]_{t+\delta} \geq S[\bar{\rho}]_t$ for $\delta \geq 0$. In other words [21], one cannot show that the entropy is a monotonously growing function ultimately reaching quantum equilibrium (i.e., corresponding to the maximum of the entropy function [32]). Importantly, in his work on the "subquantum heat-death" (i.e., illustrated with many numerical calculations [35,36] often connected with cosmological studies [37,38]), Valentini and coworkers stressed the central role of deterministic chaos in the mixing processes, and this indeed leads to an increase of the entropy function in the examples considered. Moreover, deterministic chaos in BBQT is a research topic in itself (for a recent review, see [39,40]) and many authors (including Bohm [14] and Valentini [35,36]) have stressed the role of nodal-lines associated with phase-singularities of the wave-function for steering deterministic chaos in the BBQT [41–43]. However, it has also been pointed out [39,44] that this chaos is not generic enough to force the quantum relaxation $\rho(X) = |\Psi(X)|^2$ for any arbitrary initial conditions $\rho(X) \neq |\Psi(X)|^2$ (a reversibility objection à la Kelvin–Loschmidt is already sufficient to see the impossibility of such an hypothetical deduction [21,45]). Therefore, this analysis ultimately shows that the H-theorem can only makes sense if we complete it with a discussion of the notion of typicality [45–47].

In the present work, we emphasize the role of an additional ingredient that (together with chaos and coarse graining) helps and steers the quantum dynamical relaxation $\rho(X) \to |\Psi(X)|^2$: quantum entanglement with the environment. The idea that quantum correlations must play a central role in BBQT for justifying Born's rule is not new of course. Bohm already emphasized the role of entanglement in his work [13,14,23]. It has been shown that entanglement could lead to Born's rule using ergodicity [48]. Moreover, in recent studies motivated by the Vigier–Bohm analysis, we developed a Fokker–Planck [22] and Langevin-like [49] description of relaxation to quantum equilibrium $\rho(X) = |\Psi(X)|^2$ by coupling a small system S to a thermal bath or reservoir T inducing a Brownian motion on S. We showed that, under reasonable assumptions, we can justify a version of the H-theorem where quantum equilibrium appears as a natural attractor. Furthermore, at the end of [22], we sketched an even simpler strategy based on mixing together with entanglement and involving deterministic chaotic iterative maps. After the development of such an idea, it came to our attention that a similar strategy has been already developed in an elegant work by Philbin [50], and therefore we did not include too much detail concerning our model in [22]. Here, we present the missing part and provide a more complete and quantitative description of our scenario, which is presented as an illustration of a more general scheme. More precisely, we (i) analyze the chaotic character of the specific de Broglie–Bohm dynamics associated with our toy model, (ii) build a Boltzmann diffusion equation for the probability distribution and finally (iii) derive a simple H-theorem from which Born's rule turns out to be an attractor. We emphasize that our work, like the one of Philbin, suggests interesting future developments for justifying Born's rule and recovering standard quantum mechanics within BBQT.

2. The Status of Born's Rule in the de Broglie–Bohm Theory

We start with the wave-function $\psi(\mathbf{x},t) = R(\mathbf{x},t)e^{iS(\mathbf{x},t)/\hbar}$ obeying Schrödinger's equation

$$i\hbar\frac{\partial}{\partial t}\psi(\mathbf{x},t) = \frac{-\hbar^2\nabla^2}{2m}\psi(\mathbf{x},t) + V(\mathbf{x},t)\psi(\mathbf{x},t) \tag{2}$$

for a single nonrelativistic particle with mass m in the external potentials $V(\mathbf{x},t)$ (we limit the analysis to a single particle, but the situation is actually generic). BBQT leads to the first-order "guidance" law of motion

$$\frac{d}{dt}\mathbf{x}^\psi(t) = \mathbf{v}^\psi(\mathbf{x}^\psi(t),t) \tag{3}$$

where $\mathbf{v}^\psi(\mathbf{x},t) = \frac{1}{m}\nabla S(\mathbf{x},t)$ defines an Eulerian velocity field and $\mathbf{x}^\psi(t)$ is a de Broglie–Bohm particle trajectory. Furthermore, from Equation (2), we obtain the conservation rule:

$$-\frac{\partial}{\partial t}R^2(\mathbf{x},t) = \nabla \cdot [R^2(\mathbf{x},t)\mathbf{v}^\psi(\mathbf{x},t)] \tag{4}$$

where we recognize $R^2(\mathbf{x},t) = |\psi(\mathbf{x},t)|^2$ as the distribution which is usually interpreted as Born's probability density. Now, in the abstract probability theory, we assign to every point $\mathbf{x}$ a density $\rho(\mathbf{x},t)$ corresponding to a fictitious conservative fluid obeying the constraint

$$-\frac{\partial}{\partial t}\rho(\mathbf{x},t) = \nabla \cdot [\rho(\mathbf{x},t)\mathbf{v}^\psi(\mathbf{x},t)]. \tag{5}$$

Comparing with Equation (4), we deduce that the normalized distribution $f(\mathbf{x},t) = \frac{\rho(\mathbf{x},t)}{R^2(\mathbf{x},t)}$ satisfies the equation

$$[\frac{\partial}{\partial t} + \mathbf{v}^\psi(\mathbf{x},t) \cdot \nabla]f(\mathbf{x},t) := \frac{d}{dt}f(\mathbf{x},t) = 0. \tag{6}$$

This actually means [23] that f is an integral of motion along any trajectory $\mathbf{x}^\psi(t)$. In particular, if $f(\mathbf{x},t_{in}) = 1$ at a given time t_{in} and for any point $\mathbf{x}$, this holds true at any time t. Therefore, Born's rule being valid at a given time will be preserved at any other time [11,12,23]. It is also important to see that the relation $\frac{d}{dt}f(\mathbf{x}^\psi(t),t) = 0$ plays the same role in BBQT for motions in the configuration space as Liouville's theorem $\frac{d}{dt}\eta(q(t),p(t),t) = 0$ in classical statistical mechanics (where $\eta(q,p,t)$ is the probability density in phase space q,p). Therefore, with respect to the measure $d\Gamma = |\psi(\mathbf{x},t)|^2 d^3\mathbf{x}$ (which is preserved in time along trajectories since $\frac{d}{dt}d\Gamma_t = 0$), the condition $f = 1$ is equivalent to the postulate of equiprobability used in standard statistical mechanics for the microcanonical ensemble. Clearly, we see that the inherent difficulties existing in classical statistical mechanics to justify the microcanonical ensemble are transposed in BBQT to justify Born's rule; i.e., $f = 1$.

At that stage, the definition of the probability $\rho(\mathbf{x},t)d^3\mathbf{x}$ of finding a particle in the infinitesimal volume $d^3\mathbf{x}$ is rather formal and corresponds to a Bayesian–Laplacian interpretation where probabilities are introduced as a kind of measure of chance. Moreover, in BBQT, the actual and measurable density of particles must be defined using a "collective" or ensemble of N-independent systems prepared in similar quantum states $\psi(\mathbf{x}_i,t)$ with $i = 1,\ldots,N$. However, the concept of independency in quantum mechanics imposes the whole statistical ensemble with N particles to be described by the total factorized wave-function:

$$\Psi_N(\mathbf{x}_1,\ldots,\mathbf{x}_N,t) = \prod_{i=1}^{i=N}\psi(\mathbf{x}_i,t) \tag{7}$$

as a solution of the equation

$$i\hbar \frac{\partial}{\partial t}\Psi_N = [\sum_{i=1}^{i=N} \frac{-\hbar^2 \nabla_i^2}{2m} + V(\mathbf{x}_i, t)]\Psi_N. \tag{8}$$

For this quantum state Ψ_N, BBQT allows us to build the velocity fields $\frac{d}{dt}\mathbf{x}_i^\psi(t) = \mathbf{v}^\psi(\mathbf{x}_i^\psi(t), t)$, where $\mathbf{x}_i^\psi(t) := \mathbf{x}_i^{\Psi_N}(t)$ define the de Broglie–Bohm paths for the uncorrelated particles (i.e., guided by the individual and independent wave functions $\psi(\mathbf{x}_i, t)$ and Eulerian flows $\mathbf{v}_i^{\Psi_N}(\mathbf{x}_1, \ldots, \mathbf{x}_N, t) = \mathbf{v}^\psi(\mathbf{x}_i, t)$). Within this framework, the actual density of particles $P(\mathbf{r}, t)$ at point $\mathbf{r}$ is given by

$$P(\mathbf{r}, t) = \frac{1}{N}\sum_{k=1}^{k=N} \delta^3(\mathbf{r} - \mathbf{x}_k^\psi(t)) \tag{9}$$

which clearly obeys the conservation rule

$$-\frac{\partial}{\partial t}P(\mathbf{x}, t) = \nabla \cdot [P(\mathbf{x}, t)\mathbf{v}^\psi(\mathbf{x}, t)]. \tag{10}$$

Comparing with Equation (6), we see that if $\rho(\mathbf{x}, t) = f(\mathbf{x}, t)|\psi(\mathbf{x}, t)|^2$ plays the role of an abstract Laplacian probability, $P(\mathbf{r}, t)$ instead represents the frequentist statistical probability. Both concepts are connected by the weak law of large numbers (WLLN), which is demonstrated in the limit $N \to +\infty$ and leads to the equality $\rho(\mathbf{x}, t) = P(\mathbf{r}, t)$; i.e.,

$$f(\mathbf{r}, t)|\psi(\mathbf{r}, t)|^2 = \equiv \lim_{N \to +\infty} \frac{1}{N}\sum_{k=1}^{k=N} \delta^3(\mathbf{r} - \mathbf{x}_k^\psi(t)) \tag{11}$$

where the equality must be understood in the sense of a "limit in probability" based on typicality and not as the more usual "point-wise limit". We stress that the application of the WLLN already relies on the Laplacian notion of measure of chance since by definition in a multinomial Bernoulli process, the abstract probability density $\rho_N(\mathbf{x}_1, \ldots, \mathbf{x}_N, t) = \prod_{i=1}^{i=N} \rho(\mathbf{x}_i, t)$ is used for weighting an infinitesimal volume of the N-particle configuration space $d\tau_N := \prod_{i=1}^{i=N} d^3\mathbf{x}_i$. It can be shown that in the limit $N \to +\infty$ with the use of this measure $\rho_N d\tau_N$, almost all possible configurations $\mathbf{x}_1^\psi(t), \ldots, \mathbf{x}_N^\psi(t)$ obey the generalized Born's rule $P(\mathbf{r}, t) = \rho(\mathbf{x}, t) = f(\mathbf{x}, t)|\psi(\mathbf{x}, t)|^2$ (the fluctuation varying as $\frac{1}{\sqrt{N}}$). It is in that sense that Equation (11) is said to be typical, where typical means valid for "overwhelmingly many" cases; i.e., almost all states in the whole configuration space weighted by $\rho_N d\tau_N$. The application of the law of large numbers to BBQT is well known and well established [33,46,47] but has been the subject of intense controversies [45,46,51,52]. Issues concern (1) the interpretation of ρ_N as a probability density—i.e., in relation with the notion of typicality—and (2) the choice of $f = 1$ as natural and guided by the notion of equivariance [53]. To paraphrase David Wallace, the only thing the law of large numbers proves is that relative frequency tends to weight ... with high weight [54]. However, there is a certain circularity in the reasoning that at least shows that the axiomatic nature of the probability calculus allows us to identify an abstract probability such as $\rho d^3\mathbf{x}$ to a frequency of occurrence such as $Pd^3\mathbf{x}$. However, the WLLN alone is unable to guide us in selecting a good measure for weighting typical configurations (the condition on equivariance [53] is only a convenient mathematical recipe based on elegant symmetries, not a physical consequence of a fundamental principle). Therefore, the value of the f function is unconstrained by the typicality reasoning without already assuming the result [51]. In other words, it is impossible to deduce Born's rule directly from the WLLN.

However, it must be perfectly clear that our aim here is not to criticize the concept of typicality. Typicality, associated with the names of physicists such as Boltzmann or mathematicians such as Cournot and Borel, is, we think, at the core of any rigorous formulation of objective probability [55]. Our goal in the next section is to understand how natural and how stable the Born rule $f = 1$ is. For this purpose, our method is to consider entanglement between an environment of pointers, already in quantum equilibrium, and a not yet equilibrated system driven by chaotic Bohmian dynamics to the quantum equilibrium regime.

3. A Deterministic and Chaotic Model for Recovering Born's Rule within the de Broglie–Bohm Quantum Theory

3.1. The Basic Dynamics

As a consequence of the previous discussion, we now propose a simple toy model where the condition $f = 1$ appears as an attractor; i.e, $f_t \to 1$ during a mixing process. We consider a single electron wave-packet impinging on a beam-splitter. To simplify the discussion, we consider an incident wave-train with one spatial dimension x characterized by the wave-function

$$\psi_0(x,t) \simeq \Phi_0(x - v_x t) e^{i(k_x x - \omega_k t)} \tag{12}$$

where we have the dispersion relation $E_k := \hbar \omega_k = \frac{\hbar^2 k_x^2}{2m}$ and the (negative) group velocity components $v_x = \frac{\hbar k_x}{m} < 0$ with $k_x = -|k_x|$. Furthermore, for mathematical consistency, we impose $\Phi_0 \simeq const. = C$ in the spatial support region, where the wave-packet is not vanishing and the typical wavelength $\lambda = 2\pi/|k_x| \ll L$, where L is a typical wave-packet spatial extension. If we assume Born's rule, $|C|^2$ must be identified with a probability density, and by normalization this implies $C = 1/\sqrt{L}$ (this point will be relevant only in Section 3). The beam-splitter is a rectangular potential barrier or well $V(x) = V_0$ with V_0 a constant in the region $|x| < \epsilon/2 \ll L$ and $V(x) = 0$ otherwise. During the interaction with the beam-splitter, the whole wave-function approximately reads

$$\psi(x,t) \simeq \psi_0(x,t) + R_k \psi_1(x,t)$$
$$\text{if } x > \epsilon/2$$
$$\psi(x,t) \simeq \Phi_0(-v_x t)[A_k e^{i q_x x} + B_k e^{-i q_x x}] e^{-i \omega_k t}$$
$$\text{if } |x| < \epsilon/2$$
$$\psi(x,t) \simeq T_k \psi_0(x,t)$$
$$\text{if } x < -\epsilon/2 \tag{13}$$

where $\psi_1(x,t) = \Phi_0(x + v_x t) e^{-i k_x x} e^{-i \omega_k t} = \psi_0(-x,t)$ and R_k (reflection amplitude), T_k (transmission amplitude) and A_k, B_k are Fabry–Perot coefficients computed in the limit where the wave-packet is infinitely spatially extended. We have

$$T_k = \frac{4 q_x k_x}{(q_x + k_x)^2} \frac{1}{e^{i(q_x - k_x)\epsilon} - \frac{(q_x - k_x)^2}{(q_x + k_x)^2} e^{-i(k_x + q_x)\epsilon}}$$

$$R_k = i T_k \frac{k_x^2 - q_x^2}{2 q_x k_x} \sin(q_x \epsilon)$$

$$A_k = R_k [\frac{q_x + k_x}{2 q_x} e^{-i(q_x - k_x)\epsilon/2} + \frac{q_x - k_x}{2 q_x} e^{-i(q_x + k_x)\epsilon/2}]$$

$$B_k = R_k [\frac{q_x - k_x}{2 q_x} e^{i(q_x + k_x)\epsilon/2} + \frac{q_x + k_x}{2 q_x} e^{i(q_x - k_x)\epsilon/2}] \tag{14}$$

where q_x is given by the dispersion relation $E_k := \hbar \omega_k = \frac{\hbar^2 q_x^2}{2m} + V_0$, i.e., $q_x^2 - k_x^2 = -2m V_0/\hbar$. As an illustration, we choose $\epsilon = \frac{1}{2}\frac{\lambda}{2\pi}$ and $q_x \simeq 2.5 k_x$ (i.e., $V_0 < 0$) which leads to $T_k \simeq \frac{1}{\sqrt{2}} e^{i 0.267\pi}$ and $R_k = i T_k$ corresponding to a balanced 50/50 beam-splitter.

We consider the problem from the point of view of the scattering matrix theory. First, for negative time $t_{in} < 0$ (with $|t_{in}| \gg L/|v_x|$), the incident wave-packet $\psi_0(x, t_{in})$ given by Equation (12), which is coming from the $x > 0$ region with a negative group velocity, is transformed for large positive times $t_f > 0$ (with $|t_f| \gg L/|v_x|$) into the two non overlapping wave-packets:

$$\psi(x, t_f) \simeq R_k \psi_1(x, t_f) \quad \text{if } x > 0$$
$$\psi(x, t_f) \simeq T_k \psi_0(x, t_f) \quad \text{if } x < 0 \,. \tag{15}$$

Since the wave packets are non-overlapping we write:

$$\psi(x, t_f) \simeq R_k \psi_1(x, t_f) + T_k \psi_0(x, t_f). \tag{16}$$

Of course, the situation is symmetric: if an incident wave-packet $\psi_1(x, t_{in})$ comes from the $x < 0$ region with a positive group velocity for $t_{in} < 0$, we will finally obtain, i.e., for $t_f > 0$,

$$\psi(x, t_f) \simeq T_k \psi_1(x, t_f) + R_k \psi_0(x, t_f). \tag{17}$$

The general case can thus be treated by superposition: an arbitrary initial state $\psi(x, t_{in}) = a_+ \psi_0(x, t_{in}) + a_- \psi_1(x, t_{in})$ for negative times t_{in} (with $|t_{in}| \gg L/|v_x|$) will evolve into

$$\psi(x, t_f) \simeq (a_+ R_k + a_- T_k) \psi_1(x, t_f)$$
$$+ (a_+ T_k + a_- R_k) \psi_0(x, t_f) \tag{18}$$

for positive times t_f (with $|t_f| \gg L/|v_x|$). Writing $a'_+ = a_+ R_k + a_- T_k$ and $a'_- = a_+ T_k + a_- R_k$ as the different mode amplitudes, we define a 2×2 unitary transformation

$$\begin{pmatrix} a'_+ \\ a'_- \end{pmatrix} = \begin{pmatrix} R_k & T_k \\ T_k & R_k \end{pmatrix} \begin{pmatrix} a_+ \\ a_- \end{pmatrix}$$
$$= \frac{e^{i 0.267 \pi}}{\sqrt{2}} \begin{pmatrix} i & 1 \\ 1 & i \end{pmatrix} \begin{pmatrix} a_+ \\ a_- \end{pmatrix}. \tag{19}$$

Moreover, consider now the point of view of BBQT. Following this theory, the dynamics of the material point are obtained by the integration of the guidance equation

$$\frac{d}{dt} x^{\psi}(t) = v^{\psi}(x^{\psi}(t), t) = \frac{\hbar}{m} \text{Im}[\frac{\partial}{\partial x} \psi(x, t)|_{x = x^{\psi}(t)}] \tag{20}$$

that can easily be computed numerically. We illustrate in Figure 1 the interaction with the 50/50 beam-splitter characterized by Equation (19) of a rectangular wave-packet (i.e., $\Phi_0(x) = C$ if $|x| < L/2$, where L is the width of the wave-packet) incident from the $x > 0$ region (i.e., $a_+ = 1, a_- = 0$). As a remarkable feature, we can see the Wiener fringes [11] existing in the vicinity of the beam-splitter and that strongly alter the de Broglie–Bohm trajectories. What is also immediately visible is that the de Broglie–Bohm trajectories $x^{\psi}(t)$ never cross each other. This is a general property of the first-order dynamics [14,15], which play a central role in our analysis.

An interesting feature of this example concerns the density of "probability" $|\psi(x,t)|^2$. Indeed, consider a time t_{in} in the remote past before the wave-packet from the positive region (i.e., like in Figure 1) interacts with the potential well. At that time, the center of the wave-packet is located at $x_{in} = v_x t_{in} > 0$. However, since trajectories cannot cross each other, we know that the ensemble $\gamma_+(t_{in})$ of all possible particle positions at time t_{in}—i.e., $x^{\psi}(t_{in}) \in [x_{in} - \frac{L}{2}, x_{in} + \frac{L}{2}]$—is divided into two parts. In the first part, $\gamma_+^{(+)}(t_{in})$—i.e., $x^{\psi}(t_{in}) \in [x_{in} + H, x_{in} + \frac{L}{2}]$ with $|H| < \frac{L}{2}$—all particles evolve in the future (i.e., at time t_f) into the $\psi_1(x, t_f)$ reflected wave-packet (corresponding to the support $\gamma_+(t_f)$, i.e., $x^{\psi}(t_f) \in [x_f - \frac{L}{2}, x_f - \frac{L}{2}]$ with $x_f = -v_x t_f > 0$). In the second part $\gamma_+^{(-)}(t_{in})$—i.e.,

$x^\psi(t_{in}) \in [x_{in} - \frac{L}{2}, x_{in} + H]$—all the particles necessarily end their journey in the $\psi_0(x, t_f)$ transmitted wave-packet (corresponding to the support $\gamma_-(t_f)$, i.e., $x^\psi(t_f) \in [-x_f - \frac{L}{2}, -x_f - \frac{L}{2}]$). Now, remember that from the de Broglie–Bohm–Liouville theorem, the measure $d\Gamma(x, t) = |\psi(x, t)|^2 dx$ is preserved in time; i.e., $\frac{d}{dt} d\Gamma_t = 0$. Therefore, the measure

$$\Gamma_+(t_f) = \int_{\gamma_+} |\psi(x,t)|^2 dx = LC^2/2 \qquad (21)$$

associated with the reflected wave necessarily equals the measure associated with the segment $\gamma_+^{(+)}(t_{in})$; i.e.,

$$\Gamma_+^{(+)}(t_{in}) = (L/2 - H)C^2 = \Gamma_+(t_f). \qquad (22)$$

This leads to $H = 0$, which in turn means that $\gamma_+^{(+)}(t_{in})$ corresponds to $x^\psi(t_{in}) \in [x_{in}, x_{in} + \frac{L}{2}]$ and $\gamma_+^{(-)}(t_{in})$ to $x^\psi(t_{in}) \in [x_{in} - \frac{L}{2}, x_{in}]$. This result is actually general and holds for any symmetric wave-packet $\Phi_0(x) = \Phi_0(-x)$ if we can neglect the overlap between $\Phi_0(x - v_x t_f)$ and $\Phi_0(x + v_x t_f)$).

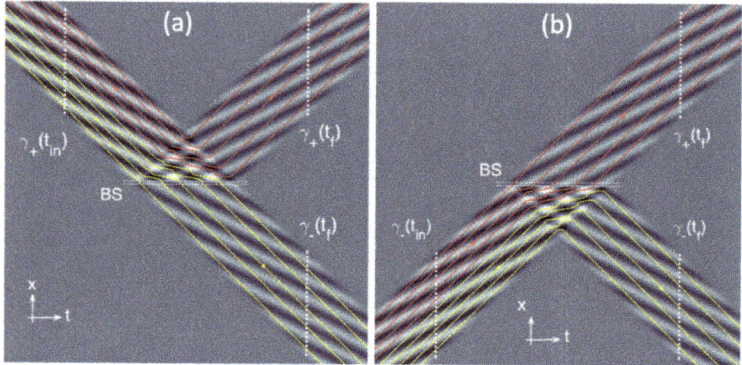

Figure 1. (a) Scattering of a 1D wave-packet impinging on a 50/50 beam-splitter (BS). The colormap shows $Re[\Psi(x,t)]$ in the t, x plane. The color (red and yellow) lines are de Broglie–Bohm trajectories associated with this wave-function (red and yellow trajectories are ending in two different wave-packets. The dotted white lines are crosscuts, as discussed in the main text. (b) A similar situation when a wave-packet impinges on the other input gate.

Moreover, for the rectangular wave-packet, we deduce from the de Broglie–Bohm–Liouville theorem $\frac{d}{dt} d\Gamma_t = 0$ that any infinitesimal-length element $\delta x^\psi(t_{in})$ surrounding a point $x^\psi(t_{in})$ in $\gamma_+(t_{in})$ evolves to the infinitesimal length $\delta x^\psi(t_f) = 2\delta x^\psi(t_{in})$ surrounding the point $x^\psi(t_f)$ located in $\gamma_\pm(t_f)$. This property can be used to define a simple mapping between the initial coordinates $x^\psi(t_{in}) \in \gamma_+(t_{in})$ and the final outcome $x^\psi(t_f) \in \gamma_+(t_f) \cup \gamma_-(t_f)$. It is simpler to introduce the normalized variables:

$$\begin{aligned}
y(t_{in}) &= \frac{x^\psi(t_{in}) - x_{in}}{2L} + \frac{3}{4} \in [\frac{1}{2}, 1] & \text{if } x^\psi(t_{in}) \in \gamma_+(t_{in}) \\
y(t_f) &= \frac{x^\psi(t_f) - x_f}{2L} + \frac{3}{4} \in [\frac{1}{2}, 1] & \text{if } x^\psi(t_f) \in \gamma_+(t_f) \\
y(t_f) &= \frac{x^\psi(t_f) + x_f}{2L} + \frac{1}{4} \in [0, \frac{1}{2}] & \text{if } x^\psi(t_f) \in \gamma_-(t_f).
\end{aligned} \qquad (23)$$

The mapping between the two new ensembles (which we will continue to name $\gamma_+(t_{in})$ and $\gamma_+(t_f) \cup \gamma_-(t_f)$) is thus simply written as

$$y(t_f) = 2y(t_{in}) - 1. \tag{24}$$

The result of this mapping is illustrated using the x coordinates in Figure 2a or the y coordinates in Figure 2b. In particular, it is visible that the correspondence $y(t_f) = F(y(t_{in}))$ is not always univocally defined. This occurs at $x^\psi(t_{in}) = x_{in}$ (i.e., $y(t_{in}) = \frac{3}{4}$), which evolves either as $x^\psi(t_f) = x_f - L/2 \in \gamma_+(t_f)$ or $x^\psi(t_f) = -x_f + L/2 \in \gamma_-(t_f)$ corresponding to the single value $y(t_f) = \frac{1}{2}$. Physically, as shown in Figure 2a, this means that a point located at the center of the wave-packet $\psi_0(x, t_{in})$ is unable to decide whether it should move into the reflected or transmitted wave-packets: this is a point of instability. This apparently violates the univocity of the de Broglie–Bohm dynamics in Equation (20), which imposes that at a given point—i.e., $x^\psi(t_{in}) = x_{in}$—one and only one trajectory is defined. However, we stress that this pathology is actually a consequence of the oversimplification of our model consisting in assuming an idealized rectangular wave packet $\Phi_0(x) = C$ if $|x| < L/2$ with abrupt boundaries at $|x| = L/2$. In a real experiment with a Gaussian wave-packet, the point $x^\psi(t_{in}) = x_{in}$ would be mapped at the internal periphery of the two wave-packets constituting $\psi(x, t_f)$ (this would correspond to the points $x^\psi(t_f) = \pm \epsilon/2 \sim 0$ where the beam splitter is located). In this regime, our assumption of a finite support for $\Phi_0(x)$ is no longer acceptable.

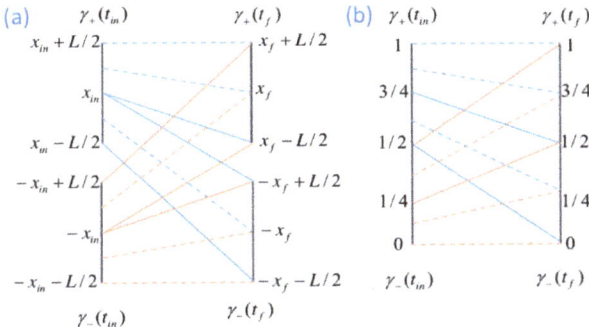

Figure 2. (a) Transformation from the initial $\gamma_\pm(t_{in})$ x-space to the final $\gamma_\pm(t_{ou})$ x-space for the two situations shown in Figure 1a,b, respectively (depicted as blue lines and red lines, respectively). (b) The same transformation using the y coordinate instead of the x coordinate (as explained in the main text).

The previous analysis was limited to the case of the wave-packet $\psi_0(x, t_{in})$ coming from the $x > 0$ region. However, in the symmetric case of a wave-packet $\psi_1(x, t_{in})$ coming from the $x < 0$ region (i.e., $a_+ = 0, a_- = 1$), the situation is very similar (as shown in Figure 2), with the only differences being that the $\gamma_+(t_{in})$ space is changed into $\gamma_-(t_{in})$, i.e., $x^\psi(t_{in}) \in [-x_{in} - \frac{L}{2}, -x_{in} + \frac{L}{2}]$ and the roles of $\gamma_+(t_f)$ and $\gamma_-(t_f)$ (the previous definitions are let unchanged) are now permuted (i.e., $\gamma_+(t_f)$ is now associated with the transmitted wave-packet and $\gamma_-(t_f)$ with the reflected one). From the point of view of BBQT, the trajectories of Figure 1b are obtained by a mirror symmetry $x \to -x$ from Figure 1a. The new mapping $x^\psi(t_{in}) \to x^\psi(t_f)$ is now well described by the variable transformation:

$$\begin{aligned} y(t_{in}) &= \frac{x^\psi(t_{in}) + x_{in}}{2L} + \frac{1}{4} \in [0, \tfrac{1}{2}] & \text{if } x^\psi(t_{in}) \in \gamma_-(t_{in}) \\ y(t_f) &= \frac{x^\psi(t_f) - x_f}{2L} + \frac{3}{4} \in [\tfrac{1}{2}, 1] & \text{if } x^\psi(t_f) \in \gamma_+(t_f) \\ y(t_f) &= \frac{x^\psi(t_f) + x_f}{2L} + \frac{1}{4} \in [0, \tfrac{1}{2}] & \text{if } x^\psi(t_f) \in \gamma_-(t_f). \end{aligned} \qquad (25)$$

which lets the definition of $y(t_f)$ unchanged with respect to Equation (24). The mapping between the two ensembles $\gamma_-(t_{in})$ and $\gamma_+(t_f) \cup \gamma_-(t_f)$ is now written as

$$y(t_f) = 2y(t_{in}) \qquad (26)$$

which is very similar to Equation (24).

3.2. Entanglement and Bernoulli's Shift

If we regroup Equations (24) and (26) together with Equations (24) and (26), we are tempted to recognize the well known Bernoulli map:

$$y(t_f) = 2y(t_{in}) \mod(1), \qquad (27)$$

which actually means

$$\begin{aligned} y(t_f) &= 2y(t_{in}) - 1 & \text{if } y(t_{in}) > \tfrac{1}{2} \\ y(t_f) &= 2y(t_{in}) & \text{if } y(t_{in}) < \tfrac{1}{2} \end{aligned} \qquad (28)$$

for $y(t_f)$ and $y(t_{in}) \in [0, 1]$. This would physically correspond to a mapping $\gamma_+(t_{in}) \cup \gamma_-(t_{in}) \to \gamma_+(t_f) \cup \gamma_-(t_f)$. In classical physics, such a mapping would be unproblematic since the two dynamics given by Equations (24) and (26) could be superposed without interference. However, in quantum mechanics, and specially in BBQT, the dynamics is contextually guided by the whole wave-function $\psi(x,t)$ and a general superposition of states $\psi(x, t_{in}) = a_+ \psi_0(x, t_{in}) + a_- \psi_1(x, t_{in})$ evolves at t_f to the state $\psi(x, t_{in})$ given by Equation (18). Consider for example with Equation (19) the unitary evolution

$$\frac{\psi_0(x, t_{in}) + i\psi_1(x, t_{in})}{\sqrt{2}} \to ie^{i0.267\pi} \psi_1(x, t_f). \qquad (29)$$

From the point of view of BBQT (as illustrated in Figure 3), we have a mapping $\gamma_+(t_{in}) \cup \gamma_-(t_{in}) \to \gamma_+(t_f)$ which has nothing to do with either Equations (24) and (26) or even Equation (27). More precisely, the mapping associated with Equation (29) reads

$$y(t_f) = \frac{y(t_{in})}{2} + \frac{1}{2} \qquad (30)$$

Therefore, the high contextuality of the BBQT leads (in agreement with wave–particle duality) to new features induced by the coherence of the different branches of the input wave-function.

In order to make sense of the Bernoulli shift in Equation (27) in a simple way, we modify the properties of our beam-splitter by adding phase plates in the input and output channels. From here on, we consider instead of Equation (19) the unitary relation

$$\begin{pmatrix} a'_+ \\ a'_- \end{pmatrix} = \frac{1}{\sqrt{2}} \begin{pmatrix} 1 & 1 \\ 1 & -1 \end{pmatrix} \begin{pmatrix} a_+ \\ a_- \end{pmatrix}. \qquad (31)$$

Furthermore, in order to break the coherence between the two input waves $\psi_0(x,t_{in})$ and $\psi_1(x,t_{in})$, we introduce entanglement with an external pointer qubit before entering the beam splitter. The pointer must represent unambiguous "which-path" information concerning the moving particle in the context of BBQT. We represent the initial state of the pointer by a wave-function $\varphi_{in}^1(Z_1)$ associated with the coordinate Z_1 of the pointer (we assume $\int dZ_1 |\varphi_{in}^1(Z_1)|^2 = 1$). The interaction leading to entanglement works in the following way: starting with an arbitrary state such as $A\psi_0(x,t_0) + B\psi_1(x,t_0)$ at time t_0 and a fixed initial pointer state $\varphi_{in}^1(Z_1)$, we obtain

$$(A\psi_0(x,t_0) + B\psi_1(x,t_0))\varphi_{in}^1(Z_1) \to A\psi_0(x,t_0)\varphi_\uparrow^1(Z_1) + B\psi_1(x,t_0)\varphi_\downarrow^1(Z_1). \tag{32}$$

Here, we assume $\int dZ_1|\varphi_\uparrow^1(Z_1)|^2 = \int dZ_1|\varphi_\downarrow^1(Z_1)|^2 = 1$ and $\int dZ_1 \varphi_\uparrow^1(Z_1)(\varphi_\downarrow^1(Z_1))^* = 0$. Additionally, in order to simplify the analysis, we suppose the pointer–particle interaction to be quasi-instantaneous and act only at time $t \simeq t_0$. Moreover, in BBQT, the positions of the particle and pointer play a fundamental, ontic role. In order to have genuine Bohmian which-path information, we thus require that the two pointer wave-functions are well localized and are not overlapping; i.e., $\varphi_\downarrow^1(Z_1)\varphi_\uparrow^1(Z_1) = 0\ \forall Z_1$.

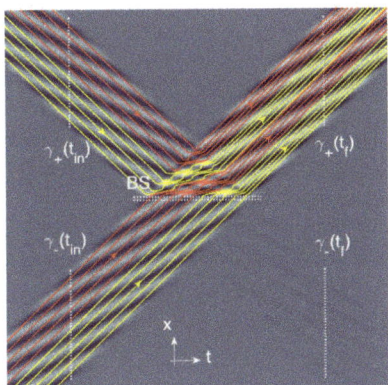

Figure 3. Same as in Figure 1 but for a symmetric superposition of the two wave-functions impinging from the two input gates of BS. The superposition principle forces the resulting wave-packet to end its journey in the exit gate $\gamma_+(t_f)$. The pilot-wave dynamics are strongly impacted by the linearity of the superposition (compare with Figure 1).

We now consider the following sequences of processes, which are sketched in Figure 4. First, we prepare a non-entangled quantum system in the initial state $\psi_0(x,t'_0)\varphi_{in}(Z)$ with $t'_0 \ll t_0$. Before interacting with the qubit, the particle wave-packet interacts with a first beam-splitter BS$_0$, as in the previous subsection. Using Equations (31) and (32), this leads to

$$\psi_0(x,t'_0)\varphi_{in}^1(Z_1) \to \frac{\psi_1(x,t_0) + \psi_0(x,t_0)}{\sqrt{2}}\varphi_{in}^1(Z_1) \to \frac{\psi_1(x,t_0)\varphi_\uparrow^1(Z_1) + \psi_0(x,t_0)\varphi_\downarrow^1(Z_1)}{\sqrt{2}}. \tag{33}$$

In order to use a probabilistic interpretation—i.e., Born's rule—we impose the normalization $C = 1/\sqrt{L}$ associated with the wave-packet Φ_0 (see Equation (12)). Second, as shown in Figure 4, the two wave-packets are moving in free space and interact with two mirrors which reflect the beams into the direction of a second beam-splitter BS$_1$, where they cross (BS$_1$ is the time translation of the same beam-splitter, but we continue to use this notation for simplicity). The main effect of the mirrors is to reverse the direction of propagation of $\psi_0(x,t_0)$ and $\psi_1(x,t_0)$—i.e., $\psi_0(x,t_0) \to -\psi_1(x,t'_1 + \frac{2D}{v_x})e^{i\chi}$ and $\psi_1(x,t_0) \to -\psi_0(x,t'_1 + \frac{2D}{v_x})e^{i\chi}$—with t'_1 a time after the interaction and $\chi = \frac{2D}{v_x}(\omega_k - k_x v_x)$

a phase shift depending on the distance D between BS_0 and any of the two mirrors ($-\frac{2D}{v_x} > 0$ is the travel time taken by the center of the wave-packet for moving from BS_0 to BS_1). At a time t'_1 before crossing BS_1, the quantum state reads

$$-e^{i\chi}\frac{\psi_0(x,t'_1+\frac{2D}{v_x})\varphi^1_\uparrow(Z_1)+\psi_1(x,t'_1+\frac{2D}{v_x})\varphi^1_\downarrow(Z_1)}{\sqrt{2}}. \tag{34}$$

At a time $t_1 \gg -\frac{2D+L}{v_x}$ after the interaction with BS_1 the quantum state reads (omitting the irrelevant phase factor)

$$\frac{\psi_0(x,t'_1+\frac{2D}{v_x})\varphi^1_\uparrow(Z_1)+\psi_1(x,t'_1+\frac{2D}{v_x})\varphi^1_\downarrow(Z_1)}{\sqrt{2}}$$
$$\to \frac{\psi_1(x,t_1+\frac{2D}{v_x})\varphi^1_\to(Z_1)+\psi_0(x,t_1+\frac{2D}{v_x})\varphi^1_\leftarrow(Z_1)}{\sqrt{2}} \tag{35}$$

where $\varphi^1_\to = \frac{\varphi^1_\uparrow+\varphi^1_\downarrow}{\sqrt{2}}$ and $\varphi^1_\leftarrow = \frac{\varphi^1_\uparrow-\varphi^1_\downarrow}{\sqrt{2}}$ are two orthogonal eigenstates. Now, if we write this quantum state during the interaction with BS_1 as $\Psi(x,Z,t)=\psi_\uparrow(x,t)\varphi^1_\uparrow(Z_1)+\psi_\downarrow(x,t)\varphi^1_\downarrow(Z_1)$ we can define the Bohmian particle velocity $\frac{d}{dt}x^\Psi(t) = v(x,Z,t)$ as:

$$\frac{d}{dt}x^\Psi(t) = \frac{v_\uparrow(x,t)|\psi_\uparrow(x,t)\varphi^1_\uparrow(Z_1)|^2+v_\downarrow(x,t)|\psi_\downarrow(x,t)\varphi^1_\downarrow(Z_1)|^2}{|\psi_\uparrow(x,t)\varphi^1_\uparrow(Z_1)|^2+|\psi_\downarrow(x,t)\varphi^1_\downarrow(Z_1)|^2} \tag{36}$$

where we introduced the two velocities $v_{\uparrow/\downarrow}(x,t) = \frac{1}{m}\partial_x S_{\uparrow/\downarrow}(x,t)$ associated with the two wave-functions $\psi_{\uparrow/\downarrow}(x,t)$. Equation (36) relies on the "which-path" constraint $\varphi^1_\uparrow(Z_1)\varphi^1_\downarrow(Z_1) = 0$ and therefore we have here two different dynamics depending on the pointer position Z_1. If Z_1 lies in the support of $\varphi^1_\uparrow(Z_1)$, we have the dynamics $\frac{d}{dt}x^\Psi(t) = v_\uparrow(x,t)$ corresponding to Figure 1a, whereas if Z_1 lies in the support of $\varphi^1_\downarrow(Z_1)$, we have the dynamics $\frac{d}{dt}x^\Psi(t) = v_\downarrow(x,t)$ corresponding to Figure 1b.

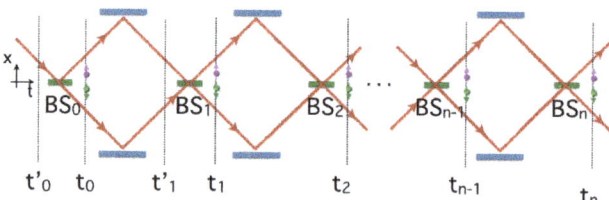

Figure 4. Drawing of the iterative procedure for entangling an initial wave-packet with "Bohmian" pointers providing unambiguous which-path information on the pilot-wave particle motion (as explained in the main text). The various pointers interacting at time $t_0, t_1 \ldots$ are sketched as qubit states.

The previous procedure for generating decohered Bohmian paths can be repeated iteratively at the times $t_2, t_3, \ldots$ after interaction with the beam-splitter BS_2, $BS_3 \ldots$ (see Figure 4). For this purpose, we consider at time t_1 entanglement with a an additional pointer initially in the state $\varphi^2_{in}(Z)$, and we assume the transformation

$$\frac{\psi_1(x,t_1+\frac{2D}{v_x})\varphi^1_\to(Z_1)+\psi_0(x,t_1+\frac{2D}{v_x})\varphi^1_\leftarrow(Z_1)}{\sqrt{2}}\varphi^2_{in}(Z_2)$$
$$\to \frac{\psi_1(x,t_1+\frac{2D}{v_x})\varphi^1_\to(Z_1)\varphi^2_\uparrow(Z_2)+\psi_0(x,t_1+\frac{2D}{v_x})\varphi^1_\leftarrow(Z_1)\varphi^2_\downarrow(Z_2)}{\sqrt{2}}. \tag{37}$$

The wave-packets propagate into the interferometer, and between times t'_2 and t_2, we obtain

$$\frac{\psi_0(x, t'_2 + \frac{4D}{v_x})\varphi^1_\rightarrow(Z_1)\varphi^2_\uparrow(Z_2) + \psi_1(x, t'_2 + \frac{4D}{v_x})\varphi^1_\leftarrow(Z_1)\varphi^2_\downarrow(Z_2)}{\sqrt{2}}$$

$$\rightarrow \frac{\psi_1(x, t_2 + \frac{4D}{v_x})\varphi^{12}_\rightarrow(Z_1, Z_2) + \psi_0(x, t_2 + \frac{4D}{v_x})\varphi^{12}_\leftarrow(Z_1, Z_2)}{\sqrt{2}} \quad (38)$$

with the orthonormal states $\varphi^{12}_\rightarrow = \frac{1}{\sqrt{2}}(\varphi^1_\rightarrow\varphi^2_\uparrow + \varphi^1_\leftarrow\varphi^2_\downarrow)$ and $\varphi^{12}_\leftarrow(Z_1, Z_2) = \frac{1}{\sqrt{2}}(\varphi^1_\rightarrow\varphi^2_\uparrow - \varphi^1_\leftarrow\varphi^2_\downarrow)$.

This can be generalized at any time t_n after interaction with BS_n:

$$\frac{\psi_0(x, t'_n + \frac{2nD}{v_x})\varphi^{1,\dots,n-1}_\rightarrow(Z_1, \dots, Z_{n-1})\varphi^n_\uparrow(Z_n) + \psi_1(x, t'_n + \frac{2nD}{v_x})\varphi^{1,\dots,n-1}_\leftarrow(Z_1, \dots, Z_{n-1})\varphi^n_\downarrow(Z_n)}{\sqrt{2}}$$

$$\rightarrow \frac{\psi_1(x, t_n + \frac{2nD}{v_x})\varphi^{1,\dots,n}_\rightarrow(Z_1, \dots, Z_n) + \psi_0(x, t_n + \frac{2nD}{v_x})\varphi^{1,\dots,n}_\leftarrow(Z_1, \dots, Z_n)}{\sqrt{2}}, \quad (39)$$

with the orthonormal states $\varphi^{1,\dots,n}_{\rightarrow/\leftarrow} = \frac{1}{\sqrt{2}}(\varphi^{1,\dots,n-1}_\rightarrow\varphi^n_\uparrow \pm \varphi^{1,\dots,n-1}_\leftarrow\varphi^n_\downarrow)$. Like for the interaction at BS_1 (between t'_1 and t_1), we can define a Bohmian dynamical evolution similar to Equation (36) but based on the wave-function

$$\Psi(x, Z1, \dots, Z_n, t) = \psi_\uparrow(x,t)\varphi^{1,\dots,n-1}_\rightarrow(Z_1, \dots, Z_{n-1})\varphi^n_\uparrow(Z_n)$$
$$+ \psi_\downarrow(x,t)\varphi^{1,\dots,n-1}_\leftarrow(Z_1, \dots, Z_{n-1})\varphi^2_\downarrow(Z_n). \quad (40)$$

We obtain the velocity

$$\frac{d}{dt}x^\Psi(t) = \frac{v_\uparrow(x,t)|\psi_\uparrow(x,t)\varphi^{1,\dots,n-1}_\rightarrow(Z_1, \dots, Z_{n-1})\varphi^n_\uparrow(Z_n)|^2}{|\psi_\uparrow(x,t)\varphi^{1,\dots,n-1}_\rightarrow(Z_1, \dots, Z_{n-1})\varphi^n_\uparrow(Z_n)|^2 + |\psi_\downarrow(x,t)\varphi^{1,\dots,n-1}_\leftarrow(Z_1, \dots, Z_{n-1})\varphi^2_\downarrow(Z_n)|^2}$$
$$+ \frac{v_\downarrow(x,t)|\psi_\downarrow(x,t)\varphi^{1,\dots,n-1}_\leftarrow(Z_1, \dots, Z_{n-1})\varphi^2_\downarrow(Z_n)|^2}{|\psi_\uparrow(x,t)\varphi^{1,\dots,n-1}_\rightarrow(Z_1, \dots, Z_{n-1})\varphi^n_\uparrow(Z_n)|^2 + |\psi_\downarrow(x,t)\varphi^{1,\dots,n-1}_\leftarrow(Z_1, \dots, Z_{n-1})\varphi^2_\downarrow(Z_n)|^2} \quad (41)$$

which like Equation (36) reduces to one of the two dynamics (i) $\frac{d}{dt}x^\Psi(t) = v_\uparrow(x,t)$ if Z_n lies in the support of $\varphi^n_\uparrow(Z_n)$ (i.e., corresponding to Figure 1a) or (ii) $\frac{d}{dt}x^\Psi(t) = v_\downarrow(x,t)$ if Z_n lies in the support of $\varphi^n_\downarrow(Z_n)$ (i.e., corresponding to Figure 1b). The full history of the particle in the interferometer depends on the positions $Z_1, \dots, Z_n$ taken by the various Bohmian pointers. In turn, this deterministic iterative process allows us to define a Bernoulli map for the evolution.

3.3. Mixing, Chaos and Relaxation to Quantum Equilibrium

The Bernoulli map is clearly defined from Equations (27) and (28) after introducing the variable $y(t)$ replacing $x(t)$. Between t'_n and t_n, this reads

$$y(t_n) = 2y(t'_n) \quad \mathrm{mod}(1). \quad (42)$$

Moreover, the $y(t'_n)$ coordinate at time t'_n is obviously equal to $y(t_{n-1})$ at time t_{n-1} (see Figure 4), and therefore we have the map

$$y(t_n) = 2y(t_{n-1}) \quad \mathrm{mod}(1). \quad (43)$$

This iterative Bernoulli map $y_n = F(y_{n-1})$ is one of the simplest chaotic maps discussed in the literature [56,57]. In particular, its chaotic nature has been already studied in the context of BBQT [58,59] (for different purposes than those considered here), and an attempt to use it for deriving Born's rule has been worked out [60] (without the entanglement used here and in [22,50]).

The chaotic nature of the map is easy to obtain; consider for example Figure 5.

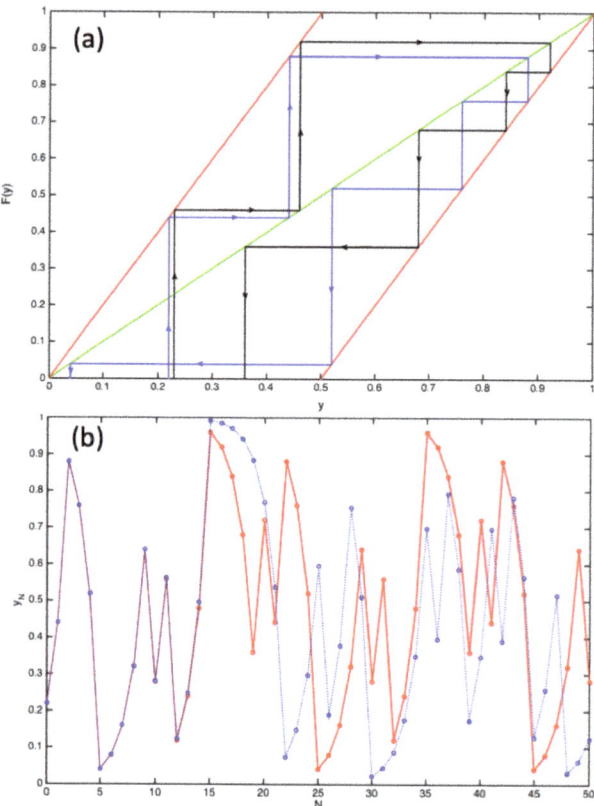

Figure 5. (a) Bernoulli map $y_n = F(y_{n-1})$ in the y, y' plane where the function $y' = F(y)$ acts iteratively. The red and green lines are acting as mirrors during the process. The black and blue trajectories correspond to different initial coordinates $y_0 = 0.22$ and $y_0 = 0.23$. (b) The same Bernoulli map is shown as a function $y = y(n)$ of the iteration steps $n = 0, 1, \ldots$. The two chaotic trajectories shown in red and blue correspond to $y_0 = 0.22$ and $y_0 = 0.220001$, respectively (see main text).

In Figure 5a, we show a standard representation of the iterative function $y_n = F(y_{n-1})$ for two paths initially starting at $y_0 = 0.22$ and $y_0 = 0.23$, and after a few iterations, the coordinates are apparently diverging in an unpredictable way. This is even more clear in the representation of Figure 5b, where two trajectories $y(t_n) := y_n$ are shown with $y_0 = 0.22$ and $y_0 = 0.220001$. Again, the motions become chaotic after a few iterations, and the trajectories are strongly diverging. Mathematically, any number y in the interval $[0, 1]$ is represented in binary notation as $0.u_1 u_2 \ldots u_n \ldots$, i.e., $y = \frac{u_1}{2} + \frac{u_2}{4} + \ldots + \frac{u_n}{2^n} + \ldots$ where $u_n = 0$ or 1. The Bernoulli transformation $y' = F(y)$ with $y' = \frac{u'_1}{2} + \frac{u'_2}{4} + \ldots + \frac{u'_n}{2^n} + \ldots$ corresponds to the shift $u'_n = u_{n-1}$; i.e., to the binary number $0.u_2 u_3 \ldots u_{n-1} \ldots$. Iteratively, this generates chaos since if the nth term in $y = \frac{u_1}{2} + \frac{u_2}{4} + \ldots + \frac{u_n}{2^n} + \ldots$ is known with an uncertainty $\delta y_i = \frac{1}{2^n}$ after n iterations, this uncertainty will grow to $\delta y_f = 1/2$. For example, if $n = 133$ and $\delta y_i = 2^{-133} \simeq 10^{-40}$, we have after only 40 iterations completely lost any predictability in the dynamics (note that rational numbers are periodical in the binary representation and therefore the sequence will reappear periodically for rational numbers representing a null measure in the segment $[0,1]$). It can be shown that this feature leads to randomness in close analogy with ideal probabilistic coin tossing [61]. Therefore, any uncertainty will ultimately lead to chaos. The Lyapunov divergence of this Bernoulli map is readily obtained by considering as in Figure 5 two trajectories $y_n^{(A)}$ and $y_n^{(B)} = y_n^{(A)} + \delta y_n$ differing by a infinitesimal number such that

$$\delta y_n = 2\delta y_{n-1} = 2^n \delta y_0 = e^{n \ln 2} \delta y_0 \tag{44}$$

where the positive Lyapunov exponent $\ln 2$ characterizes the chaotic dynamics. If we introduce the time delay $\delta t = -2D/v_x > 0$ and define the evolution time as $t_n = n\delta t$, we can rewrite the exponential divergence in Equation (44) as $e^{+t/\tau}$ where $\tau = \frac{\delta t}{\ln 2}$ defines a Lyapunov time.

Most importantly, the Bernoulli shift allows us to define a mixing property for the probability distribution $\rho(y)$. More precisely, we can consider at any time t_n the probability density $\rho(x, t_n) = \int \ldots \int \rho(x, Z_1, \ldots, Z_n, t_n) dZ_1 \ldots dZ_n$, where according to BBQT we have $\rho(x, Z_1, \ldots, Z_n, t_n) = f(x, Z_1, \ldots, Z_n, t_n)|\Psi(x, Z_1, \ldots Z_n, t_n)|^2$. In this framework, $\rho(x, t_n)$ is a coarse-grained probability involving a form of classical ignorance. In the following, we suppose that the pointers are all in quantum equilibrium, and we have $f(x, Z_1, \ldots, Z_n, t_n) := f(x, t_n)$ and $\rho(x, t_n) dx = f(x, t_n) d\Gamma(x, t_n)$ with $d\Gamma(x, t_n) = dx \int \ldots \int |\Psi(x, Z_1, \ldots Z_n, t_n)|^2 dZ_1 \ldots dZ_n$.

For the present purpose, a key result of deterministic maps such as $y_n = F(y_{n-1})$ is the Perron–Frobenius theorem [56,57] allowing us to introduce the operator $\hat{U}_{PF}$; i.e., $\mu(y, t_{n+1}) = \hat{U}_{PF} \mu(y, t_n)$ with the definition $\rho(x, t) dx = \mu(y, t) dy$. For this, we use the property for a trajectory

$$\delta(y - y_{n+1}) = \delta(y - F(y_n)) = \int_0^1 dY \delta(y - F(Y)) \delta(Y - y_n) \tag{45}$$

and the fact that any density $\mu(w, t_n)$ reads

$$\int_0^1 dy(t_n) \mu(y(t_n), t_n) \delta(w - y(t_n)) = \int_0^1 dy(t_0) \mu(y(t_0), t_0) \delta(w - y(t_n)) \tag{46}$$

(where we used Liouville's theorem $dy(t_n)\mu(y(t_n), t_n) = dy(t_0)\mu(y(t_0), t_0)$). Therefore, from Equation (45), we obtain

$$\mu(y, t_{n+1}) = \hat{U}_{PF} \mu(y, t_n) = \int_0^1 dY \delta(y - F(Y)) \mu(Y, t_n) \tag{47}$$

which for the Bernoulli map means

$$\mu(y, t_{n+1}) = \hat{U}_{PF} \mu(y, t_n) = \frac{1}{2} \left[\mu(\frac{y}{2}, t_n) + \mu(\frac{y+1}{2}, t_n) \right]. \tag{48}$$

Moreover, for the present wave-function defined in term of the wave-packet $\Phi_0(x)$ which is constant in amplitude in its support, we can also write

$$\tilde{f}(y, t_{n+1}) = \hat{U}_{PF} \tilde{f}(y, t_n) = \frac{1}{2} \left[\tilde{f}(\frac{y}{2}, t_n) + \tilde{f}(\frac{y+1}{2}, t_n) \right] \tag{49}$$

with $f(x, t) = \tilde{f}(y, t)$ using the transformation $x \to y$ (see Equations (24) and (26)) by definition and where $\int_{\gamma_+(t_n) \cup \gamma_-(t_n)} dx \frac{|C|^2}{2} f(x, t_n) = \int_0^1 dy \tilde{f}(y, t_n) = 1$ involving the normalization $C = 1/\sqrt{L}$. This iterative Perron–Frobenius relation admits Bernoulli polynomial eigenstates defined by $\frac{1}{2^n} B_n(y) = \hat{U}_{PF} B_n(y)$ with $B_0(y) = 1$, $B_1(y) = y - 1/2$, $B_2(y) = y^2 - y + 1/6, \ldots$ [56].

It can be shown [56] that the $B_m(y)$ polynomials form a basis for the probability function $\tilde{f}(y,t)$, and therefore we write $\tilde{f}(y,t_0) = \sum_{m=0}^{m=+\infty} A_m B_m(y)$, which we obtain after n iterations of the $\hat{U}_{PF}$–operator:

$$\tilde{f}(y,t_n) = \sum_{m=0}^{m=+\infty} A_m e^{-n\cdot m \ln 2} B_m(y). \qquad (50)$$

In this formula, we have [56,62]

$$A_m = \int_0^1 dy \tilde{f}(y,t_0) \tilde{B}_m(y) \qquad (51)$$

where $\tilde{B}_0(y) = 1$ and $\tilde{B}_m(y) = \lim_{\varepsilon \to 0^+} \frac{(-1)^{m-1}}{m!} \frac{d^{m-1}}{dy^{m-1}}[\delta(y-1+\varepsilon) - \delta(y-\varepsilon)]$ for $m \geq 1$. This leads to $A_0 = \int_0^1 \tilde{f}(y,t_0) dy$ and $A_m = \lim_{\varepsilon \to 0^+} \frac{1}{m!} \frac{d^{m-1}}{dy^{m-1}}[\tilde{f}(1-\varepsilon,t_0) - \tilde{f}(0+\varepsilon,t_0)]$. Equation (50) is important as it shows that in the limit $n \to +\infty$, we necessarily have $\tilde{f}(y,t_n) \to A_0 B_0(y) = A_0$. Moreover, from the properties of the Bernoulli polynomials and the normalization of the probability density, we necessarily have $\int_0^1 \tilde{f}(y,t) dy = A_0 = 1$ (with $\int_0^1 dy B_m(y) = \delta_{0,m}$). Therefore, we deduce

$$\lim_{n \to +\infty} \tilde{f}(y,t_n) = \lim_{n \to +\infty} f(x,t_n) = 1. \qquad (52)$$

This result says that quantum equilibrium, and therefore Born's rule, is a statistical attractor in BBQT. Importantly, Equation (50) shows that each term in the sum is characterized by an exponential decay $e^{-mt_n/\tau}$, which is a signature of stability (negative Lyapunov exponent) whereas the trajectories (as we have shown in Equation (44)) have a positive Lyapunov exponent associated with dynamical instability and chaos. These two pictures are thus clearly complementary. This was already emphasized long ago by Prigogine in a different context [62,63]. As an illustration, we show in Figure 6 the transformation of an arbitrary (normalized) density $\tilde{f}(y,t_0)$: after only three applications of the Perron–Frobenius operator, the density is indistinguishable from the quantum equilibrium $\tilde{f} = f = 1$, which acts as a very efficient attractor.

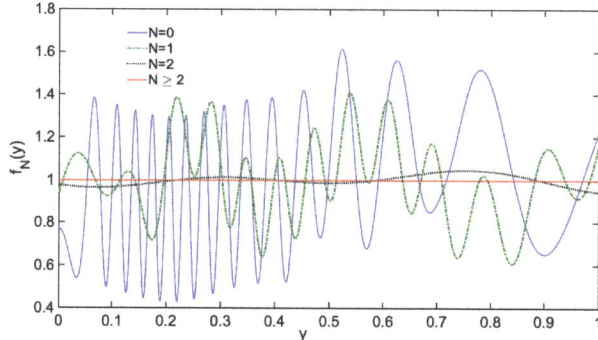

Figure 6. Evolution of $\tilde{f}(y,t_n) := \tilde{f}_n(y)$ as a function of y for a few n values (using the Perron–Frobenius operator Equation (49)). The initial distribution $\tilde{f}_0(y)$ (blue curve) was chosen to be arbitrarily irregular. After a few iterations $n \geq 2$, the function $\tilde{f}_n(y)$ cannot be distinguished from the line $\tilde{f} = f = 1$ associated with quantum equilibrium (i.e., Born's rule).

We emphasize that the iterative process sketched in Figure 4 and associated with states such as Equations (39) and (40) ultimately involves the two branches $\psi_0(x,t_n)$ and $\psi_1(x,t_n)$ entangled with an environment of Bohmian pointers characterized by $\varphi^{1,...,n}_{\to/\leftarrow} = \frac{1}{\sqrt{2}}(\varphi^{1,...,n-1}_{\to} \varphi^n_{\uparrow} \pm \varphi^{1,...,n-1}_{\leftarrow} \varphi^n_{\downarrow})$. Moreover, because of the orthogonality of these pointer states, the two branches $\psi_0(x,t_n)$ and $\psi_1(x,t_n)$ cannot interfere: they are decohered. Still, in each of the two final wave-packets $\psi_0(x, t_N)$ and $\psi_1(x, t_N)$ (after a large number of iterations N), we have $f(x, t_N) \simeq 1$ with a high accuracy. Therefore, supposing that we now make a pinhole to select one of these two branches, we have prepared a quantum system satisfying Born's rule $\rho(x, t) \simeq |\psi(x, t)|^2$. Fundamentally, this means that if an entangled system such as the system we discussed is post-selected by a filtering procedure, we can define subsystems for which Born's rule is true and where quantum coherence is maintained (this is the case with our two wave-functions ψ_1 and ψ_0 taken separately). For example, the wave-function $\psi_0(x, t)$ can be collimated and sent into an interferometer in order to observe wave–particle duality. All systems following this guiding wave belong to a statistical ensemble of particles obeying Born's rule $f \simeq 1$. Therefore, all the predictions of standard quantum mechanics are reproduced with these systems.

Although the present model is rudimentary, it allows us to obtain precious information on relaxation to quantum equilibrium. Indeed, observe that in the continuous time approximation, we have $\tilde{f}(y, t) \simeq 1 + A_1 e^{-t/\tau} B_1(y)$, which is a solution of the differential equation

$$\frac{\partial \tilde{f}(y, t)}{\partial t} = -\frac{\tilde{f}(y, t) - 1}{\tau} \tag{53}$$

This suggests a collision term in a Boltzmann-like equation and therefore an extension of our model by writing

$$\frac{df(x, t)}{dt} := \partial_t f(x, t) + v_\psi(x, t) \partial_x f(x, t) = -\frac{f(x, t) - 1}{\tau} \tag{54}$$

or equivalently with $\rho(x, t) = f(x, t)|\psi(x, t)|^2$ and $\partial_t |\psi(x, t)|^2 + \partial_x (v_\psi(x, t)|\psi(x, t)|^2) = 0$:

$$\partial_t \rho(x, t) + \partial_x (v_\psi(x, t) \rho(x, t)) = -\frac{\rho(x, t) - |\psi(x, t)|^2}{\tau}. \tag{55}$$

With such dynamics (with an effective broken time symmetry), it is useful to introduce the Valentini entropy [32]:

$$S_t := -\int f(x, t) \ln(f(x, t)) d\Gamma(x, t) \tag{56}$$

with $d\Gamma(x, t) = |\psi(x, t)|^2$. From the previous equation, we deduce

$$\frac{d}{dt} S_t = -\int \frac{df_t}{dt}(1 + \ln f_t) d\Gamma_t = \int \frac{(f_t - 1)}{\tau}(1 + \ln f_t) d\Gamma_t = \int \frac{(f_t - 1)}{\tau} \ln f_t d\Gamma_t. \tag{57}$$

This kinetic equation leads to a quantum version of the Boltzmann H-theorem, as can be shown easily: first, we have by definition $a \ln b + \frac{a}{b} - a \geq 0$ (with $a, b > 0$) leading to $(f - 1) \ln f + \frac{f-1}{f} - f - 1 \geq 0$ if $f - 1 > 0$; i.e., we obtain $(f - 1) \ln f \geq \frac{(f-1)^2}{f}$ if $f - 1 > 0$. Moreover, $\ln f \leq f - 1$, and thus if $f - 1 < 0$, we have $(f - 1) \ln f \geq (f - 1)^2$. Now, separating the full $\Gamma-$ space into two parts Γ_+ and Γ_- where $f - 1 \geq 0$ and $1 - f \geq 0$, respectively, we have

$$\frac{d}{dt} S_t = \int \frac{(f_t - 1)}{\tau} \ln f_t d\Gamma_t \geq \int_{\Gamma_+} \frac{(f_t - 1)^2}{f_t \tau} d\Gamma_t + \int_{\Gamma_-} \frac{(f_t - 1)^2}{\tau} d\Gamma_t \geq 0. \tag{58}$$

Therefore, Valentini's entropy S_t cannot decrease, and the equality $\frac{d}{dt} S_t = 0$ occurs iff $f = 1$ corresponding to the quantum equilibrium. This defines an H-theorem for BBQT.

4. Conclusions and Perspectives

The proposal discussed in this work is certainly schematic but it leads to several interesting conclusions. First, since the dynamics maps used here are deterministic and chaotic, this shows that randomness is unavoidable in BBQT. As stressed by Prigogine [62,63], we have two complementary descriptions: one with trajectories that can be associated with the evolution map $y_{n+1} = F(y_n)$ and the second with a probability density; i.e., as given by the Perron–Frobenius transformation $\tilde{f}(y, t_{n+1}) = \hat{U}_{PF}\tilde{f}(y, t_n)$. The two pictures are of course not independent since for a single trajectory we have $\delta(y - y_{n+1}) = \hat{U}_{PF}\delta(y - y_n)$ (i.e., $\tilde{f}(y, t_n) = \delta(y - y_n) = f(x, t_n) = \frac{2}{|C|^2}\delta(x - x_n) = 2L\delta(x - x_n)$). Moreover, for a trajectory, the probability distribution is singular and the convergence to equilibrium is infinitely slow (this is connected to the fact that the coefficients A_m in Equation (51) are given by an integral which is badly defined for the singular Dirac distribution $\tilde{f}(y, t_0) = \delta(y - y_0)$). Therefore, the infinite precision required to compute such a chaotic path (due to the exponentially growing deviation errors with time) leads all practical computations to the strong randomness previously mentioned. To quote Ford [61], "a chaotic orbit is random and incalculable; its information content is both infinite and incompressible". Subsequently, because of the extreme sensitivity in the initial conditions associated with the predictability horizon and the positive Lyapunov exponent, the use of probability distributions in BBQT seems (at least in our model) unavoidable if we follow Prigogine's reasoning. Indeed, Prigogine dynamic instability (and thus deterministic chaos) leads to probability. The necessarily finite precision δy_0 used to determine the position of a particle will grow exponentially with time to ultimately cover the whole segment $[0, 1]$. Therefore, if we assign a uniform ignorance probability $\tilde{f}_0$ over the segment δy_0 (in which the particle is located) then—i.e., subsequently after a few iterations—we will have $\tilde{f}_t = 1$ over the whole segment.

However, we stress that we do not share all the conclusions obtained by Prigogine concerning determinism and probability here (for related and much more detailed criticisms, see e.g., [64]). Indeed, BBQT (as with the classical mechanic considered by Prigogine in [62,63]) is a fully deterministic theory with a clear ontology in the 3D and configuration space. Therefore, while a trajectory could be incalculable by any finite mean or algorithm, the path still fundamentally exists for an idealized Laplacian daemon; i.e., having access to an infinite computing power and precision for locating and defining the particle motion. This metaphor is the core idea of Einstein's realism: postulating the existence of a world independent of the presence or absence of observers (even if the observers can be part of the world). From this ontic perspective, we need more than simply ignorance in order to justify the use of probability in statistical physics. Indeed, as emphasized long ago by Poincaré, the laws of the kinetic theory of gases still hold true even if we exactly know the positions of all molecules—[65]. There is something objective in the laws of statistical mechanics that goes beyond mere ignorance: otherwise, how could parameters such as diffusion constants have objective physical contents? This point was emphasized by Prigogine from the very beginning, and this constitutes the motivation for his program in order to justify the objectivity of thermodynamics in general and the second law—i.e., irreversibility—in particular.

However, in our opinion, the missing point in Prigogine's implication—"instability $\rightarrow$ probability $\rightarrow$ irreversibility"—is the recognition that in a deterministic theory, the laws (chaotic or not) are not complete but must be supplemented by specific initial conditions, ultimately with a cosmological origin. Indeed, if we suppose a universe made of only one electron described initially by the wave-function $\psi_0(x, t)$ and all the pointers involved in the iterative procedure sketched in Figure 4, then we must use the chaotic Bernoulli map $y_{n+1} = F(y_n)$ for this system or equivalently the Perron–Frobenius evolution $\delta(y - y_{n+1}) = \hat{U}_{PF}\delta(y - y_n)$. As we have explained, this system is unstable due to the presence of a positive Lyapunov exponent. Moreover, if we want to make sense of the formulas (49) and (50) with the rapid convergence to $\tilde{f} = f = 1$, we must consider a sufficiently regular distribution $\tilde{f}(y, t_0) \neq \delta(y - y_0)$. Now, as mentioned in Section 2, the application of the WLLN to a statistical ensemble requires a "metric" of typicality associated with the Laplacian definition of probability. In BBQT, this metric reads $\rho(\mathbf{r}, t) = f(\mathbf{r}, t)|\psi(\mathbf{r}, t)|^2$, and the law of large numbers leads to Equation (11)—i.e., $\rho(\mathbf{r}, t) \equiv \lim_{N \to +\infty} \frac{1}{N}\sum_{k=1}^{k=N} \delta^3(\mathbf{r} - \mathbf{x}_k^{\psi}(t))$—defined probabilistically in the long term; i.e, for an infinitely long sequence or infinite system. In our problem, this means that we consider an infinite Gibbs ensemble of copies similar to our system, as described in Figure 4. Here, the presence of an infinite sum of Dirac distributions is expected to lead to difficulties in connection with the chaotic map $\delta(y - y_{n+1}) = \hat{U}_{PF}\delta(y - y_n)$. In our problem, if the WLLN $\rho(\mathbf{r}, t) \equiv \lim_{N \to +\infty} \frac{1}{N} \sum_{k=1}^{k=N} \delta^3(\mathbf{r} - \mathbf{x}_k^{\psi}(t))$ is used to specify the initial distribution at time t_0, this preserves the chaotic description associated with the positive Lyapunov exponent; therefore, Dirac distributions become problematic. In order to remove this unpleasant feature, one must introduce coarse-graining as proposed by Valentini [32,51]. In our case, this can be done by using a regular weighting function $\Delta(u)$ such that $\bar{\rho}(x, t) = \int du \delta(u)\rho(x - u, t)$, which in connection with the WLLN leads to $\bar{\rho}(x, t) \equiv \lim_{N \to +\infty} \frac{1}{N} \sum_{k=1}^{k=N} \Delta(x - x_k^{\psi}(t))$. The coarse-graining of cells in the configuration space plays a central role in the work of Valentini for defining a "subquantum H-theorem" [32,33]. Here, we see that in connection with Prigogine's work, coarse-graining must be supplemented with a dose of deterministic chaos and entanglement in order to reach the quantum equilibrium regime. We believe that these two pictures complete each other very well.

Before summarizing our work, it is important to go back to Zurek's envariance as discussed in the introduction in order to see connections with the derivation of Born's rule as presented in this article. We remind the reader that in 2003, Zurek [66] proposed an alternative proof of Born's rule based on envariance—a neologism for environment-assisted invariance—with a purely quantum symmetry based on the entanglement of a system with its environment. The importance of this elegant proof could perhaps only be compared with that presented by Gleason [67] in 1957. As stressed by Zurek, "Envariance of entangled quantum states follows from the nonlocality of joint states and from the locality of systems, or, put a bit differently, from the coexistence of perfect knowledge of the whole and complete ignorance of the parts" [66]. The proof is remarkably general and does not rely on any specific ontology, even though it has been used by advocates of the many-world interpretation to justify or recover Born's rule (for a review and a comparison to the decision-theoretic deduction [5], see [6]).

In order to have a vague idea of the whole derivation, consider a Bell state $|\Psi\rangle_{\mathcal{SE}} = |\heartsuit\rangle_{\mathcal{S}}|\diamondsuit\rangle_{\mathcal{E}} + |\spadesuit\rangle_{\mathcal{S}}|\clubsuit\rangle_{\mathcal{E}}$ between a system $\mathcal{S}$ and environment $\mathcal{E}$. Now, the main idea of envariance concerns symmetry: a local "swapping" (for example, on $\mathcal{S}$ for the two possible outcomes $|\heartsuit\rangle_{\mathcal{S}}/|\spadesuit\rangle_{\mathcal{S}}$) in the entanglement is irrelevant for the local physics of $\mathcal{E}$ (this is obvious a priori, since $\mathcal{E}$ is untouched by the swap). This (unitary) swap reads

$$|\Psi\rangle_{\mathcal{SE}} = |\heartsuit\rangle_{\mathcal{S}}|\diamondsuit\rangle_{\mathcal{E}} + |\spadesuit\rangle_{\mathcal{S}}|\clubsuit\rangle_{\mathcal{E}} \to |\spadesuit\rangle_{\mathcal{S}}|\diamondsuit\rangle_{\mathcal{E}} + |\heartsuit\rangle_{\mathcal{S}}|\clubsuit\rangle_{\mathcal{E}} = |\Psi'\rangle_{\mathcal{SE}} \tag{59}$$

The symmetry of the swap should a priori also impact probabilities associated with outcomes (whatever the definition used for a probability). In other words, if we are allowed to define a probability function $\mathcal{P}_\Psi(|\heartsuit\rangle_{\mathcal{S}}|\diamondsuit\rangle_{\mathcal{E}})$ for the two correlated outcomes $\heartsuit$ and $\diamondsuit$ before the swap, then the previous equation imposes

$$\mathcal{P}_\Psi(|\heartsuit\rangle_{\mathcal{S}}|\diamondsuit\rangle_{\mathcal{E}}) = \mathcal{P}_{\Psi'}(|\spadesuit\rangle_{\mathcal{S}}|\diamondsuit\rangle_{\mathcal{E}}) \tag{60}$$

where $\mathcal{P}_{\Psi'}(|\spadesuit\rangle_{\mathcal{S}}|\diamondsuit\rangle_{\mathcal{E}})$ is a probability after the swap (i.e., defined for the state $|\Psi'\rangle_{\mathcal{SE}}$). Moreover, the swap on $\mathcal{S}$ can be compensated by a "counterswap" acting locally on the subsystem $\mathcal{E}$:

$$|\Psi'\rangle_{\mathcal{SE}} = |\spadesuit\rangle_{\mathcal{S}}|\diamondsuit\rangle_{\mathcal{E}} + |\heartsuit\rangle_{\mathcal{S}}|\clubsuit\rangle_{\mathcal{E}} \to |\spadesuit\rangle_{\mathcal{S}}|\clubsuit\rangle_{\mathcal{E}} + |\heartsuit\rangle_{\mathcal{S}}|\diamondsuit\rangle_{\mathcal{E}} = |\Psi\rangle_{\mathcal{SE}}. \tag{61}$$

Now, again from symmetry, we must have the relation

$$\mathcal{P}_{\Psi'}(|\spadesuit\rangle_{\mathcal{S}}|\diamondsuit\rangle_{\mathcal{E}}) = \mathcal{P}_\Psi(|\spadesuit\rangle_{\mathcal{S}}|\clubsuit\rangle_{\mathcal{E}}). \tag{62}$$

However, by comparing Equation (60) and Equation (62), we clearly deduce

$$\mathcal{P}_\Psi(|\spadesuit\rangle_\mathcal{S}|\clubsuit\rangle_\mathcal{E}) = \mathcal{P}_\Psi(|\heartsuit\rangle_\mathcal{S}|\diamondsuit\rangle_\mathcal{E}) = \frac{1}{2} \qquad (63)$$

which implies equiprobability for the two branches in the state $|\Psi\rangle_{\mathcal{SE}}$. This equiprobablity is clearly an illustration of Born's rule for the entangled state $|\Psi\rangle_{\mathcal{SE}}$. Therefore, envariance can be used to derive Born's rule (more general reasonings and deductions are given in [66]).

It is important to remark that the reasoning depends on the a priori existence of a probability function, and in order to justify this point, we should rely on a more precise definition of probability in a given ontology. Moreover, in the de Broglie–Bohm ontology, as in classical statistical mechanics, the concept of probability is related to a distribution of particles in ensembles or collectives and is therefore strongly rooted in the concepts of frequency and population. In other words, if we consider a large ensemble of copies for the entangled systems prepared in the quantum state $|\Psi\rangle_{\mathcal{SE}}$, then according to the Bernoulli WLLN, the probability $\mathcal{P}_\Psi(|\heartsuit\rangle_\mathcal{S}|\diamondsuit\rangle_\mathcal{E})$ is simply a measure of the fraction of systems prepared in the states $|\heartsuit\rangle_\mathcal{S}|\diamondsuit\rangle_\mathcal{E}$. Now, in the de Broglie–Bohm theory (like in classical physics), x-coordinates for particles define a "preferred basis" in the sense that particles are really located at some positions $x_\Psi(t)$ defining trajectories. Zurek's envariance can thus be applied to the de Broglie–Bohm ontology if we consider systems $\mathcal{S}$ and $\mathcal{E}$ that are well located in the configuration. Therefore, like in the model used in the present article, we can consider two non-overlapping wave-functions $\heartsuit(X_\mathcal{S})_\mathcal{S}$ and $\spadesuit(X_\mathcal{S})_\mathcal{S}$ associated with the coordinates $X_\mathcal{S}$ in the configuration space of the $\mathcal{S}$-subsystem and similarly for the non-overlapping wave-functions $\diamondsuit(X_\mathcal{E})_\mathcal{E}$ and $\clubsuit(X_\mathcal{E})_\mathcal{E}$ of the $\mathcal{E}$-subsystem. In this ontology, we can give a physical meaning to the invariance under swap or counterswap conditions.

It is indeed possible to postulate that there areas many copies of the systems prepared in the $|\Psi\rangle_{\mathcal{SE}}$ state as in the $|\Psi'\rangle_{\mathcal{SE}}$ state in the universe. The situation is similar to the one found in a classical gas of molecules were correlated pairs can be defined by exchanging some properties and are present in equal numbers before and after the swap (this kind of symmetry played a key role in the deduction made by Maxwell and Boltzmann justifying the canonical ensemble distribution). Fundamentally, this symmetry in the population is related to some choices in the initial conditions of the whole ensemble. The full deduction of Zurek based on envariance is thus preserved, and this must lead to Born's rule (at least if we assume that the population of de Broglie–Bohm particles is uniformly distributed in the spatial supports of the various wave functions).

Furthermore, it is important to stress that the envariance deduction is linked to the no-signaling theorem as shown by Barnum [68]. This no-signaling theorem was also emphasized by Valentini [69] in the de Broglie–Bohm theory in order to protect macroscopic causality and to prohibit faster-than-light signaling. Crucially, Born's rule appears as a necessary condition for the validity of the no-signaling theorem (this was also related to the second law of thermodynamics by Elitzur [70]). Interestingly, in the present work, we considered regimes of quantum-nonequilibrium where the symmetry of the entangled wave-functions was not present in the particle distribution characterized by the $f(X_t, t)$ function. However, in the end, we showed that if the environment of pointers was already in quantum equilibrium, then the system would be driven to the quantum equilibrium $f = 1$ acting as an attractor under the chaotic Bohmian dynamics. In the end, this also shows that the quantum equilibrium in the de Broglie–Bohm dynamics is natural and also how fragile and unstable physical deviations to the Born rule are. We believe that this confirms the deductions made by Zurek concerning the fundamental role of envariance.

There is another way to express the same concept: going back to our discussion about typicality at the end of Section 2, we see that in this article, we indeed developed a model that does not assume quantum equilibrium for all particles. The system moving in the interferometer is initially out of quantum equilibrium $f = 1$. However, it is quickly driven to quantum equilibrium due to (1) entanglement with pointers already relaxed in the regime $f = 1$ and (2) the presence of chaotic dynamics inducing fast mixing and thus a fast relaxation $f \to 1$. It is interesting that the number of iterations N and therefore the number of pointers involved in the process does not have to be large (i.e., we do not have to go to the thermodynamic limit $N \to +\infty$ associated with a quantum bath). As we have shown, the chaotic Bernoulli map drives the system to quantum equilibrium already for $N \simeq 3$. This demonstrates, we think, the robustness of this attractor leading to Born's rule.

To summarize, in this work, we have proposed a mechanism for relaxation to quantum equilibrium in order to recover Born's rule in BBQT. The proposed mechanism relies on entanglement with an environment of "Bohmian pointers" allowing the system to mix. The scenario was developed for the case of a single particle in 1D motion interacting with beam splitters and mirrors, but the model could be generalized to several situations involving collisions between quanta and scattering with defects or other particles. The general proposal is thus to consider the quantum relaxation to Born's rule as a genuine process in phases of matter where interactions between particles play a fundamental role. This involves usual condensed matter or even plasma or gases where collisions are mandatory. For example, based on our toy model, we consider that interaction with the beam splitter and entanglement with Bohmian pointers is a good qualitative model for discussing collisions between molecules in the atmosphere, and if we remember that nitrogen molecules at a temperature of 293 K and at a pressure of 1 bar involve typically a collision frequency of 7×10^9 /s (which implies fast dynamics for reaching quantum equilibrium), we thus have a huge number n of collisions per second corresponding to a huge number of iterations in our Bernoulli-like process based on the Perron–Frobenius operator $f(y, t_{n+1}) = \hat{U}_{PF} f(y, t_n)$. Compared to Valentini's framework [32,33] where mixing and relaxation to quantum equilibrium are associated with coarse-graining à la Gibbs, our approach emphasizes the role of information losses due to entanglement with a local environment. In both cases, we obtain an increase of entropy and a formulation of the H−theorem for BBQT. These two views are certainly complementary, in the same way that Gibbs and Boltzmann perspectives on entropy are related. This could have an impact on the efficiency of quantum relaxation in the early stages of the evolution of the universe [37,38].

Funding: This research received no external funding.

Institutional Review Board Statement: Not applicable.

Informed Consent Statement: Not applicable.

Data Availability Statement: Not applicable.

Acknowledgments: I thank Wojciech H. Zurek for interesting discussions concerning entanglement, envariance and probability. I also thank Sebastian Deffner for organizing this Special Issue celebrating the work of Zurek. I thank Serge Huant and Guillaume Bachelier for helping me during the manuscript preparation, as well as Cristian Mariani for organizing very stimulating discussions at the reading group of the Institut Neel in Grenoble.

Conflicts of Interest: The author declares no conflict of interest.

References and Note

1. Zurek, W.H. Decoherence and the transition from quantum to classical. *Phys. Today* **1991**, *44*, 36–44. [CrossRef]
2. Zurek, W.H. Quantum Darwinism, Classical reality and the Randomness of Quantum Jumps. *Phys. Today* **2014**, *67*, 44–50. [CrossRef]

3. Zurek, W.H. Decoherence, the measurement problem, and interpretations of quantum mechanics. *Rev. Mod. Phys.* **2004**, *76*, 1267–1305.
4. Zurek, W.H. Emergence of the Classical from within the Quantum Universe. *arXiv* **2107**, arXiv:2107.03378v1.
5. Wallace, D. *The Ermerging Multiverse*; Oxford University Press: Oxford, UK, 2012.
6. Drezet, A. Making sense of Born's rule $p_\alpha = |\Psi_\alpha|^2$ with the many-minds interpretation. *Quantum Stud. Math. Found.* **2021**, *8*, 315–336.
7. Zurek, W. Preferred Sets of States, Predictability, Classicality, and Environement Induced Decoherence. In *Physical Origins of Time Asymmetry*; Halliwell, J.J., Pérez-Mercader, J., Zurek, W.H., Eds.; Cambridge University Press: Cambridge, UK, 1996; pp. 175–212.
8. Appleby, D.M. Bohmian Trajectories Post-Decoherence. *Found. Phys.* **1999**, *29*, 1885–1916. [CrossRef]
9. De Broglie, L. La Mécanique Ondulatoire et la Structure Atomique de la Matière et du Rayonnement. *J. Phys. Radium* **1927**, *8*, 225–241. [CrossRef]
10. Bacciagaluppi, G.; Valentini, A. *Quantum Theory at the Crossroads: Reconsidering the 1927 Solvay Conference*; Cambridge University Press: Cambridge, UK, 2009.
11. De Broglie, L. *Introduction à L'étude de la Mécanique Ondulatoire*; Hermann: Paris, France, 1930.
12. Bohm, D. A suggested Interpretation of the Quantum Theory in Terms of Hidden Variables I. *Phys. Rev.* **1952**, *85*, 166–179. [CrossRef]
13. Bohm, D. A suggested Interpretation of the Quantum Theory in Terms of Hidden Variables II. *Phys. Rev.* **1952**, *85*, 180–193. [CrossRef]
14. Bohm, D.; Hiley, B.J. *The Undivided Universe*; Routledge: London, UK, 1993.
15. Holland, P. *The Quantum Theory of Motion*; Cambridge University Press: London, UK, 1993.
16. Sanz, A.S. Bohm's approach to quantum mechanics: Alternative theory or practical picture? *Front. Phys.* **2019**, *14*, 11301 [CrossRef]
17. Pauli, W. *Louis de Broglie Physicien et Penseur*; Albin Michel: Paris, France, 1953; pp. 33–42.
18. Keller, J.B. Bohm's Interpretation of the Quantum Theory in Terms of "Hidden" Variables. *Phys. Rev.* **1953**, *89*, 1040. [CrossRef]
19. Uffink, J. Compendium of the foundations of classical statistical physics. In *Philosophy of Physics (Handbook of the Philosophy of Science)*; Butterfield, J., Earman, J., Eds.; Elsevier: Amsterdam, The Netherlands, 2007; pp. 923–1074.
20. Barret, J.A. Introduction to Quantum Mechanics and the Measurement Problem. *Topoi* **1995**, *14*, 45–54.
21. Callender, C. The Emergence and Interpretation of Probability in Bohmian Mechanics. *Stud. Hist. Philos. Sci. Part B Stud. Hist. Philos. Mod. Phys.* **2007**, *38*, 351–370. [CrossRef]
22. Drezet, A. How to Justify Born's Rule using the Pilot Wave Theory of de Broglie? *Ann. Fond. Broglie* **2017**, *42*, 103–131.
23. Bohm, D. Proof that Probability Density Approaches $|\Psi|^2$ in Causal Interpretation of the Quantum Theory. *Phys. Rev.* **1953**, *89*, 458–466. [CrossRef]
24. Potel, G.; Muñoz-Aleñar, M.; Barranco, F.; Vigezzi, E. Stability properties of $|\Psi|^2$ in Bohmian dynamics. *Phys. Lett. A* **2002**, *299*, 125–130. [CrossRef]
25. Bohm, D.; Schützer, W. The General Statistical Problem in Physics and the Theory of Probability. *Nuovo Cim.* **1995**, *2*, 1004–1047. [CrossRef]
26. Drezet, A.; Stock, B. A causal and continuous interpretation of the quantum theory: About an original manuscript by David Bohm sent to Louis de Broglie in 1951. *Ann. Fond. Broglie* **2017**, *42*, 169–195.
27. Bohm, D.; Vigier, J.P. Model of the Causal Interpretation of Quantum Theory in Terms of a Fluid with Irregular Fluctuations. *Phys. Rev.* **1954**, *96*, 208–217. [CrossRef]
28. Mousavi, S.V.; Miret-Artès, S. Stochastic Bohmian mechanics within the Schrödinger-Langevin framework: A trajectory analysis of wave-packet dynamics in a fluctuative-dissipative medium. *Eur. Phys. J. Plus* **2019**, *134*, 311. [CrossRef]
29. Nassar, A.B.; Miret-Artès, S. *Bohmian Mechanics, Open Quantum Systems and Continuous Measurements*; Springer: Berlin/Heidelberg, Germany, 2017.
30. Yamano, T. Modulational instability for a logarithmic nonlinear Schrödinger with mixed data equation. *Appl. Math. Lett.* **2015**, *48*, 124–127. [CrossRef]
31. Bohm, D. *Causality and Chance in Modern Physics*; Routledge: London, UK, 1957.
32. Valentini, A. Signal-locality, uncertainty, and the subquantum H-theorem. I. *Phys. Lett. A* **1991**, *156*, 5–11. [CrossRef]
33. Valentini, A. On the Pilot-Wave Theory of Classical, Quantum and Subquantum Physics. Ph.D. Thesis, International School for Advanced Studies, Trieste, Italy, 1992.
34. Tolman, R.C. *The Principles of Statistical Mechanics*; Clarendon Press: Oxford, UK, 1938.
35. Valentini, A.; Westman, H. Dynamical Origin of Quantum Probabilities. *Proc. R. Soc. A* **2005**, *461*, 253–272. [CrossRef]
36. Towler, M.D.; Russell, N.J.; Valentini, A. Time scales for dynamical relaxation to the Born rule. *Proc. R. Soc. A* **2012**, *468*, 990–1013. [CrossRef]
37. Valentini, A. Astrophysical and cosmological tests of quantum theory. *J. Phys. A: Math. Theor.* **2007**, *40*, 3285–3303. [CrossRef]
38. Colin, S.; Valentini, A. Primordial quantum nonequilibrium and large-scale cosmic anomalies. *Phys. Rev. D* **2015**, *92*, 043520. [CrossRef]

39. Efthymiopoulos, C.; Contopoulos, G.; Tzemos, A.C. Chaos in de Broglie—Bohm quantum mechanics and the dynamics of quantum relaxation. *Ann. Fond. Broglie* **2017**, *45*, 133–159.
40. Contopoulos, G.; Tzemos, A.C. Chaos in Bohmian Quantum Mechanics: A Short Review. *Regul. Chaotic Dyn.* **2020**, *25*, 476–495. [CrossRef]
41. Frisk, H. Properties of the trajectories in Bohmian mechanics. *Phys. Lett. A* **1997**, *227*, 139–142. [CrossRef]
42. Falsaperla, P.; Fonte, G. On the motion of a single particle near a nodal line in the de Broglie–Bohm interpretation of quantum mechanics. *Phys. Lett. A* **2003**, *316*, 382–390. [CrossRef]
43. Wisniacki, D.A.; Pujals, E.R. Motion of vortices implies chaos in Bohmian mechanics. *Europhys. Lett.* **2005**, *71*, 159–165. [CrossRef]
44. Contopoulos, G.; Delis, N.; Efthymiopoulos, C. Order in de Broglie—Bohm quantum mechanics. *J. Phys. A Math. Theor.* **2012**, *45*, 165301. [CrossRef]
45. Norsen, T. On the Explanation of Born-Rule Statistics in the de Broglie-Bohm Pilot-Wave Theory. *Entropy* **2018**, *20*, 422. [CrossRef]
46. Dürr, D.; Goldstein, S.; Zanghí, N. Quantum mechanics, randomness, and deterministic reality. *Phys. Lett. A* **1992**, *172*, 6–12. [CrossRef]
47. Dürr, D.; Goldstein, S.; Zanghí, N. Quantum equilibrium and the origin of absolute uncertainty. *J. Stat. Phys.* **1992**, *67*, 843–907. [CrossRef]
48. Tzemos, A.C.; Contopoulos, G. Ergodicity and Born's rule in an entangled two-qubit Bohmian system. *Phys. Rev. E* **2020**, *102*, 042205. [CrossRef]
49. Drezet, A. Brownian motion in the pilot wave interpretation of de Broglie and relaxation to quantum equilibrium. *Ann. Fond. Broglie* **2018**, *43*, 23–50.
50. Philbin, T.G. Derivation of quantum probabilities from deterministic evolution. *Int. J. Quantum Found.* **2015**, *1*, 175–184.
51. Valentini, A. Foundations of Statistical Mechanics and the Status of the Born Rule in de Broglie-Bohm Pilot-Wave Theory. In *Statistical Mechanics and Scientific Explanation: Determinism, Indeterminism and Laws of Nature*; World Scientific: Singapore, 2020; pp. 423–477.
52. Dürr, D.; Struyve, W. Typicality in the foundations of statistical physics and Born's rule. *arXiv* **1910**, arXiv:1910.08049v1.
53. Equivariance means here that the density ρ must be an explicit function of R, i.e., $\rho = F(R)$ which admits the only solution $\rho = R^2$.
54. Wallace, D. What Is Probability? Difficulties Understanding Probability. 2015. Available online: https://www.youtube.com/watch?v=9ApjAYTRilo (accessed on 5 June 2021).
55. Drezet, A. Collapse of the many-worlds interpretation: Why Everett's theory is typically wrong. *arXiv* **2021**, arXiv:2109.10646.
56. Driebe, D.J. *Fully Chaotic Maps and Broken Time Symmetry*; Springer: Dordrecht, The Netherlands, 1999.
57. Schuster, H.G. *Deterministic Chaos: An Introduction*; Physik-Verlag: Weinheim, Germany, 1984.
58. Dürr, D.; Goldstein, S.; Zanghí, N. Quantum Chaos, Classical Randomness, and Bohmian Mechanics. *J. Stat. Phys.* **1992**, *68*, 259–270. [CrossRef]
59. Dewdney, C.; Malik, Z. Measurement, decoherence and chaos in quantum pinball. *Phys. Lett. A* **1996**, *220*, 183–188. [CrossRef]
60. Geiger, H.; Obermair, G.; Helm, C. Quantum mechanics without statistical postulates. In *Quantum Communications, Computing and Measurement 3*; Springer: Berlin/Heidelberg, Germany, 2002; pp. 139–142.
61. Ford, J. How random is a coin toss? *Phys. Today* **1983**, *36*, 40–47. [CrossRef]
62. Prigogine, I. *Les Lois du Chaos*; Flamarion: Paris, France, 1993.
63. Prigogine, I. *The End of Certainty: Time, Chaos, and the New Laws of Nature*; Free Press/Simon and Schuster: New York, NY, USA, 1997.
64. Bricmont, J. Science of Chaos or Chaos in Science. *Phys. Mag.* **1995**, *17*, 159–208. [CrossRef]
65. Poincaré, H. Le hasard. *Revue du Mois* **1907**, *3*, 257–276.
66. Zurek, W.H. Environment-Assisted Invariance, Entanglement, and Probabilities in Quantum Physics. *Phys. Rev. Lett.* **2003**, *90*, 120404. [CrossRef] [PubMed]
67. Gleason, A.M. Measures on the closed subspaces of a Hilbert space. *Indiana Univ. Math. J.* **1957**, *6*, 885–893. [CrossRef]
68. Barnum, H. No-signalling-based version of Zurek's derivation of quantum probabilities: A note on 'Environment-assisted invariance, entanglement, and probabilities in quantum physics'. *arXiv* **2003**, arXiv:quant-ph/0312150v1.
69. Valentini, A. Signal-locality, uncertainty, and the subquantum H-theorem. II. *Phys. Lett. A* **1991**, *158*, 1–8. [CrossRef]
70. Elitzur, A. Locality and indeterminism preserve the second law. *Phys. Lett. A* **1992**, *167*, 335–340. [CrossRef]

Article

Many-Body Localization and the Emergence of Quantum Darwinism

Nicolás Mirkin *,† and Diego A. Wisniacki †

Departamento de Física "J. J. Giambiagi" and IFIBA, FCEyN, Universidad de Buenos Aires,
Buenos Aires 1428, Argentina; wisniacki@df.uba.ar
* Correspondence: mirkin@df.uba.ar
† These authors contributed equally to this work.

Abstract: Quantum Darwinism (QD) is the process responsible for the proliferation of redundant information in the environment of a quantum system that is being decohered. This enables independent observers to access separate environmental fragments and reach consensus about the system's state. In this work, we study the effect of disorder in the emergence of QD and find that a highly disordered environment is greatly beneficial for it. By introducing the notion of lack of redundancy to quantify objectivity, we show that it behaves analogously to the entanglement entropy (EE) of the environmental eigenstate taken as an initial state. This allows us to estimate the many-body mobility edge by means of our Darwinistic measure, implicating the existence of a critical degree of disorder beyond which the degree of objectivity rises the larger the environment is. The latter hints the key role that disorder may play when the environment is of a thermodynamic size. At last, we show that a highly disordered evolution may reduce the spoiling of redundancy in the presence of intra-environment interactions.

Keywords: decoherence; Quantum Darwinism; many-body localization; disorder

1. Introduction

The question of how our classical experience emerges from the quantum nature of reality is a fascinating problem that has been a matter of controversy since the origin of quantum mechanics. In this context, the theory of decoherence constitutes the most accepted framework to bridge the gap between the classical and the quantum world [1–4]. Classicality is here interpreted as an emergent property that arises as a quantum system coupled to an environment losses its coherence and becomes diagonal in its pointer states, which survive the harmful interaction.

However, decoherence is not enough to explain the emergence of an objective reality. To do so, a possibility is to introduce the concept of redundancy and assume that during the interaction the information about the pointer states of the system is redundantly imprinted in the many degrees of freedom of the environment. Thereby, by measuring separate environmental fragments, independent observers can reach consensus about the classical state of the system without perturbing its pointer states, which are not subjected to direct measurements. The fact that some particular states of the system are the ones that survive among all the others and are able to procreate despite of the detrimental effects of its surrounding, is what gives this process the name of Quantum Darwinism (QD) [5–13].

In general, QD has been studied in the simplest scenario, where the fragments of the environment do not interact with each other. However, this may not be the most realistic situation in an experimental setup, where the intrinsic dynamics of the environment can play a significant role in the decoherent dynamics of the open system [14,15]. For this reason, it is essential to understand how different environmental properties influence the emergence of QD and which are the mechanisms that may enhance the proliferation of redundancy. For instance, it has been shown that non-Markovianity hinders objectivity by suppressing the redundant records on the environment due to information backflows [16–19]. In addition, the degree of redundancy may be worsened by small changes in the microscopic description of the environment [20–26]. More recently, a distinction between classicality and objectivity has been proposed for bipartite open quantum systems [27] and stronger conditions for classical objectivity were considered [28–33]. It is interesting to note that the quantities involved in the theory of QD, such as redundancy and objectivity, are not just mathematical abstractions but have been experimentally measured through photonic setups, nitrogen-vacancy centers [34–36] and more recently also simulated in NISQ devices [37]. Nonetheless, as it is challenging to keep track of both the system and the environment, it is not yet fully understood which specific environmental features are the ones responsible for boosting objectivity in a realistic classical circumstance.

Based on the intuition that in the most realistic scenario a many-body environment should exhibit some degree of disorder as well as intra-environment interactions, our main goal in this work is to study how both of these environmental conditions influence the proliferation of redundancy. To do so, we use as an environmental model a disordered spin chain widely studied in the context of many-body localization (MBL) [38–44]. This system exhibits an ergodic or a localized behaviour, depending on its energy and disorder strength, which sets a many-body mobility edge that has been estimated both theoretically and experimentally [45–47]. Thereby, by coupling a two-level quantum system to this disordered environment, we study the proliferation of redundant information both in the ergodic and localized phase. To this end, we introduce the notion of lack of redundancy and find that a high degree of disorder is hugely beneficial for the emergence of QD. This is related to the low entanglement that the eigenstates of the environment have in the localized regime, which enhances the capability of each fragment to store and retain information about the system. In fact, we show that the lack of redundancy exhibits the same scaling behaviour as the entanglement entropy of the initial state of the environment, which allows us to estimate the many-body mobility edge by means of our Darwinistic measure. A remarkable implication of the latter is the existence of a critical degree of disorder beyond which the degree of objectivity increases the larger the environment is, evidencing the key role that disorder may play when the environment is of a thermodynamic size. At last, while previous works have shown that allowing a small interaction between the bath registers usually spoils the stored information in the environment [16,48], we find that a highly disordered evolution reduces this detrimental effect and enhances objectivity.

This manuscript is organized as follows. In Section 2 we present the general framework, where we first introduce the physical system under consideration and then we present the main ideas behind the theory of QD. In addition, we define the Darwinistic measure that is used to quantify the degree of classical objectivity. In Section 3, we begin by illustrating our Darwinistic measure with a representative example and then we present our main results relating the degree of disorder, localization and QD. We conclude in Section 4 with some final remarks.

2. General Framework
2.1. Physical Model

To analyze the effect of disorder in the emergence of QD, we will consider a two-level quantum system $\mathcal{S}$ coupled to a disordered environment E. The total Hamiltonian describing the system plus environment is given by

$$\hat{H} = \hat{H}_{int} + \lambda \hat{H}_E, \tag{1}$$

where $\hat{H}_{int}$ and $\hat{H}_E$ are the interaction and environmental Hamiltonian, respectively, and λ is a parameter that regulates the influence of the intrinsic dynamics of E with respect to the interaction with $\mathcal{S}$. In general, we remark that QD is studied in the limit where $\lambda \ll 1$, given that a small interaction between the bath registers usually spoils the stored information [16,48]. In addition, for simplicity, we will neglect the intrinsic Hamiltonian of $\mathcal{S}$ (assuming a dephasing interaction, where $[\hat{H}_\mathcal{S}, \hat{H}_{int}] = 0$, the system time scales are not relevant and thus $\hat{H}_S$ can be neglected). The open quantum system is coupled to the environment through a global interaction, given by

$$\hat{H}_{int} = \hat{\sigma}_z^{(S)} \otimes \sum_{k=1}^{L} \hat{\sigma}_y^{(k)}, \tag{2}$$

where $\hat{\sigma}_z^{(S)}$ refers to the Pauli operator with direction $\hat{z}$ acting on S, $\hat{\sigma}_j^{(k)}$ is the Pauli operator at site $k = \{1, 2, \ldots, L\}$ with direction $j = \{x, y, z\}$ and L is the number of spins in the environment. The latter consists on a spin chain with nearest-neighbor interaction coupled to a random magnetic field in the $\hat{z}$ direction at each site. The environmental Hamiltonian is described by

$$\hat{H}_E = \frac{1}{4} \sum_{k=1}^{L} \left(\hat{\sigma}_x^{(k)} \hat{\sigma}_x^{(k+1)} + \hat{\sigma}_y^{(k)} \hat{\sigma}_y^{(k+1)} + \hat{\sigma}_z^{(k)} \hat{\sigma}_z^{(k+1)} \right) + \frac{1}{2} \sum_{k=1}^{L} h_z^{(k)} \hat{\sigma}_z^{(k)}, \tag{3}$$

where $\{h_z^{(k)}\}$ is a set of random variables uniformly distributed within the interval $[-h, h]$ and periodic boundary conditions $\hat{\sigma}_{x,y,z}^{(1)} = \hat{\sigma}_{x,y,z}^{(L+1)}$ are considered. In this model, the $\hat{z}$ component of the total spin $\hat{S}_z = \frac{1}{2} \sum_{k=1}^{L} \hat{\sigma}_z^{(k)}$ is a conserved quantity. This conservation allows the separation of the spanned space into smaller subspaces of dimension D_n, where n is a fixed quantity of spins up or down. The dimension of each subspace is given by

$$D_n = \binom{L}{n} = \frac{L!}{n!(L-n)!}. \tag{4}$$

We emphasize the fact that this system was widely studied in the context of MBL and the existence of a many-body mobility edge separating an ergodic and a localized phase has been demonstrated both theoretically and experimentally [43,45,46]. More specifically, while for weak disorder the system is chaotic and satisfies the eigenstate thermalization hypothesis (ETH), if the amount of disorder surpasses a certain critical threshold there is a transition to an MBL phase and the system does not thermalize.

Given that we are interested in the proliferation of redundancy and this is a dynamical phenomenon involving actively both the system and each individual fragment of the environment, first we will simulate the unitary dynamics of the entire system and then trace over the reduced part in which we need to focus. For this purpose, we will consider a separable initial state of the form

$$\hat{\rho}(0) = |+, x\rangle_S \langle +, x|_S \otimes |\xi\rangle_\epsilon \langle \xi|_\epsilon \tag{5}$$

where $|+, x\rangle_S$ is the eigenstate of $\hat{\sigma}_x^{(S)}$ with positive projection and $|\xi\rangle_\epsilon$ refers to the eigenstate of $\hat{H}_E$ closest to a normalized energy target ϵ. This energy target is defined as $\epsilon = (E - E_{min})/(E_{max} - E_{min})$, where E_{max} and E_{min} are the maximum and the minimum energies within a subspace with a fixed quantity of spins up or down. In particular, we restrict to the subspace of zero magnetization for even-sized chains and to the sector of n = 1 for the odd ones, such as to avoid the effect of the symmetry related with the conservation of $\hat{S}_z$ when computing $|\xi\rangle_\epsilon$ [49]. Consequently, given an initial state predetermined by a normalized energy target ϵ in the corresponding symmetric subspace, the procedure will consist of averaging over several disorder realizations for each fixed value of h.

Considering the dephasing interaction between S and the environment, the reduced density matrix of S can be solved analytically. To do so, we can rewrite the initial state of the system in the privileged basis of $\hat{\sigma}_z^{(S)}$, obtaining $\hat{\rho}(0) = \frac{1}{2} \sum_{i,j} |i, z\rangle_S \langle j, z|_S \otimes |\xi\rangle_\epsilon \langle \xi|_\epsilon$, where $|i,z\rangle_S$ refers to the eigenstate of $\hat{\sigma}_z^{(S)}$ with eigenvalue s_i. If we now evolve the full system plus environment, we have

$$\hat{\rho}(t) = e^{-i\hat{H}t}\left(\frac{1}{2}\sum_{i,j}|i,z\rangle_S\langle j,z|_S \otimes |\xi\rangle_\epsilon\langle\xi|_\epsilon\right)e^{i\hat{H}t}$$
$$= \frac{1}{2}\sum_{i,j}\left(|i,z\rangle_S\langle j,z|_S e^{-it\left(s_i\hat{H}_{int}^{(E)}+\lambda\hat{H}_E\right)}|\xi\rangle_\epsilon\langle\xi|_\epsilon e^{+it\left(s_j\hat{H}_{int}^{(E)}+\lambda\hat{H}_E\right)}\right), \quad (6)$$

where $\hat{H}_{int}^{(E)}$ refers to the term of $\hat{H}_{int}$ acting solely over the environmental degrees of freedom (in our case $\sum_{k=1}^L \hat{\sigma}_y^{(k)}$). The reduced density matrix of the system can then be obtained by tracing over the environmental degrees of freedom,

$$\hat{\rho}_S(t) = \frac{1}{2}\sum_{i,j}|i,z\rangle_S\langle j,z|_S \text{Tr}_E\left[e^{-it\left(s_i\hat{H}_{int}^{(E)}+\lambda\hat{H}_E\right)}|\xi\rangle_\epsilon\langle\xi|_\epsilon e^{+it\left(s_j\hat{H}_{int}^{(E)}+\lambda\hat{H}_E\right)}\right]$$
$$= \frac{1}{2}\sum_{i,j}|i,z\rangle_S\langle j,z|_S\langle\xi|_\epsilon e^{-it\left(s_i\hat{H}_{int}^{(E)}+\lambda\hat{H}_E\right)}e^{+it\left(s_j\hat{H}_{int}^{(E)}+\lambda\hat{H}_E\right)}|\xi\rangle_\epsilon \quad (7)$$
$$= \frac{1}{2}\left(|+,z\rangle_S\langle+,z|_S + |-,z\rangle_S\langle-,z|_S + r(t)|+,z\rangle_S\langle-,z|_S + r^*(t)|-,z\rangle_S\langle+,z|_S\right),$$

where $r(t)$ is known as the decoherence factor and in our situation is given by

$$r(t) = \langle\xi_\epsilon|e^{-it\left[\lambda\hat{H}_E+\hat{H}_{int}^{(E)}\right]}e^{it\left[\lambda\hat{H}_E-\hat{H}_{int}^{(E)}\right]}|\xi_\epsilon\rangle. \quad (8)$$

In the traditional limit of QD, we can take as a first approximation the case where $\lambda \ll 1$, which simplifies the expression of the decoherence factor to

$$r(t) \simeq \langle\xi_\epsilon|e^{-2it\hat{H}_{int}^{(E)}}|\xi_\epsilon\rangle$$
$$= \cos(2t) - i\sin(2t)\langle\xi_\epsilon|\hat{H}_{int}^{(E)}|\xi_\epsilon\rangle. \quad (9)$$

Under this simple assumption, it is straightforward to calculate the purity of S as

$$\mathcal{P}_S(t) = \frac{1+r^2(t)}{2}$$
$$= \frac{1}{2} + \frac{\cos^2(2t)+\sin^2(2t)\langle\xi_\epsilon|\hat{H}_{int}^{(E)}|\xi_\epsilon\rangle}{2}. \quad (10)$$

Consequently, as far as the information content of the state of S is considered [16], the first revival occurs at $t = \pi/2$, where we have $\mathcal{P}_S = 1$. On the contrary, $t = \pi/4$ is the moment when the influence of E over S is maximized before the first revival occurs. For this reason, we also expect QD to be more evident at this particular time.

2.2. Quantum Darwinism

The main ambition of QD is to elucidate how much information a fragment $\mathcal{F}$ of the environment acquires during the interaction with the system S and how redundant this information is. In this framework, it is useful to focus on the mutual information between S and $\mathcal{F}$, which is defined as

$$\mathcal{I}(S:\mathcal{F}) = S_S(t) + S_\mathcal{F}(t) - S_{S\mathcal{F}}(t), \quad (11)$$

where $S_S(t)$ and $S_\mathcal{F}(t)$ refer to the von Neumann entropies at time t of S and $\mathcal{F}$, respectively, and $S_{S\mathcal{F}}(t)$ is the joint entropy between the two. In the case where S and $\mathcal{F}$ are initially uncorrelated, the mutual information quantifies the total information the fragment $\mathcal{F}$ gains about the state of the system $\mathcal{S}$. In order to quantify the degree of redundancy achieved during the interaction, we will define the notion of perfect redundancy as the ideal case where the mutual information between $\mathcal{S}$ and $\mathcal{F}$ is equal to the entropy of $\mathcal{S}$ for any possible fraction f of the environment considered, i.e., $\mathcal{I}(\mathcal{S}:\mathcal{F}_l) = S_\mathcal{S}\, \forall f = l/L < 1$, where $\mathcal{F}_l$ is an environmental fragment composed of l different components (spins) and L is the total number of spins of the entire environment. Consistently, in the case where the fragment is the whole environment ($f = 1$), then $S_{\mathcal{SF}} = 0$ and we have $\mathcal{I}(\mathcal{S}:\mathcal{F}_L) = 2S_\mathcal{S}$. It is important to notice that to avoid any possible bias when selecting the environmental fragment, we must compute an averaged mutual information $\overline{\mathcal{I}}(\mathcal{S}:\mathcal{F}_l)$, where the average is taken over all possible ways of composing the fragment of l components given the environment of L spins (there are $\frac{L!}{l!(L-l)!}$ possible combinations). With the definitions above, it is straightforward to define the lack of redundancy ($\mathcal{LR}$) as the difference between perfect redundancy and the averaged mutual information achieved during the dynamics, i.e.,

$$\mathcal{LR} = \sum_{l=1}^{L-1} \frac{|S_\mathcal{S} - \overline{\mathcal{I}}(\mathcal{S}:\mathcal{F}_l)|}{S_\mathcal{S}}. \tag{12}$$

This constitutes the measure of objectivity that we will use from now on. We remark that different measures have also been previously used in the literature to quantify redundancy [20,21], but the one proposed in this work is more reliable for comparing environments with slightly different sizes. This is due to the fact that given the fractional nature of the fragment size ($f = l/L$), the possible set of values that f can take is different depending on the particular size of the chain.

3. Darwinism, MBL and Interactions

In this section, we present our main results that shed light on the relationship between disorder and QD. As a first illustrative example to clarify the definitions of the previous section, we start by plotting in Figure 1 the rescaled averaged mutual information $\overline{\mathcal{I}}(\mathcal{S}:\mathcal{F}_l)/S_\mathcal{S}$ as a function of the size of the environmental fragment for an environment composed of $L = 14$ spins. Additionally, in the same plot we show the averaged lack of redundancy $\mathcal{LR}$ as a blue light (dark) filled area in the case with low (high) disorder. It is important to point out that in this simulation the intra-environment interactions are completely neglected in the evolution by setting $\lambda = 0$. Hence, disorder only comes into play in the particular eigenstate of the environment that is taken as an initial state for the spins of the environment (see Equation (5)).

From Figure 1 we can notice that the presence of high disorder seems to enhance the emergence of objectivity, leading to a better plateau in the averaged mutual information shared between the system and the environment. Beyond this qualitative result, it is well-known that in disordered spin chains, such as our environmental model, the degree of disorder is strictly related to the localization of the system. In particular, if the disorder is weak enough the system is ergodic and its eigenstates are highly entangled. On the contrary, as the degree of disorder increases, the system reaches a localized phase and its eigenstates exhibit much less entanglement. Taking into account this fact, in what follows we will delve into the qualitative result obtained in Figure 1. To do so, in the following subsection we will perform a systematic analysis exploring the role that the localization in the initial state of the environment plays in its capability of enabling redundancy.

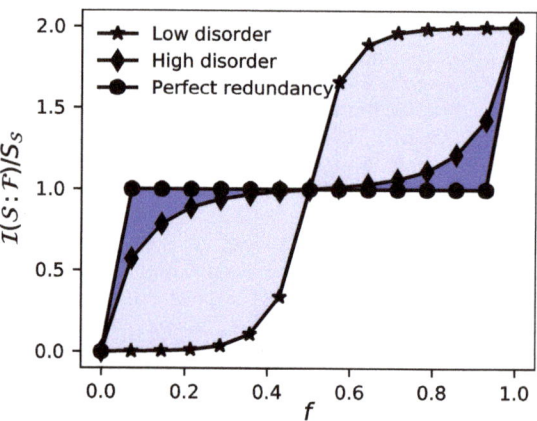

Figure 1. Rescaled averaged mutual information $\overline{\mathcal{I}}(\mathcal{S}:\mathcal{F})/S_\mathcal{S}$ as a function of the environmental fragment size f for an environment composed of $L=14$ spins. Given a fixed environmental size and disorder strength, the filled area between perfect redundancy and the averaged mutual information obtained constitutes the lack of redundancy ($\mathcal{LR}$) and our measure of objectivity. The parameters are set as $\epsilon = 0.5$, $t = \pi/4$, $\lambda = 0$, $h = 0.01$ for low disorder and $h = 5.0$ for high disorder. In both situations, 1000 realizations for different sets of $\{h_z^{(k)}\} \in [-h,h]$ were considered.

3.1. Localization in the Initial State

To further explore how the localization in the initial state of the environment influences the emergence of QD, we will now focus on the half-chain entanglement entropy $S_E = -\text{Tr}_A(\hat{\rho}_A \ln \hat{\rho}_A)$ of the reduced density matrix of the environment $\hat{\rho}_A = \text{Tr}_B|\xi\rangle\langle\xi|$, where the traces are over the left and right half-chain Hilbert spaces, respectively, and $|\xi\rangle$ is an eigenstate of $\hat{H}_E$. In the localized regime, the reduced density matrix $\hat{\rho}_A$ of a typical eigenstate $|\xi\rangle$ possesses low entanglement entropy and an area-law scaling. Conversely, in a chaotic regime satisfying ETH, eigenstates are highly entangled and exhibit a volume-law scaling. Thereby, it is possible to distinguish both regimes by analyzing the scaling behavior of S_E. To do so, in Figure 2 we plot the entanglement entropy per site S_E/L (lower panel), together with the lack of redundancy $\mathcal{LR}$ (upper panel), as a function of the disorder strength h for different environmental sizes. As before, we restrict ourselves to the zero magnetization sector and entirely focus on the eigenstate $|\xi\rangle_\epsilon$, i.e., the one with energy closest to the normalized target ϵ in each disorder realization. Once again, for computing $\mathcal{LR}$, we neglect the influence of the internal dynamics of the environment in the evolution by setting $\lambda = 0$.

The first conclusion we can extract from Figure 2 is that both $\mathcal{LR}$ and S_E/L exhibit a similar behavior as a function of disorder. In particular, we can observe that if the disorder strength h is lower than a critical value h_c, both $\mathcal{LR}$ and S_E/L increase with increasing L. On the contrary, if $h > h_c$ the behavior of both quantities is the opposite. What does this mean in terms of QD? Interestingly, this means that there is a critical value of disorder beyond which the degree of objectivity rises the larger the environment is. We emphasize that this critical value of h_c has been estimated by looking at the intersection between the two curves of largest dimension (see inset in the upper panel of Figure 2).

To provide further insight about this transition, we perform a finite size scaling analysis by collapsing all the data to the form $g[L^{1/\nu}(h-h_c)]$, similarly to what was done by previous works dealing with the same disordered quantum system [43,45]. The results of the scaling are shown in Figure 3. In particular, in the lower panel we can see that the transition is characterized by a change in the entanglement entropy scaling from an area law for $h > h_c$ (where $S_E/L \to 0$) to a volume law for $h < h_c$ (where $S_E/L \to$ constant). As was claimed before, the same scaling behavior is observed for the lack of redundancy $\mathcal{LR}$, as we show in the upper panel of Figure 3.

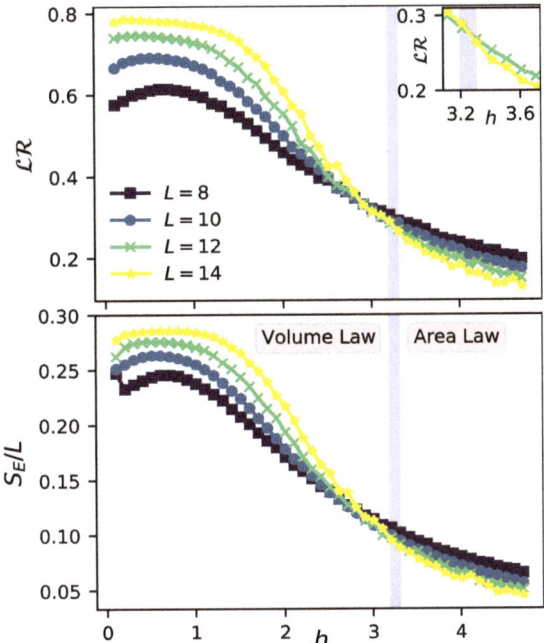

Figure 2. Upper panel: Lack of redundancy $\mathcal{LR}$ for different environmental sizes as a function of the disorder strength h. Inset: Zoom into the transition of $\mathcal{LR}$, signaled by the intersection between the two curves with the largest environmental size. The parameters are set as $\epsilon = 0.5$, $t = \pi/4$ and $\lambda = 0$. **Lower panel**: Entanglement entropy per site S_E/L of a single eigenstate of $\hat{H}_E$ ($|\xi\rangle_{\epsilon=0.5}$) for different environmental sizes as a function of the disorder strength h. A crossover between a volume and area law is observed for a critical disorder $h_c \simeq 3.2$ (blue separation). In both panels, all curves are averaged over at least 1000 different realizations of disorder.

Despite that in this first part we have shown a close relationship between the entanglement of the initial state of the environment and its capability of enabling redundancy, it is important to notice that until now we have restricted entirely to the middle of the spectrum by considering the eigenstate with energy closest to $\epsilon = 0.5$. However, the value of the critical disorder h_c depends on the energy under consideration, which determines what is called a many-body mobility edge [40–47,50,51]. For this reason, it is worthy to study how our Darwinistic measure $\mathcal{LR}$ behaves when considering different eigenstates of $\hat{H}_E$ as initial states. This is precisely what is shown in Figure 4, where we compare our measure of objectivity $\mathcal{LR}$ with the entanglement entropy S_E in the same region of parameters set both by h and ϵ.

Once again, it is clear that both quantities exhibit almost the same structure, which means that a low S_E in the initial state of the environment implies a better capacity to store redundant information and thus greater objectivity. Thereby, taking into account that the region of low entanglement is always linked to a high degree of disorder, we can conclude that disorder is beneficial for the emergence of QD. As a complement, in both panels of Figure 4 we have estimated the many-body mobility edge with the same procedure followed before for $\epsilon = 0.5$, finding a very good agreement between both measures. This mobility edge is shown with black squares for $\mathcal{LR}$ and with black diamonds for S_E.

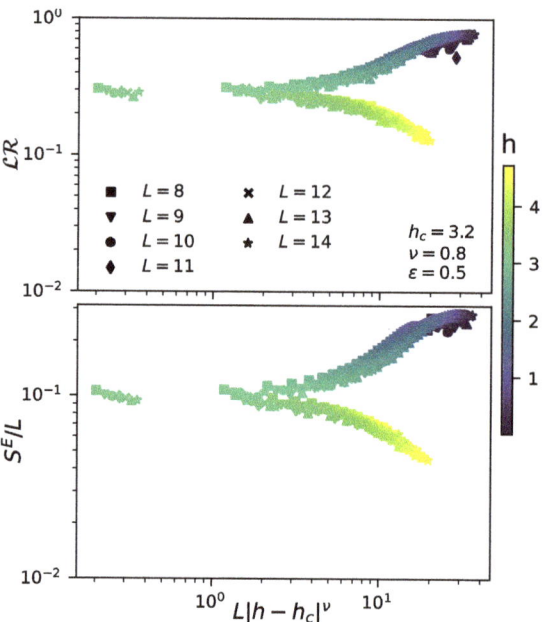

Figure 3. Upper panel: Lack of redundancy $\mathcal{LR}$ as a function of $L|h-h_c|^\nu$. The parameters are set as $\epsilon = 0.5$, $t = \pi/4$ and $\lambda = 0$. **Lower panel**: Entanglement entropy per site S_E/L of a single eigenstate of $\hat{H}_E$ ($|\xi\rangle_{\epsilon=0.5}$) as a function of $L|h-h_c|^\nu$. For weak disorder, there is a volume-law scaling that leads to a constant S_E/L, while for strong disorder we have an area law characterized by a decreasing S_E/L. For the odd-sized chains, only the subspace $\hat{S}_1$ was considered. All curves are averaged over at least 1000 different realizations of disorder.

After all the simulations shown in this subsection, we can conjecture that the reason why objectivity is boosted by using an eigenstate of a highly disordered environment as initial state, is strictly related to the low entanglement that eigenstates have in the MBL phase. This low entanglement enables each environmental fragment to store more information about the system since its initial state is much closer to a pure state. On the contrary, if the disorder is too low, eigenstates are highly entangled due to the ergodic nature of the system and consequently the initial state of each fragment is much nearer to a maximally mixed state. In this situation, the storing of information is shrunk and redundancy cannot be achieved.

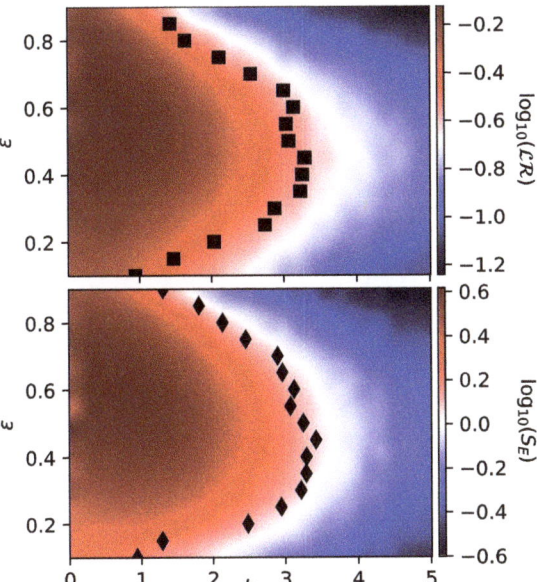

Figure 4. **Upper panel**: Lack of redundancy $\mathcal{LR}$ as a function of the disorder strength h for different eigenstates with energy ϵ taken as initial states. Since this quantity is much harder to calculate, a smaller environment of $L = 12$ was considered. The black squares refer to the critical values of h_c, that were estimated by looking at the intersection between the data obtained for $L = 12$ and $L = 10$, respectively. Parameters are set as $t = \pi/4, \lambda = 0$. **Lower panel**: Entanglement entropy S_E as a function of the disorder strength h and for different eigenstates of $\hat{H}_E$ with normalized energies ϵ (i.e., $|\xi\rangle_\epsilon$). An environment composed of $L = 14$ was considered in this case. The black diamonds refer to the critical values of h_c that were estimated by looking at the intersection between the data obtained for $L = 14$ and $L = 12$, respectively. Both panels are averaged over 1000 different realizations of disorder.

3.2. Influence of Intra-Environment Interaction

A key point that we have not analyzed yet is the following: what if we allow a mixing of the bath records by setting $\lambda \neq 0$ in the evolution? Based on our previous analysis, we already know that the initial states of the environment belonging to the ergodic regime are incapable of storing redundant information and thus of enabling objectivity. On the contrary, how robust are the MBL initial states to the mixing due to the internal dynamics of the environment? Is it still possible to distinguish both regimes in the presence of this effect? To address these questions, we will first take as initial state an eigenstate of the environment with a given disorder h and energy ϵ, evolve the system with the same amount of disorder (i.e., $\hat{H}_{int} + \lambda \hat{H}_E|_h$) and finally average over several realizations. The results of this analysis are shown in Figure 5, where we plot $\mathcal{LR}$ for different values of λ (the parameter that regulates the influence of the intra-environment interactions in the evolution).

For instance, in the upper panel of Figure 5, where we set $\lambda = 0.3$, we can observe that the same structure obtained before for $\lambda = 0$ holds. Despite that the degree of objectivity is slightly worsened in this case for the MBL region, we can still distinguish the ergodic from the localized regime by means of our Darwinistic measure. Additionally, in the lower panel of Figure 5 we show how the lack of redundancy behaves for different values of λ as a function of the disorder strength h. It is clear from here that for weak disorder the intra-environment interactions have no influence at all on the redundancy. This is not surprising given that even in the case of $\lambda = 0$ objectivity was not possible in this region. On the contrary, as the amount of disorder increases and we approach the MBL regime, the influence of the intra-environment dynamics is more notorious and we can appreciate how objectivity is slightly spoiled as λ increases.

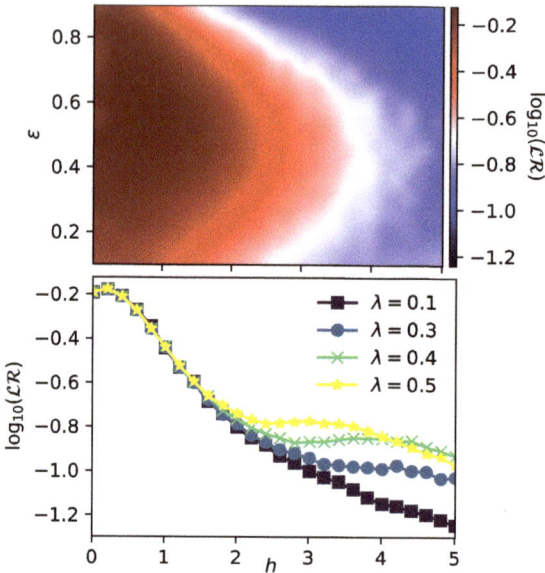

Figure 5. **Upper panel**: Lack of redundancy $\mathcal{LR}$ as a function of the disorder strength h and using as initial states different eigenstates with energy ϵ. In this panel, parameters are set as $L = 12$, $t = \pi/4$ and $\lambda = 0.3$. **Lower panel**: Lack of redundancy $\mathcal{LR}$ as a function of the disorder strength h for different values of λ. In this panel, parameters are set as $L = 12$, $t = \pi/4$ and $\epsilon = 0.9$. In both panels, 1000 different realizations of disorder were considered.

Finally, let us now restrict ourselves to the most favorable situation by fixing the initial state of the environment as a MBL eigenstate. Unlike our previous analysis, we will now evolve the same highly localized initial state with different amounts of disorder. Is the internal dynamics of a highly disordered environment still advantageous in this situation? To address this important question, in Figure 6 we show the results of a simulation where we fix the initial state of the environment as $|\xi\rangle\,|_{h=5.0,\epsilon=0.5}$ and then evolve the entire system considering different values of disorder strength, $(\hat{H}_{int} + \lambda \hat{H}_E\,|_{h'})$. From this simulation we can conclude that the presence of disorder is still beneficial for the appearance of objectivity, even in the presence of intra-environment interactions and independently of the initial state under consideration.

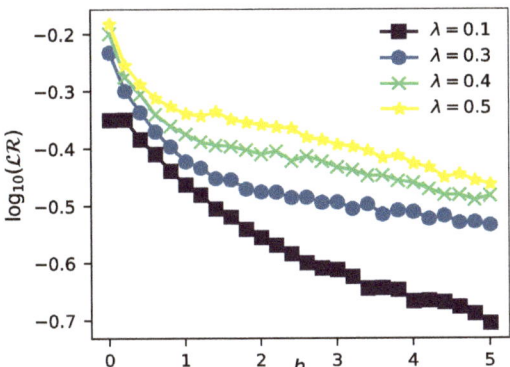

Figure 6. Lack of redundancy $\mathcal{LR}$ as a function of the disorder strength h for different values of λ. Parameters are set as $L = 10$, $t = \pi$ and the initial state of the environment is always fixed as $|\xi\rangle|_{h=5.0, \epsilon=0.5}$. As usual, 1000 different realizations of disorder were considered.

4. Conclusions

The theory of QD studies how classical objectivity emerges from a quantum realm. It poses that besides washing out the coherences of the open quantum system to which it is coupled, the environment also acts as an active witness by redundantly storing the information about the system's state. Hence, independent observers can reach consensus on the actual state of the system by measuring separate environmental fragments. Based on the intuition that in a realistic scenario a many-body environment should exhibit some degree of disorder, in this work we have explored the role that this disorder plays in the emergence of QD.

By modeling the environment as a 1D disordered spin chain, we have found that a high degree of disorder is greatly beneficial for the emergence of classical objectivity. We have shown that this is a consequence of the low entanglement that the eigenstates of the environment, which are taken as the initial states, exhibit in the localized regime. This enables each individual fragment to store a greater amount of redundant information, in comparison to the highly entangled environmental eigenstates that belong to the ergodic regime at low disorder. In particular, we have shown that the EE of the initial state not only exhibits the same structure as the lack of redundancy but also shares the same scaling behavior. This fact allowed us to estimate the many-body mobility edge by means of our Darwinistic measure, yielding a consistent agreement in comparison to the EE. In regards to QD, this result means that if the degree of disorder is higher (lower) than a critical value, the redundancy increases (decreases) the larger the environment is. Therefore, our findings evidence the important role that disorder can play in a realistic situation where the environment is of a thermodynamic size.

In addition, we have analyzed the mixing of the redundant records by allowing intra-environment interactions. Despite that low disorder is associated to an ergodic dynamics and ergodicity usually yields to a markovian evolution [15], we have found that a highly disordered evolution is less harmful for the appearance of classical objectivity. Hence, a high amount of disorder is not only beneficial for the initial state under consideration; it also reduces the mixing of the redundant records in the presence of intra-environment interactions. At last, we sincerely hope our findings shed new light on how classical objectivity emerges from a quantum world and we look forward to the possibility of implementing our ideas on some of the experimental platforms recently used in the study of the MBL transition [47].

Author Contributions: All authors contributed equally to this work. All authors have read and agreed to the published version of the manuscript.

Funding: The work was partially supported by CONICET (PIP 112201 50100493CO), UBACyT (20020130100406BA) and ANPCyT (PICT-2016-1056).

Institutional Review Board Statement: Not applicable.

Informed Consent Statement: Not applicable.

Data Availability Statement: Not applicable.

Conflicts of Interest: The authors declare no conflict of interest.

References

1. Breuer, H.P.; Petruccione, F. *The Theory of Open Quantum Systems*; Oxford University Press on Demand: Oxford, UK, 2002.
2. Zurek, W.H. Decoherence, einselection, and the quantum origins of the classical. *Rev. Mod. Phys.* **2003**, *75*, 715. [CrossRef]
3. Schlosshauer, M. Decoherence, the measurement problem, and interpretations of quantum mechanics. *Rev. Mod. Phys.* **2005**, *76*, 1267. [CrossRef]
4. Schlosshauer, M.A. *Decoherence: And the Quantum-to-Classical Transition*; Springer Science & Business Media: Berlin/Heidelberg, Germany, 2007.
5. Ollivier, H.; Poulin, D.; Zurek, W.H. Objective properties from subjective quantum states: Environment as a witness. *Phys. Rev. Lett.* **2004**, *93*, 220401. [CrossRef]
6. Ollivier, H.; Poulin, D.; Zurek, W.H. Environment as a witness: Selective proliferation of information and emergence of objectivity in a quantum universe. *Phys. Rev. A* **2005**, *72*, 042113. [CrossRef]
7. Blume-Kohout, R.; Zurek, W.H. A simple example of "Quantum Darwinism": Redundant information storage in many-spin environments. *Found. Phys.* **2005**, *35*, 1857–1876. [CrossRef]
8. Zurek, W.H. Quantum darwinism. *Nat. Phys.* **2009**, *5*, 181–188. [CrossRef]
9. Paz, J.P.; Roncaglia, A.J. Redundancy of classical and quantum correlations during decoherence. *Phys. Rev. A* **2009**, *80*, 042111. [CrossRef]
10. Brandao, F.G.; Piani, M.; Horodecki, P. Generic emergence of classical features in quantum Darwinism. *Nat. Commun.* **2015**, *6*, 1–8. [CrossRef] [PubMed]
11. García-Pérez, G.; Chisholm, D.A.; Rossi, M.A.; Palma, G.M.; Maniscalco, S. Decoherence without entanglement and quantum darwinism. *Phys. Rev. Res.* **2020**, *2*, 012061. [CrossRef]
12. Zurek, W.H. Emergence of the Classical from within the Quantum Universe. *arXiv* **2021**, arXiv:2107.03378.
13. Touil, A.; Yan, B.; Girolami, D.; Deffner, S.; Zurek, W.H. Eavesdropping on the Decohering Environment: Quantum Darwinism, Amplification, and the Origin of Objective Classical Reality. *arXiv* **2021**, arXiv:2107.00035.
14. Mirkin, N.; Wisniacki, D. Quantum chaos, equilibration, and control in extremely short spin chains. *Phys. Rev. E* **2021**, *103*, L020201. [CrossRef]
15. Mirkin, N.; Wisniacki, D.; Villar, P.I.; Lombardo, F.C. Sensing quantum chaos through the non-unitary geometric phase. *arXiv* **2021**, arXiv:2104.06367.
16. Giorgi, G.L.; Galve, F.; Zambrini, R. Quantum Darwinism and non-Markovian dissipative dynamics from quantum phases of the spin-1/2 X X model. *Phys. Rev. A* **2015**, *92*, 022105. [CrossRef]
17. Galve, F.; Zambrini, R.; Maniscalco, S. Non-markovianity hinders quantum darwinism. *Sci. Rep.* **2016**, *6*, 1–7. [CrossRef]
18. Pleasance, G.; Garraway, B.M. Application of quantum Darwinism to a structured environment. *Phys. Rev. A* **2017**, *96*, 062105. [CrossRef]
19. Milazzo, N.; Lorenzo, S.; Paternostro, M.; Palma, G.M. Role of information backflow in the emergence of quantum Darwinism. *Phys. Rev. A* **2019**, *100*, 012101. [CrossRef]
20. Zwolak, M.; Quan, H.; Zurek, W.H. Quantum Darwinism in a mixed environment. *Phys. Rev. Lett.* **2009**, *103*, 110402. [CrossRef] [PubMed]
21. Zwolak, M.; Quan, H.; Zurek, W.H. Redundant imprinting of information in nonideal environments: Objective reality via a noisy channel. *Phys. Rev. A* **2010**, *81*, 062110. [CrossRef]
22. Balanesković, N. Random unitary evolution model of quantum Darwinism with pure decoherence. *Eur. Phys. J. D* **2015**, *69*, 1–17. [CrossRef]
23. Campbell, S.; Çakmak, B.; Müstecaplıoğlu, Ö.E.; Paternostro, M.; Vacchini, B. Collisional unfolding of quantum Darwinism. *Phys. Rev. A* **2019**, *99*, 042103. [CrossRef]
24. Ryan, E.; Paternostro, M.; Campbell, S. Quantum Darwinism in a structured spin environment. *arXiv* **2020**, arXiv:2011.13385.
25. Lorenzo, S.; Paternostro, M.; Palma, G.M. Anti-Zeno-based dynamical control of the unfolding of quantum Darwinism. *Phys. Rev. Res.* **2020**, *2*, 013164. [CrossRef]
26. Le, T.P.; Winter, A.; Adesso, G. Thermality versus objectivity: can they peacefully coexist? *arXiv* **2021**, arXiv:2109.13265.
27. Çakmak, B.; Müstecaplıoğlu, Ö.E.; Paternostro, M.; Vacchini, B.; Campbell, S. Quantum Darwinism in a composite system: Objectivity versus classicality. *Entropy* **2021**, *23*, 995. [CrossRef] [PubMed]
28. Horodecki, R.; Korbicz, J.; Horodecki, P. Quantum origins of objectivity. *Phys. Rev. A* **2015**, *91*, 032122. [CrossRef]

29. Lampo, A.; Tuziemski, J.; Lewenstein, M.; Korbicz, J.K. Objectivity in the non-Markovian spin-boson model. *Phys. Rev. A* **2017**, *96*, 012120. [CrossRef]
30. Le, T.P.; Olaya-Castro, A. Objectivity (or lack thereof): Comparison between predictions of quantum Darwinism and spectrum broadcast structure. *Phys. Rev. A* **2018**, *98*, 032103. [CrossRef]
31. Le, T.P.; Olaya-Castro, A. Strong quantum darwinism and strong independence are equivalent to spectrum broadcast structure. *Phys. Rev. Lett.* **2019**, *122*, 010403. [CrossRef]
32. Korbicz, J. Roads to objectivity: Quantum darwinism, spectrum broadcast structures, and strong quantum darwinism. *arXiv* **2020**, arXiv:2007.04276.
33. Le, T.P.; Olaya-Castro, A. Witnessing non-objectivity in the framework of strong quantum Darwinism. *Quantum Sci. Technol.* **2020**, *5*, 045012. [CrossRef]
34. Ciampini, M.A.; Pinna, G.; Mataloni, P.; Paternostro, M. Experimental signature of quantum Darwinism in photonic cluster states. *Phys. Rev. A* **2018**, *98*, 020101. [CrossRef]
35. Chen, M.C.; Zhong, H.S.; Li, Y.; Wu, D.; Wang, X.L.; Li, L.; Liu, N.L.; Lu, C.Y.; Pan, J.W. Emergence of classical objectivity of quantum Darwinism in a photonic quantum simulator. *Sci. Bull.* **2019**, *64*, 580–585. [CrossRef]
36. Unden, T.K.; Louzon, D.; Zwolak, M.; Zurek, W.H.; Jelezko, F. Revealing the emergence of classicality using nitrogen-vacancy centers. *Phys. Rev. Lett.* **2019**, *123*, 140402. [CrossRef]
37. Chisholm, D.A.; García-Pérez, G.; Rossi, M.A.C.; Maniscalco, S.; Palma, G.M. Witnessing Objectivity on a Quantum Computer. *arXiv* **2021**, arXiv:2110.06243.
38. Avishai, Y.; Richert, J.; Berkovits, R. Level statistics in a Heisenberg chain with random magnetic field. *Phys. Rev. B* **2002**, *66*, 052416. [CrossRef]
39. Santos, L. Integrability of a disordered Heisenberg spin-1/2 chain. *J. Phys. Math. Gen.* **2004**, *37*, 4723. [CrossRef]
40. Žnidarič, M.; Prosen, T.; Prelovšek, P. Many-body localization in the heisenberg x x z magnet in a random field. *Phys. Rev. B* **2008**, *77*, 064426. [CrossRef]
41. Pal, A.; Huse, D.A. Many-body localization phase transition. *Phys. Rev. B* **2010**, *82*, 174411. [CrossRef]
42. De Luca, A.; Scardicchio, A. Ergodicity breaking in a model showing many-body localization. *EPL (Europhys. Lett.)* **2013**, *101*, 37003. [CrossRef]
43. Luitz, D.J.; Laflorencie, N.; Alet, F. Many-body localization edge in the random-field Heisenberg chain. *Phys. Rev. B* **2015**, *91*, 081103. [CrossRef]
44. Solórzano, A.; Santos, L.F.; Torres-Herrera, E.J. Multifractality and self-averaging at the many-body localization transition. *arXiv* **2021**, arXiv:2102.02824.
45. Alet, F.; Laflorencie, N. Many-body localization: An introduction and selected topics. *Comptes Rendus Phys.* **2018**, *19*, 498–525. [CrossRef]
46. Gong, M.; de Moraes Neto, G.D.; Zha, C.; Wu, Y.; Rong, H.; Ye, Y.; Li, S.; Zhu, Q.; Wang, S.; Zhao, Y.; et al. Experimental characterization of the quantum many-body localization transition. *Phys. Rev. Res.* **2021**, *3*, 033043. [CrossRef]
47. Guo, Q.; Cheng, C.; Sun, Z.H.; Song, Z.; Li, H.; Wang, Z.; Ren, W.; Dong, H.; Zheng, D.; Zhang, Y.R.; et al. Observation of energy-resolved many-body localization. *Nat. Phys.* **2021**, *17*, 234–239. [CrossRef]
48. Riedel, C.J.; Zurek, W.H.; Zwolak, M. The rise and fall of redundancy in decoherence and quantum Darwinism. *New J. Phys.* **2012**, *14*, 083010. [CrossRef]
49. Stöckmann, H.J. *Quantum Chaos: An Introduction*; American Association of Physics Teachers: College Park, MD, USA, 2000.
50. Kjäll, J.A.; Bardarson, J.H.; Pollmann, F. Many-body localization in a disordered quantum Ising chain. *Phys. Rev. Lett.* **2014**, *113*, 107204. [CrossRef] [PubMed]
51. Zhang, L.; Ke, Y.; Liu, W.; Lee, C. Mobility edge of Stark many-body localization. *Phys. Rev. A* **2021**, *103*, 023323. [CrossRef]

Article

Environment-Assisted Shortcuts to Adiabaticity

Akram Touil [1,*] and Sebastian Deffner [1,2]

1. Department of Physics, University of Maryland, Baltimore County, Baltimore, MD 21250, USA; deffner@umbc.edu
2. Instituto de Física 'Gleb Wataghin', Universidade Estadual de Campinas, Campinas, São Paulo 13083-859, Brazil
* Correspondence: akramt1@umbc.edu

Abstract: Envariance is a symmetry exhibited by correlated quantum systems. Inspired by this "quantum fact of life," we propose a novel method for shortcuts to adiabaticity, which enables the system to evolve through the adiabatic manifold at all times, solely by controlling the environment. As the main results, we construct the unique form of the driving on the environment that enables such dynamics, for a family of composite states of arbitrary dimension. We compare the cost of this environment-assisted technique with that of counterdiabatic driving, and we illustrate our results for a two-qubit model.

Keywords: shortcuts to adiabaticity; counterdiabatic driving; envariance; branching states

1. Introduction

An essential step in the development of viable quantum technologies is to achieve precise control over quantum dynamics [1,2]. In many situations, optimal performance relies on the ability to create particular target states. However, in dynamically reaching such states, the quantum adiabatic theorem [3] poses a formidable challenge since finite-time driving inevitably causes parasitic excitations [4–7]. Acknowledging and addressing this issue, the field of "shortcuts to adiabaticity" (STA) [8–11] has developed a variety of techniques that permit to facilitate effectively adiabatic dynamics in finite time.

Recent years have seen an explosion of work on, for instance, counterdiabatic driving [12–19], the fast-forward method [20–23], time-rescaling [24,25], methods based on identifying the adiabatic invariant [26–29], and even generalizations to classical dynamics [30–32]. For comprehensive reviews of the various techniques, we refer to the recent literature [9–11].

Among these different paradigms, counterdiabatic driving (CD) stands out, as it is the only method that forces evolution through the adiabatic manifold at all times. However, experimentally realizing the CD method requires applying a complicated control field, which often involves non-local terms that are hard to implement in many-body systems [15,17]. This may be particularly challenging if the system is not readily accessible, due to, for instance, geometric restrictions of the experimental set-up.

In the present paper, we propose an alternative method to achieve transitionless quantum driving by leveraging the system's (realistically) inevitable interaction with the environment. Our novel paradigm is inspired by "envariance," which is short for entanglement-assisted invariance. Envariance is a symmetry of composite quantum systems, first described by Wojciech H. Zurek [33]. Consider a quantum state $|\psi_{\mathcal{SE}}\rangle$ that lives on a composite quantum universe comprising the system, $\mathcal{S}$, and its environment, $\mathcal{E}$. Then, $|\psi_{\mathcal{SE}}\rangle$ is called envariant under a unitary map $u_{\mathcal{S}} \otimes \mathbb{I}_{\mathcal{E}}$ if and only if there exists another unitary $\mathbb{I}_{\mathcal{S}} \otimes u_{\mathcal{E}}$ acting on $\mathcal{E}$ such that the composite state remains unaltered after applying both maps, i.e., $(u_{\mathcal{S}} \otimes \mathbb{I}_{\mathcal{E}})|\psi_{\mathcal{SE}}\rangle = |\phi_{\mathcal{SE}}\rangle$ and $(\mathbb{I}_{\mathcal{S}} \otimes u_{\mathcal{E}})|\phi_{\mathcal{SE}}\rangle = |\psi_{\mathcal{SE}}\rangle$. In other words, the state is envariant if the action of a unitary on $\mathcal{S}$ can be inverted by applying a unitary on $\mathcal{E}$.

Citation: Touil, A.; Deffner, S. Environment-Assisted Shortcuts to Adiabaticity. *Entropy* **2021**, *23*, 1479. https://doi.org/10.3390/e23111479

Academic Editor: Ronnie Kosloff

Received: 16 October 2021
Accepted: 5 November 2021
Published: 9 November 2021

Publisher's Note: MDPI stays neutral with regard to jurisdictional claims in published maps and institutional affiliations.

Copyright: © 2021 by the authors. Licensee MDPI, Basel, Switzerland. This article is an open access article distributed under the terms and conditions of the Creative Commons Attribution (CC BY) license (https://creativecommons.org/licenses/by/4.0/).

Envariance was essential to derive Born's rule [33,34], and in formulating a novel approach to the foundations of statistical mechanics [35]. Moreover, experiments [36,37] showed that this inherent symmetry of composite quantum states is indeed a physical reality, or rather a "quantum fact of life" with no classical analog [34]. Drawing inspiration from envariance, we develop a novel method for transitionless quantum driving. In the following, we will see that instead of inverting the action of a unitary on $\mathcal{S}$, we can suppress undesirable transitions in the energy eigenbasis of $\mathcal{S}$ by applying a control field on the environment $\mathcal{E}$. In particular, we consider the unitary evolution of an ensemble of composite states $\{|\psi_{\mathcal{SE}}\rangle\}$ on a Hilbert space $\mathcal{H}_{\mathcal{S}} \otimes \mathcal{H}_{\mathcal{E}}$ of arbitrary dimension, and we determine the general analytic form of the time-dependent driving on $\mathcal{H}_{\mathcal{E}}$, which suppresses undesirable transitions in the system of interest $\mathcal{S}$. This general driving on the environment $\mathcal{E}$ guarantees that the system $\mathcal{S}$ evolves through the adiabatic manifold at all times. We dub this technique environment-assisted shortcuts to adiabaticity, or "EASTA" for short. In addition, we prove that the cost associated with the EASTA technique is exactly equal to that of counterdiabatic driving. We illustrate our results in a simple two-qubit model, where the system and the environment are each described by a single qubit. Finally, we conclude with discussing a few implications of our results in the general context of decoherence theory and quantum Darwinism.

2. Counterdiabatic Driving

We start by briefly reviewing counterdiabatic driving to establish notions and notations. Consider a quantum system $\mathcal{S}$, in a Hilbert space $\mathcal{H}_{\mathcal{S}}$ of dimension $d_{\mathcal{S}}$, driven by the Hamiltonian $H_0(t)$ with instantaneous eigenvalues $\{E_n(t)\}_{n\in[\![0,\,d_{\mathcal{S}}-1]\!]}$ and eigenstates $\{|n(t)\rangle\}_{n\in[\![0,\,d_{\mathcal{S}}-1]\!]}$. For slowly varying $H_0(t)$, according to the quantum adiabatic theorem [3], the driving of $\mathcal{S}$ is transitionless. In other words, if the system starts in the eigenstate $|n(0)\rangle$, at $t=0$, it evolves into the eigenstate $|n(t)\rangle$ at time t (with a phase factor) as follows:

$$|\psi_n(t)\rangle \equiv U(t)|n(0)\rangle = e^{-\frac{i}{\hbar}\int_0^t E_n(s)ds - \int_0^t \langle n|\partial_s n\rangle ds}|n(t)\rangle \equiv e^{-\frac{i}{\hbar}f_n(t)}|n(t)\rangle. \qquad (1)$$

For arbitrary driving $H_0(t)$, namely for driving rates larger than the typical energy gaps, the system undergoes transitions. However, it was shown [12–14] that the addition of a counterdiabatic field $H_{\text{CD}}(t)$ forces the system to evolve through the adiabatic manifold. Using the following total Hamiltonian,

$$H = H_0(t) + H_{\text{CD}}(t) = H_0(t) + i\hbar \sum_n (|\partial_t n\rangle\langle n| - \langle n|\partial_t n\rangle|n\rangle\langle n|), \qquad (2)$$

the system evolves with the corresponding unitary $U_{\text{CD}}(t) = \sum_n |\psi_n(t)\rangle\langle n(0)|$ such that the following holds:

$$U_{\text{CD}}(t)|n(0)\rangle = e^{-\frac{i}{\hbar}f_n(t)}|n(t)\rangle. \qquad (3)$$

This evolution is exact no matter how fast the system is driven by the total Hamiltonian. However, the counterdiabatic driving (CD) method requires adding a complicated counterdiabatic field $H_{\text{CD}}(t)$ involving highly non-local terms that are hard to implement in a many-body set-up [15,17]. Constructing this counterdiabatic field requires determining the instantaneous eigenstates $\{|n(t)\rangle\}_{n\in[\![0,\,d_{\mathcal{S}}-1]\!]}$ of the time-dependent Hamiltonian $H_0(t)$. Moreover, changing the dynamics of the system of interest (i.e., adding the counterdiabatic field) requires direct access and control on $\mathcal{S}$.

In the following, we will see how (at least) the second issue can be circumvented by relying on the environment $\mathcal{E}$ that inevitably couples to the system of interest. In particular, we make use of the entanglement between system and environment to avoid any transitions in the system. To this end, we construct the unique driving of the environment $\mathcal{E}$ that counteracts the transitions in $\mathcal{S}$.

3. Open System Dynamics and STA for Mixed States

We start by stating three crucial assumptions: (i) the joint state of the system $\mathcal{S}$ and the environment $\mathcal{E}$ is described by an initial wave function $|\psi_{\mathcal{SE}}(0)\rangle$ evolving unitarily, according to the Schrödinger equation; (ii) the environment's degrees of freedom do not interact with each other; (iii) the $\mathcal{S}$-$\mathcal{E}$ joint state belongs to the ensemble of singly branching states [38]. These branching states have the following general form:

$$|\psi_{\mathcal{SE}}\rangle = \sum_{n=0}^{N-1} \sqrt{p_n} |n\rangle \bigotimes_{l=1}^{N_{\mathcal{E}}} |\mathcal{E}_n^l\rangle, \tag{4}$$

where $p_n \in [0, 1]$ is the probability associated with the nth branch of the wave function, with orthonormal states $|n\rangle \in \mathcal{H}_{\mathcal{S}}$ and $\bigotimes_{l=1}^{N_{\mathcal{E}}} |\mathcal{E}_n^l\rangle \in \mathcal{H}_{\mathcal{E}}$.

Without loss of generality, we can further assume $\sqrt{p_n} = 1/\sqrt{N}$ for all $n \in [\![0, N-1]\!]$ since if $\sqrt{p_n} \neq 1/\sqrt{N}$ we can always find an extended Hilbert space [33,34] such that the state $|\psi_{\mathcal{SE}}\rangle$ becomes even. Thus, we can consider branching states $|\psi_{\mathcal{SE}}\rangle$ of the simpler form as follows:

$$|\psi_{\mathcal{SE}}\rangle = \frac{1}{\sqrt{N}} \sum_{n=0}^{N-1} |n\rangle \bigotimes_{l=1}^{N_{\mathcal{E}}} |\mathcal{E}_n^l\rangle. \tag{5}$$

In the following, we will see that EASTA can actually only be facilitated for even states (5). In Appendix B, we show that EASTA cannot be implemented for arbitrary probabilities (i.e., $(\exists\, n);\ \sqrt{p_n} \neq 1/\sqrt{N}$).

3.1. Two-Level Environment $\mathcal{E}$

We start with the instructive case of a two-level environment, cf. Figure 1. To this end, consider the following branching state:

$$|\psi_{\mathcal{SE}}(0)\rangle = \frac{1}{\sqrt{2}} |g(0)\rangle \otimes |\mathcal{E}_g(0)\rangle + \frac{1}{\sqrt{2}} |e(0)\rangle \otimes |\mathcal{E}_e(0)\rangle, \tag{6}$$

where the states $|\mathcal{E}_g(0)\rangle$ and $|\mathcal{E}_e(0)\rangle$ form a basis on the environment $\mathcal{E}$, and the states $|g(0)\rangle$ and $|e(0)\rangle$ represent the ground and excited states of $\mathcal{S}$ at $t = 0$, respectively.

It is then easy to see that there exists a unique unitary U' such that the system evolves through the adiabatic manifold in each branch of the wave function as follows:

$$(\exists!\, U');\ (U \otimes U')|\psi_{\mathcal{SE}}(0)\rangle = (U_{\text{CD}} \otimes \mathbb{I}_{\mathcal{E}})|\psi_{\mathcal{SE}}(0)\rangle. \tag{7}$$

Starting from the above equality, we obtain the following:

$$U|g(0)\rangle \otimes U'|\mathcal{E}_g(0)\rangle + U|e(0)\rangle \otimes U'|\mathcal{E}_e(0)\rangle = e^{-\frac{i}{\hbar}f_g(t)}|g(t)\rangle \otimes |\mathcal{E}_g(0)\rangle \\ + e^{-\frac{i}{\hbar}f_e(t)}|e(t)\rangle \otimes |\mathcal{E}_e(0)\rangle. \tag{8}$$

Projecting the environment $\mathcal{E}$ into the state "$|\mathcal{E}_g(0)\rangle$", we have

$$U|g(0)\rangle\langle \mathcal{E}_g(0)|U'|\mathcal{E}_g(0)\rangle + U|e(0)\rangle\langle \mathcal{E}_g(0)|U'|\mathcal{E}_e(0)\rangle = e^{-\frac{i}{\hbar}f_g(t)}|g(t)\rangle, \tag{9}$$

equivalently written as

$$(U'_{g,g})U|g(0)\rangle + (U'_{g,e})U|e(0)\rangle = e^{-\frac{i}{\hbar}f_g(t)}|g(t)\rangle, \tag{10}$$

which implies the following:

$$(U'_{g,g})|g(0)\rangle + (U'_{g,e})|e(0)\rangle = e^{-\frac{i}{\hbar}f_g(t)} U^{\dagger}|g(t)\rangle. \tag{11}$$

Therefore,

$$U'_{g,g} = e^{-\frac{i}{\hbar}f_g(t)}\langle g(0)|U^\dagger|g(t)\rangle, \text{ and } U'_{g,e} = e^{-\frac{i}{\hbar}f_g(t)}\langle e(0)|U^\dagger|g(t)\rangle. \quad (12)$$

Additionally, by projecting $\mathcal{E}$ into the state "$|\mathcal{E}_e(0)\rangle$" we obtain the following:

$$U'_{e,g} = e^{-\frac{i}{\hbar}f_e(t)}\langle g(0)|U^\dagger|e(t)\rangle, \text{ and } U'_{e,e} = e^{-\frac{i}{\hbar}f_e(t)}\langle e(0)|U^\dagger|e(t)\rangle. \quad (13)$$

It is straightforward to check that the operator U', which reads as follows:

$$U' = \begin{pmatrix} U'_{g,g} & U'_{g,e} \\ U'_{e,g} & U'_{e,e} \end{pmatrix}, \quad (14)$$

is indeed a unitary on $\mathcal{E}$.

In conclusion, we have constructed a unique unitary map that acts only on $\mathcal{E}$, but counteracts transitions in $\mathcal{S}$. Note that coupling the system and environment implies that the state of the system is no longer described by a wave function. Hence the usual counterdiabatic scheme evolves the density matrix $\rho_S(0)$ to another density $\rho_S(t)$ such that both matrices have the same populations and coherence in the instantaneous eigenbasis of $H_0(t)$ (which is what EASTA accomplishes, as well).

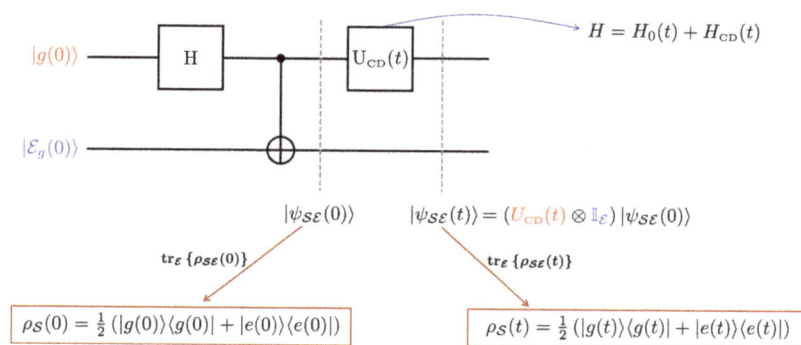

(a) Counterdiabatic scheme for open system dynamics.

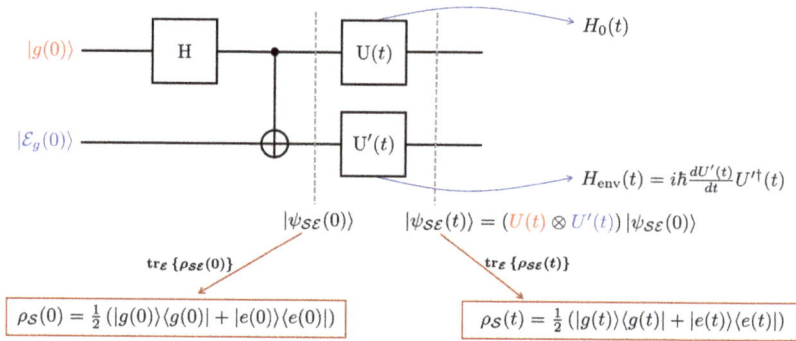

(b) Environment-assisted shortcut scheme.

Figure 1. Sketch of the two different schemes of applying STA in a branching state of the form presented in Equation (6). In both panels, the state preparation involves a Hadamard gate (H) applied on $\mathcal{S}$, and coupling with the environment through a c-not operation. In panel (a), we describe the "usual" counterdiabatic scheme. As shown in Section 3, local driving on $\mathcal{E}$ suppresses any transitions of $\mathcal{S}$ in the instantaneous eigenbasis of $H_0(t)$. The latter scheme is illustrated in panel (b).

3.2. N-Level Environment $\mathcal{E}$

We can easily generalize the two-level analysis to an N-level environment. Similar to the above description, coupling the system to the environment leads to a branching state of the following form:

$$|\psi_{S\mathcal{E}}(0)\rangle = \frac{1}{\sqrt{N}} \sum_{n=0}^{N-1} |n(0)\rangle \otimes |\mathcal{E}_n(0)\rangle, \tag{15}$$

where the states $\{|\mathcal{E}_n(0)\rangle\}_n$ form a basis on the environment $\mathcal{E}$. We can then construct a unique unitary U' such that the system evolves through the adiabatic manifold in each branch of the wave function as follows:

$$(\exists! \, U'); \; (U \otimes U')|\psi_{S\mathcal{E}}(0)\rangle = (U_{\text{CD}} \otimes \mathbb{I}_{\mathcal{E}})|\psi_{S\mathcal{E}}(0)\rangle. \tag{16}$$

The proof follows the exact same strategy as the two-level case, and we find the following:

$$(\forall \, (m,n) \in [\![0, N-1]\!]^2); \; U'_{m,n} = e^{-\frac{i}{\hbar} f_m(t)} \langle n(0)|U^{\dagger}|m(t)\rangle. \tag{17}$$

The above expression of the elements of the unitary U' is our main result, which holds for any driving $H_0(t)$ and any N-dimensional system.

3.3. Process Cost

Having established the general analytic form of the unitary applied on the environment, the next logical step is to compute and compare the cost of both schemes: (a) the usual counterdiabatic scheme and (b) the environment-assisted shortcut scheme presented above (cf. Figure 1). More specifically, we now compare the time integral of the instantaneous cost [39] for both driving schemes [39–43], (a) $C_{\text{CD}}(t) = (1/\tau) \int_0^t \|H_{\text{CD}}(s)\| ds$ and (b) $C_{\text{env}}(t) = (1/\tau) \int_0^t \|H_{\text{env}}(s)\| ds$ ($\|.\|$ is the operator norm), where the driving Hamiltonian on the environment can be determined from the expression of $U'(t)$, $H_{\text{env}}(t) = i\hbar \frac{dU'(t)}{dt} U'^{\dagger}(t)$.

In fact, from Equation (17) it is not too hard to see that the field applied on the environment $H_{\text{env}}(t)$ has the same eigenvalues as the counterdiabatic field $H_{\text{CD}}(t)$, since there exists a similarity transformation between $H_{\text{env}}(t)$ and $H_{\text{CD}}^*(t)$. Therefore, the cost of both processes is exactly the same, $C_{\text{CD}} = C_{\text{env}}$, for any arbitrary driving $H_0(t)$. Details of the derivation can be found in Appendix A. Note that for $t = \tau$, the above definition of the cost becomes the total cost for the duration "τ" of the process.

3.4. Illustration

We illustrate our results in a simple two-qubit model, where the system and and the environment are each described by a single qubit. Note that the environment can live in a larger Hilbert space while still being characterized as a virtual qubit [44]. The aforementioned virtual qubit notion simply means that the state of the environment is of rank equal to two.

We choose a driving Hamiltonian $H_0(t)$, such that

$$H_0(t) = \frac{B}{2}\sigma_x + \frac{J(t)}{2}\sigma_z, \tag{18}$$

where $J(t)$ is the driving/control field, B is a constant, and σ_z and σ_x are Pauli matrices. Depending on the physical context, B and $J(t)$ can be interpreted in various ways. In particular, as noted in ref. [45], in some contexts, the constant B can be regarded as the energy splitting between the two levels [46–48], and in others, the driving $J(t)$ can be interpreted as a time-varying energy splitting between the states [49–52]. To illustrate our results we choose the following:

$$(\forall\, t \in [0,\, \tau]);\ J(t) = B \cos^2\left(\frac{\pi t}{2\tau}\right). \tag{19}$$

The above driving evolves the system beyond the adiabatic manifold, and we quantify this by plotting, in Figure 2, the overlap between the evolved state $|\phi_n(t)\rangle \equiv U(t)|n(0)\rangle$ and the instantaneous eigenstate $|n(t)\rangle$ of the Hamiltonian $H_0(t)$, for $n \in \{g, e\}$. To illustrate our main result, we also plot the overlap between the states resulting from the two shortcut schemes (illustrated in Figure 1): the first scheme is the usual counterdiabatic (CD) driving, where we add a counterdiabatic field H_{CD} to the system of interest, and we note the resulting composite state as "$|\psi_{S\mathcal{E}}^{\mathrm{CD}}\rangle$". The second scheme is the environment-assisted shortcut to adiabaticity (EASTA), and we note the resulting composite state as "$|\psi_{S\mathcal{E}}^{\mathrm{EASTA}}\rangle$". Confirming our analytic results, the local driving on the environment ensures that the system evolves through the adiabatic manifold at all times since the state overlap is equal to one for all $t \in [0, \tau]$.

Finally, we compute and plot the cost of both shortcut schemes and verify that they are both equal to each other for all times "t" (cf. Figure 2b), and for all "τ" (cf. Figure 2c).

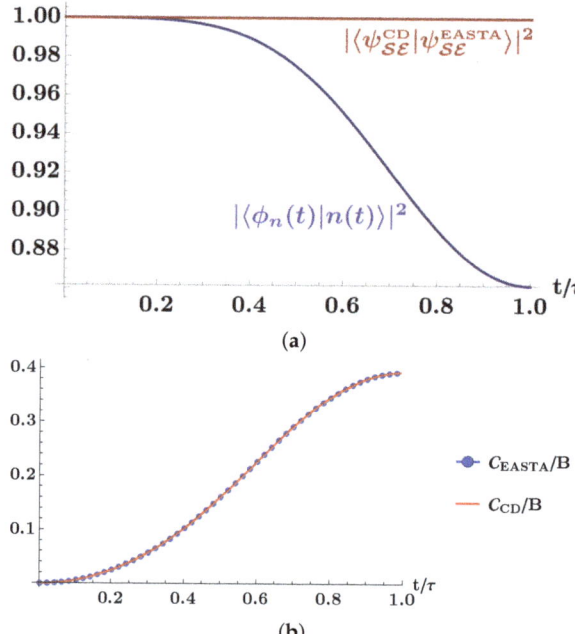

Figure 2. Cont.

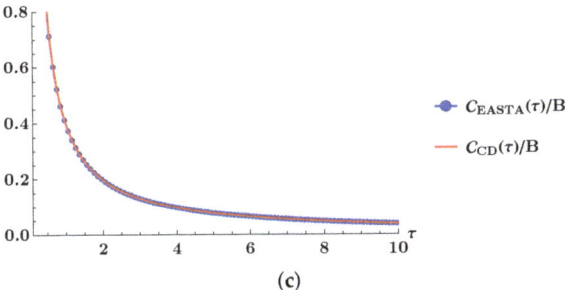

Figure 2. In panel (**a**), the blue curve illustrates the overlap between the nth evolved state $|\phi_n(t)\rangle$ and the nth instantaneous eigenstate $|n(t)\rangle$ of the Hamiltonian $H_0(t)$. This curve shows that the driving $H_0(t)$ evolves the system beyond the adiabatic manifold. The red curve illustrates that EASTA guarantees an exact evolution through the adiabatic manifold. In panel (**b**), we illustrate the cost of both the EASTA and the CD schemes, and numerically verify that they are equal $\mathcal{C} = \mathcal{C}_{\text{CD}} = \mathcal{C}_{\text{env}}$ for all $t/\tau \in [0,1]$, and $\tau = 1$. Note that in the illustrations we pick the driving field $J(t) = B\cos^2(\frac{\pi t}{2\tau})$ and $B = 1$. In panel (**c**), we illustrate the costs for different values of τ. For infinitely fast processes ($\tau \to 0$) the cost diverges and it tends to zero for infinitely slow processes ($\tau \to \infty$).

4. Concluding Remarks

4.1. Summary

In the present manuscript, we considered branching states $\{|\psi_{S\mathcal{E}}\rangle\}$, on a Hilbert space $\mathcal{H}_S \otimes \mathcal{H}_\mathcal{E}$ of arbitrary dimension, and we derived the general analytic form of the time-dependent driving on $\mathcal{H}_\mathcal{E}$, which guarantees that the system $\mathcal{S}$ evolves through the adiabatic manifold at all times. Through this environment-assisted shortcuts to adiabaticity scheme, we explicitly showed that the environment can act as a proxy to control the dynamics of the system of interest. Moreover, for branching states $|\psi_{S\mathcal{E}}\rangle$ with equal branch probabilities, we further proved that the cost associated with the EASTA technique is exactly equal to that of counterdiabatic driving. We illustrated our results in a simple two-qubit model, where the system and the environment are each described by a single qubit.

It is interesting to note that while we focused in the present manuscript on counterdiabatic driving, the technique can readily be generalized to any type of control unitary map "U_{control}", resulting in a desired evolved state $|\kappa_n(t)\rangle \equiv U_{\text{control}}|n(0)\rangle$. The corresponding unitary U' on $\mathcal{H}_\mathcal{E}$ has then the following form:

$$(\forall (m,n) \in [\![0, N-1]\!]^2); \quad U'_{m,n} = \langle n(0)|U^\dagger|\kappa_m(t)\rangle. \tag{20}$$

In the special case, for which the evolved state is equal to the nth instantaneous eigenstate of $H_0(t)$ (with a phase factor),

$$|\kappa_n(t)\rangle = e^{-\frac{i}{\hbar}f_n(t)}|n(t)\rangle, \tag{21}$$

we recover the main result of the manuscript. The above generalization illustrates the broad scope of our results. Any control unitary on the system $\mathcal{S}$ can be realized solely by acting on the environment $\mathcal{E}$, without altering the dynamics of the system of interest $\mathcal{S}$ (i.e., for any arbitrary driving $H_0(t)$ and thus, any driving rate).

4.2. Envariance and Pointer States

In the present work, we leveraged the presence of an environment to induce the desired dynamics in a quantum system. Interestingly, our novel method for shortcuts to adiabaticity relies on branching states, which play an essential role in decoherence theory and in the framework of quantum Darwinism.

In open system dynamics [53–55], the interaction between system and environment superselects states that survive the decoherence process, also known as the pointer states [56,57]. It is exactly these pointer states that are the starting point of our analysis, and for which EASTA is designed. While previous studies [58–60] have explored STA methods for open quantum systems, to the best of our understanding, the environment was only considered a passive source of additional noise described by quantum master equations. In our paradigm, we recognize the active role that an environment plays in quantum dynamics, which is inspired by envariance and reminiscent of the mindset of quantum Darwinism. In this framework [44,61–77], the environment is understood as a communication channel through which we learn about the world around us, i.e., we learn about the state of systems of interest by eavesdropping on environmental degrees of freedom [44].

Thus, in true spirit of the teachings by Wojciech H. Zurek, we have understood the agency of quantum environments and the useful role they can assume. To this end, we have applied a small part of the many lessons we learned from working with Wojciech, to connect and merge tools from seemingly different areas of physics to gain a deeper and more fundamental understanding of nature.

Author Contributions: Conceptualization, A.T. and S.D.; Formal analysis, A.T.; Funding acquisition, S.D.; Supervision, S.D.; Writing—original draft, A.T. and S.D.; Writing—review & editing, A.T. and S.D. All authors have read and agreed to the published version of the manuscript.

Funding: S.D. acknowledges support from the U.S. National Science Foundation under Grant No. DMR-2010127. This research was supported by grant number FQXi-RFP-1808 from the Foundational Questions Institute and Fetzer Franklin Fund, a donor advised fund of Silicon Valley Community Foundation (SD).

Institutional Review Board Statement: Not applicable.

Informed Consent Statement: Not applicable.

Data Availability Statement: Not applicable.

Acknowledgments: We would like to thank Wojciech H. Zurek for many years of mentorship and his unwavering patience and willingness to teach us how to think about the mysteries of the quantum universe. Enlightening discussions with Agniva Roychowdhury are gratefully acknowledged.

Conflicts of Interest: The authors declare no conflict of interest.

Appendix A. Cost of Environment-Assisted Shortcuts to Adiabaticity

In this appendix, we show that CD and EASTA have the same cost. Generally, we have the following:

$$\begin{aligned} H_{\text{env}}(t) &= i\hbar \frac{dU'(t)}{dt} U'^{\dagger}(t), \\ &= i\hbar \sum_{i,j} \sum_k \frac{dU'_{i,k}}{dt} (U'_{j,k})^* |\mathcal{E}_i(0)\rangle\langle \mathcal{E}_j(0)|. \end{aligned} \quad \text{(A1)}$$

From the main result in Equation (17), we obtain the following:

$$H_{\text{env}}(t) = \sum_{i,j} \left(\sum_k \left(\langle k(0)|i\hbar \partial_t U^{\dagger}|\psi_i(t)\rangle (U'_{j,k})^* + i\hbar \langle k(0)|U^{\dagger}|\partial_t \psi_i(t)\rangle (U'_{j,k})^* \right) \right) \\ \times |\mathcal{E}_i(0)\rangle\langle \mathcal{E}_j(0)|. \quad \text{(A2)}$$

Given that $H_0(t) = i\hbar \frac{dU(t)}{dt} U^{\dagger}(t)$, we also have

$$H_{\text{env}}(t) = \sum_{i,j} \left(\sum_k \left(\langle k(0)|(-U^{\dagger} H_0)|\psi_i(t)\rangle (U'_{j,k})^* + i\hbar \langle k(0)|U^{\dagger}|\partial_t \psi_i(t)\rangle (U'_{j,k})^* \right) \right) \\ \times |\mathcal{E}_i(0)\rangle\langle \mathcal{E}_j(0)|, \quad \text{(A3)}$$

which implies

$$H_{\text{env}}(t) = \sum_{i,j} \left(\sum_k \left(\langle k(0)|(-U^\dagger H_0)|\psi_i(t)\rangle (U'_{j,k})^* + \langle k(0)|U^\dagger H|\psi_i(t)\rangle (U'_{j,k})^* \right) \right) \quad \text{(A4)}$$
$$\times |\mathcal{E}_i(0)\rangle\langle \mathcal{E}_j(0)|,$$

and hence,

$$H_{\text{env}}(t) = \sum_{i,j} \left(\sum_k \langle k(0)|U^\dagger H_{\text{CD}}|\psi_i(t)\rangle (U'_{j,k})^* \right) |\mathcal{E}_i(0)\rangle\langle \mathcal{E}_j(0)|. \quad \text{(A5)}$$

Using $|\phi_k(t)\rangle \equiv U(t)|k(0)\rangle$ we can write the following:

$$H_{\text{env}}(t) = \sum_{i,j} \left(\sum_k \langle \psi_j(t)|\phi_k(t)\rangle\langle \phi_k(t)|H_{\text{CD}}|\psi_i(t)\rangle \right) |\mathcal{E}_i(0)\rangle\langle \mathcal{E}_j(0)|. \quad \text{(A6)}$$

Therefore, the following holds:

$$H_{\text{env}}(t) = \sum_{i,j} (\langle \psi_j(t)|H_{\text{CD}}|\psi_i(t)\rangle) |\mathcal{E}_i(0)\rangle\langle \mathcal{E}_j(0)|. \quad \text{(A7)}$$

By definition, we also have the following:

$$H_{\text{CD}} = \sum_{i,j} (\langle \psi_i(t)|H_{\text{CD}}|\psi_j(t)\rangle) |\psi_i(t)\rangle\langle \psi_j(t)|, \quad \text{(A8)}$$

and hence,

$$H_{\text{CD}}^T = H_{\text{CD}}^* = \sum_{i,j} (\langle \psi_j(t)|H_{\text{CD}}|\psi_i(t)\rangle) |\psi_i(t)\rangle\langle \psi_j(t)|. \quad \text{(A9)}$$

Thus, there exists a similarity transformation between H_{CD}^* and H_{env}, and $C_{\text{CD}} = C_{\text{env}}$ for any arbitrary driving $H_0(t)$. The similarity transformation is given by the matrix $S = \sum_j |\mathcal{E}_j(0)\rangle\langle \psi_j(t)|$, such that $SH_{\text{CD}}^* S^{-1} = H_{\text{env}}$. Since we proved that the Hamiltonians H_{CD} and H_{env} have the same eigenvalues, our result can be valid for other definitions of the cost function $\mathcal{C}$, which might involve other norms (e.g., the Frobenius norm).

It is noteworthy that in the above analysis, we do not consider the effect of quantum fluctuations [78] in the control fields, since their energetic contribution to the cost function is negligible in our context.

Appendix B. Generalization to Arbitrary Branching Probabilities

Finally, we briefly inspect the case of non-even branching states. We begin by noting the consequences of our assumptions. In particular, we have assumed that the state of system+environment evolves unitarly. Thus, consider a joint map of the form $U \otimes M$, where U is a unitary on $\mathcal{S}$. Then, it is a simple exercise to show that the map M, on $\mathcal{E}$, is also unitary, $MM^\dagger = M^\dagger M = \mathbb{I}$. In what follows, we prove by contradiction that there exists no unitary map M that suppresses transitions in $\mathcal{S}$, for branching states with arbitrary probabilities.

Consider the following:

$$|\psi_{S\mathcal{E}}(0)\rangle = \sum_{n=0}^{N-1} \sqrt{p_n}|n(0)\rangle \bigotimes_{l=1}^{N_\mathcal{E}} |\mathcal{E}_n^l(0)\rangle, \quad \text{(A10)}$$

and assume that there exists a unitary map M on $\mathcal{E}$ that suppresses transitions in $\mathcal{S}$, i.e.,

$$\sum_{n=0}^{N-1} \sqrt{p_n} U|n(0)\rangle \otimes \left(M \bigotimes_{l=1}^{N_\mathcal{E}} |\mathcal{E}_n^l(0)\rangle \right) = \sum_{n=0}^{N-1} \sqrt{p_n} e^{-\frac{i}{\hbar} f_n(t)} |n(t)\rangle \otimes \left(\bigotimes_{l=1}^{N_\mathcal{E}} |\mathcal{E}_n^l(0)\rangle \right). \quad \text{(A11)}$$

Following the same steps of Section 3, we obtain the following:

$$(\forall \, (m,n) \in [\![0, N-1]\!]^2); \quad M_{m,n} = \sqrt{\frac{p_m}{p_n}} e^{-\frac{i}{\hbar} f_m(t)} \langle n(0)|U^\dagger|m(t)\rangle. \tag{A12}$$

Comparing the above map with our main result in Equation (17), we conclude that the additional factor $\sqrt{\frac{p_m}{p_n}}$ violates unitarity, and hence we conclude that EASTA cannot work for non-even branching states (A10).

This can be seen more explicitly from the form of the matrices $MM^\dagger$ and $M^\dagger M$. Generally, and by dropping the superscript in environmental states $\otimes_{l=1}^{N_\mathcal{E}} |\mathcal{E}_n^l(0)\rangle \equiv |\mathcal{E}_n(0)\rangle$, we have the following:

$$MM^\dagger = \sum_{i,j,k} M_{i,k} M_{j,k}^* |\mathcal{E}_i(0)\rangle\langle \mathcal{E}_j(0)|, \tag{A13}$$

from the expression of the elements of M (cf. Equation (A12)), and by adopting the notation $|\phi_n\rangle \equiv U(t)|n(0)\rangle$, we obtain the following:

$$MM^\dagger = \sum_{i,j,k} \frac{\sqrt{p_i p_j}}{p_k} \langle \phi_k|\psi_i\rangle\langle \psi_j|\phi_k\rangle |\mathcal{E}_i(0)\rangle\langle \mathcal{E}_j(0)|, \tag{A14}$$

which implies

$$MM^\dagger = \mathbb{I} + \sum_{i,j} \sqrt{\frac{p_j}{p_i}} \langle \psi_j|D_{(i)}|\psi_i\rangle |\mathcal{E}_i(0)\rangle\langle \mathcal{E}_j(0)|, \tag{A15}$$

such that the matrix

$$D_{(i)} = \sum_k \frac{p_i}{p_k} |\phi_k\rangle\langle \phi_k| - \mathbb{I} \tag{A16}$$

is diagonal in the basis spanned by the orthonormal vectors $\{|\phi_k\rangle\}_k$. This matrix is generally (for any choice of $H_0(t)$ and initial state of $\mathcal{S}$) different from the null matrix for non-equal branch probabilities. A similar decomposition can be made for the matrix $M^\dagger M$, such that

$$M^\dagger M = \mathbb{I} + \sum_{i,j} \sqrt{\frac{p_i}{p_j}} \langle \phi_j|\mathcal{D}_{(i)}|\phi_i\rangle |\mathcal{E}_i(0)\rangle\langle \mathcal{E}_j(0)|, \tag{A17}$$

where

$$\mathcal{D}_{(i)} = \sum_k \frac{p_k}{p_i} |\psi_k\rangle\langle \psi_k| - \mathbb{I}. \tag{A18}$$

In conclusion, for branching states with non-equal probabilities, there is no unitary map that guarantees that the system evolves through the adiabatic manifold at all times and for any arbitrary driving $H_0(t)$. Hence, we can realize the EASTA technique only for a system maximally entangled with its environment (cf. Equation (A10) with $\sqrt{p_n} = 1/\sqrt{N}$ for all $n \in [\![0, N-1]\!]$), or in the general case (non-equal branch probabilities) when we can access an extended Hilbert space.

References

1. Deutsch, I.H. Harnessing the Power of the Second Quantum Revolution. *PRX Quantum* **2020**, *1*, 020101. [CrossRef]
2. Dowling, J.P.; Milburn, G.J. Quantum technology: The second quantum revolution. *Philos. Trans. R. Soc. Lond. Ser. A Math. Phys. Eng. Sci.* **2003**, *361*, 1655–1674. [CrossRef] [PubMed]
3. Born, M.; Fock, V. Beweis des adiabatensatzes. *Z. Phys.* **1928**, *51*, 165–180. [CrossRef]
4. Messiah, A. *Quantum Mechanics*; John Wiley & Sons: Amsterdam, The Netherlands, 1966; Volume II.
5. Nenciu, G. On the adiabatic theorem of quantum mechanics. *J. Phys. A Math. Gen.* **1980**, *13*, L15–L18. [CrossRef]
6. Nenciu, G. On the adiabatic limit for Dirac particles in external fields. *Commun. Math. Phys.* **1980**, *76*, 117. [CrossRef]
7. Nenciu, G. Adiabatic theorem and spectral concentration. *Commun. Math. Phys.* **1981**, *82*, 121. [CrossRef]
8. Torrontegui, E.; Ibáñez, S.; Martínez-Garaot, S.; Modugno, M.; del Campo, A.; Guéry-Odelin, D.; Ruschhaupt, A.; Chen, X.; Muga, J.G. Shortcuts to Adiabaticity. *Adv. At. Mol. Opt. Phys.* **2013**, *62*, 117. [CrossRef]

9. Guéry-Odelin, D.; Ruschhaupt, A.; Kiely, A.; Torrontegui, E.; Martínez-Garaot, S.; Muga, J.G. Shortcuts to adiabaticity: Concepts, methods, and applications. *Rev. Mod. Phys.* **2019**, *91*, 045001. [CrossRef]
10. del Campo, A.; Kim, K. Focus on Shortcuts to Adiabaticity. *New J. Phys.* **2019**, *21*, 050201. [CrossRef]
11. Deffner, S.; Bonança, M.V.S. Thermodynamic control —An old paradigm with new applications. *EPL (Europhys. Lett.)* **2020**, *131*, 20001. [CrossRef]
12. Demirplak, M.; Rice, S.A. Assisted adiabatic passage revisited. *J. Phys. Chem. B* **2005**, *109*, 6838. [CrossRef]
13. Demirplak, M.; Rice, S.A. Adiabatic Population Transfer with Control Fields. *J. Chem. Phys. A* **2003**, *107*, 9937. [CrossRef]
14. Berry, M.V. Transitionless quantum driving. *J. Phys. A Math. Theor.* **2009**, *42*, 365303. [CrossRef]
15. Campbell, S.; De Chiara, G.; Paternostro, M.; Palma, G.M.; Fazio, R. Shortcut to Adiabaticity in the Lipkin-Meshkov-Glick Model. *Phys. Rev. Lett.* **2015**, *114*, 177206. [CrossRef] [PubMed]
16. del Campo, A. Shortcuts to Adiabaticity by Counterdiabatic Driving. *Phys. Rev. Lett.* **2013**, *111*, 100502. [CrossRef] [PubMed]
17. del Campo, A.; Rams, M.M.; Zurek, W.H. Assisted Finite-Rate Adiabatic Passage Across a Quantum Critical Point: Exact Solution for the Quantum Ising Model. *Phys. Rev. Lett.* **2012**, *109*, 115703. [CrossRef] [PubMed]
18. Deffner, S.; Jarzynski, C.; del Campo, A. Classical and Quantum Shortcuts to Adiabaticity for Scale-Invariant Driving. *Phys. Rev. X* **2014**, *4*, 021013. [CrossRef]
19. An, S.; Lv, D.; Del Campo, A.; Kim, K. Shortcuts to adiabaticity by counterdiabatic driving for trapped-ion displacement in phase space. *Nat. Commun.* **2016**, *7*, 1–5. [CrossRef]
20. Masuda, S.; Nakamura, K. Acceleration of adiabatic quantum dynamics in electromagnetic fields. *Phys. Rev. A* **2011**, *84*, 043434. [CrossRef]
21. Masuda, S.; Nakamura, K. Fast-forward of adiabatic dynamics in quantum mechanics. *Proc. R. Soc. A* **2010**, *466*, 1135. [CrossRef]
22. Masuda, S.; Rice, S.A. Fast-Forward Assisted STIRAP. *J. Phys. Chem. A* **2015**, *119*, 3479. [CrossRef]
23. Masuda, S.; Nakamura, K.; del Campo, A. High-Fidelity Rapid Ground-State Loading of an Ultracold Gas into an Optical Lattice. *Phys. Rev. Lett.* **2014**, *113*, 063003. [CrossRef] [PubMed]
24. Bernardo, B.d.L. Time-rescaled quantum dynamics as a shortcut to adiabaticity. *Phys. Rev. Res.* **2020**, *2*, 013133. [CrossRef]
25. Roychowdhury, A.; Deffner, S. Time-Rescaling of Dirac Dynamics: Shortcuts to Adiabaticity in Ion Traps and Weyl Semimetals. *Entropy* **2021**, *23*, 81. [CrossRef] [PubMed]
26. Chen, X.; Ruschhaupt, A.; Schmidt, S.; del Campo, A.; Guéry-Odelin, D.; Muga, J.G. Fast Optimal Frictionless Atom Cooling in Harmonic Traps: Shortcut to Adiabaticity. *Phys. Rev. Lett.* **2010**, *104*, 063002. [CrossRef] [PubMed]
27. Torrontegui, E.; Martínez-Garaot, S.; Muga, J.G. Hamiltonian engineering via invariants and dynamical algebra. *Phys. Rev. A* **2014**, *89*, 043408. [CrossRef]
28. Kiely, A.; McGuinness, J.P.L.; Muga, J.G.; Ruschhaupt, A. Fast and stable manipulation of a charged particle in a Penning trap. *J. Phys. B At. Mol. Opt. Phys.* **2015**, *48*, 075503. [CrossRef]
29. Jarzynski, C.; Deffner, S.; Patra, A.; Subaş ı, Y.b.u. Fast forward to the classical adiabatic invariant. *Phys. Rev. E* **2017**, *95*, 032122. [CrossRef] [PubMed]
30. Patra, A.; Jarzynski, C. Classical and Quantum Shortcuts to Adiabaticity in a Tilted Piston. *J. Phys. Chem. B* **2017**, *121*, 3403–3411. [CrossRef] [PubMed]
31. Patra, A.; Jarzynski, C. Shortcuts to adiabaticity using flow fields. *New J. Phys.* **2017**, *19*, 125009. [CrossRef]
32. Iram, S.; Dolson, E.; Chiel, J.; Pelesko, J.; Krishnan, N.; Güngör, Ö.; Kuznets-Speck, B.; Deffner, S.; Ilker, E.; Scott, J.G.; et al. Controlling the speed and trajectory of evolution with counterdiabatic driving. *Nat. Phys.* **2021**, *17*, 135–142. [CrossRef]
33. Zurek, W.H. Environment-Assisted Invariance, Entanglement, and Probabilities in Quantum Physics. *Phys. Rev. Lett.* **2003**, *90*, 120404. [CrossRef] [PubMed]
34. Zurek, W.H. Probabilities from entanglement, Born's rule $p_k = | \psi_k |^2$ from envariance. *Phys. Rev. A* **2005**, *71*, 052105. [CrossRef]
35. Deffner, S.; Zurek, W.H. Foundations of statistical mechanics from symmetries of entanglement. *New J. Phys.* **2016**, *18*, 063013. [CrossRef]
36. Vermeyden, L.; Ma, X.; Lavoie, J.; Bonsma, M.; Sinha, U.; Laflamme, R.; Resch, K.J. Experimental test of environment-assisted invariance. *Phys. Rev. A* **2015**, *91*, 012120. [CrossRef]
37. Harris, J.; Bouchard, F.; Santamato, E.; Zurek, W.H.; Boyd, R.W.; Karimi, E. Quantum probabilities from quantum entanglement: Experimentally unpacking the Born rule. *New J. Phys.* **2016**, *18*, 053013. [CrossRef]
38. Blume-Kohout, R.; Zurek, W.H. Quantum Darwinism: Entanglement, branches, and the emergent classicality of redundantly stored quantum information. *Phys. Rev. A* **2006**, *73*, 062310. [CrossRef]
39. Abah, O.; Puebla, R.; Kiely, A.; De Chiara, G.; Paternostro, M.; Campbell, S. Energetic cost of quantum control protocols. *New J. Phys.* **2019**, *21*, 103048. [CrossRef]
40. Zheng, Y.; Campbell, S.; De Chiara, G.; Poletti, D. Cost of counterdiabatic driving and work output. *Phys. Rev. A* **2016**, *94*, 042132. [CrossRef]
41. Campbell, S.; Deffner, S. Trade-Off Between Speed and Cost in Shortcuts to Adiabaticity. *Phys. Rev. Lett.* **2017**, *118*, 100601. [CrossRef]
42. Abah, O.; Puebla, R.; Paternostro, M. Quantum State Engineering by Shortcuts to Adiabaticity in Interacting Spin-Boson Systems. *Phys. Rev. Lett.* **2020**, *124*, 180401. [CrossRef]

43. Ilker, E.; Güngör, Ö.; Kuznets-Speck, B.; Chiel, J.; Deffner, S.; Hinczewski, M. Counterdiabatic control of biophysical processes. *arXiv* **2021**, arXiv:2106.07130.
44. Touil, A.; Yan, B.; Girolami, D.; Deffner, S.; Zurek, W.H. Eavesdropping on the Decohering Environment: Quantum Darwinism, Amplification, and the Origin of Objective Classical Reality. *arXiv* **2021**, arXiv:2107.00035.
45. Barnes, E.; Das Sarma, S. Analytically Solvable Driven Time-Dependent Two-Level Quantum Systems. *Phys. Rev. Lett.* **2012**, *109*, 060401. [CrossRef] [PubMed]
46. Greilich, A.; Economou, S.E.; Spatzek, S.; Yakovlev, D.; Reuter, D.; Wieck, A.; Reinecke, T.; Bayer, M. Ultrafast optical rotations of electron spins in quantum dots. *Nat. Phys.* **2009**, *5*, 262–266. [CrossRef]
47. Poem, E.; Kenneth, O.; Kodriano, Y.; Benny, Y.; Khatsevich, S.; Avron, J.E.; Gershoni, D. Optically Induced Rotation of an Exciton Spin in a Semiconductor Quantum Dot. *Phys. Rev. Lett.* **2011**, *107*, 087401. [CrossRef]
48. Martinis, J.M.; Cooper, K.B.; McDermott, R.; Steffen, M.; Ansmann, M.; Osborn, K.D.; Cicak, K.; Oh, S.; Pappas, D.P.; Simmonds, R.W.; et al. Decoherence in Josephson Qubits from Dielectric Loss. *Phys. Rev. Lett.* **2005**, *95*, 210503. [CrossRef]
49. Petta, J.R.; Johnson, A.C.; Taylor, J.M.; Laird, E.A.; Yacoby, A.; Lukin, M.D.; Marcus, C.M.; Hanson, M.P.; Gossard, A.C. Coherent manipulation of coupled electron spins in semiconductor quantum dots. *Science* **2005**, *309*, 2180–2184. [CrossRef]
50. Foletti, S.; Bluhm, H.; Mahalu, D.; Umansky, V.; Yacoby, A. Universal quantum control of two-electron spin quantum bits using dynamic nuclear polarization. *Nat. Phys.* **2009**, *5*, 903–908. [CrossRef]
51. Maune, B.M.; Borselli, M.G.; Huang, B.; Ladd, T.D.; Deelman, P.W.; Holabird, K.S.; Kiselev, A.A.; Alvarado-Rodriguez, I.; Ross, R.S.; Schmitz, A.E.; et al. Coherent singlet-triplet oscillations in a silicon-based double quantum dot. *Nature* **2012**, *481*, 344–347. [CrossRef]
52. Wang, X.; Bishop, L.S.; Kestner, J.; Barnes, E.; Sun, K.; Sarma, S.D. Composite pulses for robust universal control of singlet–triplet qubits. *Nat. Commun.* **2012**, *3*, 1–7. [CrossRef] [PubMed]
53. Zeh, H.D. On the interpretation of measurement in quantum theory. *Found. Phys.* **1970**, *1*, 69–76. [CrossRef]
54. Zurek, W.H. Decoherence, einselection, and the quantum origins of the classical. *Rev. Mod. Phys.* **2003**, *75*, 715–775. [CrossRef]
55. Zurek, W.H. Preferred States, Predictability, Classicality and the Environment-Induced Decoherence. *Prog. Theo. Phys.* **1993**, *89*, 281–312. [CrossRef]
56. Zurek, W.H. Pointer basis of quantum apparatus: Into what mixture does the wave packet collapse? *Phys. Rev. D* **1981**, *24*, 1516–1525. [CrossRef]
57. Zurek, W.H. Environment-induced superselection rules. *Phys. Rev. D* **1982**, *26*, 1862–1880. [CrossRef]
58. Alipour, S.; Chenu, A.; Rezakhani, A.T.; del Campo, A. Shortcuts to adiabaticity in driven open quantum systems: Balanced gain and loss and non-Markovian evolution. *Quantum* **2020**, *4*, 336. [CrossRef]
59. Santos, A.C.; Sarandy, M.S. Generalized transitionless quantum driving for open quantum systems. *arXiv* **2021**, arXiv:2109.11695.
60. Yin, Z.; Li, C.; Zhang, Z.; Zheng, Y.; Gu, X.; Dai, M.; Allcock, J.; Zhang, S.; An, S. Shortcuts to Adiabaticity for Open Systems in Circuit Quantum Electrodynamics. *arXiv* **2021**, arXiv:2107.08417.
61. Riedel, C.J.; Zurek, W.H. Quantum Darwinism in an Everyday Environment: Huge Redundancy in Scattered Photons. *Phys. Rev. Lett.* **2010**, *105*, 020404. [CrossRef] [PubMed]
62. Riedel, C.J.; Zurek, W.H. Redundant information from thermal illumination: Quantum Darwinism in scattered photons. *New J. Phys.* **2011**, *13*, 073038. [CrossRef]
63. Zurek, W.H. Quantum Darwinism. *Nat. Phys.* **2009**, *5*, 181. [CrossRef]
64. Zurek, W.H. Quantum Darwinism, classical reality, and the randomness of quantum jumps. *arXiv* **2014**, arXiv:1412.5206.
65. Zurek, W.H. Quantum origin of quantum jumps: Breaking of unitary symmetry induced by information transfer in the transition from quantum to classical. *Phys. Rev. A* **2007**, *76*, 052110. [CrossRef]
66. Brandao, F.G.; Piani, M.; Horodecki, P. Generic emergence of classical features in quantum Darwinism. *Nat. Commun.* **2015**, *6*, 1–8. [CrossRef]
67. Riedel, C.J.; Zurek, W.H.; Zwolak, M. The rise and fall of redundancy in decoherence and quantum Darwinism. *New J. Phys.* **2012**, *14*, 083010. [CrossRef]
68. Milazzo, N.; Lorenzo, S.; Paternostro, M.; Palma, G.M. Role of information backflow in the emergence of quantum Darwinism. *Phys. Rev. A* **2019**, *100*, 012101. [CrossRef]
69. Kiciński, M.; Korbicz, J.K. Decoherence and objectivity in higher spin environments. *arXiv* **2021**, arXiv:2105.09093.
70. Korbicz, J. Roads to objectivity: Quantum Darwinism, Spectrum Broadcast Structures, and Strong quantum Darwinism. *arXiv* **2020**, arXiv:2007.04276.
71. Blume-Kohout, R.; Zurek, W.H. Quantum Darwinism in Quantum Brownian Motion. *Phys. Rev. Lett.* **2008**, *101*, 240405. [CrossRef]
72. Zwolak, M.; Riedel, C.J.; Zurek, W.H. Amplification, Redundancy, and Quantum Chernoff Information. *Phys. Rev. Lett.* **2014**, *112*, 140406. [CrossRef] [PubMed]
73. Zwolak, M.; Quan, H.T.; Zurek, W.H. Quantum Darwinism in a Mixed Environment. *Phys. Rev. Lett.* **2009**, *103*, 110402. [CrossRef]
74. Paz, J.P.; Roncaglia, A.J. Redundancy of classical and quantum correlations during decoherence. *Phys. Rev. A* **2009**, *80*, 042111. [CrossRef]
75. Riedel, C.J.; Zurek, W.H.; Zwolak, M. Objective past of a quantum universe: Redundant records of consistent histories. *Phys. Rev. A* **2016**, *93*, 032126. [CrossRef]

76. Riedel, C.J. Classical Branch Structure from Spatial Redundancy in a Many-Body Wave Function. *Phys. Rev. Lett.* **2017**, *118*, 120402. [CrossRef] [PubMed]
77. Fu, H.F. Uniqueness of the observable leaving redundant imprints in the environment in the context of quantum Darwinism. *Phys. Rev. A* **2021**, *103*, 042210. [CrossRef]
78. Calzetta, E. Not-quite-free shortcuts to adiabaticity. *Phys. Rev. A* **2018**, *98*, 032107. [CrossRef]

Article

Thermality versus Objectivity: Can They Peacefully Coexist?

Thao P. Le [1,*], Andreas Winter [2,3] and Gerardo Adesso [1]

1 School of Mathematical Sciences, University of Nottingham, University Park, Nottingham NG7 2RD, UK; gerardo.adesso@nottingham.ac.uk
2 Institució Catalana de Recerca i Estudis Avançats (ICREA), Pg. Lluis Companys, 23, 08001 Barcelona, Spain; andreas.winter@uab.cat
3 Grup d'Informació Quàntica, Departament de Física, Universitat Autònoma de Barcelona, 08193 Barcelona, Spain
* Correspondence: thao.le.16@ucl.ac.uk

Abstract: Under the influence of external environments, quantum systems can undergo various different processes, including decoherence and equilibration. We observe that macroscopic objects are both objective and thermal, thus leading to the expectation that both objectivity and thermalisation can peacefully coexist on the quantum regime too. Crucially, however, objectivity relies on distributed classical information that could conflict with thermalisation. Here, we examine the overlap between thermal and objective states. We find that in general, one cannot exist when the other is present. However, there are certain regimes where thermality and objectivity are more likely to coexist: in the high temperature limit, at the non-degenerate low temperature limit, and when the environment is large. This is consistent with our experiences that everyday-sized objects can be both thermal and objective.

Keywords: Quantum Darwinism; objectivity; thermalisation; open quantum systems

1. Introduction

While fundamental quantum mechanics describes how isolated quantum systems evolve under unitary evolution, realistic quantum systems are open, as they interact with external environments that are typically too large to exactly model. In order to account for large external environments without directly simulating them, the theory of open quantum systems has developed tools that allow us to study a variety of quantum processes [1,2], including decoherence [3] (the loss of phase information to the environment) and dissipation (the loss of energy to the environment) [4].

The environment, when acting as a heat bath, can lead to the equilibration and thermalisation of quantum systems [5–9]. Meanwhile, in an approach to the quantum-to-classical transition called *Quantum Darwinism* [10–14], the environment plays a key role in the process of how quantum systems appear classically objective [13,14]—whereby classical objective systems have properties that are equivalently independently verifiable by independent observers. In the realm of open quantum systems, whether one process or another occurs depends on multiple factors, including details of the system–environment interactions, initial states, time regimes, averaging, etc.

The (classical) second law of thermodynamics generally states that entropy increases over time. Following this strictly, we may imagine that in the far distant future, the entire universe will reach an equilibrium where entropy can no longer increase: this concept is known as "heat death", which can be found in early writings of Bailly, Kelvin, Clausius and von Helmholtz (see references in [15]). An alternative, recent, version of heat death would see a universe composed mostly of vacuum and very far separated particles such that no work is done: this is "cosmological heat death" [16]. There are some caveats to the concept of heat death of the universe: beyond whether or not thermodynamics can be applied at the universal level, it is known that after a sufficiently long time, Poincaré recurrences

will return the system/universe to its prior states [17]. Furthermore, the discovery of dark energy and the accelerating rate of expansion of the universe [18] leads to other theories of the universe's ultimate fate such as the "big rip" [19].

These caveats aside, on more familiar temporal and spatial human scales, both classical and quantum objects can thermalise. In fact, thermalisation is quite fundamental: in fairly generic conditions, a local subsystem (of a greater state) will likely be close to thermal [20]. We also see that many everyday physical objects have the same approximate temperature as their environment. This thermality appears to contradict with *objectivity*. In Quantum Darwinism, a system state is considered objective if multiple copies of its information exist, which is mathematically expressed as (classical) correlations between the system and its environment [11,12]. The quintessential example is of the visual information carried in the photon environment. However, information and correlations have an associated *energy* [21,22], and naively, this information should not survive under the process of thermalisation. For example, in the model analysed by Riedel et al. [23], some level of objectivity emerges at finite time, before equilibration sets in; in the model analysed by Mirkin and Wisniacki [24], tuning certain parameters produces either objectivity or thermalisation, but not both.

Furthermore, there is a distance-scale difference. Quantum Darwinism requires strong (classical) correlations between two or indeed many more systems, some of which will invariably be very distant from each other—for example, we can view galaxies billions of light years away. In contrast, thermalisation favours realistic settings that have no or rapidly decaying correlations between distant subsystems of the universe.

In this paper, we investigate this apparent conflict between thermalisation and objectivity and consider whether or not these two can co-exist. To do this, we analyse the overlap between the set of states that are thermal versus the set of states that are objective—if there is no intersection, then there cannot exist any process that produces jointly thermal-objective states. We examine three different sets of thermal states where either: (1) there is system thermalisation, (2) local system and local environment thermalisation, or (3) global system–environment thermalisation. As greater parts of the system-environment become thermal, the overlap between objectivity and thermalisation reduces, often becoming non-existent for many system–environment Hamiltonians. We also find that large environments have better potential to support both thermality and objectivity simultaneously.

This paper is organised as follows. In Section 2, we introduce the mathematical structure of objective states, and in Section 3, we introduce thermalised microcanonical states (for finite systems). Then, in Section 4 we consider the intersection between objective states versus states with a thermal system. In Section 5, we consider states with a locally thermal system and a locally thermal environment. In Section 6, we consider a globally thermal system-environment state. We discuss and conclude in Section 7.

2. Objective States

In our day-to-day experience, we typically perceive the classical world as being "objective": objects appear to exist regardless of whether we personally look at them, and the properties of these objects can be agreed upon by multiple observers. More formally, we can describe objective states as satisfying the following:

Definition 1. Objectivity *[10,11,25]: A system state is* objective *if it is (1) simultaneously accessible to many observers (2) who can all determine the state independently without perturbing it and (3) all arrive at the same result.*

The process of emergent objectivity may be described by Quantum Darwinism [10,26]: as a system interacts and decoheres due to the surrounding environment, information about the system can spread into the environment. The "fittest" information that can be copied tends to record itself in the environment at the expense of other information, thus the name Quantum Darwinism. The paradigmatic example is the photonic environment: multiple photons interact with a physical object and gain information about its physical features, such as position, colour, size, etc. Multiple independent observers can then sample a small part of this photonic environment to find very similar information about the same system state, thus deeming it objective. We depict this in Figure 1a.

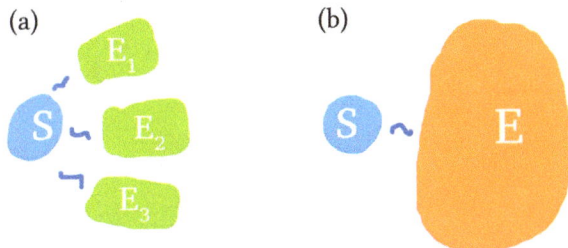

Figure 1. (**a**) Objectivity scenario, where a system interacts with multiple sub-environments, such that those sub-environments contain information about the system. (**b**) Thermalisation scenario, where a system interacts with a large heat bath environment and subsequently thermalises to the environment temperature.

There are a number of frameworks to mathematically describe objective states: in order of increasing restriction one has (Zurek's) Quantum Darwinism [10], Strong Quantum Darwinism [12] and Spectrum Broadcast Structure [11] (and invariant spectrum broadcast structure [27]). In this work, we will be focusing primarily on a bipartite system-environment, in which case Strong Quantum Darwinism and Spectrum Broadcast Structure coincide. In particular, Spectrum Broadcast Structure gives us a clear geometric state structure which is ideal for state analysis.

Objective states with spectrum broadcast structure can all be written in the following form [11]:

$$\rho_{\mathcal{SE}} = \sum_i p_i |i\rangle\langle i| \otimes \bigotimes_{k=1}^{N} \rho_{\mathcal{E}_k|i}, \quad \rho_{\mathcal{E}_k|i}\rho_{\mathcal{E}_k|j} = 0 \;\forall i \neq j, \quad (1)$$

where $\mathcal{E}$ is the accessible environment and $\mathcal{E}_k$ are the sub-environments. The conditional states $\{\rho_{\mathcal{E}_k|i}\}$ can be used to perfectly distinguish index i, where $\{|i\rangle\}$ is some diagonal basis of the system and $\{p_i\}$ its spectrum. In general, there is no basis dependence in both the system and the environments, and so the overall set of all objective states is non-convex.

3. Thermal States

Systems can exchange energy and heat through interactions with an external environment that functions as a heat bath. Over time, systems can reach thermal equilibrium. Canonically, the thermal state of a quantum system is the Gibbs state [8]. For a given energy/Hamiltonian expectation value, the thermal Gibbs state maximises the von Neumann entropy [28].

The Gibbs state, which we denote as γ, is defined with reference to its Hamiltonian $\hat{H}$ and inverse temperature $\beta = 1/k_B T$:

$$\gamma = \frac{e^{-\beta \hat{H}}}{Z_{\beta,\hat{H}}}, \quad (2)$$

where $Z_{\beta,\hat{H}} = \mathrm{tr}\left[e^{-\beta \hat{H}}\right]$ is the partition function.

If the Hamiltonian has the spectral decomposition $\hat{H} = \sum_i E_i |i\rangle\langle i|$, then we can write the canonical thermal state as

$$\gamma = \frac{\sum_i e^{-\beta E_i} |i\rangle\langle i|}{\left(\sum_j e^{-\beta E_j}\right)}. \tag{3}$$

Remark 1. *For any state ρ of full rank, there exists a Hamiltonian $\hat{H}_\rho$ and an inverse temperature β_ρ such that ρ can be considered a thermal state, i.e., we can write $\rho = \frac{1}{Z} \exp[-\beta \hat{H}_\rho]$. To see this, suppose the state ρ has the spectral decomposition $\rho = \sum_i p_i |\psi_i\rangle\langle\psi_i|$ ($p_i > 0$). Then, consider a Hamiltonian with the same eigenvectors, $\hat{H}_\rho = \sum_i E_i |\psi_i\rangle\langle\psi_i|$, with unknown eigenenergies $\{E_i\}$. We want to find $\{\beta_\rho, E_i\}$ such that*

$$\frac{e^{-\beta_\rho E_i}}{\left(\sum_j e^{-\beta_\rho E_j}\right)} \stackrel{!}{=} p_i, \quad \forall\, i. \tag{4}$$

As there is an extra variable in the set $\{\beta_\rho, E_i\}$ compared to the number of conditions, $|\{p_i\}|$, this forms an underdetermined set of equations and there can be infinitely many solutions formed by scaling β_ρ and E_i inversely.

Objective states are not globally full-rank, but we could add in a very small (non-objective) perturbation to make it full-rank. Then, from this perspective, for any full-rank approximately objective state, we can post-select system-environment Hamiltonians and a temperature at which that objective state is also thermal. In a controlled scenario (e.g., with control of the system Hamiltonian and reservoir engineering [29], or in quantum simulators [30]), it is possible to engineer an approximately objective-and-thermal state by choosing system-environment Hamiltonians based on the objective state itself.

In the rest of this paper, we will be considering the reverse scenario, i.e., *given* some system and environment Hamiltonians and inverse temperature β, can the subsequent thermal state(s) also support objectivity? By answering this question, we will better understand whether or not objectivity and thermalisation can coexist, and what conditions would allow any coexistence.

In order to answer whether or not there is any overlap between thermalisation and objectivity, we consider the precise state structure. If there is no state overlap, then both properties cannot exist simultaneously, in which case there cannot be any dynamics that produces a non-existent state. More generally, if the two set of states are sufficiently close, then perhaps a compromise is possible.

We will be examining three different types of thermal states:

1. States with system-only thermalisation. This reflects many applications and research where the system thermality is key, and the environment is assumed inaccessible, or when we have multiple environment baths of different temperatures that are independent and serve different functions.
2. States with local-system thermalisation and with local-environment thermalisation. This corresponds to the common move to describe a system and the environment as being thermal relative to the local Hamiltonians. This situation typically assumes that either the interaction is removed by the time thermality happens, or that the interaction Hamiltonian commutes with all local Hamiltonians, or that the interaction is weak.
3. Global system–environment thermalisation. This is particularly important when there are continued non-trivial, non-commuting interactions between the system and environment.

Examining thermal *states* rather than some time-averaged or instantaneous values of observables means that we are considering thermalisation in a strong sense (or that we have assumed that averaging has already been done). The results are also therefore suitable for more static applications of thermal states, e.g., resource theories.

In order to find the overlap between objective and thermal states, our main method is to start with objective states and successively restrict them to satisfy thermality. As thermal states are full-rank, we will be restricting to objective states where the reduced system and environment states are also full-rank.

Note that if the local system state thermalises, e.g., relative to its energy eigenbasis, then it can also be said to have decohered (relative to that energy eigenbasis). However, whether or not objectivity—an extension of decoherence—arises depends on whether the system thermal information can be encoded in the environment.

4. Objective States with Thermal System

In this section, we describe the system–environment states that are both objective and have a locally thermal system (and no requirements on the environment thermality or lack thereof).

Consider the situation where a system with self Hamiltonian $\hat{H}_S$ is put in thermal contact with a bath with some temperature T_B, is left to thermalise, and then de-coupled from the bath. Writing the system Hamiltonian's spectral decomposition as $\hat{H}_S = \sum_i E_i |i\rangle\langle i|$ and with fixed inverse temperature β, the system thermal state is then

$$\gamma_S = \frac{e^{-\beta \hat{H}_S}}{Z_{\beta,\hat{H}_S}} = \frac{1}{Z_{\beta,\hat{H}_S}} \sum_i e^{-E_i \beta} |i\rangle\langle i|. \quad (5)$$

This implies that objective system-environment states with locally thermal system states must have the following form:

$$\frac{1}{Z_{\beta,\hat{H}_S}} \sum_i e^{-E_i \beta} |i\rangle\langle i| \otimes \rho_{\mathcal{E}|i}, \quad \rho_{\mathcal{E}|i} \rho_{\mathcal{E}|j} = 0 \,\forall i \neq j, \quad (6)$$

where the conditional $\rho_{\mathcal{E}|i}$ are perfectly distinguishable.

As we can immediately see, these objective states describe fixed thermal-state information about the system, encoded in the probabilities $\left\{\frac{e^{-E_i \beta}}{Z_{\beta,\hat{H}_S}}\right\}_i$. Furthermore, as there are no thermal conditions imposed on the information-carrying environment, the size of set of states satisfying Equation (6) is non-empty, as we have freedom to choose any set of mutually distinguishable environment states $\{\rho_{\mathcal{E}|i}\}_i$. Therefore, objectivity and thermalisation overlap: both can occur at the same time.

The set of exact objective states with thermal system in Equation (6) is nowhere dense, as it is a subset of zero-discord states [31]. The set of states in Equation (6) is also non-convex in general, though convex subsets can be formed by restricting the conditional subspaces on the environment.

Approximate cases would correspond to imperfect information spreading into the environment and/or imperfect system thermalisation before the information spreading stage. As we have a fairly well-defined set of states (Equation (6)), any distance measure to that set can be used to describe approximately objective-with-thermal-system states, e.g.,

$$[\mathsf{T}_S\mathsf{O}]_\delta = \left\{ \rho \,\Big|\, \min_{\rho_{obj,th} \in \mathsf{T}_S\mathsf{O}} \|\rho - \rho_{obj,th}\|_1 \leq \delta \right\}, \quad (7)$$

where $\mathsf{T}_S\mathsf{O}$ (thermal-system objective) denotes the set of states satisfying Equation (6), and $\|\cdot\|_1$ is the trace norm. The convex hull of objective-with-thermal-system states are simply zero-discord states with a local thermal system:

$$\left\{ \frac{1}{Z_{\beta,\hat{H}_S}} \sum_i e^{-E_i \beta} |i\rangle\langle i| \otimes \rho_{\mathcal{E}|i} \,\Big|\, \rho_{\mathcal{E}|i} \in \mathcal{H}_\mathcal{E} \right\}, \quad (8)$$

i.e., there are no longer any restrictions on the conditional environment states $\rho_{\mathcal{E}|i}$.

Creating Objective States with Thermal Systems

A two-step process that produces objective-with-thermal-system states is first system thermalisation followed by information broadcasting. Physically, this can occur if the system was first thermalised using one bath, and then we had a fresh environment interact with the system with intent to gain information. As environments in low-entropy state $|0\rangle$ are typically better for quantum Darwinism [32–36], this second 'information-storing' environment could be a very cold bath with states close to the ground state.

The point channel can produce perfectly thermalised states:

$$\Phi_{S,th}(\cdot) = \text{tr}[\cdot]\gamma_S. \tag{9}$$

One simple method to broadcast information from system to environment is to start with the information-carrying environment in state $|0\rangle$ (e.g., zero temperature bath). Then, controlled-NOT (CNOT) operations with control system to each individual environment will perfectly broadcast the system information [14,35]:

$$\Phi_{\text{CNOT}}^{\mathcal{E}_k}(\rho_{S\mathcal{E}_k}) = U_{\text{CNOT}}^{S\mathcal{E}_k}\rho_{S\mathcal{E}_k}U_{\text{CNOT}}^{S\mathcal{E}_k\dagger}, \tag{10}$$

where $U_{\text{CNOT}}^{S\mathcal{E}_k}$ is the CNOT gate between system $\mathcal{S}$ and environment $\mathcal{E}_k$.

In general, quantum channels that can create the exact objective-with-thermal-system states from Equation (6) are point channels which thermalise the system combined with information broadcasting channels:

$$\Phi_{T_sO}(\rho_{S\mathcal{E}}) = \frac{1}{Z_{\beta,\hat{H}_S}} \sum_i e^{-E_i\beta}|i\rangle\langle i| \otimes \Phi_{\mathcal{E}|i}(\rho_{S\mathcal{E}}), \tag{11}$$

where $\left\{\Phi_{\mathcal{E}|i} : \mathcal{H}_S \otimes \hat{\mathcal{H}}_\mathcal{E} \to \hat{\mathcal{H}}_\mathcal{E}\right\}_i$ are channels on the environment such that the output states for different i are orthogonal.

This process can be performed on a quantum simulator by dividing the available qubits into 'system', 'thermal environment' and 'information-carrying environment', and enacting the suitable gate operations [37].

We can also consider partial thermalisation channels Λ_{p-th}, such that *repeated application* brings the system closer and closer to thermalisation, i.e.,

$$\Lambda_{p-th} \circ \cdots \circ \Lambda_{p-th}(\cdot) \to \gamma_S. \tag{12}$$

If the system is a qubit, then we can, without loss of generality, consider the system qubit Hamiltonian to be $H = \sigma_z/2$. One channel which, through repeated application, will lead to the system thermalising is the generalised amplitude damping channel [38]

$$\rho(t) = \Phi_t^T(\rho_0) = \sum_{i=1}^{4} E_i\rho_0 E_i^*, \tag{13}$$

with Kraus operators

$$E_1 = \sqrt{p}\begin{bmatrix} 1 & 0 \\ 0 & \sqrt{\eta} \end{bmatrix}, \qquad E_2 = \sqrt{p}\begin{bmatrix} 0 & \sqrt{1-\eta} \\ 0 & 0 \end{bmatrix}, \tag{14}$$

$$E_3 = \sqrt{1-p}\begin{bmatrix} \sqrt{\eta} & 0 \\ 0 & 1 \end{bmatrix}, \qquad E_4 = \sqrt{1-p}\begin{bmatrix} 0 & 0 \\ \sqrt{1-\eta} & 0 \end{bmatrix}, \tag{15}$$

where $p \in [0,1]$ depends on the temperature of the environment, and $\eta_t = 1 - e^{-(1+2\tilde{N})t}$, where $\tilde{N} = \frac{1}{e^{1/T}-1}$ is the boson occupation number. The equivalent Bloch sphere representation is [38,39]

$$\begin{bmatrix} x' \\ y' \\ z' \end{bmatrix} = \begin{bmatrix} \sqrt{\eta} & & \\ & \sqrt{\eta} & \\ & & \sqrt{\eta} \end{bmatrix} \begin{bmatrix} x \\ y \\ z \end{bmatrix} + \begin{bmatrix} 0 \\ 0 \\ (2p-1)(1-\eta) \end{bmatrix}, \tag{16}$$

with stationary state

$$\sigma_\infty = \begin{bmatrix} p & 0 \\ 0 & 1-p \end{bmatrix}, \tag{17}$$

where $x = \text{tr}[\sigma_x \rho_0]$, $y = \text{tr}[\sigma_y \rho_0]$ and $z = \text{tr}[\sigma_z \rho_0]$.

More generally, the following channel, in the Bloch sphere representation, will partially thermalise the system:

$$\Lambda_{p-th}(\vec{r}) = A\vec{r} + (1-A)\vec{t}_S, \tag{18}$$

where $\vec{t}_S$ is the Bloch vector of the system thermal state γ_S, $\|A\| < 1$ (under matrix norm) and $\|A\vec{r} + (1-A)\vec{t}_S\|_2 \leq 1$ for all $\|\vec{r}\|_2 \leq 1$ (under Euclidean norm). Under repeated application, the state will converge towards the Bloch vector $\vec{t}_S$, i.e., to the thermal state.

Aside from the specific model-dependent methods to produce objective-thermal states, it is possible to produce a quantum circuit that will prepare that state [40,41]. Alternatively, one could also construct a Lindblad generator $\mathcal{L}$ (with an unobserved environment) that simulates a chosen quantum channel (in the infinite time limit) [42]. In general, the specific timescales will depend on the situation and also the size of the "unobserved" environment in comparison with the system and observed environment [43–46].

5. Objective States with Thermal System and Thermal Environment

Thermal environments play a large role in thermodynamics and open quantum systems. In this section, we suppose that both the system and the environment are locally thermal.

As in the previous section, we take the system local Hamiltonian to have some general spectral decomposition $\hat{H}_S = \sum_i E_i |i\rangle\langle i|$. Suppose that the environment's self-Hamiltonian has this spectral decomposition: $\hat{H}_\mathcal{E} = \sum_k h_k |\psi_k\rangle\langle\psi_k|$. This leads to the environment thermal state

$$\gamma_\mathcal{E} = \frac{e^{-\beta \hat{H}_\mathcal{E}}}{Z_{\beta, \hat{H}_\mathcal{E}}}. \tag{19}$$

States that are locally thermal in the system and the environment can be written generally as

$$\rho_{S\mathcal{E}} = \gamma_S \otimes \gamma_\mathcal{E} + \chi_{S\mathcal{E}}, \tag{20}$$

where $\chi_{S\mathcal{E}}$ is a correlation matrix where $\text{tr}_S \chi_{S\mathcal{E}} = 0$ and $\text{tr}_\mathcal{E} \chi_{S\mathcal{E}} = 0$ [47]. Our aim is to determine whether this correlation matrix can hold objective correlations.

If the system and environment have *pure* thermal states, then the combined system–environment thermal state $|\gamma_S\rangle\langle\gamma_S| \otimes |\gamma_\mathcal{E}\rangle\langle\gamma_\mathcal{E}|$ is also trivially objective, because there is only one index on the system that the environment needs to distinguish. This can happen if the system and environment only have one energy level, or if the temperature is zero (or very low) and the system and environment both have non-degenerate ground states.

In general though, the system will not have a pure thermal state. With the added restriction of thermal environments, exact co-existence of states that are simultaneously objective and thermal becomes difficult to achieve: the thermality of the environment comes in conflict with the strong condition of classical correlations required by objectivity.

5.1. Equal System and Environment Dimension

In the scenario where the system and the individual environments have the same dimension, an exact thermal and bipartite-objective state can only exist for highly fine-tuned system and environment Hamiltonians, i.e., the energy spacing of both must be the same.

Remark 2. *If the system and individual environments have the same dimension, there exists a joint state that is both locally-thermal and objective only if they have the same thermal eigen-energies, i.e., the system Hamiltonian eigen-energies $\{E_i\}$ differ from the environment Hamiltonian eigen-energies $\{h_i\}$ by a constant shift, $E_i = h_i + c \; \forall i$.*

Proof of Remark 2. To see this, consider the objective state structure in Equation (1) and enforce the requirement of local thermality. As the environment has the same dimension, the conditional environment states of the objective state must be pure, and orthogonal for $i \neq j$, i.e., have form $\rho_{\mathcal{E}_k|i} = |\phi_{i|k}\rangle\langle\phi_{i|k}|$. This leads to the following state which is objective:

$$\rho_{S\mathcal{E}} = \sum_i p_i |i\rangle\langle i| \bigotimes_k |\phi_{i|k}\rangle\langle\phi_{i|k}|, \quad \langle\phi_{i|k}|\phi_{j|k}\rangle = 0 \; \forall i \neq j, \; \forall k, \qquad (21)$$

where $\left\{|\phi_{i|k}\rangle\right\}$ are the eigenvectors of the individual environments. This objective structure corresponds to invariant spectrum broadcast structure [27], as the environment states are also objective.

Local thermality of the system and environments means that

$$\rho_S = \sum_i p_i |i\rangle\langle i| \stackrel{!}{=} \gamma_S \text{ and } \rho_{\mathcal{E}_k} = \sum_i p_i |\phi_{i|k}\rangle\langle\phi_{i|k}| \stackrel{!}{=} \gamma_{\mathcal{E}_k}. \qquad (22)$$

In order for this to be true, the eigenvalues of both the system thermal state γ_S and the environment thermal states $\gamma_{\mathcal{E}_k}$ must be identical and equalling $\{p_i\}$, i.e.,

$$\frac{e^{-\beta E_i}}{Z_{\beta,\hat{H}_S}} = \frac{e^{-\beta h_i}}{Z_{\beta,\hat{H}_{\mathcal{E}_k}}} \quad \forall i, \qquad (23)$$

with appropriate labelling of "i" on the system and the environment.

As the inverse temperature is fixed at some β, this means that the Hamiltonian eigenenergies of the system and environment must also be the same, $\{E_i\}$ and $\{h_i\}$, respectively, up to a constant shift. That is, the environment eigenenergies are $h_i = E_i + c$, thus

$$\frac{e^{-(E_i+c)\beta}}{\sum_j e^{-(E_j+c)\beta}} = \frac{e^{-c\beta}e^{-E_i\beta}}{\sum_j e^{-c\beta}e^{-E_j\beta}} = \frac{e^{-E_i\beta}}{Z_{\beta,\hat{H}_S}}, \qquad (24)$$

as required. □

Realistically, the scenario of system and environments having identical dimension and equal eigenenergies can occur if both are made out of the same *material*, e.g., they are all photons, all spins, etc. with the same internal and external Hamiltonians up to a constant energy shift.

This shows that randomly independently chosen individual Hamiltonians for the system and the environment, will, in general, *not* support an exact thermal and objective system–environment state. Once a particular system Hamiltonian is chosen, say $\hat{H}_S = \sum_i E_i |i\rangle\langle i|$, an exact thermal-objective system-environment state (with identical system and sub-environment dimensions) can only exist if the environment Hamiltonians have form $\hat{H}_{\mathcal{E}_k} = \sum_i (E_i + c_k) U_k |i\rangle\langle i| U_k^\dagger$, with freedom in real value energy c_k and unitary rotation U_k

that produces various sets of orthogonal eigenvectors, in order to give rise to the exact thermal-objective state:

$$\rho_{S\mathcal{E}}^{obj,th} = \frac{1}{Z_{\beta,\hat{H}_S}} \sum_i e^{-E_i \beta} |i\rangle\langle i| \otimes \bigotimes_{k=1}^{N} |\phi_{i|k}\rangle\langle\phi_{i|k}|, \quad (25)$$

where $|\phi_{i|k}\rangle = U_k |i\rangle_{\mathcal{E}_k}$.

5.1.1. Approximate Thermal-Objective States

As noted, an exact thermal-objective state can only emerge when the system and environment Hamiltonians have a very particular relationship. More generally, we can look for the existence of a state that is *approximately* thermal and objective.

Suppose we allow a deviation in the environment Hamiltonian from the ideal Hamiltonian, i.e., where $\hat{H}_{\mathcal{E}} = \sum_i (E_i + c + \delta_i)|\phi_i\rangle\langle\phi_i|_{\mathcal{E}}$, where $\{\delta_i\}_i$ are different for at least two i's (we work with one environment for simplicity). In this situation, while the state in Equation (25) is objective, it no longer has local thermal environments. We can measure the minimum distance between the set of thermal states and the set of objective states with the trace norm as follows:

$$D_{\text{obj-thm}}(\hat{H}_S, \hat{H}_{\mathcal{E}}, \beta) = \min_{\rho_{obj}, \gamma_{S\mathcal{E}}} \left\| \rho_{obj} - \gamma_{S\mathcal{E}} \right\|_1, \quad (26)$$

where ρ_{obj} are objective states, and $\gamma_{S\mathcal{E}} = \gamma_S \otimes \gamma_{\mathcal{E}} + \chi_{S\mathcal{E}}$ have locally thermal system and environment and variable correlation matrix $\chi_{S\mathcal{E}}$.

Taking the ansatz

$$\rho_{obj}^* = \frac{1}{Z_{\beta,\hat{H}_S}} \sum_i e^{-E_i\beta} |i\rangle\langle i| \otimes |\phi_i\rangle\langle\phi_i|_{\mathcal{E}}, \quad (27)$$

from Equation (25), the distance of this objective state to the set of locally thermal states can be bounded above:

$$D_{\text{obj-thm}}(\hat{H}_S, \hat{H}_{\mathcal{E}_k}, \beta)$$
$$\leq \min_{\chi_{S\mathcal{E}} \text{ traceless}} \left\| \begin{array}{l} \frac{1}{Z_{\beta,\hat{H}_S}} \sum_i e^{-E_i\beta}|i\rangle\langle i| \otimes |\phi_i\rangle\langle\phi_i|_{\mathcal{E}} \\ -\frac{1}{Z_{\beta,\hat{H}_S}} \sum_i e^{-E_i\beta}|i\rangle\langle i| \otimes \frac{1}{Z_{\beta,\hat{H}_{\mathcal{E}}}} \sum_j e^{-(E_j+c+\delta_j)\beta}|\phi_j\rangle\langle\phi_j|_{\mathcal{E}} - \chi_{S\mathcal{E}} \end{array} \right\|_1. \quad (28)$$

By picking a sample matrix,

$$\chi_{S\mathcal{E}} = \frac{1}{Z_{\beta,\hat{H}_S}} \sum_i e^{-E_i\beta}|i\rangle\langle i| \otimes |\phi_i\rangle\langle\phi_i|_{\mathcal{E}} - \gamma_S \otimes \frac{1}{Z_{\beta,\hat{H}_S}} \sum_i e^{-E_i\beta}|\phi_i\rangle\langle\phi_i|_{\mathcal{E}}, \quad (29)$$

the distance is then bounded as

$$D_{\text{obj-thm}}(\hat{H}_S, \hat{H}_{\mathcal{E}_k}, \beta)$$
$$\leq \left\| \gamma_S \otimes \frac{1}{Z_{\beta,\hat{H}_{\mathcal{E}}}} \sum_j e^{-(E_j+c+\delta_j)\beta}|\phi_j\rangle\langle\phi_j|_{\mathcal{E}} - \gamma_S \otimes \frac{1}{Z_{\beta,\hat{H}_S}} \sum_i e^{-E_i\beta}|\phi_i\rangle\langle\phi_i|_{\mathcal{E}} \right\|_1 \quad (30)$$

$$= \left\| \frac{1}{Z_{\beta,\hat{H}_{\mathcal{E}}}} \sum_j e^{-(E_j+c+\delta_j)\beta}|\phi_j\rangle\langle\phi_j|_{\mathcal{E}} - \frac{1}{Z_{\beta,\hat{H}_S}} \sum_i e^{-E_i\beta}|\phi_i\rangle\langle\phi_i|_{\mathcal{E}} \right\|_1 \quad (31)$$

$$= \sum_i \left| \frac{e^{-(E_i+c+\delta_i)\beta}}{Z_{\beta,\hat{H}_{\mathcal{E}}}} - \frac{e^{-E_i\beta}}{Z_{\beta,\hat{H}_S}} \right|. \quad (32)$$

The distance is bounded by the difference between the thermal-state eigenenergies, which here is a nonlinear function of the deviations $\{\delta_i\}$.

In Figure 2, we consider if this error is Normal-distributed $\delta_i \sim \mathcal{N}(0, \sigma)$ with mean zero and standard deviation σ. We see that, on average, increasing the spread σ linearly increases the upper bound on the distance measure of Equation (32) in the domain considered.

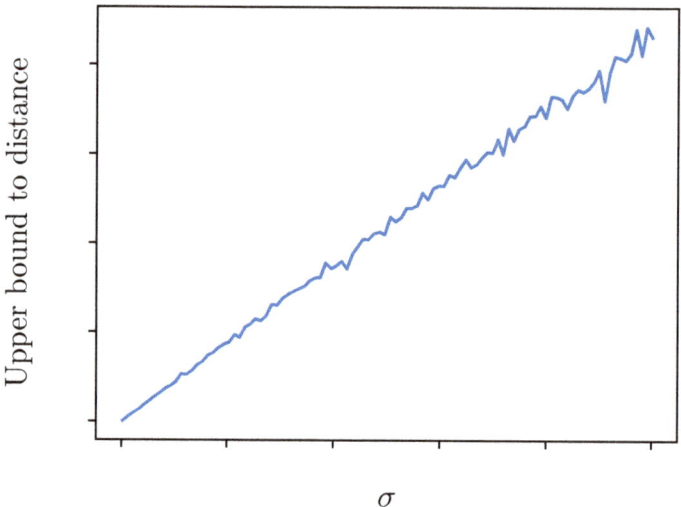

Figure 2. Averaged upper bound to the distance (Equation (32)) between the set of objective states vs. the set of thermal states (locally thermal system and environment) versus standard deviation σ of the deviations δ_i. That is, the environment Hamiltonian is less-than-optimal: for a system Hamiltonian energy distribution $\{E_i\}$, the environment Hamiltonian energies are $\{E_i + \delta_i\}$, where the deviations are $\delta_i \sim \mathcal{N}(0, \sigma)$ (normal distribution). The inverse temperature is $\beta = 1$, with qubit system and qubit environment. Averaged across 1000 random instances.

5.1.2. Employing Macrofractions

A known technique for improving distinguishability of environments is the use of macrofractions, i.e., grouping multiple subenvironments into a greater environment fragment [48–50]. By doing this, even if the deviation of the environment Hamiltonian energies from the system Hamiltonian energies is large, we may be able to construct an approximate objective-thermal state.

Consider the distance between the set of objective states and the set of states with locally thermal subsystems similarly as above:

$$D_{\text{obj-thm}}\left(\hat{H}_{\mathcal{S}}, \{\hat{H}_{\mathcal{E}_k}\}_{k=1}^{N}, \beta\right) = \min_{\rho_{\text{obj}}, \gamma_{\mathcal{S}\mathcal{E}}} \left\| \rho_{\text{obj}} - \gamma_{\mathcal{S}\mathcal{E}} \right\|_1, \tag{33}$$

where the following state consists of locally thermal system and environments: $\gamma_{\mathcal{S}\mathcal{E}} = \gamma_{\mathcal{S}} \otimes \gamma_{\mathcal{E}_1} \otimes \cdots \otimes \gamma_{\mathcal{E}_N} + \chi_{\mathcal{S}\mathcal{E}}$, with correlation matrix $\chi_{\mathcal{S}\mathcal{E}}$ such that $\text{tr}_{\mathcal{S}}[\chi_{\mathcal{S}\mathcal{E}}] = 0$ and $\text{tr}_{\mathcal{E}_k}[\chi_{\mathcal{S}\mathcal{E}}] = 0$ for all k.

Using $\rho^*_{obj} = \frac{1}{Z_{\beta,\hat{H}_S}} \sum_i e^{-E_i\beta}|i\rangle\langle i| \otimes \bigotimes_{k=1}^N |\phi_i\rangle\langle\phi_i|_{\mathcal{E}_k}$ as an example close-by objective state, and with matrix

$$\chi^*_{S\mathcal{E}} = \rho^*_{obj} - \gamma_S \otimes \bigotimes_{k=1}^N \left(\frac{1}{Z_{\beta,\hat{H}_S}} \sum_i e^{-E_i\beta}|\phi_i\rangle\langle\phi_i|_{\mathcal{E}_k} \right), \quad (34)$$

the distance is then bounded as

$$D_{\text{obj-thm}}(\hat{H}_S, \hat{H}_{\mathcal{E}_1}, \ldots, \hat{H}_{\mathcal{E}_N}, \beta)$$

$$\leq \left\| \bigotimes_{k=1}^N \left(\frac{1}{Z_{\beta,\hat{H}_{\mathcal{E}_k}}} \sum_i e^{-(E_i + c + \delta_{i|k})\beta}|\phi_i\rangle\langle\phi_i|_{\mathcal{E}_k} \right) \right.$$
$$\left. - \bigotimes_{k=1}^N \left(\frac{1}{Z_{\beta,\hat{H}_S}} \sum_i e^{-E_i\beta}|\phi_i\rangle\langle\phi_i|_{\mathcal{E}_k} \right) \right\|_1 \quad (35)$$

$$= \sum_{i_1,\ldots,i_N} \left| \frac{e^{-(E_{i_1} + c + \delta_{i_1|1})\beta}}{Z_{\beta,\hat{H}_{\mathcal{E}_1}}} + \cdots + \frac{e^{-(E_{i_N} + c + \delta_{i_N|N})\beta}}{Z_{\beta,\hat{H}_{\mathcal{E}_N}}} - \frac{e^{-E_{i_1}\beta} \cdots e^{-E_{i_N}\beta}}{\left(Z_{\beta,\hat{H}_S}\right)^N} \right|. \quad (36)$$

We plot the behaviour of the bound Equation (36) in Figure 3. As expected, the figure shows that increasing the number of environments included into a macrofraction leads to a decreasing distance between the set of thermal states versus the set of objective states. This is essentially as though we considered increasingly larger environments, which is the focus of the next subsection.

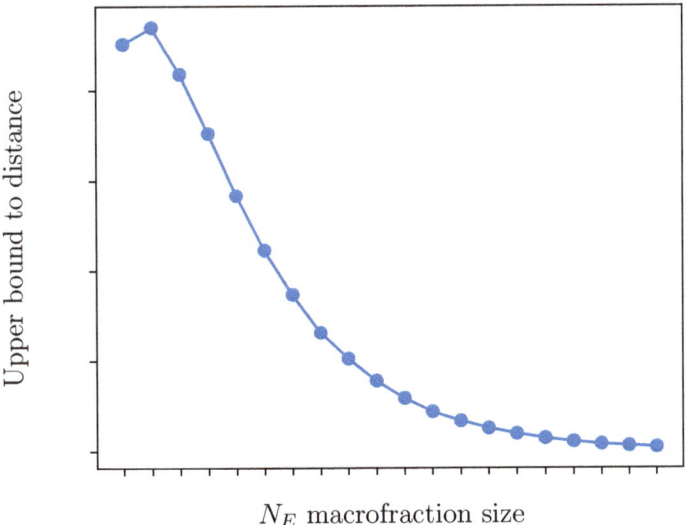

Figure 3. Upper bound to the distance (Equation (36)) between the set of objective states and the set of thermal states (locally thermal system and environment) versus macrofractions of size N_E. A macrofraction is collection of environments. Here, the environment Hamiltonians are less-than-optimal, i.e., for a system Hamiltonian energy distribution $\{E_i\}$, the environment Hamiltonians energies are $\{E_i + \delta_{i|k}\}$, $k = 1, \ldots, N_E$, where the "error" is $\delta_i \sim \mathcal{N}(0, \sigma = 0.05)$ (Normal distribution). The inverse temperature is $\beta = 1$, with qubit system and qubit environments. Averaged across 500 random instances.

5.2. Environment Dimension Larger than System Dimension

In common situations, environments are much larger than the system. Intuitively, larger environment dimensions should give greater flexibility to form approximately objective-thermal states. In this section, we find that the existence of exact thermal-objective states requires very fine tuned system and environment Hamiltonians. However, we will also find that as the dimension of the environment goes up (e.g., towards the classical/thermodynamic limit), there will exist states that are close to both objectivity and local thermality.

Theorem 1. *The distance between the set of objective states and the set of states with locally thermal system and environment goes to zero as the dimension of the environment goes to infinity.*

Proof of Theorem 1. Consider the distance between these two sets for some given system thermal state γ_S and environment thermal state $\gamma_\mathcal{E}$:

$$D_{\text{obj-thm}}(\gamma_S, \gamma_\mathcal{E}) = \min_{\substack{\rho_{obj} \\ \chi_{S\mathcal{E}}}} \left\| \rho_{obj} - (\gamma_S \otimes \gamma_\mathcal{E} + \chi_{S\mathcal{E}}) \right\|_1, \qquad (37)$$

where ρ_{obj} are objective states and $\chi_{S\mathcal{E}}$ are correlation matrices. Decomposing the system thermal state as $\gamma_S = \sum_i p_i |i\rangle\langle i|$, where $p_i = \dfrac{e^{-E_i\beta}}{Z_{\beta, \hat{H}_S}}$, we can bound Equation (37) by fixing the local state on the system in the objective states ρ_{obj} as

$$D_{\text{obj-thm}}(\gamma_S, \gamma_\mathcal{E}) \leq \min_{\substack{\rho_{\mathcal{E}|i} \perp \rho_{\mathcal{E}|i'} \\ \chi_{S\mathcal{E}}}} \left\| \sum_i p_i |i\rangle\langle i| \otimes \rho_{\mathcal{E}|i} - (\gamma_S \otimes \gamma_\mathcal{E} + \chi_{S\mathcal{E}}) \right\|_1, \qquad (38)$$

where $\rho_{\mathcal{E}|i} \perp \rho_{\mathcal{E}|i'}$ denotes that the conditional environment states should be perfectly distinguishable as per objectivity.

By picking a sample matrix $\chi_{S\mathcal{E}} = \sum_i p_i |i\rangle\langle i| \otimes \rho_{\mathcal{E}|i} - \gamma_S \otimes \sum_i p_i \rho_{\mathcal{E}|i}$, the distance Equation (38) is then bounded as

$$D_{\text{obj-thm}}(\gamma_S, \gamma_\mathcal{E}) \leq \min_{\rho_{\mathcal{E}|i} \perp \rho_{\mathcal{E}|i'}} \left\| \sum_i p_i \rho_{\mathcal{E}|i} - \gamma_\mathcal{E} \right\|_1. \qquad (39)$$

Write the environment thermal state as $\gamma_\mathcal{E} = \sum_j \dfrac{e^{-h_j\beta}}{Z_{\beta, \hat{H}_\mathcal{E}}} |\psi_j\rangle\langle\psi_j|$. Suppose that the states $\rho_{\mathcal{E}|i}$ are diagonal in the same eigenstates as $\{|\psi_j\rangle\}$, i.e., take $\rho_{\mathcal{E}|i} = \sum_j c_{j|i} |\psi_j\rangle\langle\psi_j|$, where $\sum_j c_{j|i} = 1$, and $c_{j|i} c_{j|i'} = 0$ for $i \neq i'$ for orthogonality. Then,

$$D_{\text{obj-thm}}(\gamma_S, \gamma_\mathcal{E}) \leq \min_{c_{j|i} \text{ orthogonal}} \sum_j \left| \sum_i p_i c_{j|i} - \frac{e^{-h_j\beta}}{Z_{\beta, \hat{H}_\mathcal{E}}} \right|. \qquad (40)$$

As $c_{j|i} c_{j|i'} = 0$ (i.e., for orthogonality), we can define disjoint sets C_i where $j \in C_i$ means $c_{j|i} \neq 0$ and $c_{j|i'} = 0$ if $i \neq i'$. We are essentially partitioning the environment eigenvectors $|\psi_j\rangle_\mathcal{E}$ into groups labelled by the *system* eigenvectors $|i\rangle_S$.

$$D_{\text{obj-thm}}(\gamma_S, \gamma_\mathcal{E}) \leq \min_{\{C_i\} \text{disjoint}} \sum_{k=1}^{d_S} \sum_{j \in C_k} \left| p_k c_{j|k} - \frac{e^{-h_j\beta}}{Z_{\beta, \hat{H}_\mathcal{E}}} \right|. \qquad (41)$$

Naively, the minimum would occur if $c_{j|i}^* = \left(\dfrac{e^{-h_j\beta}}{Z_{\beta, \hat{H}_\mathcal{E}}} \right) / p_i$. However, such $c_{j|i}$ may not lead to a real state, due to lack of normalisation. Instead, we can upperbound this with the candidate $\tilde{c}_{j|i} = \dfrac{c^*_{j|i}}{\sum_{k \in C_i} c^*_{k|i}}$, which *is* normalised. In the optimal case, $\tilde{c}_{j|i} = c^*_{j|i}$ and the distance would go to zero. Simplifying, then our candidates are

$$\tilde{c}_{j|i} = \frac{e^{-h_j \beta}}{\sum_{k \in C_i} e^{-h_k \beta}}, \tag{42}$$

leading to

$$D_{\text{obj-thm.}}(\gamma_S, \gamma_\mathcal{E}) \leq \min_{\{C_i\}\text{disjoint}} \sum_{k=1}^{d_S} \left| p_k - \frac{\left(\sum_{j \in C_k} e^{-h_j \beta}\right)}{Z_{\beta, \hat{H}_\mathcal{E}}} \right|. \tag{43}$$

Without loss of generality, we can consider the smallest h_j to be zero, and therefore $\max_j \dfrac{e^{-h_j \beta}}{Z_{\beta, \hat{H}_\mathcal{E}}} = \dfrac{1}{Z_{\beta, \hat{H}_\mathcal{E}}}$.

Consider the following algorithm for picking j indices to include in C_k. Every time we include in another index $\tilde{j}$ into C_k, the value of $\dfrac{\left(\sum_{j \in C_k} e^{-h_j \beta}\right)}{Z_{\beta, \hat{H}_\mathcal{E}}}$ increases by at most $\dfrac{1}{Z_{\beta, \hat{H}_\mathcal{E}}}$. Therefore, a basic procedure is to start with $C_k = \{\cdot\}$ (empty) and randomly add in $j_1, j_2, \ldots$ until we are close to the value of p_k. We stop adding more j's when $\dfrac{\left(\sum_{j \in C_k} e^{-h_j \beta}\right)}{Z_{\beta, \hat{H}_\mathcal{E}}}$ exceeds the value of p_k, and can choose to either keep or remove the last j depending on whether its inclusion or exclusion leads to a value closer to p_k.

Because the maximum step-change is $\dfrac{1}{Z_{\beta, \hat{H}_\mathcal{E}}}$, this means that the maximum difference is bounded:

$$\left| p_k - \frac{\left(\sum_{j \in C_k} e^{-h_j \beta}\right)}{Z_{\beta, \hat{H}_\mathcal{E}}} \right| \leq \frac{1}{2} \frac{1}{Z_{\beta, \hat{H}_\mathcal{E}}}. \tag{44}$$

We depict this in Figure 4.

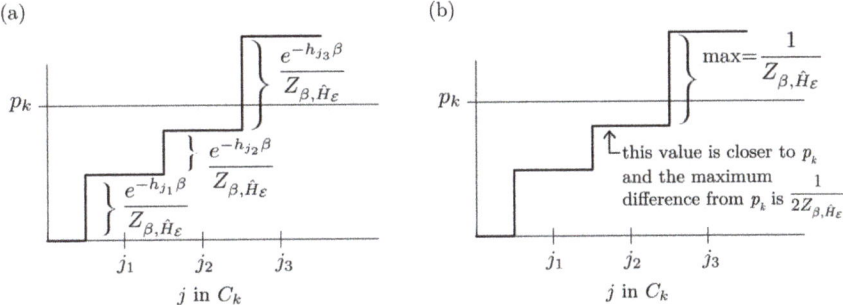

Figure 4. Illustration of part of the proof for Theorem 1, following after Equation (43). The aim is to assign environment indices j to groups labelled by system indices k. As we add in more indices j into C_k, the sum $\dfrac{\left(\sum_{j \in C_k} e^{-h_j \beta}\right)}{Z_{\beta, \hat{H}_\mathcal{E}}}$ increases. In this example, in (**a**), we stop adding more indices after j_3, as j_3 leads to overshooting the value of p_k. We either keep the last j_3 if the sum with j_3 is closer to p_k or we do not include it if the sum is closer to p_k without it. In (**b**), we have decided not to keep the last j_3 term as the sum is closer to p_k without it.

Repeat this for all p_k. In a random procedure, it may happen that some C_k have been overassigned, leading to many sums which are large $\frac{\left(\sum_{j \in C_k} e^{-h_j \beta}\right)}{Z_{\beta, \hat{H}_{\mathcal{E}}}} > p_k$, thus leading to a shortage of indices j left for the remaining p_k. Therefore, we may have to suboptimally remove earlier indices $\tilde{j}$, leading to a greater maximum difference:

$$\left| p_k - \frac{\left(\sum_{j \in C_k} e^{-h_j \beta}\right)}{Z_{\beta, \hat{H}_{\mathcal{E}}}} \right| \leq \frac{1}{Z_{\beta, \hat{H}_{\mathcal{E}}}}. \tag{45}$$

Therefore,

$$D_{\text{obj-thm}}(\gamma_S, \gamma_{\mathcal{E}}) \leq \sum_{k=1}^{d_S} \frac{1}{Z_{\beta, \hat{H}_{\mathcal{E}}}} = \frac{d_S}{Z_{\beta, \hat{H}_{\mathcal{E}}}}. \tag{46}$$

As the dimension of the environment, d_E, increases, this leads to more environment Hamiltonian eigenvalues $\{h_j\}$. This in turn increases the value of the partition function $Z_{\beta, \hat{H}_{\mathcal{E}}} = \sum_{j=1}^{d_E} e^{-h_j \beta} \to \infty$ as $d_E \to \infty$. Thus, the distance between the set of thermal states and the set of objective states goes to zero: $D_{\text{obj-thm}}(\gamma_S, \gamma_{\mathcal{E}}) \to 0$ (provided the system dimension remains fixed). □

5.3. Low Temperature and High Temperature Limits

Provided that the Hamiltonian of the *system* has a non-degenerate ground state, then in the low temperature limit, the thermal state of the system will be (approximately) pure. At $T = 0$, we will have the trivial objective and thermal state $|\psi_{S\text{ground}}\rangle\langle\psi_{S\text{ground}}| \otimes \gamma_{\mathcal{E}}$ ground (trivially objective in the sense that there is only one index/single piece of information available).

In contrast, in the high temperature limit, the thermal states of the system and environment will approach maximally mixed states. If the dimension of the environment, d_E is the same as the system $d = d_S = d_E$, then at the infinite temperature limit, the following state satisfies both local thermality and objectivity:

$$\rho_{T \to \infty} = \frac{1}{d} \sum_i |i\rangle\langle i|_S \otimes |\psi_i\rangle\langle\psi_i|_{\mathcal{E}}, \tag{47}$$

along with any other local permutation of indices. This leads to $d!$ different objective-thermal states.

If the dimension of the environment is a *multiple* of the system dimension, then it is also possible to have an exact locally-thermal and objective state: Suppose $d_E = M d_S$ where $M \in \mathbb{N}$ is a positive integer. Note that the system thermal state at this infinite temperature is $\gamma_S = \sum_{i=1}^{d_S} \frac{1}{d_S} |i\rangle\langle i|$. The environment thermal state can be written as

$$\gamma_{\mathcal{E}} = \sum_{i=1}^{d_E} \frac{1}{d_E} |\psi_i\rangle\langle\psi_i| = \sum_{i=1}^{M d_S} \frac{1}{M d_S} |\psi_i\rangle\langle\psi_i| = \sum_{i=1}^{d_S} \frac{1}{d_S} \rho_{\mathcal{E}|i}, \tag{48}$$

$$\rho_{\mathcal{E}|i} := \sum_{k=M(i-1)+1}^{Mi} \frac{1}{M} |\psi_k\rangle\langle\psi_k|. \tag{49}$$

Therefore, the joint state

$$\rho_{S\mathcal{E}} = \sum_{i=1}^{d_S} \frac{1}{d_S} |i\rangle\langle i| \otimes \rho_{\mathcal{E}|i} \tag{50}$$

is both objective *and* satisfies local thermality. We can also see that this state is not unique, i.e., permutations of $|\psi_k\rangle$ in each $\rho_{\mathcal{E}|i}$ are possible, thus there is more than one state that is both objective and satisfies local thermality. To be precise, there are $\frac{(Md_S)!}{(M!)^{d_S}}$ such exactly objective-thermal states.

However, in general, the environment dimension is not an exact multiple of the system dimension. Then, in the high temperature limit, there does not exist an *exact* objective-thermal state. We can apply Theorem 1 to bound the distance between the set of thermal states (at $T \to \infty$) and the set of objective states:

$$D_{\text{obj-thm}}(\gamma_S, \gamma_{\mathcal{E}})|_{T \to \infty} \leq \frac{d_S}{Z_{\beta, \hat{H}_{\mathcal{E}}}} = \frac{d_S}{d_{\mathcal{E}}}. \tag{51}$$

That is, the higher the environment dimension relative to the system dimension, the more likely it is to have a state that is both closely thermal and closely objective.

6. Objective States That Are Globally Thermal

When the system–environment interaction is strong and/or non-commuting with the local Hamiltonians, the thermal state cannot be described by just the local Hamiltonian. Instead, the joint-system environment thermal state is given by the total Hamiltonian, $\hat{H}_{\text{total}} = \hat{H}_S + \hat{H}_{\mathcal{E}} + \hat{H}_{\text{int}}$, where $\hat{H}_{\text{int}}$ is the interaction Hamiltonian:

$$\gamma_{S\mathcal{E}} = \frac{e^{-\beta \hat{H}_{\text{total}}}}{Z_{\beta, \hat{H}_{\text{total}}}}. \tag{52}$$

This type of scenario assumes that the system and environment continue to interact for all time, in all the relevant time frames. As there is only one such thermal state for finite systems, we do not have the extra degrees of freedom for forming objective states as we did in the previous two sections. As such, it is highly unlikely that this one global thermal state is also exactly objective. Furthermore, thermal states are full-rank, but exact objective states are not globally full-rank. So at best, there could only an approximately objective-thermal state.

The global thermal state $\gamma_{S\mathcal{E}}$ will only be approximately objective if the relevant total Hamiltonian structure itself fits a very particular form such that its thermal state is also objective at the appropriate energy scale. The eigenstates of the total Hamiltonian become the eigenstates of the thermal state. Therefore, the Hamiltonians must have a particular *system-environment correlated* eigenstate structure. We give two examples:

Example 1. *Consider the Hamiltonian*

$$\hat{H}_{\text{total}} = \sum_i E_i |i\rangle\langle i| \otimes |\phi_i\rangle\langle\phi_i| + \hat{H}_{\text{high-energy}}, \tag{53}$$

where $\hat{H}_{\text{high-energy}}$ is an orthogonal addition with eigenenergies much higher than the energy scale given by the temperature T and with eigenstates such that $\hat{H}_{\text{total}}$ is full-rank. This produces the following global thermal state that is also approximately objective:

$$\gamma_{S\mathcal{E}} = \frac{1}{Z_{\beta, \hat{H}_{\text{total}}}} \sum_i e^{-\beta E_i} |i\rangle\langle i| \otimes |\phi_i\rangle\langle\phi_i| + \delta_{\text{high-energy}}, \tag{54}$$

where $\delta_{\text{high-energy}}$ is a perturbative term corresponding to high-energy states.

Example 2. *Consider Hamiltonians of the following form:*

$$\hat{H}_{total} = \sum_i E_i |i\rangle\langle i| \otimes \sum_a q_{a|i} |\phi_a\rangle\langle \phi_a| + \hat{H}_{high\text{-}energy}, \tag{55}$$

where $q_{a|i}q_{a|j} = 0\ \forall i \neq j$, and where $\hat{H}_{high\text{-}energy}$ is an orthogonal addition with eigenenergies much higher than the energy scale given by the temperature T and with eigenstates such that $\hat{H}_{total}$ is full-rank. These give rise to a Gibbs thermal state that is also approximately objective:

$$\gamma_{S\mathcal{E}} = \frac{1}{Z_{\beta,\hat{H}_{total}}} \sum_{i,a} e^{-\beta E_i q_{a|i}} |i\rangle\langle i| \otimes |\phi_a\rangle\langle \phi_a| + \delta_{high\text{-}energy} \tag{56}$$

$$= \sum_i p_i |i\rangle\langle i| \otimes \sum_a c_{a|i} |\phi_a\rangle\langle \phi_a| + \delta_{high\text{-}energy}, \tag{57}$$

$$p_i := \frac{\sum_b e^{-\beta E_i q_{b|i}}}{Z_{\beta,\hat{H}_{total}}}, \quad c_{a|i} = \frac{e^{-\beta E_i q_{a|i}}}{\left(\sum_b e^{-\beta E_i q_{b|i}}\right)}, \quad c_{a|i} c_{a|j} = 0\ \forall i \neq j, \tag{58}$$

where $\delta_{high\text{-}energy}$ is a perturbative term corresponding to high-energy states.

Remark 3. *Recall Remark 1 where, for any given state of full rank, a Hamiltonian and temperature can be found such that it can be considered thermal. As such, for any full rank approximately objective state, a Hamiltonian and temperature can be found such that it can be considered also thermal. However, the objective states form a set of measure zero (as discord-free states have zero measure [31]). Thus, the set of sub-component Hamiltonians directly corresponding to those objective states (up to a mutiplicative coefficient, and not including high-energy terms) is also zero measure.*

Since objective states are not globally full-rank, there are no objective states that are also exactly globally thermal, and most Hamiltonians will not produce an approximately objective state either. The Hamiltonians that do give rise to (approximately) objective thermal states such as those given in Equations (53) and (55) consist of strong, constant, interactions between the system and the environments, which is unrealistic.

7. Conclusions

In our everyday experience, there are a number of phenomena which appear natural to us. One of them is *thermalisation*, in which physical objects eventually reach thermal equilibrium with the surrounding environment, e.g., an ice cream melting in hot weather. We also typically take for granted that physical objects are *objective*, i.e., their existence and properties can be agreed upon by many people. On the quantum mechanical level, thermalisation and objectivisation of quantum systems can arise through their interaction with external environments.

Thermalisation itself is thought to be a generic process and will occur approximately in general scenarios [20], more so than objectivity [50,51]. In contrast, objectivity requires classical correlations that are more sensitive to the situation, though components of objectivity can occur generically [50–53].

In general, the set of objective states does not have a preferred basis. Imposing (approximate) thermality can help select a preferred basis on the system and environment, which also leads to a preferred arrangement of classical correlations. If the system local Hamiltonian commutes with the interaction Hamiltonian (among the more straight forward scenarios in which quantum Darwinism has been explored [48,54–57]), then the preferred basis of objectivity would coincide with the "thermal" basis. The joint analysis of objectivity and thermalisation is further motivated by the fact that we observe everyday classical objects that are both objective and thermal.

In this paper, we examined the intersection of thermalisation and objectivity, especially when a single environment is required to fulfil both roles. In particular, we examined whether they can exist simultaneously by exploring whether a system-environment state can be both thermal (having the microcanonical Gibbs form) and objective (having state structure that satisfies spectrum broadcast structure).

By sequentially considering whether only the local system is thermal, or the local system and local environment, or the joint system-environment is thermal, we are able to characterise how rare it is for thermality and objectivity to coincide. This is summarised in Table 1. As we increased the thermalisation requirement from local system to global system and environment, the likelihood of an overlapping objectivity-thermal state existing decreases. This shows that in general, thermality and objectivity *are* at odds.

Table 1. Summary table. $\hat{H}_S$ is the system Hamiltonian, $\hat{H}_\mathcal{E}$ is the environment Hamiltonian and β is the inverse temperature.

Setting	Coexistence
Thermal system only	Yes, for all $\hat{H}_S$ and β
Local-thermal system and environment	Only for some $\hat{H}_S$, $\hat{H}_\mathcal{E}$; an approximate state exists for large environments
Global thermal system and environment	Only approximate state possible, *extremely* rare and fine-tuned

By studying the intersection of the sets of thermal and objective states, we can therefore also give a statement about the dynamics that have either objective states or thermal states as their fixed points or as their asymptotic state(s): due to the fine-tuned structure of thermal-objective states, only finely tuned dynamics would produce those states.

Quantum Darwinism can be hindered by numerous factors, such as non-Markovianity [32,58–64], non-ideal environments [33,34], initial system–environment correlations [32,35], environment–environment interactions [23,24,32,62,65], etc. It was shown that environment-environment interactions can lead to thermalisation at the detriment of objectivity in [23,24], but it is still open whether the other factors would lead to similar behaviour.

Based on these results, we conclude that if the hypothetical entropic death of the universe is characterised by the global thermalisation of the entire (observable) universe, then it is extremely unlikely for objectivity to remain. This is consistent with our intuition that, at thermalisation (heat death), there should be no work left to be done. In contrast, objectivity implies information about one system in another, which usually contains extractable work [22].

That said, there are (very) rare situations where a global thermal state can still support objective correlations, at least theoretically. *If* objectivity and information does remain, then this implies that there are highly nonlocal, strong interactions, as such giving rise to Hamiltonians like in Equation (55), which are required to maintain correlations in the global thermal state. While this is unrealistic that the entire universe can have such strong interactions, it may be possible for smaller parts of the universe to maintain interactions and thus have subcomponents that are objective.

Another possibility is that the system alone thermalises on the short time scale, while on more intermediate timescales the system and (information-carrying) environment locally thermalises. Meanwhile, perhaps only at long time scales does the global system-environment thermalise, achieving an ultimate "heat death". We found that objectivity is more likely to be able to coexist with thermality in the first two situations. This suggests that objectivity can survive in the short and intermediate timescales, before fading away at the long timescale.

The following narrative feels intuitive: e.g., decoherence occurs first as a loss of phase information, followed by the classical information spread that characterises objectivity; the classical information fades, followed by thermalisation in which all information is lost (aside from select information such as temperature) [23]. Whether this is 'common' remains an open question.

Author Contributions: Conceptualisation, T.P.L.; methodology, T.P.L.; formal analysis, T.P.L., A.W. and G.A.; writing—original draft preparation, T.P.L.; writing—review and editing, T.P.L., A.W. and G.A.; visualisation, T.P.L. All authors have read and agreed to the published version of the manuscript.

Funding: TPL acknowledges financial support from the UKRI Engineering and Physical Sciences Research Council (EPSRC) under the Doctoral Prize Award (Grant No. EP/T517902/1) hosted by the University of Nottingham. GA acknowledges financial support from the Foundational Questions Institute (FQXi) under the Intelligence in the Physical World Programme (Grant No. RFP-IPW-1907). AW was supported by the Spanish MINECO (projects FIS2016-86681-P and PID2019-107609GB-I00/AEI/10.13039/501100011033), both with the support of FEDER funds, and by the Generalitat de Catalunya (project 2017-SGR-1127).

Conflicts of Interest: The authors declare no conflict of interest.

References

1. Breuer, H.P.; Petruccione, F. *The Theory of Open Quantum Systems*; Oxford University Press: Oxford, UK, 2007.
2. Rivas, A.; Huelga, S.F. *Open Quantum Systems*; Springer: Berlin/Heidelberg, Germany, 2012. [CrossRef]
3. Schlosshauer, M. Quantum decoherence. *Phys. Rep.* **2019**, *831*, 1–57. [CrossRef]
4. Dittrich, T.; Hänggi, P.; Ingold, G.L.; Kramer, B.; Schön, G.; Zwerger, W. *Quantum Transport and Dissipation*; Wiley-Vch: Weinheim, Germany, 1998; Volume 3.
5. Yukalov, V. Equilibration and thermalization in finite quantum systems. *Laser Phys. Lett.* **2011**, *8*, 485–507. [CrossRef]
6. Linden, N.; Popescu, S.; Short, A.J.; Winter, A. Quantum mechanical evolution towards thermal equilibrium. *Phys. Rev. E* **2009**, *79*, 061103. [CrossRef]
7. Riera, A.; Gogolin, C.; Eisert, J. Thermalization in Nature and on a Quantum Computer. *Phys. Rev. Lett.* **2012**, *108*, 080402. [CrossRef]
8. Gogolin, C.; Eisert, J. Equilibration, thermalisation, and the emergence of statistical mechanics in closed quantum systems. *Rep. Prog. Phys.* **2016**, *79*, 056001. [CrossRef]
9. Goold, J.; Huber, M.; Riera, A.; del Rio, L.; Skrzypczyk, P. The role of quantum information in thermodynamics—A topical review. *J. Phys. A Math. Theor.* **2016**, *49*, 143001. [CrossRef]
10. Zurek, W.H. Quantum Darwinism. *Nat. Phys.* **2009**, *5*, 181–188. [CrossRef]
11. Horodecki, R.; Korbicz, J.K.; Horodecki, P. Quantum origins of objectivity. *Phys. Rev. A* **2015**, *91*, 032122. [CrossRef]
12. Le, T.P.; Olaya-Castro, A. Strong Quantum Darwinism and Strong Independence are Equivalent to Spectrum Broadcast Structure. *Phys. Rev. Lett.* **2019**, *122*, 010403. [CrossRef] [PubMed]
13. Çakmak, B.; Müstecaplıoğlu, Ö.E.; Paternostro, M.; Vacchini, B.; Campbell, S. Quantum Darwinism in a Composite System: Objectivity versus Classicality. *Entropy* **2021**, *23*, 995. [CrossRef] [PubMed]
14. Touil, A.; Yan, B.; Girolami, D.; Deffner, S.; Zurek, W.H. Eavesdropping on the Decohering Environment: Quantum Darwinism, Amplification, and the Origin of Objective Classical Reality. *arXiv* **2021**, arXiv:2107.00035.
15. Brush, S.G. *A History of Modern Planetary Physics: Nebulous Earth*; Cambridge University Press: Cambridge, UK, 1996; p. 77.
16. Adams, F.C.; Laughlin, G. A dying universe: The long-term fate and evolution of astrophysical objects. *Rev. Mod. Phys.* **1997**, *69*, 337–372. [CrossRef]
17. Dyson, L.; Lindesay, J.; Susskind, L. Is There Really a de Sitter/CFT Duality. *J. High Energy Phys.* **2002**, *2002*, 45. [CrossRef]
18. Riess, A.G.; Filippenko, A.V.; Challis, P.; Clocchiatti, A.; Diercks, A.; Garnavich, P.M.; Gilliland, R.L.; Hogan, C.J.; Jha, S.; Kirshner, R.P.; et al. Observational Evidence from Supernovae for an Accelerating Universe and a Cosmological Constant. *Astron. J.* **1998**, *116*, 1009–1038. [CrossRef]
19. Caldwell, R.R.; Kamionkowski, M.; Weinberg, N.N. Phantom Energy: Dark Energy with w < −1 Causes a Cosmic Doomsday. *Phys. Rev. Lett.* **2003**, *91*, 071301. [CrossRef]
20. Popescu, S.; Short, A.J.; Winter, A. Entanglement and the foundations of statistical mechanics. *Nat. Phys.* **2006**, *2*, 754–758. [CrossRef]
21. Huber, M.; Perarnau-Llobet, M.; Hovhannisyan, K.V.; Skrzypczyk, P.; Klöckl, C.; Brunner, N.; Acín, A. Thermodynamic cost of creating correlations. *New J. Phys.* **2015**, *17*, 065008. [CrossRef]
22. Perarnau-Llobet, M.; Hovhannisyan, K.V.; Huber, M.; Skrzypczyk, P.; Brunner, N.; Acín, A. Extractable Work from Correlations. *Phys. Rev. X* **2015**, *5*, 041011. [CrossRef]
23. Riedel, C.J.; Zurek, W.H.; Zwolak, M. The rise and fall of redundancy in decoherence and quantum Darwinism. *New J. Phys.* **2012**, *14*, 083010. [CrossRef]
24. Mirkin, N.; Wisniacki, D.A. Many-Body Localization and the Emergence of Quantum Darwinism. *Entropy* **2021**, *23*, 1377. [CrossRef]
25. Ollivier, H.; Poulin, D.; Zurek, W.H. Objective Properties from Subjective Quantum States: Environment as a Witness. *Phys. Rev. Lett.* **2004**, *93*, 220401. [CrossRef] [PubMed]
26. Zurek, W.H. Decoherence, einselection, and the quantum origins of the classical. *Rev. Mod. Phys.* **2003**, *75*, 715–775. [CrossRef]

27. Le, T.P.; Olaya-Castro, A. Witnessing non-objectivity in the framework of strong quantum Darwinism. *Quantum Sci. Technol.* **2020**, *5*, 045012. [CrossRef]
28. Jaynes, E.T. Information Theory and Statistical Mechanics. *Phys. Rev.* **1957**, *106*, 620–630. [CrossRef]
29. Schirmer, S.G.; Wang, X. Stabilizing open quantum systems by Markovian reservoir engineering. *Phys. Rev. A* **2010**, *81*, 062306. [CrossRef]
30. Barreiro, J.T.; Müller, M.; Schindler, P.; Nigg, D.; Monz, T.; Chwalla, M.; Hennrich, M.; Roos, C.F.; Zoller, P.; Blatt, R. An open-system quantum simulator with trapped ions. *Nature* **2011**, *470*, 486–491. [CrossRef]
31. Ferraro, A.; Aolita, L.; Cavalcanti, D.; Cucchietti, F.M.; Acín, A. Almost all quantum states have nonclassical correlations. *Phys. Rev. A* **2010**, *81*, 052318. [CrossRef]
32. Giorgi, G.L.; Galve, F.; Zambrini, R. Quantum Darwinism and non-Markovian dissipative dynamics from quantum phases of the spin-1/2 XX model. *Phys. Rev. A* **2015**, *92*, 022105. [CrossRef]
33. Zwolak, M.; Quan, H.T.; Zurek, W.H. Quantum Darwinism in a Mixed Environment. *Phys. Rev. Lett.* **2009**, *103*, 110402. [CrossRef]
34. Zwolak, M.; Quan, H.T.; Zurek, W.H. Redundant imprinting of information in nonideal environments: Objective reality via a noisy channel. *Phys. Rev. A* **2010**, *81*, 062110. [CrossRef]
35. Balanesković, N. Random unitary evolution model of quantum Darwinism with pure decoherence. *Eur. Phys. J. D* **2015**, *69*, 232. [CrossRef]
36. Balanesković, N.; Mendler, M. Dissipation, dephasing and quantum Darwinism in qubit systems with random unitary interactions. *Eur. Phys. J. D* **2016**, *70*, 177. [CrossRef]
37. Chisholm, D.A.; García-Pérez, G.; Rossi, M.A.C.; Maniscalco, S.; Palma, G.M. Witnessing Objectivity on a Quantum Computer. *arXiv* **2021**, arXiv:2110.06243.
38. Nielsen, M.A.; Chuang, I. *Quantum Computation and Quantum Information*; Cambridge University Press: Cambridge, UK, 2010.
39. Fujiwara, A. Estimation of a generalized amplitude-damping channel. *Phys. Rev. A* **2004**, *70*, 012317. [CrossRef]
40. Plesch, M.; Brukner, Č. Quantum-state preparation with universal gate decompositions. *Phys. Rev. A* **2011**, *83*, 032302. [CrossRef]
41. Araujo, I.F.; Park, D.K.; Petruccione, F.; da Silva, A.J. A divide-and-conquer algorithm for quantum state preparation. *Sci. Rep.* **2021**, *11*, 6329. [CrossRef]
42. Albert, V.V.; Bradlyn, B.; Fraas, M.; Jiang, L. Geometry and Response of Lindbladians. *Phys. Rev. X* **2016**, *6*, 041031. [CrossRef]
43. Short, A.J.; Farrelly, T.C. Quantum equilibration in finite time. *New J. Phys.* **2012**, *14*, 013063. [CrossRef]
44. Brandão, F.G.S.L.; Ćwikliński, P.; Horodecki, M.; Horodecki, P.; Korbicz, J.K.; Mozrzymas, M. Convergence to equilibrium under a random Hamiltonian. *Phys. Rev. E* **2012**, *86*, 031101. [CrossRef]
45. Cramer, M. Thermalization under randomized local Hamiltonians. *New J. Phys.* **2012**, *14*, 053051. [CrossRef]
46. Hutter, A.; Wehner, S. Dependence of a quantum-mechanical system on its own initial state and the initial state of the environment it interacts with. *Phys. Rev. A* **2013**, *87*, 012121. [CrossRef]
47. Cheong, S.A.; Henley, C.L. Correlation density matrix: An unbiased analysis of exact diagonalizations. *Phys. Rev. B* **2009**, *79*, 212402. [CrossRef]
48. Mironowicz, P.; Korbicz, J.; Horodecki, P. Monitoring of the Process of System Information Broadcasting in Time. *Phys. Rev. Lett.* **2017**, *118*, 150501. [CrossRef]
49. Mironowicz, P.; Należyty, P.; Horodecki, P.; Korbicz, J.K. System information propagation for composite structures. *Phys. Rev. A* **2018**, *98*, 022124. [CrossRef]
50. Korbicz, J.K.; Aguilar, E.A.; Ćwikliński, P.; Horodecki, P. Generic appearance of objective results in quantum measurements. *Phys. Rev. A* **2017**, *96*, 032124. [CrossRef]
51. Brandão, F.G.S.L.; Piani, M.; Horodecki, P. Generic emergence of classical features in quantum Darwinism. *Nat. Commun.* **2015**, *6*, 7908. [CrossRef]
52. Knott, P.A.; Tufarelli, T.; Piani, M.; Adesso, G. Generic Emergence of Objectivity of Observables in Infinite Dimensions. *Phys. Rev. Lett.* **2018**, *121*, 160401. [CrossRef]
53. Colafranceschi, E.; Lami, L.; Adesso, G.; Tufarelli, T. Refined diamond norm bounds on the emergence of objectivity of observables. *J. Phys. A Math. Theor.* **2020**, *53*, 395305. [CrossRef]
54. Tuziemski, J.; Korbicz, J.K. Dynamical objectivity in quantum Brownian motion. *Europhys. Lett.* **2015**, *112*, 40008. [CrossRef]
55. Tuziemski, J.; Lampo, A.; Lewenstein, M.; Korbicz, J.K. Reexamination of the decoherence of spin registers. *Phys. Rev. A* **2019**, *99*, 022122. [CrossRef]
56. Roszak, K.; Korbicz, J.K. Entanglement and objectivity in pure dephasing models. *Phys. Rev. A* **2019**, *100*, 062127. [CrossRef]
57. Roszak, K.; Korbicz, J.K. Glimpse of objectivity in bipartite systems for nonentangling pure dephasing evolutions. *Phys. Rev. A* **2020**, *101*, 052120. [CrossRef]
58. Galve, F.; Zambrini, R.; Maniscalco, S. Non-Markovianity hinders Quantum Darwinism. *Sci. Rep.* **2016**, *6*, 19607. [CrossRef] [PubMed]
59. Pleasance, G.; Garraway, B.M. Application of quantum Darwinism to a structured environment. *Phys. Rev. A* **2017**, *96*, 062105. [CrossRef]
60. Le, T.P.; Olaya-Castro, A. Objectivity (or lack thereof): Comparison between predictions of quantum Darwinism and spectrum broadcast structure. *Phys. Rev. A* **2018**, *98*, 032103. [CrossRef]

61. Lorenzo, S.; Paternostro, M.; Palma, G.M. Reading a Qubit Quantum State with a Quantum Meter: Time Unfolding of Quantum Darwinism and Quantum Information Flux. *Open Syst. Inf. Dyn.* **2019**, *26*, 1950023. [CrossRef]
62. Milazzo, N.; Lorenzo, S.; Paternostro, M.; Palma, G.M. Role of information backflow in the emergence of quantum Darwinism. *Phys. Rev. A* **2019**, *100*, 012101. [CrossRef]
63. Lorenzo, S.; Paternostro, M.; Palma, G.M. Anti-Zeno-based dynamical control of the unfolding of quantum Darwinism. *Phys. Rev. Res.* **2020**, *2*, 013164. [CrossRef]
64. García-Pérez, G.; Chisholm, D.A.; Rossi, M.A.C.; Palma, G.M.; Maniscalco, S. Decoherence without entanglement and quantum Darwinism. *Phys. Rev. Res.* **2020**, *2*, 012061(R). [CrossRef]
65. Ryan, E.; Paternostro, M.; Campbell, S. Quantum Darwinism in a structured spin environment. *Phys. Lett. A* **2021**, *416*, 127675. [CrossRef]

Article

Limits to Perception by Quantum Monitoring with Finite Efficiency

Luis Pedro García-Pintos [1,2,*] **and Adolfo del Campo** [1,3,4,5,*]

[1] Department of Physics, University of Massachusetts, Boston, MA 02125, USA
[2] Joint Center for Quantum Information and Computer Science and Joint Quantum Institute, NIST/University of Maryland, College Park, MD 20742, USA
[3] Department of Physics and Materials Science, University of Luxembourg, L-1511 Luxembourg, Luxembourg
[4] Donostia International Physics Center, E-20018 San Sebastián, Spain
[5] IKERBASQUE, Basque Foundation for Science, E-48013 Bilbao, Spain
* Correspondence: lpgp@umd.edu (L.P.G.-P.); adolfo.delcampo@uni.lu (A.d.C.)

Abstract: We formulate limits to perception under continuous quantum measurements by comparing the quantum states assigned by agents that have partial access to measurement outcomes. To this end, we provide bounds on the trace distance and the relative entropy between the assigned state and the actual state of the system. These bounds are expressed solely in terms of the purity and von Neumann entropy of the state assigned by the agent, and are shown to characterize how an agent's perception of the system is altered by access to additional information. We apply our results to Gaussian states and to the dynamics of a system embedded in an environment illustrated on a quantum Ising chain.

Keywords: quantum monitoring; Quantum Darwinism; continuous quantum measurements

Quantum theory rests on the fact that the *quantum state* of a system encodes all predictions of possible measurements as well as the system's posterior evolution. However, in general, different agents may assign different states to the same system, depending on their knowledge of it. Complete information of the physical state of a system is equated to pure states, mathematically modeled by unit vectors in Hilbert space. By contrast, mixed states correspond to a lack of complete descriptions of the system, either due to uncertainties in the preparation, or due to the system being correlated with secondary systems. In this paper, we address how the perception of a system differs among observers with different levels of knowledge. Specifically, we quantify how different the effective descriptions that two agents provide of the same system can be, when acquiring information through continuous measurements.

Consider a monitored quantum system, that is, a system being continuously measured in time. An omniscient agent $\mathcal{O}$ is assumed to know all interactions and measurements that occur to the system. In particular, she has access to all outcomes of measurements that are performed. As such, $\mathcal{O}$ has a complete description of the *pure state* $\rho_t^{\mathcal{O}} = \left(\rho_t^{\mathcal{O}}\right)^2$ of the system.

While not necessary for subsequent results, we model such a monitoring process by continuous quantum measurements [1–3] as a natural test-bed with experimental relevance [4–6]. For ideal continuous quantum measurements, the state $\rho_t^{\mathcal{O}}$ satisfies a stochastic equation dictating its change,

$$d\rho_t^{\mathcal{O}} = -i\left[H, \rho_t^{\mathcal{O}}\right]dt + \Lambda\left[\rho_t^{\mathcal{O}}\right]dt + \sum_\alpha I_{A_\alpha}\left[\rho_t^{\mathcal{O}}\right]dW_t^\alpha. \tag{1}$$

The dephasing superoperator $\Lambda[\rho_t^\mathcal{O}]$ is of Lindblad form,

$$\Lambda[\rho_t^\mathcal{O}] = -\sum_\alpha \frac{1}{8\tau_m^\alpha}\left[A_\alpha, \left[A_\alpha, \rho_t^\mathcal{O}\right]\right] \quad (2)$$

for the set of measured physical observables $\{A_\alpha\}$, and the "innovation terms" are given by

$$I_{A_\alpha}[\rho_t^\mathcal{O}] = \frac{1}{\sqrt{4\tau_m^\alpha}}\left(\{A_\alpha, \rho_t^\mathcal{O}\} - 2\operatorname{Tr}\left(A_\alpha \rho_t^\mathcal{O}\right)\rho_t^\mathcal{O}\right). \quad (3)$$

The latter account for the information about the system acquired during the monitoring process, and model the quantum back-action on the state during a measurement. The *characteristic measurement times* τ_m^α depend on the strength of the measurement, and characterize the time over which information of the observable A_α is acquired. The terms dW_t^α are independent random Gaussian variables of zero mean and variance dt.

An agent $\mathcal{A}$ without access to the measurement outcomes possesses a different–incomplete description of the state of the system. The need to average over the unknown results implies that the state $\rho_t^\mathcal{A}$ assigned by $\mathcal{A}$ satisfies the master equation

$$d\rho_t^\mathcal{A} = -i\left[H, \rho_t^\mathcal{A}\right]dt + \Lambda\left[\rho_t^\mathcal{A}\right]dt, \quad (4)$$

obtained from (1) by using that $\langle dW_t^\alpha \rangle = 0$, where $\langle \cdot \rangle$ denote averages over realizations of the measurement process [1]. Assuming that agent $\mathcal{A}$ knows the initial state of the system before the measurement process, $\rho_0^\mathcal{O} = \rho_0^\mathcal{A}$, the state that she assigns at later times is $\rho_t^\mathcal{A} \equiv \langle \rho_t^\mathcal{O} \rangle$.

As a result of the incomplete description of the state of the system, agent $\mathcal{A}$ suffers from a growing uncertainty in the predictions of measurement outcomes. We quantify this by means of two figures of merit: the trace distance and the relative entropy.

The trace distance between states σ_1 and σ_2 is defined as

$$\mathcal{D}(\sigma_1, \sigma_2) = \frac{\|\sigma_1 - \sigma_2\|_1}{2}, \quad (5)$$

where the trace norm for an operator with a spectral decomposition $A = \sum_j \lambda_j |j\rangle\langle j|$ is $\|A\|_1 = \sum_j |\lambda_j|$. Its operational meaning derives from the fact that the trace distance characterizes the maximum difference in probability of outcomes for any measurement on the states σ_1 and σ_2:

$$\mathcal{D}(\sigma_1, \sigma_2) = \max_{0 \leq P \leq \mathbb{1}} |\operatorname{Tr}(P\sigma_1) - \operatorname{Tr}(P\sigma_2)|, \quad (6)$$

where P is a positive-operator valued measure. It also quantifies the probability p of successfully guessing, with a single measurement instance, the correct state in a scenario where one assumes equal prior probabilities for having state σ_1 or σ_2. Then, the best conceivable protocol gives $p = \frac{1}{2}(1 + \mathcal{D}(\sigma_1, \sigma_2))$. Thus, if two states are close in trace distance they are hard to distinguish under any conceivable measurement [7–9].

The relative entropy also serves as a figure of merit to quantify the distance between probability distributions, in particular characterizing the extent to which one distribution can encode information contained in the other one [10]. In the quantum case, the relative entropy is defined as:

$$S(\sigma_1 \| \sigma_2) \equiv \operatorname{Tr}(\sigma_1 \log \sigma_1) - \operatorname{Tr}(\sigma_1 \log \sigma_2). \quad (7)$$

In a hypothesis testing scenario between states σ_1 and σ_2, the probability p_N of wrongly believing that σ_2 is the correct state scales as $p_N \sim e^{-NS(\sigma_1\|\sigma_2)}$ in the limit of large N, where N is the number of copies of the state that are available to measure on [11,12]. That is, σ_2 is easily confused with σ_1 if $S(\sigma_1\|\sigma_2)$ is small [13,14].

1. Quantum Limits to Perception

Lack of knowledge of the outcomes from measurements performed on the system induces $\mathcal{A}$ to assign an incomplete, mixed, state to the system. This hinders the agent's perception of the system (see illustration in Figure 1). We quantify this by the trace distance and the relative entropy.

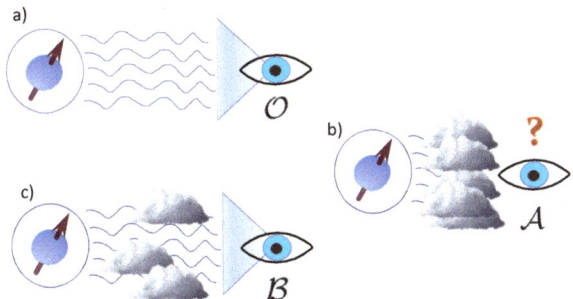

Figure 1. Illustration of the varying degrees of perception by different agents. The amount of information that an agent possesses of a system can drastically alter its perception, as the expectations of outcomes for measurements performed on the system can differ. (**a**) The state $\rho_t^{\mathcal{O}}$ assigned by omniscient agent $\mathcal{O}$, who has full access to the measurement outcomes, corresponds to a complete pure-state description of the system. O thus has the most accurate predictive power. (**b**) An agent $\mathcal{A}$ completely ignorant of measurement outcomes possesses the most incomplete description of the system. (**c**) A continuous transition between the two descriptions, corresponding to the worst and most complete perceptions of the system respectively, is obtained by considering an agent $\mathcal{B}$ with partial access to the measurement outcomes of the monitoring process.

We are interested in comparing $\mathcal{A}$'s incomplete description to the pure state $\rho_T^{\mathcal{O}}$ assigned by $\mathcal{O}$, i.e., to the complete description. Under ideal monitoring of a quantum system, the pure state $\rho_T^{\mathcal{O}}$ remains pure. Therefore, the following holds [7]:

$$1 - \text{Tr}\left(\rho_T^{\mathcal{O}} \rho_T^{\mathcal{A}}\right) \leq \mathcal{D}\left(\rho_T^{\mathcal{O}}, \rho_T^{\mathcal{A}}\right) \leq \sqrt{1 - \text{Tr}(\rho_T^{\mathcal{O}} \rho_T^{\mathcal{A}})}. \tag{8}$$

One can then directly relate the average trace distance to the purity $\mathcal{P}\left(\rho_T^{\mathcal{A}}\right) \equiv \text{Tr}\left(\rho_T^{\mathcal{A}^2}\right)$ of state $\rho_T^{\mathcal{A}}$ as

$$1 - \mathcal{P}\left(\rho_T^{\mathcal{A}}\right) \leq \left\langle \mathcal{D}\left(\rho_T^{\mathcal{O}}, \rho_T^{\mathcal{A}}\right) \right\rangle \leq \sqrt{1 - \mathcal{P}(\rho_T^{\mathcal{A}})}, \tag{9}$$

by using Jensen's inequality and the fact that the square root is concave. The level of mixedness of the state $\rho_T^{\mathcal{A}}$ that $\mathcal{A}$ assigns to the system provides lower and upper bounds to the average probability of error that she has in guessing the actual state of the system $\rho_T^{\mathcal{O}}$. This provides an operational meaning to the purity of a quantum state, as a quantifier of the average trace distance between a state $\rho_t^{\mathcal{O}}$ and post-measurement (average) state $\rho_t^{\mathcal{A}}$.

To appreciate the dynamics in which the average trace distance evolves, we note that at short times

$$\frac{T}{\tau_D} \leq \left\langle \mathcal{D}\left(\rho_T^{\mathcal{O}}, \rho_T^{\mathcal{A}}\right) \right\rangle \leq \sqrt{\frac{T}{\tau_D}}, \tag{10}$$

where the decoherence rate is given by [15,16]

$$\frac{1}{\tau_D} = \sum_\alpha \frac{1}{4\tau_m^\alpha} \mathrm{Var}_{\rho_0^A}(A_\alpha), \qquad (11)$$

in terms of the variance $\mathrm{Var}_{\rho_0^A}(A_\alpha)$ of the measured observables over the initial pure state ρ_0^A. Analogous bounds can be derived at arbitrary times of evolution for the difference of perceptions among various agents (see Appendix A).

For the case of the quantum relative entropy between states of complete and incomplete knowledge, the following identity holds:

$$\langle S(\rho_t^\mathcal{O}||\rho_t^\mathcal{A})\rangle = S(\rho_t^\mathcal{A}), \qquad (12)$$

proven by using that $\rho_t^\mathcal{O}$ is pure and that the von Neumann entropy of a state σ is $S(\sigma) := -\mathrm{Tr}(\sigma \log \sigma)$. Thus, the entropy of the state assigned by the agent $\mathcal{A}$ fully determines the average relative entropy with respect to the complete description $\rho_t^\mathcal{O}$ (alternative interpretations to this quantity have been given in [17,18]).

Similar calculations allow to bound the variances of $\mathcal{D}(\rho_T^\mathcal{O},\rho_T^\mathcal{A})$ and of $S(\rho_t^\mathcal{O}||\rho_t^\mathcal{A})$ as well. The variance of the trace distance, $\Delta\mathcal{D}_T^2 \equiv \langle \mathcal{D}^2(\rho_T^\mathcal{O},\rho_T^\mathcal{A})\rangle - \langle\mathcal{D}(\rho_T^\mathcal{O},\rho_T^\mathcal{A})\rangle^2$, satisfies

$$\Delta\mathcal{D}_T^2 \leq \mathcal{P}(\rho_T^\mathcal{A}) - \mathcal{P}(\rho_T^\mathcal{A})^2, \qquad (13)$$

while for the variance of the relative entropy it holds that

$$\Delta S^2(\rho_t^\mathcal{O}||\rho_t^\mathcal{A}) \leq \mathrm{Tr}(\rho_t^\mathcal{A} \log^2 \rho_t^\mathcal{A}) - S^2(\rho_t^\mathcal{A}). \qquad (14)$$

The right-hand side of this inequality admits a classical interpretation in terms of the variance of the surprisal $(-\log p_j)$ over the eigenvalues p_j of $\rho_t^\mathcal{A}$ [14]. We thus find that, at the level of a single realization, the dispersion of the relative entropy between the states assigned by the agents $\mathcal{O}$ and $\mathcal{A}$ is upper bounded by the variance of the surprise in the description of $\mathcal{A}$. The later naturally vanishes when $\rho_t^\mathcal{A}$ is pure, and increases as the state becomes more mixed.

2. Transition to Complete Descriptions

So far we considered the extreme case of comparing the states assigned by $\mathcal{A}$, who is in complete ignorance of the measurement outcomes, and by an omniscient agent $\mathcal{O}$. One can in fact consider a continuous transition between these limiting cases, i.e., as the accuracy in the perception of the monitored system by an agent is enhanced, as illustrated in Figure 1. Consider a third agent $\mathcal{B}$, with access to a fraction of the measurement output. This can be modeled by introducing a filter function $\eta(\alpha) \in [0,1]$ characterizing the efficiency of the measurement channels in Equation (1) [1]. Then, the dynamics of state $\rho_t^\mathcal{B}$ is dictated by

$$d\rho_t^\mathcal{B} = -i[H,\rho_t^\mathcal{B}]dt + \Lambda[\rho_t^\mathcal{B}]dt + \sum_\alpha \sqrt{\eta(\alpha)} I_{A_\alpha}[\rho_t^\mathcal{B}]dV_t^\alpha, \qquad (15)$$

with dV_t^α Wiener noises for observer $\mathcal{B}$. It holds that $\rho_t^\mathcal{B} \equiv \langle\rho_t^\mathcal{O}\rangle_\mathcal{B}$, where the average is now over the outcomes obtained by $\mathcal{O}$ that are unknown to $\mathcal{B}$ [1].

Note that the case with null measurement efficiencies $\eta(j) = 0$ gives the exact same dynamics as that of a system in which the monitored observables $\{A_\alpha\}$ are coupled to environmental degrees of freedom, producing dephasing [19,20]. Equations (15) and (1) then correspond to unravellings in which partial or full access to environmental degrees of freedom allow learning the state of the system by conditioning on the state observed in the environment. Therefore, knowing how $\mathcal{D}(\rho_t^\mathcal{B},\rho_t^\mathcal{O})$ and $S(\rho_t^\mathcal{O}||\rho_t^\mathcal{B})$ decrease as η increases directly informs of how much the description of an open system can be improved by observing a fraction of the environment. This is reminiscent of the Quantum Darwinism approach, whereby fractions of the environment encode objective approximate descriptions of the system. While in the Darwinistic framework the focus is on environmental correlations, we focus on the state of the system itself.

The results of the previous section hold for partial-ignorance state ρ_t^B as well:

$$1 - \mathcal{P}\left(\rho_T^B\right) \leq \left\langle \mathcal{D}\left(\rho_T^\mathcal{O}, \rho_T^B\right)\right\rangle_\mathcal{B} \leq \sqrt{1 - \mathcal{P}(\rho_T^B)} \tag{16a}$$

$$\left\langle S\left(\rho_t^\mathcal{O} || \rho_t^B\right)\right\rangle_\mathcal{B} = S\left(\rho_t^B\right). \tag{16b}$$

Similar extensions are obtained for the variances. This allows exploring the transition from the incomplete description of $\mathcal{A}$, to a complete description of the state of the system as $\eta \to 1$. Note that these results hold for each realization of a trajectory of $\mathcal{B}$'s state ρ_t^B, and that if one averages over the measurement outcomes unknown to both agents $\mathcal{A}$ and $\mathcal{B}$, Equation (16b) gives $\langle S(\rho_t^\mathcal{O} || \rho_t^B)\rangle = \langle S(\rho_t^B)\rangle$.

These results allow to compare the descriptions of different agents that jointly monitor a system [1,20–23]. We show in Appendix A that

$$\left|\text{Tr}\left(\rho_T^{A2}\right) - \text{Tr}\left(\rho_T^{B2}\right)\right| \leq \left\langle \mathcal{D}\left(\rho_T^A, \rho_T^B\right)\right\rangle_{\mathcal{AB}} \leq \sqrt{1 - \text{Tr}\left(\rho_T^{A2}\right)} + \sqrt{1 - \text{Tr}\left(\rho_T^{B2}\right)}. \tag{17}$$

The joint monitoring of a system by independent observers has been realized experimentally in [24,25].

3. Illustrations

3.1. Evolution of the Limits to Perception

Consider a 1D transverse field Ising model, with the Hamiltonian

$$H = -h\sum_j^N \sigma_j^x - J\sum_j^{N-1} \sigma_j^z \sigma_{j+1}^z, \tag{18}$$

where σ_j^x and σ_j^z denote Pauli matrices on the x and z directions, and $\{h, J\}$ denote coupling strengths.

We study the case of observer $\mathcal{O}$ monitoring the individual spin z components. Equation (1) thus governs the evolution of the state $\rho_t^\mathcal{O}$, with $\{A_\alpha\} = \{\sigma_j^z\}$. Meanwhile, the state assigned by observers with partial access to measurement outcomes follows Equation (15). The case $\eta(j) = 0$ gives equivalent dynamics to that of an Ising chain in which individual spins couple to environmental degrees of freedom via σ_j^z, producing dephasing.

Figure 2 illustrates the evolution of the averaged relative entropy $\langle S(\rho_t^\mathcal{O} || \rho_t^B)\rangle$ between the complete description and $\mathcal{B}$'s partial one, for different values of the monitoring efficiency η. The average $\langle \cdot \rangle$ is over all measurement outcomes. Analogous results for the average trace distance can be found in Appendix A. The dynamics are simulated by implementation of the monitoring process as a sequence of weak measurements, which can be modeled by Kraus operators acting on the state of the system. Specifically, the evolution of $\rho_t^\mathcal{O}$ and corresponding state ρ_t^B with partial measurements is numerically obtained from assuming two independent measurement processes, as in [1].

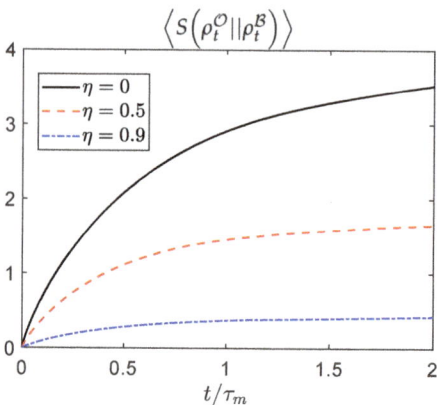

Figure 2. Evolution of the average relative entropy. Simulated evolution of the average $\langle S(\rho_t^\mathcal{O} \| \rho_t^\mathcal{B}) \rangle = \langle S(\rho_t^\mathcal{B}) \rangle$ of the relative entropy between complete and incomplete descriptions for a spin chain initially in a paramagnetic state on which individual spin components σ_j^z are monitored. Here $\langle \cdot \rangle$ denotes an average over all measurement outcomes, and $\rho_t^\mathcal{B} = \langle \rho_t^\mathcal{O} \rangle_\mathcal{B}$ is the state assigned by agent $\mathcal{B}$ after discarding the outcomes unknown to him. The simulation corresponds to $N = 6$ spins, with couplings $J\tau_m = h\tau_m = 1/2$. For $\eta = 0$ (black continuous curve), agent $\mathcal{A}$, without any access to the measurement outcomes, has the most incomplete description of the system. For $\eta = 0.5$ (red dashed curve), $\mathcal{B}$ gets closer to the complete description of the state of the system, after gaining access to partial measurement results. Finally, when $\eta = 0.9$ (blue dotted curve), access to enough information provides $\mathcal{B}$ with an almost complete description of the state. Importantly, in all cases the agent can estimate how far the description possessed is from the complete one solely in terms of the entropy $S(\rho_t^\mathcal{B})$.

3.2. Transition to Complete Descriptions

Consider the case of a one-dimensional harmonic oscillator with position and momentum operators X and P. We assume agent $\mathcal{B}$ is monitoring the position of the oscillator with an efficiency η. The dynamics is dictated by Equation (15) for the case of a single monitored observable X, and can be determined by a set of differential equations on the moments of the Gaussian state $\rho_t^\mathcal{B}$ [1,21].

We prove in Appendix A that the purity of the density matrix for long times has a simple expression in terms of the measurement efficiency, satisfying $\mathcal{P}(\rho_T^\mathcal{B}) \longrightarrow \sqrt{\eta}$ for long times. Equation (16) and properties of Gaussian states [22–26] then imply

$$1 - \sqrt{\eta} \leq \langle \mathcal{D}(\rho_T^\mathcal{O}, \rho_T^\mathcal{B}) \rangle_\mathcal{B} \leq \sqrt{1 - \sqrt{\eta}}, \tag{19}$$

and

$$\langle S(\rho_t^\mathcal{O} \| \rho_t^\mathcal{B}) \rangle_\mathcal{B} = \left(\frac{1}{2\sqrt{\eta}} + \frac{1}{2}\right) \log\left(\frac{1}{2\sqrt{\eta}} + \frac{1}{2}\right) - \left(\frac{1}{2\sqrt{\eta}} - \frac{1}{2}\right) \log\left(\frac{1}{2\sqrt{\eta}} - \frac{1}{2}\right). \tag{20}$$

See [27] for further results on the gains in purity that can be obtained from conditioning on measurement outcomes in Gaussian systems. Figure 3 depicts the trace distance $\langle \mathcal{D}(\rho_t^\mathcal{B}, \rho_t^\mathcal{O}) \rangle_\mathcal{B}$ and the relative entropy $\langle S(\rho_t^\mathcal{O} \| \rho_t^\mathcal{B}) \rangle_\mathcal{B}$ as a function of the measurements efficiency of $\mathcal{B}$'s measurement process, illustrating the transition from least accurate perception to most accurate perception and optimal predictive power as $\eta \to 1$. Note that, since both the bounds on the trace distance and relative entropy are independent of the parameters of the model in this example, the transition to most accurate perceptions of the system is solely a function of the measurement efficiency. The figures show that a high knowledge of the state of the system is gained for $\eta \sim 0$ as η increases. This gain decreases for larger values of η. This observation is confirmed by explicit computation using the relative entropy, which satisfies $\frac{d}{d\eta}\langle S(\rho_t^{\mathcal{O}}||\rho_t^{\mathcal{B}})\rangle_{\mathcal{B}} = \log\left(\frac{1-\sqrt{\eta}}{1+\sqrt{\eta}}\right)/(4\eta^{3/2})$. Thus, its rate of change and the information gain diverges for $\eta \to 0$ as a power law $\frac{d}{d\eta}\langle S(\rho_t^{\mathcal{O}}||\rho_t^{\mathcal{B}})\rangle_{\mathcal{B}} = -(1/6 + 1/2\eta) + \mathcal{O}(\eta^2)$, while it becomes essentially constant for intermediate values of η. In the transition to most accurate perception the effective description of the system changes from a mixed to a pure state, and the information gain becomes divergent as well as $\eta \to 1$.

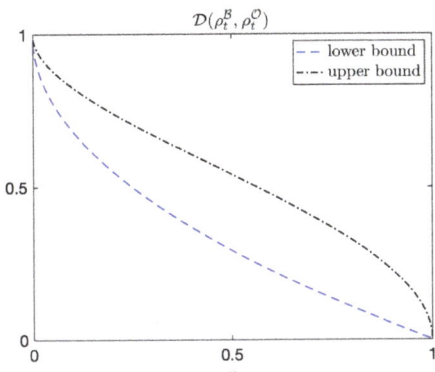
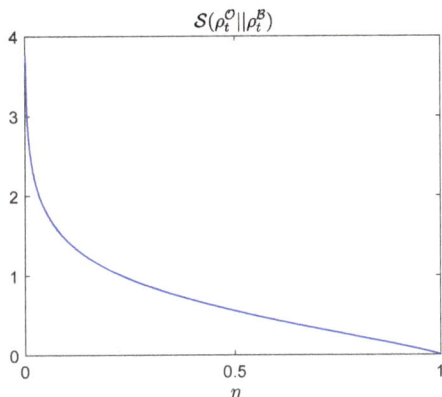

Figure 3. **Transition between levels of perception.** Bounds on average trace distance (**left**) and average relative entropy (**right**) as function of measurement efficiency for a harmonic oscillator undergoing monitoring of its position. For such a system the purity of the state $\rho_t^{\mathcal{B}}$ depends solely on the measurement efficiency with which observer $\mathcal{B}$ monitors the system. This illustrates the transition from complete ignorance of the outcomes of measurements performed ($\eta = 0$), to the most complete description as $\eta \to 1$—the situation with the most accurate perception. Efficient use of information happens when a small fraction of the measurement output is incorporated at $\eta \ll 1$, as then both $\mathcal{D}\left(\rho_t^{\mathcal{B}}, \rho_t^{\mathcal{O}}\right)$ and the relative entropy $S\left(\rho_t^{\mathcal{O}}||\rho_t^{\mathcal{B}}\right)$ decay rapidly.

4. Discussion

Different levels of information of a system amount to different effective descriptions. We studied these different descriptions for the case of a system being monitored by an observer, and compared this agent's description to that of other agents with a restricted access to the measurement outcomes. With continuous measurements as an illustrative case study, we put bounds on the average trace distance between states that different agents assign to the system, and obtained exact results for the average quantum relative entropy. The expressions solely involve the state assigned by the less-knowledgeable agent, providing estimates for the distance to the exact state that can be calculated by the agent without knowledge of the latter.

The setting we presented here has a natural application to the case of a system interacting with an environment. For all practical purposes, one can view the effect of an environment as effectively monitoring the system with which it interacts [28,29]. Without access to the environmental degrees of freedom, the master equation that governs the state of the system takes a Lindblad form with Hermitian operators, as in Equation (4). However, access to the degrees of freedom of the environment can provide information of the state of the system, effectively leading to a dynamics governed by Equation (15). Access to a high fraction of the environment leads to a dynamics as in Equation (1), providing complete description of the state of the system by conditioning on the observed state of the environmental degrees of freedom. With this in mind, our results shed light on how much one can improve the description of a given system by incorporating information encoded in an environment [29–35], as experimentally explored in [36,37]. Note that since our bounds depend on the state assigned by the agent with less information, the above is independent of the unraveling chosen. It would also be interesting to extend our results and the connections to the dynamics of open systems to more general monitoring dynamics (e.g., non-Hermitian operators or other noise models).

As brought up by an analysis of a continuously-monitored harmonic oscillator, a large gain of information about the state of the system occurs when an agent has access to a small fraction of the measurement output, when quantified both by the trace distance and by the relative entropy. Our results thus complement the Quantum Darwinism program and related approaches [29–35], where the authors compare the state of a system interacting with an environment and the state of fractions of such an environment. While those works focused on the correlation buildup between the system and the environment, we instead address the subjective description that observers assign to the state of the system, conditioned on the information encoded in a given measurement record.

Author Contributions: Formal analysis, L.P.G.-P. and A.d.C.; Investigation, L.P.G.-P. and A.d.C.; Writing—original draft, L.P.G.-P. and A.d.C. All authors have read and agreed to the published version of the manuscript.

Funding: This work was funded by the John Templeton Foundation, UMass Boston (project P20150000 029279), and DOE grant DE-SC0019515.

Data Availability Statement: Not Applicable.

Conflicts of Interest: The authors declare no conflict of interest.

Appendix A.

Appendix A.1. Derivation of Bounds to Average Trace Distance

Using Equations (2) and (4) in the main text and that $\rho_0^O = \rho_0^A$, we find

$$\left\langle 1 - \text{Tr}\left(\rho_T^O \rho_T^A\right)\right\rangle = -\left\langle \int_{\text{Tr}(\rho_0^O \rho_0^A)}^{\text{Tr}(\rho_T^O \rho_T^A)} d\,\text{Tr}\left(\rho_t^O \rho_t^A\right)\right\rangle \quad (A1)$$

$$= -\int_{F_0}^{F_T} d\,\text{Tr}\left(\rho_t^A \rho_t^A\right)$$

$$= -2\int_0^T \text{Tr}\left(\rho_t^A \Lambda\left[\rho_t^A\right]\right) dt$$

$$= +2\sum_\alpha \frac{1}{8\tau_m^\alpha} \int_0^T \text{Tr}\left(\left[A_\alpha, \left[A_\alpha, \rho_t^A\right]\right]\rho_t^A\right) dt$$

$$= \sum_\alpha \frac{1}{4\tau_m^\alpha} \int_0^T \text{Tr}\left(\left[\rho_t^A, A_\alpha\right]\left[A_\alpha, \rho_t^A\right]\right) dt.$$

This identity can be conveniently expressed in terms of the 2-norm of the commutator $[\rho_t^A, A]$ as

$$\left\langle 1 - \text{Tr}\left(\rho_T^O \rho_T^A\right)\right\rangle = \sum_\alpha \frac{1}{4\tau_m^\alpha} \int_0^T \left\|\left[\rho_t^A, A_\alpha\right]\right\|_2^2 dt = \sum_\alpha \frac{T}{4\tau_m^\alpha} \overline{\left\|\left[\rho_t^A, A_\alpha\right]\right\|_2^2}, \quad (A2)$$

where we denote the time-average of a function f by $\overline{f} \equiv \int_0^T f(t)dt/T$. Note that the expression $\sum_\alpha \frac{1}{4\tau_m^\alpha} \overline{\left\|\left[\rho_t^A, A_\alpha\right]\right\|_2^2}$ plays the role of a time-averaged decoherence time [15,16], generalizing Equation (11) in the main text.

This sets alternative bounds on the average distance between the state ρ_t^A assigned by $\mathcal{A}$ and the actual state of the system $\rho_t^\mathcal{O}$, in terms of the effect of the Lindblad dephasing term acting on the incomplete-knowledge state ρ_t^A,

$$T \sum_\alpha \tfrac{1}{4\tau_m^\alpha} \overline{\|[\rho_t^A, A_\alpha]\|_2^2} \leq \left\langle \mathcal{D}\left(\rho_T^\mathcal{O}, \rho_T^A\right) \right\rangle \leq \sqrt{T \sum_\alpha \tfrac{1}{4\tau_m^\alpha} \overline{\|[\rho_t^A, A_\alpha]\|_2^2}}.$$

A short time analysis provides a sense of the evolution of the upper and lower bounds on the trace distance and how they compare to its variance. To leading order in a Taylor series expansion,

$$\mathcal{P}\left(\rho_\tau^A\right) \approx 1 + 2\operatorname{Tr}\left(\rho_0^A \Lambda\left[\rho_0^A\right]\right)\tau = 1 - \sum_\alpha \frac{1}{4\tau_m^\alpha} \operatorname{Tr}\left(\left[\rho_0^A, A_\alpha\right]\left[A_\alpha, \rho_0^A\right]\right)\tau, \quad (A3)$$

and one finds

$$\tau \sum_\alpha \tfrac{1}{4\tau_m^\alpha} \left\|\left[\rho_0^A, A_\alpha\right]\right\|_2^2 \leq \left\langle \mathcal{D}\left(\rho_\tau^\mathcal{O}, \rho_\tau^A\right) \right\rangle \leq \sqrt{\tau \sum_\alpha \tfrac{1}{4\tau_m^\alpha} \|[\rho_0^A, A_\alpha]\|_2^2}. \quad (A4)$$

Note that the behavior of the trace distance is determined by the timescale in which decoherence occurs.

Using Equation (9) in the main text and Jensen's inequality, one obtains

$$\left\langle \mathcal{D}^2\left(\rho_T^\mathcal{O}, \rho_T^A\right) \right\rangle \leq 1 - \mathcal{P}\left(\rho_T^A\right), \quad (A5)$$

which implies that the variance $\Delta \mathcal{D}_T^2 \equiv \left\langle \mathcal{D}^2(\rho_T^\mathcal{O}, \rho_T^A) \right\rangle - \left\langle \mathcal{D}(\rho_T^\mathcal{O}, \rho_T^A) \right\rangle^2$ satisfies

$$\Delta \mathcal{D}_T^2 \leq \mathcal{P}\left(\rho_T^A\right) - \mathcal{P}\left(\rho_T^A\right)^2. \quad (A6)$$

In the short time limit this becomes

$$\Delta \mathcal{D}_\tau^2 \leq -2\operatorname{Tr}\left(\rho_0^A \Lambda\left[\rho_0^A\right]\right)\tau. \quad (A7)$$

Appendix A.2. Derivation of the Average and Variance of the Quantum Relative Entropy

Using that $\rho_t^\mathcal{O}$ is pure, and that the von Neumann entropy is given by $S(\rho) \equiv -\operatorname{Tr}(\rho \log \rho)$, we obtain that the average over the results unknown to agent $\mathcal{A}$ satisfy

$$\left\langle S\left(\rho_t^\mathcal{O} \| \rho_t^A\right) \right\rangle = \left\langle \operatorname{Tr}\left(\rho_t^\mathcal{O} \log \rho_t^\mathcal{O}\right) \right\rangle - \left\langle \operatorname{Tr}\left(\rho_t^\mathcal{O} \log \rho_t^A\right) \right\rangle \quad (A8)$$
$$= 0 - \operatorname{Tr}\left(\rho_t^A \log \rho_t^A\right) = S\left(\rho_t^A\right).$$

This sets a direct connection between the average error induced by assigning state ρ_t^A instead of the exact state $\rho_t^\mathcal{O}$, as quantified by the relative entropy, in terms of the von Neumann entropy of the state accessible to agent $\mathcal{A}$.

In turn, the variance of the relative entropy satisfies

$$\Delta S^2\left(\rho_t^\mathcal{O} \| \rho_t^A\right) = \left\langle S^2\left(\rho_t^\mathcal{O} \| \rho_t^A\right) \right\rangle - \left\langle S\left(\rho_t^\mathcal{O} \| \rho_t^A\right) \right\rangle^2 \quad (A9)$$
$$= \left\langle \operatorname{Tr}\left(\rho_t^\mathcal{O} \log \rho_t^A\right)^2 \right\rangle - S^2\left(\rho_t^A\right)$$
$$\leq \left\langle \operatorname{Tr}\left(\rho_t^\mathcal{O}\right) \operatorname{Tr}\left(\rho_t^\mathcal{O} \log^2 \rho_t^A\right) \right\rangle - S^2\left(\rho_t^A\right)$$
$$= \operatorname{Tr}\left(\rho_t^A \log^2 \rho_t^A\right) - S^2\left(\rho_t^A\right),$$

using the Cauchy–Schwarz inequality in the third line. Note that this expression is identical to the variance of the operator $(-\log \rho_t^A)$, which can be thought of as the quantum extension to the notion of the "information content" or "surprisal" $(-\log p)$ in classical information theory.

Appendix A.3. Bounds to the Difference between Perceptions of Multiple Agents

Consider two agents $\mathcal{A}$ and $\mathcal{B}$ who simultaneously monitor different observables on a system. Each one has access to the measurement outcomes of their devices, but not to the results obtained by the other agent. The states ρ_T^A and ρ_T^B that $\mathcal{A}$ and $\mathcal{B}$ assign to the system differ from the actual pure state $\rho_T^\mathcal{O}$ that corresponds to the complete description of the system. For simplicity let us consider that $\mathcal{A}$ monitors a single observable A and $\mathcal{B}$ monitors a single observable B. The complete-description state of the system assigned by all-knowing agent $\mathcal{O}$ evolves according to

$$d\rho_t^\mathcal{O} = L\left[\rho_t^\mathcal{O}\right]dt + I_A\left[\rho_t^\mathcal{O}\right]dW_t^A + I_B\left[\rho_t^\mathcal{O}\right]dW_t^B, \tag{A10}$$

with the Lindbladian $L[\rho_t^\mathcal{O}] \equiv -i[H, \rho_t^\mathcal{O}] + \Lambda_A[\rho_t^\mathcal{O}] + \Lambda_B[\rho_t^\mathcal{O}]$, with corresponding dephasing terms on observables A and B. The innovation terms I_A and I_B are defined as in Equation (3) in the main text, and dW_t^A and dW_t^B are independent noise terms.

The states of both observers satisfy

$$d\rho_t^A = L\left[\rho_t^A\right]dt + I_A\left[\rho_t^A\right]dV_t^A \tag{A11}$$

$$d\rho_t^B = L\left[\rho_t^B\right]dt + I_B\left[\rho_t^B\right]dV_t^B. \tag{A12}$$

Consistency between observers implies that their noises are related to the ones appearing in Equation (A10) by [1,3]:

$$dW_t^A = \left(\text{Tr}\left(\rho_t^A A\right) - \text{Tr}\left(\rho_t^\mathcal{O} A\right)\right)\frac{dt}{\tau_m} + dV_t^A$$

$$dW_t^B = \left(\text{Tr}\left(\rho_t^B B\right) - \text{Tr}\left(\rho_t^\mathcal{O} B\right)\right)\frac{dt}{\tau_m} + dV_t^B. \tag{A13}$$

As the state of each observer satisfies Equation (9), the triangle inequality provides the upper bound

$$\langle \mathcal{D}\left(\rho_T^A, \rho_T^B\right)\rangle_{AB} \leq \sqrt{1 - \text{Tr}\left(\rho_T^{A^2}\right)} + \sqrt{1 - \text{Tr}\left(\rho_T^{B^2}\right)}, \tag{A14}$$

and the lower bound

$$\langle \mathcal{D}\left(\rho_T^A, \rho_T^B\right)\rangle_{AB} \geq \left|\text{Tr}\left(\rho_T^{A^2}\right) - \text{Tr}\left(\rho_T^{B^2}\right)\right|. \tag{A15}$$

Appendix A.4. Illustration—Evolution of Limits to Perception

We consider the case of observer $\mathcal{O}$ monitoring the spin components σ_j^z on a 1D transverse field Ising model, with the Hamiltonian defined in Equation (18) of the main text. Figure A1 shows the evolution of the average trace distance $\langle \mathcal{D}(\rho_T^\mathcal{O}, \rho_T^B)\rangle$ between the complete description and $\mathcal{B}$'s partial one, along with the bounds (16), for different values of the monitoring efficiency η. Figure A2 shows the evolution of the average relative entropy $\langle S(\rho_T^\mathcal{O}||\rho_T^B)\rangle$. The dynamics are simulated by implementation of the monitoring process as a sequence of weak measurements modeled by Kraus operators acting on the state of the system. Specifically, the evolution of $\rho_t^\mathcal{O}$ and corresponding state ρ_t^B with partial measurements is numerically obtained from assuming two independent measurement processes, as in [1].

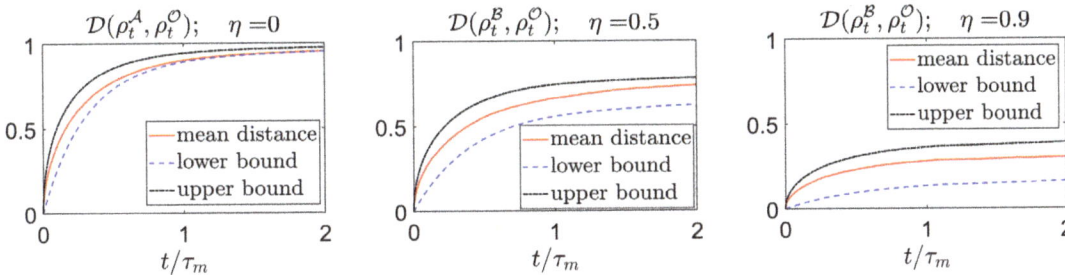

Figure A1. Evolution of the average trace distance and its bounds. Simulated evolution of the average trace distance $\left\langle \mathcal{D}\left(\rho_T^{\mathcal{O}}, \rho_T^{\mathcal{B}}\right) \right\rangle$ between complete and incomplete descriptions for a spin chain initially in a paramagnetic state on which individual spin components σ_j^z are monitored. The simulation corresponds to $N = 6$ spins, with couplings $J\tau_m = h\tau_m = 1/2$. The upper and lower bounds (16) on the average trace distance is depicted by dashed lines, while the shaded area represents the (one standard deviation) confidence region obtained from the upper bound (13) on the standard deviation in the main text, calculated with respect to the mean distance. For $\eta = 0$ (**left**), agent $\mathcal{A}$, without any access to the measurement outcomes, has the most incomplete description of the system. After gaining access to partial measurement results, with $\eta = 0.5$ (**center**) $\mathcal{B}$ gets closer to the complete description of the state of the system. Finally, when $\eta = 0.9$ (**right**), access to enough information provides $\mathcal{B}$ with an almost complete description of the state. Importantly, in all cases the agent can bound how far the description possessed is from the complete one solely in terms solely of the purity $\mathcal{P}\left(\rho_T^{\mathcal{B}}\right)$.

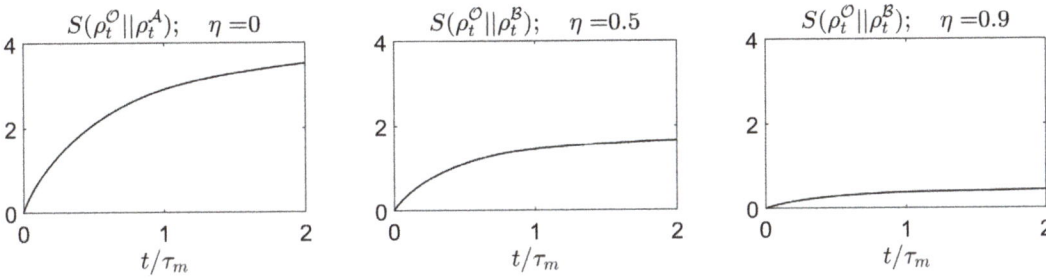

Figure A2. Evolution of the average relative entropy and its bounds. Simulated evolution of the average relative entropy $\left\langle S\left(\rho_T^{\mathcal{O}} \| \rho_T^{\mathcal{B}}\right) \right\rangle$ between complete and incomplete descriptions for a spin chain on which the z components of individual spins are monitored. The shaded area represents the (one standard deviation) confidence region obtained from the upper bound on the standard deviation of the relative entropy, Equation (14) in the main text. As in the case of the trace distance, access to more information leads to a more accurate state assigned by the agent.

Appendix A.5. Illustration—Transition to Complete Descriptions

Consider the case of a one-dimensional harmonic oscillator with position and momentum operators X and P, respectively. We assume agent $\mathcal{B}$ is monitoring the position of the harmonic oscillator, with an efficiency η. The dynamics of state $\rho_t^{\mathcal{B}}$ is dictated by Equation (15) in the main text for the case of a single monitored observable, with

$$\Lambda\left[\rho_t^{\mathcal{B}}\right] = \frac{1}{8\tau_m}\left[X,\left[X,\rho_t^{\mathcal{B}}\right]\right]; \quad \mathcal{I}_X\left[\rho_t^{\mathcal{B}}\right] = \frac{1}{\sqrt{4\tau_m}}\left(\{X,\rho_t^{\mathcal{B}}\} - 2\,\mathrm{Tr}\left(X\rho_t^{\mathcal{B}}\right)\rho_t^{\mathcal{B}}\right). \quad \text{(A16)}$$

Such a dynamics preserves the Gaussian property of states. For these, the variances

$$v_x \equiv \mathrm{Tr}\left(\rho_t^{\mathcal{B}} X^2\right) - \mathrm{Tr}\left(\rho_t^{\mathcal{B}} X\right)^2, \quad \text{(A17)}$$

$$v_p \equiv \mathrm{Tr}\left(\rho_t^{\mathcal{B}} P^2\right) - \mathrm{Tr}\left(\rho_t^{\mathcal{B}} P\right)^2, \quad \text{(A18)}$$

and covariance
$$c_{xp} \equiv \text{Tr}\left(\rho_t^B \frac{\{X,P\}}{2}\right) - \text{Tr}\left(\rho_t^B X\right) \text{Tr}\left(\rho_t^B P\right), \tag{A19}$$

satisfy the following set of differential equations (in natural units) [1,21]:

$$\frac{d}{dt} v_x = 2\omega c_{xp} - \frac{\eta}{\tau_m} v_x^2, \tag{A20a}$$

$$\frac{d}{dt} v_p = -2\omega c_{xp} + \frac{1}{4\tau_m} - \frac{\eta}{\tau_m} c_{xp}^2, \tag{A20b}$$

$$\frac{d}{dt} c_{xp} = \omega v_p - \omega v_x - \frac{\eta}{\tau_m} v_x c_{xp}. \tag{A20c}$$

While the first moments do evolve stochastically, the second moments above satisfy a set of deterministic coupled differential equations. This in turn implies that the purity of the state, which can be obtained from the covariance matrix [22–26]

$$\sigma(t) \equiv \begin{bmatrix} v_x & c_{xp} \\ c_{xp} & v_p \end{bmatrix} \tag{A21}$$

as

$$\mathcal{P}\left(\rho_T^B\right) = \frac{1}{2\sqrt{\det[\sigma(t)]}}, \tag{A22}$$

evolves deterministically as well.

The solution for long times can be derived from Equations (A20), giving

$$c_{xp}^{ss} = -\frac{\omega \tau_m \pm \sqrt{\omega^2 \tau_m^2 + \eta/4}}{\eta}, \tag{A23a}$$

$$v_x^{ss} = \sqrt{\frac{2\omega \tau_m}{\eta} c_{xp}^{ss}}, \tag{A23b}$$

$$v_p^{ss} = v_x^{ss}\left(1 + \frac{\eta}{\omega \tau_m} c_{xp}^{ss}\right), \tag{A23c}$$

which provides the long-time asymptotic value of the purity as a function of the measurement efficiency. The latter turns out to have the following simple expression

$$\mathcal{P}\left(\rho_T^B\right) = \frac{1}{2\sqrt{v_x^{ss} v_p^{ss} - (c_{xp}^{ss})^2}} \tag{A24}$$

$$= \frac{1}{2\sqrt{\frac{2\omega \tau_m}{\eta} c_{xp}^{ss}\left(1 + \frac{\eta}{\omega \tau_m} c_{xp}^{ss}\right) - (c_{xp}^{ss})^2}}$$

$$= \frac{1}{2\sqrt{\frac{2\omega \tau_m}{\eta} c_{xp}^{ss} + (c_{xp}^{ss})^2}}$$

$$= \frac{1}{2\sqrt{\frac{\tau_m}{\eta}\left(\frac{1}{4\tau_m} - \frac{\eta}{\tau_m}(c_{xp}^{ss})^2\right) + (c_{xp}^{ss})^2}} = \frac{1}{2\sqrt{\frac{1}{4\eta}}} = \sqrt{\eta}. \tag{A25}$$

Using that

$$1 - \mathcal{P}\left(\rho_T^B\right) \leq \left\langle \mathcal{D}\left(\rho_T^O, \rho_T^B\right) \right\rangle_B \leq \sqrt{1 - \mathcal{P}(\rho_T^B)}, \tag{A26}$$

then implies

$$1 - \sqrt{\eta} \leq \left\langle \mathcal{D}\left(\rho_T^{\mathcal{O}}, \rho_T^{\mathcal{B}}\right) \right\rangle_{\mathcal{B}} \leq \sqrt{1 - \sqrt{\eta}}. \tag{A27}$$

The entropy of a 1-mode Gaussian state can be expressed in terms of the purity of the state as

$$S\left(\rho_T^{\mathcal{B}}\right) = \left(\frac{1}{2\mathcal{P}(\rho_T^{\mathcal{B}})} + 1/2\right) \log\left(\frac{1}{2\mathcal{P}(\rho_T^{\mathcal{B}})} + 1/2\right) \tag{A28}$$
$$- \left(\frac{1}{2\mathcal{P}(\rho_T^{\mathcal{B}})} - 1/2\right) \log\left(\frac{1}{2\mathcal{P}(\rho_T^{\mathcal{B}})} - 1/2\right).$$

Then, using that $\left\langle S(\rho_t^{\mathcal{O}} \| \rho_t^{\mathcal{B}}) \right\rangle_{\mathcal{B}} = S(\rho_t^{\mathcal{B}})$ and Equation (A25), we obtain that for long times,

$$\left\langle S\left(\rho_t^{\mathcal{O}} \| \rho_t^{\mathcal{B}}\right) \right\rangle_{\mathcal{B}} = S\left(\rho_T^{\mathcal{B}}\right) \tag{A29}$$
$$= \left(\frac{1}{2\sqrt{\eta}} + \frac{1}{2}\right) \log\left(\frac{1}{2\sqrt{\eta}} + \frac{1}{2}\right)$$
$$- \left(\frac{1}{2\sqrt{\eta}} - \frac{1}{2}\right) \log\left(\frac{1}{2\sqrt{\eta}} - \frac{1}{2}\right).$$

References

1. Jacobs, K.; Steck, D. A straightforward introduction to continuous quantum measurement. *Contemp. Phys.* **2006**, *47*, 279–303. [CrossRef]
2. Wiseman, H.M.; Milburn, G.J. *Quantum Measurement and Control*; Cambridge University Press: Cambridge, UK, 2009.
3. Jacobs, K. *Quantum Measurement Theory and Its Applications*; Cambridge University Press: Cambridge, UK, 2014.
4. Murch, K.W.; Weber, S.J.; Macklin, C.; Siddiqi, I. Observing single quantum trajectories of a superconducting quantum bit. *Nature* **2013**, *502*, 211–214. [CrossRef]
5. Devoret, M.H.; Schoelkopf, R.J. Superconducting Circuits for Quantum Information: An Outlook. *Science* **2013**, *339*, 1169–1174. [CrossRef]
6. Weber, S.J.; Chantasri, A.; Dressel, J.; Jordan, A.N.; Murch, K.W.; Siddiqi, I. Mapping the optimal route between two quantum states. *Nature* **2014**, *511*, 570. [CrossRef]
7. Nielsen, M.A.; Chuang, I.L. *Quantum Computation and Quantum Information: 10th Anniversary Edition*; Cambridge University Press: Cambridge, UK, 2010. [CrossRef]
8. Wilde, M.M. *Quantum Information Theory*; Cambridge University Press: Cambridge, UK, 2013. [CrossRef]
9. Watrous, J. *The Theory of Quantum Information*; Cambridge University Press: Cambridge, UK, 2018. [CrossRef]
10. Cover, T.M.; Thomas, J.A. *Elements of Information Theory*; John Wiley & Sons: Hoboken, NJ, USA, 2012. [CrossRef]
11. Hiai, F.; Petz, D. The proper formula for relative entropy and its asymptotics in quantum probability. *Commun. Math. Phys.* **1991**, *143*, 99–114. [CrossRef]
12. Ogawa, T.; Nagaoka, H. Strong converse and Stein's lemma in quantum hypothesis testing. In *Asymptotic Theory of Quantum Statistical Inference: Selected Papers*; World Scientific: Singapore, 2005; pp. 28–42. [CrossRef]
13. Schumacher, B.; Westmoreland, M.D. Relative entropy in quantum information theory. *Contemp. Math.* **2002**, *305*, 265–290. [CrossRef]
14. Vedral, V. The role of relative entropy in quantum information theory. *Rev. Mod. Phys.* **2002**, *74*, 197–234. [CrossRef]
15. Chenu, A.; Beau, M.; Cao, J.; del Campo, A. Quantum Simulation of Generic Many-Body Open System Dynamics Using Classical Noise. *Phys. Rev. Lett.* **2017**, *118*, 140403. [CrossRef] [PubMed]
16. Beau, M.; Kiukas, J.; Eguskiza, I.L.; del Campo, A. Nonexponential Quantum Decay under Environmental Decoherence. *Phys. Rev. Lett.* **2017**, *119*, 130401. [CrossRef] [PubMed]
17. Barchielli, A. Entropy and information gain in quantum continual measurements. In *Quantum Communication, Computing, and Measurement 3*; Springer: Berlin/Heidelberg, Germany, 2002; pp. 49–57. [CrossRef]
18. Barchielli, A.; Gregoratti, M. *Quantum Trajectories and Measurements in Continuous Time: The Diffusive Case*; Springer: Berlin/Heidelberg, Germany, 2009; Volume 782. [CrossRef]
19. Zurek, W.H. Decoherence and the Transition from Quantum to Classical. *Phys. Today* **1991**, *44*, 36–44. [CrossRef]

20. Schlosshauer, M.A. *Decoherence: And the Quantum-to-Classical Transition*; Springer Science & Business Media: Berlin/Heidelberg, Germany, 2007. [CrossRef]
21. Doherty, A.C.; Jacobs, K. Feedback control of quantum systems using continuous state estimation. *Phys. Rev. A* **1999**, *60*, 2700–2711. [CrossRef]
22. Paris, M.G.A.; Illuminati, F.; Serafini, A.; De Siena, S. Purity of Gaussian states: Measurement schemes and time evolution in noisy channels. *Phys. Rev. A* **2003**, *68*, 012314. [CrossRef]
23. Ferraro, A.; Olivares, S.; Paris, M. *Gaussian States in Quantum Information*; Napoli Series on physics and Astrophysics; Bibliopolis: Pittsburgh, PA, USA, 2005.
24. Wang, X.B.; Hiroshima, T.; Tomita, A.; Hayashi, M. Quantum information with Gaussian states. *Phys. Rep.* **2007**, *448*, 1–111. [CrossRef]
25. Weedbrook, C.; Pirandola, S.; García-Patrón, R.; Cerf, N.J.; Ralph, T.C.; Shapiro, J.H.; Lloyd, S. Gaussian quantum information. *Rev. Mod. Phys.* **2012**, *84*, 621–669. [CrossRef]
26. Adesso, G.; Ragy, S.; Lee, A.R. Continuous variable quantum information: Gaussian states and beyond. *Open Syst. Inf. Dyn.* **2014**, *21*, 1440001. [CrossRef]
27. Laverick, K.T.; Chantasri, A.; Wiseman, H.M. Quantum State Smoothing for Linear Gaussian Systems. *Phys. Rev. Lett.* **2019**, *122*, 190402. [CrossRef]
28. Schlosshauer, M. Decoherence, the measurement problem, and interpretations of quantum mechanics. *Rev. Mod. Phys.* **2005**, *76*, 1267–1305. [CrossRef]
29. Zurek, W.H. Quantum darwinism. *Nat. Phys.* **2009**, *5*, 181. [CrossRef]
30. Zwolak, M.; Quan, H.T.; Zurek, W.H. Redundant imprinting of information in nonideal environments: Objective reality via a noisy channel. *Phys. Rev. A* **2010**, *81*, 062110. [CrossRef]
31. Jess Riedel, C.; Zurek, W.H.; Zwolak, M. The rise and fall of redundancy in decoherence and quantum Darwinism. *New J. Phys.* **2012**, *14*, 083010. [CrossRef]
32. Zwolak, M.; Zurek, W.H. Complementarity of quantum discord and classically accessible information. *Sci. Rep.* **2013**, *3*, 1729. [CrossRef]
33. Brandão, F.G.S.L.; Piani, M.; Horodecki, P. Generic emergence of classical features in quantum Darwinism. *Nat. Commun.* **2015**, *6*, 7908. [CrossRef] [PubMed]
34. Horodecki, R.; Korbicz, J.K.; Horodecki, P. Quantum origins of objectivity. *Phys. Rev. A* **2015**, *91*, 032122. [CrossRef]
35. Le, T.P.; Olaya-Castro, A. Strong Quantum Darwinism and Strong Independence are Equivalent to Spectrum Broadcast Structure. *Phys. Rev. Lett.* **2019**, *122*, 010403. [CrossRef] [PubMed]
36. Ciampini, M.A.; Pinna, G.; Mataloni, P.; Paternostro, M. Experimental signature of quantum Darwinism in photonic cluster states. *Phys. Rev. A* **2018**, *98*, 020101. [CrossRef]
37. Chen, M.C.; Zhong, H.S.; Li, Y.; Wu, D.; Wang, X.L.; Li, L.; Liu, N.L.; Lu, C.Y.; Pan, J.W. Emergence of classical objectivity of quantum Darwinism in a photonic quantum simulator. *Sci. Bull.* **2019**, *64*, 580–585. [CrossRef]

Quantifying Decoherence via Increases in Classicality

Shuangshuang Fu [1] and Shunlong Luo [2,3,*]

1. School of Mathematics and Physics, University of Science and Technology Beijing, Beijing 100083, China; shuangshuang.fu@ustb.edu.cn
2. Academy of Mathematics and Systems Science, Chinese Academy of Sciences, Beijing 100190, China
3. School of Mathematical Sciences, University of Chinese Academy of Sciences, Beijing 100049, China
* Correspondence: luosl@amt.ac.cn

Abstract: As a direct consequence of the interplay between the superposition principle of quantum mechanics and the dynamics of open systems, decoherence is a recurring theme in both foundational and experimental exploration of the quantum realm. Decoherence is intimately related to information leakage of open systems and is usually formulated in the setup of "system + environment" as information acquisition of the environment (observer) from the system. As such, it has been mainly characterized via correlations (e.g., quantum mutual information, discord, and entanglement). Decoherence combined with redundant proliferation of the system information to multiple fragments of environment yields the scenario of quantum Darwinism, which is now a widely recognized framework for addressing the quantum-to-classical transition: the emergence of the apparent classical reality from the enigmatic quantum substrate. Despite the half-century development of the notion of decoherence, there are still many aspects awaiting investigations. In this work, we introduce two quantifiers of classicality via the Jordan product and uncertainty, respectively, and then employ them to quantify decoherence from an information-theoretic perspective. As a comparison, we also study the influence of the system on the environment.

Keywords: decoherence; classicality; channel; open system; interference

1. Introduction

A fundamental hallmark of quantum mechanics is the superposition principle [1,2], which leads naturally to coherence and interference [3]. Although reduced coherence (e.g., Landau's study of wave damping [4]) and suppression of interference (e.g., Mott's analysis of α-particle tracking [5]) have featured early studies ever since the beginning of quantum mechanics, the modern conceptualization of the idea of decoherence as a subject in its own right started only in the 1970s, as initiated by Zeh and Zurek [6–10]. The influential and seminal work of Zurek has led further to the development of quantum Darwinism. Nowadays, decoherence has been a subject of many studies after surprising neglect at the initial stage and has gained increasingly importance with the deep investigations of quantum measurement and the emergence of quantum information.

Decoherence provides an elegant mechanism for exploring the boundary between classical and quantum behaviors and imposes technological limits for quantum devices. An ultimate goal of quantum information science is to construct quantum computers, which are notoriously fragile and prone to decoherence, and they call for combating decoherence for quantum information processing [11]. Decoherence also plays a significant role in designing error correction codes, as the notion of decoherence-free schemes (subspace) indicates. Of course, decoherence actually has many more applications to quantum science than to quantum computing per se.

Formally, decoherence usually refers to the decay of the off-diagonal entries of the system density matrix (in the basis of the pointer observable) caused by evolution of the combined "system + environment". Alternatively, it is also characterized as the establishing of correlations between the system and the environment, which causes the system to behave in a classical manner. In this context, the environment effectively measures (monitors) the system. This relational scenario indicates that decoherence is a relative concept and has to be characterized with respect to a reference basis and an environment. In a more pedantic and rigorous fashion, when we talk about decoherence, we should bear in mind (explicitly/implicitly) three ingredients:

(1) Decoherence of which (state)?
(2) Decoherence relative to which (basis, or more generally, channel)?
(3) Decoherence caused by which (environment or observation)?

Decoherence is intimately related to a range of fundamental quantum issues such as the measurement problem [12–17], entanglement and nonlocality [18], irreversibility (the arrow of time) [19], and the quantum-to-classical transition [8–10,12–18]. The later seeks an explanation of the apparent transition from the quantum realm to the classical realm (i.e., the emergence of a classical objective reality from the quantum substrate) as described by quantum Darwinism [20–30]. Decoherence serves as a natural arena for the interplay among wave–particle duality [31–36], wave-packet collapse [8,9,37,38], information transferring [39–41], state broadcasting [42–47], and quantum correlations (quantum discord) [48–54]. Decoherence is also employed in the theory of decoherent histories (consistent histories) approach to quantum mechanics [55–59].

Coherence and decoherence are complementary to each other, or, phrased alternatively, they are the two sides of the same coin: decoherence is just loss of coherence. Coherence arises from the superposition principle and means that a state is in superposition of several states operating together in a coherent way, and decoherence means the loss of this behavior or, more precisely, the loss of definite phase relation between the constituent states for the superposition and thus results in classical mixture of states. Coherence and decoherence play a pivotal role in studying the theoretical issue of the quantum-to-classical transition and in investigating the practical issue concerning physical realization of quantum information processing.

Decoherence is intimately related to loss of quantumness or, put alternatively, an increase in classicality. The quantumness of states and ensembles were studied from various perspectives [60–72]. In particular, the use of non-commutativity as a quantumness witness for a single system was proposed and experimentally confirmed in Refs. [64–67]. An explicit relation between the Jordan product of operators and quantumness was discussed in [70]. A method for measuring quantumness in interferometric setups was presented in [72].

In this work, motivated by previous studies, and following quantitative investigations of coherence and superposition [73–84], we aimed at quantifying decoherence induced by the environment, which may be helpful for quantitatively characterizing certain features of the quantum-to-classical transition and quantum Darwinism.

The remainder of the article is arranged as follows. In Section 2, we present some preliminary results. In particular, we introduce two quantifiers of classicality in terms of operator anti-commutators (symmetric and the Jordan product of operators) and a modified variance in a general setup, which, apart from their use in quantifying decoherence, may be of independent interest. Two inequalities for monotonicity of classicality are established. In Section 3, we introduce two quantifiers of decoherence by exploiting the monotonicity of classicality and reveal their basic features. In Section 4, we discuss the influence on the environment caused by the system, which stands in contrast to decoherence of the system induced by the environment. In Section 5, we illustrate the quantifiers of decoherence in a two-path interferometer. Finally, we summarize the results and present some discussions in Section 6. For simplicity, we consider only finite dimensional systems, although it seems that many results can be readily extended to infinite dimensional cases.

2. Preliminaries

In this section, we consider a general setup of state–channel interaction and discuss two quantifiers of classicality, which will be used to quantify decoherence in the next section.

The first quantifier involves the Jordan product of operators and is intimately connected to the Wigner–Yanase skew information [84]. The second is defined via variance of a state, which stands in some sense dual to the conventional variance of an observable [85,86].

Decoherence is sometimes also called dephasing, dynamical decoherence, or environment-induced decoherence. Here, we emphasize the role of the environment in inducing decoherence. In the conventional approach, decoherence is often read from the off-diagonal entries of the reduced system density matrix after it interacts with the environment, which provide a rather complete picture of the effect of decoherence. However, since all these off-diagonal entries still constitute a matrix with vanishing diagonals, one may be interested in summarizing decoherence by a single numerical quantity, just like although a quantum state provides a complete description of a system, one still seeks certain functionals of the state, such as the von Neumann entropy and purity, to capture some essential features of the state.

Decoherence is usually studied in the context of an open system, which is coupled with the environment. When we focus on the system and ignore the environment, the dynamics of a state ρ of a d-dimensional quantum system is mathematically described by a quantum channel (here we only consider the case with the same input and output system) in the Kraus representation form [11,87]

$$\mathcal{K}(\rho) = \sum_i K_i \rho K_i^\dagger, \tag{1}$$

where K_i are the Kraus operators (effects) satisfying $\sum_i K_i^\dagger K_i = \mathbf{1}$ (the identity operator), which ensures trace-preservation of the channel $\mathcal{K}$. If moreover $\sum_i K_i K_i^\dagger = \mathbf{1}$, then the channel is called unital: it leaves the maximally mixed state (proportional to the identity operator) invariant. We remark that in Equation (1) if we replace ρ by any operator X, the above operation still makes sense as a map. This channel will serve as a reference channel when we talk about decoherence (with respect to $\mathcal{K}$) and actually may be regarded as a generalization of an orthonormal basis, which induces a von Neumann measurement. Consequently, a general notion of decoherence goes beyond that based on an orthonormal basis (pointer observable).

2.1. Classicality in Terms of the Jordan Product

In order to establish notation and to motivate our approach to decoherence, we first recall certain information-theoretical features of state–channel interaction [84]. For the channel determined by Equation (1), let

$$J(\rho, \mathcal{K}) = \frac{1}{2} \sum_i \mathrm{tr}(\{\sqrt{\rho}, K_i\}\{\sqrt{\rho}, K_i\}^\dagger), \tag{2}$$

which will be interpreted as a kind of measure of classicality for the state–channel interaction (or as the classicality of the state with respect to the channel), as will be elucidated later. Here,

$$\{X, Y\} = XY + YX$$

denotes the anti-commutator (the Jordan product or the symmetric product) of operators X and Y acting on the system Hilbert space. This commutative product indicates certain features of classicality. Indeed, decoherence is intimately related to the appearance or increasing of classicality, and the symmetric Jordan product, as a commutative operation, is also intimately related to classicality. Consequently, it is plausible and reasonable that decoherence may be quantified via the Jordan product of states and observables, just like that quantumness of states can be characterized via the Jordan product of observables [70]. After simple manipulation, we have

$$J(\rho, \mathcal{K}) = \frac{1}{2} \mathrm{tr}(\mathcal{K}(\rho) + \mathcal{K}^\dagger(\rho) + 2\sqrt{\rho}\mathcal{K}^\dagger(\sqrt{\rho})), \tag{3}$$

where
$$\mathcal{K}^\dagger(X) = \sum_i K_i^\dagger X K_i$$

is the dual channel of $\mathcal{K}$. We notice that $\mathrm{tr}(\sqrt{\rho}\mathcal{K}^\dagger(\sqrt{\rho})) = \mathrm{tr}(\mathcal{K}^\dagger(\sqrt{\rho})\sqrt{\rho}) = \mathrm{tr}(\sqrt{\rho}\mathcal{K}(\sqrt{\rho}))$.

It is well known that the Kraus operators for the operator-sum representation in Equation (1) are not unique, and the question arises as to whether the defining Equation (2) for the classicality quantifier $J(\rho, \mathcal{K})$ is well defined. Indeed, the Kraus operators K_i for different representations of the channel $\mathcal{K}$ are related by unitary transformations (the unitary freedom in the operator-sum representation of a channel) [11], and it can be readily shown that $J(\rho, \mathcal{K})$ is independent of the choice of the Kraus operators and is thus unambiguously defined.

For comparison, we also introduce

$$I(\rho, \mathcal{K}) = \frac{1}{2}\sum_i \mathrm{tr}\big([\sqrt{\rho}, K_i][\sqrt{\rho}, K_i]^\dagger\big), \tag{4}$$

where
$$[X, Y] = XY - YX$$

denotes the commutator (the Lie product or the anti-symmetric product) of the operators X and Y. Clearly,

$$I(\rho, \mathcal{K}) = \frac{1}{2}\mathrm{tr}\big(\mathcal{K}(\rho) + \mathcal{K}^\dagger(\rho) - 2\sqrt{\rho}\mathcal{K}^\dagger(\sqrt{\rho})\big). \tag{5}$$

It is remarkable that if K_i is a Hermitian operator, then the summand

$$\frac{1}{2}\mathrm{tr}\big([\sqrt{\rho}, K_i][\sqrt{\rho}, K_i]^\dagger\big) = -\frac{1}{2}\mathrm{tr}\big([\sqrt{\rho}, K_i]^2\big)$$

in Equation (4) is precisely the celebrated Wigner–Yanase skew information

$$I(\rho, K_i) = -\frac{1}{2}\mathrm{tr}\big([\sqrt{\rho}, K_i]^2\big) \tag{6}$$

of ρ (with K_i serving as a conserved observable) [88], which is now playing an increasingly interesting and important role in quantum theory [89–97]. In particular, the Wigner–Yanase skew information is monotone in the sense that [98,99]

$$I(\Phi(\rho), K) \leq I(\rho, K) \tag{7}$$

for any channel Φ that does not disturb the observable K (i.e., $\Phi^\dagger(K) = K$, $\Phi^\dagger(K^2) = K^2$). This will be used to establish Proposition 1.

It is well recognized that the Wigner–Yanase skew information is a particular version of quantum Fisher information [90], which is quite different from the quantum (von Neumann) entropy. Actually, the original motivation for Wigner and Yanase introducing the skew information was to seek an alternative quantity for quantifying information contents of quantum states in the presence of conserved observables.

By Equations (3) and (5) and the fact that $\mathrm{tr}\rho = 1$, if the channel $\mathcal{K}$ is unital in the sense that $\mathcal{K}(\mathbf{1}) = \mathbf{1}$ (equivalently, $\sum_i K_i K_i^\dagger = \mathbf{1}$), then

$$J(\rho, \mathcal{K}) + I(\rho, \mathcal{K}) = 2, \tag{8}$$

which shows that $J(\rho, \mathcal{K})$ (involving the symmetric Jordan product) and $I(\rho, \mathcal{K})$ (involving the anti-symmetric Lie product) are complementary to each other. Moreover,

$$2 \geq J(\rho, \mathcal{K}) \geq 1 \geq I(\rho, \mathcal{K}) \geq 0.$$

We first list some basic properties of $J(\rho, \mathcal{K})$.

(a) $1 \leq J(\rho, \mathcal{K}) \leq 2$. Moreover, $J(\rho, \mathcal{K}) = 2$ if and only if $[\sqrt{\rho}, K_i] = 0$ for all i.
(b) $J(\rho, \mathcal{K})$ is concave in ρ.
(c) $J(\rho, \mathcal{K})$ is covariant in the sense that

$$J(U\rho U^\dagger, \mathcal{K}) = J(\rho, U^\dagger \mathcal{K} U)$$

for any unitary operator U on the system Hilbert space. Here $U^\dagger \mathcal{K} U(\rho) = \sum_i (U^\dagger K_i U) \rho (U^\dagger K_i U)^\dagger$.

Item (a) is apparent from the definition, and item (b) follows from Equation (3) and the celebrated Lieb concavity [100,101], which states that the functional $\mathrm{tr}(\rho^s X \rho^{1-s} X^\dagger)$ is concave in the state ρ for any $s \in (0,1)$ and any operator X. Here we only used the case $s = 1/2$. Item (c) can be readily checked.

Recall that the dual of the channel $\Phi(\rho) = \sum_i K_i \rho K_i^\dagger$ is defined as $\Phi^\dagger(X) = \sum_i K_i^\dagger X K_i$ for any operator X. The following monotonicity of $J(\rho, \mathcal{K})$ under certain channels Φ plays a crucial role in our approach to decoherence.

Proposition 1. *Let Φ be a unital channel that does not disturb the Kraus operators of the reference channel $\mathcal{K}$ defined by Equation (1) in the sense that $\Phi^\dagger(K_i) = K_i$ and $\Phi^\dagger(K_i K_i^\dagger) = K_i K_i^\dagger$ for all i, then*

$$J(\rho, \mathcal{K}) \leq J(\Phi(\rho), \mathcal{K}). \tag{9}$$

Noting the complementarity relation (8), the above monotonicity may be directly derived from the corresponding property of the Wigner–Yanase skew information, as described in Equation (7).

In view of the above increasing behavior (under certain channels) and the properties specified by items (a)–(c), we may interpret $J(\rho, \mathcal{K})$ as a quantifier of classicality of the state ρ (with reference to the channel $\mathcal{K}$). Indeed, a reasonable measure of classicality should be concave in the state ρ (classical mixing of states should not decrease classicality on average), which is in accordance with item (b). Operations on the state that leave the reference channel undisturbed also should not decrease classicality, which is guaranteed by inequality (9). In contrast, $I(\rho, \mathcal{K})$ may be regarded as a quantity of coherence or quantumness of ρ (with reference to $\mathcal{K}$). This is consistent with Equation (8), which may be regarded as an information-theoretic manifestation of the Bohr complementarity from the perspective of the asymmetry–symmetry trade-off [84]: $I(\rho, \mathcal{K})$ characterizes the asymmetry (of ρ with respect to $\mathcal{K}$) and can be related to the path feature in an interferometric setup, while $J(\rho, \mathcal{K})$ characterizes the symmetry (of ρ with respect to $\mathcal{K}$) and can be related to fringe visibility.

2.2. Classicality in Terms of Uncertainty

Although the quantity $J(\rho, \mathcal{K})$ has nice information-theoretic features, it involves the square root of a state and thus may be difficult to calculate. For simplicity and comparison, we also introduce an alternative measure of classicality without the square root, which is directly based on a modification of the ubiquitous notion of variance (uncertainty).

Recall that any state, as a Hermitian operator, can also be formally regarded as an observable, and thus one may consider its variance with respect to another state (or, more generally, any operator) [85,86]. Following this consideration, we introduce the variance of a state ρ in a channel $\mathcal{K}$ defined by Equation (1) as

$$V_\mathcal{K}(\rho) = \sum_i V_{K_i}(\rho), \tag{10}$$

where

$$V_K(\rho) = \mathrm{tr}\big((\rho - \mathrm{tr}(\rho K^\dagger K))^2 K^\dagger K\big) \tag{11}$$

is the generalized variance of ρ (considered as an observable) in K (not necessarily a Hermitian operator). It turns out that

$$V_K(\rho) = \text{tr}(\rho^2 K^\dagger K) - (\text{tr}(\rho K^\dagger K))^2 (2 - \text{tr}(K^\dagger K)) \tag{12}$$

and in particular, if $\text{tr}(K^\dagger K) = 1$, then

$$V_K(\rho) = \text{tr}(\rho^2 K^\dagger K) - (\text{tr}(\rho K^\dagger K))^2.$$

In a d-dimensional system, the variance of ρ in $\mathcal{K}$ is upper bounded as

$$V_\mathcal{K}(\rho) = \text{tr}(\rho^2) - \sum_i (\text{tr}(\rho K_i^\dagger K_i))^2 (2 - \text{tr}(K_i^\dagger K_i)) \tag{13}$$

$$\leq \text{tr}(\rho^2) - \sum_i (\text{tr}(\rho K_i^\dagger K_i))^2 (2 - d)$$

$$\leq 1 + (d-2) \sum_i (\text{tr}(\rho K_i^\dagger K_i))^2$$

$$\leq 1 + (d-2)$$

$$= d - 1.$$

Furthermore, if $\text{tr}(K_i^\dagger K_i) = 1$ for all i, then we actually have

$$V_\mathcal{K}(\rho) = \text{tr}(\rho^2) - \sum_i (\text{tr}(\rho K_i^\dagger K_i))^2 \leq 1. \tag{14}$$

For some applications and intuitions of the above quantities, see Refs. [85,86]. In Equation (10), we have put K in the subscript, i.e., with the notation $V_K(\rho)$ rather than $V(\rho, K)$; we are emphasizing that the above variance is quite different from the conventional variance $V(\rho, K) = \text{tr}(\rho(K - \text{tr}\rho K)^2)$ of the observable K (in the state ρ). Indeed, $V_K(\rho)$ is convex in ρ, while $V(\rho, K)$ is concave in ρ.

To introduce an alternative quantifier of classicality, noting that $V_\mathcal{K}(\rho) \leq d - 1$, we define

$$C(\rho, \mathcal{K}) = d - 1 - V_\mathcal{K}(\rho) = S_2(\rho) + \sum_i (\text{tr}(\rho K_i^\dagger K_i))^2 (2 - \text{tr}(K_i^\dagger K_i)) + d - 2, \tag{15}$$

where

$$S_2(\rho) = 1 - \text{tr}(\rho^2)$$

is the Tsallis 2-entropy. The quantity $C(\rho, \mathcal{K})$ has the following properties.
(a) $0 \leq C(\rho, \mathcal{K}) \leq d - 1$.
(b) $C(\rho, \mathcal{K})$ is concave in ρ.
(c) $C(\rho, \mathcal{K})$ is covariant in the sense that

$$C(U\rho U^\dagger, \mathcal{K}) = C(\rho, U^\dagger \mathcal{K} U)$$

for any unitary operator U on the system Hilbert space. Here the channel $U^\dagger \mathcal{K} U$ is defined as $U^\dagger \mathcal{K} U(\rho) = \sum_i (U^\dagger K_i U)\rho(U^\dagger K_i U)^\dagger$.

Similar to $J(\rho, \mathcal{K})$, we have the following monotonicity property.

Proposition 2. *Let Φ be a unital channel that does not disturb the Kraus operators of the reference channel $\mathcal{K}$ defined by Equation (1) in the sense that $\Phi^\dagger(K_i^\dagger K_i) = K_i^\dagger K_i$ for all i, then*

$$C(\rho, \mathcal{K}) \leq C(\Phi(\rho), \mathcal{K}). \tag{16}$$

In order to prove the above statement and to characterize the effect of the channel Φ, we first recall the notion of majorization for vectors [102–104]. For any real vector $x = (x_1, x_2, \cdots, x_d) \in \mathbb{R}^d$, let $x^\downarrow = (x_1^\downarrow, x_2^\downarrow, \cdots, x_d^\downarrow)$ be the vector obtained by rearranging the components of x in a non-increasing order. The weak majorization relation $x \preccurlyeq_w y$ (i.e., x is weakly majorized by y, or y weakly majorizes x) means that [103]

$$\sum_{i=1}^k x_i^\downarrow \leq \sum_{i=1}^k y_i^\downarrow, \quad k = 1, 2, \cdots, d.$$

If furthermore $\sum_{i=1}^d x_i^\downarrow = \sum_{i=1}^d y_i^\downarrow$ (which is always satisfied for probability vectors), then it is said that x is majorized by y, denoted as $x \preccurlyeq y$. Intuitively, $x \preccurlyeq y$ means that x is more chaotic (more flat, more uniform, more mixed, and more spread out) than y. For example,

$$\left(\frac{1}{d}, \frac{1}{d}, \cdots, \frac{1}{d}\right) \preccurlyeq (x_1, x_2, \cdots, x_d) \preccurlyeq (1, 0, \cdots, 0)$$

for any $x_i \geq 0, \sum_{i=1}^d x_i = 1$. It is well known that $x \preccurlyeq y$ if and only if $x = My$ for some doubly stochastic matrix M (i.e., square matrix with non-negative entries and all row and column sums equal to 1) [102]. We will be only concerned with probability vectors arising from eigenvalues of a quantum state (density matrix).

Now, by the condition $\Phi^\dagger(K_i^\dagger K_i) = K_i^\dagger K_i$ we obtain

$$\mathrm{tr}\big(\Phi(\rho) K_i^\dagger K_i\big) = \mathrm{tr}\big(\rho \Phi^\dagger(K_i^\dagger K_i)\big) = \mathrm{tr}\big(\rho K_i^\dagger K_i\big).$$

Consequently, under the above condition, inequality (16) is equivalent to

$$\mathrm{tr}(\Phi(\rho)^2) \leq \mathrm{tr}(\rho^2),$$

which is true for any unital channel.

3. Quantifying Decoherence of System Induced by Environment

With the above preparation, which is a rather general setup, we now proceed to quantify decoherence of system induced by environment. In order to obtain more concrete and explicit results, we have to specify the system-environment coupling. For simplicity, we study the important case when the reference channel $\mathcal{K}$ is induced by a von Neumann measurement $\Pi = \{\Pi_i = |i\rangle\langle i| : i = 1, 2, \cdots, d\}$ in a d-dimensional system with $\{|i\rangle : i = 1, 2, \cdots, d\}$ being an orthonormal basis of the system Hilbert space. In this case, we write the corresponding reference channel as

$$\Pi(\rho) = \sum_{i=1}^d \Pi_i \rho \Pi_i = \sum_{i=1}^d \langle i|\rho|i\rangle |i\rangle\langle i|.$$

By specifying $\mathcal{K}$ to Π and noting Equation (3), we have

$$J(\rho, \Pi) = 1 + \mathrm{tr}\big(\sqrt{\rho}\Pi^\dagger(\sqrt{\rho})\big) = 1 + \sum_{i=1}^d \langle i|\sqrt{\rho}|i\rangle^2. \tag{17}$$

Consider a quantum system with a d-dimensional Hilbert space H_S, which interacts with an environment consisting of d parts described by the Hilbert space $H_E = H_{E_1} \otimes H_{E_2} \otimes \cdots \otimes H_{E_d}$ through the controlled unitary operation

$$\Pi_U = \Pi_1 \otimes U_{E_1} + \Pi_2 \otimes U_{E_2} + \cdots + \Pi_d \otimes U_{E_d} \tag{18}$$

on the combined system

$$H_S \otimes H_E = H_S \otimes (H_{E_1} \otimes H_{E_2} \otimes \cdots \otimes H_{E_d}).$$

Here $\mathcal{U} = \{U_{E_i} : i = 1, 2, \cdots, d\}$ denotes the collection of unitary operators on the various sub-environments, with U_{E_i} acting only on H_{E_i}. This scenario is schematically depicted in Figure 1, and will be further discussed in the next section. In this context, one may wonder why the dimension of the quantum system is the same as the number of environments. This arises naturally in a multi-path interferometer, in which we are only concerned with the path degree of freedoms, and thus the associated system Hilbert space is spanned by the path basis. Consequently, the system is d-dimensional when we have d paths. In order to study the decoherence of the system (consisting of the d paths as an orthonormal basis), we attach a detector to each path, and thus we have d sub-environments (corresponding to the d detectors).

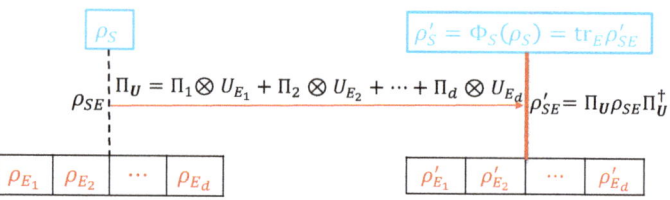

Figure 1. Schematic illustration of decoherence of the system (initially in the state ρ_S) induced by the environment consisting of d sub-environments (initially in the state $\rho_E = \rho_{E_1} \otimes \rho_{E_2} \otimes \cdots \otimes \rho_{E_d}$). The combined initial system–environment state is $\rho_{SE} = \rho_S \otimes \rho_E$. The system and environment is coupled via the combined unitary operator $\Pi_{\mathcal{U}} = \sum_{i=1}^{d} \Pi_i \otimes U_{E_i}$, and the final combined system–environment state is $\rho'_{SE} = \Pi_{\mathcal{U}} \rho_{SE} \Pi_{\mathcal{U}}^\dagger$ with final system state $\rho'_S = \mathrm{tr}_E \rho'_{SE}$. The decoherence of ρ_S (with respect to Π) induced by the environment is quantified by $D(\rho_S|\Pi, \mathcal{U}) = J(\rho'_S, \Pi) - J(\rho_S, \Pi)$ (see Equation (27)) and $F(\rho_S|\Pi, \mathcal{U}) = C(\rho'_S, \Pi) - C(\rho_S, \Pi)$ (see Equation (31)), both of which may be interpreted as increases in classicality of the system caused by the environment.

The initial combined system–environment state is

$$\rho_{SE} = \rho_S \otimes \rho_E,$$

where ρ_S is the initial system state, and $\rho_E = \rho_{E_1} \otimes \rho_{E_2} \otimes \cdots \otimes \rho_{E_d}$ is the initial environment state. When expressed as a density matrix with respect to the orthonormal basis $\{|i\rangle : i = 1, 2, \cdots, d\}$, the initial system state ρ_S has the matrix form

$$\rho_S = \left(\langle i|\rho_S|j\rangle\right) = \begin{pmatrix} \langle 1|\rho_S|1\rangle & \langle 1|\rho_S|2\rangle & \cdots & \langle 1|\rho_S|d\rangle \\ \langle 2|\rho_S|1\rangle & \langle 2|\rho_S|2\rangle & \cdots & \langle 2|\rho_S|d\rangle \\ \vdots & \vdots & \ddots & \vdots \\ \langle d|\rho_S|1\rangle & \langle d|\rho_S|2\rangle & \cdots & \langle d|\rho_S|d\rangle \end{pmatrix}. \qquad (19)$$

After the system–environment interaction through the unitary operation (18), the final state of the combined system is

$$\begin{aligned} \rho'_{SE} &= \Pi_{\mathcal{U}} \rho_{SE} \Pi_{\mathcal{U}}^\dagger \\ &= (\Pi_1 \otimes U_{E_1} + \cdots + \Pi_d \otimes U_{E_d})(\rho_S \otimes \rho_E)(\Pi_1 \otimes U_{E_1} + \cdots + \Pi_d \otimes U_{E_d})^\dagger \\ &= \sum_{i,j=1}^{d} (\Pi_i \rho_S \Pi_j) \otimes (U_{E_i} \rho_E U_{E_j}^\dagger). \end{aligned} \qquad (20)$$

Here we emphasize that U_{E_i} acts only nontrivially on H_{E_i}. From the above expression, we obtain the final (reduced) system state

$$\rho'_S = \mathrm{tr}_E \rho'_{SE} = \sum_{i,j=1}^{d} \mathrm{tr}(U_{E_i} \rho_E U_{E_j}^\dagger) \cdot \Pi_i \rho_S \Pi_j \qquad (21)$$

after the interaction, which can be represented as the $d \times d$ matrix (noting that $\Pi_i = |i\rangle\langle i|$)

$$\rho'_S = \left(\langle i|\rho_S|j\rangle\omega_{ij}\right) = \begin{pmatrix} \langle 1|\rho_S|1\rangle & \langle 1|\rho_S|2\rangle\omega_{12} & \cdots & \langle 1|\rho_S|d\rangle\omega_{1d} \\ \langle 2|\rho_S|1\rangle\omega_{21} & \langle 2|\rho_S|2\rangle & \cdots & \langle 2|\rho_S|d\rangle\omega_{2d} \\ \vdots & \vdots & \ddots & \vdots \\ \langle d|\rho_S|1\rangle\omega_{d1} & \langle d|\rho_S|2\rangle\omega_{d2} & \cdots & \langle d|\rho_S|d\rangle \end{pmatrix} = \rho_S \circ \Omega \quad (22)$$

with respect to the orthonormal basis $\{|i\rangle : i = 1, 2, \cdots, d\}$. Here the symbol $\circ$ denotes the Hadamard product (also called the Schur product or the entry-wise product) of matrices defined as $(a_{ij}) \circ (b_{ij}) = (a_{ij}b_{ij})$, and $\Omega = (\omega_{ij})$ with

$$\omega_{ij} = \text{tr}(U_{E_i}\rho_E U^\dagger_{E_j})$$

being a correlation matrix, i.e., a non-negative definite matrix with diagonal entries all equal to 1. By casting ω_{ij} as

$$\omega_{ij} = \text{tr}(U_{E_i}\rho_E U^\dagger_{E_j}) = \text{tr}(X_i X^\dagger_j),$$

with $X_i = U_{E_i}\sqrt{\rho_E}$, we readily see that the matrix $\Omega = (\omega_{ij})$ is a Gram matrix of the family of operators $\{X_i : i = 1, 2, \cdots, d\}$ as vectors in the Hilbert space consisting of operators (with the Hilbert–Schmidt product) acting on the environment. Moreover,

$$\omega_{ij} = \begin{cases} 1, & i = j \\ \omega_i \omega^*_j, & i \neq j \end{cases}$$

with $\omega_i = \text{tr}(U_{E_i}\rho_{E_i})$, and ω^*_j denotes the complex conjugation of the complex number ω_j. Since Ω is a non-negative definite matrix, it has a square root, which may be symbolically expressed as

$$\sqrt{\Omega} = \left(\alpha_{ij}\right) = \begin{pmatrix} \langle \boldsymbol{\alpha}_1| \\ \langle \boldsymbol{\alpha}_2| \\ \vdots \\ \langle \boldsymbol{\alpha}_d| \end{pmatrix} = (|\boldsymbol{\alpha}_1\rangle, |\boldsymbol{\alpha}_2\rangle, \cdots, |\boldsymbol{\alpha}_d\rangle), \quad (23)$$

where the bra $\langle \boldsymbol{\alpha}_i| = \sum_{j=1}^d \alpha_{ij}\langle j|$ is identified with the row vector $(\alpha_{i1}, \alpha_{i2}, \cdots, \alpha_{id})$, while the corresponding adjoint vector (ket) $|\boldsymbol{\alpha}_i\rangle = \sum_{j=1}^d \alpha^*_{ij}|j\rangle = \sum_{j=1}^d \alpha_{ji}|j\rangle$ is identified with the column vector $(\alpha^*_{i1}, \alpha^*_{i2}, \cdots, \alpha^*_{id})^T = (\alpha_{1i}, \alpha_{2i}, \cdots, \alpha_{di})^T$. Consequently, Ω can be expressed as the following Gram matrix

$$\Omega = \begin{pmatrix} \langle \boldsymbol{\alpha}_1| \\ \langle \boldsymbol{\alpha}_2| \\ \vdots \\ \langle \boldsymbol{\alpha}_d| \end{pmatrix} (|\boldsymbol{\alpha}_1\rangle, |\boldsymbol{\alpha}_2\rangle, \cdots, |\boldsymbol{\alpha}_d\rangle) = (\langle \boldsymbol{\alpha}_i|\boldsymbol{\alpha}_j\rangle), \quad (24)$$

which will be used later.

We write the operation determined by Equation (22) as the channel

$$\Phi_S(\rho_S) = \rho'_S = \rho_S \circ \Omega, \quad (25)$$

which may be called a Hadamard channel due to the involvement of the Hadamard product. This channel has some nice properties.

(a) The dual of the channel $\Phi_S(\rho_S) = \rho_S \circ \Omega$ is $\Phi^\dagger_S(X) = X \circ \Omega^T$, where Ω^T denotes the transposition of the matrix Ω. In particular, if Ω is a real symmetric matrix and thus $\Omega^T = \Omega^* = \Omega$, then the corresponding channel $\Phi_S(\rho_S)$ is self-dual. Here Ω^* denotes complex conjugation of each entry of the matrix Ω.

(b) The channel $\Phi_S(\rho_S) = \rho_S \circ \Omega$ can be expressed as the Kraus operator-sum form

$$\Phi_S(\rho_S) = \sum_{j=1}^d \Omega_j \rho_S \Omega_j^\dagger \qquad (26)$$

with the diagonal matrices (Kraus operators)

$$\Omega_j = \mathrm{diag}\{\alpha_{1j}, \alpha_{2j}, \cdots, \alpha_{dj}\} = \begin{pmatrix} \alpha_{1j} & 0 & \cdots & 0 \\ 0 & \alpha_{2j} & \cdots & 0 \\ \vdots & \vdots & \ddots & \vdots \\ 0 & 0 & \cdots & \alpha_{dj} \end{pmatrix}$$

with α_{ij} determined by Equation (23).

(c) If $|\omega_{ij}| < 1$ for $i \neq j$, then the repeated iteration of the channel Φ_S tends to the completely decohering channel in the sense that $\lim_{n \to \infty} \Phi_S^n(\rho_S) = \mathrm{diag}(\rho_S)$. Here the convergence is for any norm on the operator space of a finite dimensional Hilbert space.

All the above properties can be directly verified.

Compared with the initial system state ρ_S given by Equation (19), the off-diagonal entries of the final system state $\rho_S' = \Phi_S(\rho_S)$ in Equation (22) is multiplied by ω_{ij}. This is the conventional meaning of decoherence as decaying of off-diagonal entries of the density matrix. In order to use a single numerical quantity to summarize certain amount of decoherence, we introduce the following quantity

$$D(\rho_S | \Pi, \mathbf{U}) = J(\rho_S', \Pi) - J(\rho_S, \Pi), \qquad (27)$$

which is our first key character for quantifying decoherence induced by the environment. The above quantifier of decoherence can be more explicitly expressed as

$$D(\rho_S | \Pi, \mathbf{U}) = \sum_{i=1}^d \left(\langle i | \sqrt{\rho_S'} | i \rangle^2 - \langle i | \sqrt{\rho_S} | i \rangle^2 \right).$$

The physical intuition of the above quantity is the increase in classicality caused by the interaction with the environment (the channel Φ_S). This notation indicates clearly and precisely that we are talking about the decoherence of the initial system state ρ_S (with respect to Π) induced by the environment (symbolized by the collection $\mathbf{U} = \{U_{E_i} : i = 1, 2, \cdots, d\}$ of unitary operators acting on the environment).

The quantifier of decoherence $D(\rho_S | \Pi, \mathbf{U})$ possesses the following properties.

Proposition 3. $0 \leq D(\rho_S | \Pi, \mathbf{U}) \leq 1$. Moreover, $D(\rho_S | \Pi, \mathbf{U}) = 0$ if $U_{E_i} = c_i \mathbf{1}_{E_i}$ (proportional to the identity operator on the i-th sub-environment for all i).

We conjecture that $D(\rho_S | \Pi, \mathbf{U})$ is convex in ρ. It seems that a proof may require some deep mathematics.

To prove Proposition 3, first noting that $\Phi_S^\dagger(\rho_S) = \rho_S \circ \Omega^T$, it is easy to verify $\Phi_S^\dagger(\Pi_i) = \Pi_i$. Now, from $\Pi_i^2 = \Pi_i$ and inequality (9) in Proposition 1, we conclude that

$$J(\rho_S', \Pi) = J(\Phi_S(\rho_S), \Pi) \leq J(\rho_S, \Pi), \qquad (28)$$

which implies the desired inequality $0 \leq D(\rho_S | \Pi, \mathbf{U})$. The upper bound $D(\rho_S | \Pi, \mathbf{U}) \leq 1$ follows readily from the property of $J(\rho, \Pi)$.

For the decoherence channel Φ_S, we have

$$\lambda(\Phi_S(\rho_S)) \prec \lambda(\rho_S), \qquad (29)$$

where $\lambda(\rho_S)$ is the probability vector consisting of the eigenvalues (spectrum, in any order) of the quantum state ρ_S. The heuristic and intuitive meaning of the above inequality is that the decoherence renders the state flatter in the sense that the probability vector consisting of the eigenvalues of the final state is more uniform (more mixing, more spread out) than that of the initial system state, as mathematically defined by the majorization relation of probability vectors.

Recall that a unitarily invariant norm $||\cdot||$ is an operator norm with the unitary invariance $||X|| = ||UXW||$ for all X and all unitary operators U and W. Prototypical examples of such norms include the trace norm, the Frobenius norm, the p-norm (with $p \geq 1$), and the Ky Fan norm [104]. Equation (29) implies that

$$||\Phi_S(\rho_S)|| \geq ||\rho_S|| \tag{30}$$

for any unitarily invariant norm $||\cdot||$. In particular, if Φ_S is the completely decohering channel in the sense that $\Omega = (\omega_{ij}) = \mathbf{1}$, that is

$$\Phi_S(\rho_S) = \begin{pmatrix} \langle 1|\rho_S|1\rangle & 0 & \cdots & 0 \\ 0 & \langle 2|\rho_S|2\rangle & \cdots & 0 \\ \vdots & \vdots & \ddots & \vdots \\ 0 & 0 & \cdots & \langle d|\rho_S|d\rangle \end{pmatrix} = \mathrm{diag}(\rho_S),$$

then we come to the well-known fact that the vector formed by the diagonal entries of a density matrix is majorized by the vector formed by the eigenvalues of the matrix [102], that is, $\lambda(\mathrm{diag}(\rho_S)) \preccurlyeq \lambda(\rho_S)$. By taking the trace norm of the logarithm of the states, we obtain $\Pi_{i=1}^d \langle i|\rho_S|i\rangle \geq \det(\rho_S) = \Pi_{i=1}^d \lambda_i(\rho_S)$, which is precisely the celebrated Hadamard determinant inequality [105]. Here $\lambda_i(\rho_S)$ are eigenvalues of ρ_S, and $\lambda(\rho_S) = (\lambda_1(\rho_S), \lambda_2(\rho_S), \cdots, \lambda_d(\rho_S))$.

In terms of classicality defined via variance of states, we introduce an alternative quantifier for decoherence as

$$F(\rho_S|\Pi, \boldsymbol{U}) = C(\rho_S', \Pi) - C(\rho_S, \Pi), \tag{31}$$

which can be explicitly expressed as

$$F(\rho_S|\Pi, \boldsymbol{U}) = \mathrm{tr}(\rho_S^2) - \mathrm{tr}(\rho_S'^2) = \sum_{i=1}^d \left(\langle i|\rho_S^2|i\rangle - \langle i|\rho_S'^2|i\rangle \right). \tag{32}$$

The intuition of the above measure is similar to that of $D(\rho_S|\Pi, \boldsymbol{U})$: The increase in classicality of the system caused by the environment captures some essential features of decoherence.

Proposition 4.

(a) $0 \leq F(\rho_S|\Pi, \boldsymbol{U}) \leq 1$. Moreover, $F(\rho_S|\Pi, \boldsymbol{U}) = 0$ if $U_{E_i} = c_i \mathbf{1}_{E_i}$ (proportional to the identity operator on the i-th sub-environment for all i).

(b) $F(\rho_S|\Pi, \boldsymbol{U})$ is convex in ρ.

For item (a), the non-negativity of $F(\rho_S|\Pi, \boldsymbol{U})$ follows from inequality (16) in Proposition 2. The upper bound is evident in view of inequality (32).

For item (b), let $c \in [0,1]$, ρ_S and σ_S be two states with $\rho_S' = \Phi_S(\rho_S), \sigma_S' = \Phi_S(\sigma_S)$. Straightforward manipulation yields

$$cF(\rho_S|\Pi, \boldsymbol{U}) + (1-c)F(\sigma_S|\Pi, \boldsymbol{U}) - F(c\rho_S + (1-c)\sigma_S|\Pi, \boldsymbol{U})$$
$$= c(1-c)\left(\mathrm{tr}((\rho_S - \sigma_S)^2) - \mathrm{tr}((\rho_S' - \sigma_S')^2) \right)$$
$$\geq 0.$$

The last inequality follows from

$$\lambda(\rho'_S - \sigma'_S) \preccurlyeq \lambda(\rho_S - \sigma_S).$$

We see that, on the one hand, $D(\rho_S|\Pi, U)$ and $F(\rho_S|\Pi, U)$ share some similar properties, and, on the other hand, they have different advantages and disadvantages. This is reminiscent of the comparison between the conventional variance and Fisher information.

4. Influence on Environment Caused by System

The interaction between the system and the environment is mutual. While we are focusing on the decoherence of the system caused by the environment, it may also be useful to investigate the influence on the environment caused by the system. In a formal fashion, this may also be interpreted as the decoherence of the environment caused by the system. Due to the asymmetry of the system–environment interaction, there are subtle differences between the influence on the environment caused by the system and that on the system caused by the environment.

From Equation (20), we obtain the final environment state

$$\rho'_E = \mathrm{tr}_S \rho'_{SE} = \sum_{i=1}^d \mathrm{tr}(\Pi_i \rho_S) U_{E_i} \rho_E U^\dagger_{E_i} = \sum_{i=1}^d p_i U_{E_i} \rho_E U^\dagger_{E_i}$$

after the system–environment interaction. Here $p_i = \mathrm{tr}(\rho_S \Pi_i) = \langle i|\rho_S|i\rangle$. We denote the above operation as

$$\Phi_E(\rho_E) = \rho'_E = \sum_{i=1}^d p_i U_{E_i} \rho_E U^\dagger_{E_i},$$

which is a random unitary channel with Kraus operators $\sqrt{p_i} U_{E_i}$. Moreover, noting that $\rho_E = \rho_{E_1} \otimes \rho_{E_2} \otimes \cdots \otimes \rho_{E_d}$, we have

$$J(\rho_E, \Phi_E) = 1 + \mathrm{tr}(\sqrt{\rho_E} \Phi^\dagger_E(\sqrt{\rho_E})) = 1 + \sum_{i=1}^d p_i \mathrm{tr}(\sqrt{\rho_E} U^\dagger_{E_i} \sqrt{\rho_E} U_{E_i})$$

$$= 1 + \sum_{i=1}^d p_i \mathrm{tr}(\sqrt{\rho_{E_i}} U^\dagger_{E_i} \sqrt{\rho_{E_i}} U_{E_i}) \tag{33}$$

and

$$J(\rho'_E, \Phi_E) = 1 + \mathrm{tr}(\sqrt{\rho'_E} \Phi^\dagger_E(\sqrt{\rho'_E})) = 1 + \sum_{i=1}^d p_i \mathrm{tr}(\sqrt{\rho'_E} U^\dagger_{E_i} \sqrt{\rho'_E} U_{E_i})$$

The final state of the i-th sub-environment reads

$$\rho'_{E_i} = \mathrm{tr}_{\hat{E}_i} \rho'_E = \mathrm{tr}_{\hat{E}_i} \Big(\sum_{i=1}^d p_i U_{E_i} \rho_E U^\dagger_{E_i} \Big) = p_i U_{E_i} \rho_{E_i} U^\dagger_{E_i} + (1 - p_i) \rho_{E_i},$$

where the notation $\mathrm{tr}_{\hat{E}_i}$ denotes the partial trace over all sub-environments except for E_i. We denote the corresponding operation as the channel

$$\Phi_{E_i}(\rho_{E_i}) = \rho'_{E_i} = p_i U_{E_i} \rho_{E_i} U^\dagger_{E_i} + (1 - p_i) \rho_{E_i},$$

which is also a random unitary channel. The classicality of the environment can be evaluated as

$$J(\rho_{E_i}, \Phi_{E_i}) = 1 + \mathrm{tr}(\sqrt{\rho_{E_i}} \Phi^\dagger_{E_i}(\sqrt{\rho_{E_i}})) = 2 - p_i + p_i \mathrm{tr}(\sqrt{\rho_{E_i}} U^\dagger_{E_i} \sqrt{\rho_{E_i}} U_{E_i}) \tag{34}$$

and

$$J(\rho'_{E_i}, \Phi_{E_i}) = 1 + \mathrm{tr}(\sqrt{\rho'_{E_i}} \Phi^\dagger_{E_i}(\sqrt{\rho'_{E_i}})) = 2 - p_i + p_i \mathrm{tr}(\sqrt{\rho'_{E_i}} U^\dagger_{E_i} \sqrt{\rho'_{E_i}} U_{E_i}).$$

Comparing Equations (33) and (34), we get

$$2 - J(\rho_E, \Phi_E) = \sum_{i=1}^{d} (2 - J(\rho_{E_i}, \Phi_{E_i})),$$

or equivalently,

$$I(\rho_E, \Phi_E) = \sum_{i=1}^{d} I(\rho_{E_i}, \Phi_{E_i}),$$

which shows a kind of additivity property, as intuitively expected since the initial environment is in a product state $\rho_E = \rho_{E_1} \otimes \rho_{E_2} \otimes \cdots \otimes \rho_{E_d}$.

In terms of the classicality $J(\rho_E, \Phi_E)$ of the environment, we define the influence on the total environment caused by the system as

$$D(\rho_E | U, \Pi) = J(\rho'_E, \Phi_E) - J(\rho_E, \Phi_E) \tag{35}$$

and the influence on the i-th sub-environment caused by the system as

$$D(\rho_{E_i} | U, \Pi) = J(\rho'_{E_i}, \Phi_{E_i}) - J(\rho_{E_i}, \Phi_{E_i}), \tag{36}$$

respectively. Compared with Equation (27), we have deliberately swapped the place of U and Π to indicate the difference of the reference channels. The influence on the environment caused by the system can be explicitly evaluated as

$$D(\rho_E | U, \Pi) = \sum_{i=1}^{d} p_i \mathrm{tr}\left(\sqrt{\rho'_E} U^\dagger_{E_i} \sqrt{\rho'_E} U_{E_i} - \sqrt{\rho_E} U^\dagger_{E_i} \sqrt{\rho_E} U_{E_i} \right).$$

Similarly,

$$D(\rho_{E_i} | U, \Pi) = p_i \mathrm{tr}\left(\sqrt{\rho'_{E_i}} U^\dagger_{E_i} \sqrt{\rho'_{E_i}} U_{E_i} - \sqrt{\rho_{E_i}} U^\dagger_{E_i} \sqrt{\rho_{E_i}} U_{E_i} \right).$$

If we use the alternative quantifier of classicality $C(\rho, \mathcal{K})$, then the classicality of the initial and final environment states with respect to the reduced environment channel can be evaluated as

$$C(\rho_E, \Phi_E) = 1 - \mathrm{tr}(\rho_E^2) + \sum_{i=1}^{d} p_i^2 (2 - p_i d_i) + d - 2$$

$$C(\rho'_E, \Phi_E) = 1 - \mathrm{tr}(\rho'^2_E) + \sum_{i=1}^{d} p_i^2 (2 - p_i d_i) + d - 2.$$

where d_i is the dimension of the i-th sub-environment. In terms of the classicality of the environment $C(\rho_E, \Phi_E)$, we have an alternative measure of influence on the total environment caused by the system as

$$F(\rho_E | U, \Pi) = C(\rho'_E, \Phi_E) - C(\rho_E, \Phi_E)$$

and the influence on the i-th environment caused by the system as

$$F(\rho_{E_i} | U, \Pi) = C(\rho'_{E_i}, \Phi_{E_i}) - C(\rho_{E_i}, \Phi_{E_i}),$$

respectively. It turns out that

$$F(\rho_E | U, \Pi) = \mathrm{tr}(\rho_E^2) - \mathrm{tr}(\rho'^2_E)$$
$$F(\rho_{E_i} | U, \Pi) = \mathrm{tr}(\rho_{E_i}^2) - \mathrm{tr}(\rho'^2_{E_i}).$$

These quantities of influence on the environment (caused by the system) may be compared with the quantifiers of decoherence of the system (caused by the environment), and they should be correlated due to the system-environment coupling.

5. Illustrating Decoherence in Interferometry

We illustrate the effectiveness of the quantifiers proposed in the preceding section with a two-path interferometer, as depicted in Figure 2. The system Hilbert space of interest here is effectively a qubit space with the two paths labeled as $\Pi_1 = |0\rangle\langle 0|$ and $\Pi_2 = |1\rangle\langle 1|$. Let the initial system state (the path degree part of the physical state) be

$$\rho_S = \frac{1}{2}\left(1 + \sum_{i=1}^{3} r_j \sigma_j\right) = \frac{1}{2}\begin{pmatrix} 1+r_3 & r_1 - ir_2 \\ r_1 + ir_2 & 1 - r_3 \end{pmatrix} \tag{37}$$

with the Bloch vector $\boldsymbol{r} = (r_1, r_2, r_3) \in \mathbb{R}^3$ satisfying $|r| = \sqrt{r_1^2 + r_2^2 + r_3^2} \leq 1$ and σ_j being the Pauli spin matrices. The eigenvalues of ρ_S are $(1 \pm |r|)/2$. It can be directly evaluated that

$$\sqrt{\rho_S} = \frac{1}{2\sqrt{\gamma}}\begin{pmatrix} \gamma + r_3 & r_1 - ir_2 \\ r_1 + ir_2 & \gamma - r_3 \end{pmatrix}$$

with

$$\gamma = 1 + \sqrt{1 - |r|^2}. \tag{38}$$

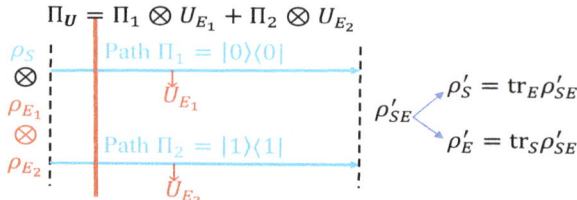

Figure 2. Schematic illustration of decoherence induced by the array of path detectors $\boldsymbol{U} = \{U_{E_i} : i = 1, 2\}$ (serving as the environment of the system state ρ_S) attached to the collection of path $\Pi = \{\Pi_i : i = 1, 2\}$. Each path Π_i is probed by a detector U_{E_i}. The initial system state is ρ_S, while the initial array of detector state is $\rho_E = \rho_{E_1} \otimes \rho_{E_2}$. The combined initial state is $\rho_{SE} = \rho_S \otimes \rho_E$. The system–detector coupling is via the combined unitary operator $\Pi_{\boldsymbol{U}} = \sum_{i=1}^{2} \Pi_i \otimes U_{E_i}$, and the final combined system is $\rho'_{SE} = \Pi_{\boldsymbol{U}} \rho_{SE} \Pi_{\boldsymbol{U}}^{\dagger}$ with final system state $\rho'_S = \mathrm{tr}_E \rho'_{SE}$. The decoherence of ρ_S (with respect to Π) induced by the path detectors are quantified by $D(\rho_S|\Pi, \boldsymbol{U}) = J(\rho'_S, \Pi) - J(\rho_S, \Pi)$ and $F(\rho_S|\Pi, \boldsymbol{U}) = C(\rho'_S, \Pi) - C(\rho_S, \Pi)$, which are the increasing amount of classicality of the system state caused by the path detectors.

For a two-path interferometer with a detector attached to each path, let ρ_{E_i} be the initial detector state attached to path i; the system and detector evolve under the controlled-$\boldsymbol{U}$ operation

$$\Pi_{\boldsymbol{U}} = \Pi_1 \otimes U_{E_1} + \Pi_2 \otimes U_{E_2}. \tag{39}$$

From an information-theoretic point of view, this controlled-$\boldsymbol{U}$ operation correlates the quantum system and the detector and leads to the combined final state

$$\begin{aligned}\rho'_{SE} &= \Pi_{\boldsymbol{U}}(\rho_S \otimes \rho_E)\Pi_{\boldsymbol{U}}^{\dagger} \\ &= (\Pi_1 \rho_S \Pi_1) \otimes (U_{E_1} \rho_E U_{E_1}^{\dagger}) + (\Pi_1 \rho_S \Pi_2) \otimes (U_{E_1} \rho_E U_{E_2}^{\dagger}) \\ &\quad + (\Pi_2 \rho_S \Pi_1) \otimes (U_{E_2} \rho_E U_{E_1}^{\dagger}) + (\Pi_2 \rho_S \Pi_2) \otimes (U_{E_2} \rho_E U_{E_2}^{\dagger}).\end{aligned} \tag{40}$$

The final system state can be obtained by taking the partial trace over the detector as

$$\rho'_S = \mathrm{tr}_E \rho'_{SE}$$
$$= \Pi_1 \rho_S \Pi_1 + \Pi_1 \rho_S \Pi_2 \mathrm{tr}(U_{E_1} \rho_E U_{E_2}^\dagger) + \Pi_2 \rho_S \Pi_1 \mathrm{tr}(U_{E_2} \rho_E U_{E_1}^\dagger) + \Pi_2 \rho_S \Pi_2$$
$$= \frac{1}{2} \begin{pmatrix} 1 + r_3 & (r_1 - ir_2)\mathcal{V}^* \\ (r_1 + ir_2)\mathcal{V} & 1 - r_3 \end{pmatrix}.$$

with

$$\mathcal{V} = \mathrm{tr}(U_{E_2} \rho_E U_{E_1}^\dagger) = \mathrm{tr}(U_{E_2} \rho_E) \cdot \mathrm{tr}(\rho_{E_1} U_{E_1}^\dagger)$$

being a complex number. By the Cauchy–Schwarz inequality, we have

$$|\mathcal{V}|^2 = |\mathrm{tr}((U_{E_2}\sqrt{\rho_E})(U_{E_1}\sqrt{\rho_E})^\dagger)|^2$$
$$\leq \mathrm{tr}((U_{E_2}\sqrt{\rho_E})(U_{E_2}\sqrt{\rho_E})^\dagger) \cdot \mathrm{tr}((U_{E_1}\sqrt{\rho_E})(U_{E_1}\sqrt{\rho_E})^\dagger)$$
$$= 1.$$

The eigenvalues of $\rho'_S = \Phi_S(\rho_S)$ are

$$\lambda_1(\rho'_S) = \frac{1}{2}\left(1 + \sqrt{r_3^2 + (r_1^2 + r_2^2)|\mathcal{V}|^2}\right) \tag{41}$$

$$\lambda_2(\rho'_S) = \frac{1}{2}\left(1 - \sqrt{r_3^2 + (r_1^2 + r_2^2)|\mathcal{V}|^2}\right). \tag{42}$$

Consequently, we see that

$$\lambda(\rho'_S) \preccurlyeq \lambda(\rho_S),$$

as it should be by Proposition 2.

Noting that

$$\sqrt{\rho'_S} = \frac{1}{2\sqrt{\gamma'}} \begin{pmatrix} \gamma' + r_3 & (r_1 - ir_2)\mathcal{V}^* \\ (r_1 + ir_2)\mathcal{V} & \gamma' - r_3 \end{pmatrix},$$

where

$$\gamma' = 1 + \sqrt{1 - (r_1^2 + r_2^2)|\mathcal{V}|^2 - r_3^2}, \tag{43}$$

we obtain

$$D(\rho_S|\Pi, \mathbf{U}) = J(\rho'_S, \Pi) - J(\rho_S, \Pi)$$
$$= \left(\frac{\gamma' + r_3}{2\sqrt{\gamma'}}\right)^2 + \left(\frac{\gamma' - r_3}{2\sqrt{\gamma'}}\right)^2 - \left(\frac{\gamma + r_3}{2\sqrt{\gamma}}\right)^2 - \left(\frac{\gamma - r_3}{2\sqrt{\gamma}}\right)^2$$
$$= \frac{1}{2}(\gamma' - \gamma)\left(1 - \frac{r_3^2}{\gamma'\gamma}\right). \tag{44}$$

Since $\gamma' \geq \gamma, \gamma \geq 1 \geq r_3$, we see readily that the above quantity is non-negative. Moreover, because γ' is a decreasing function of $|\mathcal{V}|^2$, from Equation (44) we see that $D(\rho_S|\Pi, \mathbf{U})$ is a decreasing function of $|\mathcal{V}|^2$.

Similarly, we can evaluate

$$C(\rho'_S, \Pi) = 1 - \frac{1}{4}((1 + r_3)^2 + (r_1^2 + r_2^2)|\mathcal{V}|^2 + (1 - r_3)^2 + (r_1^2 + r_2^2)|\mathcal{V}|^2)$$
$$+ \frac{1}{4}((1 + r_3)^2 + (1 - r_3)^2)$$
$$= 1 - \frac{1}{2}(r_1^2 + r_2^2)|\mathcal{V}|^2,$$

from which we obtain

$$F(\rho_S|\Pi, \boldsymbol{U}) = C(\rho'_S, \Pi) - C(\rho_S, \Pi) = \frac{1}{2}(r_1^2 + r_2^2)(1 - |\mathcal{V}|^2), \qquad (45)$$

which is also apparently a decreasing function of $|\mathcal{V}|$.

It can be easily verified that both the decoherence quantifiers $D(\rho_S|\Pi, \boldsymbol{U})$ and $F(\rho_S|\Pi, \boldsymbol{U})$ are decreasing functions of $|\mathcal{V}|$, and achieve the minimal value 0 when $|\mathcal{V}| = 1$, which corresponds to the situation when the detector does not obtain the path information. In this case, coherence is preserved, and there is no decoherence. This is consistent with our intuition since decoherence can be regarded as the washing out of interference, while $D(\rho_S|\Pi, \boldsymbol{U})$ and $F(\rho_S|\Pi, \boldsymbol{U})$ can be regarded as measures of path information leakage to the detectors (classical path information). The detectors, from which we can obtain the path information of the quantum system, would inevitably reduce the interference ability of the quantum system.

The quantity $\mathcal{V} = \text{tr}(U_{E_2}\rho_E U_{E_1}^\dagger)$ arises naturally in at least two other contexts:

(a) If we take $U_{E_1} = \mathbf{1}$ and $U_{E_2} = U$, then we come to the setup of Englert [34], in which $|\mathcal{V}|$ is the fringe visibility in the complementarity relation

$$|\mathcal{V}|^2 + \mathcal{D}^2 \leq 1,$$

with $\mathcal{D} = \frac{1}{2}\text{tr}|U\rho_E U^\dagger - \rho_E|$ being the quantitative measure of distinguishability. In this context, $\mathcal{V}$ is also called the interference function.

(b) If we define the generalized variance of measuring any operator X in state σ as

$$V(\sigma, X) = \text{tr}\big(\sigma(X - \text{tr}(\sigma X))(X - \text{tr}(\sigma X))^\dagger\big),$$

and consider the unitary operator $U_{E_1}^\dagger U_{E_2} = U_{E_1}^\dagger \otimes U_{E_2}$, then we have

$$V(\rho_E, U_{E_1}^\dagger U_{E_2}) = \text{tr}\big(\rho_E(U_{E_1}^\dagger U_{E_2} - \text{tr}(\rho_E U_{E_1}^\dagger U_{E_2}))(U_{E_1}^\dagger U_{E_2} - \text{tr}(\rho_E U_{E_1}^\dagger U_{E_2}))^\dagger\big)$$
$$= 1 - |\text{tr}(U_{E_2}\rho_E U_{E_1}^\dagger)|^2$$
$$= 1 - |\mathcal{V}|^2,$$

which is a kind of measure of path detecting capability. The above relation immediately leads to

$$V(\rho_E, U_{E_1}^\dagger U_{E_2}) + |\mathcal{V}|^2 = 1,$$

which is apparently a complementary relation between the path information and fringe visibility. Furthermore, combined with Equation (45), we have

$$F(\rho_S|\Pi, \boldsymbol{U}) = \frac{1}{2}(r_1^2 + r_2^2)V(\rho_E, U_{E_1}^\dagger U_{E_2}),$$

which relates the decoherence directly with the path-detecting information. This is consistent with our intuitive understanding of decoherence as the information leakage to the detectors (environment).

Now we make some comparison of our quantifiers of decoherence with existing ones. Since, in general, decoherence is also regarded as the establishment of correlations between the system and environment, it is expected that decoherence should be related to correlations, as quantified by the mutual information between the system and the environment. For simplicity, we consider the setup described by Figure 2 and assume that the initial system state and environment state are both pure. In this case, the final system–environment state ρ'_{SE} is pure since the coupling Π_U is unitary. Consequently, the mutual information of the final system–environment state is

$$I(\rho'_{SE}) = S(\rho'_S) + S(\rho'_E) - S(\rho'_{SE}) = 2S(\rho'_S) = 2\big(-\lambda_1(\rho'_S)\ln\lambda_1(\rho'_S) - \lambda_2(\rho'_S)\ln\lambda_2(\rho'_S)\big),$$

where $\lambda_j(\rho'_S)$ are determined by Equations (41) and (42), and $S(\sigma) = -\mathrm{tr}\sigma\ln\sigma$ is the von Neumann entropy of the state σ. Since the initial system state ρ_S defined by Equation (37) is pure, we have $r_1^2 + r_2^2 + r_3^2 = 1$. Therefore by Equations (41), (42) and (45), we have

$$\lambda_1(\rho'_S) = \frac{1}{2}\Big(1 + \sqrt{1 - (r_1^2 + r_2^2)(1 - |\mathcal{V}|^2)}\Big) = \frac{1}{2}\Big(1 + \sqrt{1 - 2F(\rho_S|\Pi, U)}\Big),$$
$$\lambda_2(\rho'_S) = \frac{1}{2}\Big(1 - \sqrt{1 - (r_1^2 + r_2^2)(1 - |\mathcal{V}|^2)}\Big) = \frac{1}{2}\Big(1 - \sqrt{1 - 2F(\rho_S|\Pi, U)}\Big).$$

Now the mutual information can be expressed as

$$I(\rho'_{SE}) = 2H\Big(\frac{1}{2}\big(1 + \sqrt{1 - 2F(\rho_S|\Pi, U)}\big)\Big),$$

where $H(p) = -p\ln p - (1-p)\ln(1-p)$ is the binary Shannon entropy function, $0 \leq p \leq 1$. From the above equation, we see that the mutual information is monotonically related to the decoherence: when decoherence increases, the mutual information increases, which is consistent with the intuition that larger decoherence corresponds to larger amount of correlations established between the system and the environment (larger information leakage to the environment). Although the above result is proved for initial pure states and $F(\rho_S|\Pi, U)$, the general cases concerning mixed initial states and the decoherence quantifier $D(\rho_S|\Pi, U)$ are similar, but the calculations are more complicated. It will be also interesting to make a more comprehensive comparative studies between various quantities related to decoherence and correlations.

6. Summary

In order to quantify decoherence induced by environment, we reviewed two quantifiers of classicality in a general setup of state–channel interaction by exploiting the Jordan symmetric product and a modified notion of variance. These quantifiers may be of independent interest in addressing the classical–quantum interplay. We also elucidated some simple yet useful features of the decoherence channel (Hadamard channel).

Employing the above quantifiers of classicality, we introduced two quantifiers of decoherence induced by environment in the combined "system + environment" setup. These quantifiers have some nice properties and can be used to summarize the decoherence strength of an open system. Connections with complementarity were discussed. The results were illustrated via a two-path interferometer.

A natural approach to quantifying decoherence is via correlations between the system and the environment. There are various quantifiers for correlations such as the quantum mutual information, entanglement, quantum discord, measurement-induced disturbance, measurement-induced nonlocality, classical correlations, etc. In particular, decoherence is quantified from a decorrelating perspective in Refs. [106,107]. However, correlations are generally hard to evaluate. Our present approaches differ from the conventional approach to decoherence via correlations such as quantum mutual information. Our quantifiers of decoherence are relatively easier to calculate and have intimate relations with the Wigner–Yanase skew information, uncertainty, and the resource theory of coherence. This indicates certain operational significance of the quantities. However, it remains to further study the operational meaning of these quantifiers of decoherence and to investigate their implications for foundational issues and experimental practices.

For open quantum systems, apart from decoherence, another prominent characteristic is quantum Markovianity/non-Markovianity [108–116]. Although the classical Markovianity is uniquely defined and well understood, there is not a single universally accepted definition of quantum Markovianity. A host of quantum Markovianity-related concepts coexist, such as GKS–Lindblad master equations, distinguishability, divisibility, no-information backflow, monotonic decreasing in correlations, etc. However, just like decoherence is related to the decaying of off-diagonal entries of the density matrix, a general common feature of the various Markovianities is related to information loss and memoryless effects. This indicates that there are intimate relations between decoherence and Markovianity. We remark that the feature of decoherence as information monotonically flowing into the environment is deeply related to the Markovian approximation. In non-Markovian dynamics, in contrast to decoherence, recoherence may occur. The interplay and relations between decoherence and quantum Markovianity/non-Markovianity are worth further investigations.

Author Contributions: All authors contributed equally to the work. All authors have read and agreed to the published version of the manuscript.

Funding: This research was supported by the National Key R&D Program of China, Grant No. 2020YFA0712700; the Fundamental Research Funds for the Central Universities, Grant No. FRF-TP-19-012A3; and the National Natural Science Foundation of China, Grant Nos. 11875317 and 61833010.

Data Availability Statement: Not appliable.

Conflicts of Interest: The authors declare no conflict of interest.

References

1. Dirac, P.A.M. *The Principles of Quantum Mechanics*, 4th ed.; Clarendon Press: Oxford, UK, 1958.
2. von Neumann, J. *Mathematical Foundations of Quantum Mechanics*; Princeton University Press: Princeton, NJ, USA, 1955.
3. Ficek, Z.; Swain, S. *Quantum Interference and Coherence: Theory and Experiments*; Springer: Berlin, Germany, 2005.
4. Landau, L.D. The damping problem in wave mechanics. *Z. Phys.* **1927**, *45*, 430–441.
5. Mott, N.F. The wave mechanics of α-ray tracks. *Proc. R. Soc. Lond. A* **1929**, *126*, 79–84.
6. Zeh, H.D. On the interpretation of measurement in quantum theory. *Found. Phys.* **1970**, *1*, 69–76. [CrossRef]
7. Zeh, H.D. Toward a quantum theory of observation. *Found. Phys.* **1973**, *3*, 109–116. [CrossRef]
8. Zurek, W.H. Pointer basis of quantum apparatus: Into what mixture does the wave packet collapse? *Phys. Rev. D* **1981**, *24*, 1516. [CrossRef]
9. Zurek, W.H. Environment-induced superselection rules. *Phys. Rev. D* **1982**, *26*, 1862. [CrossRef]
10. Zurek, W.H. Decoherence and the transition from quantum to classical. *Phys. Today* **1991**, *44*, 36–44. [CrossRef]
11. Nielsen, M.A.; Chuang, I.L. *Quantum Computation and Quantum Information*; Cambrideg University Press: Cambridge, UK, 2000.
12. Joos, E.; Zeh, H.D. The emergence of classical properties through interaction with the environment. *Z. Phys. B* **1985**, *59*, 223–243. [CrossRef]
13. Giulini, D.; Joos, E.; Kiefer, C.; Kupsch, J.; Stamatescu, I.-O.; Zeh, H.D. *Decoherence and the Appearance of a Classical World in Quantum Theory*; Springer: Berlin, Germany, 1996.
14. Zurek, W.H. Decoherence, einselection, and the quantum origins of the classical. *Rev. Mod. Phys.* **2003**, *75*, 715. [CrossRef]
15. Schlosshauer, M. Decoherence, the measurement problem and interpretations of quantum mechanics. *Rev. Mod. Phys.* **2004**, *76*, 1267. [CrossRef]
16. Schlosshauer, M. *Decoherence and the Quantum-to-Classical Transition*; Springer: Berlin, Germany, 2007.
17. Schlosshauer, M. Quantum decoherence. *Phys. Rep.* **2019**, *831*, 1–57. [CrossRef]
18. Duplantier, B.; Raimond, J.M.; Rivasseau, V. Quantum Decoherence. In *Poincaré Seminar 2005*; Springer: Berlin, Germany, 2007.
19. Zeh, H.D. *The Physical Basis of The Direction of Time*; Springer: Berlin, Germany, 2007.
20. Ollivier, H.; Poulin, D.; Zurek, W.H. Objective properties from subjective quantum states: Environment as a witness. *Phys. Rev. Lett.* **2004**, *93*, 220401. [CrossRef] [PubMed]
21. Blume-Kohout, R.; Zurek, W.H. Quantum Darwinism: Entanglement, branches, and the emergent classicality of redundantly stored quantum information. *Phys. Rev. A* **2006**, *73*, 062310. [CrossRef]
22. Zurek, W.H. Quantum Darwinism. *Nat. Phys.* **2009**, *5*, 181–188. [CrossRef]
23. Zwolak, M.; Quan, H.T.; Zurek, W.H. Quantum Darwinism in a hazy environment. *Phys. Rev. Lett.* **2009**, *103*, 110402. [CrossRef] [PubMed]
24. Riedel, C.J.; Zurek, W.H.; Zwolak, M. The rise and fall of redundancy in decoherence and quantum Darwinism. *New J. Phys.* **2012**, *14*, 083010. [CrossRef]
25. Korbicz, J.K.; Horodecki, P.; Horodecki, R. Objectivity in the photonic environment through state information broadcasting. *Phys. Rev. Lett.* **2014**, *112*, 120402. [CrossRef]
26. Horodecki, R.; Korbicz, J.K.; Horodecki, P. Quantum origins of objectivity. *Phys. Rev. A* **2015**, *91*, 032122. [CrossRef]

27. Brandaö, F.G.S.L.; Piani, M.; Horodecki, P. Generic emergence of classical features in quantum Darwinism. *Nat. Commun.* **2015**, *6*, 7908. [CrossRef]
28. Knott, P.A.; Tufarelli, T.; Piani, M.; Adesso, G. Generic emergence of objectivity of observables in infinite dimensions. *Phys. Rev. Lett.* **2018**, *121*, 160401. [CrossRef] [PubMed]
29. Zurek, W.H. Quantum theory of the classical: Quantum jumps, Born's rule and objective classical reality via quantum Darwinism. *Philos. Trans. R. Soc. A* **2018**, *376*, 20180107. [CrossRef]
30. Le, T.P.; Olaya-Castro, A. Strong quantum darwinism and strong independence are equivalent to spectrum broadcast structure. *Phys. Rev. Lett.* **2019**, *122*, 010403. [CrossRef] [PubMed]
31. Wootters, W.K.; Zurek, W.H. Complementarity in the double-slit experiment: Quantum nonseparability and a quantitative statement of Bohr's principle. *Phys. Rev. D* **1979**, *19*, 473. [CrossRef]
32. Greenberger, D.M.; Yasin, A. Simultaneous wave and particle knowledge in a neutron interferometer. *Phys. Lett. A* **1988**, *128*, 391–394. [CrossRef]
33. Scully, M.O.; Englert, B.G.; Walther, H. Quantum optical tests of complementarity. *Nature* **1991**, *351*, 111–116. [CrossRef]
34. Englert, B.-G. Fringe visibility and which-way information: An inequality. *Phys. Rev. Lett.* **1996**, *77*, 2154. [CrossRef] [PubMed]
35. Dürr, S. Quantitative wave-particle duality in multibeam interferometers. *Phys. Rev. A* **2001**, *64*, 042113. [CrossRef]
36. Englert, B.-G.; Kaszlikowsk, D.; Kwek, L.C.; Chee, W.H. Wave-particle duality in multi-path interferometers: General concepts and three-path interferometers. *Int. J. Quantum Inf.* **2008**, *06*, 129–157. [CrossRef]
37. Luo, S. From quantum no-cloning to wave-packet collapse. *Phys. Lett. A* **2010**, *374*, 1350–1353. [CrossRef]
38. Zurek, W.H. Wave-packet collapse and the core quantum postulates: Discreteness of quantum jumps from unitarity, repeatability, and actionable information. *Phys. Rev. A* **2013**, *87*, 052111. [CrossRef]
39. Janssens, B.; Maassen, H. Information transfer implies state collapse. *J. Phys. A* **2006**, *39*, 9845–9860. [CrossRef]
40. Janssens, B. Unifying decoherence and the Heisenberg principle. *Lett. Math. Phys.* **2017**, *107*, 1557–1579. [CrossRef]
41. Wu, Z.; Zhu, C.; Luo, S.; Wang, J. Information transfer in generalized probabilistic theories. *Phys. Lett. A* **2015**, *379*, 2694–2697. [CrossRef]
42. Wootters, W.K.; Zurek, W.H. A single quantum cannot be cloned. *Nature* **1982**, *299*, 802–803. [CrossRef]
43. Barnum, H.; Caves, C.M.; Fuchs, C.A.; Jozsa, R.; Schumacher, B. Noncommuting mixed states cannot be broadcast. *Phys. Rev. Lett.* **1996**, *76*, 2818. [CrossRef]
44. Chiribella, G.; D'Ariano, G.M. Quantum information becomes classical when distributed to many users. *Phys. Rev. Lett.* **2006**, *97*, 250503. [CrossRef]
45. Piani, M.; Horodecki, P.; Horodecki, R. No-local-broadcasting theorem for multipartite quantum correlations. *Phys. Rev. Lett.* **2008**, *100*, 090502. [CrossRef]
46. Luo, S.; Sun, W. Decomposition of bipartite states with applications to quantum no-broadcasting theorems. *Phys. Rev. A* **2010**, *82*, 012338. [CrossRef]
47. Scandolo, C.M.; Salazar, R.; Korbicz, J.K.; Horodecki, P. Universal structure of objective states in all fundamental causal theories. *Phys. Rev. Res.* **2021**, *3*, 033148. [CrossRef]
48. Ollivier, H.; Zurek, W.H. Quantum discord: A measure of the quantumness of correlations. *Phys. Rev. Lett.* **2001**, *88*, 017901. [CrossRef]
49. Henderson, L.; Vedral, V. Classical, quantum and total correlations. *J. Phys. A* **2001**, *34*, 6899–6905. [CrossRef]
50. Luo, S. Quantum discord for two-qubit systems. *Phys. Rev. A* **2008**, *77*, 042303. [CrossRef]
51. Luo, S.; Fu, S. Geometric measure of quantum discord. *Phys. Rev. A* **2010**, *82*, 034302. [CrossRef]
52. Modi, K.; Brodutch, A.; Cable, H.; Paterek, T.; Vedral, V. The classical-quantum boundary for correlations: Discord and related measures. *Rev. Mod. Phys.* **2012**, *84*, 1655. [CrossRef]
53. Chang, L.; Luo, S. Remedying the local ancilla problem with geometric discord. *Phys. Rev. A* **2013**, *87*, 062303. [CrossRef]
54. Streltsov, A.; Zurek, W.H. Quantum discord cannot be shared. *Phys. Rev. Lett.* **2013**, *111*, 040401. [CrossRef] [PubMed]
55. Griffiths, R.B. Consistent histories and the interpretation of quantum mechanics. *J. Stat. Phys.* **1984**, *36*, 219–272. [CrossRef]
56. Paz, J.P.; Zurek, W.H. Environment-induced decoherence, classicality and consistency of quantum histories. *Phys. Rev. D* **1993**, *48*, 2728. [CrossRef]
57. Griffiths, R.B. Consistent histories and quantum reasoning. *Phys. Rev. A* **1996**, *54*, 2759. [CrossRef] [PubMed]
58. Griffiths, R.B. *Consistent Quantum Theory*; Cambridge University Press: Cambridge, UK, 2002.
59. Riedel, C.J.; Zurek, W.H.; Zwolak, M. Objective past of a quantum universe: Redundant records of consistent histories. *Phys. Rev. A* **2016**, *93*, 032126. [CrossRef]
60. Fuchs, C.A. Just two nonorthogonal quantum states. *arXiv* **1998**, arXiv:quant-ph/9810032.
61. Fuchs, C.A.; Sasaki, M. The quantumness of a set of quantum states. *arXiv* **2003**, arXiv:quant-ph/0302108.
62. Fuchs, C.A.; Sasaki, M. Squeezing quantum information through a classical channel: Measuring the "quantumness" of a set of quantum states. *Quantum Inf. Comput.* **2003**, *3*, 377–404. [CrossRef]
63. Horodecki, M.; Horodecki, P.; Horodecki, R.; Piani, M. Quantumness of ensemble from nobroadcasting principle. *Int. J. Quantum Inf.* **2006**, *4*, 105–118. [CrossRef]
64. Alicki, R.; Van Ryn, N. A simple test of quantumness for a single system. *J. Phys. A* **2008**, *41*, 062001. [CrossRef]

65. Alicki, R.; Piani, M.; Van Ryn, N. Quantumness witnesses. *J. Phys. A* **2008**, *41*, 495303. [CrossRef]
66. Brida, G.; Degiovanni, I.P.; Genovese, M.; Schettini, V.; Polyakov, S.V.; Migdall, A. Experimental test of nonclassicality for a single particle. *Opt. Express* **2008**, *16*, 11750. [CrossRef]
67. Brida, G.; Degiovanni, I.P.; Genovese, M.; Piacentini, F.; Schettini, V.; Gisin, N.; Polyakov, S.V.; Migdall, A. Improved implementation of the Alicki-Van Ryn nonclassicality test for a single particle using Si detectors. *Phys. Rev. A* **2009**, *79*, 044102. [CrossRef]
68. Luo, S.; Li, N.; Sun, W. How quantum is a quantum ensemble. *Quantum Inf. Process.* **2010**, *9*, 711–726. [CrossRef]
69. Luo, S.; Li, N.; Fu, S. Quantumness of quantum ensembles. *Theor. Math. Phys.* **2011**, *169*, 1724–1739. [CrossRef]
70. Facchi, P.; Ferro, L.; Marmo, G.; Pascazio, S. Defining quantumness via the Jordan product. *J. Phys. A* **2014**, *47*, 035301. [CrossRef]
71. Li, N.; Luo, S.; Mao, Y. Quantifying the quantumness of quantum ensembles. *Phys. Rev. A* **2017**, *96*, 022132. [CrossRef]
72. Ferro, L.; Fazio, R.; Illuminati, F.; Marmo, G.; Pascazio, S.; Vedral, V. Measuring quantumness: From theory to observability in interferometric setups. *Eur. Phys. J. D* **2018**, *72*, 219. [CrossRef]
73. Herbut, F. A quantum measure of coherence and incompatibility. *J. Phys. A* **2005**, *38*, 2959–2974. [CrossRef]
74. Åberg, J. Quantifying superposition. *arXiv* **2016**, arXiv:Quant-ph/0612146.
75. Levi, F.; Mintert, F. A quantitative theory of coherent delocalization. *New J. Phys.* **2014**, *16*, 033007. [CrossRef]
76. Baumgratz, T.; Cramer, M.; Plenio, M.B. Quantifying coherence. *Phys. Rev. Lett.* **2014**, *113*, 140401. [CrossRef]
77. Streltsov, A.; Singh, U.; Dhar, H.S.; Bera, M.N.; Adesso, G. Measuring quantum coherence with entanglement. *Phys. Rev. Lett.* **2015**, *115*, 020403. [CrossRef]
78. Yuan, X.; Zhou, H.; Cao, Z.; Ma, X. Intrinsic randomness as a measure of quantum coherence. *Phys. Rev. A* **2015**, *92*, 022124. [CrossRef]
79. Winter, A.; Yang, D. Operational resource theory of coherence. *Phys. Rev. Lett.* **2016**, *116*, 120404. [CrossRef]
80. Streltsov, A.; Adesso, G.; Plenio, M.B. Quantum coherence as a resource. *Rev. Mod. Phys.* **2017**, *89*, 041003. [CrossRef]
81. Luo, S.; Sun, Y. Partial coherence with application to the monotonicity problem of coherence involving skew information. *Phys. Rev. A* **2017**, *96*, 022136. [CrossRef]
82. Luo, S.; Sun, Y. Quantum coherence versus quantum uncertainty. *Phys. Rev. A* **2017**, *96*, 022130. [CrossRef]
83. Sun, Y.; Mao, Y.; Luo, S. From quantum coherence to quantum correlations. *Europhys. Lett.* **2017**, *118*, 60007. [CrossRef]
84. Luo, S.; Sun, Y. Coherence and complementarity in state-channel interaction. *Phys. Rev. A* **2018**, *98*, 012113. [CrossRef]
85. Zhang, Y.; Luo, S. Quantum states as observables: Their variance and nonclassicality. *Phys. Rev. A* **2020**, *102*, 062211. [CrossRef]
86. Sun, Y.; Luo, S. Coherence as uncertainty. *Phys. Rev. A* **2021**, *103*, 042423. [CrossRef]
87. Kraus, B. *States, Effects, and Operations: Fundamental Notions of Quantum Theory*; Springer: Berlin, Germany, 1983.
88. Wigner, E.P.; Yanase, M.M. Information contents of distributions. *Proc. Natl. Acad. Sci. USA* **1963**, *49*, 910–918. [CrossRef]
89. Luo, S. Wigner-Yanase skew information and uncertainty relations. *Phys. Rev. Lett.* **2003**, *91*, 180403. [CrossRef]
90. Luo, S. Winger-Yanase skew information versus quantum Fisher information. *Proc. Am. Math. Soc.* **2003**, *132*, 885–890. [CrossRef]
91. Luo, S. Heisenberg uncertainty relation for mixed states. *Phys. Rev. A* **2005**, *72*, 042110. [CrossRef]
92. Luo, S. Quantum versus classical uncertainty. *Theor. Math. Phys.* **2005**, *143*, 681–688. [CrossRef]
93. Luo, S.; Fu, S.; Oh, C.H. Quantifying correlations via the Wigner-Yanase skew information. *Phys. Rev. A* **2012**, *85*, 032117. [CrossRef]
94. Marvian, I.; Spekkens, R.W. Extending Noether's theorem by quantifying the asymmetry of quantum states. *Nat. Commun.* **2014**, *5*, 3821. [CrossRef]
95. Girolami, D. Observable measure of quantum coherence in finite dimensional systems. *Phys. Rev. Lett.* **2014**, *113*, 170401. [CrossRef] [PubMed]
96. Lostaglio, M.; Korzekwa, K.; Jennings, D.; Rudolph, T. Quantum coherence, time-translation symmetry, and thermodynamics. *Phys. Rev. X* **2015**, *5*, 021001. [CrossRef]
97. Marvian, I.; Spekkens, R.W.; Zanardi, P. Quantum speed limits, coherence and asymmetry. *Phys. Rev. A* **2016**, *93*, 052331. [CrossRef]
98. Luo, S.; Zhang, Q. Skew information decreases under quantum measurements. *Theor. Math. Phys.* **2007**, *151*, 529–538. [CrossRef]
99. Li, W. Monotonicity of skew information and its applications in quantum resource theory. *Quantum Inf. Process.* **2019**, *18*, 166. [CrossRef]
100. Lieb, E.H. Convex trace functions and the Wigner-Yanase-Dyson conjecture. *Adv. Math.* **1973**, *11*, 267–288. [CrossRef]
101. Luo, S.; Zhang, Y. Detecting nonclassicality of light via Lieb's concavity. *Phys. Lett. A* **2019**, *383*, 125836. [CrossRef]
102. Horn, R.A. *Topics in Matrix Analysis*; Cambridge University Press: Cambridge, UK, 1991.
103. Marshall, A.W. *Inequalities: Theory of Majorization and Its Applications*; Springer: New York, NY, USA, 2011.
104. Bhatia, R. *Matrix Analysis*; Springer: Berlin, Germany, 2013.
105. Hadamard, J. Résolution d'une question relative aux determinants. *Bull. Sci. Math.* **1893**, *17*, 240–246.
106. Luo, S.; Fu, S.; Li, N. Decorrelating capabilities of operations with application to decoherence. *Phys. Rev. A* **2010**, *82*, 052122. [CrossRef]
107. Luo, S.; Li, N. Decoherence and measurement-induced correlations. *Phys. Rev. A* **2011**, *84*, 052309. [CrossRef]

108. Gorini, V.; Kossakowski, A.; Sudarshan, E.C.G. Completely positive dynamical semigroups of n-level systems. *J. Math. Phys.* **1976**, *17*, 821–825. [CrossRef]
109. Lindblad, G. On the generators of quantum dynamical semigroups. *Commun. Math. Phys.* **1976**, *48*, 119–130. [CrossRef]
110. Breuer, H.-P.; Laine, E.-M.; Piilo, J. Measure for the degree of non-Markovian behavior of quantum processes in open systems. *Phys. Rev. Lett.* **2009**, *103*, 210401. [CrossRef] [PubMed]
111. Luo, S.; Fu, S.; Song, H. Quantifying non-Markovianity via correlations. *Phys. Rev.* **2012**, *86*, 044101. [CrossRef]
112. Jiang, M.; Luo, S. Comparing quantum Markovianities: Distinguishability versus correlations. *Phys. Rev. A* **2013**, *88*, 034101. [CrossRef]
113. Rivas, Á.; Huelga, S.F.; Plenio, M.B. Quantum non-Markovianity: Characterization, quantification and detection. *Rep. Prog. Phys.* **2014**, *77*, 09400. [CrossRef]
114. Song, H.; Luo, S.; Hong, Y. Quantum non-Markovianity based on the Fisher information matrix. *Phys. Rev. A* **2015**, *91*, 042110. [CrossRef]
115. Li, L.; Hall, M.J.W.; Wiseman, H.M. Concepts of quantum non-Markovianity: A hierarchy. *Phys. Rep.* **2018**, *759*, 1–51. [CrossRef]
116. Wu, K.-D.; Hou, Z.; Xiang, G.-Y.; Li, C.-F.; Guo, G.-C.; Dong, D.; Nori, F. Detecting non-Markovianity via quantified coherence: Theory and experiments. *NPJ Quantum Inf.* **2020**, *6*, 55. [CrossRef]

Article

Quantum–Classical Correspondence Principle for Heat Distribution in Quantum Brownian Motion

Jin-Fu Chen [1], Tian Qiu [1] and Hai-Tao Quan [1,2,3,*]

1. School of Physics, Peking University, Beijing 100871, China; chenjinfu@pku.edu.cn (J.-F.C.); tianqiu2016@pku.edu.cn (T.Q.)
2. Collaborative Innovation Center of Quantum Matter, Beijing 100871, China
3. Frontiers Science Center for Nano-Optoelectronics, Peking University, Beijing 100871, China
* Correspondence: htquan@pku.edu.cn

Abstract: Quantum Brownian motion, described by the Caldeira–Leggett model, brings insights to the understanding of phenomena and essence of quantum thermodynamics, especially the quantum work and heat associated with their classical counterparts. By employing the phase-space formulation approach, we study the heat distribution of a relaxation process in the quantum Brownian motion model. The analytical result of the characteristic function of heat is obtained at any relaxation time with an arbitrary friction coefficient. By taking the classical limit, such a result approaches the heat distribution of the classical Brownian motion described by the Langevin equation, indicating the quantum–classical correspondence principle for heat distribution. We also demonstrate that the fluctuating heat at any relaxation time satisfies the exchange fluctuation theorem of heat and its long-time limit reflects the complete thermalization of the system. Our research study justifies the definition of the quantum fluctuating heat via two-point measurements.

Keywords: open quantum systems; phase-space formulation; quantum Brownian motion; heat statistics

1. Introduction

In the past few decades, the discovery of fluctuation theorems [1–4] and the establishment of the framework of stochastic thermodynamics [5–7] deepened our understanding of the fluctuating nature of thermodynamic quantities (such as work, heat and entropy production) in microscopic systems [8–13]. Among various fluctuation theorems, the non-equilibrium work relation [2] sharpens our understanding of the second law of thermodynamics by presenting an elegant and precise equality associating the free energy change with the fluctuating work. Such a relation was later extended to the quantum realm based on the two-point measurement definition of the quantum fluctuating work [14,15], soon after its discovery in the classical regime. The work statistics has been widely studied in various microscopic classical and quantum systems [16–26]. Historically, the quantum–classical correspondence principle played an essential role in the development of the theory of quantum mechanics and the interpretation of the transition from quantum to classical world [27,28]. In Refs. [19,22,24], it is demonstrated that the existence of the quantum–classical correspondence principle for work distribution brings justification for the definition of quantum fluctuating work via two-point measurements.

Compared to work statistics, heat statistics relevant to thermal transport associated with a nonequilibrium stationary state has been extensively studied [29–38], but the heat statistics in a finite-time quantum thermodynamic process [39–41] and its quantum–classical correspondence have been less explored. A challenge is that the precise description of the bath dynamics requires handling a huge number of degrees of freedom of the heat bath. Different approaches have been proposed to calculate the quantum fluctuating heat and its statistics, such as the non-equilibrium Green's function approach

to quantum thermal transport [29,32,36,42–44] and the path-integral approach to quantum thermodynamics [45–49]. However, very few analytical results about the heat statistics have been obtained for the relaxation processes in open quantum systems. These analytical results are limited to either the relaxation dynamics described by the Lindblad master equation [39,40] or the long-time limit independent of the relaxation dynamics [50]. On the other hand, some results about the heat statistics in the classical Brownian motion model have been reported [51–59]. How the quantum and the classical heat statistics (especially associated with the relaxation dynamics in finite time) are related to each other has not been explored so far, probably due to the difficulty in studying the heat statistics in open quantum systems [60–62].

In this article, we study the heat statistics of a quantum Brownian motion model described by the Caldeira–Leggett Hamiltonian [48,63–68], where the heat bath is modeled as a collection of harmonic oscillators. Although it is well known that the dynamics of such an open quantum system can approach that of the classical Brownian motion in the classical limit $\hbar \to 0$ [64], less is known about the heat statistics of this model during the finite-time relaxation process. Here, we focus on the relaxation process without external driving (the Hamiltonian of the system is time-independent); thus, the quantum fluctuating heat can be defined as the difference of the system energy between the initial and the final measurements [69]. Under the Ohmic spectral density, the dynamics of the composite system is exactly solvable in the continuum limit of the bath oscillators [70]. By employing the phase-space formulation approach [71–73], we obtain analytical results of the characteristic function of heat for the Caldeira–Leggett model at any relaxation time τ with an arbitrary friction coefficient κ. Previously, such an approach was employed to study the quantum corrections to work [74–76] and entropy [77,78]. Analytical results of the heat statistics bring important insights to understand the fluctuating property of heat. By taking the classical limit $\hbar \to 0$, the heat statistics of the Caldeira–Leggett model approaches that of the classical Brownian motion model. Thus, our results verify the quantum–classical correspondence principle for heat distribution, and provide justification for the definition of the quantum fluctuating heat via two-point measurements. We also verify, from the analytical results, that the heat statistics satisfies the exchange fluctuation theorem of heat [4].

The rest of this article is organized as follows. In Section 2, we introduce the Caldeira–Leggett model and define the quantum fluctuating heat. In Section 3, the analytical results of the characteristic function of heat are obtained by employing the phase-space formulation approach. We show the quantum–classical correspondence of the heat distribution and discuss the heat distribution in the long-time limit or with the extremely weak or strong coupling strength. The conclusion is given in Section 4.

2. The Caldeira–Leggett Model and the Heat Statistics

2.1. The Caldeira–Leggett Model

The quantum Brownian motion is generally described by the Caldeira–Leggett model [64,65], where the system is modeled as a single particle moving in a specific potential and the heat bath is a collection of harmonic oscillators. For simplicity, we choose the harmonic potential for the system [66,79–81], where the dynamics of such an open quantum system can be solved analytically. The system relaxes to the equilibrium state at the temperature of the heat bath. We study the heat distribution of such a quantum relaxation process and analytically obtain the characteristic function of heat and its classical correspondence based on the phase-space formulation of quantum mechanics.

The total Hamiltonian of the composite system is $H_{\text{tot}} = H_S + H_B + H_{SB}$ with each term being

$$H_S = \frac{1}{2}\frac{\hat{p}_0^2}{m_0} + \frac{1}{2}m_0\omega_0^2\hat{q}_0^2 \tag{1}$$

$$H_B = \sum_{n=1}^{N}\left(\frac{1}{2}\frac{\hat{p}_n^2}{m_n} + \frac{1}{2}m_n\omega_n^2\hat{q}_n^2\right) \tag{2}$$

$$H_{SB} = -\hat{q}_0\sum_{n=1}^{N}(C_n\hat{q}_n) + \sum_{n=1}^{N}\left(\frac{C_n^2}{2m_n\omega_n^2}\hat{q}_0^2\right), \tag{3}$$

where m_0, ω_0, $\hat{q}_0$ and $\hat{p}_0$ (m_n, ω_n, $\hat{q}_n$ and $\hat{p}_n$ with $n=1,2,3,...,N$) are the mass, frequency, position and momentum of the system (the n-th bath harmonic oscillator) and C_n is the coupling strength between the system and the n-th bath harmonic oscillator. The counter-term $\sum_n[C_n^2/(2m_n\omega_n^2)]\hat{q}_0^2$ is included in the interaction Hamiltonian H_{SB} to cancel the frequency shift of the system.

The spectral density is defined as $J(\omega) := \sum_n[C_n^2/(2m_n\omega_n)]\delta(\omega-\omega_n)$. We adopt an Ohmic spectral density with the Lorentz–Drude cutoff [67]

$$J(\omega) = \frac{m_0\kappa}{\pi}\omega\frac{\Omega_0^2}{\Omega_0^2+\omega^2}, \tag{4}$$

where κ is the friction coefficient. A sufficiently large cutoff frequency Ω_0 ($\Omega_0 \gg \omega_0$) is applied to ensure a finite counter-term and the dynamics with the timescale exceeding $1/\Omega_0$ is Markovian. Under such a spectral density, the dissipation dynamics of the Caldeira–Leggett model with a weak coupling strength $\kappa \ll \omega_0$ reproduces that of the classical underdamped Brownian motion when taking the classical limit $\hbar \to 0$ [64].

We assume the initial state to be a product state of the system and the heat bath

$$\rho(0) = \rho_S(0) \otimes \rho_B^G, \tag{5}$$

which makes it possible to define the quantum fluctuating heat via two-point measurements. Here, $\rho_S(0)$ is the initial state of the system and $\rho_B^G = \exp(-\beta H_B)/Z_B(\beta)$ is the Gibbs distribution of the heat bath with the inverse temperature β and the partition function $Z_B(\beta) = \text{Tr}[\exp(-\beta H_B)]$.

2.2. The Quantum Fluctuating Heat in the Relaxation Process

We study the heat distribution of the relaxation process based on the two-point measurement definition of the quantum fluctuating heat. When no external driving is applied to the system, the Hamiltonian of the system is time-independent. Since no work is performed during the relaxation process, the quantum fluctuating heat can be defined as

$$Q_{l'l} = E_{l'}^S - E_l^S, \tag{6}$$

where E_l^S ($E_{l'}^S$) is the eigenenergy of the system corresponding to the outcome l (l') at the initial (final) time $t=0$ ($t=\tau$). The two-point measurements over the heat bath can be hardly realized due to a huge number of degrees of freedom of the heat bath [20], while the measurements over the small quantum system are much easier in principle. The positive sign corresponds to the energy flowing from the heat bath to the system.

For the system prepared in an equilibrium state, no coherence exists in the initial state and the initial density matrix of the system commutes with the Hamiltonian of the system, $[\rho(0), H_S] = 0$. The probability of observing the transition from l and l' is

$$p_{\tau,l'l} = \gamma_{\tau,l'l}p_l, \tag{7}$$

with the conditional transition probability $\gamma_{\tau,l'l} = \text{Tr}\big[(\hat{P}^S_{l'} \otimes I_B)U_{\text{tot}}(\tau)(\hat{P}^S_l \otimes \rho^G_B)U^\dagger_{\text{tot}}(\tau)\big]$ and the initial probability $p_l = \text{Tr}[\rho(0)\hat{P}^S_l]$. Here, $\hat{P}^S_l = |l\rangle\langle l|$ is the projection operator corresponding to the outcome l. The heat distribution is defined as

$$P_\tau(q) := \sum_{l',l} \delta(q - Q_{l'l}) p_{\tau,l'l}. \tag{8}$$

The characteristic function of heat $\chi_\tau(\nu)$ is defined as the Fourier transform of the heat distribution $\chi_\tau(\nu) := \sum_{l',l} \exp[i\nu(E^S_{l'} - E^S_l)] p_{\tau,l'l}$, which can be rewritten explicitly as

$$\chi_\tau(\nu) = \text{Tr}\Big[e^{i\nu H_S} U_{\text{tot}}(\tau)\big(e^{-i\nu H_S}\rho(0)\big)U^\dagger_{\text{tot}}(\tau)\Big], \tag{9}$$

where $U_{\text{tot}}(\tau) = \exp(-iH_{\text{tot}}\tau/\hbar)$ is the unitary time-evolution operator of the composite system.

Our goal is to analytically calculate the characteristic function $\chi_\tau(\nu)$. Previously, the quantum–classical correspondence principle for heat statistics has been analyzed with the path-integral approach to quantum thermodynamics [48], yet the explicit result of the characteristic function (or generating function) of heat has not been obtained so far. We employ the phase-space formulation approach to solve this problem and rewrite the characteristic function Equation (9) into

$$\chi_\tau(\nu) = \text{Tr}\Big[e^{i\nu H^H_S(\tau)} \eta(0)\Big], \tag{10}$$

where the system Hamiltonian in the Heisenberg picture is

$$H^H_S(\tau) = U^\dagger_{\text{tot}}(\tau) H_S U_{\text{tot}}(\tau), \tag{11}$$

and the density matrix-like operator $\eta(0)$ is

$$\eta(0) = \Big[e^{-i\nu H_S}\rho_S(0)\Big] \otimes \rho^G_B. \tag{12}$$

We express Equation (10) with the phase-space formulation of quantum mechanics [71–76]:

$$\chi_\tau(\nu) = \frac{1}{(2\pi\hbar)^{N+1}} \int d\mathbf{z} \Big[e^{i\nu H^H_S(\tau)}\Big]_w(\mathbf{z}) \cdot P(\mathbf{z}), \tag{13}$$

where $\mathbf{z}$ represents a point $\mathbf{z} = [\mathbf{q}, \mathbf{p}] = [q_0, ..., q_N, p_0, ..., p_N]$ in the phase space of the composite system and the integral is performed over the whole phase space. The subscript "w" indicates the Weyl symbol of the corresponding operator and $P(\mathbf{z})$ is the Weyl symbol of the operator $\eta(0)$, which is explicitly defined as [71]

$$P(\mathbf{z}) := \int d\mathbf{y} \Big\langle \mathbf{q} - \frac{\mathbf{y}}{2}\Big|\eta(0)\Big|\mathbf{q} + \frac{\mathbf{y}}{2}\Big\rangle e^{\frac{i\mathbf{p}\cdot\mathbf{y}}{\hbar}}. \tag{14}$$

In the following, we calculate the heat statistics Equation (13) by employing the phase-space formulation approach.

3. Results of the Characteristic Function of Heat

We show a sketch of the derivation of the heat statistics $\chi_\tau(\nu)$ with the details left in Appendix A. We specifically consider the system is initially prepared at an equilibrium state $\rho_S(0) = \exp(-\beta' H_S)/Z_S(\beta')$ with the inverse temperature β' and the partition function $Z_S(\beta') = 1/[2\sinh(\beta'\hbar\omega_0/2)]$. The heat bath is at the inverse temperature β, which is different from β'. In Equation (13), the two Weyl symbols $\big[e^{i\nu H^H_S(\tau)}\big]_w(\mathbf{z})$ and $P(\mathbf{z})$ are obtained as

$$\left[e^{iv H_S^H(\tau)}\right]_w(\mathbf{z}) = \frac{1}{\cos\left(\frac{v\hbar\omega_0}{2}\right)} \exp\left[\frac{i}{2\hbar}\mathbf{z}^T \tilde{\mathbf{\Lambda}}_{vz}(\tau)\mathbf{z}\right], \tag{15}$$

and

$$P(\mathbf{z}) = \frac{2\sinh\left(\frac{\beta'\hbar\omega_0}{2}\right)}{\cosh\left[\frac{(\beta'+iv)\hbar\omega_0}{2}\right]} \cdot \left[\prod_{n=1}^{N} 2\tanh\left(\frac{\beta\hbar\omega_n}{2}\right)\right] \cdot \exp\left(-\frac{1}{2\hbar}\mathbf{z}^T \mathbf{\Lambda}_{\beta z}\mathbf{z}\right), \tag{16}$$

where the explicit expressions of the matrices $\tilde{\mathbf{\Lambda}}_{vz}(\tau)$ and $\mathbf{\Lambda}_{\beta z}$ are given in Equations (A10) and (A36), respectively.

Substituting Equations (15) and (16) into Equation (13), the characteristic function of heat at any relaxation time τ with an arbitrary friction coefficient κ is finally obtained as

$$\chi_\tau(v) = \left\{ \left[(1+i\Xi)(1-i\Theta\Xi) - i\Xi(1-\Theta-i\Theta\Xi)\frac{\kappa^2 \cos(2\hat{\omega}_0\tau) - 4\omega_0^2}{(\kappa^2 - 4\omega_0^2)e^{\kappa\tau}}\right]^2 \right.$$
$$\left. + \Xi^2(1-\Theta-i\Theta\Xi)^2 \left[\left(\frac{\kappa^2\cos(2\hat{\omega}_0\tau)-4\omega_0^2}{(\kappa^2-4\omega_0^2)e^{\kappa\tau}}\right)^2 - e^{-2\kappa\tau}\right]\right\}^{\frac{1}{2}}, \tag{17}$$

where the quantities Ξ and Θ are

$$\Xi = \frac{\tan\left(\frac{v\hbar\omega_0}{2}\right)}{\tanh\left[\frac{(\beta'+iv)\hbar\omega_0}{2}\right] - i\tan\left(\frac{v\hbar\omega_0}{2}\right)}, \tag{18}$$

$$\Theta = \frac{\tanh\left[\frac{(\beta'+iv)\hbar\omega_0}{2}\right] - i\tan\left(\frac{v\hbar\omega_0}{2}\right)}{\tanh\left(\frac{\beta\hbar\omega_0}{2}\right)}. \tag{19}$$

Induced by the friction, the frequency of the system harmonic oscillator is shifted to $\hat{\omega}_0 = \sqrt{\omega_0^2 - \kappa^2/4}$.

From the analytical results of the heat statistics Equation (17), the average heat $\langle Q \rangle(\tau) = -i\partial_v[\ln \chi_\tau(v)]|_{v=0}$ is immediately obtained as

$$\langle Q \rangle(\tau) = \frac{\omega_0 \hbar}{2}\left[\coth\left(\frac{\beta\omega_0\hbar}{2}\right) - \coth\left(\frac{\beta'\omega_0\hbar}{2}\right)\right]\left[1 - \frac{\kappa^2 \cos(2\hat{\omega}_0\tau) - 4\omega_0^2}{(\kappa^2 - 4\omega_0^2)e^{\kappa\tau}}\right], \tag{20}$$

and the variance $\mathrm{Var}(Q)(\tau) = -\partial_v^2[\ln \chi_\tau(v)]|_{v=0}$ is

$$\mathrm{Var}(Q)(\tau) = \mathrm{I} + \mathrm{II}\cdot e^{-\kappa\tau} + \mathrm{III}\cdot e^{-2\kappa\tau}, \tag{21}$$

with

$$\mathrm{I} = \frac{\omega_0^2\hbar^2\left[\mathrm{csch}^2\left(\frac{\beta\omega_0\hbar}{2}\right) + \mathrm{csch}^2\left(\frac{\beta'\omega_0\hbar}{2}\right)\right]}{4}, \tag{22}$$

$$\mathrm{II} = \frac{\kappa^2\cos(2\hat{\omega}_0\tau) - 4\omega_0^2}{2\omega_0^2} \cdot \frac{\omega_0^2\hbar^2\left[\coth^2\left(\frac{\beta\omega_0\hbar}{2}\right) + \mathrm{csch}^2\left(\frac{\beta'\omega_0\hbar}{2}\right) - \coth\left(\frac{\beta\omega_0\hbar}{2}\right)\coth\left(\frac{\beta'\omega_0\hbar}{2}\right)\right]}{4}, \tag{23}$$

$$\mathrm{III} = \frac{\kappa^4\cos(4\hat{\omega}_0\tau) + 8\omega_0^2\kappa^2[1 - 2\cos(2\hat{\omega}_0\tau)] + 16\omega_0^4}{16\hat{\omega}_0^4} \cdot \frac{\omega_0^2\hbar^2\left[\coth\left(\frac{\beta\omega_0\hbar}{2}\right) - \coth\left(\frac{\beta'\omega_0\hbar}{2}\right)\right]^2}{4}. \tag{24}$$

Similarly, one can calculate the higher cumulants from the analytical results of the heat statistics. In the following, we examine the properties of the heat statistics of the quantum Brownian motion.

3.1. Quantum–Classical Correspondence Principle for Heat Statics and the Exchange Fluctuation Theorem of Heat

We further take the classical limit $\hbar \to 0$ or, more rigorously, $\beta\hbar\omega_0 \to 0$. The two quantities approach $\Xi \to \nu/\beta'$ and $\Theta \to \beta'/\beta$ and the characteristic function of heat (Equation (17)) becomes

$$\chi_\tau^{\text{cl}}(\nu) = \left\{ \left[(1+i\frac{\nu}{\beta'})(1-i\frac{\nu}{\beta}) - \frac{i\nu(\beta-\beta'-i\nu)}{\beta\beta'} \frac{(\kappa^2 \cos(2\hat{\omega}_0\tau) - 4\omega_0^2)}{(\kappa^2 - 4\omega_0^2)e^{\kappa\tau}} \right]^2 \right.$$
$$\left. + \nu^2 \left(\frac{\beta-\beta'-i\nu}{\beta\beta'} \right)^2 \left[\left(\frac{\kappa^2 \cos(2\hat{\omega}_0\tau) - 4\omega_0^2}{(\kappa^2 - 4\omega_0^2)e^{\kappa\tau}} \right)^2 - e^{-2\kappa\tau} \right] \right\}^{-\frac{1}{2}}, \quad (25)$$

which is consistent with the results obtained from the classical Brownian motion described by the Kramers equation (see Ref. [58] or Appendix C). The average heat is

$$\left\langle Q^{\text{cl}} \right\rangle(\tau) = \frac{\beta'-\beta}{\beta\beta'} \left[1 - \frac{\kappa^2 \cos(2\hat{\omega}_0\tau) - 4\omega_0^2}{(\kappa^2 - 4\omega_0^2)e^{\kappa\tau}} \right], \quad (26)$$

and the variance $\text{Var}\left(Q^{\text{cl}}\right)(\tau) = -\partial_\nu^2[\ln\chi_\tau^{\text{cl}}(\nu)]\big|_{\nu=0}$ is

$$\text{Var}\left(Q^{\text{cl}}\right)(\tau) = \text{I}^{\text{cl}} + \text{II}^{\text{cl}} \cdot e^{-\kappa\tau} + \text{III}^{\text{cl}} \cdot e^{-2\kappa\tau}, \quad (27)$$

with

$$\text{I}^{\text{cl}} = \frac{\beta^2 + \beta'^2}{\beta^2 \beta'^2} \quad (28)$$

$$\text{II}^{\text{cl}} = \frac{\kappa^2 \cos(2\hat{\omega}_0\tau) - 4\omega_0^2}{2\omega_0^2} \cdot \frac{\beta^2 - \beta\beta' + \beta'^2}{\beta^2 \beta'^2} \quad (29)$$

$$\text{III}^{\text{cl}} = \frac{\kappa^4 \cos(4\hat{\omega}_0\tau) + 8\omega_0^2\kappa^2[1 - 2\cos(2\hat{\omega}_0\tau)] + 16\omega_0^4}{16\omega_0^4} \cdot \frac{(\beta-\beta')^2}{\beta^2\beta'^2}. \quad (30)$$

From Equation (17) (or the classical counterpart Equation (25)), one can see the characteristic function of heat exhibits the following symmetry:

$$\chi_\tau(\nu) = \chi_\tau[-i(\beta-\beta') - \nu], \quad (31)$$

which shows that the heat distribution satisfies the exchange fluctuation theorem of heat in the differential form $P_\tau(Q)/P_\tau(-Q) = \exp[-(\beta-\beta')Q]$ [4]. By setting $\nu = 0$, we obtain the relation $\chi_\tau[-i(\beta-\beta')] = \chi_\tau(0) = 1$, which is exactly the exchange fluctuation theorem of heat in the integral form $\langle\exp[(\beta-\beta')Q]\rangle = 1$.

3.2. Long-Time Limit

In the long-time limit $\tau \to \infty$, the characteristic functions of heat (Equations (17) and (25)) become

$$\chi_\infty(\nu) = \frac{\left(1 - e^{-\beta'\omega_0\hbar}\right)\left(1 - e^{-\beta\omega_0\hbar}\right)}{\left(1 - e^{-(\beta'+i\nu)\omega_0\hbar}\right)\left(1 - e^{-(\beta-i\nu)\omega_0\hbar}\right)}, \tag{32}$$

and

$$\chi_\infty^{cl}(\nu) = \frac{\beta'\beta}{(\beta' + i\nu)(\beta - i\nu)}. \tag{33}$$

Such results, independent of the relaxation dynamics, are in the form

$$\chi_{th}(\nu) = \frac{Z_S(\beta' + i\nu)Z_S(\beta - i\nu)}{Z_S(\beta')Z_S(\beta)}, \tag{34}$$

reflecting complete thermalization of the system [53]. For example, the relaxation of a harmonic oscillator governed by the quantum–optical master equation gives the identical characteristic function of heat in the long-time limit [39]. In Appendix D, we demonstrate that the characteristic function of heat for any relaxation process with complete thermalization is always in the form of Equation (34). With the simple expressions (32) and (33) of the characteristic functions, the heat distributions are obtained from the inverse Fourier transform as

$$P_\infty(q) = \begin{cases} \frac{\left(1-e^{-\beta'\omega_0\hbar}\right)\left(1-e^{-\beta\omega_0\hbar}\right)}{1-e^{-(\beta'+\beta)\omega_0\hbar}} \sum_{j=0}^{\infty} \delta(q - j\omega_0\hbar)e^{-\beta q} & q \geq 0 \\ \frac{\left(1-e^{-\beta'\omega_0\hbar}\right)\left(1-e^{-\beta\omega_0\hbar}\right)}{1-e^{-(\beta'+\beta)\omega_0\hbar}} \sum_{j=1}^{\infty} \delta(q + j\omega_0\hbar)e^{\beta' q} & q < 0 \end{cases}, \tag{35}$$

and

$$P_\infty^{cl}(q) = \begin{cases} \frac{\beta'\beta}{\beta'+\beta}e^{-\beta q} & q \geq 0 \\ \frac{\beta'\beta}{\beta'+\beta}e^{\beta' q} & q < 0 \end{cases}, \tag{36}$$

which are exactly the same as the long-time results obtained in Ref. [39].

3.3. Weak/Strong Coupling Limit in Finite Time

In the weak coupling limit $\kappa \ll \omega_0$, the characteristic function of heat Equation (17) becomes

$$\chi_\tau^w(\nu) = \frac{1}{(1 + i\Xi)(1 - i\Xi\Theta)(1 - e^{-\kappa\tau}) + e^{-\kappa\tau}}. \tag{37}$$

There is only one relaxation timescale associated to κ. Such situation corresponds to the highly underdamped regime of the classical Brownian motion and a systematic method has been proposed to study the heat distribution [56], as well as the work distribution, under an external driving [82,83].

In the strong coupling limit $\kappa \gg \omega_0$, the characteristic function of heat Equation (17) becomes

$$\chi_\tau^s(\nu) = \frac{1}{\sqrt{(1 + i\Xi)(1 - i\Xi\Theta)(1 - e^{-2\kappa\tau}) + e^{-2\kappa\tau}}} \times \frac{1}{\sqrt{(1 + i\Xi)(1 - i\Xi\Theta)\left(1 - e^{-\frac{2\omega_0^2}{\kappa}\tau}\right) + e^{-\frac{2\omega_0^2}{\kappa}\tau}}}. \tag{38}$$

The relaxation timescales of the momentum (the first factor) and the coordinate (the second factor) are separated. The long-time limits of both Equations (37) and (38) are equal to Equation (32). In classical thermodynamics, the usual overdamped approximation neglects the motion of the momentum; hence, the heat statistics derived under such an approximation is incomplete [52]. Actually, the momentum degree of freedom also contributes to the heat statistics.

3.4. Numerical Results

In Figure 1, we show the cumulative heat distribution function $\Pr(Q < q) := \int_{-\infty}^{q} P_\tau(q')dq'$ with different friction coefficients $\kappa = 0.01, 1$ and 100, at the rescaled relaxation time $\tilde{\tau} = \kappa\tau = 1$ and 10. We set the mass $m_0 = 1$ and the frequency $\omega_0 = 1$ for the system harmonic oscillator, the inverse temperatures $\beta = 1$ and $\beta' = 2$ for the initial equilibrium states of the heat bath and the system, respectively. The Planck constant is set to be $\hbar = 1, 0.5, 0.1$. With the decrease in $\hbar$, the quantum result Equation (17) approaches the classical result Equation (25). Thus, the quantum–classical correspondence of the heat distribution is demonstrated for generic values of the friction coefficient κ.

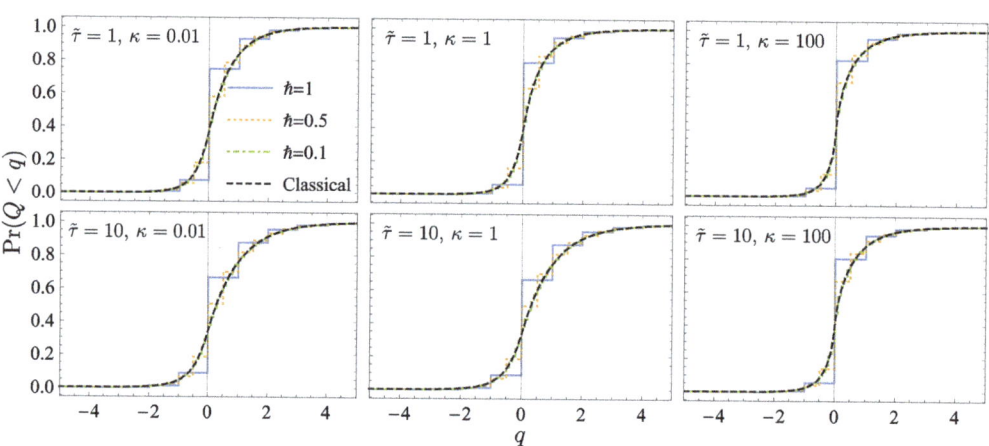

Figure 1. The cumulative heat distribution function $\Pr(Q < q)$. The choices of the parameters are given in the main text. We compare the results of the Caldeira–Leggett model (blue solid, orange dotted and green dot-dashed curves) in Equation (17) and those of the classical Brownian motion (black dashed curve) in Equation (25). The rescaled relaxation time is $\tilde{\tau} = \kappa\tau = 1$ in the upper subfigures and $\tilde{\tau} = 10$ in the lower subfigures. The left, middle and right subfigures illustrate the results for the weak ($\kappa = 0.01$), intermediate ($\kappa = 1$) and strong coupling strength ($\kappa = 100$).

For $\kappa = 0.01$ and 1, complete thermalization is achieved at $\tilde{\tau} = 10$. The left-lower and middle-lower subfigures show the identical distribution characterized by Equations (35) and (36). For $\kappa = 100$, the momentum degree of freedom is thermalized $\exp(-2\tilde{\tau}) \approx 0$ in Equation (38), while the coordinate degree of freedom remains frozen $\exp[-2(\omega_0^2/\kappa^2)\tilde{\tau}] \approx 1$ in Equation (38). Thus, the distribution in the right-lower subfigure is different from the middle-lower subfigure.

In Figure 2, we illustrate the results of the mean value $\langle Q \rangle(\tau)$ and the variance $\text{Var}(Q)(\tau)$ with different friction coefficients $\kappa = 0.01, 1$ and 100. The parameters are the same as those in Figure 1. The quantum results approach the classical results with the decrease in $\hbar$. For $\kappa = 0.01$ and 1 (left and middle subfigures), complete thermalization is reached when $\tilde{\tau} > 5$. The mean value and the variance approach $\lim_{\tau\to\infty}\langle Q^{\text{cl}} \rangle(\tau) = 1/\beta - 1/\beta'$ and $\lim_{\tau\to\infty}\text{Var}(Q^{\text{cl}})(\tau) = 1/\beta^2 + 1/\beta'^2$ (gray horizontal lines). For $\kappa = 100$ (right subfigures), only the momentum degree of freedom is thermalized at this timescale. Thus, the mean value and the variance take half value of their long-time limits. When the coordinate degree of freedom is also thermalized in the long-time limit ($\tilde{\tau} \gg \kappa^2/\omega_0^2 = 10^4$), the mean value and the variance are expected to approach the same values as those in the middle subfigures.

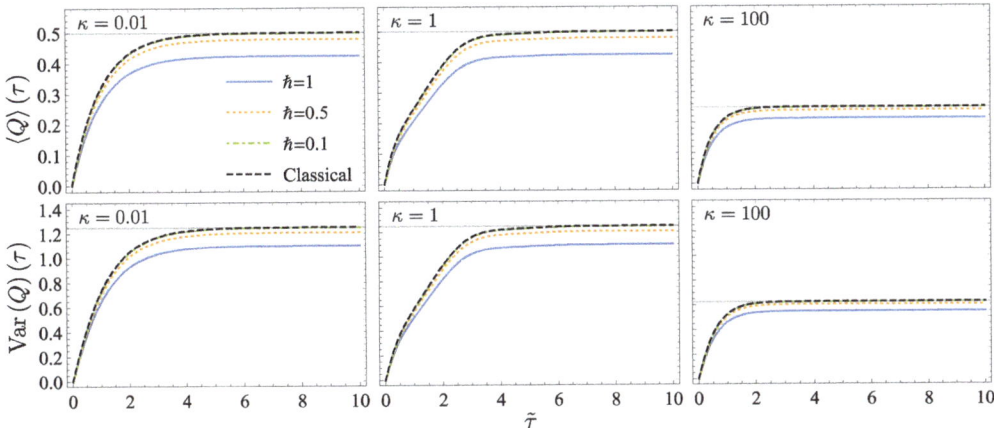

Figure 2. The evolution of the mean value $\langle Q \rangle(\tau)$ (**upper subfigures**) and the variance $\text{Var}(Q)(\tau)$ (**lower subfigures**) of the heat statistics as functions of the rescaled time $\tilde{\tau} = \kappa \tau$.

4. Conclusions

Previously, the heat statistics of the relaxation processes has been studied analytically in open quantum systems described by the Lindblad master equation [39,40,50]. However, due to the rotating wave approximation and other approximations, such quantum systems do not possess a well-defined classical counterpart. Hence, the quantum–classical correspondence principle for heat distribution has not been well established.

In this paper, we study the heat statistics of the quantum Brownian motion model described by the Caldeira–Leggett Hamiltonian, in which the bath dynamics is explicitly considered. By employing the phase-space formulation approach, we obtain the analytical expressions of the characteristic function of heat at any relaxation time τ with an arbitrary friction coefficient κ. The analytical results of heat statistics bring important insights to the studies of quantum thermodynamics. For example, in the classical limit, our results approach the heat statistics of the classical Brownian motion. Thus, the quantum–classical correspondence principle for heat statistics is verified in this model. Our analytical results provide justification for the definition of quantum fluctuating heat via two-point measurements.

We also discuss the characteristic function of heat in the long-time limit or with the extremely weak/strong coupling strength. In the long-time limit, the form of the characteristic function of heat reflects complete thermalization of the system. In addition, from the analytical expressions of the heat statistics, we can immediately verify the exchange fluctuation theorem of heat. The phase-space formulation can be further utilized to study the joint statistics of work and heat in a driven open quantum system, which would be beneficial in exploring the fluctuations of power and efficiency in finite-time quantum heat engines.

Author Contributions: Conceptualization, J.-F.C. and H.-T.Q.; Formal analysis, J.-F.C.; Funding acquisition, H.-T.Q.; Investigation, J.-F.C.; Methodology, J.-F.C.; Supervision, H.-T.Q.; Validation, T.Q. and H.-T.Q.; Visualization, J.-F.C.; Writing—original draft, J.-F.C.; Writing—review & editing, T.Q. and H.-T.Q. All authors have read and agreed to the published version of the manuscript.

Funding: H. T. Quan acknowledges support from the National Natural Science Foundation of China under Grants No. 11775001, No. 11534002 and No. 11825001.

Data Availability Statement: Not applicable.

Acknowledgments: This paper is dedicated to Wojciech Zurek on the occasion of his 70th birthday for his mentorship as well as his kind and generous supports to one of the authors (H. T. Quan), and for his many insightful contributions to our understanding about the quantum-to-classical transition.

Conflicts of Interest: The authors declare no conflict of interest.

Appendix A. Derivation to the Characteristic Function of Heat (17)

We show the detailed derivation to the characteristic function of heat $\chi_\tau(\nu)$. First, we calculate the two Wigner functions $\left[e^{i\nu H_S^H(t)}\right]_w(\mathbf{z})$ and $P(\mathbf{z})$. Then, the final result Equation (17) is obtained from Equation (13).

Appendix A.1. $\left[e^{i\nu H_S^H(t)}\right]_w(\mathbf{z})$

With the quadratic Hamiltonian $H_S^H(t)$, the Wigner function $\left[e^{i\nu H_S^H(t)}\right]_w(\mathbf{z})$ is [78,81]

$$\left[e^{i\nu H_S^H(t)}\right]_w(\mathbf{z}) = \frac{1}{\cos\left(\frac{\omega_0 \hbar \nu}{2}\right)} \exp\left[i\frac{m_0 \omega_0}{\hbar}\tan\left(\frac{\omega_0 \hbar \nu}{2}\right)q_0^2(t) + i\frac{1}{m_0 \hbar \omega_0}\tan\left(\frac{\omega_0 \hbar \nu}{2}\right)p_0^2(t)\right] \quad (A1)$$

$$= \frac{1}{\cos\left(\frac{\omega_0 \hbar \nu}{2}\right)} \exp\left[\frac{i}{2\hbar}\mathbf{z}^T(t)\mathbf{\Lambda}_{\nu z}\mathbf{z}(t)\right], \quad (A2)$$

where $\mathbf{z}(t)$ gives the trajectory in the phase space determined by the initial point $\mathbf{z}(0) = \mathbf{z}$ and $\mathbf{\Lambda}_{\nu z}$ is a rank-2 diagonal matrix

$$\mathbf{\Lambda}_{\nu z} = \begin{pmatrix} 2m_0\omega_0 \tan\left(\frac{\omega_0 \hbar \nu}{2}\right) & & & \\ & \mathbf{O} & & \\ & & \frac{2}{m_0 \omega_0}\tan\left(\frac{\omega_0 \hbar \nu}{2}\right) & \\ & & & \mathbf{O} \end{pmatrix}, \quad (A3)$$

with an $N \times N$ zero matrix $\mathbf{O}$. The unlisted elements are zeros. The trajectory $\mathbf{z}(t)$ satisfies the classical equation of motion (also the equation of motion in the Heisenberg picture).

$$\dot{q}_0 = \frac{p_0}{m_0}, \quad (A4)$$

$$\dot{q}_n = \frac{p_n}{m_n}, \quad (A5)$$

$$\dot{p}_0 = -m_0 \tilde{\omega}_0^2 q_0 + \sum_n C_n q_n, \quad (A6)$$

$$\dot{p}_n = -m_n \omega_n^2 q_n + C_n q_0, \quad (A7)$$

with $\tilde{\omega}_0^2 = \omega_0^2 + \sum_{n=1}^N C_n^2/(m_0 m_n \omega_n^2)$. The above differential equations can be rewritten into a compact form $\dot{\mathbf{z}}(t) = \mathbf{L}\mathbf{z}(t)$. The trajectory $\mathbf{z}(t) = [\mathbf{q}(t), \mathbf{p}(t)]$ in the phase space characterizes the evolution of the composite system with the positions $\mathbf{q}(t) = [q_0(t), ..., q_N(t)]$ and the momenta $\mathbf{p}(t) = [p_0(t), ..., p_N(t)]$ and is related to the initial point by the dynamical map $\mathbf{z}(t) = \exp(\mathbf{L}t)\mathbf{z}(0)$. The $(2N+2) \times (2N+2)$ matrix $\mathbf{L}$ is explicitly

$$\mathbf{L} = \begin{pmatrix} & & & & & \frac{1}{m_0} & & & & \\ & & & & & & \frac{1}{m_1} & & & \\ & & & & & & & \frac{1}{m_2} & & \\ & & & & & & & & \ddots & \\ & & & & & & & & & \frac{1}{m_N} \\ -m_0\tilde{\omega}_0^2 & C_1 & C_2 & \cdots & C_N & & & & & \\ C_1 & -m_1\omega_1^2 & & & & & & & & \\ C_2 & & -m_2\omega_2^2 & & & & & & & \\ \cdots & & & \cdots & & & & & & \\ C_N & & & & -m_N\omega_N^2 & & & & & \end{pmatrix}, \quad \text{(A8)}$$

and the matrix exponential is formally written as

$$\exp(\mathbf{L}t) = \begin{pmatrix} \alpha_0 & \alpha_1 & \cdots & \alpha_N & \frac{\beta_0}{m_0} & \frac{\beta_1}{m_1} & \cdots & \frac{\beta_N}{m_N} \\ \gamma_1 & \Lambda_{11} & \cdots & \Lambda_{1N} & \frac{\xi_1}{m_0} & \frac{\Delta_{11}}{m_1} & \cdots & \frac{\Delta_{1N}}{m_N} \\ \cdots & \cdots & \cdots & \cdots & \cdots & \cdots & \cdots & \cdots \\ \gamma_N & \Lambda_{N1} & \cdots & \Lambda_{NN} & \frac{\xi_N}{m_0} & \frac{\Delta_{N1}}{m_1} & \cdots & \frac{\Delta_{NN}}{m_N} \\ m_0\dot\alpha_0 & m_0\dot\alpha_1 & \cdots & m_0\dot\alpha_N & \frac{m_0}{m_0}\dot\beta_0 & \frac{m_0}{m_1}\dot\beta_1 & \cdots & \frac{m_0}{m_N}\dot\beta_N \\ m_1\dot\gamma_1 & m_1\dot\Lambda_{11} & \cdots & m_1\dot\Lambda_{1N} & \frac{m_1}{m_0}\dot\xi_1 & \frac{m_1}{m_1}\dot\Delta_{11} & \cdots & \frac{m_1}{m_N}\dot\Delta_{1N} \\ \cdots & \cdots & \cdots & \cdots & \cdots & \cdots & \cdots & \cdots \\ m_N\dot\gamma_N & m_N\dot\Lambda_{N1} & \cdots & m_N\dot\Lambda_{NN} & \frac{m_N}{m_0}\dot\xi_N & \frac{m_N}{m_1}\dot\Delta_{N1} & \cdots & \frac{m_N}{m_N}\dot\Delta_{NN} \end{pmatrix}. \quad \text{(A9)}$$

We rewrite the quadratic form into $\mathbf{z}^T(t)\mathbf{\Lambda}_{vz}\mathbf{z}(t) = \mathbf{z}^T(0)\tilde{\mathbf{\Lambda}}_{vz}(t)\mathbf{z}(0)$ with

$$\tilde{\mathbf{\Lambda}}_{vz}(t) = \exp\left(\mathbf{L}^T t\right)\mathbf{\Lambda}_{vz}\exp(\mathbf{L}t). \quad \text{(A10)}$$

We next carry out every element in Equation (A9) through the Laplace transforms of Equations (A4)–(A7):

$$s\tilde{q}_0(s) - q_0(0) = \frac{\tilde{p}_0(s)}{m_0}, \quad \text{(A11)}$$

$$s\tilde{q}_n(s) - q_n(0) = \frac{\tilde{p}_n(s)}{m_n}, \quad \text{(A12)}$$

$$s\tilde{p}_0(s) - p_0(0) = -m_0\tilde{\omega}_0^2\tilde{q}_0(s) + \sum_n C_n\tilde{q}_n(s), \quad \text{(A13)}$$

$$s\tilde{p}_n(s) - p_n(0) = -m_n\omega_n^2\tilde{q}_n(s) + C_n\tilde{q}_0(s). \quad \text{(A14)}$$

Representing $\tilde{q}_n(s)$ and $\tilde{p}_n(s)$ with $\tilde{q}_0(s)$ and the initial conditions, we obtain

$$\left\{s^2 + \tilde{\omega}_0^2 - \sum_n \left[\frac{C_n^2}{m_0 m_n(s^2 + \omega_n^2)}\right]\right\}\tilde{q}_0(s) = \dot{q}_0(0) + sq_0(0) + \sum_n \frac{C_n}{m_0}\left[\frac{\dot{q}_n(0) + sq_n(0)}{s^2 + \omega_n^2}\right]. \quad \text{(A15)}$$

Under the Ohmic spectral density Equation (4), the above equation is simplified to

$$(s^2 + \kappa s + \omega_0^2)\tilde{q}_0(s) = \dot{q}_0(0) + sq_0(0) + \sum_n \frac{C_n}{m_0}\left[\frac{\dot{q}_n(0) + sq_n(0)}{s^2 + \omega_n^2}\right], \quad \text{(A16)}$$

where the summation on the left-hand side of Equation (A15) can be approximately expressed as

$$\sum_n \left[\frac{C_n^2}{m_0 m_n (s^2 + \omega_n^2)} \right] \approx -\kappa s + \sum_n \frac{C_n^2}{m_0 m_n \omega_n^2}, \tag{A17}$$

with a large cutoff frequency Ω_0. The inverse Laplace transform gives the differential equation of $q_0(t)$ as

$$\ddot{q}_0(t) + \kappa \dot{q}_0(t) + \omega_0^2 q_0(t) = \underbrace{-\kappa q_0(0)\delta(t)}_{\text{initial velocity change}} + \underbrace{\sum_n \frac{C_n}{m_0}\left[\dot{q}_n(0)\frac{\sin(\omega_n t)}{\omega_n} + q_n(0)\cos(\omega_n t)\right]}_{\text{stochastic force}}. \tag{A18}$$

On the right-hand side, the second term presents the stochastic force induced by the heat bath; the first term indicates an abrupt velocity change $-\kappa q_0(0)$ of the system particle at the initial time $t = 0$ [63,84,85]. The sudden change in velocity occurs for the system harmonic oscillator when the coupling between the system and the heat bath is switched on. Such an initial slippage is caused by the assumption of the initial product state. To avoid such an initial discontinuous problem, we drop the first term by considering the particle motion as starting at $t = 0+$ [70]. Under such a modification, the Caldeira–Leggett model can reproduce the complete Langevin equation with an arbitrary friction coefficient κ for both the underdamped and the overdamped regimes and the heat distribution of the Caldeira–Leggett model approaches that of the classical Brownian motion described by the Kramers equation [86]. In Appendix B, for the classical counterpart of the Caldeira–Leggett model, we show that the initial slippage can be naturally eliminated by choosing another initial state.

After dropping the first term, Equation (A16) becomes

$$(s^2 + \kappa s + \omega_0^2)\tilde{q}_0(s) = \dot{q}_0(0) + (\kappa + s)q_0(0) + \sum_n \frac{C_n}{m_0}\left[\frac{\dot{q}_n(0) + sq_n(0)}{s^2 + \omega_n^2}\right]. \tag{A19}$$

The solutions to $\tilde{q}_0(s)$ and $\tilde{q}_n(s)$ follow immediately as

$$\tilde{q}_0(s) = \frac{\dot{q}_0(0) + (\kappa + s)q_0(0) + \sum_n \frac{C_n}{m_0}\frac{\dot{q}_n(0) + sq_n(0)}{s^2 + \omega_n^2}}{s^2 + \kappa s + \omega_0^2}, \tag{A20}$$

$$\tilde{q}_n(s) = \frac{\dot{q}_n(0) + sq_n(0)}{s^2 + \omega_n^2} + \frac{C_n}{m_n} \cdot \frac{\dot{q}_0(0) + (\kappa + s)q_0(0) + \sum_l \frac{C_l}{m_0}\frac{\dot{q}_l(0) + sq_l(0)}{s^2 + \omega_l^2}}{(s^2 + \omega_n^2)(s^2 + \kappa s + \omega_0^2)}. \tag{A21}$$

With the inverse Laplace transform, the elements in the matrix $\exp(\mathbf{L}t)$ Equation (A9) are determined by

$$\begin{pmatrix} q_0(t) \\ q_1(t) \\ \dots \\ q_N(t) \end{pmatrix} = \begin{pmatrix} \alpha_0 & \alpha_1 & \alpha_2 & \dots & \alpha_N & \beta_0 & \beta_1 & \beta_2 & \dots & \beta_N \\ \gamma_1 & \Lambda_{11} & \Lambda_{12} & \dots & \Lambda_{1N} & \xi_1 & \Delta_{11} & \Delta_{12} & \dots & \Delta_{1N} \\ \dots & \dots & \dots & & \dots & \dots & \dots & \dots & & \dots \\ \gamma_N & \Lambda_{N1} & \Lambda_{N2} & \dots & \Lambda_{NN} & \xi_N & \Delta_{N1} & \Delta_{N2} & \dots & \Delta_{NN} \end{pmatrix} \begin{pmatrix} q_0(0) \\ q_1(0) \\ \dots \\ q_N(0) \\ \dot{q}_0(0) \\ \dot{q}_1(0) \\ \dots \\ \dot{q}_N(0) \end{pmatrix}, \tag{A22}$$

where the elements in the matrix of the right-hand side are explicitly solved as [70]

$$\alpha_0 = e^{-\frac{\kappa t}{2}} \left[\cos(\hat{\omega}_0 t) + \frac{\kappa}{2\hat{\omega}_0} \sin(\hat{\omega}_0 t) \right], \quad (A23)$$

$$\beta_0 = \frac{e^{-\frac{\kappa t}{2}}}{\hat{\omega}_0} \sin(\hat{\omega}_0 t), \quad (A24)$$

$$\alpha_n = \frac{C_n}{m_0} f_n(t), \quad (A25)$$

$$\beta_n = \frac{C_n}{m_0} g_n(t), \quad (A26)$$

$$\gamma_n = \frac{C_n}{m_n} [f_n(t) + \kappa g_n(t)], \quad (A27)$$

$$\zeta_n = \frac{C_n}{m_n} g_n(t), \quad (A28)$$

$$\Lambda_{nl} = \delta_{nl} \cos(\omega_n t) + \frac{C_n C_l}{m_n m_0} F_{nl}(t), \quad (A29)$$

$$\Delta_{nl} = \frac{\delta_{nl}}{\omega_n} \sin(\omega_n t) + \frac{C_n C_l}{m_n m_0} G_{nl}(t). \quad (A30)$$

The functions $f_n(t)$, $g_n(t)$, $F_{nl}(t)$ and $G_{nl}(t)$ are, explicitly,

$$f_n(t) = \mathscr{L}^{-1} \left[\frac{s}{(s^2 + \kappa s + \omega_0^2)(s^2 + \omega_n^2)} \right], \quad (A31)$$

$$g_n(t) = \mathscr{L}^{-1} \left[\frac{1}{(s^2 + \kappa s + \omega_0^2)(s^2 + \omega_n^2)} \right], \quad (A32)$$

$$F_{nl}(t) = \mathscr{L}^{-1} \left[\frac{s}{(s^2 + \kappa s + \omega_0^2)(s^2 + \omega_n^2)(s^2 + \omega_l^2)} \right], \quad (A33)$$

$$G_{nl}(t) = \mathscr{L}^{-1} \left[\frac{1}{(s^2 + \kappa s + \omega_0^2)(s^2 + \omega_n^2)(s^2 + \omega_l^2)} \right], \quad (A34)$$

where $\mathscr{L}^{-1}(\cdot)$ denotes the inverse Laplace transform with $\mathscr{L}(\cdot) = \int_0^\infty (\cdot) e^{-st} dt$.

Appendix A.2. P(z)

$P(\mathbf{z})$ is the Wigner function of the state $\eta(0)$ for the composite system [78,81]:

$$P(\mathbf{z}) = \frac{2 \sinh\left(\frac{\beta'\hbar\omega_0}{2}\right)}{\cosh\left[\frac{(\beta'+i\nu)\hbar\omega_0}{2}\right]} \cdot \left[\prod_{n=1}^{N} 2 \tanh\left(\frac{\beta\hbar\omega_n}{2}\right) \right] \cdot \exp\left[-\frac{1}{2\hbar} \mathbf{z}^T \Lambda_{\beta z} \mathbf{z}\right], \quad (A35)$$

where $\Lambda_{\beta z}$ is a $(2N+2) \times (2N+2)$ diagonal matrix

$$\Lambda_{\beta z} = \text{diag}(\lambda_{\beta' q_0}, \theta_1, ..., \theta_N, \lambda_{\beta' p_0}, \mu_1, ..., \mu_N), \quad (A36)$$

with the elements

$$\theta_n = 2m_n\omega_n \tanh\left(\frac{\beta\hbar\omega_n}{2}\right), \tag{A37}$$

$$\mu_n = \frac{2}{m_n\omega_n}\tanh\left(\frac{\beta\hbar\omega_n}{2}\right), \tag{A38}$$

$$\lambda_{\beta'q_0} = 2m_0\omega_0 \tanh\left[\frac{(\beta'+i\nu)\hbar\omega_0}{2}\right], \tag{A39}$$

$$\lambda_{\beta'p_0} = \frac{2}{m_0\omega_0}\tanh\left[\frac{(\beta'+i\nu)\hbar\omega_0}{2}\right]. \tag{A40}$$

Appendix A.3. Calculation of the Integral

With the explicit expressions of $\left[e^{i\nu H_S^H(\tau)}\right]_w(\mathbf{z})$ and $P(\mathbf{z})$, we perform the integral in Equation (13) and obtain the result of the characteristic function of heat

$$\chi_\tau(\nu) = \sqrt{\frac{\det(\mathbf{\Lambda}_{\beta z} - i\mathbf{\Lambda}_{\nu z})}{\det[\mathbf{\Lambda}_{\beta z} - i\tilde{\mathbf{\Lambda}}_{\nu z}(\tau)]}}. \tag{A41}$$

We use the following integral formula:

$$\int d\mathbf{x}\, e^{-\frac{1}{2}\mathbf{x}^T \mathbf{T} \mathbf{x}} = \sqrt{\frac{(2\pi)^{\dim(\mathbf{T})}}{\det(\mathbf{T})}}, \tag{A42}$$

where all the eigenvalues of $\mathbf{T}$ have positive real parts.

By introducing a diagonal matrix $\mathbf{A} = \mathbf{\Lambda}_{\beta z} - i\mathbf{\Lambda}_{\nu z}$, we rewrite Equation (A41) as

$$\chi_\tau(\nu) = \sqrt{\frac{1}{\det\left(\mathbf{I} + i\sqrt{\mathbf{A}^{-1}}[\mathbf{\Lambda}_{\nu z} - \tilde{\mathbf{\Lambda}}_{\nu z}(\tau)]\sqrt{\mathbf{A}^{-1}}\right)}}. \tag{A43}$$

Since $\tilde{\mathbf{\Lambda}}_{\nu z}(\tau)$ is a rank-2 matrix, we rewrite it as

$$\tilde{\mathbf{\Lambda}}_{\nu z}(\tau) = 2m_0\omega_0 \tan\left(\frac{\omega_0 \hbar \nu}{2}\right)\left[\mathbf{v}_{q_0}(\tau)\mathbf{v}_{q_0}^T(\tau) + \frac{1}{m_0^2\omega_0^2}\mathbf{v}_{p_0}(\tau)\mathbf{v}_{p_0}^T(\tau)\right], \tag{A44}$$

with the vectors

$$\mathbf{v}_{q_0}(\tau) = \left(\alpha_0, \alpha_1, ..., \alpha_N, \frac{\beta_0}{m_0}, \frac{\beta_1}{m_1}, ..., \frac{\beta_N}{m_N}\right)^T, \tag{A45}$$

$$\mathbf{v}_{p_0}(\tau) = \left(m_0\dot{\alpha}_0, m_0\dot{\alpha}_1, ..., m_0\dot{\alpha}_N, \dot{\beta}_0, \frac{m_0}{m_1}\dot{\beta}_1, ..., \frac{m_0}{m_N}\dot{\beta}_N\right)^T. \tag{A46}$$

where the evolution time t in the terms α_n and β_n is set to τ. We rewrite the matrix in the determinant (see Equation (A43)) as

$$\sqrt{\mathbf{A}^{-1}}(\mathbf{\Lambda}_{\nu z} - \tilde{\mathbf{\Lambda}}_{\nu z}(\tau))\sqrt{\mathbf{A}^{-1}} = \mathbf{M}\mathbf{M}^T, \tag{A47}$$

with the matrix

$$\mathbf{M}^{\mathrm{T}} = \begin{pmatrix} \sqrt{2m_0\omega_0 \tan\frac{\omega_0\hbar\nu}{2}} \mathbf{v}_{q_0}^{\mathrm{T}}(0) \\ \sqrt{\frac{2}{m_0\omega_0} \tan\frac{\omega_0\hbar\nu}{2}} \mathbf{v}_{p_0}^{\mathrm{T}}(0) \\ i\sqrt{2m_0\omega_0 \tan\frac{\omega_0\hbar\nu}{2}} \mathbf{v}_{q_0}^{\mathrm{T}}(\tau) \\ i\sqrt{\frac{2}{m_0\omega_0} \tan\frac{\omega_0\hbar\nu}{2}} \mathbf{v}_{p_0}^{\mathrm{T}}(\tau) \end{pmatrix} \sqrt{\mathbf{A}^{-1}}. \qquad (A48)$$

The determinant in Equation (A43) can be simplified to

$$\det\left(\mathbf{I} + i\sqrt{\mathbf{A}^{-1}}[\mathbf{\Lambda}_{\nu z} - \tilde{\mathbf{\Lambda}}_{\nu z}(\tau)]\sqrt{\mathbf{A}^{-1}}\right) = \det\left(\mathbf{I}_4 + i\mathbf{M}^{\mathrm{T}}\mathbf{M}\right), \qquad (A49)$$

where the right-hand side is the determinant of a 4 × 4 matrix and $\mathbf{I}_4$ is the 4 × 4 identity matrix. Notice that the initial values of the two vectors are

$$\mathbf{v}_{q_0}(0) = (1, 0, ...0, 0, 0, ..., 0)^{\mathrm{T}}, \qquad (A50)$$
$$\mathbf{v}_{p_0}(0) = (0, 0, ...0, 1, 0, ..., 0)^{\mathrm{T}}. \qquad (A51)$$

The explicit result of $\mathbf{M}^{\mathrm{T}}\mathbf{M}$ is obtained as

$$\mathbf{M}^{\mathrm{T}}\mathbf{M} = \Xi \begin{pmatrix} 1 & 0 & i\alpha_0 & i\dot{\alpha}_0/\omega_0 \\ 0 & 1 & i\omega_0\beta_0 & i\dot{\beta}_0 \\ i\alpha_0 & i\omega_0\beta_0 & -h_{11}(\tau) & -h_{12}(\tau) \\ i\dot{\alpha}_0/\omega_0 & i\dot{\beta}_0 & -h_{12}(\tau) & -h_{22}(\tau) \end{pmatrix}, \qquad (A52)$$

where the elements are functions of the final time τ and the functions $h_{11}(\tau)$, $h_{12}(\tau)$ and $h_{22}(\tau)$ are

$$h_{11}(\tau) = \frac{2m_0\omega_0}{\Xi} \tan\left(\frac{\omega_0\hbar\nu}{2}\right) \mathbf{v}_{q_0}^{\mathrm{T}}(\tau)\mathbf{A}^{-1}\mathbf{v}_{q_0}(\tau), \qquad (A53)$$

$$h_{22}(\tau) = \frac{2}{m_0\omega_0\Xi} \tan\left(\frac{\omega_0\hbar\nu}{2}\right) \mathbf{v}_{p_0}^{\mathrm{T}}(\tau)\mathbf{A}^{-1}\mathbf{v}_{p_0}(\tau), \qquad (A54)$$

$$h_{12}(\tau) = \frac{2}{\Xi} \tan\left(\frac{\omega_0\hbar\nu}{2}\right) \mathbf{v}_{q_0}^{\mathrm{T}}(\tau)\mathbf{A}^{-1}\mathbf{v}_{p_0}(\tau), \qquad (A55)$$

with

$$\mathbf{v}_{q_0}^{\mathrm{T}}(t)\mathbf{A}^{-1}\mathbf{v}_{q_0}(t) = \frac{\alpha_0^2 + \omega_0^2\beta_0^2}{2m_0\omega_0\left\{\tanh\left[\frac{(\beta'+i\nu)\hbar\omega_0}{2}\right] - i\tan\left(\frac{\omega_0\hbar\nu}{2}\right)\right\}} + \sum_{n=1}^{N}\left(\frac{\alpha_n^2}{\theta_n} + \frac{1}{\mu_n}\frac{\beta_n^2}{m_n^2}\right), \qquad (A56)$$

$$\mathbf{v}_{p_0}^{\mathrm{T}}(t)\mathbf{A}^{-1}\mathbf{v}_{p_0}(t) = \frac{m_0(\dot{\alpha}_0^2 + \omega_0^2\dot{\beta}_0^2)}{2\omega_0\left\{\tanh\left[\frac{(\beta'+i\nu)\hbar\omega_0}{2}\right] - i\tan\left(\frac{\omega_0\hbar\nu}{2}\right)\right\}} + m_0^2\sum_{n=1}^{N}\left(\frac{\dot{\alpha}_n^2}{\theta_n} + \frac{1}{\mu_n}\frac{\dot{\beta}_n^2}{m_n^2}\right), \qquad (A57)$$

$$\mathbf{v}_{q_0}^{\mathrm{T}}(t)\mathbf{A}^{-1}\mathbf{v}_{p_0}(t) = \frac{\frac{d}{dt}(\alpha_0^2 + \omega_0^2\beta_0^2)}{4\omega_0\left\{\tanh\left[\frac{(\beta'+i\nu)\hbar\omega_0}{2}\right] - i\tan\left(\frac{\omega_0\hbar\nu}{2}\right)\right\}} + \frac{m_0}{2}\sum_{n=1}^{N}\frac{d}{dt}\left(\frac{\alpha_n^2}{\theta_n} + \frac{1}{\mu_n}\frac{\beta_n^2}{m_n^2}\right). \qquad (A58)$$

The summations are replaced by the integral with the Ohmic spectral density and every element in Equation (A52) is carried out as

$$\alpha_0(\tau) = e^{-\frac{\kappa\tau}{2}}\left[\cos(\hat{\omega}_0\tau) + \frac{\kappa\sin(\hat{\omega}_0\tau)}{2\hat{\omega}_0}\right], \tag{A59}$$

$$\beta_0(\tau) = \frac{e^{-\frac{\kappa\tau}{2}}\sin(\hat{\omega}_0\tau)}{\hat{\omega}_0}, \tag{A60}$$

$$h_{11}(\tau) = \Theta + e^{-\kappa\tau}\left[\frac{\omega_0^2}{\hat{\omega}_0^2} + \frac{\kappa\sin(2\hat{\omega}_0\tau)}{2\hat{\omega}_0} - \frac{\kappa^2\cos(2\hat{\omega}_0\tau)}{4\hat{\omega}_0^2}\right](1-\Theta), \tag{A61}$$

$$h_{22}(\tau) = \Theta + e^{-\kappa\tau}\left[\frac{\omega_0^2}{\hat{\omega}_0^2} - \frac{\kappa\sin(2\hat{\omega}_0\tau)}{2\hat{\omega}_0} - \frac{\kappa^2\cos(2\hat{\omega}_0\tau)}{4\hat{\omega}_0^2}\right](1-\Theta), \tag{A62}$$

$$h_{12}(\tau) = \frac{\kappa\omega_0 e^{-\kappa\tau}}{2\hat{\omega}_0^2}(\Theta-1)[1-\cos(2\hat{\omega}_0\tau)]. \tag{A63}$$

Then, Equation (17) is obtained by directly calculating the determinant of a 4×4 matrix in Equation (A49).

Appendix B. Classical Caldeira–Leggett Model

We consider the classical Caldeira–Leggett model, where coordinates and momenta commute with each other. To eliminate the initial slippage, the initial state is amended as a coupled state,

$$\rho^{\text{cl}}(\mathbf{z};0) = \frac{e^{-\beta' H_S(0) - \beta[H_B(0) + H_{SB}(0)]}}{Z^{\text{cl}}(\beta',\beta)}, \tag{A64}$$

which represents the probability density in the phase space of the composite system. The classical partition function is obtained by performing the integral in the phase space

$$Z^{\text{cl}}(\beta',\beta) = \iint e^{-\beta' H_S(0) - \beta[H_B(0) + H_{SB}(0)]} dq_0 dq_1 ... dq_N dp_0 dp_1 ... dp_N \tag{A65}$$

$$= \frac{2\pi}{\beta'\omega_0}\prod_{n=1}^{N}\left(\frac{2\pi}{\beta\omega_n}\right), \tag{A66}$$

which is independent of the interaction (notice that the partition function of the quantum model relies on the interaction strength [68,87]).

We also define the classical fluctuating heat as the energy difference of the initial and the final system energy. For classical dynamics, the initial and the final states are directly represented by the points in the phase space and the measurements over the system can be applied without disturbing the composite system. Therefore, the characteristic function of heat is

$$\chi_\tau^{\text{cl}}(\nu) = \frac{\iint e^{i\nu H_S(\tau) - (\beta' + i\nu)H_S(0) - \beta[H_B(0) + H_{SB}(0)]} dq_0 dq_1 ... dq_N dp_0 dp_1 ... dp_N}{Z^{\text{cl}}(\beta',\beta)}, \tag{A67}$$

where the energy of the system $H_S(t) = [p_0(t)]^2/(2m_0) + m_0\omega_0^2[q_0(t)]^2/2$ is determined by $p_0(t)$ and $q_0(t)$ associated with the initial point $\mathbf{z}$. We choose a new set of initial variables q_0, $\mathfrak{q}_n := q_n - C_n q_0/(m_n\omega_n^2)$, p_0 and p_n in the following calculation.

We rewrite the evolution of the coordinate $q_0(t)$ of the system Equation (A16) as

$$(s^2 + \kappa s + \omega_0^2)\tilde{q}_0(s) = \dot{q}_0(0) + \left(s + \sum_n \frac{C_n^2}{m_0 m_n \omega_n^2}\frac{s}{s^2 + \omega_n^2}\right)q_0(0) + \sum_n \frac{C_n}{m_0}\frac{\dot{\mathfrak{q}}_n(0) + s\mathfrak{q}_n}{s^2 + \omega_n^2}. \tag{A68}$$

For the Ohmic spectral density, the summation in the second term is

$$\sum_n \frac{c_n^2}{m_0 m_n \omega_n^2} \frac{s}{s^2 + \omega_n^2} = \kappa. \tag{A69}$$

Thus, Equation (A68) naturally leads to Equation (A19) by substituting $q_n(0)$ into q_n. The initial slippage is rationally eliminated by choosing a coupled initial state Equation (A64). In reality, the interaction between the system and the heat bath always exists and one cannot prepare the initial state of the composite system without the influence of the interaction. The initial state of the composite system is more likely in the coupled form Equation (A64). The heat bath encodes partial information of the system due to the interaction.

Similar to Equation (A10), the system energy at time t can be represented by the dynamical map as

$$H_S(t) = \frac{1}{2} \mathbf{z}^\mathsf{T}(t) \mathbf{\Lambda}_{H_S} \mathbf{z}(t) \tag{A70}$$

$$= \frac{1}{2} \mathbf{z}^\mathsf{T}(0) \tilde{\mathbf{\Lambda}}_{H_S}(t) \mathbf{z}(0), \tag{A71}$$

with the following matrices [88]

$$\mathbf{\Lambda}_{H_S} = \begin{pmatrix} m_0 \omega_0^2 & & \mathbf{0} \\ & & \\ & \frac{1}{m_0} & \\ \mathbf{0} & & \end{pmatrix}, \tag{A72}$$

and

$$\tilde{\mathbf{\Lambda}}_{H_S}(t) = \exp(\mathbf{L}^\mathsf{T} t) \mathbf{\Lambda}_{H_S} \exp(\mathbf{L} t). \tag{A73}$$

The initial vector is now amended to

$$\mathbf{z}(0) = (q_0(0), q_1, ..., q_n, p_0(0), ..., p_N(0))^\mathsf{T}. \tag{A74}$$

The initial Hamiltonians $H_S(0)$ and $H_B(0) + H_{SB}(0)$ are

$$H_S(0) = \frac{1}{2} \mathbf{z}^\mathsf{T}(0) \mathbf{\Lambda}_{H_S} \mathbf{z}(0), \tag{A75}$$

$$H_B(0) + H_{SB}(0) = \sum_{n=1}^{N} \left(\frac{1}{2} \frac{p_n^2}{m_n} + \frac{1}{2} m_n \omega_n^2 q_n^2 \right)$$

$$= \frac{1}{2} \mathbf{z}^\mathsf{T}(0) \mathbf{\Lambda}_{H_B} \mathbf{z}(0), \tag{A76}$$

with the matrix

$$\mathbf{\Lambda}_{H_B} = \mathrm{diag}(0, m_1 \omega_1^2, ..., m_N \omega_N^2, 0, \frac{1}{m_1}, ..., \frac{1}{m_N}). \tag{A77}$$

According to the integral Formula (A42), we carry out the characteristic function Equation (A67) into

$$\chi_\tau^{\mathrm{cl}}(\nu) = \sqrt{\frac{\det[\beta' \mathbf{\Lambda}_{H_S} + \beta \mathbf{\Lambda}_{H_B}]}{\det[\beta' \mathbf{\Lambda}_{H_S} + \beta \mathbf{\Lambda}_{H_B} - i\nu(\tilde{\mathbf{\Lambda}}_{H_S}(\tau) - \mathbf{\Lambda}_{H_S})]}}. \tag{A78}$$

For the classical limit $\hbar \to 0$, we can verify

$$\lim_{\hbar \to 0} \frac{\Lambda_{\beta z}}{\hbar} = (\beta' + i\nu)\Lambda_{H_S} + \beta \Lambda_{H_B}, \tag{A79}$$

$$\lim_{\hbar \to 0} \frac{\Lambda_{\nu z}}{\hbar} = \nu \Lambda_{H_S}, \tag{A80}$$

$$\lim_{\hbar \to 0} \frac{\tilde{\Lambda}_{\nu z}(t)}{\hbar} = \nu \tilde{\Lambda}_{H_S}(t), \tag{A81}$$

and obtain

$$\lim_{\hbar \to 0} \chi_\tau(\nu) = \chi_\tau^{\text{cl}}(\nu), \tag{A82}$$

with $\chi_\tau(\nu)$ given in Equation (A41). The final result Equation (A78) is the same as Equation (25). Hence, we use the same notation.

Appendix C. The Characteristic Function of Heat for the Classical Brownian Motion

We derive the characteristic function of heat for the classical Brownian motion. For an underdamped Brownian particle moving in a potential $V(x)$, the stochastic dynamics is described by the complete Langevin equation

$$\ddot{x} + \kappa \dot{x} + \frac{1}{m}\frac{\partial V}{\partial x} = \frac{1}{m} F_{\text{fluc}}(t). \tag{A83}$$

The fluctuating force $F_{\text{fluc}}(t)$ is a Gaussian white noise satisfying the fluctuation–dissipation relation

$$\langle F_{\text{fluc}}(t) F_{\text{fluc}}(t') \rangle = 2m\kappa k_B T \delta(t - t'). \tag{A84}$$

The evolution of the system state is characterized by the probability density function $\rho(x, p; t)$ in the phase space. The stochastic dynamics is then described by the Kramers equation [86]

$$\frac{\partial \rho}{\partial t} = \mathscr{L}[\rho], \tag{A85}$$

with the Liouville operator

$$\mathscr{L}[\rho] = -\frac{\partial}{\partial x}\left(\frac{p}{m}\rho\right) + \frac{\partial}{\partial p}\left[\kappa p \rho + \frac{\partial V(x)}{\partial x}\rho + \frac{\kappa m}{\beta}\frac{\partial \rho}{\partial p}\right]. \tag{A86}$$

Similarly, in the phase space, we calculate the characteristic function of heat for the classical Brownian motion

$$\chi_\tau^{\text{cl}}(\nu) = \iint dx\, dp\, e^{i\nu\left[\frac{p^2}{2m} + V(x)\right]} \eta(x, p; \tau), \tag{A87}$$

where a probability-density-like function $\eta(x, p; t)$ also satisfies the dynamic Equation (A85) with the initial condition

$$\eta(x, p; 0) = e^{-i\nu\left[\frac{p^2}{2m} + V(x)\right]} \rho(x, p; 0). \tag{A88}$$

We consider the system potential as a harmonic potential $V(x) = m\omega_0^2 x^2 / 2$ and the initial system state as an equilibrium state

$$\rho(x, p; 0) = \frac{1}{Z_S^{\text{cl}}(\beta')} e^{-\beta'\left(\frac{p^2}{2m} + \frac{1}{2}m\omega_0^2 x^2\right)}, \tag{A89}$$

with the inverse temperature β' and the classical partition function $Z_S^{cl}(\beta') = 2\pi/(\beta'\omega_0)$. Under such conditions, the probability-density-like function $\eta(x, p; t)$ is always in a quadratic form, assumed as

$$\eta(x, p; t) = \frac{1}{Z_S^{cl}(\beta')} e^{-\left[a(t)\frac{p^2}{2m} + b(t)\frac{1}{2}m\omega_0^2 x^2 + c(t)\omega_0 x p + \Lambda(t)\right]}. \tag{A90}$$

The Kramers Equation (A85) for $\eta(x, p; t)$ leads to the following ordinary differential equations:

$$\dot{\Lambda} = -\kappa\left(1 - \frac{a}{\beta}\right), \tag{A91}$$

$$\dot{a} = 2\kappa a\left(1 - \frac{a}{\beta}\right) - 2\omega_0 c, \tag{A92}$$

$$\dot{b} = 2c\left(\omega_0 - \frac{\kappa}{\beta}c\right), \tag{A93}$$

$$\dot{c} = \omega_0(a - b) + \kappa c - 2\frac{\kappa}{\beta}ac, \tag{A94}$$

with the initial conditions $a(0) = b(0) = \beta' + i\nu$, $c(0) = 0$ and $\Lambda(0) = 0$. According to the conservation of the probability $\iint \eta(x, p; t) dx dp = \text{const}$, the coefficient $\Lambda(t)$ is obtained as

$$e^{-\Lambda(t)} = \frac{\sqrt{a(t)b(t) - c(t)^2}}{\beta' + i\nu}. \tag{A95}$$

Substituting Equation (A90) into Equation (A87), we obtain the characteristic function for the classical Brownian motion as

$$\chi_\tau^{cl}(\nu) = \frac{\beta'}{\beta' + i\nu}\sqrt{\frac{a(\tau)b(\tau) - c(\tau)^2}{[a(\tau) - i\nu][b(\tau) - i\nu] - c(\tau)^2}}. \tag{A96}$$

To solve the nonlinear differential Equations (A92)–(A94), we introduce a new set of variables,

$$A = \frac{a}{ab - c^2}, \tag{A97}$$

$$B = \frac{b}{ab - c^2}, \tag{A98}$$

$$C = \frac{c}{ab - c^2}, \tag{A99}$$

and obtain the linear differential equations

$$\frac{dA}{dt} = -2\omega_0 C, \tag{A100}$$

$$\frac{dB}{dt} = 2\omega_0 C - 2\kappa B + 2\frac{\kappa}{\beta}, \tag{A101}$$

$$\frac{dC}{dt} = \omega_0(A - B) - \kappa C, \tag{A102}$$

with the initial conditions $A(0) = B(0) = 1/(\beta' + i\nu)$ and $C(0) = 0$. The characteristic function Equation (A96) becomes

$$\chi_\tau^{cl}(\nu) = \frac{\beta'}{\beta' + i\nu} \sqrt{\frac{1}{1 - i\nu(A + B) - \nu^2(AB - C^2)}}. \tag{A103}$$

The solutions to Equations (A100)–(A102) are

$$A(t) = -\frac{e^{-\kappa t}[\kappa^2 \cos(2\hat{\omega}_0 t) - 2\hat{\omega}_0 \kappa \sin(2\hat{\omega}_0 t) - 4\omega_0^2]}{4\beta \hat{\omega}_0^2} \frac{\beta - \beta' - i\nu}{\beta' + i\nu} + \frac{1}{\beta'}, \tag{A104}$$

$$B(t) = -\frac{e^{-\kappa t}[\kappa^2 \cos(2\hat{\omega}_0 t) + 2\hat{\omega}_0 \kappa \sin(2\hat{\omega}_0 t) - 4\omega_0^2]}{4\beta \hat{\omega}_0^2} \frac{\beta - \beta' - i\nu}{\beta' + i\nu} + \frac{1}{\beta'}, \tag{A105}$$

$$C(t) = -\frac{2e^{-\kappa t}\kappa \omega_0[\cos(2\hat{\omega}_0 t) - 1]}{4\beta \hat{\omega}_0^2} \frac{\beta - \beta' - i\nu}{\beta' + i\nu}, \tag{A106}$$

with $\hat{\omega}_0 = \sqrt{\omega_0^2 - \kappa^2/4}$. Plugging the solutions into Equation (A103), we immediately obtain Equation (25). We remark that the heat distribution of the classical Brownian motion was obtained by the path-integral method in Ref. [58], but they only consider the initial temperature of the system to be the same as that of the bath.

Appendix C.1. The Long-Time Limit

After sufficiently long relaxation time, the solutions $a(t)$, $b(t)$ and $c(t)$ to Equations (A92)–(A94) eventually approach $a(\infty) = b(\infty) = \beta$ and $c(\infty) = 0$. The long-time limit of Equation (A96) reproduces Equation (33).

Appendix C.2. The Underdamped Limit

In the underdamped limit $\kappa/\omega_0 \to 0$, the differential Equations (A92)–(A94) are reduced to

$$\dot{a} = \kappa a\left(1 - \frac{a}{\beta}\right), \tag{A107}$$

with $b = a$ and $c = 0$. The solution is

$$a(t) = \frac{\beta(\beta' + i\nu)}{\beta' + i\nu + (\beta - \beta' - i\nu)e^{-\kappa t}}, \tag{A108}$$

and Equation (A96) becomes

$$\chi_\tau^{w,cl}(\nu) = \frac{\beta \beta'}{(\beta - i\nu)(\beta' + i\nu)(1 - e^{-\kappa \tau}) + \beta \beta' e^{-\kappa \tau}}. \tag{A109}$$

It can be checked that Equation (37) reproduces Equation (A109) in the classical limit $\hbar \to 0$.

Appendix C.3. The Overdamped Limit

In the overdamped limit $\kappa/\omega_0 \to \infty$, the differential Equations (A92)–(A94) are reduced to

$$\dot{a} = 2\kappa a\left(1 - \frac{a}{\beta}\right), \tag{A110}$$

$$\dot{b} = 2\omega_0 c\left(1 - \frac{\kappa}{\beta \omega_0}c\right), \tag{A111}$$

$$0 = (\kappa c + \omega_0 a) - 2\frac{\kappa}{\beta}ac - b\omega_0. \tag{A112}$$

Eliminating c in Equation (A112), Equation (A111) becomes

$$\dot{b} = \frac{2\omega_0^2}{\kappa} \frac{(\beta - a - b)(b - a)}{(\beta - 2a)\left(1 - 2\frac{a}{\beta}\right)}. \tag{A113}$$

Notice that, in the overdamped limit, the relaxation timescales of the momentum and the coordinate are separated. We can substitute $a = \beta$ in Equation (A113) and obtain

$$\dot{b} = \frac{2\omega_0^2}{\kappa} b \left(1 - \frac{b}{\beta}\right). \tag{A114}$$

With the initial condition $a(0) = \beta' + i\nu$ and $b(0) = \beta' + i\nu$, the solutions are

$$a(t) = \frac{(\beta' + i\nu)\beta}{\beta' + i\nu + (\beta - \beta' - i\nu)e^{-2\kappa t}}, \tag{A115}$$

$$b(t) = \frac{(\beta' + i\nu)\beta}{\beta' + i\nu + (\beta - \beta' - i\nu)e^{-\frac{2\omega_0^2}{\kappa}t}}. \tag{A116}$$

We substitute Equations (A115), (A116) and $c(t) \approx 0$ into Equation (A96) and obtain

$$\chi_\tau^{s,cl}(\nu) = \frac{\beta\beta'}{\sqrt{(\beta - i\nu)(\beta' + i\nu)(1 - e^{-2\kappa\tau}) + \beta\beta'e^{-2\kappa\tau}}}$$
$$\times \frac{1}{\sqrt{(\beta - i\nu)(\beta' + i\nu)\left(1 - e^{-\frac{2\omega_0^2}{\kappa}\tau}\right) + \beta\beta'e^{-\frac{2\omega_0^2}{\kappa}\tau}}}. \tag{A117}$$

It can be checked that Equation (38) reproduces Equation (A117) in the classical limit $\hbar \to 0$.

Appendix D. The Characteristic Function of Heat for Complete Thermalization

We derive the characteristic function of heat for a complete thermalization process, Equation (34), in the main content. For a complete thermalization process (typically with infinite relaxation time), the information of the initial state is completely forgotten and the final state is always an equilibrium state at the inverse temperature β of the heat bath,

$$\gamma_{th,l'l} = p_{l'}^{eq}, \tag{A118}$$

regardless of the initial state l. Therefore, the characteristic function of heat for complete thermalization is $\chi_{th}(\nu) = \sum_{l',l} \exp[i\nu(E_{l'}^S - E_l^S)]p_l p_{l'}^{eq}$. We immediately obtain Equation (34) by plugging into the initial distribution $p_l = \exp(-\beta' E_l^S)/Z_S(\beta')$ and the final distribution $p_{l'}^{eq} = \exp(-\beta E_{l'}^S)/Z_S(\beta)$, where $Z_S(\beta') = \sum_l \exp(-\beta' E_l^S)$ is the partition function of the system at the inverse temperature β'.

References and Notes

1. Gallavotti, G.; Cohen, E.G.D. Dynamical Ensembles in Nonequilibrium Statistical Mechanics. *Phys. Rev. Lett.* **1995**, *74*, 2694–2697. [CrossRef] [PubMed]
2. Jarzynski, C. Nonequilibrium Equality for Free Energy Differences. *Phys. Rev. Lett.* **1997**, *78*, 2690–2693. [CrossRef]
3. Crooks, G.E. Entropy production fluctuation theorem and the nonequilibrium work relation for free energy differences. *Phys. Rev. E* **1999**, *60*, 2721–2726. [CrossRef] [PubMed]
4. Jarzynski, C.; Wójcik, D.K. Classical and Quantum Fluctuation Theorems for Heat Exchange. *Phys. Rev. Lett.* **2004**, *92*, 230602. [CrossRef]
5. Jarzynski, C. Equalities and Inequalities: Irreversibility and the Second Law of Thermodynamics at the Nanoscale. *Annu. Rev. Condens. Matter Phys.* **2011**, *2*, 329–351. [CrossRef]
6. Sekimoto, K. *Stochastic Energetics*; Springer: Berlin/Heidelberg, Germany, 2010. [CrossRef]
7. Seifert, U. Stochastic thermodynamics, fluctuation theorems and molecular machines. *Rep. Prog. Phys.* **2012**, *75*, 126001. [CrossRef] [PubMed]

8. Seifert, U. Entropy Production along a Stochastic Trajectory and an Integral Fluctuation Theorem. *Phys. Rev. Lett.* **2005**, *95*, 040602. [CrossRef] [PubMed]
9. Esposito, M.; Harbola, U.; Mukamel, S. Nonequilibrium fluctuations, fluctuation theorems, and counting statistics in quantum systems. *Rev. Mod. Phys.* **2009**, *81*, 1665–1702. [CrossRef]
10. Campisi, M.; Hänggi, P.; Talkner, P. Colloquium: Quantum fluctuation relations: Foundations and applications. *Rev. Mod. Phys.* **2011**, *83*, 771–791. [CrossRef]
11. Klages, R. *Nonequilibrium Statistical Physics of Small Systems: Fluctuation Relations and Beyond*; Wiley-VCH: Weinheim, Germany, 2013.
12. Horodecki, M.; Oppenheim, J. Fundamental limitations for quantum and nanoscale thermodynamics. *Nat Commun* **2013**, *4*, 2059. [CrossRef]
13. Ciliberto, S. Experiments in Stochastic Thermodynamics: Short History and Perspectives. *Phys. Rev. X* **2017**, *7*, 021051. [CrossRef]
14. Tasaki, H. Jarzynski Relations for Quantum Systems and Some Applications. *arXiv* **2000**, arXiv:cond-mat.stat-mech/cond-mat/0009244.
15. Kurchan, J. A Quantum Fluctuation Theorem. *arXiv* **2000**, arXiv: cond-mat.stat-mech/cond-mat/0007360
16. Talkner, P.; Lutz, E.; Hänggi, P. Fluctuation theorems: Work is not an observable. *Phys. Rev. E* **2007**, *75*, 050102. [CrossRef] [PubMed]
17. Deffner, S.; Lutz, E. Nonequilibrium work distribution of a quantum harmonic oscillator. *Phys. Rev. E* **2008**, *77*, 021128. [CrossRef] [PubMed]
18. Liu, F. Calculating work in adiabatic two-level quantum Markovian master equations: A characteristic function method. *Phys. Rev. E* **2014**, *90*, 032121. [CrossRef] [PubMed]
19. Zhu, L.; Gong, Z.; Wu, B.; Quan, H.T. Quantum-classical correspondence principle for work distributions in a chaotic system. *Phys. Rev. E* **2016**, *93*, 062108. [CrossRef]
20. Funo, K.; Quan, H. Path Integral Approach to Quantum Thermodynamics. *Phys. Rev. Lett.* **2018**, *121*, 040602. [CrossRef]
21. Salazar, D.S.P.; Lira, S.A. Stochastic thermodynamics of nonharmonic oscillators in high vacuum. *Phys. Rev. E* **2019**, *99*, 062119. [CrossRef]
22. Jarzynski, C.; Quan, H.; Rahav, S. Quantum-Classical Correspondence Principle for Work Distributions. *Phys. Rev. X* **2015**, *5*, 031038. [CrossRef]
23. Deffner, S.; Paz, J.P.; Zurek, W.H. Quantum work and the thermodynamic cost of quantum measurements. *Phys. Rev. E* **2016**, *94*, 010103(R). [CrossRef]
24. García-Mata, I.; Roncaglia, A.J.; Wisniacki, D.A. Quantum-to-classical transition in the work distribution for chaotic systems. *Phys. Rev. E* **2017**, *95*, 050102. [CrossRef]
25. Fei, Z.; Quan, H. Nonequilibrium Green's Function's Approach to the Calculation of Work Statistics. *Phys. Rev. Lett.* **2020**, *124*, 240603. [CrossRef] [PubMed]
26. Qiu, T.; Fei, Z.; Pan, R.; Quan, H.T. Path-integral approach to the calculation of the characteristic function of work. *Phys. Rev. E* **2020**, *101*, 032111. [CrossRef] [PubMed]
27. Zurek, W.H. Decoherence and the Transition from Quantum to Classical. *Phys. Today* **1991**, *44*, 36–44. [CrossRef]
28. Zurek, W.H. Decoherence, einselection, and the quantum origins of the classical. *Rev. Mod. Phys.* **2003**, *75*, 715–775. [CrossRef]
29. Saito, K.; Dhar, A. Fluctuation Theorem in Quantum Heat Conduction. *Phys. Rev. Lett.* **2007**, *99*, 180601. [CrossRef] [PubMed]
30. Dubi, Y.; Ventra, M.D. Colloquium: Heat flow and thermoelectricity in atomic and molecular junctions. *Rev. Mod. Phys.* **2011**, *83*, 131–155. [CrossRef]
31. Thingna, J.; García-Palacios, J.L.; Wang, J.S. Steady-state thermal transport in anharmonic systems: Application to molecular junctions. *Phys. Rev. B* **2012**, *85*, 195452. [CrossRef]
32. Wang, J.S.; Agarwalla, B.K.; Li, H.; Thingna, J. Nonequilibrium Green's function method for quantum thermal transport. *Front. Phys.* **2014**, *9*, 673–697. [CrossRef]
33. Thingna, J.; Manzano, D.; Cao, J. Dynamical signatures of molecular symmetries in nonequilibrium quantum transport. *Sci. Rep.* **2016**, *6*, 28027. [CrossRef]
34. He, D.; Thingna, J.; Wang, J.S.; Li, B. Quantum thermal transport through anharmonic systems: A self-consistent approach. *Phys. Rev. B* **2016**, *94*, 155411. [CrossRef]
35. Segal, D.; Agarwalla, B.K. Vibrational Heat Transport in Molecular Junctions. *Ann. Phys. Chem.* **2016**, *67*, 185–209. [CrossRef]
36. Kilgour, M.; Agarwalla, B.K.; Segal, D. Path-integral methodology and simulations of quantum thermal transport: Full counting statistics approach. *J. Chem. Phys.* **2019**, *150*, 084111. [CrossRef]
37. Wang, C.; Ren, J.; Cao, J. Unifying quantum heat transfer in a nonequilibrium spin-boson model with full counting statistics. *Phys. Rev. A* **2017**, *95*, 023610. [CrossRef]
38. Aurell, E.; Donvil, B.; Mallick, K. Large deviations and fluctuation theorem for the quantum heat current in the spin-boson model. *Phys. Rev. E* **2020**, *101*, 052116. [CrossRef] [PubMed]
39. Denzler, T.; Lutz, E. Heat distribution of a quantum harmonic oscillator. *Phys. Rev. E* **2018**, *98*, 052106. [CrossRef]
40. Salazar, D.S.P.; Macêdo, A.M.S.; Vasconcelos, G.L. Quantum heat distribution in thermal relaxation processes. *Phys. Rev. E* **2019**, *99*, 022133. [CrossRef]

41. Popovic, M.; Mitchison, M.T.; Strathearn, A.; Lovett, B.W.; Goold, J.; Eastham, P.R. Quantum Heat Statistics with Time-Evolving Matrix Product Operators. *PRX Quantum* **2021**, *2*, 020338. [CrossRef]
42. Karsten Balzer, M.B. *Nonequilibrium Green's Functions Approach to Inhomogeneous Systems*; Springer: Berlin Heidelberg, 2012.
43. Esposito, M.; Ochoa, M.A.; Galperin, M. Quantum Thermodynamics: A Nonequilibrium Green's Function Approach. *Phys. Rev. Lett.* **2015**, *114*, 080602. [CrossRef] [PubMed]
44. Polanco, C.A. Nonequilibrium Green's functions (NEGF) in vibrational energy transport: a topical review. *Nanoscale Microscale Thermophys. Eng.* **2021**, *25*, 1–24. [CrossRef]
45. Aron, C.; Biroli, G.; Cugliandolo, L.F. Symmetries of generating functionals of Langevin processes with colored multiplicative noise. *J. Stat. Mech.* **2010**, *2010*, P11018. [CrossRef]
46. Mallick, K.; Moshe, M.; Orland, H. A field-theoretic approach to non-equilibrium work identities. *J. Phys. A* **2011**, *44*, 095002. [CrossRef]
47. Carrega, M.; Solinas, P.; Braggio, A.; Sassetti, M.; Weiss, U. Functional integral approach to time-dependent heat exchange in open quantum systems: general method and applications. *New J. Phys.* **2015**, *17*, 045030. [CrossRef]
48. Funo, K.; Quan, H.T. Path integral approach to heat in quantum thermodynamics. *Phys. Rev. E* **2018**, *98*, 012113. [CrossRef] [PubMed]
49. Yeo, J. Symmetry and its breaking in a path-integral approach to quantum Brownian motion. *Phys. Rev. E* **2019**, *100*, 062107. [CrossRef]
50. Fogedby, H.C. Heat fluctuations in equilibrium. *J. Stat. Mech. Theory Exp.* **2020**, *2020*, 083208. [CrossRef]
51. van Zon, R.; Cohen, E.G.D. Extended heat-fluctuation theorems for a system with deterministic and stochastic forces. *Phys. Rev. E* **2004**, *69*, 056121. [CrossRef]
52. Imparato, A.; Peliti, L.; Pesce, G.; Rusciano, G.; Sasso, A. Work and heat probability distribution of an optically driven Brownian particle: Theory and experiments. *Phys. Rev. E* **2007**, *76*, 050101. [CrossRef]
53. Fogedby, H.C.; Imparato, A. Heat distribution function for motion in a general potential at low temperature. *J. Phys. A Math. Theor.* **2009**, *42*, 475004. [CrossRef]
54. Chatterjee, D.; Cherayil, B.J. Exact path-integral evaluation of the heat distribution function of a trapped Brownian oscillator. *Phys. Rev. E* **2010**, *82*, 051104. [CrossRef]
55. Gomez-Solano, J.R.; Petrosyan, A.; Ciliberto, S. Heat Fluctuations in a Nonequilibrium Bath. *Phys. Rev. Lett.* **2011**, *106*, 200602. [CrossRef]
56. Salazar, D.S.P.; Lira, S.A. Exactly solvable nonequilibrium Langevin relaxation of a trapped nanoparticle. *J. Phys. A Math. Theor.* **2016**, *49*, 465001. [CrossRef]
57. Pagare, A.; Cherayil, B.J. Stochastic thermodynamics of a harmonically trapped colloid in linear mixed flow. *Phys. Rev. E* **2019**, *100*, 052124. [CrossRef] [PubMed]
58. Paraguassú, P.V.; Aquino, R.; Morgado, W.A.M. The Heat Distribution of the Underdamped Langevin Equation *arXiv* **2021**. arXiv:cond-mat.stat-mech/2102.09115
59. Gupta, D.; Sivak, D.A. Heat fluctuations in a harmonic chain of active particles. *Phys. Rev. E* **2021**, *104*, 024605. [CrossRef]
60. Esposito, M.; Ochoa, M.A.; Galperin, M. Nature of heat in strongly coupled open quantum systems. *Phys. Rev. B* **2015**, *92*, 235440. [CrossRef]
61. Talkner, P.; Hänggi, P. Open system trajectories specify fluctuating work but not heat. *Phys. Rev. E* **2016**, *94*, 022143. [CrossRef] [PubMed]
62. Talkner, P.; Hänggi, P. Colloquium : Statistical mechanics and thermodynamics at strong coupling: Quantum and classical. *Rev. Mod. Phys.* **2020**, *92*, 041002. [CrossRef]
63. Bez, W. Microscopic preparation and macroscopic motion of a Brownian particle. *Z. Phys. B* **1980**, *39*, 319–325. [CrossRef]
64. Caldeira, A.; Leggett, A. Path integral approach to quantum Brownian motion. *Phys. A* **1983**, *121*, 587–616. [CrossRef]
65. Caldeira, A.; Leggett, A. Quantum tunnelling in a dissipative system. *Ann. Phys.* **1983**, *149*, 374–456. [CrossRef]
66. Unruh, W.G.; Zurek, W.H. Reduction of a wave packet in quantum Brownian motion. *Phys. Rev. D* **1989**, *40*, 1071–1094. [CrossRef] [PubMed]
67. Breuer, H.P.; Petruccione, F. *The Theory of Open Quantum Systems*; Oxford University Press: Oxford, UK, 2007. [CrossRef]
68. Weiss, U. *Quantum Dissipative Systems*; World Scientific Publishing Company: Singapore, 2008.
69. Usually the quantum fluctuating heat is defined via two-point measurements over the heat bath. When the Hamiltonian of the system is time-independent, the internal energy change of the system is completely caused by the heat exchange. The quantum fluctuating heat can thus be alternatively defined via two-point measurements over the system, whose number of degrees of freedom is much smaller than that of the heat bath. Hence, the calculation of the heat statistics can be significantly simplified under this definition.
70. Yu, L.H.; Sun, C.P. Evolution of the wave function in a dissipative system. *Phys. Rev. A* **1994**, *49*, 592–595. [CrossRef]
71. Wigner, E. On the Quantum Correction For Thermodynamic Equilibrium. *Phys. Rev.* **1932**, *40*, 749–759. [CrossRef]
72. Hillery, M.; O'Connell, R.; Scully, M.; Wigner, E. Distribution functions in physics: Fundamentals. *Phys. Rep.* **1984**, *106*, 121–167. [CrossRef]
73. Polkovnikov, A. Phase space representation of quantum dynamics. *Ann. Phys.* **2010**, *325*, 1790–1852. [CrossRef]

74. Fei, Z.; Quan, H.T.; Liu, F. Quantum corrections of work statistics in closed quantum systems. *Phys. Rev. E* **2018**, *98*, 012132. [CrossRef]
75. Qian, Y.; Liu, F. Computing characteristic functions of quantum work in phase space. *Phys. Rev. E* **2019**, *100*, 062119. [CrossRef]
76. Brodier, O.; Mallick, K.; de Almeida, A.M.O. Semiclassical work and quantum work identities in Weyl representation. *J. Phys. A Math. Theor.* **2020**, *53*, 325001. [CrossRef]
77. Qiu, T.; Fei, Z.; Pan, R.; Quan, H.T. Quantum corrections to the entropy and its application in the study of quantum Carnot engines. *Phys. Rev. E* **2020**, *101*, 032113. [CrossRef]
78. Qiu, T.; Quan, H.T. Quantum corrections to the entropy in a driven quantum Brownian motion model. *Commun. Theor. Phys.* **2021**, *73*, 095602. [CrossRef]
79. Hu, B.L.; Paz, J.P.; Zhang, Y. Quantum Brownian motion in a general environment: Exact master equation with nonlocal dissipation and colored noise. *Phys. Rev. D* **1992**, *45*, 2843–2861. [CrossRef]
80. Karrlein, R.; Grabert, H. Exact time evolution and master equations for the damped harmonic oscillator. *Phys. Rev. E* **1997**, *55*, 153–164. [CrossRef]
81. Ford, G.W.; O'Connell, R.F. Exact solution of the Hu-Paz-Zhang master equation. *Phys. Rev. D* **2001**, *64*, 105020. [CrossRef]
82. Salazar, D.S.P. Work distribution in thermal processes. *Phys. Rev. E* **2020**, *101*, 030101. [CrossRef] [PubMed]
83. Chen, Y.H.; Chen, J.F.; Fei, Z.; Quan, H.T. A microscopic theory of Curzon-Ahlborn heat engine. *arXiv* **2021**, arXiv:cond-mat.stat-mech/2108.04128
84. Cañizares, J.S.; Sols, F. Translational symmetry and microscopic preparation in oscillator models of quantum dissipation. *Phys. A* **1994**, *212*, 181–193. [CrossRef]
85. Ju, K.K.; Guo, C.X.; Pan, X.Y. Initial-Slip Term Effects on the Dissipation-Induced Transition of a Simple Harmonic Oscillator. *Chin. Phys. Lett.* **2017**, *34*, 010301. [CrossRef]
86. Kramers, H.A. Brownian motion in a field of force and the diffusion model of chemical reactions. *Physica* **1940**, *7*, 284–304. [CrossRef]
87. Grabert, H.; Weiss, U.; Talkner, P. Quantum theory of the damped harmonic oscillator. *Z. Phys. B* **1984**, *55*, 87–94. [CrossRef]
88. Strictly, the substitution requires to amend $\gamma_n, \Lambda_{nm}, \xi_n, \Delta_{nm}$ accordingly, but we only require $q_0(t)$ and $p_0(t)$ to calculate the characteristic function of heat, so we skip the further amendment.

Article

Does Decoherence Select the Pointer Basis of a Quantum Meter?

Abraham G. Kofman * and Gershon Kurizki *

Department of Chemical and Biological Physics, Weizmann Institute of Science, Rehovot 761001, Israel
* Correspondence: kofmana@gmail.com or abraham.kofman@weizmann.ac.il (A.G.K.); gershon.kurizki@weizmann.ac.il (G.K.)

Abstract: The consensus regarding quantum measurements rests on two statements: (i) von Neumann's standard quantum measurement theory leaves undetermined the basis in which observables are measured, and (ii) the environmental decoherence of the measuring device (the "meter") unambiguously determines the measuring ("pointer") basis. The latter statement means that the environment *monitors* (measures) *selected* observables of the meter and (indirectly) of the system. Equivalently, a measured quantum state must end up in one of the "pointer states" that persist in the presence of the environment. We find that, unless we restrict ourselves to projective measurements, decoherence does not necessarily determine the pointer basis of the meter. Namely, generalized measurements commonly allow the observer to choose from a multitude of alternative pointer bases that provide the same information on the observables, regardless of decoherence. By contrast, the measured observable does not depend on the pointer basis, whether in the presence or in the absence of decoherence. These results grant further support to our notion of Quantum Lamarckism, whereby the observer's choices play an indispensable role in quantum mechanics.

Keywords: quantum measurements; decoherence; pointer states; Quantum Lamarckism; the observer in quantum mechanics

Citation: Kofman, A.G.; Kurizki, G. Does Decoherence Select the Pointer Basis of a Quantum Meter? *Entropy* **2022**, *24*, 106. https://doi.org/10.3390/e24010106

Academic Editors: Sebastian Deffner, Raymond Laflamme, Juan Pablo Paz and Michael Zwolak

Received: 13 December 2021
Accepted: 6 January 2022
Published: 10 January 2022

Publisher's Note: MDPI stays neutral with regard to jurisdictional claims in published maps and institutional affiliations.

Copyright: © 2022 by the authors. Licensee MDPI, Basel, Switzerland. This article is an open access article distributed under the terms and conditions of the Creative Commons Attribution (CC BY) license (https://creativecommons.org/licenses/by/4.0/).

1. Introduction

Attempts to banish the observer from quantum mechanics have motivated approaches [1–4] whereby the *environment observes* a quantum system. These approaches "objectivize" quantum measurement theory by substituting the environment-induced decoherence of a quantum observable for its unread (nonselective) measurement. In the simplest version of these approaches introduced by von Neumann [5], the environment and the system are entangled by their interaction, and the environment is then ignored (traced out), decohering the reduced state of the system. Subsequent theory, notably Zurek's, has pleaded the case for "the environment as the observer" by stressing the importance of system-environment correlations in determining the information obtainable on the system through the notions of "einselection" [4,6] and "the environment as a witness" [7,8] and the mechanism of enforcing classicality [9–11].

These approaches must cope with the issue that *the decomposition of a (closed) "supersystem" into an open quantum system and its environment is often neither unique nor inevitable, but rather a matter of expediency and choice for the observer:* Depending on the computational and experimental resources, the observer can choose which degrees of freedom pertain to the system to be measured (or otherwise manipulated) and which ones are part of the inaccessible environment ("bath"). However, even after this choice has been made, the observer must choose what observable of the system to measure and how frequently. We have long stressed that einselection, which singles out the states of a quantum system that are resilient to decoherence, is restricted to long time scales compatible with the Markovian (memoryless) assumption concerning the environment (bath) response [12]. Conversely, it excludes much shorter non-Markovian time scales that are restricted to the memory or correlation time of the bath response [13], a time scale that is often overlooked.

However, as we have shown, *this division of time scales is invalid* when the quantum system is subject to monitoring by the observer, even if such monitoring is considered non-intrusive, corresponding to quantum nondemolition (QND) measurements that leave the quantum observable of the system intact [12,13]. Nevertheless, the ensuing system–bath dynamics may drastically deviate from the course prescribed by decoherence or dissipation or even from the course prescribed by dynamical control [14–20].

Such measurement-induced dynamics may steer the system to a final state where it is heated up (in the Zeno regime) or cooled down (in the anti-Zeno regime [21]) irrespective of the bath temperature [22,23]. The observer's ability to steer the evolution of open systems is the basis for our fundamental approach we have dubbed Quantum Lamarckism [24] whereby the system evolution is dictated not merely by decoherence or bath effects but by its functional adaptation to the observer's choices.

Here we seek further support for the view embodied by Quantum Lamarckism that the observer cannot be banished from quantum mechanics. We do so by exploring the choices available to the observer in selecting the pointer basis of a meter in the presence of decoherence.

In the standard (von Neumann) quantum-measurement theory [5] an observable of a system S is measured by coupling the system S to a "meter" M and then measuring the latter. Namely, S is observed via M. von Neumann's theory is moot concerning the choice of basis for M and the effects of decoherence on M. By venturing beyond von Neumann's theory, Zurek investigated [3,4,6] what happens when the observable (pointer) of M differs from the "standard pointer", which commutes with the state of M after the S-M interaction, and what are the consequences of decoherence of M. His investigations can be briefly summarized by the following points:

(a) The measured observable of S is uniquely determined by the measured observable of M.
(b) Decoherence "dynamically selects" the pointer basis of M.
(c) As a consequence of (a) and (b), the decoherence of M "dynamically selects" the measurable observables of S and M [3], which leads to Zurek's notion of einselection [4,6].

Our analysis shows that the pointer-basis selection for a quantum meter in the presence of decoherence is not necessarily restricted by einselection. We find that, unless we restrict ourselves to projective measurements of the observable by the meter, decoherence does not in general select the pointer basis of M (Section 2). Under mild conditions, there is a multitude of alternative pointer bases the observer can choose from, all of which are capable of providing the same information on the observable by means of generalized measurements, regardless of decoherence. By contrast, the selection of the pointer basis of M does not affect the measured observable, which remains unique, whether in the absence or in the presence of decoherence (Section 3). We illustrate these results for the case of a qubit meter decohered by a bath when this meter measures a two-level system (Section 4). These results are discussed as arguments in favor of the central role of the observer in quantum mechanics in the spirit of Quantum Lamarckism [24] (Section 5).

2. Quantum Pointer Resilient to Decoherence

Let us consider a measurement of an observable $\hat{S}$ of system S by a meter M that is subject to decoherence by a bath B. Although our analysis can be completely general, we choose for simplicity the S-M interaction (via Hamiltonian H_{SM}) to be much stronger (hence faster) than that of M-B (via Hamiltonian H_{MB}). The measurement process then consists of three distinct stages:

(1) S and M interact over time interval τ_M that is long enough to entangle the two, but short enough to ignore the effects of B. The observable of the system S to be measured is represented in the basis of its (orthonormal) eigenstates $|S_n\rangle$, as

$$\hat{S} = \sum_n \epsilon_n |S_n\rangle\langle S_n|, \quad (1)$$

whereas the *unknown* initial state of the system S is

$$|\psi_S(0)\rangle = \sum_n c_n |S_n\rangle. \qquad (2)$$

The initial factorized state of S and M then evolves over the time interval $(0, \tau_M)$ to a state that obeys the Schmidt decomposition,

$$|\psi_{SM}(0)\rangle = \sum_n c_n |S_n\rangle \otimes |M\rangle \rightarrow |\psi_{SM}(\tau_M)\rangle = \sum_n c_n |S_n\rangle \otimes |P_n\rangle, \qquad (3)$$

where the meter states also satisfy orthonormality.

For a proper measurement of the observable $\hat{S}$ we impose the back-action evasion (quantum non-demolition) condition [25],

$$[\hat{S}, H_{SM}(t)] = 0, \qquad (4)$$

on the system-meter (SM) coupling Hamiltonian $H_{SM}(t)$. Moreover, we assume that τ_M is sufficiently short, so that the system Hamiltonian H_S can be neglected during the S-M interaction (the impulsive limit). We also neglect the meter Hamiltonian.

A measurement in the basis of the meter states $|P_n\rangle$ collapses the system state to an eigenstate $|S_n\rangle$ and thereby yields the eigenvalue ϵ_n of $\hat{S}$ with the probability $|c_n|^2$. The meter observable has then the form

$$\hat{P} = \sum_n b_n |P_n\rangle\langle P_n|, \qquad (5)$$

which we dub the *standard pointer*, since it effects ideal (projective) measurements of the system. The corresponding meter state, obtained from Equation (3) upon tracing over S, is then

$$\rho_M(\tau_M) = \sum_n |c_n|^2 |P_n\rangle\langle P_n|. \qquad (6)$$

(2) On a much longer time scale, $t \gg 1/\gamma \gg t_c$ where $1/\gamma$ is the decoherence time of the meter (M) and t_c is the correlation (memory) time of the decohering bath (B) [12,13], we choose a nondegenerate meter variable $\hat{Q}$ which satisfies the back-action evasion condition for the M-B interaction,

$$[\hat{Q}, H_{MB}(t)] = 0, \qquad (7)$$

where $H_{MB}(t)$ is the M-B coupling Hamiltonian. This condition ensures that the eigenstates $|Q_n\rangle$ of $\hat{Q}$ are invariant under decoherence. In order to conform to Zurek's analysis [3,6–8], we take H_{MB} to commute with H_{SM}. Then the standard pointer $\hat{P}$ of stage 1 can be shown to be identical with $\hat{Q}$. Upon tracing out B, we then arrive at the S-M state that is stationary and diagonal in the bases $\{|S_n\rangle\}$ and $\{|Q_n\rangle\}$ as $t \to \infty$,

$$\rho_{SM}(t) \to \rho_{SM}^\infty = \sum_n |c_n|^2 |S_n\rangle|Q_n\rangle\langle S_n|\langle Q_n|. \qquad (8)$$

Namely, decoherence eliminates the off-diagonal elements of the joint S-M state and acts as a nonselective measurement without a readout of the measurement results of the meter by the bath. Since now the standard pointer coincides with $\hat{Q}$, this means that the bath performs a non-selective measurement of the system.

(3) At stage 3, which follows the decoherence stage 2, projective measurement of the meter is performed on ρ_{SM}^∞ in the $\{|Q_n\rangle\}$ basis. This measurement is assumed to be fast (impulsive), so that the evolution of the meter during the measurement may be neglected. Then, a measurement of $\hat{Q}$ yields a selective projective measurement of the observable $\hat{S}$. Namely, an eigenvalue ϵ_n of $|S_n\rangle$ is obtained with probability $|c_n|^2$.

These results adhere to Zurek's view regarding the pointer basis [3,6–8]: They show that decoherence determines a meter state that is diagonal in the basis $\{|Q_n\rangle\}$, and only this basis can yield projective measurements of the system. Decoherence dynamically selects a unique "resilient" basis $\{|Q_n\rangle\}$, whereas any pointer basis differing from $\{|Q_n\rangle\}$ cannot yield projective measurements of the system. The question we raise is: Does this advantageous property single out $\hat{Q}$ as the only appropriate pointer?

3. Alternative Quantum Pointers

To answer this question, consider the general case where the standard pointer $\hat{P}$ does not commute with $\hat{Q}$, which is invariant under the action of H_{MB}. This means that $\hat{P}$ and $\hat{Q}$ are determined independently, by the non-commuting Hamiltonians H_{SM} and H_{MB}. Moreover, we consider a selective measurement of a meter variable $\hat{R}$ arbitrarily chosen by the observer. Generally, $\hat{R}$ commutes neither with $\hat{P}$ nor with $\hat{Q}$. Whereas in von Neumann's theory the S-M correlation (stage 1) is directly followed by a selective measurement of the meter (stage 3), we here adopt Zurek's procedure whereby stage 3 is preceded by a nonselective measurement of the meter caused by decoherence (stage 2)

At $t \to \infty$, i.e., after the completion of decoherence, we then have

$$\rho_{SM}(\infty) = \sum_{k,l,n} c_n c_l^* \langle Q_k | P_n \rangle \langle P_l | Q_k \rangle |S_n\rangle\langle S_l| \otimes |Q_k\rangle\langle Q_k|. \tag{9}$$

Now the meter state becomes

$$\rho_M' = \text{Tr}_S \, \rho_{SM}(\infty) = \sum_n p_n' |Q_n\rangle\langle Q_n|. \tag{10}$$

The column vector of the probabilities $\vec{p}' = \{p_n'\}$ is given by

$$\vec{p}' = \mathbf{E}' \vec{c}, \tag{11}$$

$\mathbf{E}'$ being the decoherence matrix with the elements

$$\mathbf{E}' = \{E_{mn}'\} = \{|\langle Q_m | P_n \rangle|^2\}. \tag{12}$$

The matrix $\mathbf{E}'$ is doubly stochastic, i.e., it satisfies

$$\sum_m E_{mn}' = \sum_n E_{mn}' = 1. \tag{13}$$

A comparison of the state (10) at stage 2 with the state (6) at stage 1 shows that decoherence rotates the eigenbasis of the meter state from $\{|P_n\rangle\}$ to $\{|Q_n\rangle\}$ and changes the eigenvalues from $|c_n|^2$ to p_n'. Since $\mathbf{E}'$ is doubly stochastic, $\vec{p}'$ is majorized by $\vec{c}$. As a result, the state (10) is more mixed with a higher von Neumann entropy (i.e., is more randomized) than (6), unless $\{|Q_n\rangle\}$ coincides with $\{|P_n\rangle\}$. Yet, does this randomization preclude the use of $\hat{P}$, the standard pointer, or any other pointer, for measuring the system observable $\hat{S}$?

To find out, consider that at stage 3 subsequent to stage 2, the meter undergoes a projective measurement in some basis $\{|R_n\rangle\}$ of an observable $\hat{R}$ arbitrarily chosen by the observer. An observation of the mth outcome in this basis results in the (unnormalized) post-measurement state of the system that is generally mixed. It can be written in the operator-sum representation, as

$$\rho_{S,m}' = \sum_k \hat{M}_{mk} |\psi_S(0)\rangle\langle\psi_S(0)| \hat{M}_{mk}^\dagger, \tag{14}$$

in terms of the Kraus operators

$$\hat{M}_{mk} = \langle R_m | Q_k \rangle \sum_n \langle Q_k | P_n \rangle |S_n\rangle\langle S_n|. \tag{15}$$

The measurement probabilities are then

$$p_m = \text{Tr}\,\rho'_{S,m} = \langle \psi_S(0)|\hat{E}_m|\psi_S(0)\rangle, \qquad (16)$$

with

$$\hat{E}_m = \sum_k \hat{M}^\dagger_{mk}\hat{M}_{mk} = \sum_n E_{mn}|S_n\rangle\langle S_n|. \qquad (17)$$

The set of operators $\hat{E}_m$ is known as a POVM (positive operator-valued measure) [26]. Here the POVM matrix $\mathbf{E} = \{E_{mn}\}$ is given by

$$\mathbf{E} = \mathbf{E}''\mathbf{E}', \qquad (18)$$

where

$$\mathbf{E}'' = \{\,|\langle R_m|Q_n\rangle|^2\,\}. \qquad (19)$$

The POVM operators (17) are diagonal in the basis $\{|S_n\rangle\}$, which means that the system observable that is measured is invariably $\hat{S}$, *irrespective of the choice of the meter basis* $\{|P_n\rangle\}$, $\{|Q_n\rangle\}$, or $\{|R_n\rangle\}$. This result stands contrary to the notion that the measurable system observable depends on the pointer.

Among the multitude of alternative pointer bases, the basis that conforms to Zurek's analysis is the one that coincides with the decoherence-invariant basis,

$$|R_n\rangle = |Q_n\rangle. \qquad (20)$$

Equations (12), (18) and (19) then yield the POVM matrix

$$\mathbf{E} = \{\,|\langle R_m|P_n\rangle|^2\,\}, \qquad (21)$$

whereas Equations (14) and (15) entail a pure post-measurement state, $\rho'_{S,m} = |\psi'_{S,m}\rangle\langle \psi'_{S,m}|$, where [3]

$$|\psi'_{S,m}\rangle = \hat{M}_m|\psi_S(0)\rangle = \sum_n \langle R_m|P_n\rangle c_n |S_n\rangle \qquad (22)$$

with $\hat{M}_m = \sum_n \langle R_m|P_n\rangle |S_n\rangle\langle S_n|$.

Only under condition (20), decoherence gives rise to a nonselective measurement that does not affect the results of a subsequent selective projective measurement of the meter, since both are performed in the same basis. In all other pointer bases $\{|R_n\rangle\}$, decoherence affects the measurement results and/or the post-measurement states of the system, usually (partially or completely) randomizing them. However, as shown below, in most cases decoherence does not erase the information on the system, whereas in some cases it can even be beneficial for measurements.

Returning to the general case, we can rewrite (16) in the form

$$\vec{p} = \mathbf{E}\vec{c}, \qquad (23)$$

where $\vec{p}$ and $\vec{c}$ are column vectors with the components p_n and $|c_n|^2$, respectively. Then $\vec{c}$ can be obtained by inverting (23),

$$\vec{c} = \mathbf{E}^{-1}\vec{p}, \qquad (24)$$

i.e., *all $|c_n|^2$ can be extracted from the measurement results, provided $\mathbf{E}^{-1}$ exists.*

This inversion condition holds iff the rows (or, equivalently, columns) of $\mathbf{E}$ are linearly independent, or, equivalently, iff the POVM operators $\hat{E}_m$ are linearly independent. Then decoherence does not degrade the information obtainable on the system observable. The inversion condition holds iff the determinants of both $\mathbf{E}'$ and $\mathbf{E}''$ are nonzero. We can then fully recover the original vector $\vec{c}$ prior to the decoherence, even though the vector $\vec{p}$ has been generally affected by decoherence.

Conversely, when all the POVM operators $\hat{E}_m$ are proportional to each other, we find that they are proportional to the identity operator with the coefficient $1/d$, where d is the system dimensionality. This means that

$$E_{mn} = 1/d. \tag{25}$$

Inserting (25) into (23) yields that in such cases the measurement results are completely random, $p_m = 1/d$, and reveal no information on the system.

In particular, *in the absence of decoherence* measurements provide no information on the system, when [cf. (21) and (25)]

$$|\langle R_m | P_n \rangle|^2 = 1/d, \tag{26}$$

namely, the actual ($\{|R_n\rangle\}$) and standard ($\{|P_n\rangle\}$) pointer bases (5) are *mutually unbiased*.

In the presence of decoherence, Equations (12), (18), (19) and (25) imply that the decoherence can completely erase the information on the system, but only when the decoherence-invariant $\{|Q_n\rangle\}$ basis is mutually unbiased with either the standard pointer $\{|P_n\rangle\}$ or the actual-pointer $\{|R_n\rangle\}$ basis.

Surprisingly, decoherence is advantageous for measurements in mutually unbiased bases $\{|P_n\rangle\}$ and $\{|R_n\rangle\}$. In the absence of decoherence, a pair of such bases provides improper measurements that do not yield information on the system. However, *when decoherence occurs in the basis $\{|Q_n\rangle\}$, which is mutually biased with both $\{|P_n\rangle\}$ and $\{|R_n\rangle\}$, information is not erased by a measurement in the latter two bases*. This effect is counter-intuitive, since decoherence in the meter obliterates information on the system, at least partially. Nevertheless, *decoherence can turn improper measurements into proper ones*, since decoherence rotates the meter-state eigenbasis $\{|P_n\rangle\}$ into the basis $\{|Q_n\rangle\}$, which is not mutually unbiased (and thus can be dubbed mutually biased) with $\{|R_n\rangle\}$.

There can be intermediate cases, where the number of linearly independent POVM operators is greater than 1 but smaller than d. In such cases, the results of projective measurements cannot be completely reconstructed, but the POVM still provides *partial information* on the system by restricting the values of $|c_n|^2$.

4. Qubit Meter Decohered by a Bath

As an illustration of the foregoing general analysis, let us consider a two-level system (TLS) that is being measured by a qubit meter, having degenerate energy eigenstates $|0\rangle$, $|1\rangle$. Measurements in the basis of TLS energy eigenstates $\{|g\rangle, |e\rangle\}$ are performed via a time-dependent TLS-meter interaction Hamiltonian of the form

$$H_{\text{SM}} = (\pi/2) h(t) |e\rangle\langle e| (\hat{I}_{\text{M}} - \hat{\sigma}_x^{\text{M}}). \tag{27}$$

Here $\hat{I}_{\text{M}}$ is the identity operator of the meter, $\hat{\sigma}_x^{\text{M}} = |0\rangle\langle 1| + |1\rangle\langle 0|$, and $h(t)$, satisfying $\int_{-\infty}^{\infty} h(t) = 1$, is a smooth temporal profile of the TLS coupling to the qubit meter during the measurement that occurs in the interval centered at $t = 0$ with duration τ_{M}. A possible (but not unique) choice is the form [22]

$$h(t) = \frac{1}{2\tau_{\text{M}} \cosh^2(t/\tau_{\text{M}})}. \tag{28}$$

This form of H_{SM} corresponds to the controlled-not (CNOT) entangling operation [26]

$$\hat{U}_{\text{CN}} = e^{-i \int_{-\infty}^{\infty} dt H_{\text{SM}}(t)}. \tag{29}$$

If the measurement duration τ_{M} is much shorter than all other time scales, tending to the impulsive limit $\tau_{\text{M}} \to 0$, then its action is well approximated by the operator $\hat{U}_{\text{CN}}$.

The meter–bath interaction is taken to be

$$H_{\text{MB}} = |1\rangle\langle 1| \otimes \hat{B}_1 + |0\rangle\langle 0| \otimes \hat{B}_0, \tag{30}$$

where $\hat{B}_1$ and $\hat{B}_0$ are bath operators that have orthogonal eigenstates. We may then describe stages (1) and (2) of the measurement process in Section 2 as follows:
(1) Stage 1 yields in a Schmidt-decomposed S-M correlated state:

$$(c_e|e\rangle + c_g|g\rangle)|0\rangle \rightarrow c_e|e\rangle|1\rangle + c_g|g\rangle|0\rangle. \tag{31}$$

(2) Stage 2 produces the reduced S-M density matrix. This state pertains to the standard pointer basis of M $\{|0\rangle, |1\rangle\}$, which satisfies the back-action evasion condition (7), and hence its states are invariant under the decoherence. At times much longer than the decoherence times, this state attains the diagonal form,

$$\rho_{\text{SM}} \rightarrow |c_e|^2 |e\rangle\langle e||1\rangle\langle 1| + |c_g|^2 |g\rangle\langle g||0\rangle\langle 0|. \tag{32}$$

(3) At stage 3, the following cases merit consideration:
(i) The actual pointer basis $\{|R_n\rangle\}$ coincides with $\{|P_n\rangle\}$ and $\{|Q_n\rangle\}$. The measurements of the system are then projective, and decoherence does not affect them, as shown in Section 2.
(ii) $\{|R_n\rangle\}$ is an arbitrary pointer basis, given by

$$|R_0\rangle = a|0\rangle + b|1\rangle, \quad |R_1\rangle = b^*|0\rangle - a^*|1\rangle, \quad |a|^2 + |b|^2 = 1. \tag{33}$$

In the present case, $|P_n\rangle = |Q_n\rangle$, Equations (12), (18) and (19) yield again (21), which for a qubit meter becomes

$$\mathbf{E} = \begin{pmatrix} |a|^2 & |b|^2 \\ |b|^2 & |a|^2 \end{pmatrix}. \tag{34}$$

In this case, the measurement results are *the same as in the absence of decoherence*, although the meter decoherence affects the possible post-measurement states of the system, which are now mixed. In the present case, they are

$$\begin{aligned} \rho'_0 &= |a|^2|c_g|^2|g\rangle\langle g| + |b|^2|c_e|^2|e\rangle\langle e|, \\ \rho'_1 &= |b|^2|c_g|^2|g\rangle\langle g| + |a|^2|c_e|^2|e\rangle\langle e|. \end{aligned} \tag{35}$$

When $|a| \neq |b|$, $\mathbf{E}$ has a nonzero determinant, and $\vec{c}$ in (11) can be evaluated from the POVM probabilities p_0, p_1,

$$|c_g|^2 = \frac{p_0 - |b|^2}{1 - 2|b|^2}, \quad |c_e|^2 = \frac{p_1 - |b|^2}{1 - 2|b|^2}. \tag{36}$$

(iii) The pointer bases with $|a| = |b| = 1/\sqrt{2}$ do not provide any information on the system, since the determinant of $\mathbf{E}$ then vanishes. These pointer bases have the form

$$\left\{ (|0\rangle + e^{i\chi}|1\rangle)/\sqrt{2}, \quad (|0\rangle - e^{i\chi}|1\rangle)/\sqrt{2} \right\}, \tag{37}$$

where χ is an arbitrary phase. Such pointer bases lie in the xy-plane of the Bloch sphere and are all unbiased with respect to the standard pointer basis. These pointers yield the random probabilities

$$p_0 = p_1 = 1/2. \tag{38}$$

Result (38) contradicts the claim that a Stern–Gerlach magnet with a field gradient in the direction z can measure the spin in the direction y. In fact, since a pointer basis of the form (37) does not provide any information on the system, it is inadequate and cannot be used for a spin measurement in any direction.

5. Discussion

Pointer states have been defined by Zurek [3,6–8] as the ones that are minimally entangled with the bath following their interaction. To find them, one quantifies the entanglement generated between the system and the bath by the von Neumann entropy obtained for the reduced density matrix of the system $\rho_\Psi(t)$ [initialized from $\rho_\Psi(0) = |\Psi\rangle\langle\Psi|$]. The pointer states are then obtained by minimizing the entropy over $|\Psi\rangle$ and demanding robustness under time variation.

When the dynamics is dominated by the system Hamiltonian, the pointer states defined as above coincide with the energy eigenstates of this Hamiltonian and conform with the view that decoherence induced by the bath *"observes"* the system and selects its pointer states. Similar conclusions apply to a meter that is coupled to a bath and measures the system.

As we have shown, *a pointer basis is not uniquely selected by decoherence*: there is a broad variety of pointer bases pertaining to a meter under the influence of a bath that still allow us to extract complete or, at least, partial information on the system. The possibility to extract the full information on the system via generalized measurement, notwithstanding the randomness of the meter observable due to decoherence, is our main result.

We note that an ideal von Neumann measurement does not reveal the phases of the superposition coefficients even without decoherence, so that the resilience of the meter basis to decoherence does not resolve the fundamental issue of quantum measurements that prompted von Neumann to introduce the projection postulate [5]. However, we may rotate the meter basis at different angles, and, for each angle, repeat the measurement on unmeasured portions of the ensemble, thereby acquiring information on the phases within an accuracy limited by the Cramer–Rao bound of estimation theory [27]. As shown by us, this bound is accessible in practice by measurements of the state decoherence combined with suitably optimized dynamical control [28]. Hence, for each rotation angle of the meter we may invoke the same considerations as the ones outlined in the present analysis. Thus, our conclusions apply in general to the acquisition of quantum information in noisy or dissipative media [29].

Zurek's Quantum Darwinism [9–11] asserts that the measured information is proliferated in the environment in many copies, the observer being one of the many parts of the environment. We find, in contrast, that irrespective of the number of copies, the observer can open channels of information extraction from the system that are not constrained by the environment, by appropriately choosing the meter basis. Thus, the observer may override decoherence in almost any chosen measuring (pointer) basis. This observer's choice can deprive resilient pointer states of their privileged status.

The present analysis gives further support to our "quantum Lamarckian" thesis [24] regarding the indispensable role of the observer. By contrast, we conclude that decoherence is neither an inevitable natural order nor a fundamental selection mechanism, but merely a reflection of the limitations of the observer's resources. For a growing variety of systems and observables, the observer's manipulations of the system–bath complex may render the notion of decoherence superfluous.

Author Contributions: Conceptualization, A.G.K. and G.K.; methodology, A.G.K.; formal analysis, A.G.K. and G.K.; writing, G.K. and A.G.K. All authors have read and agreed to the published version of the manuscript.

Funding: This research was funded by DFG (FOR 2724), QUANTERA (PACE-IN) and EU FET-OPEN (PATHOS).

Institutional Review Board Statement: Not applicable.

Informed Consent Statement: Not applicable.

Data Availability Statement: Not applicable.

Conflicts of Interest: The authors declare no conflict of interest. The funders had no role in the design of the study; in the collection, analyses, or interpretation of data; in the writing of the manuscript, or in the decision to publish the results.

References

1. Joos, E.; Zeh, H.D.; Kiefer, C.; Giulini, D.; Stamatescu, J.K.I.O. *Decoherence and the Appearance of a Classical World in Quantum Theory*, 2nd ed.; Springer: Berlin/Heidelberg, Germany, 2003.
2. Schlosshauer, M.A. *Decoherence and the Quantum-to-Classical Transition*; Springer: Berlin/Heidelberg, Germany, 2007.
3. Zurek, W.H. Pointer basis of quantum apparatus: Into what mixture does the wave packet collapse? *Phys. Rev. D* **1981**, *24*, 1516–1525. [CrossRef]
4. Zurek, W.H. Environment-induced superselection rules. *Phys. Rev. D* **1982**, *26*, 1862–1880. [CrossRef]
5. von Neumann, J. *Mathematical Foundations of Quantum Mechanics*; Prinston University Press: Prinston, NJ, USA, 1955.
6. Zurek, W.H. Einselection and decoherence from an information theory perspective. *Ann. Phys.* **2000**, *11-12*, 855–864. [CrossRef]
7. Ollivier, H.; Poulin, D.; Zurek, W.H. Objective properties from subjective quantum states: Environment as a witness. *Phys. Rev. Lett.* **2004**, *93*, 220401. [CrossRef]
8. Ollivier, H.; Poulin, D.; Zurek, W.H. Environment as a witness: Selective proliferation of information and emergence of objectivity in a quantum universe. *Phys. Rev. A* **2005**, *72*, 423113. [CrossRef]
9. Blume-Kohout, R.; Zurek, W.H. Quantum Darwinism: Entanglement, branches, and the emergent classicality of redundantly stored quantum information. *Phys. Rev. A* **2006**, *73*, 062310. [CrossRef]
10. Blume-Kohout, R.; Zurek, W.H. Quantum Darwinism in quantum Brownian motion. *Phys. Rev. Lett.* **2008**, *101*, 240405. [CrossRef] [PubMed]
11. Zurek, W.H. Quantum Darwinism. *Nat. Phys.* **2009**, *5*, 181–188. [CrossRef]
12. Breuer, H.P.; Petruccione, F. *The Theory of Open Quantum Systems*; Oxford University Press: Oxford, UK, 2002.
13. Kurizki, G.; Kofman, A.G. *Thermodynamics and Control of Open Quantum Systems*; Cambridge University Press: Cambridge, UK, 2022.
14. Kofman, A.G.; Kurizki, G. Universal dynamical control of quantum mechanical decay: Modulation of the coupling to the continuum. *Phys. Rev. Lett.* **2001**, *87*, 270405. [CrossRef]
15. Kofman, A.G.; Kurizki, G. Unified theory of dynamically suppressed qubit decoherence in thermal baths. *Phys. Rev. Lett.* **2004**, *93*, 130406. [CrossRef]
16. Kurizki, G.; Zwick, A. From coherent to incoherent dynamical control of open quantum systems. *Adv. Chem. Phys.* **2016**, *159*, 137–217.
17. Gordon, G.; Erez, N.; Kurizki, G. Universal dynamical decoherence control of noisy single- and multi-qubit systems. *J. Phys. B* **2007**, *40*, S75–S93. [CrossRef]
18. Gordon, G.; Kurizki, G.; Kofman, A.G. Universal dynamical control of decay and decoherence in multilevel systems. *J. Opt. B* **2005**, *7*, S283–S292. [CrossRef]
19. Viola, L.; Lloyd, S. Dynamical suppression of decoherence in two-state quantum systems. *Phys. Rev. A* **1998**, *58*, 2733–2744. [CrossRef]
20. Vitali, D.; Tombesi, P. Heating and decoherence suppression using decoupling techniques. *Phys. Rev. A* **2001**, *65*, 012305. [CrossRef]
21. Kofman, A.G.; Kurizki, G. Acceleration of quantum decay processes by frequent observations. *Nature* **2000**, *405*, 546–550. [CrossRef] [PubMed]
22. Erez, N.; Gordon, G.; Nest, M.; Kurizki, G. Thermodynamic control by frequent quantum measurements. *Nature* **2008**, *452*, 724–727. [CrossRef] [PubMed]
23. Álvarez, G.A.A.; Rao, D.D.B.; Frydman, L.; Kurizki, G. Zeno and anti-Zeno polarization control of spin ensembles by induced dephasing. *Phys. Rev. Lett.* **2010**, *105*, 160401. [CrossRef]
24. Kurizki, G.; Kofman, A.G. Quantum Lamarckism: Observation, control and decoherence. *Phys. Scr.* **2018**, *93*, 124003. [CrossRef]
25. Scully, M.O.; Zubairy, M.S. *Quantum Optics*; Cambridge University Press: Cambridge, UK, 1997.
26. Nielsen, M.A.; Chuang, I.L. *Quantum Computation and Quantum Information*; Cambridge University Press: Cambridge, UK, 2000.
27. Paris, M.G.A. Quantum estimation for quantum technology. *Int. J. Quantum Inf.* **2009**, *07*, 125–137. [CrossRef]
28. Zwick, A.; Alvarez, G.A.; Kurizki, G. Maximizing information on the environment by dynamically controlled qubit probes. *Phys. Rev. Appl.* **2016**, *5*, 014007. [CrossRef]
29. Gordon, G.; Kurizki, G. Dynamical protection of quantum computation from decoherence in laser-driven cold-ion and cold-atom systems. *New J. Phys.* **2008**, *10*, 045005. [CrossRef]

Article

A Classical Formulation of Quantum Theory?

William F. Braasch, Jr. [1] and William K. Wootters [2,*]

1 Department of Physics and Astronomy, Dartmouth College, Hanover, NH 03755, USA; wbraasch@gmail.com
2 Department of Physics, Williams College, Williamstown, MA 01267, USA
* Correspondence: william.wootters@williams.edu

Abstract: We explore a particular way of reformulating quantum theory in classical terms, starting with phase space rather than Hilbert space, and with actual probability distributions rather than quasiprobabilities. The classical picture we start with is epistemically restricted, in the spirit of a model introduced by Spekkens. We obtain quantum theory only by combining a *collection* of restricted classical pictures. Our main challenge in this paper is to find a simple way of characterizing the allowed sets of classical pictures. We present one promising approach to this problem and show how it works out for the case of a single qubit.

Keywords: Wigner function; qubit; quasiprobability; epistemic restriction; quantum reconstruction; phase space

Citation: Braasch, W.F., Jr.; Wootters, W.K. A Classical Formulation of Quantum Theory? *Entropy* **2022**, *24*, 137. https://doi.org/10.3390/e24010137

Academic Editors: Sebastian Deffner, Raymond Laflamme, Juan Pablo Paz and Michael Zwolak

Received: 17 December 2021
Accepted: 12 January 2022
Published: 17 January 2022

Publisher's Note: MDPI stays neutral with regard to jurisdictional claims in published maps and institutional affiliations.

Copyright: © 2022 by the authors. Licensee MDPI, Basel, Switzerland. This article is an open access article distributed under the terms and conditions of the Creative Commons Attribution (CC BY) license (https://creativecommons.org/licenses/by/4.0/).

1. Introduction

Much of Wojciech Zurek's research, including his research on quantum Darwinism, has been aimed at explaining the emergence of the classical world from the quantum world. This is of course an important endeavor, partly because, as he has pointed out, quantum theory and classical physics seem almost incompatible at first sight.

"The quantum principle of superposition implies that any combination of quantum states is also a legal state. This seems to be in conflict with everyday reality: States we encounter are localized. Classical objects can be either here or there, but never *both* here and there" [1].

Indeed, it is an interesting fact that the standard formulation of quantum theory—with state vectors in Hilbert space—looks as different as it does from the emergent classical picture. In this paper, we take a step towards a reformulation of quantum theory that looks more classical from the very beginning, being based on phase space rather than Hilbert space. At the same time, we wish to avoid the negative probabilities of the Wigner-function formulation, which is the most common phase-space formulation of quantum theory.

We are motivated largely by the general observation that it is good to have alternative formulations of a well-established theory. Alternative formulations can provide novel insights and new methods of analysis. In the present case, we can also hope that our classical-like formulation will ultimately provide another perspective on the quantum-to-classical transition.

Though we intend in future work to apply our methods to continuous quantum variables such as position and momentum, in this paper, we restrict our attention to the case of systems normally described with a finite-dimensional Hilbert space. For us, this means that the phase spaces we use are *discrete*. Specifically, we use the discrete phase space introduced in [2], which is simplest when the Hilbert-space dimension d is prime. In that case, the phase space is a $d \times d$ array of points, with axes—analogous to position and momentum axes—labeled by elements of the field $\mathbb{Z}_d$, that is, the integers mod d. As we explain in the following section, in this phase space it makes sense to speak of "lines" and "parallel lines". Each line has exactly d points, and there are $d+1$ ways of dividing the d^2 points of phase space into d parallel lines.

Our work is related to a construction due to Spekkens [3–6]. Starting with the same discrete phase space, he defines an "epistemically restricted classical theory": the points of phase space are understood to be the actual, underlying states of the system, but an observer cannot know this state. The most detailed description an observer can give is a uniform probability distribution over one of the lines. Spekkens showed that many qualitative features of quantum theory can be captured by this model, but the model cannot fully imitate quantum theory because it is non-contextual.

In a recent paper, we showed how one can construct a picture that borrows some of Spekkens' ideas but that accommodates the full quantum theory of a d-state system [7]. Specifically, we found that one can decompose the quantum description of a complete experiment—a preparation, a transformation (or a sequence of transformations), and a measurement—into a collection of classical descriptions, each entailing certain epistemic restrictions similar to but subtly different from the one imposed in Spekkens' model. There is one such classical description for each possible choice of what we call a "framework." The framework defines the epistemic restrictions placed on the classical model. Within each framework, we can imagine a classical observer whose picture of the experiment is perfectly compatible with an ontological model in which the system really does occupy a definite phase-space point at every moment, and in which a transformation is represented by an ordinary set of transition probabilities in phase space. Each classical observer will compute their own prediction for the experiment, in the form of a probability assigned to each possible outcome. We showed how to combine these classical predictions to reconstruct the quantum prediction. In a slogan, we say the quantum prediction is obtained by "summing the nonrandom parts". The meaning of this slogan will become clear in the following section, but essentially, the nonrandom part of a probability value is its deviation from the value one would use under a condition of minimal knowledge. (Thus the expression, "the nonrandom part," is a kind of shorthand. We do not mean to imply that there is no element of randomness in values of a probability that differ from the minimal-knowledge value.) Intriguingly, the use of this unusual method of combining probability distributions allows us to reproduce the operational statistics of the non-commutative theory of quantum mechanics starting with ordinary (commutative) classical probability theory.

In [7], we were not able to come up with a simple set of criteria for determining precisely what sets of classical descriptions are allowed—we did specify a set of criteria, but it is not simple. Such criteria are desirable if our formulation of quantum theory is to be self-contained, that is, not dependent on concepts from the Hilbert-space formulation. The primary aim of the present paper is to identify such a set of criteria.

The rest of this paper is organized as follows. In the next section, we review the formalism of [7]: how the frameworks are defined, how one decomposes the quantum description of an experiment into epistemically restricted classical descriptions, and how the predictions based on these classical descriptions are combined to recover the quantum prediction. In Section 3, we write down four equations showing how any pair of components of an experiment—the components being preparations, transformations, and measurement outcomes—can be combined to obtain either other components or an observable probability. For example, a preparation followed by a transformation constitutes another preparation, and for a preparation followed directly by a yes-or-no test, there is an equation that yields the probability of the outcome "yes". The basis of each of these four equations is the principle that the nonrandom parts of the inputs should be summed to obtain the nonrandom part of the output. At this point, we ask our main question: To what extent do these four composition rules determine the allowed sets of classical descriptions? That is, to what extent do these equations characterize the structure of quantum theory for the d-state system? We find it useful to add a few auxiliary assumptions, but we do not know whether all these assumptions are necessary. Conceivably, a more parsimonious set of postulates is possible.

In Section 4, we specialize to the case of a single qubit and ask whether the composition rules and auxiliary postulates of Section 3 determine the quantum theory of this simple system. We find that we recover either the standard quantum theory for a qubit or a theory with a discrete set of transformations.

Of course, we would like to extend this approach to all possible Hilbert-space dimensions and to composite systems. We discuss the possibilities for doing this in the concluding section.

For the remainder of this Introduction, we review briefly some of the earlier efforts to reconstruct quantum theory from basic principles, as well as other work on quantum theory in phase space and other approaches to representing quantum theory in terms of probability distributions.

Reconstructions of quantum theory can be traced back to Birkhoff and von Neumann [8]. In these initial forays, the focus was on mathematical axiomatizations [9–12]. However, it is appealing to think that quantum mechanics might be reconstructed by stipulating a set of principles in the spirit of Einstein's principles that lead to the theory of special relativity. This more operationally oriented approach was ignited by Hardy [13]. In Hardy's axiomatization, the addition of the key word "continuous" to one of his principles differentiates quantum mechanics from classical probability theory. Although the approach we describe here is different from Hardy's, that same key word rears its head as the distinguishing feature between quantum mechanics and a simpler theory, as we will see in Section 4. Other important reconstruction efforts have likewise relied on operational or information-theoretic principles [14–19]. Recently, diagrammatic postulates have been used to reconstruct quantum theory [20].

In another vein, attempts to pinpoint essential quantumness have taken the tack of augmenting classical physics with simple rules. As we mentioned, Spekkens and collaborators have done this in a series of epistemically restricted classical theories used to support an epistemic interpretation of the quantum state [3–5]. Spekkens' model has previously been provided with a contextual extension, but without fully capturing quantum theory [21]. It has also been shown to hold strong similarities to stabilizer physics [22–24], thereby providing a link to a subtheory of quantum mechanics that plays an important role in quantum computing. Spekkens' model is naturally set in phase space, which provides the backbone for our work.

Quantum mechanics set in phase space has a history almost as long as quantum mechanics itself [25,26]. Again, the most commonly used phase-space representation of a quantum state is the Wigner function. An interesting complementary strategy is to invert the definition of the Wigner function to make classical mechanics look more like quantum theory [27,28]. A number of different discrete Wigner functions have been defined for finite-dimensional quantum systems [2,29–33]. In this paper, although our aim is to go beyond Wigner functions and use only nonnegative probabilities, we do use concepts from the Wigner-function definition of [2].

There are numerous reasons to study quantum mechanics in phase space. In quantum optics, the appearance of the negativity of the Wigner function signals the onset of quantum behavior [34,35]. The negativity of the Wigner function has also been linked to contextuality, which is another famous notion of nonclassicality [36–38], and to the power of quantum computing [24,39–41].

The tomography of quantum states is closely tied to the Wigner function. We effectively use tomographic representations of quantum states in this paper. For this reason, our work is also closely related to the "classical" approach to quantum theory found in [42–44]. The authors of these papers have successfully described a large number of quantum phenomena from this perspective. Our approach diverges from theirs in that we treat every aspect of a quantum experiment tomographically.

Certain subtheories of quantum mechanics have been proven to be nonnegative in the Wigner-function representation. The stabilizer subtheory is one of them [31], and sampling its nonnegative representation provides the basis for the classical simulation of stabilizer physics [39]. Under certain assumptions, it has been shown that the full quantum theory requires negativity in some aspect (preparation, transformation, or measurement) of a frame-theoretic generalization of the Wigner-function representation [45–47]. The Pusey–Barrett–Rudolph theorem is another expression of the limitation on representing quantum mechanics with classical probability theory [48]. Nonetheless, in the search for new ways in which to simulate quantum systems, researchers have found positive probabilistic representations of quantum theory by loosening certain assumptions upon which the theorems are built [49–54]. In another setting, Fuchs and Schack have expressed quantum states and transformations as probability distributions over the possible outcomes of a SIC-POVM [55].

Again, our approach begins by decomposing the quantum description of an experiment into a collection of classical probabilistic descriptions, as we explain more fully in the following section.

2. A Quantum Experiment as a Collection of Classical Experiments

In this section, we briefly review the formalism developed in [7]. We begin with a bit of notation and terminology.

Let us assume for now that the system we are studying has a Hilbert space with prime dimension d. We use Greek letters to label the points of the $d \times d$ phase space. Each point α can be specified by its horizontal and vertical coordinates, which we write as α_q and α_p, respectively, to emphasize the analogy with position and momentum. Here α_q and α_p both take values in $\mathbb{Z}_d$. A *line* is the set of points α satisfying an equation of the form $a\alpha_q + b\alpha_p = c$ for fixed $a, b, c \in \mathbb{Z}_d$ with a and b not both zero. Two lines are parallel if they can be specified by equations of this form differing only in the value of c. We refer to a line passing through the origin as a *ray*.

A point in phase space is not a valid quantum state, but we find it extremely helpful to associate with each point α a quasi-density matrix $\hat{A}_\alpha$, which we call a "phase point operator." This is a trace-one Hermitian matrix, but it is not a legitimate density matrix because it can have negative eigenvalues. The matrices $\hat{A}_\alpha$ that we use are the ones introduced in [2] to define a discrete Wigner function (see below). The matrix $\hat{A}_\alpha$ for any odd prime d is written as follows in terms of its components:

$$(\hat{A}_\alpha)_{kl} = \delta_{2\alpha_q, k+l} \omega^{\alpha_p(k-l)}, \tag{1}$$

where $\omega = e^{2\pi i/d}$ and the arithmetic in the subscript of the Kronecker delta is mod d. For $d = 2$, there is a special formula:

$$\hat{A}_\alpha = \tfrac{1}{2}[\hat{I} + (-1)^{\alpha_p}\hat{X} + (-1)^{\alpha_q + \alpha_p}\hat{Y} + (-1)^{\alpha_q}\hat{Z}], \tag{2}$$

where $\hat{X}, \hat{Y}, \hat{Z}$ are the Pauli matrices and $\hat{I}$ is the 2×2 identity matrix. The $\hat{A}$ matrices are orthogonal in the Hilbert–Schmidt sense:

$$\text{tr}(\hat{A}_\alpha \hat{A}_\beta) = d\delta_{\alpha\beta}, \tag{3}$$

and because there are d^2 of them, they serve as a basis for the space of all $d \times d$ matrices. In particular, we can expand a density matrix $\hat{w}$ as a linear combination of $\hat{A}$'s.

$$\hat{w} = \sum_\alpha Q(\alpha|\hat{w})\hat{A}_\alpha. \tag{4}$$

The coefficients $Q(\alpha|\hat{w})$ in this expansion constitute the *discrete Wigner function* representing the given state.

The operators $\hat{A}_\alpha$ also have the following special property, which we use immediately in the following subsection. For any line ℓ, the average of the $\hat{A}$'s over that line is a one-dimensional projection operator:

$$\frac{1}{d} \sum_{\alpha \in \ell} \hat{A}_\alpha = |\psi_\ell\rangle\langle\psi_\ell|, \tag{5}$$

where $|\psi_\ell\rangle$ is a state vector associated with the line ℓ. Since the $\hat{A}$'s are orthogonal to each other, the $|\psi\rangle$'s associated with a complete set of parallel lines—we call such a set a striation—constitute an orthonormal basis for the Hilbert space. Moreover, because any two non-parallel lines intersect in exactly one point, Equation (3) guarantees that these bases are mutually unbiased; that is, each basis vector is an equal-magnitude superposition of the vectors of any of the other bases.

2.1. Defining the Frameworks

A "framework" is a mathematical structure that determines what epistemic constraint one of our classical probability distributions must satisfy. The introduction of the concept of a framework is one way in which our work differs from Spekkens' model. In Spekkens' model, there is just one classical world, and there is one epistemic constraint that applies to it. In his model, for example, a uniform probability distribution over any line of the discrete phase space counts as a legitimate epistemic state. By contrast, what we are doing, roughly speaking, is to decompose this set of possibilities into distinct cases—one for each possible slope of a line—and to associate each of these cases with a different classical world.

We now explain specifically what kind of mathematical structure constitutes a framework for each component of an experiment—a preparation, a transformation, or a measurement—and what epistemic restriction is associated with each of these frameworks.

For either a preparation or a measurement, a framework is simply a striation of the phase space—a complete set of parallel lines. We label such a striation with the symbol B, since each striation is associated with an orthonormal basis. For a given framework B, the classical probability function representing a given preparation or measurement outcome is required to be constant along each line of the striation B—this is the epistemic restriction associated with the framework B. We define these restricted probability functions in the next subsection.

To define the framework for a transformation, we need to consider a special class of linear transformations on the discrete phase space. Let us think of a point α as represented by a column vector with components α_q and α_p. Then a linear transformation is represented by a 2×2 matrix, with elements in $\mathbb{Z}_d$, acting from the left on this column vector. A *symplectic* transformation is a linear transformation that preserves the symplectic product:

$$\langle \alpha, \beta \rangle = \alpha_p \beta_q - \alpha_q \beta_p. \quad (6)$$

For the case we consider, in which the phase space has just two discrete dimensions, the symplectic transformations are the same as the transformations whose matrices have unit determinant.

The number of symplectic matrices for any prime d is $d(d^2 - 1)$. Our formulation is simplest if, among these symplectic matrices, there exists a set $\mathcal{T}$ of just $d^2 - 1$ such matrices that has the "nonsingular difference" property: the difference between any two matrices in $\mathcal{T}$ has a nonzero determinant. It turns out that this condition allows for a particularly simple reconstruction of a quantum transformation from the classical transition probabilities, defined in the following section. In [7], the nonsingular difference is the only property we require of the set $\mathcal{T}$, and to our knowledge, it is not known whether such a set of $d^2 - 1$ matrices exists for all prime d. However, for our present purposes, we also need $\mathcal{T}$ to constitute a *group*, that is, a subgroup of the symplectic group Sp(2,d). It is known that such a special subgroup exists for the values $d = 2, 3, 5, 7, 11$ but not for larger values [56]. We can develop our formalism so as to apply to every prime dimension, regardless of whether there exists a special set $\mathcal{T}$—indeed, we did this in [7]. (If no such set exists, we use the full symplectic group and insert a factor of $1/d$ whenever we sum over the symplectic matrices.) However, in the present paper, for simplicity, we restrict our attention to those dimensions for which such a special subgroup exists. This makes the equations simpler. In Section 4, we specialize to the case of a single qubit, for which we now write down explicitly the unique special subgroup of symplectic matrices:

$$\mathcal{I} = \begin{pmatrix} 1 & 0 \\ 0 & 1 \end{pmatrix} \qquad \mathcal{R} = \begin{pmatrix} 0 & 1 \\ 1 & 1 \end{pmatrix} \qquad \mathcal{L} = \begin{pmatrix} 1 & 1 \\ 1 & 0 \end{pmatrix} \qquad (7)$$

One can verify that the difference between any two of these matrices has a nonzero determinant. The choice of symbols comes from the fact that $\mathcal{R}$ permutes the three nonzero points by rotating them to the right, whereas $\mathcal{L}$ rotates them to the left.

Now, finally, we can say what we mean by a framework for a transformation. Again, let $\mathcal{T}$ be a group of $d^2 - 1$ symplectic transformations with the nonsingular difference property. Then a framework for a transformation is simply a symplectic matrix S chosen from the set $\mathcal{T}$. (When such a group does not exist, we let every symplectic matrix define a framework.)

As we have said, for a preparation or a measurement outcome, the associated probability function—defined in the following subsection—will be required to be constant along each line of the striation B serving as the framework. Something similar happens for a transformation. However, instead of working in phase space per se, we now imagine ourselves working in the set of all *ontic transitions* from one point to another. Let us label such a transition as $\alpha \to \beta$. There are d^4 ontic transitions. Now, just as a striation B partitions the d^2 points of phase space into d sets of d points each, we can regard a symplectic transformation S as partitioning the d^4 ontic transitions into d^2 sets, each comprising d^2 transitions.

Here is how this partitioning happens. For a fixed symplectic matrix S and a given ontic transition $\alpha \to \beta$, let the *displacement* δ be defined by $\delta = \beta - S\alpha$. That is, δ is the extra displacement one needs to arrive at β, once one has applied S to α. Keeping S fixed, we define the "displacement class" associated with δ to be the set of all the ontic transitions $\alpha \to \beta$ such that $\beta - S\alpha = \delta$. For any given S, there are d^2 displacement classes, each consisting of d^2 ontic transitions. The framework S entails the following epistemic restriction: the classical transition probabilities characterizing a given transformation must be *constant* within each displacement class. In the following subsection, we show how such a set of transition probabilities is to be defined.

Consider now an entire experiment consisting of a preparation, a transformation, and a measurement. A framework for the whole experiment is obtained by choosing a framework for each component of the experiment. We express a framework $\mathcal{F}$ for this experiment as the ordered triple $\mathcal{F} = (B', S, B)$, where B and B' are the frameworks for the preparation and measurement, respectively. (We read the ordered triple from right to left, because in our equations, this is the order in which the associated probability functions will appear.)

As it turns out, we need to consider only a subset of the possible combinations (B', S, B), namely those for which the striation B' is precisely the striation obtained by applying S to the striation B. We call such a combination a *coherent* framework for the experiment. We *may* use other frameworks—ones that are not coherent—but it turns out that such frameworks will contribute nothing to our predictions for the outcome of the experiment. Similarly, if the experiment includes two or more successive transformations, so that we have a framework $(B', S_n, \ldots, S_1, B)$, we need to consider only those frameworks for which $B' = S_n \ldots S_1 B$.

We are now ready to show how the quantum description of a preparation, a transformation, or a measurement outcome can be replaced by a set of epistemically restricted classical descriptions.

2.2. Decomposing the Quantum Description of an Experiment into Classical Descriptions

We begin with the case of a preparation. The standard quantum description of a preparation is given by a density matrix $\hat{w}$. We replace this single quantum description with $d + 1$ classical descriptions $R^B(\alpha|\hat{w})$, one for each striation B. Each of these classical descriptions is simply a probability distribution over phase space, and each of these probability distributions satisfies the epistemic constraint associated with B: the distribution must be constant along each line of B.

The definition of $R^B(\alpha|\hat{w})$ in terms of the density matrix $\hat{w}$ is simple:

$$R^B(\alpha|\hat{w}) = \frac{1}{d}\langle\psi_\ell|\hat{w}|\psi_\ell\rangle, \tag{8}$$

where ℓ is the unique line in B that contains the point α. Again, $|\psi_\ell\rangle$ is the state vector associated with the line ℓ. It is not hard to show that R is a properly normalized probability distribution over phase space—that is,

$$\sum_\alpha R^B(\alpha|\hat{w}) = 1, \tag{9}$$

and it is clear that R is constant over each line in B. It is possible to reconstruct $\hat{w}$ from the whole set of R's, but in this paper, our ultimate aim is to work wholly with the classical descriptions. Therefore, we would like to think of the R's as the primary description of the preparation.

We now move on to the case of a measurement (saving the more complicated case of a transformation for later in this subsection). We are interested just in the probabilities of the outcomes of a measurement, not in any change in the system caused by the measurement. A measurement in this sense is represented in quantum theory by a POVM, that is, a set of positive semidefinite operators on the d-dimensional Hilbert space that sum to the identity. Let $\hat{E}$ be one element of such a POVM, corresponding to a particular outcome of the measurement. We now show how to replace $\hat{E}$ with a set of classical probability functions $R^B(\hat{E}|\alpha)$, one for each striation B. In keeping with the associated epistemic restriction, the function $R^B(\hat{E}|\alpha)$ will be constant along each line of B.

The definition of $R^B(\hat{E}|\alpha)$ is similar to the one in Equation (8).

$$R^B(\hat{E}|\alpha) = \langle\psi_\ell|\hat{E}|\psi_\ell\rangle, \tag{10}$$

where ℓ is again the unique line in B that contains α. Informally, we think of $R^B(\hat{E}|\alpha)$ as the probability of the outcome $\hat{E}$ when the system is at the point α (an illegal quantum state). Note that this function has a different normalization from the classical probability distributions describing a preparation. We can think of the uniform distribution over phase space—with the value $1/d^2$ for each point α—as representing the completely mixed state. (This interpretation comes from the discrete Wigner function). Therefore, we expect the following normalization:

$$\sum_\alpha \left[R^B(\hat{E}|\alpha) \times \frac{1}{d^2}\right] = \text{tr}[\hat{E}(\hat{I}/d)] = \frac{1}{d}\text{tr}\hat{E}$$
$$\implies \sum_\alpha R^B(\hat{E}|\alpha) = d\,\text{tr}\hat{E}. \tag{11}$$

One can see from Equation (10) that the function is indeed normalized in this way.

We now turn our attention to the case of a transformation. In general, the quantum description of a normalization-preserving transformation is given by a completely positive, trace-preserving map, which in turn can be specified by a set of Kraus operators. We will replace this description by a set of classical probability distributions. We restrict our attention to operations that preserve the Hilbert-space dimension, and we restrict our attention to *unital* transformations, that is, transformations that leave the completely mixed state unchanged.

We begin by defining a set of *transition quasiprobabilities* that characterize a given transformation. For an operation $\mathcal{E}$, these are defined by:

$$Q_{\mathcal{E}}(\beta|\alpha) = \frac{1}{d}\text{tr}\big[\hat{A}_\beta \mathcal{E}(\hat{A}_\alpha)\big]. \tag{12}$$

In particular, if $\mathcal{E}$ is a unitary transformation, we have:

$$Q_{\mathcal{E}}(\beta|\alpha) = \frac{1}{d}\text{tr}\big[\hat{A}_\beta \hat{U} \hat{A}_\alpha \hat{U}^\dagger\big]. \tag{13}$$

In a discrete-Wigner-function formulation, we can interpret $Q_{\mathcal{E}}(\beta|\alpha)$ as the quasiprobability that a system at the point α will move to the point β when the transformation $\mathcal{E}$ is applied. Thus, if the transformation is applied to a system described by the Wigner function $Q(\alpha|\hat{w})$, the resulting Wigner function $Q(\beta|\mathcal{E}(\hat{w}))$ is given by:

$$Q(\beta|\mathcal{E}(\hat{w})) = \sum_\alpha Q_{\mathcal{E}}(\beta|\alpha) Q(\alpha|\hat{w}). \tag{14}$$

Though $Q_{\mathcal{E}}(\beta|\alpha)$ plays the role of a probability in this equation, it is not a probability since it can take negative values [57]. It is, however, normalized as a probability distribution: $\sum_\beta Q_{\mathcal{E}}(\beta|\alpha) = 1$. Because our transformations are unital, $Q_{\mathcal{E}}$ is also normalized over its second argument: $\sum_\alpha Q_{\mathcal{E}}(\beta|\alpha) = 1$.

We use $Q_{\mathcal{E}}(\beta|\alpha)$ to define our classical transition probabilities (which are indeed nonnegative). Again, the framework for a transformation is specified by a symplectic transformation S chosen from the set $\mathcal{T}$ defined above. In the framework S, the probability that a system at point α will move to β is given by:

$$R_{\mathcal{E}}^S(\beta|\alpha) = \frac{1}{d^2} \sum_\mu Q_{\mathcal{E}}(S\mu + \delta|\mu), \tag{15}$$

where $\delta = \beta - S\alpha$. That is, we obtain $R_{\mathcal{E}}^S(\beta|\alpha)$ simply by averaging $Q_{\mathcal{E}}(\beta|\alpha)$ over the displacement class δ in which the ontic transition $\alpha \to \beta$ lies. By definition, then, $R_{\mathcal{E}}^S(\beta|\alpha)$ is constant over each displacement class.

What is much less obvious is that $R_{\mathcal{E}}^S(\beta|\alpha)$ is always nonnegative. This was proven in [7], and we do not repeat the proof here. (For the special case $d = 2$, the nonnegativity *depends* on using the special subgroup $\mathcal{T}$ of symplectic matrices. For odd primes, $R_{\mathcal{E}}^S$ is nonnegative for any symplectic S). We also showed in that paper how to reconstruct the quantum operation $\mathcal{E}$ from the entire set of $R_{\mathcal{E}}^S$'s.

We now have all the ingredients we need for a classical description of a whole experiment, within a specified framework. Let us suppose the experiment consists of a preparation, followed by a transformation, followed by a measurement. In terms of standard quantum mechanical concepts, we can compute the probability of a particular outcome via the equation:

$$P(\hat{E}|\mathcal{E}, \hat{w}) = \text{tr}\big[\hat{E}\mathcal{E}(\hat{w})\big], \tag{16}$$

where $\hat{w}$ is the initial density matrix, $\mathcal{E}$ is the transformation, and $\hat{E}$ is the POVM element representing the outcome.

Within the classical framework (B', S, B), we can try to compute the same probability by writing:

$$P(\hat{E}|\mathcal{E}, \hat{w}) \stackrel{?}{=} \sum_{\alpha\beta} R^{B'}(\hat{E}|\beta) R_{\mathcal{E}}^S(\beta|\alpha) R^B(\alpha|\hat{w}). \tag{17}$$

Note that we are combining the probabilities in the standard way. Again, every function inside the sum is nonnegative and properly normalized, so the resulting probability is at least a legitimate probability. However, it is not the correct value. This is largely because the classical story associated with a specific framework is by no means the whole story.

We need the predictions obtained from *all* the coherent frameworks in order to recover the quantum prediction. We show how this is done in the following subsection.

2.3. Recovering the Quantum Prediction: Summing the Nonrandom Parts

The formula for reconstructing the quantum prediction from the whole set of classical predictions is quite simple. As we noted in the Introduction, it depends on the concept of the "nonrandom part" of a probability, which we now explain.

For a probability distribution $R(\alpha)$ over the discrete phase space, we define the nonrandom part $\Delta R(\alpha)$ to be the deviation from the uniform distribution:

$$\Delta R(\alpha) = R(\alpha) - \frac{1}{d^2}. \tag{18}$$

For the probability of a measurement outcome $\hat{E}$, we define the nonrandom part by subtracting the probability we would assign to the outcome $\hat{E}$ if we were starting with the completely mixed state, or in phase-space language, if we were starting from the uniform distribution over phase space. Thus, we have:

$$\Delta R^B(\hat{E}|\alpha) = R^B(\hat{E}|\alpha) - \frac{1}{d^2}\sum_{\gamma} R^B(\hat{E}|\gamma), \tag{19}$$

or, for an expression using standard quantum mechanical terms,

$$\Delta P(\hat{E}|\hat{w}) = P(\hat{E}|\hat{w}) - \frac{1}{d}\mathrm{tr}\hat{E}. \tag{20}$$

For all these cases, "Δ" means that we are subtracting the "random part" of the given probability, that is, the value we would assign to the probability under a condition of minimal knowledge.

Let us now consider an experiment consisting of a preparation $\hat{w}$, a transformation $\mathcal{E}$, and a measurement, one of whose possible outcomes is $\hat{E}$. We showed in [7] that we recover the quantum mechanically predicted probability of the outcome $\hat{E}$ via the following formula:

$$\Delta P(\hat{E}|\mathcal{E},\hat{w}) = \sum_{\mathcal{F}} \Delta P^{\mathcal{F}}(\hat{E}|\mathcal{E},\hat{w}), \tag{21}$$

where the sum is over all coherent frameworks $\mathcal{F} = (B', S, B)$, and:

$$P^{\mathcal{F}}(\hat{E}|\mathcal{E},\hat{w}) = \sum_{\alpha\beta} R^{B'}(\hat{E}|\beta) R^S_{\mathcal{E}}(\beta|\alpha) R^B(\alpha|\hat{w}). \tag{22}$$

That is, within each framework, we compute the probability of $\hat{E}$ in an utterly standard way. What is nonstandard is that we then combine these various classical predictions by summing the nonrandom parts.

One component of the derivation of Equation (21) is the formula that inverts Equation (15), which was also proven in [7]:

$$\Delta Q_{\mathcal{E}}(\beta|\alpha) = \sum_{S} \Delta R^S_{\mathcal{E}}(\beta|\alpha). \tag{23}$$

We will find this equation useful in Section 4 below.

3. The Composition Rules and Their Role as Foundational Postulates

In the preceding section, we started with the standard quantum mechanical description of each component of an experiment and then defined our classical probability functions in terms of the associated quantum concepts. Our ultimate aim, though, is to develop a self-contained formulation of quantum theory, in which the basic objects are epistemically restricted classical probability functions. This means that we cannot rely on the standard concepts of quantum theory to determine which sets of classical probability functions are allowed. We must find criteria that are independent of the vectors and operators of Hilbert space. It is to this aim that we now turn our attention. In this section, therefore, we switch to an operational understanding of the symbols w, $\mathcal{E}$, and E. We use those symbols to refer to a preparation, a transformation, and a measurement outcome—processes and events one can observe in a lab—and not to any particular mathematical objects. The absence of hats on the symbols is a notational indication of this switch.

Again, the calculation in Equation (22), in which we compute the probability of the outcome E from the perspective of one of our classical observers, is quite ordinary—all the probabilities are being used in the standard way. It is only when we combine the classical predictions, via Equation (21), that we combine probabilities in a way that we would never do classically—by summing the nonrandom parts. We are inclined, then, to regard the summing of the nonrandom parts as the essentially quantum mechanical component of our formulation. We do not claim to fully understand the significance of this procedure. However, it does seem to capture what is quantum mechanical about our formalism, just as the superposition principle can be understood as the quintessential quantum mechanical feature of the usual formulation. We do not mean to imply that our rule is in any way an expression of the superposition principle, but only that we are giving our rule a fundamental status in the mathematical formalism. (The superposition principle is quite foreign to our approach, since we are working only with probabilities and not with amplitudes).

This circumstance leads us to ask whether the procedure of summing nonrandom parts can be used as a foundational principle, which could determine which sets of probability distributions are permitted.

To that end, let us consider the following four equations—the "composition rules"—all of which follow from the definitions of the preceding section, but all of which also make sense without reference to any Hilbert-space concepts. In these equations, the symbol Δ is consistently used to indicate the nonrandom part of whatever follows it:

1. Combining a preparation with a transformation to obtain another preparation:

$$\Delta R^{B'}(\beta|\mathcal{E}(w)) = \sum_{\{(S,B)|SB=B'\}} \Delta \left[\sum_{\alpha} R^S_{\mathcal{E}}(\beta|\alpha) R^B(\alpha|w) \right]; \tag{24}$$

2. Combining two transformations in sequence to obtain another transformation:

$$\Delta R^S_{\mathcal{E}_2 \circ \mathcal{E}_1}(\gamma|\alpha) = \sum_{\{(S_2,S_1)|S_2 S_1 = S\}} \Delta \left[\sum_{\beta} R^{S_2}_{\mathcal{E}_2}(\gamma|\beta) R^{S_1}_{\mathcal{E}_1}(\beta|\alpha) \right]; \tag{25}$$

3. Combining a transformation with a measurement outcome to obtain another measurement outcome:

$$\Delta R^{B'}(E'|\alpha) = \sum_{\{(B,S)|S^{-1}B=B'\}} \Delta \left[\sum_{\beta} R^B(E|\beta) R^S_{\mathcal{E}}(\beta|\alpha) \right], \tag{26}$$

where E' is the measurement outcome that is equivalent to applying $\mathcal{E}$ and then obtaining the outcome E;

4. Combining a preparation w with a measurement outcome E to obtain the probability $P(E|w)$ of the outcome E given the preparation w:

$$\Delta P(E|w) = \sum_B \Delta \left[\sum_{\alpha} R^B(E|\alpha) R^B(\alpha|w) \right]. \tag{27}$$

We can summarize all of these equations by saying that in any combination of the components of an experiment, one always sums the nonrandom parts of the classically expected results, the sum being over all frameworks that are consistent with the framework of the resulting classical probability function (or, in the last case, all frameworks that are coherent).

The equations listed above are all correct as statements within quantum theory, but our question now is whether they are *sufficient* to pick out the allowed sets of R functions.

They may not be fully sufficient. These equations set conditions on the whole system of probability distributions, describing all the components of an experiment, and there could be trade-offs among these components. It is conceivable, for example, that by being more restrictive in what we allow for measurements, we can be more generous in what we allow for preparations. In this paper, we avoid some of this worry by making the following three auxiliary assumptions, but we are not certain whether all these auxiliary assumptions are necessary:

A. For each preparation w with probability functions $R^B(\alpha|w)$, there is a corresponding measurement outcome E with probability functions $R^B(E|\alpha) = dR^B(\alpha|w)$, and the random part of $R^B(E|\alpha)$ is $1/d$;

B. For an invertible transformation $\mathcal{E}$ with probability functions $R^S_{\mathcal{E}}(\beta|\alpha)$, the probability functions of the inverse are $R^S_{\mathcal{E}^{-1}}(\beta|\alpha) = R^{S^{-1}}_{\mathcal{E}}(\alpha|\beta)$;

C. Every preparation consistent with Equation (27) and Assumption A is physically possible. Moreover, the complete system of preparations, transformations, and measurement outcomes must be *maximal*. That is, it should not be possible to add any other transformation or measurement outcome without violating Equations (24)–(27) or one of our assumptions.

Assumption A minimizes the likelihood of precisely the kind of trade-off we described above. Assumption B gives the most natural definition of the inverse in our formalism. The spirit behind Assumption C is that we are starting with a picture in which all properly normalized probability functions are allowed. The composition rules and the auxiliary assumptions are intended simply to restrict the set of such functions, and we do not want to restrict it more than necessary.

To see how a proposed set of R functions might run afoul of the composition rules and the auxiliary assumptions, suppose that for a single qubit, we were to say that there exists a preparation w such that for each striation B,

$$R^B(\alpha|w) = \begin{cases} \frac{1}{2} & \text{if } \alpha \text{ lies on the ray in } B \\ 0 & \text{otherwise} \end{cases} \quad (28)$$

Then, by Assumption A, there exists a measurement outcome E such that:

$$R^B(E|\alpha) = \begin{cases} 1 & \text{if } \alpha \text{ lies on the ray in } B \\ 0 & \text{otherwise} \end{cases} \quad (29)$$

These functions are perfectly consistent with the epistemic constraint—each is constant along each line of its striation B—but they are not consistent with Equation (27): the computed probability for the outcome E, given the preparation w, comes out to be two, which is not a legitimate value for a probability. Our question is whether similar considerations will rule out all other sets of R's that do not correspond to legitimate quantum states and processes.

We have by no means answered this question in general, but we do have some answers for the special case of a single qubit. They are the subject of the following section.

4. The Case of a Single Qubit

Here, we show how Equations (24)–(27) and Assumptions A, B, and C apply to the case $d = 2$.

4.1. The Allowed Preparations and Measurements

For now, let us continue to take d as any prime number. Let the functions $R^B(\alpha|w)$ describe a preparation w. Then, by Assumption A, there is a measurement outcome E described by $\tilde{R}^B(E|\alpha) = dR^B(\alpha|w)$. Inserting this w and E into Equation (27), we obtain:

$$\Delta P(E|w) = \sum_B \Delta \left[\sum_\alpha R^B(E|\alpha) R^B(\alpha|w) \right]. \tag{30}$$

Each term in this equation that is preceded by Δ is a probability assigned to the outcome E. Therefore, the Δ tells us to subtract $1/d$ (as is also specified in Assumption A). Collecting the constant terms on the right-hand side, we have:

$$P(E|w) = \sum_{B,\alpha} \left[R^B(E|\alpha) R^B(\alpha|w) \right] - 1. \tag{31}$$

Now, we replace $R^B(E|\alpha)$ with $dR^B(\alpha|w)$ to obtain:

$$P(E|w) = d \sum_{B,\alpha} R^B(\alpha|w)^2 - 1. \tag{32}$$

In order to prevent $P(E|w)$ from being larger than one, we need to insist that:

$$\sum_{B,\alpha} R^B(\alpha|w)^2 \leq \frac{2}{d}. \tag{33}$$

This condition must hold for every prime d. As we now show, for the case of a single qubit, it completely defines the set of allowed preparations.

For a qubit, Equation (33) becomes simply:

$$\sum_{B,\alpha} R^B(\alpha|w)^2 \leq 1. \tag{34}$$

Suppose we have a set of functions $R^B(\alpha|w)$ satisfying this inequality. Let us define the quantities r_x, r_y, and r_z as follows:

$$\begin{aligned} r_x &= \sum_\alpha (-1)^{\alpha_p} R^X(\alpha|w) \\ r_y &= \sum_\alpha (-1)^{\alpha_q + \alpha_p} R^Y(\alpha|w) \\ r_z &= \sum_\alpha (-1)^{\alpha_q} R^Z(\alpha|w), \end{aligned} \tag{35}$$

where X, Y, and Z are the horizontal, diagonal, and vertical striations, respectively. These equations can be inverted to give:

$$\begin{aligned} R^X(\alpha|w) &= \tfrac{1}{4}[1 + (-1)^{\alpha_p} r_x] \\ R^Y(\alpha|w) &= \tfrac{1}{4}[1 + (-1)^{\alpha_q + \alpha_p} r_y] \\ R^Z(\alpha|w) &= \tfrac{1}{4}[1 + (-1)^{\alpha_q} r_z]. \end{aligned} \tag{36}$$

One can see from Equation (36) that:

$$\sum_{B,\alpha} R^B(\alpha|w)^2 = \tfrac{3}{4} + \tfrac{1}{4}\left(r_x^2 + r_y^2 + r_z^2 \right). \tag{37}$$

Therefore, Equation (34) is equivalent to the condition that the vector $\vec{r} = (r_x, r_y, r_z)$ has length no greater than one.

From the definition of $R^B(\alpha|w)$ in Section 2, one can show that the R's given in Equation (36) correspond to the density matrix $\hat{w} = \frac{1}{2}(I + \vec{r} \cdot \hat{\vec{\sigma}})$, where $\hat{\vec{\sigma}}$ is the vector of Pauli matrices. We see, then, that the condition (34) is indeed sufficient to restrict the set of R's to their proper range (that is, to the range $|\vec{r}| \leq 1$). Assumption C then tells us that the entire set of such preparations is allowed. In this way, we recover the Bloch sphere.

Do our assumptions also pick out the valid measurement outcomes? In the standard quantum formalism, we can characterize the allowed POVM elements $\hat{E}$ by the following condition: an operator $\hat{E}$ is a valid POVM element if and only if the quantity:

$$P(E|w) = \text{tr}(\hat{E}\hat{w}) \tag{38}$$

lies in the interval $[0,1]$ for every density matrix $\hat{w}$. Now, Equation (27) is simply an expression of Equation (38) in our formalism. Therefore, the condition that the $P(E|w)$ appearing in Equation (27) must be in the range $[0,1]$ is equivalent to the quantum condition we have just stated. Equation (27) thus picks out the valid measurement outcomes, as long as we know what the valid preparations are. This we do know, as we have seen in the preceding paragraph.

4.2. The Allowed Invertible Transformations

Here, we aim to determine what set or sets of invertible transformations on a qubit are consistent with our assumptions.

We begin by noting that for any invertible transformation $\mathcal{E}$, we can derive from Assumption B that $R_{\mathcal{E}}^S(\beta|\alpha)$ is normalized over its second index, as well as its first. (As we noted earlier, the same is true for any unital transformation, a concept that still makes sense in our phase-space setting). We use this fact a few times in what follows.

Our next step is to derive the representation of the identity transformation $R_I^S(\beta|\alpha)$. For $d = 2$, there is a valid preparation given by the following probability distributions:

$$R^X(\alpha|w) = R^Y(\alpha|w) = \frac{1}{4}\begin{array}{|c|c|}\hline 1 & 1 \\\hline 1 & 1 \\\hline\end{array}, \quad R^Z(\alpha|w) = \frac{1}{2}\begin{array}{|c|c|}\hline 1 & 0 \\\hline 1 & 0 \\\hline\end{array}. \tag{39}$$

(The bottom left box of such a phase-space diagram corresponds to phase-space point $\alpha = (0,0)$, and the appropriate index increases by one when moving either up or right.) This corresponds to the spin-up state in the z-direction for a qubit. From the instance of Equation (24) that results from this preparation and the identity channel:

$$\Delta R^Z(\beta|w) = \sum_{\{(S,B)|SB=Z\}} \Delta\left[\sum_\alpha R_I^S(\beta|\alpha) R^B(\alpha|w)\right]. \tag{40}$$

Applying the normalization rule $\sum_\alpha R_I^S(\beta|\alpha) = 1$ to the terms with $B = X$ and $B = Y$, for which R^B is uniform, yields a null contribution. What remains is:

$$\Delta R^Z(\beta|w) = \Delta\left[\sum_\alpha R_I^{\mathcal{I}}(\beta|\alpha) R^Z(\alpha|w)\right]. \tag{41}$$

For this to hold true, the transitions of $R_I^{\mathcal{I}}(\beta|\alpha)$ must not take either of the points on the nonzero line of $R^Z(\alpha|w)$ away from that line. However, this same argument can be made for a preparation corresponding to any other line and the form of $R_I^{\mathcal{I}}(\beta|\alpha)$ should not change. This implies:

$$R_I^{\mathcal{I}}(\beta|\alpha) = \delta_{\alpha\beta}. \tag{42}$$

Therefore, whenever the identity transformation is inserted into Equation (24), the LHS of the equation will always equal the term on the RHS that includes $R_I^{\mathcal{I}}(\beta|\alpha)$. The other two terms—corresponding to the symplectic matrices $\mathcal{R}$ and $\mathcal{L}$—must sum to zero, which can only be possible for all preparations when:

$$R_I^\mathcal{R}(\beta|\alpha) = R_I^\mathcal{L}(\beta|\alpha) = \frac{1}{4}. \tag{43}$$

Equations (42) and (43) thus give us the representation of the identity transformation.

We now make use of Equation (25) specialized to the case of a transformation being combined with its inverse. Leveraging Assumption B, we find:

$$\Delta R_I^S(\gamma|\alpha) = \sum_{S'} \Delta \left[\sum_\beta R_\mathcal{E}^{SS'}(\gamma|\beta) R_\mathcal{E}^{S'}(\alpha|\beta) \right]. \tag{44}$$

We again use the fact that the sum of $R_\mathcal{E}$ over its second argument is unity. From this, it follows that we can move the Δ on the right-hand side of Equation (44) to the factors inside the sum over β (see Appendix B of [7]):

$$\sum_{S'} \Delta \left[\sum_\beta R_\mathcal{E}^{SS'}(\gamma|\beta) R_\mathcal{E}^{S'}(\alpha|\beta) \right] = \sum_{S',\beta} \Delta R_\mathcal{E}^{SS'}(\gamma|\beta) \Delta R_\mathcal{E}^{S'}(\alpha|\beta). \tag{45}$$

From Equation (23), we have that:

$$Q_\mathcal{E}(\gamma|\beta) = \frac{1}{4} + \sum_S \Delta R_\mathcal{E}^S(\gamma|\beta). \tag{46}$$

Combining Equations (44)–(46) with the inverse rule and the form of $R_I^\mathcal{T}(\beta|\alpha)$, one can show that the transition quasiprobabilities for any invertible transformation can be thought of as an orthogonal matrix:

$$\sum_\beta Q_\mathcal{E}(\gamma|\beta) Q_\mathcal{E}(\alpha|\beta) = \sum_\beta \left(\frac{1}{4} + \sum_S \Delta R_\mathcal{E}^S(\gamma|\beta) \right) \left(\frac{1}{4} + \sum_{S'} \Delta R_\mathcal{E}^{S'}(\alpha|\beta) \right) \tag{47}$$

$$= \frac{1}{4} + \sum_{S,S'} \Delta \left[\sum_\beta R_\mathcal{E}^{SS'}(\gamma|\beta) R_\mathcal{E}^{S'}(\alpha|\beta) \right] \tag{48}$$

$$= \frac{1}{4} + \sum_S \Delta R_I^S(\gamma|\alpha) \tag{49}$$

$$= \delta_{\alpha\gamma}. \tag{50}$$

Although we ultimately want to know what sets of transition probabilities $R_\mathcal{E}^S$ are allowed in our theory, the argument is less cumbersome if we work with the quasiprobabilities $Q_\mathcal{E}$ temporarily. They are of course well defined in terms of the transition probabilities $R_\mathcal{E}^S$ (by Equation (23)).

We can express the Wigner function $Q(\alpha|w)$ for a qubit as a four-component column vector $\vec{Q}_w$ on which a transition quasiprobability matrix $Q_\mathcal{E}$ acts. Thus, Equation (14) becomes:

$$\vec{Q}_{w'} = Q_\mathcal{E} \vec{Q}_w, \tag{51}$$

where $w' = \mathcal{E}(w)$. We also know that $Q_\mathcal{E}$ and its inverse both preserve normalization, which means that each row and each column of $Q_\mathcal{E}$ sums to unity. Because of this, we can write:

$$\Delta \vec{Q}_{w'} = Q_\mathcal{E} \Delta \vec{Q}_w, \tag{52}$$

where $\Delta \vec{Q}$ is defined through our usual Δ notation, that is, by subtracting $1/4$ from each component. Now, define the following orthogonal matrix:

$$M = \tfrac{1}{2}\begin{pmatrix} 1 & 1 & -1 & -1 \\ 1 & -1 & -1 & 1 \\ 1 & -1 & 1 & -1 \\ 1 & 1 & 1 & 1 \end{pmatrix}. \tag{53}$$

Then, we have:

$$\left(M\Delta\vec{Q}_{w'}\right) = MQ_{\mathcal{E}}M^T\left(M\Delta\vec{Q}_w\right). \tag{54}$$

Note that the last component of either $M\Delta\vec{Q}_w$ or $M\Delta\vec{Q}_{w'}$ is zero due to normalization. Therefore, these vectors are confined to three dimensions. Meanwhile, the matrix $MQ_{\mathcal{E}}M^T$ is still orthogonal. Moreover, it is block diagonal, consisting of a 3×3 block in the upper left and the number 1 in the lower right. Consequently, it is effectively a 3×3 orthogonal matrix acting on the three-dimensional space in which $M\Delta\vec{Q}_w$ can have nonzero components. Let us define $\hat{w}$ to be $\sum_\alpha Q(\alpha|w)\hat{A}_\alpha$. This matrix has unit trace, so we can express it as $\hat{w} = (1/2)(I + \vec{r} \cdot \hat{\vec{\sigma}})$ for some real vector $\vec{r}$. Then, one can show from the definition of $\hat{A}_\alpha$ that the three nonzero components of $M\Delta\vec{Q}_w$ are the components r_1, r_2, r_3 of $\vec{r}$. Thus, the fact that $Q_{\mathcal{E}}$ is orthogonal implies that every reversible transformation can be thought of as a rotation of the Bloch sphere, possibly combined with a reflection.

We now have a set of invertible transformations that is more permissive than that of a qubit, since it includes the possibility of reflection. That is, it includes transformations represented by 3×3 orthogonal matrices with determinant -1. (In standard quantum terms, it includes antiunitary transformations.) However, not all of the negative-determinant transformations are allowed, as we now show.

One can always decompose a negative-determinant orthogonal transformation of the sphere into an inversion through the center followed by a rotation. We denote the inversion operation as Ω. To find R_Ω^S, note that the phase point operators are defined using an expansion of Pauli operators and have unit trace, so they can be represented by points in the same three-dimensional space in which $\vec{r}$ lives. For example, $\hat{A}_{(0,0)} = \tfrac{1}{2}(I + \vec{r} \cdot \hat{\vec{\sigma}})$, where $\vec{r} = (1,1,1)$, and more generally, we can write $\hat{A}_\alpha = \tfrac{1}{2}(I + \vec{r}_\alpha \cdot \hat{\vec{\sigma}})$. Therefore, the inversion operation $\Omega(\hat{A}_\alpha)$ is well defined: extra minus signs appear before the $\hat{X}, \hat{Y}$, and $\hat{Z}$ terms. We can then use Equations (12) and (15) to find:

$$\begin{aligned} R_\Omega^\mathcal{I}(\beta|\alpha) &= \tfrac{1}{2} - \delta_{\alpha\beta}, \\ R_\Omega^\mathcal{R}(\beta|\alpha) &= R_\Omega^\mathcal{L}(\beta|\alpha) = \tfrac{1}{4}. \end{aligned} \tag{55}$$

$R_\Omega^\mathcal{I}$ has negative values and, therefore, is not compatible with our formalism.

This does not yet rule out any of the other negative-determinant transformations. (It does, however, rule out the possibility of including even a single such transformation if all the rotations are allowed, since we could then construct Ω.) Again, all negative-determinant transformations can be written as an inversion followed by a rotation $\mathcal{E}$, and we can use the combination rule in Equation (25) to show that:

$$R_{\mathcal{E} \circ \Omega}^S(\beta|\alpha) = \tfrac{1}{2} - R_\mathcal{E}^S(\beta|\alpha). \tag{56}$$

It follows that we can only allow transformations described by $\mathcal{E} \circ \Omega$, if the rotation $\mathcal{E}$ is represented by transition probabilities that never exceed $1/2$. In Appendix A, we show that this leaves us with only twelve possible rotations that can be composed with inversion to give legal transition probabilities. Let us call them $\mathcal{E}_j$. These include 90 degree right-hand rotations around each of the six cardinal directions and 180 degree rotations around each axis that forms a 45 degree angle with a pair of cardinal axes.

The twelve operations $\mathcal{E}_j \circ \Omega$ effect the permutations of the four vectors $\vec{r}_\alpha$. (Recall that these vectors correspond to the four phase point operators and thus to the four points of phase space.) Composing these operations, we obtain a set of twelve rotations of the form $\mathcal{E}_j \circ \mathcal{E}_k$. Altogether, this gives us a set of positive- and negative-determinant transformations that correspond to the twenty-four ways one can permute the four phase point operators. Although this set of twenty-four is quite different from the set of reversible transformations of a qubit, it is intriguing that it is a nontrivial set of transformations that can easily be understood classically.

We thus have two possibilities for the set of transformations: (i) a continuous set consisting of all the rotations of the Bloch sphere—the set we were aiming for—or (ii) a finite set that can be understood as comprising all possible permutations of the four ontic states. Both sets are maximal in the sense that they cannot be augmented with any other transformations.

To summarize, it appears that our composition rules and auxiliary assumptions do not uniquely lead to qubit physics. Nonetheless, our simple setup does bring us remarkably close. At this point, the best we can do is to include another assumption such as the continuity of the set of transformations that would eliminate the finite set.

5. Conclusions

For a quantum system with a prime Hilbert-space dimension, we have a way of decomposing the quantum description of an experiment into a set of classical, epistemically restricted descriptions. For each of these classical descriptions, which consist of nothing but probability functions, we can imagine an observer using these functions to compute the probability of any given outcome of the experiment. For any given classical observer, this prediction will be a bad prediction, but we know how to combine the predictions of all the classical observers to recover the correct quantum mechanical probability: we sum the nonrandom parts.

However, this picture begins with the standard formulation of quantum theory. Our aim is to develop an alternative, self-contained formulation of quantum theory in which the classical descriptions are the primary mathematical entities. The formulation we seek would thus be based entirely on actual probability functions defined on phase space. To create such a formulation, we need a set of criteria for determining when a given probabilistic description of a preparation, a transformation, or a measurement outcome is legitimate. In this paper, we have presented and begun to explore a set of equations that might serve as the basis for such criteria. These equations—our four composition rules—can all be placed under the heading, "sum the nonrandom parts." We have been led to this approach by the fact that this intriguing prescription is the only non-classical element of our formalism. We are wondering whether summing the nonrandom parts is a key to what is characteristically "quantum" about quantum theory, and we have speculated that it may play a fundamental role loosely analogous to that of the superposition principle in the standard formulation.

Summing the nonrandom parts is a strange way to combine probability distributions. It could easily lead to illegal probabilities if there were not some constraints on the probability distributions being combined. Therefore, simply by insisting that the probabilities computed via this prescription are legitimate, we are implicitly placing constraints on our classical probability distributions. This fact has led us to ask the question: Are those constraints, along with a set of intuitively plausible auxiliary assumptions, sufficient to define the structure of quantum theory?

We addressed this question for the case of a single qubit, with only reversible transformations, and we found that we can recover the usual quantum rules that determine what states are allowed and what transformations are allowed. (For the case of transformations, we need an assumption such as continuity to rule out a particular finite set of unitary and antiunitary transformations that is consistent with our other assumptions.)

However, the case of a single qubit is relatively simple. In our formalism, the set of allowed states is determined entirely by the condition that:

$$\sum_{B,\alpha} R^B(\alpha|w)^2 \leq 1. \tag{57}$$

For a general qudit, we have an analogous equation:

$$\sum_{B,\alpha} R^B(\alpha|w)^2 \leq \frac{2}{d}. \tag{58}$$

However, for $d > 2$, this is not the *only* condition required for a state to be legitimate. Therefore, any argument from our composition rules is not likely to be as simple as the one we were able to use for a single qubit.

Once we permit ourselves the extra assumption that the set of transformations is continuous, the reversible transformations on a single qubit are also relatively simple. They are equivalent to the rotations in three dimensions. Therefore, we mainly needed to show that the matrix of transition quasiprobabilities, $Q_{\mathcal{E}}(\beta|\alpha)$, is an orthogonal matrix. In higher dimensions, this matrix is again orthogonal, but other conditions must also be met in order to arrive at the unitary transformations.

However, we have by no means used all the information available in our composition rules (Equations (24)–(27)). Therefore, one can hope that these equations constitute a sufficient or nearly sufficient set of restrictions for arbitrary prime d.

Ultimately, we would like to extend our work to all Hilbert-space dimensions. In the analysis of [2], a system with composite dimension d is treated as a composite system. It would be natural for us to use the same strategy here. Thus, the phase space for a system with dimension six would be a four-dimensional space, the Cartesian product of $\mathbb{Z}_2^2$ and $\mathbb{Z}_3^2$. A framework for a preparation or a measurement outcome would consist of a striation B_2 of $\mathbb{Z}_2^2$ and a striation B_3 of $\mathbb{Z}_3^2$. In future work, we plan to use this factorization scheme to extend our treatment of preparations and measurements to arbitrary composite dimensions and, indeed, to arbitrary composite discrete systems. We see no obstacles there. The treatment of *transformations*, on the other hand, is more challenging. One can show that, if S ranges over all the 2×2 symplectic matrices with entries in $\mathbb{Z}_d$, where d is composite, then the whole set of probability distributions $R_{\mathcal{E}}^S(\beta|\alpha)$, defined in the natural way, does not contain the information needed to reconstruct the transition quasiprobabilities $Q_{\mathcal{E}}(\beta|\alpha)$. (Moreover, factoring the group of symplectic transformations into groups associated with the prime factors of d does not change the information content of the R's.) This fact does not imply that our formalism cannot be extended to composite dimensions, but it does mean that new ideas will be needed.

Of course we would also like to extend our "classical" treatment of quantum theory to the case of continuous phase space, the realm that is truly the domain of classical mechanics. The concepts of striations, displacements, and symplectic transformations are all sensible concepts for such a phase space. However, we anticipate challenges in finding the proper analogue of our notion of the sum of the nonrandom parts. For example, whereas the "random part" of a probability distribution over a discrete phase space is simply the uniform distribution, there is no such thing as a normalized uniform distribution over an infinite phase space. We plan to address this and related issues in future work.

Finally, it is interesting to ask whether our formalism lends itself to an ontological account of a quantum experiment. Each of our imagined classical observers would have no problem finding a realistic interpretation of their description of the experiment: the system is always at some location in phase space, and when a transformation occurs, the system jumps probabilistically to some other point. It is much more difficult, though, to find an ontological account that incorporates all the classical descriptions. This is not to say it cannot be done. If it is possible, it will certainly require expanding the picture beyond that of a stochastic process on phase space. It would also require making physical sense of the mathematical prescription to sum the nonrandom parts.

Author Contributions: Formal analysis, W.F.B.J. and W.K.W.; Investigation, W.F.B.J. and W.K.W.; Writing—original draft, W.F.B.J. and W.K.W.; Writing—review & editing, W.F.B.J. and W.K.W. All authors have read and agreed to the published version of the manuscript.

Funding: This research received no external funding.

Conflicts of Interest: The authors declare no conflict of interest.

Appendix A

Here, we prove that there is one possible set of transformations allowed within our scheme that includes a finite set of negative-determinant orthogonal transformations of the Bloch sphere.

Recall that we started with only our set of rules and assumptions and made no reference to Hilbert space. Using these, we found that the legal transformations can be understood as orthogonal transformations of the Bloch sphere. We now wonder what the possible rotations are that can be composed with the inversion operations Ω without generating a negative probability. We have seen that such a rotation must itself never generate a probability greater than $1/2$ for any of its R values. We could compute the R values for the orthogonal transformation $Q_\mathcal{E}$ directly from Equation (15). However, since we have established a correspondence between rotations of the sphere and unitary transformations, it is legitimate to use Equation (13), together with Equation (15), to compute these values.

The virtue of this strategy is that any unitary operation on a qubit can be expressed in a simple way:

$$\hat{U} = u_0 \hat{I} + i u_1 \hat{X} + i u_2 \hat{Y} + i u_3 \hat{Z}, \tag{A1}$$

where $\vec{u} = (u_0, u_1, u_2, u_3)$ is a real four-vector with unit length. The set of functions $R^S_\mathcal{E}$ (where $\mathcal{E}$ refers to this unitary transformation) holds twelve values that we can calculate using Equations (13) and (15). (For each of the three S's, $R^S_\mathcal{E}$ has sixteen entries, but remember that these are partitioned into four displacement classes, each of which holds a single value of $R^S_\mathcal{E}$.) These values are listed in the following phase-space diagrams, where the label on the left is the symplectic transformation S and the phase-space points correspond to the value $\delta = \beta - S\alpha$.

$$\mathcal{I}: \quad \begin{array}{|c|c|} \hline u_3^2 & u_2^2 \\ \hline u_0^2 & u_1^2 \\ \hline \end{array}$$

$$\mathcal{R}: \quad \frac{1}{4} \times \begin{array}{|c|c|} \hline (u_0 - u_1 + u_2 - u_3)^2 & (u_0 + u_1 - u_2 - u_3)^2 \\ \hline (u_0 + u_1 + u_2 + u_3)^2 & (u_0 - u_1 - u_2 + u_3)^2 \\ \hline \end{array} \tag{A2}$$

$$\mathcal{L}: \quad \frac{1}{4} \times \begin{array}{|c|c|} \hline (u_0 - u_1 + u_2 + u_3)^2 & (u_0 + u_1 + u_2 - u_3)^2 \\ \hline (u_0 - u_1 - u_2 - u_3)^2 & (u_0 + u_1 - u_2 + u_3)^2 \\ \hline \end{array}$$

Suppose for now that all the u_j's are nonnegative. Again, we have already seen in the main text that in order to be composed with the inversion operator Ω, a transformation can have no value of $R^S_\mathcal{E}(\beta|\alpha)$ greater than $1/2$. Therefore, we must have the following three relations:

$$\begin{aligned} u_0^2 + u_1^2 + u_2^2 + u_3^2 &= 1, \\ u_j &\leq \frac{1}{\sqrt{2}}, \\ u_0 + u_1 + u_2 + u_3 &\leq \sqrt{2}, \end{aligned} \tag{A3}$$

where the second line is from $R_{\mathcal{E}}^{\mathcal{T}}$ and the third line is from $R_{\mathcal{E}}^{\mathcal{R}}$. The argument is easier to see if we define $v_j = \sqrt{2}\, u_j$. Then, the conditions on v_j are:

$$v_0^2 + v_1^2 + v_2^2 + v_3^2 = 2,$$
$$v_j \leq 1, \quad\quad\quad\quad\quad\quad\quad (A4)$$
$$v_0 + v_1 + v_2 + v_3 \leq 2.$$

Because each v_j is no larger than one, $v_j^2 \leq v_j$. However, then, the only way to satisfy the first and third conditions is to make each v_j^2 equal to v_j. This means each v_j must be either zero or one. Then, the first equation tells us that exactly two v_j's are equal to one and the other two are equal to zero. Therefore, exactly two of the u_j's are equal to $1/\sqrt{2}$ and the other two are equal to zero.

Of course, we also have to deal with the possibility that one or more of the u_j's is negative. However, looking at the values of R in Equation (A2), we see that all possible combinations of the plus and minus signs appear in $R_{\mathcal{E}}^{\mathcal{R}}$ and $R_{\mathcal{E}}^{\mathcal{L}}$. Therefore, we can replace the last v condition with $|v_0| + |v_1| + |v_2| + |v_3| \leq 2$. The middle equation can be $|v_j| \leq 1$. Then, the same argument applies.

The only option we are left with is to form four-vectors where only two entries are $\pm 1/\sqrt{2}$ and the other two are zero. There are twenty-four ways to do this, but one-half of that set of vectors is just the negative of the other half. Mapping back from $\vec{u}$ to $\hat{U}$, this minus sign is just a phase that can be ignored. We are left with twelve possible rotations compatible with the inversion operator.

References

1. Zurek, W.H. Quantum Darwinism. *Nat. Phys.* **2009**, *5*, 181. [CrossRef]
2. Wootters, W.K. A Wigner-function formulation of finite-state quantum mechanics. *Ann. Phys.* **1987**, *176*, 1. [CrossRef]
3. Spekkens, R.W. Evidence for the epistemic view of quantum states: A toy theory. *Phys. Rev. A* **2007**, *75*, 032110. [CrossRef]
4. Bartlett, S.D.; Rudolph, T.; Spekkens, R.W. Reconstruction of Gaussian quantum mechanics from Liouville mechanics with an epistemic restriction. *Phys. Rev. A* **2012**, *86*, 012103. [CrossRef]
5. Spekkens, R.W. Quasi-Quantization: Classical Statistical Theories with an Epistemic Restriction. In *Quantum Theory: Informational Foundations and Foils*; Chiribella, G., Spekkens, R.W., Eds.; Springer: Dordrecht, The Netherlands, 2016.
6. Hausmann, L.; Nurgalieva, N.; del Rio, L. A consolidating review of Spekkens' toy theory. *arXiv* **2021**, arXiv:2105.03277.
7. Braasch, W.F., Jr.; Wootters, W.K. A quantum prediction as a collection of epistemically restricted classical predictions. *arXiv* **2021**, arXiv:2107.02728.
8. Rédei, M. Why John von Neumann did not like the Hilbert space formalism of quantum mechanics (and what he liked instead). *Stud. Hist. Philos. Sci. Part B* **1996**, *27*, 493–510. [CrossRef]
9. von Neumann, J. *Mathematische Grundlagen der Quantenmechanik*; Springer: Berlin/Heidelberg, Germany, 1932. Translation *Mathematical Foundations of Quantum Mechanics*; Princeton University Press: Princeton, NJ, USA, 1955.
10. Mackey, G.W. *The Mathematical Foundations of Quantum Mechanics*; W. A. Benjamin: New York, NY, USA, 1963.
11. Piron, C. Axiomatique quantique. *Helv. Phys. Acta* **1964**, *37*, 439–468.
12. Ludwig, G. *An Axiomatic Basis of Quantum Mechanics*; Derivation of Hilbert Space; Springer: Berlin/Heidelberg, Germany, 1985; Volume 1.
13. Hardy, L. Quantum Theory From Five Reasonable Axioms. *arXiv* **2001**, arXiv:quant-ph/0101012.
14. Clifton, R.; Bub, J.; Halvorson, H. Characterizing Quantum Theory in Terms of Information-Theoretic Constraints. *Found. Phys.* **2003**, *33*, 1561–1591. [CrossRef]
15. D'Ariano, G.M. How to derive the hilbert-space formulation of quantum mechanics from purely operational axioms. *AIP Conf. Proc.* **2006**, *844*, 101.
16. Goyal, P. Information-Geometric Reconstruction of Quantum Theory. *Phys. Rev. A* **2008**, *78*, 052120. [CrossRef]
17. Dakić, B.; Brukner, Č. *Quantum Theory and Beyond: Is Entanglement Special?* Cambridge University Press: Cambridge, UK, 2011; pp. 365–392.
18. Masanes, L.; Müller, M.P. A derivation of quantum theory from physical requirements. *New J. Phys.* **2011**, *13*, 063001. [CrossRef]
19. Chiribella, G.; D'Ariano, G.M.; Perinotti, P. Informational derivation of quantum theory. *Phys. Rev. A* **2011**, *84*, 012311. [CrossRef]
20. Selby, J.H.; Scandolo, C.M.; Coecke, B. Reconstructing quantum theory from diagrammatic postulates. *Quantum* **2021**, *5*, 445. [CrossRef]
21. Larsson, J. A contextual extension of Spekkens' toy model. *AIP Conf. Proc.* **2012**, *1424*, 211.

22. Catani, L.; Browne, D.E. Spekkens' toy model in all dimensions and its relationship with stabiliser quantum mechanics. *New J. Phys.* **2017**, *19*, 073035. [CrossRef]
23. Catani, L.; Browne, D.E. State-injection schemes of quantum computation in Spekkens' toy theory. *Phys. Rev. A* **2018**, *98*, 052108. [CrossRef]
24. Schmid, D.; Du, H.; Selby, J.H.; Pusey, M.F. The only noncontextual model of the stabilizer subtheory is Gross's. *arXiv* **2021**, arXiv:2101.06263.
25. Wigner, E. On the Quantum Correction For Thermodynamic Equilibrium. *Phys. Rev.* **1932**, *40*, 749–759. [CrossRef]
26. Moyal, J.E. Quantum Mechanics as a Statistical Theory. *Proc. Camb. Phil. Soc.* **1949**, *45*, 545–553. [CrossRef]
27. Groenewold, H.J. On the Principles of Elementary Quantum Mechanics. *Physica* **1946**, *12*, 405–460. [CrossRef]
28. Bracken, A.J. Quantum mechanics as an approximation to classical mechanics in Hilbert space. *J. Phys. A Math. Gen.* **2003**, *36*, L329. [CrossRef]
29. Buot, F.A. Method for calculating $\text{Tr}\mathcal{H}^n$ in solid-state theory. *Phys. Rev. B* **1974**, *10*, 3700. [CrossRef]
30. Gibbons, K.S.; Hoffman, M.J.; Wootters, W.K. Discrete phase space based on finite fields. *Phys. Rev. A* **2004**, *70*, 062101. [CrossRef]
31. Gross, D. Hudson's Theorem for finite-dimensional quantum systems. *J. Math. Phys.* **2006**, *47*, 122107. [CrossRef]
32. Gross, D. Non-negative Wigner functions in prime dimensions. *Appl. Phys. B* **2007**, *86*, 367. [CrossRef]
33. Vourdas, A. *Finite and Profinite Quantum Systems*; Springer: Cham, Switzerland, 2017.
34. Hudson, R.L. When is the Wigner quasi-probability density nonnegative? *Rep. Math. Phys.* **1974**, *6*, 249–252. [CrossRef]
35. Kenfack, A.; Zyczkowski, K. Negativity of the Wigner function as an indicator of non-classicality. *J. Opt. B Quantum Semiclass. Opt.* **2004**, *6*, 396–404. [CrossRef]
36. Spekkens, R.W. Negativity and Contextuality are Equivalent Notions of Nonclassicality. *Phys. Rev. Lett.* **2008**, *101*, 020401. [CrossRef] [PubMed]
37. Schmid, D.; Selby, J.H.; Wolfe, E.; Kunjwal, R.; Spekkens, R.W. Characterization of Noncontextuality in the Framework of Generalized Probabilistic Theories. *PRX Quantum* **2021**, *2*, 010331. [CrossRef]
38. Schmid, D.; Selby, J.H.; Pusey, M.F.; Spekkens, R.W. A structure theorem for all noncontextual ontological models of an operational theory. *arXiv* **2020**, arXiv:2005.07161.
39. Veitch, V.; Ferrie, C.; Gross, D.; Emerson, J. Negative quasi-probability as a resource for quantum computation. *New J. Phys.* **2012**, *14*, 113011. [CrossRef]
40. Bermejo-Vega, J.; Delfosse, N.; Browne, D.E.; Okay, C.; Raussendorf, R. Contextuality as a Resource for Models of Quantum Computation with Qubits. *Phys. Rev. Lett.* **2017**, *119*, 120505. [CrossRef] [PubMed]
41. Delfosse, N.; Okay, C.; Bermejo-Vega, J.; Browne, D.E.; Raussendorf, R. Equivalence between contextuality and negativity of the Wigner function for qudits. *New J. Phys.* **2017**, *19*, 123024. [CrossRef]
42. Chernega, V.N.; Man'ko, O.V.; Man'ko, V.I. Probability Representation of Quantum Observables and Quantum States. *J. Russ. Laser Res.* **2017**, *38*, 141. [CrossRef]
43. Mancini, S.; Man'ko, V.I.; Tombesi, P. Symplectic tomography as classical approach to quantum systems. *Phys. Lett. A* **1996**, *213*, 1. [CrossRef]
44. Ibort, A.; Man'ko, V.I.; Marmo, G.; Simoni, A.; Ventriglia, F. An introduction to the tomographic picture of quantum mechanics. *Phys. Scr.* **2009**, *79*, 065013. [CrossRef]
45. Ferrie, C.; Emerson, J. Frame representations of quantum mechanics and the necessity of negativity in quasi-probability representations. *J. Phys. A Math. Theor.* **2008**, *41*, 352001. [CrossRef]
46. Ferrie, C.; Emerson, J. Framed Hilbert space: Hanging the quasi-probability pictures of quantum theory. *New J. Phys.* **2009**, *11*, 063040. [CrossRef]
47. Ferrie, C.; Morris, R.; Emerson, J. Necessity of negativity in quantum theory. *Phys. Rev. A* **2010**, *82*, 044103. [CrossRef]
48. Pusey, M.F.; Barrett, J.; Rudolph, T. On the reality of the quantum state. *Nat. Phys.* **2012**, *8*, 475–478. [CrossRef]
49. Lillystone, P.; Emerson, J. A Contextual ψ-Epistemic Model of the n-Qubit Stabilizer Formalism. *arXiv* **2019**, arXiv:1904.04268.
50. Raussendorf, R.; Bermejo-Vega, J.; Tyhurst, E.; Okay, C.; Zurel, M. Phase-space-simulation method for quantum computation with magic states on qubits. *Phys. Rev. A* **2020**, *101*, 012350. [CrossRef]
51. Zurel, M.; Okay, C.; Raussendorf, R. Hidden Variable Model for Universal Quantum Computation with Magic States on Qubits. *Phys. Rev. Lett.* **2020**, *125*, 260404. [CrossRef]
52. Cohendet, O.; Combe, P.; Sirugue, M.; Sirugue-Collin, M. A stochastic treatment of the dynamics of an integer spin. *J. Phys. A Math. Gen.* **1988**, *21*, 2875. [CrossRef]
53. Cohendet, O.; Combe, P.; Sirugue-Collin, M. Fokker-Planck equation associated with the Wigner function of a quantum system with a finite number of states. *J. Phys. A Math. Gen.* **1990**, *23*, 2001. [CrossRef]
54. Hashimoto, T.; Horibe, M.; Hayashi, A. Stationary quantum Markov process for the Wigner function on a lattice phase space. *J. Phys. A Math. Theor.* **2007**, *40*, 14253. [CrossRef]
55. Fuchs, C.A.; Schack, R. Quantum-Bayesian coherence. *Rev. Mod. Phys.* **2013**, *85*, 1693. [CrossRef]
56. Chau, H.F. Unconditionally secure key distribution in higher dimensions by depolarization. *IEEE Trans. Inf. Theory* **2005**, *51*, 1451. [CrossRef]
57. Braasch, W.F., Jr.; Wootters, W.K. Transition probabilities and transition rates in discrete phase space. *Phys. Rev. A* **2020**, *102*, 052204. [CrossRef]

Revisiting Born's Rule through Uhlhorn's and Gleason's Theorems

Alexia Auffèves [1] and Philippe Grangier [2,*]

[1] Institut Néel, 25 rue des Martyrs, BP166, CEDEX 9, F38042 Grenoble, France; alexia.auffeves@neel.cnrs.fr
[2] Laboratoire Charles Fabry, Institut d'Optique Graduate School, Centre National de la Recherche Scientifique (CNRS), Université Paris Saclay, F91127 Palaiseau, France
* Correspondence: philippe.grangier@institutoptique.fr

Abstract: In a previous article we presented an argument to obtain (or rather infer) Born's rule, based on a simple set of axioms named "Contexts, Systems and Modalities" (CSM). In this approach, there is no "emergence", but the structure of quantum mechanics can be attributed to an interplay between the quantized number of modalities that is accessible to a quantum system and the continuum of contexts that are required to define these modalities. The strong link of this derivation with Gleason's theorem was emphasized, with the argument that CSM provides a physical justification for Gleason's hypotheses. Here, we extend this result by showing that an essential one among these hypotheses—the need of unitary transforms to relate different contexts—can be removed and is better seen as a necessary consequence of Uhlhorn's theorem.

Keywords: quantum mechanics; contextuality; Gleason's theorem; Uhlhorn's theorem

1. Introduction

Many recent articles have proposed derivations of Born's rule [1–4], which is clearly a major theoretical basis of quantum mechanics (QMs). In the framework of this Special Issue, let us note, in particular, the construction based on Quantum Darwinism and envariance, as proposed by Wojciech Zurek [5–8]. It will be discussed further in the conclusion, but in this article we take a different position, i.e., we start from some simple physical requirements or postulates [1], based on established (quantum) empirical evidence [9–15]; then, we infer a mathematical structure that can describe these physical requirements; and, finally, we deductively obtain Born's rule and, more generally, the probabilistic structure of QM. We note that related ideas have been discussed in the framework of quantum logic [16,17], but our approach here is a physicist's rather than a logician's. With respect to [1], the main purpose of the present article is to simplify further the required mathematical hypotheses, by showing that an essential one—the need of unitary transforms to relate different contexts—can be removed and is better seen as a necessary consequence of Uhlhorn's theorem, to be introduced below.

2. The CSM Framework

The approach of "Contexts, Systems and Modalities" (CSM) is a point of view on Quantum Mechanics based on a non-classical ontology, where physical properties are attributed to physical objects consisting of a system within a context, that is an idealized measurement apparatus. Such physical properties are called modalities, and a modality belongs to a specified system within a specified context, which is described classically (see Annex for more precise definitions). Loosely speaking, the mathematical description of a modality includes both a usual state vector $|\psi\rangle$ and a complete set of commuting operators admitting this vector as an eigenstate. Though it may appear heavier at first sight, this point of view eliminates a lot of troubles about QM, and can be seen (in some sense) as a reconciliation between Bohr and Einstein in their famous 1935 debate [18].

The main feature which makes modalities non-classical is that they are both quantized and contextual, as written above. More precisely, the empirical facts that we want to describe mathematically are:

(i) in each context a measurement provides one modality among N possible ones, that are mutually exclusive. No measurement can provide more than N mutually exclusive modalities, and once obtained in a given context, a modality corresponds to a certain and repeatable result, as long as one remains in this same context.

(ii) the certainty and repeatability of a modality can be transferred between contexts; this fundamental property is called extracontextuality of modalities. All the modalities that are related together with certainty, either in the same or in different contexts, constitute an equivalence class that we call an extravalence class.

(iii) the different contexts relevant for a given quantum system are related between themselves by transformations g that have the structure of a continuous group $\mathcal{G}$.

An essential consequence of statement (i), spelled out as Theorems 1 and 2 in [1], is that a probabilistic description is necessary. The main idea is simple: since there are, at most, N mutually exclusive modalities in any given context, as well as a continuous infinity of different contexts all carrying N modalities, the only way to relate N modality in a context to N modalities in another one must be probabilistic; otherwise, there would be a "supercontext" with more that N mutually exclusive modalities. See [1] for details. This idea is very fundamental in CSM, and it makes that probabilities are a necessary consequence of contextual quantization. From this conclusion, together with statement (ii), we can look for a probability law by using Gleason's theorem.

The third statement (iii) tells that all the different contexts relevant for a given quantum system are related between themselves by continuous transformations g, which are associative, have a neutral element (no change), and have an inverse. Therefore, this set has the structure of a continuous group $\mathcal{G}$, which is generally not commutative (such as the rotations of a macroscopic device). Our goal is then to identify a (non-classical) probabilistic framework [1] corresponding to these requirements, and to draw consequences by using suitable standard theorems.

For this purpose, the central mathematical ingredient is to associate a rank-one projector P_i (a $N \times N$ hermitian matrix, such as $P^2 = P = P^\dagger$) to each modality, with the rule that modalities associated with orthogonal projectors are mutually exclusive and modalities associated with the same projector are mutually certain. Correspondingly, a context is associated with a set of mutually orthogonal projectors, whereas an extravalence class of modalities is associated with a single projector. In addition, we assume that, given a modality in a context, the probability to get another modality in another context is a function of the two projectors associated with these two modalities (or equivalently with their two extravalence class).

The heuristic motivation for using a complete set of mutually orthogonal projectors to build up a context is that this ensures that the events associated with modalities cannot be subdivided in more elementary events, as this would be the case with classical (partition-based) probabilities. On the other hand, the construction warrants that certainty can be transferred between contexts for extravalent modalities.

Now, we want to show that the usual structure of QM follows from the above hypotheses; this means that unitary transforms between projectors as well as Born's rule are necessary in the above framework. Let us emphasize that it is easy to show these results fulfill our hypotheses; however, showing that they are necessary requires powerful (and difficult to demonstrate) mathematical theorems. Necessity also means that if one wants to give up unitary transforms or Born's rule, one has to give up one of the statements above, without contradicting empirical evidence, which is an interesting challenge [19].

3. Necessity of Unitary Transforms

As said above, the basic mathematical tool we use is to associate N mutually orthogonal projectors with the N mutually exclusive modalities within a given context. The choice of such a specific orthogonal set of projectors associated with a context is not given a priori, but once it is done, the sets of projectors in all other contexts should be obtained by a bijective map Γ reflecting the structure of the continuous group $\mathcal{G}$ of context changes. For consistency, if two orthogonal projectors are associated with two mutually exclusive modalities, they should stay orthogonal under the map Γ, whatever choice is made for the projectors associated with a "reference" (fiduciary) context. Then, let us consider the following.

Theorem 1 (Uhlhorn's theorem [20,21]). *Let $\mathcal{H}$ be a complex Hilbert space with $dim(\mathcal{H}) \geq 3$, and let $P_1(\mathcal{H})$ denote the set of all rank-one projections on $\mathcal{H}$. Then, every bijective map $\Gamma: P_1(\mathcal{H}) \to P_1(\mathcal{H})$, such that $pq = 0$ in $P_1(\mathcal{H})$ if and only if $\Gamma(p)\Gamma(q) = 0$, is induced by a unitary or anti-unitary operator on the underlying Hilbert space.*

This theorem implies that if orthogonality is conserved as required above, then the transformations between the sets of projectors associated with different contexts is unitary or anti-unitary. (As a reminder, an anti-unitary operator U is a bijective antilinear map, such that $\langle Ux|Uy\rangle = \langle x|y\rangle^*$ for all vectors x, y in $\mathcal{H}$). In the case of a continuous group of transformations, which is the case here, then the transformation must be unitary (and not anti-unitary) as long as it is continuously connected to the identity, which is the situation we are interested in (see also below).

The strength and importance of Uhlhorn's theorem is that it requires that the map keeps the orthogonality of rank-one projections, or equivalently of non-normalized vectors (or rays). A transformation mapping an orthonormal basis onto an orthonormal basis is clearly a unitary or anti-unitary transform; however, this result is far from obvious if the conservation of the norm is not required. A related (but weaker) result is Wigner's theorem, reaching the same conclusion as Uhlhorn's if the modulus of the scalar product of any two vectors is conserved by the transformation. Uhlhorn's theorem is much more powerful, since it only assumes that the scalar product is conserved when it is zero, i.e., when the two rays are orthogonal [22].

We thus get a major result: once a set of mutually orthogonal projectors associated with a fiduciary context has been chosen, the sets of projectors associated to all other contexts are obtained by unitary transformations, so we are unitarily "moving" in a Hilbert space. There are also various arguments for using unitary (complex) rather than orthogonal (real) matrices. In our framework, the simplest argument is to require that all permutations of modalities within a context are continuously connected to the identity. This is not possible with (real) orthogonal matrices, which split into two subsets with determinants ± 1, but is possible with unitary ones [12,14].

4. Necessity of Born's Rule

The next step is to consider the probability $f(P_i)$ to get a modality associated with projector P_i. By construction, a context is such that $\sum_{i=1}^{i=N} P_i = I$ and $\sum_{i=1}^{i=N} f(P_i) = 1$ for any complete set $\{P_i\}$. However, these are just the hypothesis of Gleason's theorem, so there is a density matrix ρ such that $f(P_i) = \text{Trace}(\rho P_i)$. More precisely :

Theorem 2 (Gleason's Theorem [23,24]). *Let f be a function to the real unit interval from the projection operators on a separable (real or complex) Hilbert space with a dimension at least 3. If one has $\sum_i f(P_i) = 1$ for any set $\{P_i\}$ of mutually orthogonal rank-one projectors summing to the identity, then there exists a positive-semidefinite self-adjoint operator ρ with unit trace (called a density operator), such that $f(P_i) = \text{Trace}(\rho P_i)$.*

If we start from a known modality as written in Section 2 above, then the probability value 1 is reached and ρ is also a projector Q_j, so that $f(P_i) = \text{Trace}(Q_j P_i)$ which is the usual Born's rule. As already explained in [1], we considered initial and final modalities, i.e., rank 1 projectors [14], but, more generally, Gleason's theorem provides the probability law for density operators (convex sums of projectors), interpreted as statistical mixtures.

This clarifies the link between Born's rule and the mathematical structure of density operators [25]. One, thus, can obtain the basic probabilistic framework of QM; this is enough for our purpose here, but more is needed for a full reconstruction. In particular, composite systems and tensor products should be included. See [19] for a preliminary discussion.

In addition, one must explicitly define the relevant physical properties and associated contexts that may go from space–time symmetries (Galileo group, Lorentz group) to qubits registers. Then, the unitary transforms appear as representations of the relevant group of symmetry [26]. In any case, contextual quantization applies and sets the scene where the actual physics takes place.

5. Discussion

For the sake of completeness, it is useful to reinforce the fact that some statements have already been presented in [1]. A key feature of the contextual quantification postulate (see Appendix A) is the fixed value N of the maximum number of mutually exclusive modalities, which turns out to be the dimension of Hilbert space. This provides another heuristic reason for using projectors: the projective structure of the probability law guarantees that the maximum number of mutually exclusive modalities cannot be circumvented.

This would not be the case in the usual partition-based probability theory as partitioning all modalities into N subsets for any given context would not prevent subpartitions, corresponding to additional details or hidden variables forbidden by our basic postulate. This is mathematically equivalent to the Bell's or Kochen–Specker's (KS) theorems and all their variants, which essentially demonstrate the inadequacy of probabilities based on partitions. This problem disappears when projectors are used, and then, starting from Gleason's theorem, there is no choice but Born's rule.

It should also be noted that Bell's or KS theorems consider discrete sets of contexts, while Gleason's theorem is based on the interaction between the continuum of contexts and the quantified number of accessible modalities in a given context. This feature is also fully consistent with the ideas of CSM. Therefore, Gleason's assumptions in our approach have a deep physical content that combines contextual quantification and extracontextuality of modalities. Since these features are required by empirical evidence, the usual QM formalism provides a good answer to a well-posed question.

We note, however, that our approach leads to some differences with the standard (textbook) one; in particular, the usual quantum state vector $|\psi\rangle$ is not predictively complete, since it provides a well-defined probability distribution only when "completed" by the specification of a context [27]. A complete description, also including the contexts requires the use of algebraic methods [19].

To conclude, let us come back to some epistemological difference between the approach used here and the one favored by Wojciech Zurek [5–7]. In his point of view, the role of mathematics is prescriptive. First, "Let be Ψ", and then all the rest should follow. On the contrary, in our approach its role is descriptive; there is a physical world out there, and the mathematical langage is our best tool to "speak" about it—but it is a langage, not the Tables of the Law. Additionally, in CSM, there is no "Emergence of the Classical" [7] as both classical and quantum descriptions are needed to make sense of our physical universe, where an object is a system within a context.

More specifically about Born's rule, in [8], Wojciech Zurek proposes to derive it, and to identify and analyse origins of probability and randomness in physics, based on environment-assisted invariance (envariance), i.e., a quantum symmetry of entangled systems. An interesting remark in this article is "The only known way to recognize effective classicality in a wholly quantum Universe is based on decoherence. But decoherence is 'off limits' as it employs tools dependent on Born's rule. On the other hand, when classicality was 'imposed by force' by Gleason (...), this seemed to work to a degree, although interpretational issues were left largely unaddressed and doubts have rightly persisted". The goal pursued in the present paper is to address these interpretational issues with precision and hopefully to remove the corresponding doubts.

These subtleties may appear more philosophical than practical, and they do not preclude an agreement on more down-to-the-earth issues, e.g., the management of decoherence for applications to quantum technologies. However, keeping such foundational issues opened and discussed is certainly a compost for new ideas to germinate.

Author Contributions: Writing—original draft, P.G.; Writing—review & editing, A.A. All authors have read and agreed to the published version of the manuscript.

Funding: This research received no external funding.

Acknowledgments: The authors thank Franck Laloë and Roger Balian for many useful discussions, and Nayla Farouki for continuous support.

Conflicts of Interest: The authors declare no conflict of interest.

Appendix A. CSM Definitions and Postulates

For the convenience of the reader, this Appendix summarizes the basic elements of CSM, that have already been published elsewhere, see, e.g., [1].

Hypothesis 1a (ontology). *Let us consider a quantum system S interacting with a specified set of measurement devices, called a* **context***. The best physically allowed measurement process provides a set of numbers, corresponding to the values of a complete set of jointly measurable quantities. Ideally, these values will be found again with certainty, as long as the system and context are kept the same; they define a* **modality***, belonging to a system within a context.*

We note that the free evolution of the system is omitted here; if it is present, the result of a new measurement can still be predicted with certainty, but in another context that can be deduced from the free evolution. Here, the word "context" includes the actual settings of the device, e.g., the fact that S_z is measured rather than S_x. Thus, the context must be factual, not contrafactual. On the other hand, all devices designed to measure S_z are equivalent as a context, in a (Bohrian) sense that they all define the same conditions for predicting the future behaviour of the system. Note that the modalities are not defined in the same way as the usual "quantum states of the system" since they are explicitly attached to both the context and the system. This leads to the following addition:

Hypothesis 1b (extravalence). *When S interacts in succession with different contexts, certainty and repeatability may be transferred between their modalities. This is called* **extracontextuality***, and defines an equivalence class between modalities, called* **extravalence***.*

The equivalence relation is obvious. For more details and examples of extravalence classes, see [14]. Note that extravalent modalities appear only if $N \geq 3$, which has an obvious geometrical interpretation in relation with both Gleason's and Uhlhorn's theorems. From the above postulates, one measurement provides one and only one modality. Therefore in any given context the various possible modalities are mutually exclusive, i.e., if one is true, or verified, all other ones are not true or not verified. This is formalized by

Hypothesis 2 (contextual quantization). *For a given context, i.e., a given "knob settings" of the measurement apparatus, there exist N modalities that are mutually exclusive. The value of N, called the dimension, is a characteristic property of a given quantum system and is the same in any relevant context.*

Modalities observed in different contexts are generally not mutually exclusive, they are said to be incompatible, meaning that if a result is true, or verified, one cannot tell whether the other one is true or not. The corresponding (Born's) probability law is obtained from Gleason's theorem [1]. Finally, a last statement defines the relation between contexts:

Hypothesis 3 (changing contexts). *The different contexts relevant for a given quantum system are related between themselves by (classical) transformations that have the structure of a generally non-commutative continuous group $\mathcal{G}$.*

The intuitive idea behind these statements is that making more measurements in QM (by changing the context) cannot provide "more details" about the system, because this would increase the number of mutually exclusive modalities, contradicting Hypothesis 2. One might conclude that changing context randomizes all results, but this is not true either, as some modalities may be related with certainty between different contexts.

This is why extravalence is an essential feature of the construction, both as a physical requirement, and as a justification for Gleason's hypotheses. Given also Uhlhorn's hypotheses, that changing the context must preserve the mutual exclusiveness of modalities, or the orthogonality of projectors, Born's rule appears as a necessity.

References

1. Auffèves, A.; Grangier, P. Deriving Born's rule from an Inference to the Best Explanation. *Found. Phys.* **2020**, *50*, 1781–1793. [CrossRef]
2. Adesso, G.; Franco, R.L.; Parigi, V. Foundations of quantum mechanics and their impact on contemporary society. *Philos. Trans. R. Soc. A Math. Phys. Eng. Sci.* **2018**, *376*, 20180112. [CrossRef] [PubMed]
3. Khrennikov, A.; Summhammer, J. Dialogue on Classical and Quantum between mathematician and experimenter. *arXiv* **2001**, arXiv:quant-ph/0111130.
4. Laloë, F. *Do We Really Understand Quantum Mechanics?*; Cambridge University Press: Cambridge, UK, 2012.
5. Zurek, W.H. Quantum darwinism, classical reality, and the randomness of quantum jumps. *Phys. Today* **2014**, *67*, 44–50. [CrossRef]
6. Auffèves, A.; Grangier, P.; Kastner, R.E.; Zurek, W.H. Classical selection and quantum Darwinism. *Phys. Today* **2015**, *68*, 8–10. [CrossRef]
7. Zurek, W.H. Emergence of the Classical from within the Quantum Universe. *arXiv* **2021**, arXiv:2107.03378.
8. Zurek, W.H. Probabilities from entanglement, Born's rule $p_k = |\psi_k|^2$ from envariance. *Phys. Rev. A* **2005**, *71*, 052105. [CrossRef]
9. Lipton, P. *Inference to the Best Explanation*, 2nd ed.; Routledge: London, UK, 2004.
10. Auffèves, A.; Grangier, P. Contexts, Systems and Modalities: A new ontology for quantum mechanics. *Found. Phys.* **2016**, *46*, 121. [CrossRef]
11. Auffèves, A.; Grangier, P. Violation of Bell's inequalities in a quantum realistic framework. *Int. J. Quantum Inf.* **2016**, *14*, 1640002. [CrossRef]
12. Auffèves, A.; Grangier, P. Recovering the quantum formalism from physically realist axioms. *Sci. Rep.* **2017**, *7*, 43365. [CrossRef]
13. Grangier, P.; Auffèves, A. What is quantum in quantum randomness?. *Philos. Trans. R. Soc. A Math. Phys. Eng. Sci.* **2018**, *376*, 20170322. [CrossRef] [PubMed]
14. Auffèves, A.; Grangier, P. Extracontextuality and extravalence in quantum mechanics. *Philos. Trans. R. Soc. A Math. Phys. Eng. Sci.* **2018**, *376*, 20170311. [CrossRef] [PubMed]
15. Auffèves, A.; Grangier, P. A generic model for quantum measurements. *Entropy* **2019**, *21*, 904. [CrossRef]
16. Svozil, K. *Quantum Logic*; Springer: Singapore, 1998.
17. Pitowsky, I. *Quantum Probability–Quantum Logic*; Springer: New York, NY, USA, 2006.
18. Farouki, N.; Grangier, P. The Einstein-Bohr debate: finding a common ground of understanding? *Found. Sci.* **2021**, *26*, 97–101. [CrossRef]
19. Grangier, P. Completing the quantum formalism in a contextually objective framework. *Found. Phys.* **2021**, *51*, 76. [CrossRef]
20. Uhlhorn, U. Representation of symmetry transformations in quantum mechanics. *Arkiv Fysik* **1962**, *23*, 307–340.
21. Chevalier, G. Wigner-Type Theorems for Projections. *Int. J. Theor. Phys.* **2008**, *47*, 69–80. [CrossRef]
22. Semrl, P. Wigner symmetries and Gleason's theorem. *J. Phys. A Math. Theor.* **2021**, *54*, 315301. [CrossRef]
23. Gleason, A.M. Measures on the Closed Subspaces of a Hilbert Space. *J. Math. Mech.* **1957**, *6*, 885. [CrossRef]
24. Cooke, R.; Keanes, M.; Moran, W. An elementary proof of Gleason's theorem. In *Mathematical Proceedings of the Cambridge Philosophical Society*; Cambridge University Press: Cambridge, UK, 1985; Volume 98, pp. 117–128.
25. Masanes, L.; Galley, T.D.; Müller, M.P. The Measurement Postulates of Quantum Mechanics are Redundant. *Nat. Commun.* **2019**, *10*, 1361. [CrossRef]
26. Laloë, F. Symétries continues. *Collection Savoirs Actuels-Mathématiques*; EDP Sciences: Les Ulis, France, 2021; ISBN 978-2-7598-2631-5.
27. Grangier, P. Contextual inferences, nonlocality, and the incompleteness of quantum mechanics. *Entropy* **2021**, *23*, 1660. [CrossRef] [PubMed]

Emergence of Objectivity for Quantum Many-Body Systems

Harold Ollivier

Institut National de Recherche en Informatique et en Automatique, 2 Rue Simone Iff, 75012 Paris, France; harold.ollivier@inria.fr

Abstract: We examine the emergence of objectivity for quantum many-body systems in a setting without an environment to decohere the system's state, but where observers can only access small fragments of the whole system. We extend the result of Reidel (2017) to the case where the system is in a mixed state, measurements are performed through POVMs, and imprints of the outcomes are imperfect. We introduce a new condition on states and measurements to recover full classicality for any number of observers. We further show that evolutions of quantum many-body systems can be expected to yield states that satisfy this condition whenever the corresponding measurement outcomes are redundant.

Keywords: decoherence; quantum–classical transition; many-body system; quantum Darwinism

1. Introduction

The emergence of classical reality from within a quantum mechanical universe has always been central to discussions on the foundations of quantum theory. While decoherence—through interactions of a quantum system with its environment—accounts for the disappearance of superpositions of quantum states [1–3], it does not provide an a priori explanation for all intrinsic properties of a classical world and, in particular, for the emergence of an objective classical reality.

Quantum Darwinism [4–11] proposes a solution to fill this gap. Its credo states that rather than interacting directly with systems of interest, observers intercept a small fraction of their environment to gather information about them. Classicality then emerges naturally from quantum Darwinism. First, observing the system of interest $\mathcal{S}$ indirectly, by measuring its environment $\mathcal{E}$ rather than directly with an apparatus, restricts obtainable information to observables on $\mathcal{S}$ that are faithfully recorded in the environment. In practice, these observables are commuting with the well-defined preferred pointer basis induced by decoherence due to the interaction Hamiltonian between $\mathcal{S}$ and $\mathcal{E}$. Second, requiring the observer to be able to infer the state of $\mathcal{S}$ by measuring only a small fraction of $\mathcal{E}$ implies that many such observers can do the same without modifying the state of the system. This, in turn, grants the state of the system an objective existence, as it can be discovered and agreed upon by many observers.

While early descriptions of quantum Darwinism [4,5] focused on simple models to build intuition, several subsequent works have studied the redundancy of information in more complex settings. References [8,12–15] show that quantum Darwinism—through the redundant proliferation of information about the pointer states in the environment—is a rather ubiquitous phenomenon encountered in many realistic situations.

The models used above to exemplify quantum Darwinism consider that the whole universe can be naturally split between $\mathcal{S}$, the system of interest, and $\mathcal{E}$, the environment itself subdivided into subsystems $\mathcal{E} = \cup_i \mathcal{E}_i$. As a consequence, the emergence of classicality is de facto analyzed relative to this separation. Redundant information is sought about observables on $\mathcal{S}$ in $\mathcal{E}$. Yet, this is already going beyond what seems to be the minimal requirement that should allow to recover classical features of the universe: a natural egalitarian tensor–product structure for the state space, without explicit reference to a preferred system–environment dichotomy.

Such a scenario is particularly relevant for the Consistent Histories framework [16–18]. The universe is viewed as a closed quantum system in which one wants to identify a single set of consistent histories that describe the quasi-classical domain, where emergent coarse-grained observables follow the classical equations of motion [19], and become objective for observers embedded in the quantum universe. In a similar fashion, this scenario is adapted for understanding the emergence of objective properties in many-body physics. The reason is that for such composite systems, quantum fluctuations can be recorded into complex mesoscopic regions, e.g., in the course of their amplification by classically chaotic systems. Hence, redundant information need not be relative to observables of a single subsystem or any predefined set of subsystems, but rather to observables of to-be-determined sets of subsystems. Ref. [20] examines this question and shows that, due to the absence of a fixed set of subsystems defining the system of interest $\mathcal{S}$, it is possible to construct redundant records for two mutually incompatible observables. While this gives a clear example where redundancy of information is not enough to guarantee the uniqueness of objective observables, the main result of [20] shows that this ambiguity requires the redundant records to delicately overlap with one another. In practical situations, such a delicate overlap is expected to be unlikely, thereby recovering the usual uniqueness of objective observables.

The present work shows that a similar conclusion can be expected in a more general setting, where redundant records are not required to be perfectly imprinted in the Hilbert space of the whole universe and where observables are replaced with POVMs (Throughout this paper, observable refer to sharp observables, so that POVMs are a generalization of observables). To this end, Section 2 presents an overview of [20] and outlines some of the key ingredients used implicitly when relying on perfect redundant records of observables. Section 3 generalizes the tools defining redundancy and classicality to our scenario. Section 4 provides a sufficient criterion on the approximate redundant records to recover classicality for a single set of POVMs on $\mathcal{S}$. Finally, Section 5 takes a dynamical perspective to the emergence of objectivity and shows that our criterion is expected to hold in a wide range of situations, thereby implying that quantum Darwinism is a ubiquitous explanation for the emergence of classical properties in quantum many-body systems.

2. Objectivity for Idealized Quantum Many-Body Systems

In Ref. [20], an archetypal quantum many-body system is introduced to study the emergence of objective properties. It consists of a quantum system $\mathcal{S}$ composed of a collection of microscopic quantum systems $\mathcal{S} = \cup_{i=1}^{N} \mathcal{S}_i$. As a consequence, the Hilbert space $\mathcal{H}_\mathcal{S}$ of $\mathcal{S}$ has a natural tensor–product structure, $\mathcal{H}_\mathcal{S} = \bigotimes_i \mathcal{H}_{\mathcal{S}_i}$.

Objective classical properties for $\mathcal{S}$ are expected to emerge from redundant imprints that are accessible to observers using feasible measurements on fractions of $\mathcal{S}$. More precisely, assuming $\mathcal{S}$ is in a pure state $|\psi\rangle$, redundant observables should induce a decomposition of $|\psi\rangle$ into orthogonal but un-normalized branches $|\psi_i\rangle$

$$|\psi\rangle = \sum_i |\psi_i\rangle, \qquad (1)$$

each $|\psi_i\rangle$ being a common eigenstate of the redundant observables. This implies that, for measurements on fractions of $\mathcal{S}$, this coherent superposition is indistinguishable from the incoherent classical mixture $\sum_i |\psi_i\rangle\langle\psi_i|$, thus forbidding observers to experience the quantumness of the correlations between fragments of $\mathcal{S}$.

The similarity with quantum Darwinism should be clearly apparent: for both, not all subsystems can be measured simultaneously, thus forcing partial observations. In the presence of faithful redundant imprints, this would allow several observers to agree on their measurement results, thereby granting those records and associated observables an objective existence.

However, the similarity stops here. For quantum many-body systems, one cannot readily conclude that evolutions inducing faithful redundant imprints will favor the emergence of a *single* set of redundant observables, contrarily to usual system–environment settings [21]. The reason for such difference stems from the absence, in the many-body setting, of precise localization for the redundant records themselves.

For instance, in Ref. [21], although the choice of one subsystem of the whole universe for playing the role of reference system is arbitrary—any other would be equivalent for the purpose of the conducted analysis—it is clearly identified, and the redundant imprints refer to a measurement record of an observable for this specific subsystem. Therefore, comparisons between the conclusions drawn for different choices of the reference subsystem cannot be made. Even more strikingly, Ref. [20] gives a concrete example of two redundantly recorded, yet non-commuting, observables for $\mathcal{S}$. One or the other could then equally pretend to be objective, while their combination does not allow the branch decomposition of Equation (1).

To see this, consider $\mathcal{S}$ made of qubits $\mathcal{S}_{i,j}$ where $(i,j) \in [1,N] \times [1,N]$. The state of $\mathcal{S}$ is prepared by applying a CPTP map Λ from a single qubit to $\mathcal{S}$ and defined in the following way:

$$|0\rangle \to |\bar{0}\rangle = \frac{1}{\sqrt{2^N}} \bigotimes_{i=1}^{N} \left(\bigotimes_{j=1}^{N} |0\rangle_{i,j} + \bigotimes_{j=1}^{N} |1\rangle_{i,j} \right)$$

$$|1\rangle \to |\bar{1}\rangle = \frac{1}{\sqrt{2^N}} \bigotimes_{i=1}^{N} \left(\bigotimes_{j=1}^{N} |0\rangle_{i,j} - \bigotimes_{j=1}^{N} |1\rangle_{i,j} \right).$$

Clearly, for fixed i, the measurement of the qubits labeled $\{(i,j), j \in [1,N]\}$ in the basis $(\bigotimes_{j=1}^{N} |0\rangle_{i,j} \pm \bigotimes_{j=1}^{N} |1\rangle_{i,j})/\sqrt{2}$ is equivalent to the measurement of the whole system relative to the basis $\{|\bar{0}\rangle, |\bar{1}\rangle\}$. This means that the information about the observable $\bar{Z} = |\bar{0}\rangle\langle\bar{0}| - |\bar{1}\rangle\langle\bar{1}|$ is perfectly imprinted N times in $\mathcal{S}$.

In addition, one can also rewrite the vectors $|\bar{0}\rangle$ and $|\bar{1}\rangle$:

$$|\bar{0}\rangle = \frac{1}{\sqrt{2^N}} \bigotimes_{i=1}^{N} \left(\bigotimes_{j=1}^{N} |0\rangle_{i,j} + \bigotimes_{j=1}^{N} |1\rangle_{i,j} \right)$$
$$= \frac{1}{\sqrt{2^N}} \sum_{b=0}^{2^N-1} \bigotimes_{j=1}^{N} |b_j\rangle \qquad (2)$$

$$|\bar{1}\rangle = \frac{1}{\sqrt{2^N}} \bigotimes_{i=1}^{N} \left(\bigotimes_{j=1}^{N} |0\rangle_{i,j} - \bigotimes_{j=1}^{N} |1\rangle_{i,j} \right)$$
$$= \frac{1}{\sqrt{2^N}} \sum_{b=0}^{2^N-1} \bigotimes_{j=1}^{N} (-1)^b |b_j\rangle, \qquad (3)$$

where, for a given b written as a binary string $b = (b_1, \ldots, b_N)$, $|b\rangle = \bigotimes_{i=1}^{N} |b_i\rangle_i$. Combining Equations (2) and (3), the conjugate basis has a simple expression:

$$\frac{|\bar{0}\rangle + |\bar{1}\rangle}{\sqrt{2}} = \frac{1}{\sqrt{2^N}} \sum_{\substack{b \in [0, 2^N-1] \\ h(b): \text{even}}} \bigotimes_{j=1}^{N} |b_j\rangle$$

$$\frac{|\bar{0}\rangle - |\bar{1}\rangle}{\sqrt{2}} = \frac{1}{\sqrt{2^N}} \sum_{\substack{b \in [0, 2^N-1] \\ h(b): \text{odd}}} \bigotimes_{j=1}^{N} |b_j\rangle,$$

where $h(b)$ denotes the Hamming weight of b. As a consequence of this rewrite, for fixed j, any measurement of qubits labeled $\{(i,j), i \in [0,N]\}$ that reveals the parity of the weight of b_j is equivalent to a measurement of the conjugate observable $\bar{X} = |\bar{0}\rangle\langle\bar{1}| + |\bar{1}\rangle\langle\bar{0}|$. Hence, the information about $\bar{X}$ is perfectly imprinted N times in $\mathcal{S}$, leading to an apparent paradox. Each $\bar{X}$ and $\bar{Z}$ defines a set of redundantly imprinted observables, yet each set is incompatible with the other. The measurement results that can be gathered by observers measuring the redundant imprints cannot be explained by resorting to a classical mixture of orthogonal states. Here, redundancy is not enough to imply the classicality of observables.

Nonetheless, it should be noted that both observables cannot be measured simultaneously by different observers in spite of their redundancy. This is because any redundant record of $\bar{X}$ and any reduncant record of $\bar{Z}$ overlap in exactly one qubit and require incompatible measurements for this specific qubit. Thus, it is not possible to share one redundant record of $\bar{Z}$ with one observer, and one about $\bar{X}$ with another. It is also not possible to have the first observer perform a non-destructive measurement of $\bar{Z}$ on its part of $\mathcal{S}$ and pass the overlapping qubit to the second observer so that he/she measures $\bar{X}$: the first measurement already destroys the needed coherence for the second.

This remark is the core of the main result of [20] for recovering objectivity for quantum many-body systems. A sufficient criterion is introduced to guarantee that any two redundant records in $\mathcal{S}$, possibly corresponding to different observables F and G, can always be measured in any order and yet yield compatible results. More precisely, it ensures that the state $|\psi\rangle$ of the whole system $\mathcal{S}$ can be written as $|\psi\rangle = \sum_i |\psi_i\rangle$, where each $|\psi_i\rangle$ is a simultaneous eigenstate of F and G, thereby ensuring the orthogonality of the $|\psi_i\rangle$ and the indistinguishability between $|\psi\rangle$ and $\sum_i |\psi_i\rangle\langle\psi_i|$ for feasible measurements.

To make this formal (see [20] for details), suppose $\boldsymbol{F} = \{F_f\}_{f \in \mathcal{F}}$ and $\boldsymbol{G} = \{G_g\}_{g \in \mathcal{G}}$ are two sets of redundantly recorded observables on $\mathcal{S}$ with respect to the corresponding partitions $\mathcal{F}$ and $\mathcal{G}$ of the microscopic sites $\mathcal{S}_i$ of $\mathcal{S}$. This means that for each element $f \in \mathcal{F}$, there exists an observable $F_f \in \boldsymbol{F}$ on f that can be decomposed into projectors $\{F_f^\alpha\}_\alpha$ where α is an eigenvalue of F_f such that

$$\forall \alpha,\ \forall f' \in \mathcal{F},\quad F_f^\alpha |\psi\rangle = F_{f'}^\alpha |\psi\rangle,$$

and similarly for $G_g \in \boldsymbol{G}$ on $g \in \mathcal{G}$ with projectors $\{G_g^\mu\}_\mu$ associated to eigenvalues μ of G_g. Then, a sufficient condition on $\mathcal{F}$ and $\mathcal{G}$ to ensure that results of F_f on f are compatible with those of G_g on g, for all values of f and g, is that for all $f, f' \in \mathcal{F}$, there exists $g \in \mathcal{G}$, possibly depending on f, and f' such that $f \cap g = f' \cap g = \emptyset$, and vice versa with the roles of $\mathcal{F}$ and $\mathcal{G}$ permuted. This property is called *non pair-covering* of $\mathcal{F}$ and $\mathcal{G}$ [20].

As a result, when $\mathcal{F}$ and $\mathcal{G}$ are not pair covering each other, we have

$$\forall f, f' \in \mathcal{F},\ \exists g \in \mathcal{G},\quad F_f^\alpha G_g^\mu |\psi\rangle = F_{f'}^\alpha G_g^\mu |\psi\rangle,$$
$$\forall g, g' \in \mathcal{G},\ \exists f \in \mathcal{F},\quad G_g^\mu F_f^\alpha |\psi\rangle = G_{g'}^\mu F_f^\alpha |\psi\rangle.$$

In essence, this means that not only are there redundant imprints of the observables in $\boldsymbol{F}$ in the state $|\psi\rangle$ of $\mathcal{S}$, but the redundancy remains even though $G_g \in \boldsymbol{G}$ is actively measured or $|\psi\rangle$ is decohered as a result of tracing out $g \in \mathcal{G}$ (and the same with the roles of $\boldsymbol{F}$ and $\boldsymbol{G}$ permuted).

This is indeed enough to impose the commutation on the support of $|\psi\rangle$: using the same notation, for any f and g, the non-pair covering condition gives

$$\exists g',\quad f \cap g' = \emptyset$$
$$\exists f',\quad f' \cap g = f' \cap g' = \emptyset.$$

Then,

$$F_f^\alpha G_g^\mu |\psi\rangle = F_f^\alpha G_{g'}^\mu |\psi\rangle \tag{4}$$
$$= F_{f'}^\alpha G_{g'}^\mu |\psi\rangle \tag{5}$$
$$= G_{g'}^\mu F_{f'}^\alpha |\psi\rangle \tag{6}$$
$$= G_g^\mu F_{f'}^\alpha |\psi\rangle \tag{7}$$
$$= G_g^\mu F_f^\alpha |\psi\rangle, \tag{8}$$

where Equations (4) and (8) follow from the redundancy of records, Equations (5) and (7) derive from the non-pair covering condition, and Equation (6) is a direct consequence of the absence of overlap between f' and g'.

One can now prove by induction that the same holds for multiple sets of redundantly imprinted observables $F, G, \ldots Z$. Their projectors commute over $|\psi\rangle$, allowing to define a common branch decomposition for the state of the system as prescribed by Equation (1).

3. Approximate Records and Classicality for Quantum Many-Body Systems

The significance of the non-pair covering criterion introduced in the previous section is due to the relative ease with which it is met in practice. The overlap that is required to maintain the ambiguity between redundantly recorded, yet incompatible, observables is too delicate to happen in realistic physical systems—see [20] for an extended discussion on this point.

However, this reasoning suffers from several drawbacks. First, the non-pair covering criterion is applicable only to (sharp) observables and not to the broader information gathering strategies that can be implemented using POVMs. Second, redundant observables must be perfectly imprinted in fragments of $\mathcal{S}$. Both restrictions can be ultimately traced back to how redundancy is measured and how classicality is deemed, that is, whenever projective measurements are compatible on the state $|\psi\rangle$ of the system, or equivalently, whenever they commute on the support of $|\psi\rangle$.

The paragraphs below address these two points by providing a definition of approximate redundant records of POVMs and an alternative witness for their classicality.

3.1. Approximate Copies of POVM Records

Let $\mathcal{S} = \cup_{i=1}^N \mathcal{S}_i$ be a many-body system with N microscopic sites. Denote by $\mathcal{F}$ a partition of $[1, N]$ and by $\mathcal{S}_f = \cup_{i \in f} \mathcal{S}_i$, for $f \in \mathcal{F}$.

Definition 1 (δ-approximate records). *For $f, f' \in \mathcal{F}$ with $f \neq f'$, and two POVMs $F_f = \{F_f^\alpha\}_\alpha$ and $F_{f'} = \{F_{f'}^\alpha\}_\alpha$, respectively, on S_f and $S_{f'}$. For $\delta > 0$, we say that $F_{f'}$ δ-approximately records F_f on the system state ρ if, $\forall \alpha$,*

$$\mathrm{tr}\left(F_f^\alpha \otimes F_{f'}^\alpha \rho\right) \geq (1-\delta)\,\mathrm{tr}\left(F_f^\alpha \rho\right).$$

As expected, this definition captures the fact that, given that outcome α is observed by measuring F_f on ρ, a measurement of $F_{f'}$ yields the same outcome α with a probability of at least $1 - \delta$. This is because

$$\Pr\left(F_{f'} \text{ yields outcome } \alpha \mid F_f \text{ yields outcome } \alpha \right) = \frac{\mathrm{tr}\left(F_f^\alpha \otimes F_{f'}^\alpha \rho\right)}{\mathrm{tr}\left(F_f^\alpha \rho\right)}.$$

When the above property is true for all $f, f' \in \mathcal{F}$, we say that the set of POVMs $= \{F_f\}_{f \in \mathcal{F}}$ is $|\mathcal{F}|$-*times δ-approximately redundant*.

The following lemma shows that Definition 1 falls back to that of [20] for $\delta = 0$, pure system states and (sharp) observables.

Lemma 1. *Assume F_f and $F_{f'}$ are projective measurements on disjoint subsets f and f' of $[1, N]$, and that $F_{f'}$ 0-approximately records F_f on $|\psi\rangle$. Then*

$$F_f^\alpha \otimes F_{f'}^\alpha |\psi\rangle = F_{f'}^\alpha |\psi\rangle.$$

Proof. Define the following normalized states

$$\left|\psi_{F_f^\alpha}\right\rangle = \frac{F_f^\alpha |\psi\rangle}{\text{tr}\left(F_f^\alpha |\psi\rangle\langle\psi|\right)} \text{ and } \left|\psi_{F_{f'}^\alpha}\right\rangle = \frac{F_{f'}^\alpha |\psi\rangle}{\text{tr}\left(F_{f'}^\alpha |\psi\rangle\langle\psi|\right)}.$$

By assumption, $\text{tr}\left(F_f^\alpha \otimes F_{f'}^\alpha |\psi\rangle\langle\psi|\right) = \text{tr}\left(F_f^\alpha |\psi\rangle\langle\psi|\right)$. Using the definition of $\left|\psi_{F_f^\alpha}\right\rangle$, this becomes

$$\text{tr}\left(F_{f'}^\alpha \left|\psi_{F_f^\alpha}\right\rangle\left\langle\psi_{F_f^\alpha}\right|\right) \times \text{tr}\left(F_f^\alpha |\psi\rangle\langle\psi|\right) = \text{tr}\left(F_f^\alpha |\psi\rangle\langle\psi|\right).$$

Hence, one concludes that $\text{tr}\left(F_{f'}^\alpha \left|\psi_{F_f^\alpha}\right\rangle\right) = 1$, which implies that

$$F_{f'}^\alpha \left|\psi_{F_f^\alpha}\right\rangle = \left|\psi_{F_f^\alpha}\right\rangle. \tag{9}$$

Similarly, for all α, β, we have

$$\text{tr}\left(F_f^\alpha \left|\psi_{F_{f'}^\beta}\right\rangle\left\langle\psi_{F_{f'}^\beta}\right|\right) = \frac{\text{tr}\left(F_f^\alpha \otimes F_{f'}^\beta |\psi\rangle\langle\psi|\right)}{\text{tr}\left(F_{f'}^\beta |\psi\rangle\langle\psi|\right)}.$$

Using equation (9) on the rhs above and recalling that $F_{f'}^\alpha \times F_{f'}^\beta = F_{f'}^\alpha \times \mathbb{1}_{\alpha=\beta}$, we obtain

$$\text{tr}\left(F_f^\alpha \left|\psi_{F_{f'}^\beta}\right\rangle\left\langle\psi_{F_{f'}^\beta}\right|\right) = \frac{\text{tr}\left(F_f^\alpha |\psi\rangle\langle\psi|\right)}{\text{tr}\left(F_{f'}^\beta |\psi\rangle\langle\psi|\right)} \times \mathbb{1}_{\alpha=\beta}.$$

For fixed β, taking the sum over α yields 1, because $\left|\psi_{F_{f'}^\beta}\right\rangle$ is normalized and $\sum_\alpha F_f^\alpha = \mathbb{1}$, so that we can conclude that $\text{tr}\left(F_f^\alpha \left|\psi_{F_{f'}^\alpha}\right\rangle\right) = 1$. In turn, this implies that $F_f^\alpha \left|\psi_{F_{f'}^\alpha}\right\rangle = \left|\psi_{F_{f'}^\alpha}\right\rangle$ and we arrive at

$$F_f^\alpha |\psi\rangle = F_f^\alpha \otimes F_{f'}^\alpha |\psi\rangle = F_{f'}^\alpha |\psi\rangle.$$

□

3.2. Extending the Compatibility Criterion as a Witness for Classicality

As previously argued, one expects that quantum Darwinism for a many-body system $\mathcal{S}$ implies that (i) a preferred set of POVMs emerges from the sole requirement of being approximately redundantly recorded in the state of $\mathcal{S}$, and (ii) these POVMs exhibit classicality.

The natural choice of witness for classicality is that observers accessing fragments of $\mathcal{S}$ will be able to explain all the correlations of their measurement results without the recourse to quantum correlations. In [20], this is required for arbitrary pure quantum states of the system, which translates into the ability of the preferred observables to induce a decomposition of the state $|\psi\rangle$ of $\mathcal{S}$ into a superposition of orthogonal branches $|\psi\rangle = \sum_i |\psi_i\rangle$, where each $|\psi_i\rangle$ is a common eigenstate of all observables in redundantly imprinted sets $O_1, O_2, \ldots$, i.e.,

$$\forall O \in O_1 \cup O_2 \cup \ldots, \ O|\psi_i\rangle = \omega(i, O)|\psi_i\rangle,$$

thereby defining the compatibility of all the observables of $O_1 \cup O_2 \cup \ldots$ on $|\psi\rangle$.

As anticipated, compatibility does not generalize straightforwardly to POVMs due to the absence of a meaningful equivalent to eigenstates of observables. Nonetheless, several options have been proposed in other contexts to understand and sometimes quantify the classicality of POVMs, namely through the introduction of commutativity, non-disturbance, joint-measurability and coexistence (see, for example, [22,23]). Our choice, justified below, for the substitute for compatibility is based on joint measurability.

Definition 2 (Joint-measurability). *Let O be a set of POVMs, and for $O \in \mathbf{O}$ denote its elements by $\{O^\omega\}_\omega$. The set $\mathbf{O}$ is jointly measurable if and only if there exists a POVM T with elements $\{T^\theta\}_\theta$ such that*

$$\forall O \in \mathbf{O}, \; \forall \omega, \; O^\omega = \sum_\theta p(\omega|O,\theta) T^\theta, \tag{10}$$

where $p(\omega|O,\theta)$ is a probability distribution for ω when O and θ are fixed.

This definition states that all measurements in $\mathbf{O}$ can be simulated by first measuring T and then, depending on the obtained outcome θ and the chosen $O \in \mathbf{O}$, by sampling ω according to the probability distribution $p(\omega|O,\theta)$.

This choice is motivated by the operational approach promoted by quantum Darwinism. Observers can perform measurements, accumulate statistics and investigate correlations between them. When POVMs are jointly measurable, observers are able to interpret the correlations of measurement results through a simple marginalization process.

Joint measurability is further justified as a witness of classicality, as it rules out steering—a purely quantum phenomenon—(see [24] for a review). On the contrary, coexistence can reveal steering [25], and is therefore not an appropriate choice in our context. Additionally, non-disturbance suffers from drawbacks in light of quantum Darwinism: it is usually asymmetric, meaning that measurements need to be carried out in a precise order so as to not disturb one another. This ordering requirement contradicts our everyday experience of classical features obviously robust to the precise order in which measurements are performed. Finally, commutativity is shown to imply joint measurability [22], but the converse is in general not true. Hence, without further good reasons to rule out joint measurability, witnessing classicality through commutativity risks being too restrictive and, thus, potentially missing the emergence of objectivity.

Additionally, Proposition 1 of [22] shows that when restricted to projective measurements, joint measurability is indeed equivalent to the commutativity of observables. Thus, our choice of witness for classicality reduces to that of Ref. [20], as compatibility on the state of the system reduces to commutativity on its support.

Lastly, to obtain a useful criterion for classicality in our context, it needs to account for (i) approximations and (ii) systems whose evolutions practically restrict their attainable states to a subset of all possible density matrices. To this end, we note that the operator equality of Equation (10) is equivalent to a statement on probabilities of the outcomes computed for system states ρ that span the set of density matrices for S. This is because the trace function is an inner product for the real Hilbert space of Hermitian matrices. Hence, we can deal with (i) by stating that probability distributions are close to that obtained for jointly measurable POVMs, and (ii) can be accounted for by enforcing the relation only on the set $\mathcal{D}$ of attainable states.

Definition 3 (δ-approximate joint measurability over $\mathcal{D}$). *Let $\mathcal{D}$ be a set of density matrices, $\delta \geq 0$ and $\mathbf{O}$ a set of POVMs, where the elements of $O \in \mathbf{O}$ are $\{O^\omega\}_\omega$. The set $\mathbf{O}$ is δ approximately jointly measurable over $\mathcal{D}$ if there exists a POVM T with elements $\{T^\theta\}_\theta$ such that*

$$\forall O \in \mathbf{O}, \; \forall \omega, \; \forall \rho \in \mathcal{D}, \; \left| \mathrm{tr}(O^\omega \rho) - \sum_\theta p(\omega|O,\theta) \, \mathrm{tr}\left(T^\theta \rho\right) \right| \leq \delta, \tag{11}$$

where $p(\omega|O,\theta)$ is a probability distribution for ω when O and θ are fixed.

4. Recovering Joint Measurability

As seen in Section 2, redundancy is not enough to imply classicality. The absence of a natural, or preferred, way to group microscopic sites of a quantum many-body system allows information about incompatible observables to be redundantly recorded in the whole system. Although incompatible observables cannot be read off at the same time by multiple observers—so that this statement does not violate axioms of quantum mechanics—they can still collectively decide beforehand which one to recover.

In the case of perfect redundant records of projective measurements, the non pair-covering condition ensures that only a single set of compatible observables can be accessed by observers, thus corresponding to the everyday experience. Given our definitions of approximate records and the replacement of compatibility with approximate joint measurability, the question we have to address is whether non pair-covering is enough to guarantee the joint measurability of a single set of observables.

Theorem 1. *Let S be a quantum many-body system, such that there exists $\mathcal{F}$, a partition of $[1,N]$ of the microscopic sites S_i of S. Let $\mathbf{F} = \{F_f\}_f$ be a set POVMs, where F_f acts on f only and satisfies $\forall \alpha$ and $\forall f, f' \in \mathcal{F}$,*

$$\forall \rho \in \mathcal{D}, \ \mathrm{tr}\left(F_f^\alpha \otimes F_{f'}^\alpha \rho\right) \geq (1-\delta)\,\mathrm{tr}\left(F_f^\alpha \rho\right),$$

for some $\delta > 0$, and $\mathcal{D}$ a set of density matrices. Assume there exists $\mathcal{G}$, a second partition, and $= \{G_g\}_g$ with $g \in \mathcal{G}$ a second set of POVMs satisfying the corresponding approximate redundantly recorded condition stated above. Assume that $\mathcal{F}$ and $\mathcal{G}$ do not pair-cover each other, then for all $f \in \mathcal{F}$ and $g \in \mathcal{G}$, F_f and G_g are δ-approximately jointly measurable on $\mathcal{D}$.

Proof. The non pair-covering condition imposes that

$$\forall f, f' \in \mathcal{F}, \exists g \in \mathcal{G}, \text{ s.t. } f \cap g = \emptyset \text{ and } f' \cap g = \emptyset$$
$$\forall g, g' \in \mathcal{G}, \exists f \in \mathcal{F}, \text{ s.t. } g \cap f = \emptyset \text{ and } g' \cap f = \emptyset.$$

For given $f \in \mathcal{F}$ and $g \in \mathcal{G}$, using the non pair-covering condition, it is possible to choose $f' \in \mathcal{F}$ and $g' \in \mathcal{G}$ such that

$$f \cap g' = \emptyset = f' \cap g'$$
$$g \cap f' = \emptyset = g' \cap f'.$$

Then, using redundancy and the disjointness conditions above, for all α, we obtain

$$\mathrm{tr}\left(F_f^\alpha \rho\right) \geq \mathrm{tr}\left(F_f^\alpha \otimes F_{f'}^\alpha \rho\right)$$
$$= \mathrm{tr}\left(F_f^\alpha \otimes F_{f'}^\alpha \otimes \sum_\nu G_{g'}^\nu \rho\right)$$
$$\geq (1-\delta)\,\mathrm{tr}\left(F_{f'}^\alpha \otimes \sum_\nu G_{g'}^\nu \rho\right),$$

and similarly for all ν

$$\mathrm{tr}\left(G_g^\nu \rho\right) \geq \mathrm{tr}\left(G_g^\mu \otimes G_{g'}^\mu \rho\right)$$
$$= \mathrm{tr}\left(G_g^\mu \otimes G_{g'}^\mu \otimes \sum_\beta F_{f'}^\beta \rho\right)$$
$$\geq (1-\delta)\,\mathrm{tr}\left(G_{g'}^\mu \otimes \sum_\beta F_{f'}^\beta \rho\right).$$

We also have

$$\mathrm{tr}\left(F_f^\alpha \rho\right) = 1 - \sum_{\beta\setminus\alpha} \mathrm{tr}\left(f_f^\beta \rho\right)$$

$$\leq 1 - (1-\delta) \sum_{\beta\setminus\alpha} \mathrm{tr}\left(F_{f'}^\beta \otimes \sum_\nu G_{g'}^\nu \rho\right)$$

$$= 1 - (1-\delta)\left(1 - \mathrm{tr}\left(F_{f'}^\alpha \otimes \sum_\nu G_{g'}^\nu \rho\right)\right)$$

$$= (1-\delta) \mathrm{tr}\left(F_{f'}^\alpha \otimes \sum_\nu G_{g'}^\nu \rho\right) + \delta,$$

and similarly for $\mathrm{tr}\left(G_g^\nu \rho\right)$.

Combining both inequalities, we arrive at

$$\forall \alpha, \nu, \; \left|\mathrm{tr}\left(F_f^\alpha \rho\right) - \mathrm{tr}\left(\sum_\nu F_{f'}^\alpha \otimes G_{g'}^\nu \rho\right)\right| \leq \delta, \text{ and}$$

$$\forall \beta, \mu, \; \left|\mathrm{tr}\left(G_f^\mu \rho\right) - \mathrm{tr}\left(\sum_\beta F_{f'}^\beta \otimes G_{g'}^\mu \rho\right)\right| \leq \delta.$$

This concludes the proof, as the probabilities of obtaining outcomes F_f^α and G_g^μ are δ-close to that obtained by measuring $F_{f'}^\alpha \otimes G_{g'}^\mu$ followed by the appropriate post processing, consisting of summing over the outcomes of the ignored POVM. □

Hence, any pair of approximately redundantly recorded POVMs is approximately jointly measurable. The trouble to recover a perfect analogue to the ideal case with pure states and projective measurements is that pairwise joint measurability does not imply global joint measurability [26]. That is, for three POVMs, all pairs can be jointly measurable, but all three of them might not be the marginals of a single POVM. As a consequence, one cannot claim full classicality in such a situation.

Global joint measurability can nonetheless be obtained by strengthening the non pair-covering condition into non tuple-covering.

Definition 4 (non tuple-covering). $\mathcal{F}, \mathcal{G}, \ldots, \mathcal{Z}$ partitions of $[1, N]$ are non tuple-covering each other iff, $\forall f \in \mathcal{F}, g \in \mathcal{G}, \ldots, z \in \mathcal{Z}, \exists f' \in \mathcal{F}, g' \in \mathcal{G}, \ldots, z' \in \mathcal{Z}$ s.t.

$$f' \cap g = f' \cap g' = \ldots = f' \cap z = f' \cap z' = \emptyset$$
$$g' \cap f = g' \cap f' = \ldots = g' \cap z = g' \cap z' = \emptyset$$
$$\vdots$$
$$z' \cap f = z' \cap f' = z' \cap g = z' \cap g' = \ldots = \emptyset.$$

Using this definition, the following theorem allows to recover global joint measurability.

Theorem 2. Let $\mathbf{F} = \{F_f\}_{f\in\mathcal{F}}$, $\mathbf{G} = \{G_g\}_{g\in\mathcal{G}}, \ldots \mathbf{Z} = \{Z_z\}_{z\in\mathcal{Z}}$ be sets of δ-approximate redundantly recorded POVMs on the state of a quantum many-body system $\mathcal{S}$, with $\mathcal{F}, \mathcal{G}, \ldots \mathcal{Z}$ partitions of $[1, N]$, the indices of the microscopic sites. If the partitions $\mathcal{F}, \mathcal{G}, \ldots \mathcal{Z}$ do not tuple-cover each other, then for any $f, g, \ldots z$, $F_f, G_g, \ldots Z_z$ are δ-approximately joint measurable.

Proof. Given the non tuple-covering condition, one could appropriately replace any measurement of $F_f, G_g, \ldots Z_z$ by a measurement of $F_{f'}, G_{g'}, \ldots Z_{z'}$. From there, the same proof technique as the one used for Theorem 1 applies. Using the said replacement of measurements, one arrives at a situation where all POVMs $F_{f'}, G_{g'}, \ldots, Z_{z'}$ act on different subsets of the microscopic sites. They are, thus, defining a global POVM with elements $F_{f'}^\alpha \otimes G_{g'}^\beta \otimes \ldots Z_{z'}^\zeta$ from which the probabilities of the outcomes $(\alpha, \beta, \ldots, \zeta)$ can be δ-approximated through classical post-processing. This allows to conclude about the δ-approximate joint-measurability criterion for POVMs $\{F_f\}_{f \in \mathcal{F}}, \{G_g\}_{g \in \mathcal{G}}, \ldots, \{Z_z\}_{z \in \mathcal{Z}}$. □

5. Dynamical Approach to the Emergence of Classicality

The non pair-covering condition has an appealing property of being rather simple and allowing the recovery of objectivity for usual many-body physics experiments: pair-covering is too delicate to maintain for macroscopic systems containing possibly millions or billions of microscopic sites so that they would necessarily be exhibiting only usual classical properties.

On the contrary, the non tuple-covering seems a more complex, if not harder, condition to achieve. This, in turn, weakens considerably the above argument and, as a consequence, the reach of quantum Darwinism for quantum many-body systems. Yet, we prove below that this is not the case, and that quantum Darwinism is a ubiquitous mechanism to explain the emergence of a single set of approximately jointly-measurable POVMs.

The way to address this question is to take a dynamical view at the creation of the redundant imprints into the state of the quantum many-body system. More precisely, we need to acknowledge the fact that the redundant imprints—be they perfect or approximate—are the result of an evolution from some initial state of an initial uncorrelated system $\mathcal{R}$. In other terms, it results from the transformation of a state $\sigma \in \mathcal{D}(\mathcal{R})$ to a state $\rho \in \mathcal{D}(\mathcal{S})$, where $\mathcal{D}(\mathcal{R})$ is the set of density matrices for $\mathcal{R}$ and similarly for $\mathcal{S}$. The transformation can then be represented by a CPTP map Λ so that $\rho = \Lambda(\sigma)$.

The structure of the correlations, and hence of the information, between $\mathcal{R}$ and $\mathcal{S}$ can be analyzed using the techniques pioneered in [21] and refined in [27]. Yet, these need to be recast to fit into the quantum many-body setting, as they have been developed in the system–environment context.

Theorem 3. *Let Λ be a CPTP map from $\mathcal{D}(\mathcal{R})$ to $\mathcal{D}(\mathcal{S})$, and $w_q, w_f \in [1, N]$, with $\mathcal{S} = \cup_{i=1}^N \mathcal{S}_i$ and $w_q + w_f \leq N$. For all $\sigma \in \mathcal{D}(\mathcal{R})$, consider $\varrho = \Lambda(\sigma)$ the state of a generic quantum many-body system that evolved from the initial preparation state σ through Λ. Then, there exists a subset q of $[1, N]$ of size at most w_q such that for all subsets f of $[1, N] \setminus q$ with size w_f, and for all POVMs $F_f = \{F_f^\alpha\}_\alpha$ on f*

$$\forall \alpha, \left| \mathrm{tr}\left(F_f^\alpha \varrho\right) - \sum_\theta p(\alpha | F_f, \theta) \, \mathrm{tr}\left(T_q^\theta \varrho\right) \right| \leq \delta,$$

with $\delta = d_\mathcal{R} \sqrt{2 \ln(d_\mathcal{R}) \frac{w_f}{w_q}}$, where T_q is a fixed POVM on q that does not depend on f nor σ, and where $p(\alpha | F_f, \theta)$ is a classical probability distribution for α when F_f and θ are fixed that is independent of σ. Above, $d_\mathcal{R}$ denotes the dimension of $\mathcal{R}$.

Proof. The proof will proceed in two steps. First, it will follow the steps of Theorem 2 of [27] to obtain a bound on the distance between the Choi-states of two specific channels, one being the channel Λ reduced to some sufficiently small subsets f and the other one being a measure and prepare channel from $\mathcal{R}$ to f. The second step will focus on the measurement done by the measure and prepare channel and show that it can be understood as a measurement on a subset q disjoint and independent of f.

Consider a basis $|i\rangle$ of $\mathcal{R}$ and a fiducial reference system $\mathcal{R}'$ isomorphic to $\mathcal{R}$. Define the maximally mixed state $|\psi\rangle$ of $\mathcal{R}\mathcal{R}'$ as $1/\sqrt{d_\mathcal{R}} \sum_i |ii\rangle_{\mathcal{R}\mathcal{R}'}$. The Choi-state of Λ is then $\rho = (\mathbb{1}_{\mathcal{R}'} \otimes \Lambda(|\psi\rangle\langle\psi|)$ (see, for example, [28]). We can now apply Proposition 1 of [27] to ρ.

For $w_f, w_q \in [1, N]$, there exists $q \subseteq [1, N]$ of size w_q and Ξ_q a quantum–classical channel on q such that

$$\forall f \subseteq [1, N] \setminus q, \ |f| = w_f, \ \max_{\Xi_f \in QC} I(\mathcal{R}' : f|q)_{\Xi_f \otimes \Xi_q(\rho)} \leq S(\mathcal{R}')_\rho \frac{w_f}{w_q}.$$

Above, Ξ_f is a quantum–classical channel on f such that $\Xi_f(X) = \sum_\alpha \text{tr}\left(F_f^\alpha |\alpha\rangle\langle\alpha|\right)$ for some POVM F_f on f; $S(\mathcal{R}')_\rho$ is the von Neumann entropy for the system $\mathcal{R}'$ when the global state is ρ; and $I(\mathcal{R}' : f|q)_{\Xi_f \otimes \Xi_q(\rho)}$ is the quantum mutual information between $\mathcal{R}'$ and f conditioned on q for the global state $\Xi_f \otimes \Xi_q(\rho)$—note that to ease notation, the obvious identity operators will continue to be omitted. The interest of this proposition is that it constructs a subset q of microscopic subsystems of $\mathcal{S}$ of size at most w_q such that, *irrespective* of the choice of another subset f of microscopic subsystems of size w_f disjoint from q, the correlations between $\mathcal{R}'$ and any observation on f through Ξ_f conditioned on an observation of q through Ξ_q can be made small. This means that observing q through Ξ_q extracts all there is to know about $\mathcal{R}'$ so that it becomes uncorrelated with any further observation on f. By analogy with the classical case, Ref. [27] refers to the region q as a quantum Markov blanket. We can now use this bound to arrive at a statement of closeness between two Choi-states. More precisely, for Ξ_q implementing the POVM $T_q = \{T_q^\theta\}_\theta$ on q so that $\Xi_q(X) = \sum_\theta \text{tr}\left(T_q^\theta X\right) |\theta\rangle\langle\theta|$, we have

$$\text{tr}_f(\Xi_f \otimes \Xi_q(\rho)) = \Xi_f\left(\sum_\theta p_\theta \rho_{\mathcal{R}'f}^\theta |\theta\rangle\langle\theta|\right), \text{ with} \quad (12)$$

$$p_\theta = \text{tr}\left(T_q^\theta \rho\right) \quad (13)$$

$$\rho_{\mathcal{R}'f}^\theta = \frac{1}{p_\theta} \text{tr}_{\bar{f}q}(T_q^\theta \rho), \quad (14)$$

where $\bar{f}$ is the complement of f in $[1, N] \setminus q$ so that the system $\mathcal{S}$ decomposes into $f\bar{f}q$. As a consequence, $I(\mathcal{R}' : f|q)_{\Xi_f \otimes \Xi_q(\rho)} = \sum_\theta I(\mathcal{R}' : f)_{\Xi_f(\rho_{\mathcal{R}'f}^\theta)}$. Using the quantum Pinsker inequality [29] for $I(\mathcal{R}' : f)_{\Xi_f(\rho_{\mathcal{R}'f}^\theta)}$, one obtains that

$$\frac{1}{2\ln 2}\left\|\Xi_f(\rho_{\mathcal{R}'f}^\theta - \rho_{\mathcal{R}'}^\theta \otimes \rho_f^\theta)\right\|_1^2 \leq I(\mathcal{R}' : f)_{\Xi_f(\rho_{\mathcal{R}'f}^\theta)}.$$

This being true for all θ, using the convexity of both the square function and the 1-norm, we obtain

$$\frac{1}{2\ln 2}\left\|\Xi_f(\rho_{\mathcal{R}'f} - \sum_\theta p_\theta \rho_{\mathcal{R}'}^\theta \otimes \rho_f^\theta)\right\|_1^2 \leq I(\mathcal{R}' : f|q)_{\Xi_f \otimes \Xi_q(\rho)}.$$

Now, using Equation (5) and $S(\mathcal{R}') \leq \log(d_\mathcal{R})$, we have that for all quantum–classical channels Ξ_f on f:

$$\left\|\Xi_f(\rho_{\mathcal{R}'f} - \sum_\theta p_\theta \rho_{\mathcal{R}'}^\theta \otimes \rho_f^\theta)\right\|_1 \leq \sqrt{2\ln(d_\mathcal{R})\frac{w_f}{w_q}}. \quad (15)$$

Above $\rho_{\mathcal{R}'f}$ is the Choi-state corresponding to Λ_f obtained by reducing the channel Λ to f, while $\sum_\theta p_\theta \rho_{\mathcal{R}'}^\theta \otimes \rho_f^\theta$ defines Γ_f, corresponding to a measure and prepare channel from $\mathcal{R}$ to f, as its Choi-state is separable with respect to the $\mathcal{R}'f$ partition. Note that in Γ_f, the prepared states ρ_f^θ are independent of the input of the channel.

We can define two additional channels, $\Lambda_f^{\Xi_f} = \Xi_f \circ \Lambda_f$ and $\Gamma_f^{\Xi_f} = \Xi_f \circ \Gamma_f$ that correspond to the Choi-states $\Xi_f(\rho_{\mathcal{R}'f})$ and $\Xi_f(\sum_\theta p_\theta \rho_{\mathcal{R}'}^\theta \otimes \rho_f^\theta)$, respectively, and that are realized by measuring the output states of Λ_f and Γ_f with the POVM $F_f = \{F_f^\alpha\}_\alpha$. Then, we have, for all $\Xi_f \in QC$

$$\left\|\Lambda_f^{\Xi_f} - \Gamma_f^{\Xi_f}\right\|_\diamond \leq d_\mathcal{R} \left\|\Xi_f(\rho_{\mathcal{R}'f} - \sum_\theta p_\theta \rho_{\mathcal{R}'}^\theta \otimes \rho_f^\theta)\right\|_1$$

which implies, as the diamond norm is the result of an optimization over all input states and because of Equation (15), that

$$\forall \sigma \in \mathcal{D}(\mathcal{R}), \left\|\Lambda_f^{\Xi_f}(\sigma) - \Gamma_f^{\Xi_f}(\sigma)\right\|_1 \leq d_\mathcal{R} \sqrt{2\ln(d_\mathcal{R}) \frac{w_f}{w_q}}. \quad (16)$$

We almost arrive at our result and just need to give a more explicit interpretation to both states in the above equation. $\Lambda_f^{\Xi_f}(\sigma) = \sum_\alpha \operatorname{tr}\left(F_f^\alpha \Lambda(\sigma)\right) |\alpha\rangle\langle\alpha|$ is the state obtained after measuring $\Lambda(\sigma)$ using F_f acting on subset f of size w_f. To interpret the state $\Gamma_f^{\Xi_f}(\sigma)$, recall that the output of a given channel Φ from $\mathcal{R}$ to f can be inferred from its corresponding Choi-state $\rho_{\mathcal{R}'f}^\Phi$, using the simple identity $\Phi(\sigma) = \operatorname{tr}_{\mathcal{R}'}(\rho_{\mathcal{R}'f}^\Phi \sigma^T)$. Therefore, we have

$$\Gamma_f^{\Xi_f}(\sigma) = \operatorname{tr}_{\mathcal{R}'}\left(\sum_\theta p_\theta \rho_{\mathcal{R}'}^\theta \sigma^T\right) \otimes \left(\sum_\alpha \operatorname{tr}\left(F_f^\alpha \rho_f^\theta\right)|\alpha\rangle\langle\alpha|\right)$$

$$= \operatorname{tr}_{\mathcal{R}'}\left(\sum_\theta \operatorname{tr}_{f\bar{f}q}(T_q^\theta \rho)\sigma^T\right) \otimes \left(\sum_\alpha \operatorname{tr}\left(F_f^\alpha \rho_f^\theta\right)|\alpha\rangle\langle\alpha|\right)$$

$$= \operatorname{tr}\left(\sum_\theta T_q^\theta \Lambda(\sigma)\right) \otimes \left(\sum_\alpha \operatorname{tr}\left(F_f^\alpha \rho_f^\theta\right)|\alpha\rangle\langle\alpha|\right),$$

where we use Equation (14) to replace $p_\theta \rho_{\mathcal{R}'}^\theta$ with $\operatorname{tr}_{f\bar{f}q} T_q^\theta \Lambda(\rho)$. Note that for the states ρ_f^θ for varying θ are independent of σ so that $\operatorname{tr}\left(F_f^\alpha \rho_f^\theta\right)$ can be rewritten as $p(\alpha|F_f,\theta)$, a classical probability distribution for α, given F_f and θ. Equation (16) can now be rewritten as

$$\forall \sigma \in \mathcal{D}(\mathcal{R}), \sum_\alpha \left\|\operatorname{tr}\left(F_f^\alpha \Lambda(\sigma)\right) - \operatorname{tr}\left(\sum_\theta T_q^\theta \Lambda(\sigma)\right) \operatorname{tr}\left(F_f^\alpha \rho_f^\theta\right)\right\|_1 \leq d_\mathcal{R} \sqrt{2\ln(d_\mathcal{R})\frac{w_f}{w_q}}.$$

All derivations above are independent from the choice of subset f and of quantum-classical channel Ξ_f—or, equivalently, of F_f—as long as w_f and w_q are chosen such that $\delta = d_\mathcal{R}\sqrt{2\ln(d_\mathcal{R})\frac{w_f}{w_q}}$ is small. This concludes the proof as

$$\forall \varrho \in \mathcal{D}, \forall \alpha, \left|\operatorname{tr}\left(F_f^\alpha \varrho\right) - \sum_\theta p(\alpha|F_f,\theta)\operatorname{tr}\left(T_q^\theta \varrho\right)\right| \leq \sum_{\tilde{\alpha}}\left|\operatorname{tr}\left(F_f^{\tilde{\alpha}}\varrho\right) - \sum_\theta p(\tilde{\alpha}|F_f,\theta)\operatorname{tr}\left(T_q^\theta \varrho\right)\right| \leq \delta.$$

□

In effect, Proposition 1 of [27] identifies a fraction of $\mathcal{S}$ that contains all the information that can be accessed about the initial state σ after Λ has taken place. This then decoheres all other possible smaller fractions f of $\mathcal{S}$ disjoint from q. The consequence is that any measurement on such fractions can be implemented by first measuring q and then by post processing classically the result depending on the choice of measurement F_f on f. This being true for all sufficiently small fractions f and any measurement on F_f, we recover the δ-

approximate joint measurability for such measurements over the states that are dynamically created by Λ from any initial state σ. Hence, when observers are restricted to fractions f, quantum Darwinism yields objective properties of the system that can all be understood as stemming from a single classical measurement on the Markov blanket q.

6. Conclusions

The last section shows that generic evolutions of quantum many-body systems do systematically generate Markov blankets that capture all correlations between fragments of $\mathcal{S}$. As a consequence, measurement results obtained by observers measuring fragments of $\mathcal{S}$ outside Markov blankets can be explained using classical correlations only. This implies that the non tuple-covering condition is generically satisfied for all partitions of $\mathcal{S}$ that contain the Markov blanket. Hence, while the non tuple-covering condition seemed an a priori more complex requirement to satisfy compared to the non pair-covering, as soon as Markov blankets are outside the reach of observers, quantum Darwinism can be invoked to recover robust classical objective properties of quantum many-body systems. This is a situation similar to that of system–environment settings, where Markov blankets are created generically by quantum evolutions and are responsible for objective classical reality [21,27]. Further analysis of the precise location and accessibility of Markov blankets in realistic settings is left for future work.

Funding: This research received no external funding.

Institutional Review Board Statement: Not applicable.

Informed Consent Statement: Not applicable.

Data Availability Statement: Not applicable.

Acknowledgments: I am extremely grateful to Wojciech Zurek for having introduced me to quantum information, for his guidance, stimulating discussions and the wonderful time at the Los Alamos National Laboratory.

Conflicts of Interest: The authors declare no conflict of interest.

References

1. Zurek, W.H. Pointer basis of quantum apparatus: Into what mixture does the wave packet collapse? *Phys. Rev. D.* **1981**, *24*, 1516. [CrossRef]
2. Zurek, W.H. Environment-induced superselection rules. *Phys. Rev. D.* **1982**, *26*, 1862–1880. [CrossRef]
3. Joos, E.; Zeh, H.D. The emergence of classical property through interaction with the environment. *Z. Phys. B* **1985**, *59*, 223. [CrossRef]
4. Ollivier, H.; Poulin, D.; Zurek, W.H. Objective properties from subjective quantum states: Environment as a witness. *Phys. Rev. Lett.* **2004**, *93*, 220401. [CrossRef] [PubMed]
5. Ollivier, H.; Poulin, D.; Zurek, W.H. Environment as a Witness: Selective Proliferation of Information and Emergence of Objectivity. *Phys. Rev. A* **2005**, *72*, 042113. [CrossRef]
6. Blume-Kohout, R.; Zurek, W.H. A Simple Example of "Quantum Darwinism": Redundant Information Storage in Many-Spin Environments. *Found Phys.* **2005**, *35*, 1857–1876. [CrossRef]
7. Blume-Kohout, R.; Zurek, W.H. Quantum Darwinism: Entanglement, branches, and the emergent classicality of redundantly stored quantum information. *Phys. Rev. A* **2006**, *73*, 062310. [CrossRef]
8. Blume-Kohout, R.; Zurek, W.H. Quantum Darwinism in Quantum Brownian Motion. *Phys. Rev. Lett.* **2008**, *101*, 240405. [CrossRef]
9. Zurek, W.H. Quantum Darwinism. *Nat. Phys.* **2009**, *5*, 181–188. [CrossRef]
10. Zurek, W.H. Quantum Darwinism, classical reality, and the randomness of quantum jumps. *Phys. Today* **2014**, *67*, 44. [CrossRef]
11. Zurek, W.H. Quantum theory of the classical: quantum jumps, Born's Rule and objective classical reality via quantum Darwinism. *Phil. Trans. R. Soc. A.* **2018**, *376*, 20180107–20180107. [CrossRef] [PubMed]
12. Riedel, C.J.; Zurek, W.H. Quantum Darwinism in an Everyday Environment: Huge Redundancy in Scattered Photons. *Phys. Rev. Lett.* **2010**, *105*, 020404. [CrossRef]
13. Korbicz, J.K.; Horodecki, P.; Horodecki, R. Objectivity in a Noisy Photonic Environment through Quantum State Information Broadcasting. *Phys. Rev. Lett.* **2014**, *112*, 120402. [CrossRef] [PubMed]
14. Zwolak, M.; Riedel, C.J.; Zurek, W.H. Amplification, Redundancy, and Quantum Chernoff Information. *Phys. Rev. Lett.* **2014**, *112*, 140406. [CrossRef]

15. Zwolak, M.; Riedel, C.J.; Zurek, W.H. Amplification, Decoherence and the Acquisition of Information by Spin Environments. *Sci. Rep.* **2016**, *6*, 25277. [CrossRef] [PubMed]
16. Griffiths, R.B. Consistent histories and the interpretation of quantum mechanics. *J. Stat. Phys.* **1984**, *36*, 219. [CrossRef]
17. Omnès, R. *The Interpretation of Quantum Mechanics*; Princeton University Press: Princeton, NJ, USA, 1994.
18. Griffiths, R.B.; Omnès, R. Consistent Histories and Quantum Measurements. *Phys. Today* **1999**, *52*, 26. [CrossRef]
19. Riedel, C.J.; Zurek, W.H.; Zwolak, M. Objective past of a quantum universe: Redundant records of consistent histories. *Phys. Rev. A* **2016**, *93*, 032126. [CrossRef]
20. Riedel, C.J. Classical Branch Structure from Spatial Redundancy in a Many-Body Wave Function. *Phys. Rev. Lett.* **2017**, *118*, 120402. [CrossRef]
21. Brandão, F.G.S.L.; Piani, M.; Horodecki, P. Generic emergence of classical features in quantum Darwinism. *Nat. Commun.* **2015**, *6*, 7908. [CrossRef]
22. Heinosaari, T.; Wolf, M.M. Nondisturbing quantum measurements. *J. Math. Phys.* **2010**, *51*, 092201. [CrossRef]
23. Ludwig, G. *Foundations of Quantum Mechnanics I*; Texts and Monographs in Physics; Springer: Berlin/Heidelberg, Germany, 1983. [CrossRef]
24. Uola, R.; Costa, A.C.S.; Nguyen, H.C.; Gühne, O. Quantum steering. *Rev. Mod. Phys.* **2020**, *92*, 015001. [CrossRef]
25. Uola, R.; Moroder, T.; Gühne, O. Joint Measurability of Generalized Measurements Implies Classicality. *Phys. Rev. Lett.* **2014**, *113*, 160403. [CrossRef] [PubMed]
26. Heunen, C.; Fritz, T.; Reyes, M.L. Quantum theory realizes all joint measurability graphs. *Phys. Rev. A* **2014**, *89*, 032121. [CrossRef]
27. Qi, X.L.; Ranard, D. Emergent classicality in general multipartite states and channels. *Quantum* **2021**, *5*, 555. [CrossRef]
28. Wilde, M.M. *Quantum Information Theory*, 2nd ed.; Cambridge University Press: Cambridge, UK, 2017. [CrossRef]
29. Hiai, F.; Ohya, M.; Tsukada, M. KMS condition and relative entropy in von Neumann algebras. *Pacific J. Math.* **1981**, *96*, 99–109. [CrossRef]

Article

Equilibration and "Thermalization" in the Adapted Caldeira–Leggett Model

Andreas Albrecht [1,2]

[1] Center for Quantum Mathematics and Physics, University of California at Davis, One Shields Ave., Davis, CA 95616, USA; ajalbrecht@ucdavis.edu

[2] Department of Physics and Astronomy, University of California at Davis, One Shields Ave., Davis, CA 95616, USA

Abstract: I explore the processes of equilibration exhibited by the Adapted Caldeira–Leggett (ACL) model, a small unitary "toy model" developed for numerical studies of quantum decoherence between an SHO and an environment. I demonstrate how dephasing allows equilibration to occur in a wide variety of situations. While the finite model size and other "unphysical" aspects prevent the notions of temperature and thermalization from being generally applicable, certain primitive aspects of thermalization can be realized for particular parameter values. I link the observed behaviors to intrinsic properties of the global energy eigenstates, and argue that the phenomena I observe contain elements which might be key ingredients that lead to ergodic behavior in larger more realistic systems. The motivations for this work range from curiosity about phenomena observed in earlier calculations with the ACL model to much larger questions related to the nature of equilibrium, thermalization, and the emergence of physical laws.

Keywords: equilibration; thermalization; quantum entanglement; ergodicity; closed systems; emergence; finite systems

1. Introduction

In [1], my collaborators and I introduced a toy model which adapted the Caldeira–Leggett model for numerical analysis. This "Adapted Caldeira–Leggett" (ACL) model was designed to optimize decoherence and einselection between a simple harmonic oscillator (SHO) and an environment. The SHO and environment are treated together as a closed, unitarily evolving quantum system. The ACL model naturally equilibrates when evolved for a sufficient length of time. We used equilibrium states thus obtained in [2] to study the extent to which equilibrium states can exhibit einselection [3] despite the absence of an arrow of time. That work was motivated especially by cosmological considerations.

In this paper, I dig deeper into the equilibrium behavior exhibited by the ACL model. I show that a range of equilibration behaviors is possible, some of which show attributes that might be seen as a primitive form of "thermalization," and others that definitely do not. I show how the different behaviors are controlled by parameters in the ACL Hamiltonian and relate these behaviors to properties of the global energy eigenstates.

One motivation for this work is to make sure the equilibrium states of the ACL model form a suitable foundation for the studies in [2] (they do). However, by design, the ACL model eschews a number of physically realistic features (such as locality in the environment) to allow decoherence to function efficiently with limited computational resources. One might ask, what is the point of studying equilibration in a system with significant unphysical features? While in [1], and also in [4], we do make some connection to results from Nuclear Magnetic Resonance experiments, for the purposes of this paper, I regard the physically unrealistic aspects of the ACL model as a strength.

I have long been fascinated by the question of the emergence of physical laws through the identification of (possibly multiple) semiclassical domains in large quantum systems (as discussed, for example, in [5,6]). One feature that seems to be important is the capability of large numbers of degrees of freedom to behave in very simple ways that have a semiclassical description. In physically realistic situations, this is often achieved by the processes of equilibration and thermalization. I am interested in turning the question around and learning in general terms what sorts of physical systems can achieve these behaviors. I am curious if the need to have equilibration and thermalization can help choose—in some selection process associated with their emergence—key features of the laws of physics as we know them. This paper takes a very small step in that direction by exploring the various behaviors of the ACL model.

I introduce the ACL model in Section 2 and in Section 3 demonstrate how the process of dephasing lies at the root of the wide range of equilibration processes that the model exhibits. I point out that, quite generically, the dephasing processes provide all that is needed to produce suitable equilibrium states for the work in [2]. In Section 4, I show that the processes depicted in Section 3 are missing a key feature associated with thermalization. Sections 5 scan a range of results produced by varying a parameter in the Hamiltonian. I show how an appropriate choice of this parameter allows the ACL model to include the thermalizing features, and argue that additional approximately conserved quantities are present in cases in which such features are absent. The discussion up to Section 5 has been shaped by tracking the energies of the SHO and the environment, specifically the first moments of the energy distributions for each of these subsystems. Section 6 expands the discussion to scrutinize the full energy distributions for these subsystems, starting with their initial forms and tracking them as they settle into equilibrium. I explore how these also depend on the parameters of the system and study the presence or absence of the thermalizing behavior in this context. Section 7 examines the properties of the global energy eigenstates, first establishing their general properties and then relating those to various behaviors reported earlier in the paper. The question of the tuning of parameters and the initial states is examined briefly in Section 8, and Section 9 presents some further discussion and conclusions. This is an invited paper for a special volume honoring the 70th birthday of Wojciech Zurek, and I offer some appropriate reflections in Section 10.

2. ACL Model

In [1], my collaborators and I introduced a toy model which adapted the Caldeira–Leggett model for numerical analysis. This "Adapted Caldeira–Leggett" (ACL) model has a "world" Hamiltonian H_w of the form

$$H_w = H_s \otimes \mathbf{1}^e + H^I + \mathbf{1}^s \otimes H_e \tag{1}$$

where the "system" Hamiltonian H_s represents a truncated simple harmonic oscillator (SHO).

The interaction term is given by $H^I = q_s \otimes H_e^I$, where q_s is the SHO position operator and H_e^I has the form

$$H_e^I = E_I R_I^e + E_I^0. \tag{2}$$

The matrix R_I^e is a random matrix constructed by drawing each of the real and imaginary parts of each independent matrix element of this $N_e \times N_e$ Hermitian matrix from a distribution that is uniform over the interval $[-0.5, 0.5]$. Throughout this paper, I will use $N_e = 600$ (the size of the environment Hilbert space) and $N_s = 30$ for the truncated SHO (as used in [1,2]).

The environment self-Hamiltonian is given by

$$H_e = E_e R^e + E_e^0 \tag{3}$$

where R^e is constructed in the same manner as R_I^e, but as a separate realization. In Equations (2) and (3), E_I and E_e are c-numbers which parameterize the overall energy scales. Both R_I^e and R^e are fixed initially and are not changed during the time evolution.

The full Hamiltonian of the ACL model is time independent. All the results in this paper use $E_I^0 = E_e^0 = 0$, but nonzero values for these offset parameters have been useful in other contexts such as [2].

In [1], we demonstrated how the ACL model is able to numerically reproduce decoherence phenomena typically studied with the original Caldeira–Leggett model, and argued that the specific form of H_w enables the numerical studies to reproduce these phenomena in an efficient manner. In [2], we used ACL model calculations to address the relationship between the arrow of time and the emergence of classicality (a topic we motivated with cosmological considerations), and, in [4], we explored new phenomena at the early stages of decoherence.

We made a point in [1] of demonstrating the capability of the ACL model to equilibrate, and these equilibrated states played a key role in [2]. The focus of this paper is to more fully understand the equilibration processes in the ACL model, and place them in the context of modern ideas from quantum statistical mechanics.

3. Basic Equilibration and Dephasing

The basic equilibration process of the ACL model is demonstrated in Figure 1. In this example, energy flows from the SHO to the environment for a period of time, and then the energies in both systems stabilize, up to small fluctuations.

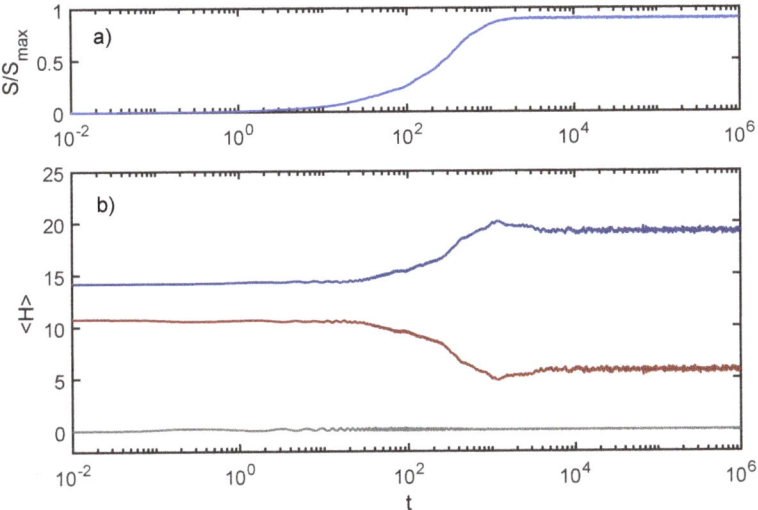

Figure 1. Equilibration in the ACL model: Entropy increases and energy flows from the environment to the SHO for a period of time, and then stabilizes up to small fluctuations. (**a**) entanglement entropy between the SHO and the environment; (**b**) subsystem energies $\langle H_s \rangle$ (blue) and $\langle H_e \rangle$ (red), and interaction energy $\langle H^I \rangle$ (grey).

For these curves, I used $E_e = 1$ and $E_I = 0.02$. Throughout this paper, I use units where $\hbar \omega_{SHO} = 1$. The initial state is a product of a coherent state for the SHO and an eigenstate of H_e, each with energies as shown in the plot.

As inferred in Appendix A of [2], the basic mechanism for this equilibration is "dephasing." When expanding the global state as

$$|\psi_w\rangle = \sum_i \alpha_w^i(t) \left| E_w^i \right\rangle \qquad (4)$$

where $|E_w^i\rangle$ are the eigenstates of H_w, special relationships are required among the $\alpha_w^i(t=0)$ to realize the initial product form of $|\psi_w\rangle$. The dimension of the global space ($N_w = N_s \times N_e = 18{,}000$) is sufficiently large, and the eigenvalues of H_w are sufficiently incommensurate that these special relationships come undone over time. The equilibrium state corresponds to the state where the phases of the $\alpha_w^i(t=0)$ are fully randomized. This is demonstrated explicitly in Figure 2 where additional curves are included from an initial state where the phases of α_w^i were randomized "by hand" at $t=0$.

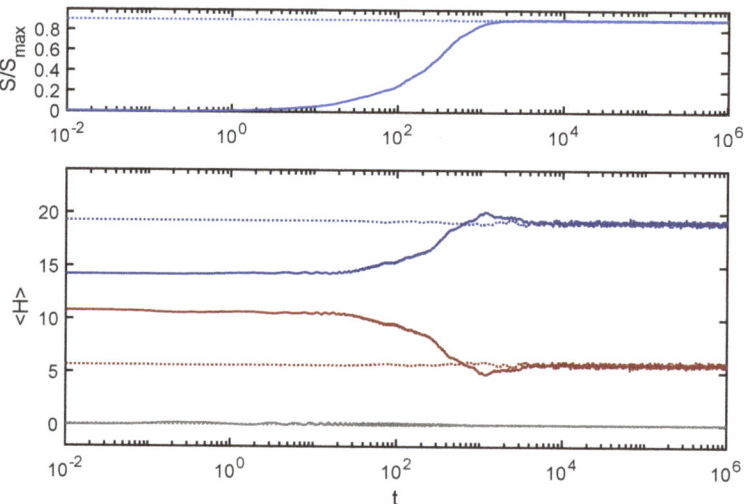

Figure 2. Dephasing: In addition to the curves shown in Figure 1, I have added dotted curves from the calculations with randomized α_w^i phases discussed in the text. The convergence of the dotted and solid curves at later times reflects the dephasing nature of the equilibration process.

This dephasing process is well-known in the quantum statistical mechanics literature (as reviewed, for example, in [7]. Some nice historical reflections can be found in [8]). Papers such as [9,10] also demonstrate its general relevance to decoherence. In Appendix B I elaborate a bit on how I used the term dephasing here, and its connection to other topics such as decoherence.

Figure 3 shows the effect of choosing different random number seeds on curves from Figure 2.

In this figure, the curves from Figure 2 are reproduced along with four additional curves. The additional curves were generated the same way, except with different seeds for the random number generator used for randomizing phases and for the random entries in H_e and H_e^I. The similarity of these sets of curves reflects the fact that artifacts of individual random number seeds show up only in the small scale fluctuations.

I note that the equilibration process driven by dephasing presented here is more than sufficient as a basis for the equilibrium states studied in [2]. For that work, the crucial piece is that detailed balance should be respected, so that fluctuations and their time reverse are equally likely to appear. Next, I turn to more nuanced aspects of equilibration in this model which I find interesting, although not specifically in the context of [2].

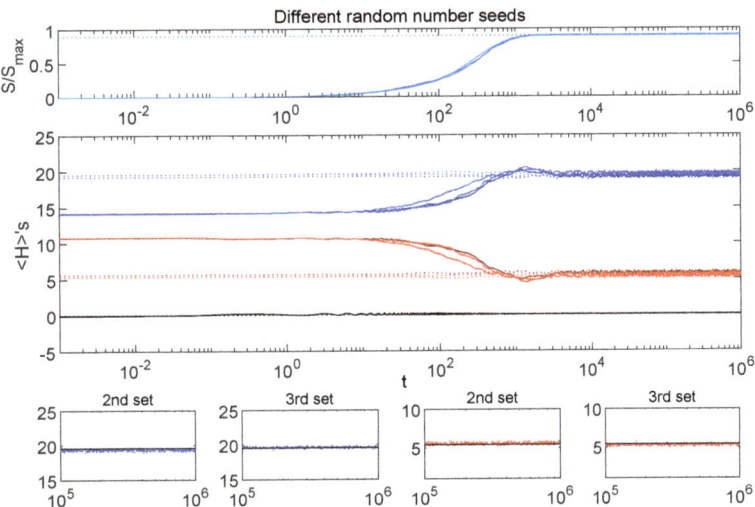

Figure 3. Random artifacts: The curves from Figure 2 are shown with additional curves (in brighter shades) giving the same calculations using different random number seeds. The small panels zoom in on the $\langle H \rangle$'s during equilibrium, and show the same state in each panel, with and without the randomized phases. The matched pairs converge tightly (supporting the dephasing picture), while subtle changes to the Hamiltonian from changing the random number seed generate a slightly larger scatter from one set to another. The small panels have black horizontal lines that are the same for both sets as a reference to aid in tracking the vertical scatter between the sets.

4. Equilibration without "Thermalization"

Figure 4 plots the entanglement entropy and subsystem energies from Figure 1 along with equivalent curves produced with different initial conditions.

In each case, the total energy was set at $\langle H_w \rangle = 25$, but the initial energy was distributed differently between the environment and the SHO. As with Figure 1, all SHO initial states were coherent states with initial energies as shown in the plot, and the environment initial states were eigenstates of H_e. More details about how the initial conditions are constructed appear in Appendix A.

One expects isolated physical systems with the same global energy to thermalize to the same distribution of energies among subsystems, regardless of initial conditions. To the extent that that has not happened in the examples shown in Figure 4, it appears that this equilibration process does not exhibit that aspect of thermalization. There appear to be interesting parallels between the behaviors of the ACL model and the behaviors associated with localization phenomena in condensed matter systems [11]. I will touch on this a couple of times in this paper but warn the reader that I use the term "thermalize" with a grain of salt since no example given here has all the features one associates with full thermalization.

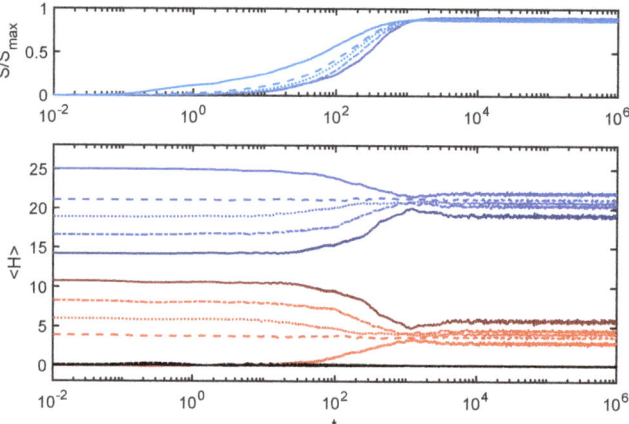

Figure 4. Varying the initial conditions: In addition to the curves from Figure 1, I have added results from different initial conditions (all with the same total energy $\langle H_w \rangle$). The new curves have a different shade of the same color and each set (S, $\langle H_s \rangle$ and $\langle H_e \rangle$) is matched by line type. Note that, while the total energy is the same, at the end of the equilibration process, the energy distribution between the environment and the SHO is different in each case. Here, $E_I = 0.02$.

5. Varying the Coupling Strength E_I

It is instructive to consider the special case of $E_I = 0$. In that case, no energy will flow between the environment and the SHO, and the energies $\langle H_e \rangle$ and $\langle H_s \rangle$ are separately conserved. When $E_I = 0$, formally, *any* initial state is already "equilibrated" in terms of the values $\langle H_e \rangle$ and $\langle H_s \rangle$, insofar as after an extended period of evolution these will be unchanged. In this section, we examine the different behaviors that emerge as E_I is varied. We will see that the $E_I = 0$ case offers a useful reference point for this exploration and helps us interpret the lack of "thermalization" discussed with Figure 4.

Figure 5 uses $E_I = 0.007$, a factor of 0.35 down from the case shown in Figure 4. The sets of initial conditions and the other parameters in H_w are identical for the two figures.

Here, the energy in each subsystem changes very little, and the equilibrium energy values achieved from different initial conditions are further apart than in Figure 4. This is as expected since one is closer to the $E_I = 0$ case. One might have the intuition that any nonzero value of E_I should allow equilibration, with smaller E_I's leading to longer equilibration times. I believe that intuition is only valid for much larger systems, and, in any case, it is certainly not valid for the results reported here.

Figure 6 corresponds to $E_I = 0.1$, considerably larger than values used for Figures 4 and 5.

The energy for each subsystem converges to the same value after equilibration, realizing the sense of "thermalization" considered in Section 4. I will further explore the ways this equilibration process is different from what is seen for other values of E_I in later sections of this article. In addition, note that the interaction energy $\langle H_I \rangle$ (black curves) shows larger fluctuations than for the previous plots, but that these curves still settle down to the same value, which is considerably smaller than the equilibrium energies in either subsystem. This allows one to still consider this a "weakly coupled" case.

Figure 7 shows a strongly coupled case, with E_I 10 times larger than the value used for Figure 6.

With such a large coupling, each subsystem has much less of an individual identity in terms of its evolution and the interpretation of $\langle H_s \rangle$ and $\langle H_e \rangle$. However, the dephasing process still leads to stable values for $\langle H_s \rangle$, $\langle H_e \rangle$ and S at later times, with only small fluctuations.

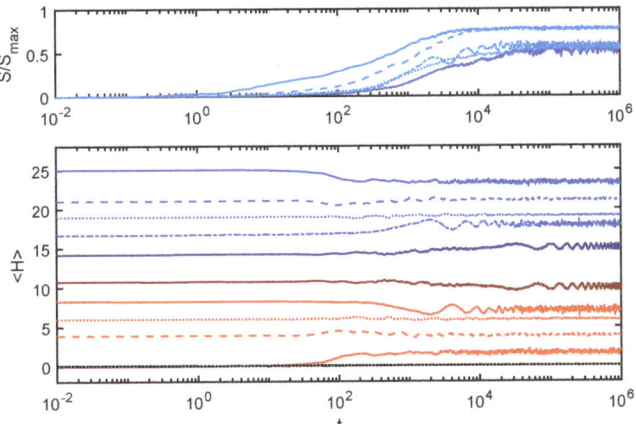

Figure 5. $E_I = 0.007$: These curves correspond to the curves in Figure 4, but evolved with a lower value of E_I, closer to the limit of complete decoupling. These curves exhibit less energy flow, and greater differences among the equilibrium values for each subsystem, despite the fixed value of the global energy. This is what one expects as one approaches the $E_I = 0$ limit.

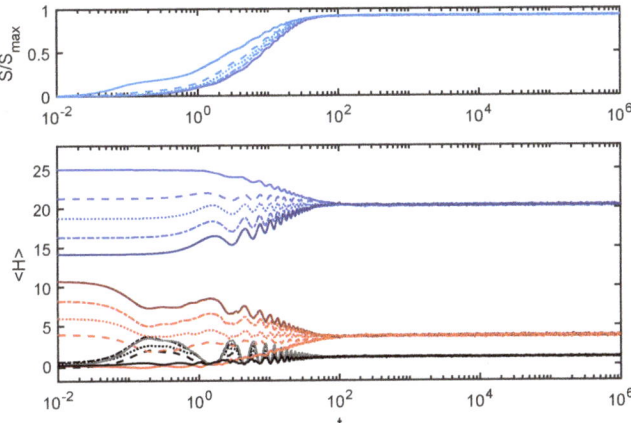

Figure 6. $E_I = 0.1$: Similar to Figures 4 and 5, but evolved with a larger value of E_I (5 times larger than for Figure 4). All the initial conditions converge to the same energy value for each subsystem, realizing the primitive notion of "thermalization" discussed in Section 4.

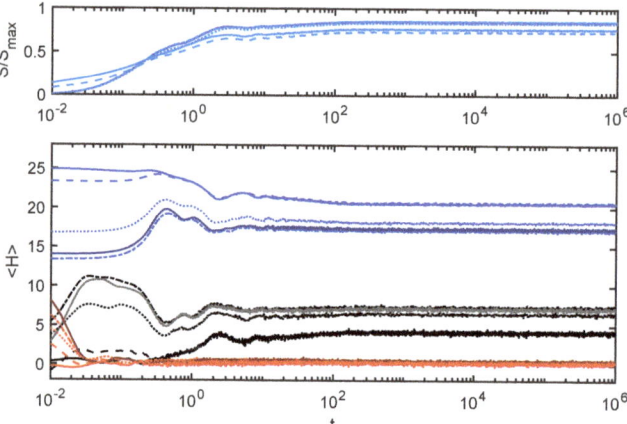

Figure 7. $E_I = 1$: This case is strongly coupled. Under such conditions, each subsystem has less of an individual identity, but the dephasing process still creates some notion of equilibration.

6. Energy Distributions

Throughout this paper, I take the global system to be in a pure quantum state $|\psi_w\rangle$. In general, each subsystem will be described by a density matrix according to

$$\rho_s \equiv Tr_e(|\psi\rangle_{ww}\langle\psi|) \tag{5}$$

and

$$\rho_e \equiv Tr_s(|\psi\rangle_{ww}\langle\psi|). \tag{6}$$

When written on the basis of eigenstates of H_s and H_e, respectively, the diagonal elements of ρ_s and ρ_e give the probabilities assigned to different values of the subsystem energies. I define

$$P_s(E) \equiv diag(\rho_s^E) \tag{7}$$

and

$$P_e(E) \equiv diag(\rho_e^E) \tag{8}$$

where the superscript E indicates that the energy eigenbasis is used. Note that, for the ACL model, the argument E on the left side of these expressions is drawn from the discrete set of energy eigenvalues.

These figures show the case for which the energies (namely, the first moments of these distributions) are shown in Figure 1. One can see that, as we have already seen in the case of the first moments, the whole distribution stabilizes at late times, up to small fluctuations.

Figures 10 and 11 show the late time distributions for the full range of initial conditions and choices of E_I considered above. It is certainly not surprising that the cases where the subsystem energies equilibrated to different values show significantly different late time forms for the overall distributions. It is interesting though that, in the case ($E_I = 0.1$) where the subsystem energies equilibrated to the same values for different initial states, the entire distribution appears to equilibrate to the same form, encompassing many more moments than just the first.

Figure 8 shows the time evolution of $P_s(E)$ and Figure 9 shows the corresponding $P_e(E)$ evolution.

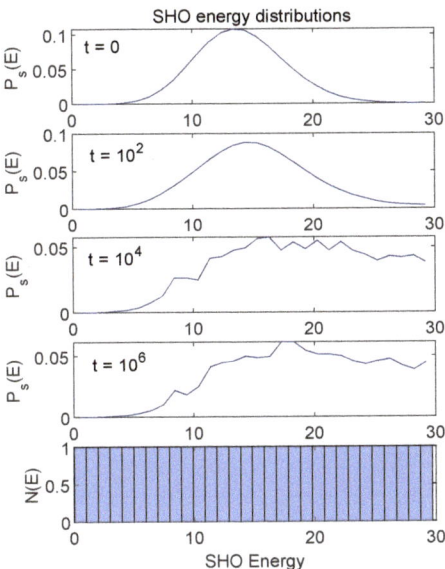

Figure 8. Time evolution of SHO energy distribution $P_s(E)$ for the case shown in Figure 1. The histogram in the lower panel is the density of energy eigenstates for the SHO (which is uniform). I have connected the discrete set of points given by $P_s(E)$ here for ease of viewing.

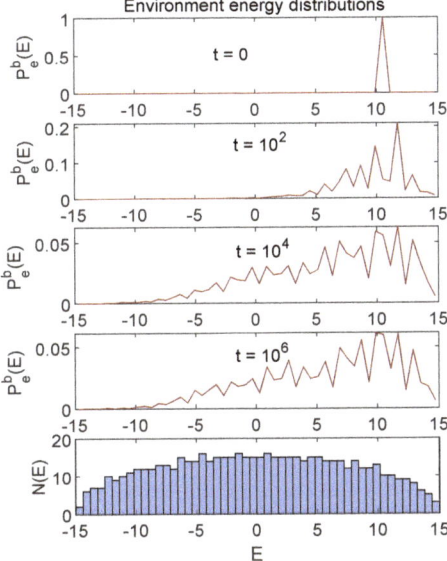

Figure 9. Time evolution of environment energy distribution $P_e(E)$ for the case shown in Figure 1. The histogram in the lower panel shows the density of energy eigenstates for the environment (which reflects the Wigner semicircle form expected for a random Hamiltonian). The $N_e = 600$ different eigenvalues have been binned as shown in the histogram and I plot $P_e^b(E)$, which is the total probability in the corresponding bin. This discrete set of points is connected for visualization purposes.

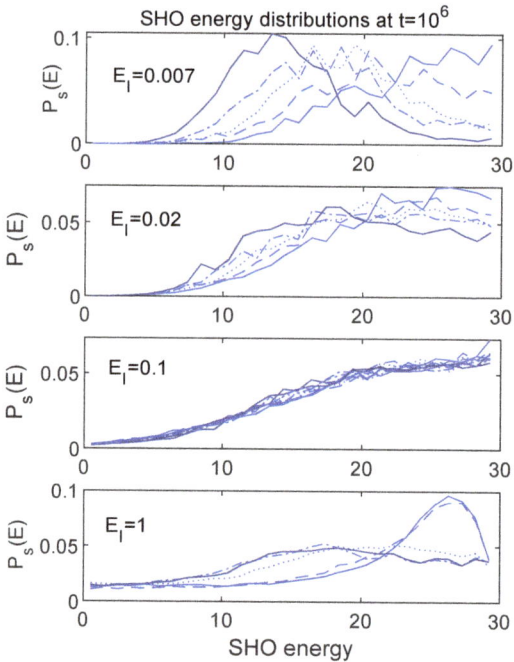

Figure 10. Late time energy distributions for the SHO. Each panel shows a set corresponding to the five different initial conditions, evolved using the value of E_I as marked. For $E_I = 0.1$, the SHO energies (first moments of $P_s(E)$) converged at late times for the different initial conditions (see Figure 6). These results indicate that many more than just the first moment converges for this value of E_I. The $E_I = 0.1$ panel includes the phase randomized version of each curve as well.

In Section 4, I discussed a primitive notion of "thermalization" based on the expectation that a thermalized system should share energies in the same proportions among different subsystems, regardless of the initial state, as long as each initial state had the same total energy. Among the cases considered in Section 5, we saw that only the $E_I = 0.1$ case met that criterion. Figures 10 and 11 show that, for $E_I = 0.1$, the system meets a stronger criterion, namely that many moments of the final energy distributions are independent of the initial state. This is certainly what one gets in the case of true thermalization of realistic physical systems, although it is worth emphasizing that none of the distributions shown are truly thermal in the sense of having the Gibbs form, as a function of an actual temperature. Still, having a parameter to dial which can turn on or off the rudimentary features of thermalization discussed here suggests that further explorations might reveal some insights into the notion of thermalization in general. I undertake such explorations in what follows.

It is tempting to make contact with the notion of "generalized canonical state" as discussed, for example, in [12]. However, in the places I have seen the generalized Gibbs distribution discussed it has taken a more idealized form. For example, a thermodynamic limit is taken or an idealized notion of "passivity" [13,14] is utilized. Those idealizations would preclude the sort of small fluctuations that appear in the my results.

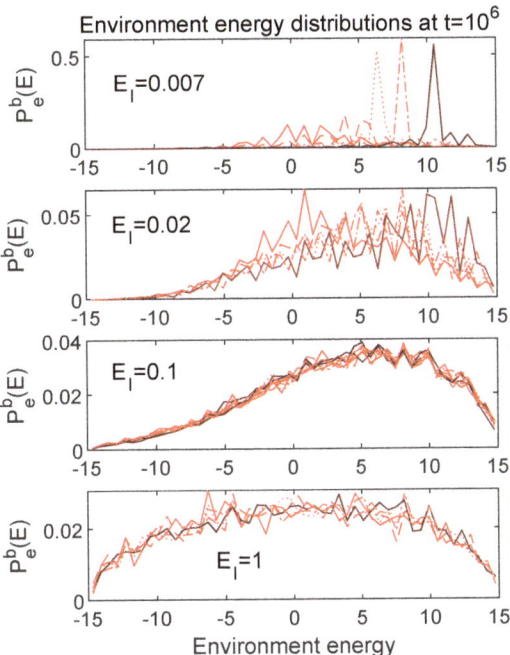

Figure 11. Late time energy distributions for the environment. Each panel shows a set corresponding to the five different initial conditions, evolved using the value of E_I as marked. For $E_I = 0.1$, the environment energies (first moments of $P_e(E)$) converged at late times for the different initial conditions (see Figure 6). These results indicate that many more than just the first moment converges for this value of E_I. The $E_I = 0.1$ panel includes the phase randomized version of each curve as well.

Before concluding this section, I want to comment about the strongly coupled $E_I = 1$ case. I have included it in this paper for completeness, but it should be emphasized that, due to the strong coupling, there is little meaning to the s and e subsystems. The quantities plotted in that case ($\langle H_s \rangle$, $\langle H_s \rangle$, $P_s(E)$ and $P_e(E)$), are mathematically well-defined, but they do not have natural physical interpretations. It seems unlikely that the $E_I = 1$ case admits a physically useful interpretation of the full space as a tensor product of any subspaces—certainly not the specific e and s ones considered here. One point one can make about this case is that it demonstrates that a rudimentary process of equilibration, driven by dephasing, is possible without any reference to energy flow, or any sense in which one subsystem is acting as a "bath" to another. Comments along these lines appear in [12].

7. The H_w Eigenstates

7.1. Energy Distributions in the Subspaces

Here, I explore the relationship between the phenomena discussed above and the form of the eigenstates of the global Hamiltonian H_w. I will focus here on the $E_I = 0.007$ and $E_I = 0.1$ cases. The $E_I = 0.02$ case exhibits behavior intermediate between those two, and, as discussed above, the $E_I = 1$ is not amenable to deeper analysis due to the strong coupling.

Recall that, for the $E_I = 0$ case, the eigenstates of H_w are products of eigenstates of H_s and H_e. Once the interaction is turned on, in general, H_w eigenstates will appear as density matrices in the s and e subspaces. I will utilize the techniques from Section 6 to focus on the energy distributions $P_s(E)$ and $P_e(E)$, given by the diagonal elements of the density matrices according to Equations (7) and (8). While these give incomplete information (only certain matrix elements will be shown, and $P_e(E)$ will appear binned as above), that information is sufficient to get a sense of what is going on. I have studied the properties of these states with more complete information than presented here and have confirmed that the information I do present gives a reasonable characterization for the points I want to make.

Figures 12 and 13 show information about a broad range of H_w eigenstates in terms of $P_s(E)$ and $P_e(E)$, respectively, for the $E_I = 0.007$ case.

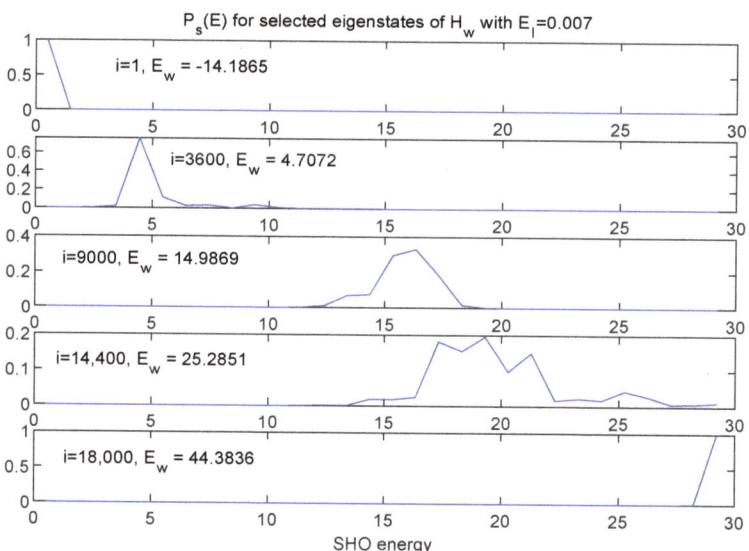

Figure 12. A selection of eigenstates of H_w (running from minimum to maximum eigenvalues) represented in terms of distributions in SHO energy. Here, $E_I = 0.007$. Note that, while these are not perfect delta functions, they are reasonably sharply peaked, as one would expect for a situation close to the $E_I = 0$ limit.

For this case, one can see that, while the eigenstates of H_w may not be perfect product states of H_s and H_e eigenstates, the energy distributions are still quite localized, as one would expect for very weak coupling.

Figure 14 shows energy distributions in both s and e subspaces for three adjacent energy eigenstates of H_w.

While the three pairs of curves represent eigenvalues of H_w which differ by at most 0.04%, the energy distribution between s and e is very different for each of the three cases. This is simply a reflection of the fact that there *are* many ways of distributing a fixed total energy among the two subsystems, and the peaked nature of the energy distributions for this very weakly coupled case allows that fact to play out in a simple and vivid way in the eigenstates of H_w.

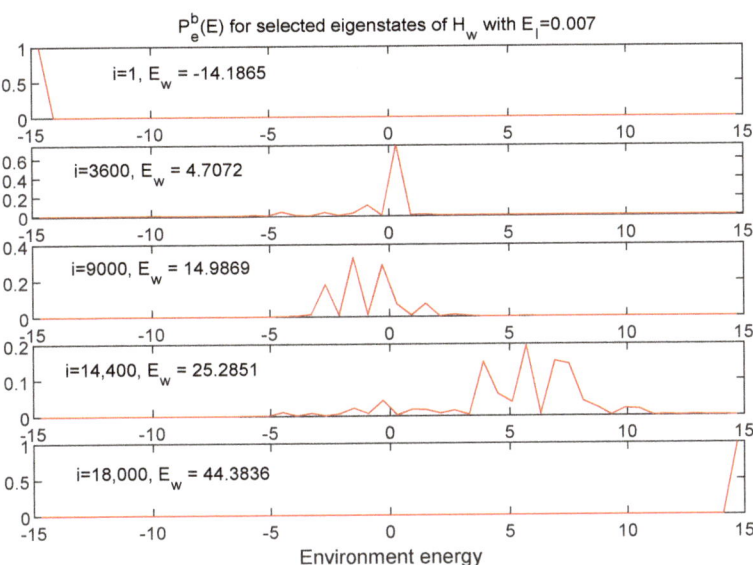

Figure 13. The same eigenstates shown in Figure 12 are shown here in terms of the (binned) distributions in environment energy. These too are reasonably sharply peaked, as expected.

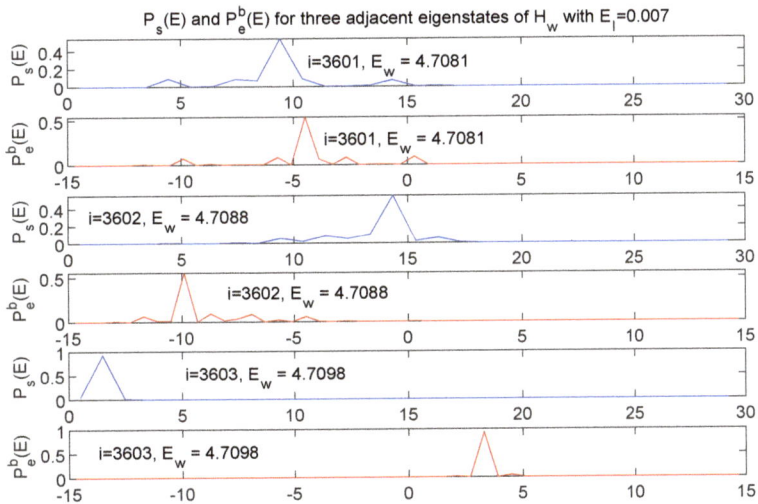

Figure 14. Energy distributions shown in both s (blue) and e (red) for three adjacent eigenstates of H_w, with $E_I = 0.007$. Although the associated values of E_w are essentially identical the energy is distributed in very different ways between the two subsystems.

Figures 15 and 16 show information about a broad range of H_w eigenstates in terms of $P_s(E)$ and $P_e(E)$, respectively, this time for the $E_I = 0.1$ case.

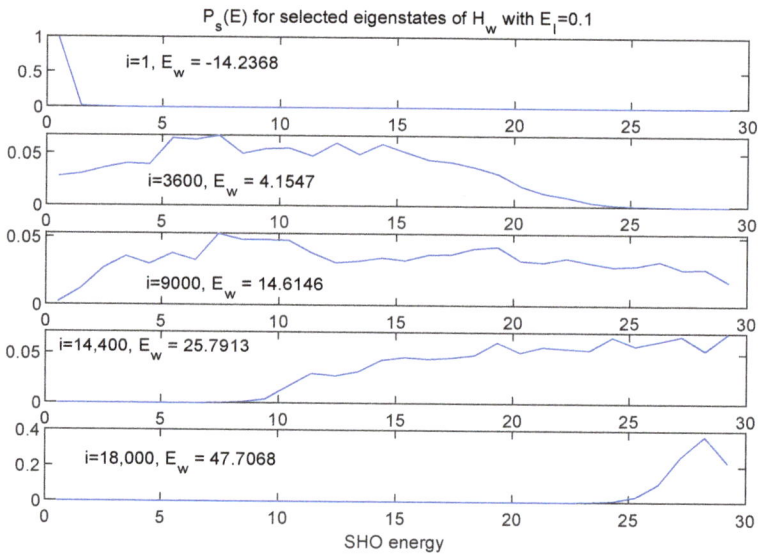

Figure 15. A selection of eigenstates of H_w (running from minimum to maximum eigenvalues) represented in terms of distributions in SHO energy. Here, $= E_I = 0.1$. While this case is weakly coupled by some measures, the interaction is strong enough to mix many of the energy eigenstates of the SHO, creating much broader distributions than seen in Figure 12 for the $E_I = 0.007$ case, at least away from the extreme ends of the spectrum.

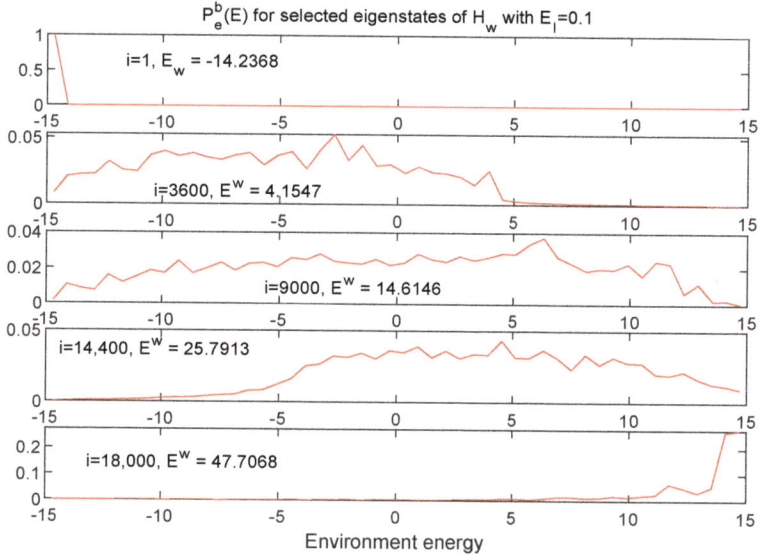

Figure 16. The same eigenstates shown in Figure 15 are shown here in terms of the distributions in environment energy. These distributions are also much more broad than those shown in Figure 13 for the $E_I = 0.07$ case.

While in many respects the $E_I = 0.1$ case might be thought of as "weakly coupled"—for example, note the small relative values of the interaction energy shown in black in

Figure 6—the interaction term is strong enough to mix many eigenstates of H_s and of H_e, leading to much broader distributions, except at the extremes of the spectrum. Note that the relevant measure for understanding the breadth of these distributions is the size of the interaction term relative to the *spacing* of the energy eigenvalues of the respective subsystems.

Figure 17 shows energy distributions in both s and e subspaces for three adjacent energy eigenstates of H_w, here with $E_I = 0.1$.

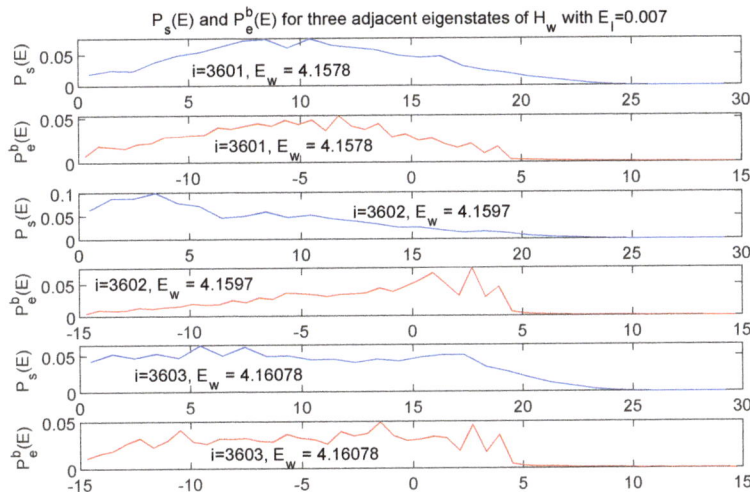

Figure 17. Energy distributions shown in both s (blue) and e (red) for three adjacent eigenstates of H_w with $E_I = 0.1$. For these broad distributions, the differences between neighboring eigenstates are more subtly compared with the more weakly coupled case shown in Figure 14.

In contrast with what was seen for the more weakly coupled case in Figure 14, the changes in the subsystem energy distributions as one steps between adjacent eigenstates of H_w are more subtle, although the differences can be discerned upon inspection.

7.2. Energy Distributions in the Global Space w

Having established significant differences between eigenstates of H_w as they appear in the subsystems, depending on the strength of the coupling E_I, I will now consider how the initial conditions are represented in these different sets of eigenstates. Figure 18 shows the distributions $P_w(E)$, defined in the same manner as P_s and P_e (Equations (7) and (8)) but in the global "world" space w using $\rho_w = |\psi\rangle_{ww}\langle\psi|$. The P_w's are time independent, and the different curves correspond to the set of five different initial conditions used to create each of Figures 4–7. (Note that I have only been using the same set of five initial conditions throughout this paper. I have been evolving and analyzing each one using H_w's with different values of E_I.)

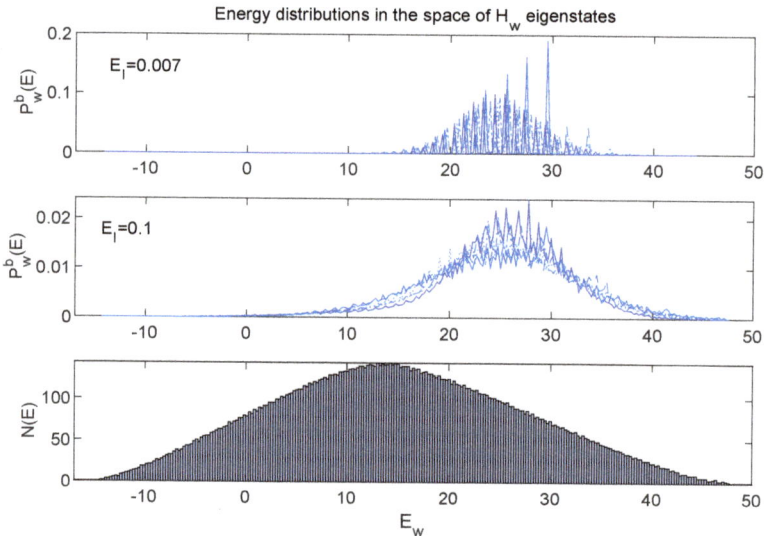

Figure 18. The (binned) global energy distributions $P_w^b(E)$ corresponding to the five initial states used throughout this paper. One can see that these curves have very different behaviors depending on the coupling strength E_I. For example, the $E_I = 0.007$ curves frequently approach zero, and the $E_I = 0.1$ curves do not. The bottom panel shows a histogram representing the density of energy eigenstates $N(E_w)$. Technically, $N(E_w)$ will be different for the two values of E_I, but both the values shown here are small enough not to change the form of $N(E_w)$ significantly.

Figure 19 shows zoomed-in portions of the top two panels of Figure 18.

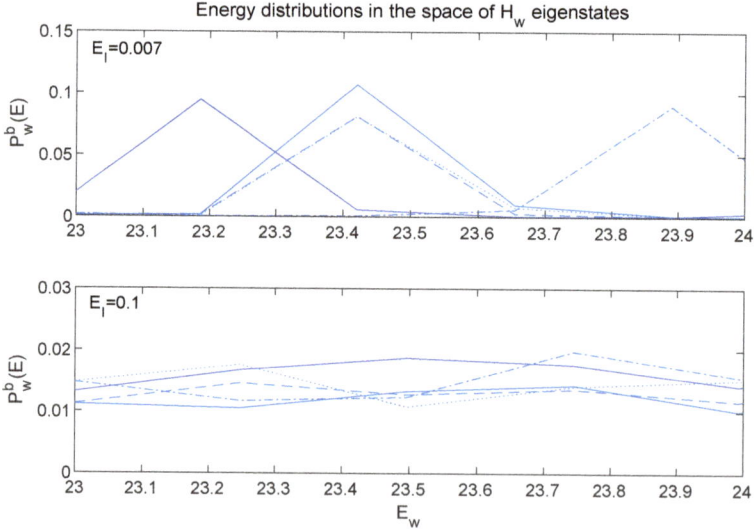

Figure 19. A zoomed-in look at the first two panels of Figure 18. One can see that not only do the $E_I = 0.007$ curves approach zero frequently, in contrast to the $E_I = 0.1$ curves, but the curves for each state exhibit very different patterns of large and small values.

The large oscillations of the $E_I = 0.007$ curves are especially clear in Figure 19, and one can see that the individual curves have very different locations of their peaks and minima.

7.3. Interpretation

I have presented information about the eigenstates of H_w using both the subsystem and global perspectives. These perspectives can be brought together in the following way. Consider the state $|E_i\rangle_s |E_j\rangle_e$, a product of eigenstates of H_s and H_e (with particular values of i and j), and consider expanding that state in eigenstates of H_w. For the $E_I = 0.007$ case, if a particular eigenstate $|E_k\rangle_w$ of H_w has a strong overlap with $|E_i\rangle_s |E_j\rangle_e$, then the $(k+1)$th state is likely to have a much weaker overlap. This is expected given the way the energy distributions shift among the subsystems as the index is incremented, as illustrated in Figure 14. (A similar situation is considered for many body systems in [15].) Expanding in eigenstates of H_w with $E_I = 0.1$ will work very differently. As illustrated in Figure 17, neighboring eigenstates will have energy distributions in the subsystems which are not radically different as the index is incremented. This suggests that the overlaps will vary much more smoothly with the index of E_k.

Similarly, the breadth of the distributions of $|E_w\rangle$'s in the s and e energy distributions for $E_I = 0.1$ suggests initial states with energy shared differently between s and e can still pick up similar overlaps with the $|E_w\rangle$'s, accounting for the overall shape similarity among the different curves in the 2nd panel of Figure 18. Furthermore, since $P_w(E)$, plus the phases, gives complete information about the global state $|\psi\rangle_w$, it is not surprising that, under equilibrium conditions (when the phases may be taken as random), states with similar $P_w(E)$'s also give similar $P_s(E)$'s and $P_e(E)$'s. (The $|E_w\rangle$ energy distributions in the s and e are not perfectly broad, so, not surprisingly, I have found examples of other initial states with particularly extreme energy distributions among s and e which have somewhat different shapes for $P_w(E)$, and even the 2nd panel of Figure 18 shows noticeable variations.)

The initial states studied here are products of coherent states in s with energy eigenstates in e. That makes the simple illustration above less rigorous, but the coherent states are somewhat localized in energy, so the main thrust of the illustration should carry through. In addition, the energy distributions in s and e only contain some of the information relevant for calculating the overlap $(_s\langle E_i|_e\langle E_j|) \cdot |E_k\rangle_w$, but again that information seems enough to capture some sense of what makes the $P_w(E)$ curves so different for the two values of E_I. Similar arguments can be used to relate my results to the Eigenstate Thermalization Hypothesis, which I do in Appendix C.

Finally, if one considers some process of extending this analysis to larger systems, one could imagine cases where the $P_w(E)$ distributions become more narrow (perhaps einselected into sharp energies through weakly coupled environments as in the "quantum limit" discussed in [16]). The smooth qualities of $P_w(E)$ we see for $E_I = 0.1$ could correspond in such a limit to a relatively flat distribution within the allowed range. This could connect with ergodic ideas which count each state equally within allowed energies, making contact with conventional statistical mechanics.

On the other hand, looking at the $E_I = 0.007$ case suggests another limit where $P_w(E)$ could remain more jagged, preventing simple statistical arguments from taking hold. By envisioning limits in this way, it does seem like the primitive "thermalized" behaviors of the $E_I = 0.1$ case discussed in Sections 5 and 6 are in some sense precursors to a full notion of thermalization for larger systems. Likewise, the alternative limit suggested by the $E_I = 0.007$ case has parallels with Anderson and many body localization in large systems. The localized systems exhibit a lack of thermalization for the same sorts of reasons as the toy model considered here, namely the lack of full access to states that should be allowed based purely on energetic reasons. In addition, just as the localized case appears to reflect additional (approximately) conserved quantities [17], I have associated the special features of the $E_I = 0.007$ case with the (partially broken) symmetry conserving $\langle H_s \rangle$ and $\langle H_e \rangle$ separately in the $E_I = 0$ limit.

7.4. The Effective Dimension as a Diagnostic

One way to characterize the different qualities of the sets of curves in Figures 18 and 19 is using the "effective dimension"

$$d^w_{eff} \equiv \frac{1}{\sum_i (P^w(E_i))^2}. \quad (9)$$

This quantity takes its minimum value of unity if $P(E_i)$ is a delta function, and reaches its maximum possible value, N_w, if all $P(E)$'s are identical. Table 1 compiles information about the d^w_{eff} values for the curves shown in Figure 18, as well as for the $P_w(E)$'s for $E_I = 1$ and $E_I = 0.02$ (which I have not displayed in graphical form and for which d_{eff} takes on intermediate values).

Table 1. The effective dimension (d^w_{eff}, from Equation (9)), evaluated for and averaged over the five sets of initial states used in this paper. The effective dimension is larger when the function $P(E)$ is broad and smooth. Comparing the curves in the top two panels of Figure 18 (as well as Figure 19) suggests it is not surprising that d_{eff} for $E_I = 0.1$ is more than 60 times greater than the $E_I = 0.007$ case. (The quantity Δ gives the variance of d_{eff} across the five solutions.)

E_I	$\langle d^w_{eff} \rangle / N_w$	Δ	% of $d^w_{eff}(E_I = 0.1)$
1	0.087	30%	27%
0.1	0.24	8%	100%
0.02	0.06	33%	25%
0.007	0.004	70%	1.6%

The extremely different natures of the $E_I = 0.1$ and $E_I = 0.007$ curves are nicely captured by the large difference between their d_{eff} values. In addition, Δ, the variance of d_{eff} across the five different states gives one measure of "scatter" among the different $P_w(E)$ curves for fixed E_I. This scatter is smallest for the $E_I = 0.1$ case, which is consistent with the observations made about energy distributions in Section 6 (although those were focused on energy distributions in the subsystems).

8. Tuning of States and Parameters

In the analysis presented here, the "thermalized"-like behavior seems to emerge as a special case for a particular value (presumably actually a small region of values) for E_I. In much larger systems exhibiting localization discussed in the literature, it is typically the non-thermalized behavior that seems special, usually associated with specific parameter choices that lead to integrability. I simply note here that it is not surprising that such matters of tuning depend on measures implicit in the model being considered. I regard the ACL model as too simplistic to draw broad conclusions about tuning of parameters, except as an illustration of how measures can turn out differently. If the "emergent laws" perspective mentioned in the introduction is ever realized, that will come with its own perspective (and probably challenges) regarding measures.

I also note that tuning of the initial state is involved in the notion of equilibration. A special choice of initial state with a low entropy is required in order to see a system dynamically approach equilibrium. The fact that the actual Universe did indeed have such a special low entropy initial state is a source of great interest and curiosity to me, and although it is not often stated that way, it is related to the notorious "tuning problems" in cosmology (see [18] for pioneering work and Section 5 of [2] for a recent summary). That is certainly not (directly) the topic of this paper, although I can not help but note with interest the very different perspective I sometimes see in the statistical mechanics literature (for example, [12] which implies that the Universe should be taken to be in a typical state).

9. Discussion and Conclusions

This research originated with my curiosity about various behaviors of the ACL model that I encountered in earlier work [1,2]. On one hand, the equilibration process seemed so robust I wondered if there was a straightforward ergodicity picture to back it up. On the other hand, examination of the energy distributions that appeared in equilibrium made it clear that no conventional notion of temperature applied. Furthermore, standard arguments would interpret the part of the environment density of states $N(E)$ that decreases with E (see Figure 9) as a "negative temperature". Would that introduce strange artifacts in our results?

In this work, I have examined the equilibration processes in the ACL model systematically. I have seen how the dephasing process is the solid foundation on which the equilibration takes place. Dephasing is able to drive equilibration under conditions where the notions of temperature and ergodicity do not apply. I have argued that this very basic form of equilibration is sufficient to support the use of the ACL model in studies of the equilibrium phenomena explored in [2].

Even though the notion of temperature does not apply, I have considered some primitive aspects of "thermalization." Specifically, I have considered the expectation that different initial states with the same global energy thermalize to the same subsystem energy distributions. The ACL model is only able to realize this expectation in equilibrium for certain values of the coupling strength. When this aspect of thermalization is realized, the energy distributions in the global space are smooth. In the other cases, the global energy distribution can be quite jagged. I have related these different behaviors to the intrinsic properties of the global energy eigenstates, and argued that the smooth behavior could be viewed as something of a precursor to ergodicity, which might take a more concrete form in the limit of larger system sizes. In addition, I have noted some rough parallels with discussions of the presence or absence of thermalization in large condensed matter systems.

Regarding negative temperature, even in the absence of a solid notion of temperature, the evolution of the energy distribution depicted in Figure 9 toward regions of lower energy but higher density of states might be seen as a more primitive version of the phenomena that can be associated with a negative temperature in other systems.

I have found it interesting to learn the degree to which the very simple ACL model is able to reflect certain familiar elements of equilibration, while still missing out on others due to its small size and other "unphysical" aspects. Understanding systems such as this one that are on the edge of familiar behaviors could prove useful in exploring selection effects in frameworks where the laws of physics themselves are emergent, one of the motivations for this research I discussed in the Introduction. Such work might ultimately help us understand the origin of the specific behaviors of the world around us that we call "physical".

10. Reflections

It is a great pleasure to contribute to this volume honoring Wojciech Zurek's 70th birthday. I first met Wojciech at an Aspen Center for Physics workshop the summer after I completed my PhD in 1983. I have had the good fortune of having numerous connections with Wojciech since then, including as his postdoc later in the 1980s. Wojciech has been an inspiration to me in many ways. For one, his unbounded and energetic curiosity has led to some of the most joyful and adventurous conversations of my entire career. It is definitely in the spirit of this adventurous style that I have pursued the topics of this paper. I am also grateful to Wojciech for helping me develop a taste for natural hot springs. It is fitting that certain advances on this project were made while partaking of some of my local favorites (experiencing temperature, but fortunately not equilibrium).

Funding: This work was supported in part by the U.S. Department of Energy, Office of Science, Office of High Energy Physics QuantISED program under Contract No. KA2401032.

Institutional Review Board Statement: Not applicable.

Informed Consent Statement: Not applicable.

Data Availability Statement: Not applicable.

Acknowledgments: I am grateful to Rose Baunach, Zoe Holmes, Veronika Hubeny, Richard Scalettar, and Rajiv Singh for helpful conversations.

Conflicts of Interest: The author declares no conflict of interest. The funders had no role in the design of the study; in the collection, analyses, or interpretation of data; in the writing of the manuscript, or in the decision to publish the results.

Appendix A. Initial Conditions

As discussed in [1], coherent states can be constructed for the truncated SHO using the standard formula

$$|\alpha\rangle = \exp\left(\alpha \hat{a}^\dagger - \alpha^* \hat{a}\right)|0\rangle. \tag{A1}$$

The five initial states used throughout this paper are constructed by selecting the ith eigenstate of H_e, with i drawn from $\{300, 400, 450, 500, 550\}$ (ordered with increasing eigenvalue). Recall that $N_e = 600$.

I then adjust α so that the initial state $|\alpha\rangle_s|i\rangle_e$ has $\langle H_w \rangle = 25$. Note that $\langle H_w \rangle$ includes the interaction term, so the value of α technically depends on E_I. Except for the strongly coupled $E_I = 1$ case, this dependence is very weak. The exact values of the different initial subsystem energies in each case can be read from Figures 4–7.

Appendix B. Dephasing, Decoherence and Dissipation

This work focuses on dissipative processes which cause energy to flow and then stabilize at equilibrium values. My focus on energy flow is natural for studying the topic of thermalization. In [1], we explored how decoherence and dissipation happen on different time scales in the ACL model, a difference which is much more pronounced for larger systems. In addition, I note here that the term dephasing can mean different things, for example, relating the phases of two different beams as discussed in [19], where the notion of depolarization is also explored and contrasted. I use dephasing to refer to the randomization of the α_w^i phases over time. The dephasing I observe is not absolute, since recurrences are to be expected eventually. However, the recurrence time lies far beyond the time ranges explored here (and in fact far outside the dynamic range of my computations, which are documented in [1]). This arrangement of the various relative time scales is well suited for the topics of this paper.

Appendix C. Eigenstate Thermalization Hypothesis

The Eigenstate Thermalization Hypothesis (ETH) [20–22] proposes that important statistical properties of thermalized systems can be expressed by single eigenstates of the global Hamiltonian. Even though the ETH is intended to apply to much larger systems, out of curiosity I have explored how the ACL behaviors might relate to the ETH. Focusing on the $P_s(E)$'s and $P_e(E)$'s, one can see from Figures 14 and 17 that the subsystem energy distributions look more similar for individual eigenstates of H_w for $E_I = 0.1$ than for $E_I = 0.007$. This similarity suggests that for the "thermalized" $E_I = 0.1$ case individual eigenstates are starting to line up behind a common statement about the subsystem energy distributions, which would be a signature of the ETH. But the fact that significant differences remain among the $E_I = 0.1$ curves suggests this signature is not expressed strongly.

Figure A1 presents a more systematic analysis of the H_w eigenstates relevant to the sets of initial conditions used here. (The selection of the eigenstates is illustrated in Figure A2.)

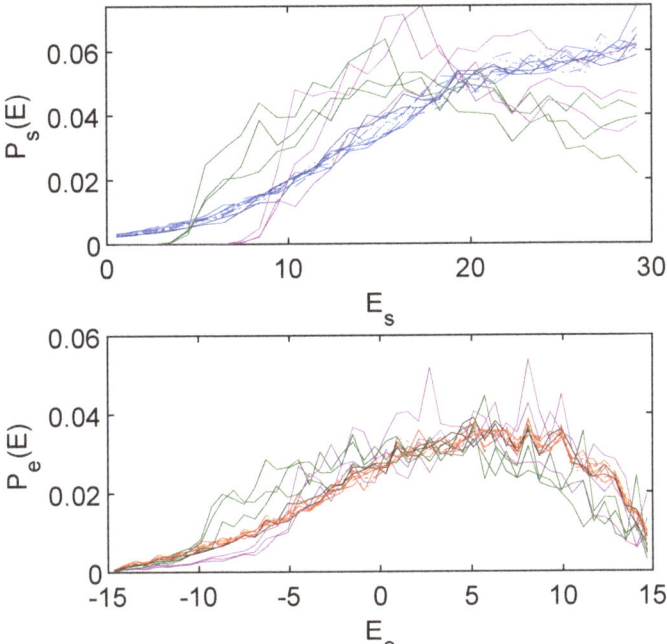

Figure A1. Exploring ETH: The energy distributions for the $E_I = 0.1$ case from Figures 10 (system) and 11 (environment) are shown (blue and red curves, respectively). In addition, the energy distributions for individual eigenstates of H_w are plotted. As depicted (and color coded) in Figure A2, the particular H_w eigenstates are chosen to be representative of the global energy distributions that correspond to the original curves from Figures 10 and 11. No single eigenstate fully characterizes the equilibrium distributions (although they are not completely off the mark), and there is significant scatter among the distributions drawn from the individual eigenstates. These results suggest only a very loose realization of the ETH.

The $P_s(E)$ and $P_e(E)$ curves for those eigenstates approach the energy distributions for our set of initial states reasonably well, but they still retain considerably greater scatter than seen for the non-H_w eigenstate states. Thus, the averaging over the entire distribution in $P_w(E)$ space appears to have a significant role in realizing the sharpness of the convergence of the $P_s(E)$ and $P_e(E)$ curves. Although one could try to argue that there are elements of the ETH being expressed here, any such expression is only an approximate one.

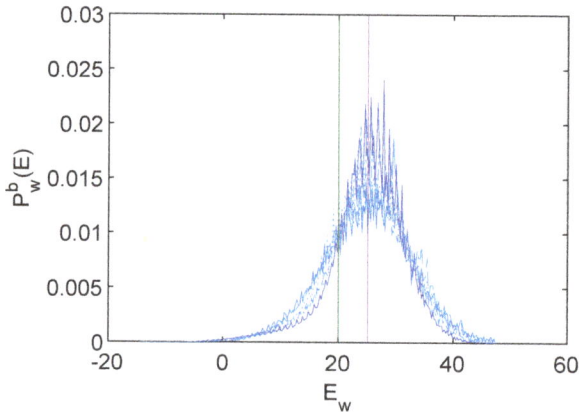

Figure A2. Selected eigenstates: The eigenvalues of the H_w eigenstates chosen for Figure A1 are shown here (vertical lines), against the backdrop of the global energy distributions from the $E_I = 0.1$ panel in Figure 18, which correspond to the original energy distributions depicted for the subsystems in Figure A1. There are three green and three purple lines, which are unresolved in the figure because they show adjacent eigenvalues (which only differ at the 0.01% level). The curves in Figure A1 are matched by color with the eigenvalues shown here.

References

1. Albrecht, A.; Baunach, R.; Arrasmith, A. Adapted Caldeira–Leggett Model. *arXiv* **2021**, arXiv:2105.14040.
2. Albrecht, A.; Baunach, R.; Arrasmith, A. Einselection, Equilibrium and Cosmology. *arXiv* **2021**, arXiv:2105.14017.
3. Zurek, W.H.; Habib, S.; Paz, J.P. Coherent states via decoherence. *Phys. Rev. Lett.* **1993**, *70*, 1187–1190. [CrossRef] [PubMed]
4. Baunach, R.; Albrecht, A.; Arrasmith, A. Copycat process in the early stages of einselection. *arXiv* **2021**, arXiv:2105.14032.
5. Albrecht, A.; Iglesias, A. The Clock ambiguity and the emergence of physical laws. *Phys. Rev. D* **2008**, *77*, 063506. [CrossRef]
6. Albrecht, A.; Iglesias, A. Lorentz symmetric dispersion relation from a random Hamiltonian. *Phys. Rev. D* **2015**, *91*, 043529. [CrossRef]
7. Binder, F.; Correa, L.; Gogolin, C.; Anders, J.; Adesso, G. *Thermodynamics in the Quantum Regime: Fundamental Aspects and New Directions*; Fundamental Theories of Physics; Springer International Publishing: Cham, Switzerland, 2019.
8. Lloyd, S. Excuse our ignorance. *Nat. Phys.* **2006**, *2*, 727–728. [CrossRef]
9. Cucchietti, F.M.; Paz, J.P.; Zurek, W.H. Decoherence from spin environments. *Phys. Rev. A* **2005**, *72*, 052113. [CrossRef]
10. Zurek, W.H.; Cucchietti, F.M.; Paz, J.P. Gaussian Decoherence and Gaussian Echo from Spin Environments. *arXiv* **2006**, arXiv:quant-ph/quant-ph/0611200.
11. Nandkishore, R.; Huse, D.A. Many-Body Localization and Thermalization in Quantum Statistical Mechanics. *Annu. Rev. Condens. Matter Phys.* **2015**, *6*, 15–38. [CrossRef]
12. Popescu, S.; Short, A.J.; Winter, A. Entanglement and the foundations of statistical mechanics. *Nat. Phys.* **2006**, *2*, 754–758. [CrossRef]
13. Rigol, M.; Dunjko, V.; Yurovsky, V.; Olshanii, M. Relaxation in a Completely Integrable Many-Body Quantum System: An Ab Initio Study of the Dynamics of the Highly Excited States of 1D Lattice Hard-Core Bosons. *Phys. Rev. Lett.* **2007**, *98*, 050405. [CrossRef] [PubMed]
14. Lenard, A. Thermodynamical proof of the Gibbs formula for elementary quantum systems. *J. Stat. Phys.* **1978**, *19*, 575–586. [CrossRef]
15. Ikeda, T.N.; Watanabe, Y.; Ueda, M. Eigenstate randomization hypothesis: Why does the long-time average equal the microcanonical average? *Phys. Rev. E* **2011**, *84*, 021130. [CrossRef] [PubMed]
16. Paz, J.P.; Zurek, W.H. Quantum limit of decoherence: Environment induced superselection of energy eigenstates. *Phys. Rev. Lett.* **1999**, *82*, 5181–5185. [CrossRef]
17. Serbyn, M.; Papić, Z.; Abanin, D.A. Local Conservation Laws and the Structure of the Many-Body Localized States. *Phys. Rev. Lett.* **2013**, *111*, 127201. [CrossRef] [PubMed]
18. Penrose, R. Singularities and time-asymmetry. In *General Relativity*; An Einstein Centenary Survey; University of Oxford: Oxford, UK, 1979.
19. Rauch, H.; Suda, M.; Pascazio, S. Decoherence, dephasing and depolarization. *Phys. Condens. Matter* **1999**, *267–268*, 277–284. [CrossRef]
20. Deutsch, J.M. Quantum statistical mechanics in a closed system. *Phys. Rev. A* **1991**, *43*, 2046–2049. [CrossRef] [PubMed]

1. Srednicki, M. Chaos and quantum thermalization. *Phys. Rev. E* **1994**, *50*, 888–901. [CrossRef] [PubMed]
2. D'Alessio, L.; Kafri, Y.; Polkovnikov, A.; Rigol, M. From quantum chaos and eigenstate thermalization to statistical mechanics and thermodynamics. *Adv. Phys.* **2016**, *65*, 239–362. [CrossRef]

Article

Non-Perfect Propagation of Information to a Noisy Environment with Self-Evolution

Piotr Mironowicz [1,2,*], Paweł Horodecki [1,3] and Ryszard Horodecki [1]

1. International Centre for Theory of Quantum Technologies, University of Gdansk, Wita Stwosza 63, 80-308 Gdansk, Poland; pawel.horodecki@pg.edu.pl (P.H.); ryszard.horodecki@ug.edu.pl (R.H.)
2. Department of Algorithms and System Modeling, Faculty of Electronics, Telecommunications and Informatics, Gdansk University of Technology, Gabriela Narutowicza 11/12, 80-233 Gdansk, Poland
3. Faculty of Applied Physics and Mathematics, Gdansk University of Technology, Gabriela Narutowicza 11/12, 80-233 Gdansk, Poland
* Correspondence: piotr.mironowicz@gmail.com

Abstract: We study the non-perfect propagation of information for evolving a low-dimensional environment that includes self-evolution as well as noisy initial states and analyse the interrelations between the degree of objectivization and environment parameters. In particular, we consider an analytical model of three interacting qubits and derive its objectivity parameters. The numerical analysis shows that the quality of the spectrum broadcast structure formed during the interaction may exhibit non-monotonicity both in the speed of self-dynamics of the environment as well as its mixedness. The former effect is particularly strong, showing that—considering part of the environment as a measurement apparatus—an increase of the external magnetic field acting on the environment may turn the vague measurement into close to ideal. The above effects suggest that quantum objectivity may appear after increasing the dynamics of the environment, although not with respect to the pointer basis, but some other, which we call the generalized pointer or indicator basis. Furthermore, it seems also that, when the objectivity is poor, it may be improved, at least by some amount, by increasing the thermal noise. We provide further evidence of this by analysing the upper bounds on distance to the set of states representing perfect objectivity in the case of a higher number of qubits.

Keywords: quantum Darwinism; decoherence; objectivity

1. Introduction

Quantum mechanics works perfectly and is reliable in an appropriate regime. Nevertheless, it leaves us with cognitive discomfort, as a theory that pretends to be fundamental should describe whole physical reality, including the classical objective properties of the systems that are inter-subjectively verifiable by independent observers. The problem is that quantum formalism does not offer a simple footbridge from the quantum world to our actual world. This issue involves many aspects; it has a long history and huge literature [1]. In particular, it involves a highly non-trivial question: Is it possible to circumvent the fundamental restrictions (no-broadcasting [2,3]) on the processing of quantum information to explain the emergence of the objective nature of information redundancy in the actual world?

Thanks to Zurek's quantum Darwinism concept [4], there are strong reasons to believe that the decoherence theory pioneered by Zeh [5] and developed by Zurek [6,7] and others [8,9] based on the system–environment (or, in the Bohr's spirit: system–context [10]) paradigm offers the most promising approach to the emergence of classicality from the quantum world.

Quantum Darwinism (QD) considers a decohering environment E as a "witness" that monitors and can reveal the information about a system S. The environment consists of multiple independent N fragments, and objectivity emerges when interacting with the

system led to redundant information proliferation about system $\mathcal{S}$ measured by quantum mutual information $I(\mathcal{S}:\mathcal{E})$ between the system and an accessible fragment of the environment, $\mathcal{E} \subset E$, where $I(\mathcal{S}:\mathcal{E}) = H(\mathcal{S}) + H(\mathcal{E}) - H(\mathcal{SE})$ is the mutual information between the system and part of the environment and $H(\cdot)$ is the von Neumann entropy (see [11] and the references therein). The term "objectivity" means that the state of the system satisfies the following:

Definition 1. *A system state $\mathcal{S}$ is objective when many independent observers can determine the state of S independently, without perturbing it, and arrive at the same result [12–14].*

The different theoretical and experimental implementations of QD have been considered and discussed based on the information-theoretic condition:

$$I(\mathcal{S}:\mathcal{E}) = H(\mathcal{S}). \tag{1}$$

In many cases, the above relation is sufficient to identify correctly emergent objective properties in a quantum system in contact with an environment. Interestingly, sometimes the nature of the quantum-classical interplay may be richer. In particular, examples have been found in which QD can falsely announce objectivity, and it has been indicated that QD can be inconsistent with the emergence of objectivity when the condition (1) is used [14–16].

In connection with the QD, a problem arises: *To identify quantum primitive information broadcasting state responsible for the emergence of the perceived objectivity*. This issue was raised in [14], where it was proven that Bohr's non-disturbance measurement, full decoherence and "strong independence" lead to the paradigmatic spectrum broadcast structure (SBS) responsible for objectivity, which can be written in the following form:

$$\varrho_{\mathcal{SE}} = \sum_i p_i |\psi_i\rangle\langle\psi_i| \otimes \varrho_i^{\mathcal{E}_1} \otimes \cdots \otimes \varrho_i^{\mathcal{E}_N}, \tag{2}$$

where $\mathcal{E}$ is the accessible environment, $\mathcal{E}_k \in \{\mathcal{E}_1, \mathcal{E}_2, \ldots, \mathcal{E}_N\}$, $\mathcal{E}_k \cap \mathcal{E}_{k'} = \emptyset$, $\mathcal{E}_k \subset \mathcal{E}$ are the subenvironments. The conditional states $\{\varrho_i^{\mathcal{E}_k}\}$ can be used to perfectly distinguish index i, where $\{|\psi_i\rangle\}$ is some diagonal basis of the $\mathcal{S}$ and $\{p_i\}$ its spectrum.

The basis $\{|\psi_i\rangle\}$ has a special role in the above picture. It represents the objective information about the quantum system. The above form (2) is agnostic about the physical mechanism leading to it. Hence, we shall call the basis $\{|\psi_i\rangle\}$ a *generalised pointer basis* (or, alternatively an *indicator basis*). In the case of quantum Darwinism, when determined by the interaction Hamiltonian, this basis becomes exactly the pointer basis. However, there may be other physical processes that lead to the above (2) structure. This is directly related to the main point of the present paper: any pointer basis is the generalized pointer basis but *not* vice versa.

The above SBS state clearly shows the meaning of the terms "objective"/inter-subjective used in Definition 1. This reveals the contextual nature of objectivity, which emerges as a property of a system dependent on the combined properties of the system and the environment. These states have a discord of zero; hence, only the "classic" spectrum of the system $\{p_i\}$ is broadcast to the environment, and therefore independent observers do not have access to quantum information.

It has been proven that SBS is a stronger condition than the QD, i.e., SBS implies QD [14]. The objective states with spectrum broadcast structure can be used as ideal "frames of reference" to which any real states can be compared. The SBS was identified in the many models of open quantum systems (see [17] and the references therein), and its simulations on a quantum computer were demonstrated [18]. It was also shown that the objectivity is subjective across quantum reference frames [19], including its dynamical aspects [20].

It was mentioned in [14] that the SBS-like states may open a "classical window" for life processes within the quantum world. Interestingly, the process of objectivization of information over time was analysed using quantum state discrimination and potential applications for the theory of evolution of senses were suggested [12]. Remarkably, in nature, there are thermal states the properties of which, seem to contradict objectivity suggesting that thermality and objectivity are mutually exclusive. Recently Le et al. [21] examined the overlap between thermal and objective states and showed that there are certain regimes in which exist states that are approximately thermal and objective.

As mentioned above, the SBS implies quantum Darwinism condition (1); however, the opposite implication does not hold. The discrepancy between the QD and SBS led to the discovery of a stronger version of quantum Darwinism (SQD) [22], where (1) is replaced by a stronger condition: A system state is objective if the following conditions hold simultaneously:

$$I(\mathcal{S}:\mathcal{E}) = \chi(\mathcal{S}:\mathcal{E}), \tag{3a}$$

$$I_{acc}(\mathcal{S}:\mathcal{E}_k) = H(\mathcal{S}), \tag{3b}$$

$$I(\mathcal{E}_1 \cdots \mathcal{E}_N | \mathcal{S}) = 0, \tag{3c}$$

where $\chi(\mathcal{S}:\mathcal{E})$ is the Holevo information in the pointer basis π, $I_{acc}(\mathcal{S}:\mathcal{E}_k)$ is the accessible information and $I(\mathcal{E}_1 \cdots \mathcal{E}_N | \mathcal{S})$ is the conditional multipartite mutual information. It has been shown that SQD is equivalent to bipartite SBS, and it is sufficient and necessary for objectivity [22–24]. Thus, SBS and SQD are two extensions of the standard QD based on the quantum state structure and information, respectively [25].

However, in the limit of a large environment the standard QD works very well. In [11], the authors investigated a model based on imperfect C-NOT gates and showed that relevant quantities for QD exhibited similar dependence on the size $|\mathcal{E}_k|$ of a fragment of environment $\mathcal{E}_k$, including scaling independent from the quality of the imperfect C-NOT gates and the size of the fragment of environment $\mathcal{E}_k$.

2. Aspects of Emergence of Objective Information on Quantum Ground

The fundamental elements of Zurek's quantum Darwinism discovery were (1) The methodological identification that classical correlations between the system and environment and redundant character of the information about the system in the environment are a constitutive feature of objectivity. (2) Proof that this objective information is very special, unambiguously determined by a system–environment interaction. More precisely, the interaction chooses a basis, called the pointer basis, and this is the information concerning the question "In which state of the pointer basis is the system in?" that is replicated by interaction in the environment in a stable way. Quite remarkably, the latter feature is responsible for the strong cognitive power of the whole process.

This is the case for the following three reasons. First, the information-theoretic correlations between the system and parts of the environment have a classical, well-understood character. Second, a subject observing a part of the environment not only knows that the system is in some particular state but also knows exactly what the system state is, since the latter belongs to a special basis—the pointer basis. Third, by a repetition of an experiment of placing the system in the same state many times into the environment and observing some part of the latter, the subject is also able to learn (via a collection of the experiment statistics) about some parameters of the initial state of the system.

These correspond to the diagonal of the state written in the pointer basis. The parameters are revealed in this process. In this sense, we may understand the quantum Darwinism process as a process of objectivization that discloses the parameters of the system state.

In the present paper, we inquire as to whether and when the dynamical emergence of objectivity is possible in a more relaxed sense—namely, when one retains only the element (1) of Zurek's program. More precisely, we only demand that the information about the system being in one of the elements of some basis is classically present in the environment—there are only classical correlations between system and environment. However neither the basis needs to be directly related to the system–environment interaction nor do the corresponding statistics need to directly correspond to some particular parameters of the initial state of the system. In this sense, the basis has only the character of the generalized pointer basis (see discussion below (2)).

Below, we show that this kind of objectivization can emerge in low-dimensional qubit systems. For this purpose, we examine the non-perfect propagation of information from system $\mathcal{S}$ to the noisy environment $\mathcal{E}$ with self-evolution and analyse interrelations between the degree of objectivization and environment parameters. We consider two different environments, the first composed of one observed and one unobserved qubit and the second one where there are seven observed qubits and one unobserved.

In particular, we consider an analytical model of three interacting qubits and derive its objectivity parameters. Then, we show that, if the imperfection of the C-NOT gate is known, the emergence of the objectivity albeit with respect to a different basis than the one associated with the gate itself—can be triggered by carefully chosen environment self-dynamics. For a seven-qubit environment, numerical calculations show that dynamics of the environment may help the emergence of relaxed objectivity to happen.

3. Analytical Model for Three Interacting Qubits

Let us now investigate a model of three interacting qubits, where we consider one of them as the observed system, and the remaining two constitute the observing environment $\mathcal{E}$. In the following, we will derive a closed analytical formula for the objectivity parameters, viz. decoherence and orthogonalization, in a scenario where the information is widespread using imperfect C-NOT gate (C-INOT gate), and where the time evolution includes self-evolution of each of the qubits and their inter-environmental interaction.

3.1. Derivation of Objectivity Parameters

We model the C-INOT gates [11] defined by the formula:

$$U_{\text{C-INOT}} \equiv \begin{bmatrix} 1 & 0 & 0 & 0 \\ 0 & 1 & 0 & 0 \\ 0 & 0 & \sin(\theta) & \cos(\theta) \\ 0 & 0 & \cos(\theta) & -\sin(\theta) \end{bmatrix}, \quad (4)$$

where $\theta \in [0, \pi/2]$ is the imperfection parameter. For $\theta = 0$, the gate reproduces the perfect C-NOT gate. It does not allow to model the two qubit identity unitary. In this work, we have chosen the Kronecker product convention where the primal structure of the matrix representation is determined by the first space involved in the product.

There is an infinite number of Hamiltonians that can realise the gate (4) after some fixed time of interaction. Here, we choose the following Hamiltonian:

$$H_{\text{C-INOT}} \equiv \begin{bmatrix} 0 & 0 & 0 & 0 \\ 0 & 0 & 0 & 0 \\ 0 & 0 & (\pi/2)(1-\sin(\theta)) & -(\pi/2)\cos(\theta) \\ 0 & 0 & -(\pi/2)\cos(\theta) & (\pi/2)(1+\sin(\theta)) \end{bmatrix}. \quad (5)$$

One may check that $\exp(-itH_{\text{C-INOT}}) = U_{\text{C-INOT}}$ for $t = 1$. We denote by $H^1_{\text{C-INOT}}$, $H^2_{\text{C-INOT}}$, the Hamiltonians of C-INOT acting on the first and second qubits of the environment, respectively, conditioned by the system bit.

We assume that the total Hamiltonian is given by:

$$H_{\text{TOTAL}} \equiv H^1_{\text{C-INOT}} + H^2_{\text{C-INOT}} + \alpha_1 H_1 + \alpha_2 H_2 + \alpha_3 H_3. \quad (6)$$

where

$$H_1 \equiv \sigma_Z \otimes \mathbb{1}_2 \otimes \mathbb{1}_2, \quad (7a)$$

$$H_2 \equiv \mathbb{1}_2 \otimes \sigma_Z \otimes \mathbb{1}_2 + \mathbb{1}_2 \otimes \mathbb{1}_2 \otimes \sigma_Z, \quad (7b)$$

$$H_3 \equiv \sigma_Z \otimes \sigma_Z \otimes \mathbb{1}_2 + \sigma_Z \otimes \mathbb{1}_2 \otimes \sigma_Z + \qquad (7c)$$
$$\mathbb{1}_2 \otimes \sigma_Z \otimes \sigma_Z + \sigma_Z \otimes \sigma_Z \otimes \sigma_Z,$$

with $\mathbb{1}_2$ denoting identity on a single qubit space. Here, H_1 is the self-evolution Hamiltonian of the central system; H_2 is the self-evolution of the environmental qubits that can be, e.g., caused by an external magnetic field; H_3 contains inter-qubit interactions, between each pair of the qubits plus the joint interaction between all three qubits via ZZ and ZZZ coupling, respectively. $\alpha_1, \alpha_2, \alpha_3 \geq 0$ are the interaction strength parameters.

Whereas (7b) easily generalizes for cases with more qubits in the environment, (7c) is specific for the two-qubit case. Further in this paper, we consider other inter-environmental interactions with larger environments.

One can rewrite $H_{\text{TOTAL}} = (\pi - \alpha_1)\mathbb{1}_8 + M$ with $\mathbb{1}_8$ being the 3-qubit identity operator, and M a block-diagonal matrix, giving $V \equiv \exp(-itM)$ also of block-diagonal form, with blocks denoted by V_0 and V_1. The explicit form of those matrices is given in Appendix A.

We assume that the initial system–environment state $\varrho_{S\mathcal{E}}$ is given by:

$$\varrho_{S\mathcal{E}} = |+\rangle\langle+| \otimes \varrho^{\mathcal{E}_1} \otimes \varrho^{\mathcal{E}_2}, \qquad (8)$$

where
$$\varrho^{\mathcal{E}_1} = \varrho^{\mathcal{E}_2} = \varrho \equiv p|0\rangle\langle 0| + (1-p)|1\rangle\langle 1| \qquad (9)$$

are the environment qubit states, $p \in [0, 0.5]$.

We note that, for $\alpha_1 = \alpha_3 = 0$ the state ϱ is the termal state of the environment and $p = \frac{e^{-\alpha_2/\beta}}{e^{-\alpha_2/\beta} + e^{\alpha_2/\beta}}$, or $1/\beta = \frac{1}{2\alpha_2}\ln((1-p)/p)$, where β is the inverse temperature. This holds because of the form of H_2, i.e. the state $|1\rangle$ is the ground state of the Hamiltonian. After the time evolution, given by $\exp(-itH_{\text{TOTAL}})$, the joint state of the system and two qubit environment *in the computational basis* of the observed system is

$$\rho_{S\mathcal{E}_1\mathcal{E}_2\text{comp}} = (1/2)\begin{bmatrix} V_0 E V_0^\dagger & V_0 E V_1^\dagger \\ V_1 E V_0^\dagger & V_1 E V_1^\dagger \end{bmatrix}, \qquad (10)$$

where each element of the 2×2 matrix is a block 4×4 matrix and $E \equiv \varrho \otimes \varrho$ and $V_k \equiv \exp(-itM_k)$, $k = 0, 1$. After tracing out the second environmental qubit, we find, again, in the computational basis, the following two qubit joint state of the system and observing qubit:

$$\rho_{S\mathcal{E}_1\text{comp}} = (1/2)\begin{bmatrix} \text{Tr}_2(V_0 E V_0^\dagger) & \text{Tr}_2(V_0 E V_1^\dagger) \\ \text{Tr}_2(V_1 E V_0^\dagger) & \text{Tr}_2(V_1 E V_1^\dagger) \end{bmatrix}, \qquad (11)$$

where Tr_2 is the second qubit partial trace operation. Hence, we obtain the collective decoherence factor in the form

$$\Gamma = \left\lVert \text{Tr}_2\left(V_0 E V_1^\dagger\right) \right\rVert_{\text{Tr}}. \qquad (12)$$

This equation is the value of the trace norm of a 2×2 upper off-diagonal block of the 4×4 matrix (11). The trace norm is defined as $||A||_{\text{Tr}} = \text{Tr}(\sqrt{A^\dagger A})$.

The probabilities c_0 and c_1 of the system being in a state 0 or 1 of the computational basis are given by $c_i = (1/2)\text{Tr}(V_i E V_i^\dagger) = 0.5$ and are revealed to be constant in time. Conditioning upon the system state in the computational basis and tracing out the second environmental qubit, we find that the conditional states of the remaining (observing) qubit, denoted ϱ_0 and ϱ_1, where $\varrho_i \equiv \langle i|_S(\rho_{S\mathcal{E}_1})|i\rangle_S$ is a single qubit. Those states are obtained by a projection of the joint state of the system and part of the environment on one of the possible states of the system in the computational basis. If there is no coherence between different states of the system, then the off-diagonal elements should vanish, as is explicitly stated in the definition of SBSs.

The (generalized) fidelity [26] (also called the Bhattacharyya coefficient), used as a measure of state overlap [12] for two matrices ϱ_0 and ϱ_1 is defined as

$$\mathcal{F}(\varrho_0, \varrho_1) \equiv \text{Tr}\sqrt{\sqrt{\varrho_0}\varrho_1\sqrt{\varrho_0}}. \tag{13}$$

The larger the value of the fidelity, the poorer the orthogonalization of the relevant observable. We provide explicit formulae for (12) and (13) in Appendix B.

The upper bound to the distance to the Spectrum Broadcast Structure [12,14] is

$$||\rho_{S\mathcal{E}_1} - \rho_{S\mathcal{E}_1}^{(SBS)}|| \leq 2(\Gamma + \sqrt{c_0 c_1}\mathcal{F}(\varrho_0, \varrho_1)), \tag{14}$$

which is true for some state $\rho_{S\mathcal{E}_1}^{(SBS)}$ having the SBS form (2). The bound (14) can be applied to any state, not only qubit-qubit states. In Appendix C, we discuss the distance of the evolved state to the thermal state.

3.2. Generalised Pointer Basis Optimal for SBS

Since the constituent Hamiltonians in (7) do not commute with the C-INOT gate Hamiltonians, one cannot follow the paradigm of [6] and determine the generalized pointer basis from the interaction Hamiltonian only. In other words, this is the case when the generalized pointer basis (which may also be called the indicator basis) is a different object from the pointer basis known from quantum Darwinism.

Above in (11), we wrote the evolved state in the computational basis, and the calculations of (A12) and (A16) refer to this basis. On the other hand, one may ask the question, whether there exists some other basis of the observed system that manifests structure closer to SBS.

For the two environmental qubit cases with one of them being traced out, we shall look for the optimal SBS state—namely, the one that is the closest to the actual system–environment state represented in the computational basis $\rho_{S\mathcal{E}_1\text{comp}}$ (see (11)). To this aim, we minimize the distance of the latter to the SBS states, which, by definition, have the form:

$$\rho_{S\mathcal{E}_1}^{SBS} = \tilde{p}|\psi\rangle\langle\psi|^S \otimes |\chi\rangle\langle\chi|^{\mathcal{E}_1} + (1-\tilde{p})|\psi^\perp\rangle\langle\psi^\perp|^S \otimes |\chi^\perp\rangle\langle\chi^\perp|^{\mathcal{E}_1}. \tag{15}$$

Note that this form easily generalizes for environments of higher dimension with $|\chi\rangle\langle\chi|^{\mathcal{E}_1}$ and $|\chi^\perp\rangle\langle\chi^\perp|^{\mathcal{E}_1}$ replaced with orthogonal $\varrho_0^{\mathcal{E}_1}$ and $\varrho_1^{\mathcal{E}_1}$:

$$\rho_{S\mathcal{E}_1}^{SBS} = \tilde{p}|\psi\rangle\langle\psi|^S \otimes \varrho_0^{\mathcal{E}_1} + (1-\tilde{p})|\psi^\perp\rangle\langle\psi^\perp|^S \otimes \varrho_1^{\mathcal{E}_1}. \tag{16}$$

In the two-qubit case, minimisation of the corresponding distance

$$\left|\left|\rho_{S\mathcal{E}_1\text{comp}} - \rho_{S\mathcal{E}_1}^{SBS}\right|\right|_{\text{Tr}} \tag{17}$$

over all probability $\tilde{p}$, and state vectors $|\psi\rangle$, and $|\chi\rangle$ defining (15) gives the optimal SBS state:

$$\rho_{S\mathcal{E}_1\text{opt}}^{SBS} = \tilde{p}^*|\psi^*\rangle\langle\psi^*|^S \otimes |\chi^*\rangle\langle\chi^*|^{\mathcal{E}_1} + (1-\tilde{p}^*)|\psi^{*\perp}\rangle\langle\psi^{*\perp}|^S \otimes |\chi^{*\perp}\rangle\langle\chi^{*\perp}|^{\mathcal{E}_1}. \tag{18}$$

The basis $\{|\psi^*\rangle, |\psi^{*\perp}\rangle\}$ for which the minimum of (17) is attained should be considered as a candidate for the generalised pointer (equiv. indicator) basis for the case when the total Hamiltonian (6) does not commute with the interaction Hamiltonians (5).

To be more specific, for $|\psi\rangle$ and $|\chi\rangle$ being qubits, as in (15), we use the standard Bloch parametrization

$$|\psi\rangle = \cos(x_\psi/2)|0\rangle + \sin(x_\psi/2)\exp(iy_\psi)|1\rangle, \tag{19}$$

with $x_\psi \in [0,\pi]$, $y_\psi \in [0, 2\pi]$, and similarly for $|\chi\rangle$. Further, without loss of generality, we assume $\tilde{p} \in [0.5, 1]$. This last assumption assures continuity of the parameters obtained in the optimization, as without it the optimization has two possible equivalent solutions, *viz.* the one from (15) and the second one with $\tilde{p}$ replaced with $1 - \tilde{p}$ and states replaced with their orthogonal complements.

In the actual numerical calculations, we used unconstrained gradient search with a continuous map $\mathbb{R} \to [0.5, 1]$ for the $\tilde{p}$ parameter, and postprocessing of the resulting optimal values $x_\psi, y_\psi, x_\chi, y_\chi \in \mathbb{R}$ to obtain angles within the proper Bloch parameter range yielding the same qubit states. We illustrate the optimization of the SBS basis in Figure 1.

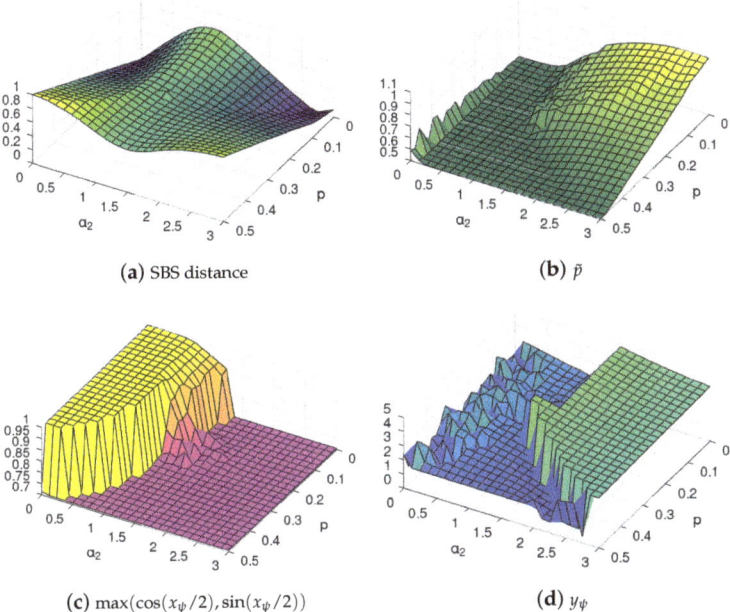

Figure 1. Sample results of SBS basis optimization (15) using the Bloch parametrization (19). We consider the state state after time $t = 1$, with Hamiltonian (6) with parameters $\alpha_1 = \alpha_3 = 0$, for different values of α_2 and environmental mixedness p, cf. (9), and perfect CNOT interaction. Figure 1a contains the minimized distance (17) obtained for $\tilde{p}$, x_ψ and y_ψ parameters shown in Figure 1b–d, respectively. Note thin Figure 1a is the same as in Figure 2a (seen from a different angle). For x_ψ in Figure 1c, we used trigonometric transformation, and thus that the value 1 refers to the computational basis. Note that the phases factor y_ψ of the Bloch qubit strongly fluctuates in the region where the computational basis is optimal, as in that case y_ψ has no impact on the state. In Figure 1c, the yellow part corresponds to the standard basis and the light purple represents bases complementary to the standard basis. The latter bases are in general different from Hadamard basis, which can be seen by examination of the phases in Figure 1d. Each of the basis in the light purple region represents some *generalised pointer basis* (see the discussion at the beginning of Section 3.2).

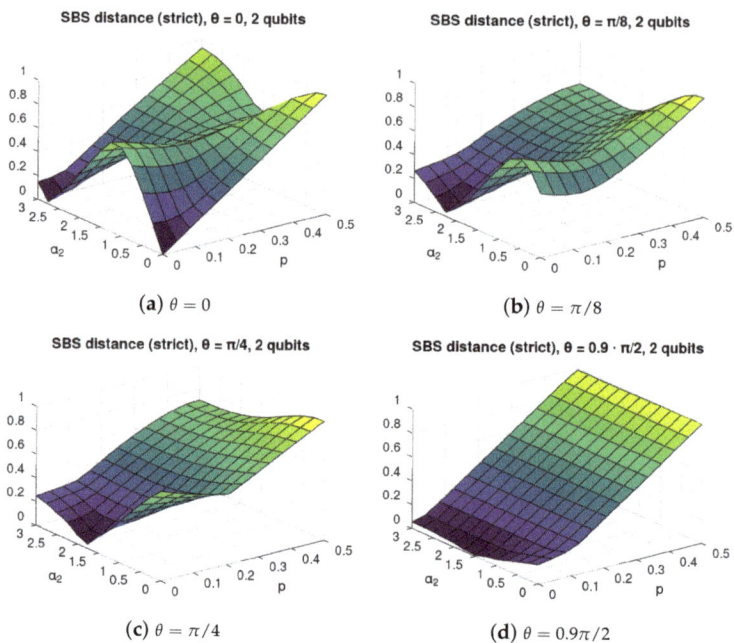

Figure 2. SBS distance for C-INOT central interaction with various values of the gate imperfection parameter θ with 2 environmental qubits. Each value of $\theta = 0, \pi/8, \pi/4, 0.9\pi/2$ refers to different interactions between the central system and each of the environmental qubits, as given in (4). The axis α_2 describes the strength of the self-evolution of the environmental qubits, see (7b), and p refers to the initial mixedness of the environmental qubits, see (9). The figure illustrates non-monotonic dependence of the distance of the evolved state from the closes SBS state of the form (15) from the parameters α_2 and p. In particular, it can be seen that, in many cases, it is not the smallest value of mixedness that leads to states close to the SBS form but the "optimal" environment mixedness p depends on the value of the self-evolution strength α_2.

3.3. Marginal Cases

Another interesting marginal case is for maximally mixed environment, i.e., for $p = 0.5$. Then, $\mu = 1/4$ and $\nu = 0$, again leading to $\mathcal{F}(\varrho_0, \varrho_1) = 1$. This is in agreement with [27], as this case refers to maximal entropy of the environment, and thus its capacity is 0.

For fixed $p \neq 0.5$ and $\theta < \pi/2$, we see from (A16) that the orthogonalization factor is a function of r_4. Thus, by changing the difference $\alpha_2 - \alpha_3$, we can adjust the total Hamiltonian so that the orthogonalization reaches its maximum. Thus, knowing the imperfections of the interaction θ, mixedness p environment, and the internal interaction H_3, we can, e.g., manipulate the magnetic field H_2 acting on the environment, to improve the quality of the measurement. We illustrate this adjustment in the following section.

4. Central Interaction: Optimization of Spectrum Broadcast Structure for 2 Environmental Qubits

We now consider the case when $\alpha_1 = \alpha_3 = 0$, and $\alpha_2, \theta \geq 0$, i.e., with imperfect central interaction and self-evolution of environmental qubits with initial mixedness parameter p after time $t = 1$, viz. at the time after which the central interaction has fully occurred.

We first note that, in the former Section 3, we considered the Spectrum Broadcast Structure obtained in the pointer basis [6], which was, in that case, equal to the computational basis of the observed system. Yet, it is possible to calculate the SBS distance for a different basis, viz. for the optimal basis, as introduced in Section 3.2.

We used the gradient method [28] to find the basis that minimizes the SBS distance. We note that the considered setup with only two qubits is very far from the one involving the macroscopic environment, and thus the objectivity present in this model can be only temporary since a single qubit is not able to induce full decoherence that is stable in time or orthogonalization of observables.

Yet, we are interested in the classical properties of the evolved system at a particular time moment, namely, the time that we denote as $t = 1$, the time at which the measurement is supposed to occur. Still, this scenario illustrates the mechanism, and we leave the actual scaling of the discussed non-monotonic phenomena for further research.

We performed the calculation of the SBS distance (17) for the case with $\alpha_1 = \alpha_3 = 0$ as a function of self-evolution of the environment parameter α_2 and environmental mixedness, or *noise*, parameter p for various C-INOT imperfection parameter θ. The results are shown in Figure 2. For better readability we show their marginal values for $p = 0$ in Figure 3a, and for $\alpha_2 = 0$ in Figure 3b.

We observe that, for $\theta > 0$, there exist values of α_2 that allow improving the SBS structure of the evolved state; thus, the self-evolution can to some extent counter-act the interaction gate imperfections.

For the perfect C-NOT depicted in Figure 2a, we observe that, for small p, the self-evolution has a destructive influence on the SBS formation. On the other hand, for large values of p, adding some self-evolution may improve the SBS structure. This reveals that, for p close to 0.5, the Hadamard basis is the actual optimal basis for SBS formation. For $\alpha_2 \approx 1.5$, we observe a surprising phenomenon—that increasing the environmental mixedness may also improve the SBS formation.

A similar situation of non-monotonicity in both α_2 and p can be clearly noticed in Figure 2b,c refering to imperfect C-NOT with $\theta = \pi/8$ and $\theta = \pi/4$, respectively. For small $\alpha_2 \approx 0$ with increasing environmental mixedness, the optimal SBS basis approaches the actual computational basis.

For large imperfections of C-NOT, with $\theta = 0.9\pi/2$, Figure 2d, we see that the SBS is being destroyed by noise in a monotonic way, but non-monotonicity in α_2 shows that the state is closest to SBS for $\alpha_2 \approx 1.5$.

To better illustrate the non-monotonic phenomena, we depicted the marginal cases in Figure 3a, where we show the SBS distance depending on α_2, and in Figure 3b, where the dependence on p is plotted.

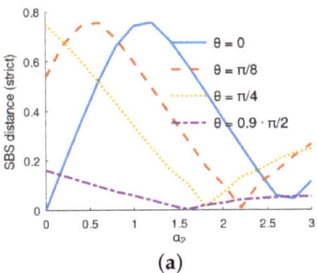
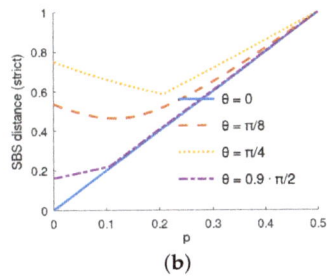

(a)   (b)

Figure 3. Illustration of non-monotonicity of SBS distance from the self-evolution of the environment parameter α_2 and environmental mixedness (noise) p. (**a**) Dependence of the SBS distance as a function of α_2 for $\alpha_1 = \alpha_3 = p = 0$ for various values of θ. (**b**) Dependence of the SBS distance as a function of p for $\alpha_1 = \alpha_2 = \alpha_3 = 0$ for various values of θ.

For the sake of completeness, let us consider another form of the interaction between the two environmental qubits—that is, the neighbour–neighbour interaction $2\mathbb{1}_2 \otimes \sigma_Z \otimes \sigma_Z$. We plot this dependence in Figure 4. The same non-monotonic pattern can be seen as in Figure 2.

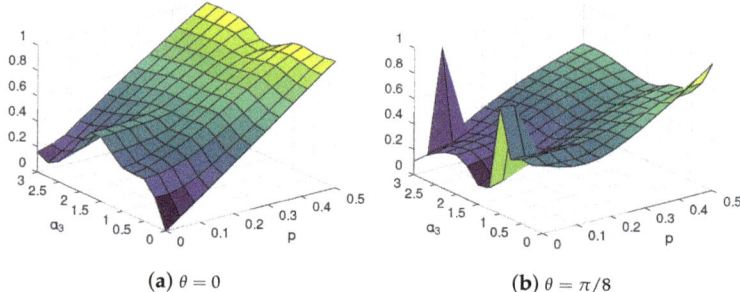

(a) $\theta = 0$ (b) $\theta = \pi/8$

Figure 4. SBS distance for interactions with C-INOT for various gate imperfection parameter θ with 2 environmental qubits. Visible is the dependence of the optimal environment mixedness p on the value of the inter-environmental-evolution strength α_3 for the Hamiltonian $H_3 = 2\mathbb{1}_2 \otimes \sigma_Z \otimes \sigma_Z$ instead of (7c).

Importance of the Basis Choice

In the present section, we illustrate the emergence of different indicator bases than the pointer basis in another way, rougher than the one performed in Section 3.2. Rather than performing full optimization, we perform a partial one, fixing the first one of the two anticipated bases (standard or Hadamard) and analysing a specific parameter that will tell us which of the bases is closer to the optimum.

To be more specific, in the optimization of the quantity (17), we allowed for *any* SBS basis $|\phi\rangle$ of the observed system in the calculation of the minimal distance of $\rho_{S\mathcal{E}_1\text{comp}}$ from the SBS set.

Now, let us assume that the basis $|\phi\rangle$ is fixed, and the optimization is performed only over pure qubits $|\chi\rangle$ and $\tilde{p} \in [0,1]$. To this end, let us define the following subset of SBS states:

$$\mathbb{S}_{|\psi\rangle} \equiv \left\{\sigma : \sigma = \tilde{p}|\psi\rangle\langle\psi| \otimes |\chi\rangle\langle\chi| + (1-\tilde{p})|\psi^{\perp}\rangle\langle\psi^{\perp}| \otimes |\chi^{\perp}\rangle\langle\chi^{\perp}|, \tilde{p} \in [0,1]\right\}. \quad (20)$$

We define the distance $\mathcal{D}$ of the state ρ from the set $\mathbb{S}$:

$$\mathcal{D}[\rho, \mathbb{S}] \equiv \min_{\sigma \in \mathbb{S}} ||\rho - \sigma||_{\text{Tr}}. \quad (21)$$

Now, we illustrate the difference between choices of different bases by comparing SBS distance if the basis of the SBS state is fixed to be either in the computational or in the Hadamard basis in (15). To this end, in Figure 5, we plot the difference between the minimized SBS-distance in the latter basis subtracted the minimized SBS distance in the former basis, viz.

$$\Delta \equiv \mathcal{D}\left[\rho_{S\mathcal{E}_1\text{comp}}, \mathbb{S}_{|+\rangle}\right] - \mathcal{D}\left[\rho_{S\mathcal{E}_1\text{comp}}, \mathbb{S}_{|0\rangle}\right]. \quad (22)$$

It can be easily seen that, even if we are not considering the optimal basis from (18) but restrict to the two simplest choices, the computational and Hadamard, the formation of the SBS structure favours either the former or the latter basis depending on the evolution and environment parameters, even though the pointer basis in quantum Darwinism sense does not change. One must remember that this is a very rough picture if compared to that of Section 3.2. However, it shows that some tendencies concerning the information about the system encoded in the environment may still be identified despite the use of less computational effort.

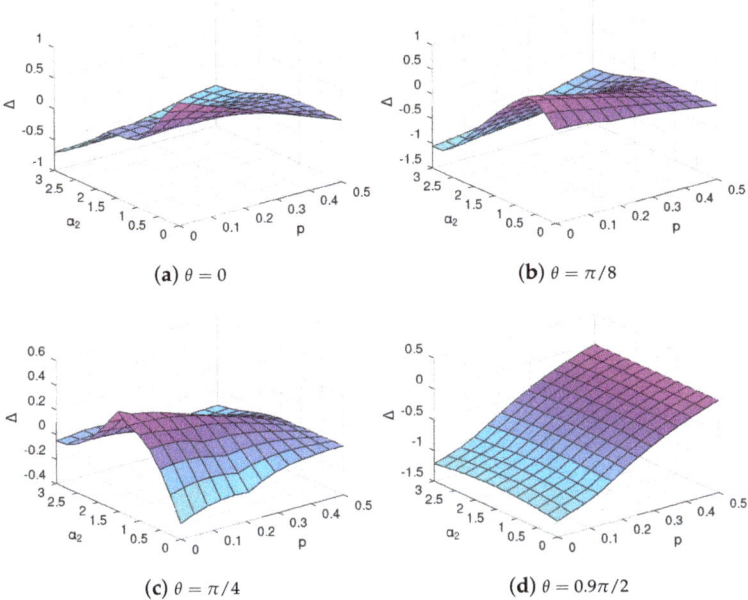

Figure 5. The difference Δ, see (22), of SBS distance for interaction with C-INOT various gate imperfection parameter θ with 2 environmental qubits if the SBS is restricted to be in the Hadamard basis subtracted with the SBS distance if the SBS is restricted to be in the computational basis. The warmer color indicates that the evolved state $\rho_{SE_1\text{comp}}$ is closer to SBS in the computational basis, and the cooler colour is in those regions, where the evolved state is closer to SBS in the Hadamard basis.

5. Central Interaction: Optimization of Spectrum Broadcast Structure for 8 Environmental Qubits

Next, we considered a case with a larger number N_{env} of environmental qubits. In this case, we consider the broadcast Hamiltonian to be a sum

$$H_{\text{int}} = \sum_{i=1}^{N_{\text{env}}} H^i_{\text{C-INOT}}, \qquad (23)$$

where $H^i_{\text{C-INOT}}$ is defined by (5) with transformation over i-th environmental qubit controlled by the central system. We consider only the self-evolution of separate environmental qubits, and thus this is a direct generalization of the three-qubits case with $\alpha_1 = \alpha_3 = 0$ and arbitrary α_2. The self-evolution Hamiltonian is (in analogy to the 3-qubit case from Section 3.1):

$$H_2 = \alpha_2 \sum_{i=1}^{N_{\text{env}}} \sigma_Z^i, \qquad (24)$$

where σ_Z^i acts on i-th environmental qubit.

We performed numerical calculations for an 8-qubit environment. We assumed that 7 of these qubits constitute the observer, with the last qubit being trace-out. In all cases in this section, we considered the optimal SBS basis.

The optimization of (17) for environments of dimension larger is much more difficult; thus, we were not able to find the state (16) exactly. Instead, we calculated the upper bound of [12], cf. (14) to check if the non-monotonic phenomena that we observed for two qubits can be expected to occur also in this case. The results of the numerical optimization are shown in Figure 6. The calculated upper bounds suggest that there exists some regime of gate imperfection θ, where both self-evolution and noise of the environment can improve the SBS structure as in the case of a two-qubit environment (see Sections 3 and 4).

We stress that the quantity (14) of [12] is only an upper bound, even though it can be applied to a state, and is easily computable. The calculation of (14) is purely algebraic and does not require any optimization procedure. On the other hand, since it provides only an upper bound, the exact results may diverge from those obtained with the bound, yet the similarity of behaviour of the plots obtained with the bound (see Figure 6) is similar to those derived using optimization of an exact formula (see Figure 2). This shows that the upper bound is able to properly grasp the non-monotonic tendencies occurring in both scenarios.

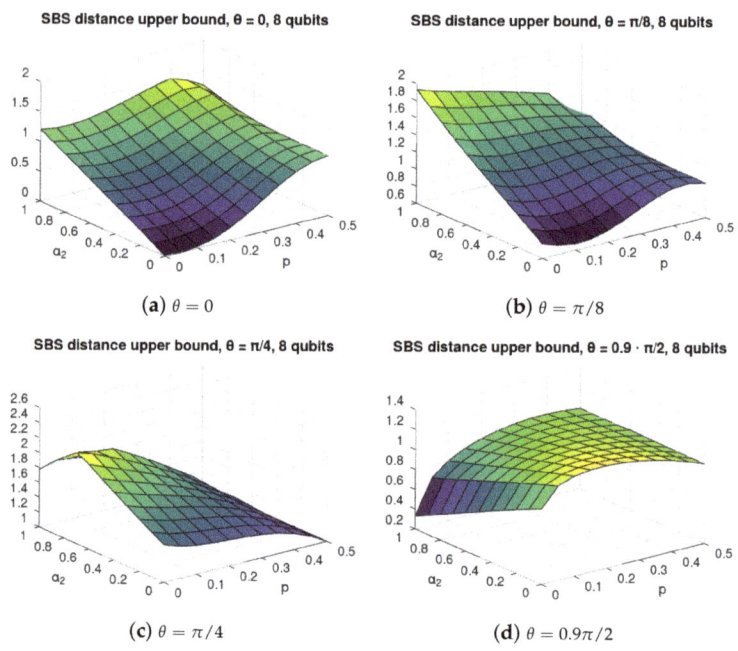

Figure 6. SBS distance for C-INOT with various gate imperfection parameters θ with 8 environmental qubits. Each value of θ refers to a different interaction between the central system and each of the environmental qubits, as given in (4). The axis α_2 describes the strength of the self-evolution of the environmental qubits, see (24), and p refers to the initial mixedness of the environmental qubits, see (9). The figure illustrate non-monotonic dependence of the *upper bound* (14) on the distance of the actually evolved state from the closes SBS state of the form (15) on the parameters α_2 and p. In particular, it can be seen that, in many cases, it is not the smallest value of mixedness, which leads to states closing (in an upper bound sense) to the SBS form, but the "optimal" environment mixedness p depends on the value of the self-evolution strength α_2.

For perfect C-NOT, see Equation (4), with $\theta = 0$, for majority values of α_2 the SBS distance is gradually growing with increasing p, approaching value close to 1 for the maximal mixedness $p \approx 0.5$. For $\alpha_2 \in [0,1]$ the SBS distance is also increasing for $p \approx 0$. Yet, for large values of α_2 and p, a slightly non-monotonic behaviour is seen in p.

For $\theta = \pi/8$, a clear improvement in SBS formation with increasing p can be seen in Figure 6b, where the optimal value of α_2 is increasing with p. For $\alpha_2 \approx 0$, it can be observed that the SBS is best formed for $p \approx 0.1$, which is also a surprising effect, confirming the previous observation that, with self-evolution of environment, it is possible that more noised (mixed) initial environment is more suitable for SBS formation that the pure environment. Even stronger effect is visible in Figure 6c. Still, it should be noted that, in those cases the SBS distance upper-bound is very large, close to 1, or even higher, and thus its behaviour may serve only as a preliminary suggestion regarding the behaviour of the actual distance to SBS of the formed states, and as such, should be followed by tight analytical approximations in the future.

In the case of large imperfections of C-INOT, viz. $\theta = 0.9\pi/2$, see Figure 6d, a clear effect of improvement in SBS formation for increasing self-evolution of environment parameter α_2 occurs, which is especially strong for small $p \approx 0$.

6. Non-Central Interaction for Eight Qubits

Now, let us consider the case with interaction between environmental qubits of the following neighbour–neighbour form:

$$H_3 = \alpha_3 \sum_{i=1}^{N_{\text{env}}} \sigma_Z^i \otimes \sigma_Z^{(i \bmod N_{\text{env}}+1)}, \qquad (25)$$

where N_{env} is the number of qubits in the environment, and σ_Z^i acts on i-th qubit of the environment. We calculated the upper bound [12] for the case with $\alpha_1 = \alpha_2 = 0$ and eight qubits as a function of the imperfection of C-INOT parameter θ and environmental noise p. The results are show in Figure 7. A strong non-monotonicity in α_3 can be observed for low values of p, e.g., in the case of $\theta = 0.9\pi/2$, where taking $\alpha_3 \approx 2$ can repair the effect of C-INOT imperfection.

The analogous situation takes place for fixed $\alpha \approx 0.75$ where the bound is decreasing with increasing initial noise for the region of $p \approx 0.1$. One should remember, however, that, in this case, the numerical values of the bound are high, and the search for possible non-monotonous behaviour of the exact distance as a function of p should be continued.

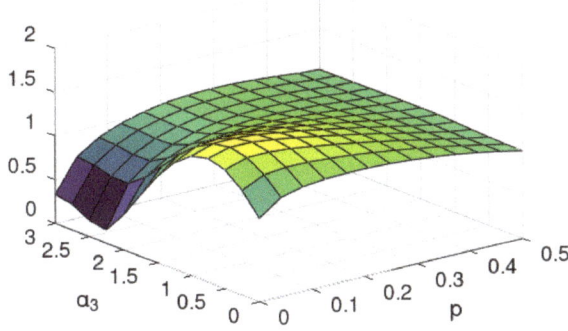

Figure 7. Upper bound on the distance to an SBS state for 8-qubit environment and $\alpha_1 = \alpha_2 = 0$ as a function of neighbour–neighbour interaction (25) strength α_3 and mixedness p of the environment.

7. Conclusions and Discussion

We examined the aspects of the emergence of objective information in the dynamic physical scenario in low-dimensional qubit systems. More precisely, we considered the non-perfect propagation of information from the system to the noisy environment with self-evolution, where the imperfect C-NOT gate [11] is accompanied by the presence of the self-dynamics of the environment, which—in general—may be in an initially mixed (thermal) state. We considered two different environments, the first composed of one observed and one unobserved qubit and the second one where there are seven observed qubits and one unobserved. In particular, we examined an analytical model of three interacting qubits, and we derived the objectivity parameters.

We considered examples with the system in the Hadamard state and showed that, if the imperfection of the C-NOT gate is known, the emergence of the objectivity—albeit with respect to a different basis than the one associated with the gate itself—can be enhanced by a carefully chosen environment self-dynamics, which may be interpreted only as an external magnetic field. The numerical optimization shows that the quality of the spectrum broadcast structure formed during the interaction may be non-monotonic both in the speed of self-dynamics of the environment as well as its mixedness. We interpret this phenomenon as the emergence of a new type of objectivity, which may be called a relaxed objectivization, since the statistics do not disclose any parameters of the initial state of the system but present to the observer some new ones, generated during the complex dynamical process.

We also discussed the case of eight qubits of environment and numerical calculations supporting the general conjecture, where the dynamics of the environment may help the emergence of objectivity to occur. This suggests that, even if the imperfectness of the C-NOT is large enough to destroy objectivity in the standard scenario [11], one may observe its "comeback" as a kind of phase transition due to the carefully tuned self-dynamics of the environment.

We believe that the above concept of the relaxed objectivization is interesting in itself because it concerns the general question of whether the system is in fully classical relation with the environment in the philosophical, purely existential sense—namely, that one is allowed to make a sensible claim that some of its property exists. In this sense, the present approach brings out the ontological aspect of emergent objectivity in a quantum world.

The possible cognitive and practical consequences lead two directions. First, if we are in the engineering paradigm, we know that objectivity (technically represented here by the SBS structure) makes the system–environment composition useless for coherent quantum information processing. This may be important in experiments monitoring a general interaction of a given system with a mesoscopic environment, including quantum memory and other coherent effects. In such cases, one should know methods to keep its state far from such an objective form.

The present analysis suggests that it can be done in a simple way—namely, by tuning an external magnetic field. Second, the present analysis may inspire several open questions concerning the possibility of the emergence of objectivity close to the original quantum Darwinism paradigm, yet more relaxed in certain physical scenarios [29].

For instance, we considered only the situation when the information was objectively "mirrored" in one environment (cf. [21]). Is it possible to observe the present, relaxed objectivity effect stable in time for a large number of environments as in the case of quantum Darwinism objectivity? If so, is it possible to find situations when, despite the "unfriendly circumstances"—environment dynamics, noise and deviation from the C-NOT gate interaction—the information about some parameters of the initial state of the system can still be easily retrieved from the environment?

Another question would be, whether and when the present objectivised basis can be exploited to read out some well-defined parameters of the whole dynamics. The original pointer basis was defined by a local element, i.e., a system–environment interaction Hamiltonian. Concerning our case: does one need to know all the global dynamics, or are there cases when knowledge of some parameters of the global dynamics (and, perhaps, its particular symmetries) is sufficient to determine our analogue of the pointer basis?

For more than two environments, the SBS structure is stronger than Strong Quantum Darwinism [22]. However, the concept of generalized pointer basis in those dynamical scenarios where interaction Hamiltonian alone does not determine objectivity may be, in full analogy, defined for Strong Quantum Darwinism, since the latter is also agnostic to the physical mechanism leading to it. The corresponding system environment state satisfying SQD is of a quite general form $\varrho_{S\mathcal{E}'} = \sum_i p_i |\psi_i\rangle\langle\psi_i| \otimes \varrho_i^{\mathcal{E}'_1 \cdots \mathcal{E}'_N}$ but with a special property.

There must exist some isometries that act *locally* on the parts of environments $U_i^{\mathcal{E}'_1} \otimes \cdots \otimes U_i^{\mathcal{E}'_N} : \mathcal{E}'_1 \otimes \cdots \otimes \mathcal{E}'_N \to \mathcal{E}_1 \mathcal{E}''_1 \otimes \cdots \otimes \mathcal{E}_N \mathcal{E}''_N$ and transform the state $\varrho_{\mathcal{S}\mathcal{E}'}$ into another state $\varrho_{\mathcal{S}\mathcal{E}\mathcal{E}''}$ in such a way that, after tracing out the $\mathcal{E}''$ parts of the environment, one finds the SBS state defined in (2) (the domains of the isometries also involve those degrees of freedom that carry possible correlations between different parts of environments but are irrelevant for objectivity). If there are interactions between different parts of the environment, it is likely that objectivity will be encoded in the above general SQD form due to correlations produced by the interactions.

Searching for a generalized pointer basis in a dynamical system may be even more demanding, especially if the environment corresponds already to so-called macrofractions (see [14]). In those cases, most likely new analytical methods will be needed due to the complexity and numerical intractability of the problem.

Finally, the observed non-monotonicity of objectivity under the parameters of the two potentially "unfriendly" elements of the scenario—the speed of the environment dynamics and mixedness of its states seems counterintuitive. We believe that this requires further investigation in more complex models—both from the SBS as well as SQD perspective—and may lead to some applications that are difficult to identify at this present, early stage of analysis.

Author Contributions: Conceptualization P.M., P.H. and R.H.; Formal analysis and visualization P.M.; Interpretation P.M., P.H. and R.H.; Writing P.M., P.H. and R.H. All authors have read and agreed to the published version of the manuscript.

Funding: The work was supported by the Foundation for Polish Science (IRAP project, ICTQT, contract No. 2018/MAB/5, co-financed by EU within Smart Growth Operational Programme). The numerical calculations were conducted using OCTAVE 6.1 [30] and packages QETLAB 0.9 [31] and Quantinf 0.5.1 [32].

Institutional Review Board Statement: Not applicable.

Informed Consent Statement: Not applicable.

Data Availability Statement: Not applicable.

Conflicts of Interest: The authors declare no conflict of interest.

Abbreviations

The following abbreviations are used in this manuscript:

SBS	spectrum broadcast structure
QD	quantum Darwinism
SQD	strong quantum Darwinism
C-NOT	controlled-NOT gate
C-INOT	controlled imperfect-NOT gate
$\mathcal{F}$	fidelity
$I(\mathcal{S}:\mathcal{E})$	mutual information between the system and part of the environment
$H(\cdot)$	von Neumann entropy
$\chi(\mathcal{S}:\mathcal{E})$	Holevo information between $\mathcal{S}$ and $\mathcal{E}$

Appendix A

Direct calculations show that $H_{\text{TOTAL}} = (\pi - \alpha_1)\mathbb{1}_8 + M$, where $\mathbb{1}_8$ is the 3-qubit identity operator, and $M \equiv \begin{bmatrix} M_0 & 0 \\ 0 & M_1 \end{bmatrix}$ is a block diagonal matrix with M_0 and M_1 given by:

$$M_0 \equiv \begin{bmatrix} \zeta_1 & 0 & 0 & 0 \\ 0 & \zeta_2 & 0 & 0 \\ 0 & 0 & \zeta_2 & 0 \\ 0 & 0 & 0 & \zeta_3 \end{bmatrix}, \qquad (A1a)$$

$$M_1 \equiv \begin{bmatrix} -y & -x/2 & -x/2 & 0 \\ -x/2 & 0 & 0 & -x/2 \\ -x/2 & 0 & 0 & -x/2 \\ 0 & -x/2 & -x/2 & y \end{bmatrix}, \tag{A1b}$$

where we denote:

$$\tilde{\zeta}_1 \equiv -\pi + 2\alpha_1 + 2\alpha_2 + 4\alpha_3, \tag{A2a}$$

$$\tilde{\zeta}_2 \equiv -\pi + 2\alpha_1 - 2\alpha_3, \tag{A2b}$$

$$\tilde{\zeta}_3 \equiv -\pi + 2\alpha_1 - 2\alpha_2, \tag{A2c}$$

$$x \equiv \pi \cos(\theta), \tag{A2d}$$

$$y \equiv \pi \sin(\theta) - 2\alpha_2 + 2\alpha_3. \tag{A2e}$$

We often use the following term:

$$w \equiv \sqrt{x^2 + y^2}. \tag{A3}$$

Calculating the eigendecomposition of (A1b), we find that $M_1 = U \cdot D \cdot U^\dagger$, where D is the diagonal matrix with elements $(0, 0, w, -w)$, and unitary U is given by:

$$U \equiv (1/2) \begin{bmatrix} 0 & \sqrt{2}x/w & (w-y)/w & (w+y)/w \\ \sqrt{2} & -\sqrt{2}y/w & -x/w & x/w \\ -\sqrt{2} & -\sqrt{2}y/w & -x/w & x/w \\ 0 & -\sqrt{2}x/w & (w+y)/w & (w-y)/w \end{bmatrix}. \tag{A4}$$

Using this formula, we can calculate $V \equiv \exp(-itM)$ to be block diagonal with blocks V_0 and V_1, where V_0 is the diagonal matrix with elements (u_1, u_2, u_2, u_3),

$$u_i \equiv \exp(-it\tilde{\zeta}_i), \tag{A5}$$

and $V_1 = R + iQ$, with R and Q defined as follows:

$$R \equiv \begin{bmatrix} r_1 & r_2 & r_2 & r_3 \\ r_2 & r_4 & r_3 & -r_2 \\ r_2 & r_3 & r_4 & -r_2 \\ r_3 & -r_2 & -r_2 & r_1 \end{bmatrix}, \tag{A6a}$$

$$Q \equiv \begin{bmatrix} -q_1 & q_2 & q_2 & 0 \\ q_2 & 0 & 0 & q_2 \\ q_2 & 0 & 0 & q_2 \\ 0 & q_2 & q_2 & q_1 \end{bmatrix}, \tag{A6b}$$

where

$$\begin{aligned} r_1 &\equiv 0.5(x^2 + (w^2 + y^2)\cos(tw))/w^2, \\ r_2 &\equiv -0.5xy(1 - \cos(tw))/w^2, \\ r_3 &\equiv -0.5x^2(1 - \cos(tw))/w^2, \\ r_4 &\equiv 0.5(x^2 \cos(tw) + w^2 + y^2)/w^2, \end{aligned} \tag{A7}$$

and

$$\begin{aligned} q_1 &\equiv -y\sin(tw)/w, \\ q_2 &\equiv 0.5x\sin(tw)/w. \end{aligned} \tag{A8}$$

One can check by direct calculations that the following identities hold:

$$\begin{aligned} r_1^2 + q_1^2 - r_4^2 &= 0, \\ q_2^2 + r_2^2 + r_3^2 + r_3 &= 0, \\ r_1 r_2 + r_2 r_3 - q_1 q_2 + r_2 &= 0, \\ q_1 r_2 + q_2 r_1 - q_2 r_3 - q_2 &= 0, \\ r_4 - r_3 - 1 &= 0, \end{aligned} \quad \text{(A9)}$$

and that $r_3 \in [-1, 0]$ and $r_4 \in [0, 1]$.

Appendix B

Using the notation of Appendix A, direct calculations show that, for Γ defined in (12), we have:

$$\Gamma = p\sqrt{s_1 + 2\Re(u_1 u_2^* s_2)} + (1-p)\sqrt{s_1 + 2\Re(u_2 u_3^* s_2)}, \quad \text{(A10)}$$

where $\Re$ is the real part of a number, and

$$s_1 \equiv (p^2 + (1-p)^2) \cdot r_4, \quad \text{(A11a)}$$

$$s_2 \equiv p(1-p) \cdot \left((r_1 + iq_1)r_4 - (r_2 - iq_2)^2 \right). \quad \text{(A11b)}$$

The states ϱ_0 and ϱ_1, obtained by conditioning upon the system state in the computational basis and tracing out the second environmental qubit, are equal,

$$\varrho_0 = \begin{bmatrix} p & 0 \\ 0 & 1-p \end{bmatrix}, \quad \text{(A12a)}$$

$$\varrho_1 = \begin{bmatrix} 1 + p(2r_4 - 1) - r_4 & (1-2p)(r_2 + iq_2) \\ (1-2p)(r_2 - iq_2) & p(1 - 2r_4) + r_4 \end{bmatrix}. \quad \text{(A12b)}$$

From the above, it follows that, for

$$\mu = -p(1-p)(2r_4 - 1) + 0.5 r_4, \quad \text{(A13)}$$

we have

$$\sqrt{\varrho_0} \varrho_1 \sqrt{\varrho_0} - \mu \mathbb{1}_2 = \begin{bmatrix} (p - 0.5) r_4 & \sqrt{p(1-p)}(1-2p)(r_2 + iq_2) \\ \sqrt{p(1-p)}(1-2p)(r_2 - iq_2) & -(p - 0.5) r_4 \end{bmatrix}. \quad \text{(A14)}$$

Using (A9), we find that the eigenvalues of (A14) are $\pm \nu$, where

$$\nu = 0.5 |1 - 2p| \sqrt{r_4 (r_4 - 4(p - p^2) \cdot (r_4 - 1))}. \quad \text{(A15)}$$

Thus, we have the following closed form for (13):

$$\mathcal{F}(\varrho_0, \varrho_1) = \sqrt{\mu + \nu} + \sqrt{\mu - \nu}. \quad \text{(A16)}$$

Appendix C

The state of an environmental qubit is given as the average of (A12), and thus it equals

$$\begin{bmatrix} 0.5 - r_4(0.5 - p) & 0.5(1 - 2p)(r_2 + iq_2) \\ 0.5(1 - 2p)(r_2 - iq_2) & 0.5 + r_4(0.5 - p) \end{bmatrix}. \quad \text{(A17)}$$

Now, let us consider how close is this state to the Gibbs state, in particular directly after the short-term C-INOT interaction, i.e., for $t = 1$?

Since the Hamiltonians (7) are diagonal in computational basis and proportional to $\sigma_Z = \begin{bmatrix} 1 & 0 \\ 0 & -1 \end{bmatrix}$, the Gibbs state will also be diagonal, with the second diagonal value greater or equal the first (for $\sigma_Z \ket{1}$ is the ground state).

Recall that from the form of the thermal environment (9), we have $p \in [0, 0.5]$. One can check that $r_4 \in [0, 1]$, and thus $r_4(0.5 - p) \geq 0$. Thereby, the second diagonal term of (A17) is greater or equal to the first, and thus the trace distance of the state (A17) from the closest thermal state is given by

$$\left\| \begin{bmatrix} 0 & 0.5(1-2p)(r_2+iq_2) \\ 0.5(1-2p)(r_2-iq_2) & 0 \end{bmatrix} \right\|_{\mathrm{Tr}}, \tag{A18}$$

where $\|\cdot\|_{\mathrm{Tr}}$ denotes the trace norm. This is equal to

$$|1-2p|\sqrt{r_2^2+q_2^2} = |(1-2p)|\sqrt{-r_4^2+r_4}. \tag{A19}$$

Direct calculations using (A9) show that either of the sides of (A19) can be rewritten also as

$$|0.5-p|x\sqrt{1-\cos\left(t\sqrt{x^2+y^2}\right)}\sqrt{\left(1+\cos\left(t\sqrt{x^2+y^2}\right)\right)x^2+2y^2}/(x^2+y^2). \tag{A20}$$

For fixed p and θ, the value of (A19) is a function of r_4 that depends on the difference $\alpha_2 - \alpha_3$. The same holds for $\mathcal{F}(\varrho_0, \varrho_1)$, cf. (A16), as μ and ν are also functions of p, θ and r_4, and thus there is a direct interplay between those two phenomena, the orthogonalization of observables and thermalization.

References

1. Landsman, N.P. Between classical and quantum. *Part Philos. Phys.* **2007**, 417–553. [CrossRef]
2. Barnum, H.; Caves, C.M.; Fuchs, C.A.; Jozsa, R.; Schumacher, B. Noncommuting mixed states cannot be broadcast. *Phys. Rev. Lett.* **1996**, *76*, 2818–2821. [CrossRef] [PubMed]
3. Piani, M.; Horodecki, P.; Horodecki, R. No-Local-Broadcasting Theorem for Multipartite Quantum Correlations. *Phys. Rev. Lett.* **2008**, *100*, 090502. [CrossRef] [PubMed]
4. Zurek, W.H. Quantum Darwinism. *Nat. Phys.* **2009**, *5*, 181. [CrossRef]
5. Zeh, H.D. On the interpretation of measurement in quantum theory. *Found. Phys.* **1970**, *1*, 69. [CrossRef]
6. Zurek, W.H. Pointer basis of quantum apparatus: Into what mixture does the wave packet collapse? *Phys. Rev. D* **1981**, *24*, 1516. [CrossRef]
7. Zurek, W.H. Decoherence, einselection, and the quantum origins of the classical. *Rev. Mod. Phys.* **2003**, *75*, 715. [CrossRef]
8. Joos, E.; Zeh, H.D.; Kiefer, C.; Giulini, D.; Kupsch, J.; Stamatescu, I.-O. *Decoherence and the Appearance of a Classical World in Quantum Theory*, 2nd ed.; Springer: New York, NY, USA, 2003.
9. Schlosshauer, M. Decoherence, the measurement problem, and interpretations of quantum mechanics. *Rev. Mod. Phys.* **2005**, *76*, 1267. [CrossRef]
10. Auffeves, A.; Philippe Grangier, P. Recovering the quantum formalism from physically realist axioms. *Sci. Rep.* **2017**, *7*, 43365. [CrossRef]
11. Touil, A.; Yan, B.; Girolami, D.; Deffner, S.; Zurek, W.H. Eavesdropping on the Decohering Environment: Quantum Darwinism, Amplification, and the Origin of Objective Classical Reality. *Phys. Rev. Lett.* **2022**, *128*, 010401. [CrossRef]
12. Mironowicz, P.; Korbicz, J.; Horodecki, P. Monitoring of the process of system information broadcasting in time. *Phys. Rev. Lett.* **2017**, *118*, 150501. [CrossRef] [PubMed]
13. Ollivier, H.; Poulin, D.; Zurek, W.H. Objective properties from subjective quantum states: Environment as a witness. *Phys. Rev. Lett.* **2004**, *93*, 220401. [CrossRef] [PubMed]
14. Horodecki, R.; Korbicz, J.K.; Horodecki, P. Quantum origins of objectivity. *Phys. Rev. A* **2015**, *91*, 032122. [CrossRef]
15. Pleasance, G.; Garraway, B.M. Application of quantum Darwinism to a structured environment. *Phys. Rev. A* **2017**, *96*, 062105. [CrossRef]
16. Le, T.P.; Olaya-Castro, A. Objectivity (or lack thereof): Comparison between predictions of quantum Darwinism and spectrum broadcast structure. *Phys. Rev. A* **2018**, *98*, 032103. [CrossRef]
17. Korbicz, J.K. Roads to objectivity: Quantum Darwinism, Spectrum Broadcast Structures, and Strong quantum Darwinism—A review. *Quantum* **2021**, *5*, 571. [CrossRef]

18. Chisholm, D.A.; Guillermo García-Pérez, D.A.; Rossi, M.A.C.; Maniscalco, S.; Palma, G.M. Witnessing Objectivity on a Quantum Computer. *arXiv* **2021**, arXiv:2110.06243.
19. Le, T.P.; Mironowicz, P.; Horodecki, P. Blurred quantum Darwinism across quantum reference frames. *Phys. Rev. A* **2020**, *102*, 062420. [CrossRef]
20. Tuziemski, J. Decoherence and information encoding in quantum reference frames. *arXiv* **2020**, arXiv:2006.07298v2.
21. Le, T.P.; Winter, A.; Adesso, G. Thermality versus objectivity: Can they peacefully coexist? *Entropy* **2021**, *23*, 1506. [CrossRef]
22. Le, T.P.; Olaya-Castro, A. Strong Quantum Darwinism and Strong Independence is equivalent to Spectrum Broadcast Structure. *Phys. Rev. Lett.* **2019**, *122*, 010403. [CrossRef] [PubMed]
23. Feller, A.; Roussel, B.; Frérot, I.; Degiovanni, P. Comment on "Strong Quantum Darwinism and Strong Independence are Equivalent to Spectrum Broadcast Structure". *Phys. Rev. Lett.* **2021**, *126*, 188901. [CrossRef] [PubMed]
24. Le, T.P.; Olaya-Castro, A. Reply to Comment on "Strong Quantum Darwinism and Strong Independence are Equivalent to Spectrum Broadcast Structure". *arXiv* **2021**, arXiv:2101.10756.
25. Le, T.P.; Olaya-Castro, A. Witnessing non-objectivity in the framework of strong quantum Darwinism. *Quantum Sci. Technol.* **2020**, *5*, 045012. [CrossRef]
26. Fuchs, C.A.; van de Graaf, J. Cryptographic distinguishability measures for quantum-mechanical states. *IEEE Trans. Inf. Theor.* **1999**, *45*, 1216. [CrossRef]
27. Zwolak, M.; Quan, H.T.; Zurek, W.H. Quantum Darwinism in a mixed environment. *Phys. Rev. Lett.* **2009**, *103*, 110402. [CrossRef]
28. Polak, E. *Optimization: Algorithms and Consistent Approximations*; Springer: Berlin/Heidelberg, Germany, 1997; ISBN 0-387-94971-2.
29. Roszak, K.; Korbicz, J.K. Glimpse of objectivity in bipartite systems for nonentangling pure dephasing evolutions. *Phys. Rev. A* **2020**, *101*, 052120. [CrossRef]
30. Eaton, J.W.; Bateman, D.; Hauberg, S.; Wehbring, R. GNU Octave Version 6.1.0 Manual: A High-Level Interactive Language for Numerical Computations. 2020. Available online: https://www.gnu.org/software/octave/doc/v6.1.0/ (accessed on 17 February 2022).
31. Johnston, N. QETLAB: A MATLAB Toolbox for Quantum Entanglement, Version 0.9. 2016. Available online: http://qetlab.com (accessed on 17 February 2022).
32. Cubitt, T. Quantinf Matlab Package, Version 0.5.1. 2013. Available online: https://www.dr-qubit.org/matlab.html (accessed on 17 February 2022).

Article
Quantum Coherences and Classical Inhomogeneities as Equivalent Thermodynamics Resources

Andrew Smith [1], Kanupriya Sinha [2,3] and Christopher Jarzynski [1,4,5,*]

1. Department of Physics, University of Maryland, College Park, MD 20742, USA; andrew.maven.smith@gmail.com
2. Department of Electrical and Computer Engineering, Princeton University, Princeton, NJ 08544, USA; kanu.sinha@asu.edu
3. School of Electrical, Computer and Energy Engineering, Arizona State University, Phoenix, AZ 85287, USA
4. Department of Chemistry and Biochemistry, University of Maryland, College Park, MD 20742, USA
5. Institute for Physical Science and Technology, University of Maryland, College Park, MD 20742, USA
* Correspondence: cjarzyns@umd.edu

Abstract: Quantum energy coherences represent a thermodynamic resource, which can be exploited to extract energy from a thermal reservoir and deliver that energy as work. We argue that there exists a closely analogous classical thermodynamic resource, namely, energy-shell inhomogeneities in the phase space distribution of a system's initial state. We compare the amount of work that can be obtained from quantum coherences with the amount that can be obtained from classical inhomogeneities, and find them to be equal in the semiclassical limit. We thus conclude that coherences do not provide a unique thermodynamic advantage of quantum systems over classical systems, in situations where a well-defined semiclassical correspondence exists.

Keywords: quantum thermodynamics; quantum coherence; work extraction

1. Introduction

This paper considers the question: How much work $\mathcal{W}$ is extracted when a quantum system S undergoes a cyclic thermodynamic process? The answer depends on details such as the duration of the process; whether or not the system exchanges energy with heat baths along the way; how the system is driven during the process; and the system's initial state, $\hat{\rho}_i$. We are specifically interested in the potential thermodynamic consequences of *energy coherences*—non-zero matrix elements $\langle m|\hat{\rho}_i|n\rangle$ for eigenstates of different energies—in the initial state. The thermodynamic utility of such coherences has been investigated in recent years [1–19], using a variety of approaches. Of particular relevance to the present paper, Kammerlander and Anders [9], using the definition of work [20,21] that we will use, have argued that if $\hat{\rho}_i$ contains coherences in the system's energy basis, then more work can be extracted than would be possible in the absence of coherences. In this sense, quantum energy coherences represent a thermodynamic resource.

It seems natural to view the presence of energy coherences in $\hat{\rho}_i$ as a uniquely *quantum* thermodynamic resource, with no classical counterpart—in much the same way that superpositions of qubit states represent a quantum computational resource unavailable to classical computers [22]. We will argue otherwise. We will identify a classical analogue of quantum energy coherences, namely energy-shell *inhomogeneities* in the initial classical phase space distribution $\rho_i(\Gamma)$. We will show that the presence of such inhomogeneities in $\rho_i(\Gamma)$ allows more work to be extracted than would be possible in their absence. Thus, both quantum energy coherences and classical energy-shell inhomogeneities can be viewed as thermodynamic resources from which work can be extracted. We will further argue that for systems that support a well-defined semiclassical limit, a fair comparison reveals that equal amounts of work can be extracted from the two resources. We therefore conclude that quantum energy coherences do not provide a quantum "thermodynamic advantage", as the same gain can be obtained from classical energy-shell inhomogeneities.

In Section 2, we introduce the framework and notation we will use to study a quantum system undergoing a cyclic thermodynamic process, in the presence of a thermal reservoir, and we analyze the work that can be extracted from energy coherences during such a process. In Section 3, we introduce the analogous classical framework and analyze the work that can be extracted from energy-shell inhomogeneities. In Section 4, we argue that when a fair comparison is made, the maximum amount of work that can be extracted in the quantum case is the same as that in the classical case. In Section 5, we extend these results to a broader class of processes. We conclude with a brief discussion in Section 6.

Throughout this paper, we will adopt an ensemble perspective, in which the state of an open quantum system is specified by a density matrix $\hat{\rho}$, and the state of a classical system is specified by a phase space distribution $\rho(\Gamma)$ rather than a phase point Γ.

2. Quantum Setup and Notation

Let S denote a quantum system of interest, and $\hat{H}$ its Hamiltonian. We consider the following situation, illustrated schematically in Figure 1: S is prepared in an initial state $\hat{\rho}_i$ at time $t = 0$, then from $t = 0$ to τ it evolves in time as its Hamiltonian is varied according to a schedule, or *protocol*, $\hat{H}(t)$. We take this process to be cyclic, in the sense that

$$\hat{H}(0) = \hat{H}(\tau) = \hat{H}_0 \tag{1}$$

where $\hat{H}_0$ is a fixed *reference Hamiltonian*. We then ask the question: How much work is extracted during this cyclic process?

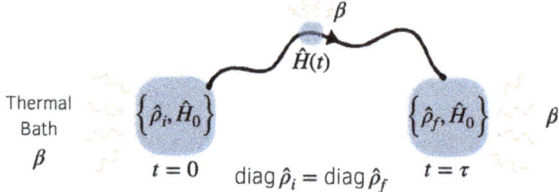

Figure 1. Schematic illustration of the quantum process described in the text. The system begins in state $\hat{\rho}_i$, then evolves in contact with a thermal bath to a final state $\hat{\rho}_f$ as the Hamiltonian is driven through a cycle from $\hat{H}(0) = \hat{H}_0$ to $\hat{H}(\tau) = \hat{H}_0$. We impose the constraint $\text{diag}\,\hat{\rho}_i = \text{diag}\,\hat{\rho}_f$, which indicates that the initial and final energy distributions are identical, while the coherences may differ.

We assume the reference Hamiltonian $\hat{H}_0$ has a discrete, non-degenerate spectrum with eigenstates $|n\rangle$ and eigenvalues ϵ_n. The assumption of non-degeneracy ensures an unambiguously defined energy basis in which coherence can be considered. It further implies that no operators commute with $\hat{H}_0$, aside from ones that are functions of $\hat{H}_0$ itself:

$$[\hat{K}, \hat{H}_0] = 0 \text{ iff } \hat{K} = k(\hat{H}_0) \tag{2}$$

for some scalar function $k(\cdot)$ of a single variable.

During the cyclic process described above, the system is in contact with a thermal bath B, at temperature β^{-1}. As a result, the evolution of S is not unitary, rather, we will say that S evolves under *isothermal dynamics*. This terminology is not meant to suggest that the system's temperature is constant, or even well-defined, merely that the system is in contact with a bath whose bulk temperature β^{-1} is well-defined. We will not specify the equations of motion for the system, as our discussion will be relatively insensitive to the exact dynamics used to model the system's evolution. However, we will demand that the isothermal dynamics of S satisfy the following thermodynamically motivated conditions: (1) if $\hat{H}$ is held fixed then the system relaxes to the canonical equilibrium state, and (2) the dynamics support a generalized second law linking suitably defined notions of free energy and work.

More precisely, condition (1) means that if $\hat{H}$ is fixed, then the isothermal dynamics cause the system to relax to the equilibrium state

$$\hat{\pi} = \frac{1}{Z^q} e^{-\beta \hat{H}} \tag{3}$$

where

$$Z^q(\hat{H}) = \operatorname{Tr} e^{-\beta \hat{H}} \quad , \quad \mathcal{F}^{q,\mathrm{eq}}(\hat{H}) = -\beta^{-1} \ln Z^q(\hat{H}) \tag{4}$$

are the partition function and free energy associated with this state. (The superscript q stands for "quantum" and distinguishes this case from the classical setup that will be introduced later. The dependence of Z^q and $\mathcal{F}^{q,\mathrm{eq}}$ on β is notationally suppressed.) We assume this relaxation occurs over a finite characteristic timescale τ_{rel}. As a consequence, if the system Hamiltonian is varied quasistatically, then the state of S tracks the instantaneous equilibrium state: $\hat{\rho}(t) = \hat{\pi}(t)$, where $\hat{\pi}(t)$ is the canonical state associated with $\hat{H}(t)$. In this quasistatic limit, the system's evolution is isothermal in the strong sense of the word: its temperature is well-defined and constant at all times. A system that evolves under a detailed balanced Lindblad master equation satisfies condition (1) [23].

By condition (2), we mean that the system obeys a generalized second law

$$\mathcal{W}^q \leq -\Delta \mathcal{F}^q = \mathcal{F}^q(0) - \mathcal{F}^q(\tau) \tag{5}$$

where the work *extracted*, non-equilibrium free energy, internal energy, and entropy are respectively defined by the following functional and functions of $\hat{\rho}(t)$ and $\hat{H}(t)$:

$$\mathcal{W}^q[\hat{\rho}(t), \hat{H}(t)] = -\int_0^\tau \operatorname{Tr}\left[\frac{d\hat{H}}{dt}\hat{\rho}\right] dt \tag{6}$$

$$\mathcal{F}^q(\hat{\rho}, \hat{H}) = \mathcal{U}^q - \mathcal{S}^q/\beta \tag{7}$$

$$\mathcal{U}^q(\hat{\rho}, \hat{H}) = \operatorname{Tr}[\hat{H}\hat{\rho}] \tag{8}$$

$$\mathcal{S}^q(\hat{\rho}) = -\operatorname{Tr}[\hat{\rho} \ln \hat{\rho}] \geq 0. \tag{9}$$

For convenience, as in Equation (5), we will often use the shorthand $\mathcal{X}(t) \equiv \mathcal{X}(\hat{\rho}(t), \hat{H}(t))$, or the even more concise $\mathcal{X}_i = \mathcal{X}(0)$ and $\mathcal{X}_f = \mathcal{X}(\tau)$, where $\mathcal{X}$ stands for $\mathcal{F}^q, \mathcal{U}^q$, or $\mathcal{S}^q$, or the classical counterparts of these quantities, defined below in Section 3.

Equations (7)–(9) generalize familiar equilibrium notions [24] of free energy, internal energy, and entropy to non-equilibrium states $\hat{\rho}$ [25]. They reduce to the usual equilibrium values when $\hat{\rho} = \hat{\pi}$. The bound given by Equation (5) is not restricted to transitions between equilibrium states, and has been derived using a variety of approaches for modeling the dynamics of a quantum system in contact with a thermal reservoir, see, e.g., Refs. [26–30]. Note that we follow engineering convention and work extraction is positive. While Equation (6) should be interpreted as the *average* work extracted from an ensemble, fluctuations will not be considered in this paper, hence we will simply refer to Equation (6) as extracted work.

The non-equilibrium free energy defined by Equation (7) can equivalently be written as

$$\mathcal{F}^q(\hat{\rho}, \hat{H}) = \mathcal{F}^{q,\mathrm{eq}}(\hat{H}) + \beta^{-1} D(\hat{\rho}|\hat{\pi}) \tag{10}$$

where $\hat{\pi}$ and $\mathcal{F}^{q,\mathrm{eq}}$ are given by Equations (3) and (4), and

$$D(\hat{\rho}_1|\hat{\rho}_2) = \operatorname{Tr}[\hat{\rho}_1(\ln \hat{\rho}_1 - \ln \hat{\rho}_2)] \geq 0 \tag{11}$$

is the quantum relative entropy, or Kullback–Leibler divergence [31], between arbitrary states $\hat{\rho}_1$ and $\hat{\rho}_2$. For a cyclic process, as defined above, Equation (5) becomes

$$\mathcal{W}^q \leq \beta^{-1}\left[D(\hat{\rho}_i|\hat{\pi}_0) - D(\hat{\rho}_f|\hat{\pi}_0)\right] \tag{12}$$

where $\hat{\rho}_{i,f}$ are the states of the system at $t = 0, \tau$, and $\hat{\pi}_0$ is the equilibrium state associated with the reference Hamiltonian $\hat{H}_0$. Although relative entropy $D(\hat{\rho}_1|\hat{\rho}_2)$ is not a proper distance measure, it vanishes when $\hat{\rho}_1 = \hat{\rho}_2$ and is strictly positive otherwise, and can be viewed as quantifying the degree to which $\hat{\rho}_1$ differs from $\hat{\rho}_2$. In this sense, Equation (12) implies that the extracted work is bounded from above by the degree to which the system is brought closer to the equilibrium state $\hat{\pi}_0$, during the cyclic process. This interpretation is in agreement with the intuition, from classical thermodynamics, that non-equilibrium states represent a thermodynamic resource: work can be extracted by cleverly facilitating a system's evolution toward equilibrium.

We take Equation (6) as our definition of work for several reasons. First, it is an established notion of thermodynamic work in quantum systems [20,21,32]. Moreover, it agrees with the notion of average work derived from the quantum work (quasi)distribution in Ref. [33], which satisfies a fluctuation theorem. Finally, this definition closely resembles those used in classical stochastic thermodynamics [34,35] and, as we will see in later sections, it allows us to establish connections with results from classical statistical physics. For the special case of isolated quantum systems, the definition given by Equation (6) is called "untouched work" in Ref. [36]. We will not discuss here how (or whether) Equation (6) connects to the traditional thermodynamic concept of raising a mass against gravity, or otherwise delivering energy to a work reservoir [24]; this question involves subtle issues related to backaction as well as potential quantum coherences in the work reservoir.

We note that other definitions of work are also commonly used in quantum thermodynamics, particularly when fluctuations in work are of interest. For instance, defining a work distribution according to the two-time energy measurement protocol [37–39] leads to a mean value that differs from Equation (6) whenever the initial state $\hat{\rho}_i$ has non-vanishing energy coherences. Additionally, some definitions of work developed in quantum resource theory [40] have a so-called work-locking property [41] which prevents the extraction of work from coherence. These resource theory definitions, which explicitly model the heat bath and demand that work be transferred deterministically, also differ from Equation (6).

Removing Coherences

To this point, we have discussed subjecting the system S to a cyclic process under isothermal dynamics. Now, following Ref. [9], we impose an additional condition:

$$\text{diag}\,\hat{\rho}_f = \text{diag}\,\hat{\rho}_i \tag{13}$$

where

$$\text{diag}\,\hat{\rho} = \sum_n |n\rangle\langle n|\hat{\rho}|n\rangle\langle n| \tag{14}$$

is the density matrix obtained from $\hat{\rho}$ by setting to zero its off-diagonal elements, in the reference energy basis. In other words, we now restrict ourselves to processes that alter the system's energy coherences $\langle m|\hat{\rho}|n\rangle$, $m \neq n$, while leaving the probabilities $\langle n|\hat{\rho}|n\rangle$ unchanged. We will refer to Equation (13), and to its classical counterpart, Equation (42), as the *isoenergetic constraint*. As in Ref. [9], our motivation for imposing this condition is to isolate and accentuate the thermodynamic implications of quantum energy coherences. From Equation (13), it follows that $\text{Tr}[\hat{H}_0\hat{\rho}_i] = \text{Tr}[\hat{H}_0\hat{\rho}_f]$, i.e.,

$$\mathcal{U}_i^q = \mathcal{U}_f^q \tag{15}$$

which in turn implies that the generalized second law, Equation (5), becomes

$$\mathcal{W}^q \leq \beta^{-1}\left(\mathcal{S}^q_f - \mathcal{S}^q_i\right). \tag{16}$$

This bound relates the maximum extractable work to the change in the system's entropy. The thermodynamic interpretation is clear: since the system's energy undergoes no net change (Equation (15)), the only way to extract work is to withdraw energy from the bath, causing the entropy of the bath to decrease by an amount $\beta \mathcal{W}^q$. This decrease in the bath's entropy must be compensated, or over-compensated, by an increase in the entropy of the system, as reflected by Equation (16).

We are now in a position to investigate the maximum amount of work that can be extracted from energy coherences. For a given reference Hamiltonian $\hat{H}_0$ and initial state $\hat{\rho}_i$, let $\mathcal{W}^{q\star}$ denote the maximum extracted work, over all protocols $\hat{H}(t)$ that begin and end in $\hat{H}_0$, subject to the isoenergetic constraint (13). Since the right side of Equation (16) is a function of $\hat{\rho}_i$ and $\hat{\rho}_f$, we can place a bound on $\mathcal{W}^{q\star}$ by maximizing that function with respect to $\hat{\rho}_f$:

$$\mathcal{W}^{q\star} \leq \beta^{-1} \max_{\hat{\rho}_f \mid \mathrm{diag}\,\hat{\rho}_f = \mathrm{diag}\,\hat{\rho}_i} \left[\mathcal{S}^q(\hat{\rho}_f) - \mathcal{S}^q(\hat{\rho}_i)\right] \tag{17}$$

For fixed diagonal elements of a density matrix $\hat{\rho}$, the value of $\mathcal{S}^q = -\mathrm{Tr}\hat{\rho}\ln\hat{\rho}$ is maximized when the off-diagonal elements are all zero. We therefore obtain

$$\mathcal{W}^{q\star} \leq \beta^{-1}[\mathcal{S}^q(\mathrm{diag}\,\hat{\rho}_i) - \mathcal{S}^q(\hat{\rho}_i)]. \tag{18}$$

This result does not yet tell us whether the bound can be saturated, that is, whether there exist protocols for extracting this amount of work. Rather, it states that under no circumstances can we extract more than this much work, in a cyclic, isothermal process satisfying Equation (13). Moreover, if a protocol for saturating this bound exists, then that protocol will result in the system ending in the state $\mathrm{diag}\,\hat{\rho}_i$ at $t = \tau$. In other words, the saturating protocol (if it exists) removes all energy coherences from the system's initial state, and effectively converts these coherences into extracted work.

In fact, protocols for saturating the bound given by Equation (18) do exist [9,28]. A simple example is given by:

$$\hat{H}(t) = \begin{cases} \hat{H}_0 & t \leq 0 \\ -\beta^{-1}\ln[(1-\lambda)\hat{\rho}_i + \lambda(\mathrm{diag}\,\hat{\rho}_i)] & 0 < t < \tau \\ \hat{H}_0 & \tau \leq t \end{cases} \tag{19}$$

where $\lambda \equiv t/\tau$ varies from 0 to 1 during the process, and τ is taken to be sufficiently large that the process is quasistatic. This protocol can be understood as follows. At the start of the process, there is a sudden change, or *quench*, in the system's Hamiltonian, from $\hat{H}_0$ at $t = 0$ to $-\beta^{-1}\ln\hat{\rho}_i$ at $t = 0^+$. Thus, at $t = 0^+$ the system's state $\hat{\rho}_i$ is in equilibrium with respect to the immediate post-quench Hamiltonian. (The term "quench" is often used in situations in which the system is in equilibrium before the quench, and out of equilibrium after it. Thus, the first step of this protocol (19) might be viewed as an *anti*-quench.) From $t = 0^+$ to τ^-, the Hamiltonian is varied quasistatically from $-\beta^{-1}\ln\hat{\rho}_i$ to $-\beta^{-1}\ln(\mathrm{diag}\,\hat{\rho}_i)$, and the system is dragged through the corresponding sequences of equilibrium states, from $\hat{\rho}_i$ to $\mathrm{diag}\,\hat{\rho}_i$—see comments after Equation (4). At $t = \tau$, a second quench abruptly returns the Hamiltonian to $\hat{H}_0$, completing the cycle. The evolution of the system's state is thus given by

$$\hat{\rho}(t) = \begin{cases} \hat{\rho}_i & t = 0 \\ (1-\lambda)\hat{\rho}_i + \lambda(\mathrm{diag}\,\hat{\rho}_i) & 0 < t < \tau \\ \mathrm{diag}\,\hat{\rho}_i & \tau \leq t. \end{cases} \tag{20}$$

We show in Appendix A that the work extracted during this process is given by the right side of Equation (18), that is the bound is saturated. Hence, under the isoenergetic constraint (13), work extraction is optimized by removing all coherences from the system's state, and the value of this optimized work is:

$$\mathcal{W}^{q\star} = \beta^{-1}[\mathcal{S}^q(\text{diag}\,\hat{\rho}_i) - \mathcal{S}^q(\hat{\rho}_i)]. \tag{21}$$

This result is equivalent to Equation (1) of Kammerlander and Anders [9].

3. Classical Setup and Notation

Now, imagine a classical system with N degrees of freedom and phase space variables

$$\Gamma = (x_1, ..., x_N, p_1, ..., p_N). \tag{22}$$

Adopting (as in the quantum case) an ensemble perspective, let the system's state at time t be described by a phase space density $\rho(\Gamma, t)$. We will consider a thermodynamic process in which the system begins in a state $\rho(\Gamma, 0) = \rho_i(\Gamma)$, then evolves from $t = 0$ to τ as its Hamiltonian is varied according to a cyclic protocol $H(\Gamma, t)$, with

$$H(\Gamma, 0) = H(\Gamma, \tau) = H_0(\Gamma) \tag{23}$$

where $H_0(\Gamma)$ specifies a reference Hamiltonian; see Figure 2. We assume that no observables commute with $H_0(\Gamma)$ under the Poisson bracket, except those that are functions of H_0:

$$\{K, H_0\} = 0 \text{ iff } K(\Gamma) = k(H_0(\Gamma)) \tag{24}$$

for some function $k(\cdot)$ (compare with Equation (2)). This assumption implies that energy is the only non-trivially conserved quantity along all trajectories $\Gamma(t)$ obeying Hamiltonian dynamics $d\Gamma/dt = \{\Gamma, H_0\}$. (This conclusion follows from the identity $(d/dt)A(\Gamma(t)) = \{A, H_0\}$, which applies to any observable $A(\Gamma)$ and any trajectory $\Gamma(t)$ obeying $d\Gamma/dt = \{\Gamma, H_0\}$). This is a necessary but not sufficient condition for the dynamics to be *ergodic* on constant-energy surfaces in phase space—an assumption often made in statistical physics. (Roughly speaking, ergodicity means that a generic Hamiltonian trajectory of energy E visits all regions of the surface $H_0 = E$, given sufficient time.) For our purposes, we do not need the assumption of ergodicity, only the weaker assumption given by Equation (24).

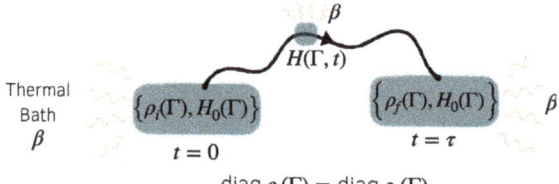

diag $\rho_i(\Gamma)$ = diag $\rho_f(\Gamma)$

Figure 2. Schematic illustration of the classical process. The system begins in state $\rho_i(\Gamma)$, then evolves in contact with a thermal bath to a final state $\rho_f(\Gamma)$ as the Hamiltonian is driven through a cycle from $H(\Gamma, 0) = H_0(\Gamma)$ to $H(\Gamma, \tau) = H_0(\Gamma)$. The constraint diag $\rho_i(\Gamma)$ = diag $\rho_f(\Gamma)$ indicates that the initial and final energy distributions are identical, while inhomogeneities may differ.

If the system were thermally isolated, then its state $\rho(\Gamma, t)$ would evolve under the Liouville equation, $\partial \rho / \partial t = \{H, \rho\}$. However, we assume that the system is in contact with a thermal bath as it undergoes the cyclic process, hence its evolution follows classical isothermal dynamics, rather than Hamiltonian dynamics. As in the quantum case, we will not specify the equations of motion that describe the isothermal dynamics, but we will make the following assumptions.

(1) If the system's Hamiltonian is held fixed, then the isothermal dynamics drive the system to the equilibrium state

$$\pi(\Gamma) = \frac{1}{Z^c} e^{-\beta H(\Gamma)} \tag{25}$$

with partition function and free energy

$$Z^c[H(\Gamma)] = \int d\Gamma \, e^{-\beta H(\Gamma)} \quad , \quad \mathcal{F}^{c,\mathrm{eq}}[H(\Gamma)] = -\beta^{-1} \ln\left(Z^c/h^N\right). \tag{26}$$

Here, h is a constant with dimensions of action that ensures the argument of the logarithm is dimensionless. We choose h to coincide with Planck's constant as this will facilitate comparisons of quantum and classical work extraction in Section 4. We assume this relaxation takes place over a finite timescale τ_{rel}. As a consequence, if $H(\Gamma, t)$ is varied quasistatically, then the system's state follows the instantaneous equilibrium state, $\rho(\Gamma, t) = \pi(\Gamma, t)$.

(2) When the system evolves over a time interval $0 \leq t \leq \tau$ under isothermal dynamics and a time-dependent Hamiltonian $H(\Gamma, t)$, it obeys a generalized second law

$$\mathcal{W}^c \leq -\Delta \mathcal{F}^c \tag{27}$$

with

$$\mathcal{W}^c[\rho(\Gamma, t), H(\Gamma, t)] = -\int_0^\tau \left(\int \frac{\partial H}{\partial t} \rho d\Gamma\right) dt \tag{28}$$

$$\mathcal{F}^c[\rho(\Gamma), H(\Gamma)] = \mathcal{U}^c - \mathcal{S}^c/\beta \tag{29}$$

$$\mathcal{U}^c[\rho(\Gamma), H(\Gamma)] = \int H(\Gamma)\rho(\Gamma) d\Gamma \tag{30}$$

$$\mathcal{S}^c[\rho(\Gamma)] = -\int \rho(\Gamma) \ln[h^N \rho(\Gamma)] d\Gamma. \tag{31}$$

Unlike the quantum von Neumann entropy (9) which is always non-negative, the classical Shannon differential (or continuous) entropy (31) can become arbitrarily negative for probability distributions that are highly concentrated in phase space, as we will see in Section 4.1. (For brevity, we will henceforth refer to the Shannon differential entropy simply as the Shannon entropy.) As with the quantum bound (Equation (5)), Equation (27) is not restricted to transitions between equilibrium states, and has been derived under a variety of modeling approaches, see, e.g., Refs. [26–30,42–44].

The classical non-equilibrium free energy (29) can be rewritten as

$$\mathcal{F}^c[\rho, H] = \mathcal{F}^{c,\mathrm{eq}}[H] + \beta^{-1} D[\rho|\pi] \tag{32}$$

where

$$D[\rho_1|\rho_2] = \int d\Gamma \, \rho_1(\Gamma) \ln \frac{\rho_1(\Gamma)}{\rho_2(\Gamma)} \geq 0 \tag{33}$$

is the classical relative entropy or Kullback–Leibler divergence. Thus, for a cyclic process, Equation (27) becomes

$$\mathcal{W}^c \leq \beta^{-1} \Big(D[\rho_i|\pi_0] - D[\rho_f|\pi_0] \Big) \tag{34}$$

where $\rho_i(\Gamma) = \rho(\Gamma, 0)$ and $\rho_f(\Gamma) = \rho(\Gamma, \tau)$ are the system's initial and final states, and $\pi_0(\Gamma)$ is the equilibrium state for the reference Hamiltonian. As in the quantum case (Equation (12)), the right side of Equation (34) provides a measure of the degree to which the process brings the system closer to equilibrium.

3.1. Energy-Shell Inhomogeneities

The evident similarity between the quantum framework for cyclic isothermal processes described by Equations (1)–(12) and the classical framework of Equations (23)–(34) motivates us to seek a classical analogue of the statement that quantum energy coherences represent a thermodynamic resource. As a step in this direction, we note that in the quantum case, density matrices that are stationary under the unitary evolution generated by $\hat{H}_0$ are exactly those that lack energy coherences in the eigenbasis of $\hat{H}_0$:

$$\frac{d\hat{\rho}}{dt} = \frac{1}{i\hbar}[\hat{H}_0, \hat{\rho}] = 0 \quad \text{iff} \quad \hat{\rho} = \text{diag}\,\hat{\rho}. \tag{35}$$

In the classical case, phase space densities that are stationary under the Hamiltonian dynamics generated by $H_0(\Gamma)$ are exactly those that are functions of $H_0(\Gamma)$:

$$\frac{\partial \rho}{\partial t} = \{H_0, \rho\} = 0 \quad \text{iff} \quad \rho(\Gamma) = k(H_0(x)) \tag{36}$$

for some function $k(\cdot)$. (Equations (2) and (24) are needed for the "only if" parts of Equations (35) and (36).) These observations suggest that we ought to view phase space distributions of the form $\rho = k(H_0)$ as analogues of density matrices that are diagonal in the eigenbasis of $\hat{H}_0$.

To pursue this idea, let $\eta(E)$ denote the distribution of energies associated with a phase space density $\rho(\Gamma)$:

$$\eta(E) = \int d\Gamma\, \rho(\Gamma)\, \delta[E - H_0(\Gamma)]. \tag{37}$$

In addition, let $\omega_E(\Gamma)$ denote the classical microcanonical density of energy E:

$$\omega_E(\Gamma) = \lim_{\Delta E \to 0} \frac{I_{[E, E+\Delta E]}(H_0(\Gamma))}{\int d\Gamma'\, I_{[E, E+\Delta E]}(H_0(\Gamma'))} = \frac{\delta[E - H_0(\Gamma)]}{\Omega(E)} \tag{38}$$

where $I_{[E, E+\Delta E]}(\cdot)$ is the indicator function over the interval $[E, E+\Delta E]$ (that is, $I_{[a,b]}(x) = 1$ when $x \in [a, b]$, otherwise $I_{[a,b]}(x) = 0$), and

$$\Omega(E) = \int d\Gamma\, \delta[E - H_0(\Gamma)] \tag{39}$$

is the classical density of states. The microcanonical density $\omega_E(\Gamma)$ is singular, uniformly distributed over the *energy shell* E (the level set $H_0 = E$), and zero elsewhere. Here, "uniformly distributed" is defined by Equation (38): as ΔE approaches zero, the phase space density remains uniform, with respect to the Liouville measure $d^N x\, d^N p$, in the region between shells E and $E + \Delta E$, and zero elsewhere.

Using Equations (37)–(39), a phase space density of the form $\rho = k(H_0)$ can be written as

$$\rho(\Gamma) = \int dE\, \eta(E)\, \omega_E(\Gamma) \tag{40}$$

with $\eta(E) = k(E)\Omega(E)$. Such a density is a statistical mixture of microcanonical ensembles (just as a diagonal density matrix is a mixture of energy eigenstates: $\hat{\rho} = \text{diag}\,\hat{\rho} = \sum_n p_n |n\rangle\langle n|$), hence $\rho(\Gamma)$ is uniform, or *homogeneous*, over any specific energy shell E, while its value differs from one shell to another. By contrast, a phase space density that is not of the form $\rho = k(H_0)$ is *inhomogeneous* on energy shells: there exist points Γ and Γ' such that $H_0(\Gamma) = H_0(\Gamma')$ but $\rho(\Gamma) \neq \rho(\Gamma')$.

We will henceforth use the terms homogeneous/inhomogeneous to distinguish between phase space densities that can/cannot be written as $\rho = k(H_0)$. For instance, the equilibrium distribution $\pi_0(\Gamma) \propto \exp -\beta H_0(\Gamma)$ is a homogeneous density. By the stationarity argument given above (Equations (35) and (36)), homogeneous phase space densities will be viewed as classical counterparts of diagonal density matrices, and inhomogeneous densities as counterparts of quantum states with energy coherences. In other words, for our purposes *the counterparts of quantum energy coherences are classical energy-shell inhomogeneities*.

We introduce the notation

$$\operatorname{diag} \rho(\Gamma) = \int dE\, \eta(E)\, \omega_E(\Gamma) \tag{41}$$

with $\eta(E)$ given by Equation (37), to denote the phase space density obtained by "homogenizing" $\rho(\Gamma)$. That is, $\operatorname{diag} \rho$ is the homogeneous density that has the same energy distribution as ρ.

3.2. Removing Inhomogeneities

Let us now focus our attention on classical, cyclic isothermal processes that satisfy the isoenergetic constraint (compare with Equation (13)):

$$\operatorname{diag} \rho_f(\Gamma) = \operatorname{diag} \rho_i(\Gamma) \tag{42}$$

where $\rho_{i,f}$ denote the system's initial and final states. Such processes leave the energy distribution undisturbed, $\eta_i(E) = \eta_f(E)$, while allowing energy-shell inhomogeneities to change. Equation (42) implies

$$\mathcal{U}_i^c = \mathcal{U}_f^c \tag{43}$$

hence, Equation (27) becomes

$$\mathcal{W}^c \leq \beta^{-1}\left(\mathcal{S}_f^c - \mathcal{S}_i^c\right). \tag{44}$$

Let $\mathcal{W}^{c\star}$ denote the maximum amount of work that can be extracted, over all conceivable cyclic protocols, for a given reference Hamiltonian $H_0(\Gamma)$ and initial state $\rho_i(\Gamma)$. Equation (44) implies

$$\begin{aligned}
\mathcal{W}^{c\star} &\leq \beta^{-1} \max_{\rho_f | \operatorname{diag} \rho_f = \operatorname{diag} \rho_i} \left(\mathcal{S}^c[\rho_f] - \mathcal{S}^c[\rho_i]\right) \\
&= \beta^{-1}(\mathcal{S}^c[\operatorname{diag} \rho_i] - \mathcal{S}^c[\rho_i])
\end{aligned} \tag{45}$$

since, among all states with a given energy distribution, the Shannon entropy is maximized by the homogeneous state (This follows from the fact that Shannon entropy increases under coarse-graining, which in turn is a consequence of Jensen's inequality, $\langle \ln x \rangle \leq \ln \langle x \rangle$).

Similarly to the quantum case (Equation (19)), the bound given by Equation (45) is saturated [27,28] by the protocol

$$H(\Gamma, t) = \begin{cases} H_0(\Gamma) & t \leq 0 \\ -\beta^{-1} \ln[(1-\lambda)\rho_i(\Gamma) + \lambda \operatorname{diag} \rho_i(\Gamma)] & 0 < t < \tau \\ H_0(\Gamma) & \tau \leq t \end{cases} \tag{46}$$

with $\lambda = t/\tau$, and τ sufficiently long that the process is effectively quasistatic. The protocol begins with a classical quench at $t = 0$. Immediately after this quench, the system's state $\rho_i(\Gamma)$ is in equilibrium with its instantaneous Hamiltonian, $H(\Gamma, 0^+) = -\beta^{-1} \ln \rho_i(\Gamma)$. During the interval $t \in (0, \tau)$, the quasistatic switching of the Hamiltonian drags the system through a sequence of equilibrium states from ρ_i to $\rho_f = \operatorname{diag} \rho_i$, and at $t = \tau$ the cyclic process is completed by suddenly returning the Hamiltonian to H_0. The evolution of the system's state $\rho(\Gamma, t)$ is entirely analogous to that given by Equation (20). Summing over the work extracted during the initial quench, the quasistatic driving, and the final quench, we find (see Appendix A) that the total extracted work is

$$\mathcal{W}^{c\star} = \beta^{-1}(\mathcal{S}^c[\operatorname{diag} \rho_i] - \mathcal{S}^c[\rho_i]), \tag{47}$$

i.e., the bound in Equation (45) is saturated. By Equation (44), any protocol satisfying Equation (42) that would bring the system to a final state $\rho_f \neq \text{diag}\, \rho_i$ would necessarily result in less work extracted.

4. Quantum–Classical Comparison

We have seen that the maximum work extracted in the quantum case, subject to the isoenergetic constraint, $\text{diag}\, \hat{\rho}_i = \text{diag}\, \hat{\rho}_f$, is achieved by quasistatically removing all energy coherences from the system's initial state: $\hat{\rho}_i \rightarrow \text{diag}\, \hat{\rho}_i$. Similarly, the maximum work extracted in the classical case is achieved by quasistatically removing all energy-shell inhomogeneities. The optimized work values $\mathcal{W}^{q\star}$ and $\mathcal{W}^{c\star}$ are given by Equations (21) and (47). The close similarity between these results supports our view that classical energy-shell inhomogeneities are thermodynamic counterparts of quantum energy coherences. Both are resources that can be leveraged to extract work.

While the expressions for $\mathcal{W}^{q\star}$ and $\mathcal{W}^{c\star}$ are nearly identical, it still remains to compare them quantitatively. Ideally, we would like to compare the values of $\mathcal{W}^{q\star}$ and $\mathcal{W}^{c\star}$ for a given quantum reference Hamiltonian $\hat{H}_0$ and initial state $\hat{\rho}_i$, and appropriately defined classical counterparts $H_0(\Gamma)$ and $\rho_i(\Gamma)$. To this end, throughout this section and the next we assume that $\hat{H}_0$ is a function of position and momentum operators $(\hat{x}_1, \cdots \hat{x}_N)$ and $(\hat{p}_1, \cdots \hat{p}_N)$, and we further assume that $\hat{H}_0$ has a well-defined counterpart $H_0(\Gamma)$. This condition is satisfied, for instance, by Hamiltonians of the kinetic-plus-potential form $\hat{H}_0 = K(\hat{p}_1, \cdots \hat{p}_N) + V(\hat{x}_1, \cdots \hat{x}_N)$, for which $H_0(\Gamma)$ is obtained by replacing momentum and position operators with classical momentum and position variables.

Identifying a correspondence between quantum and classical states $\hat{\rho}$ and $\rho(\Gamma)$ is trickier. Common approaches that map density operators into phase space distributions [45,46] suffer from undesirable properties. For instance, neither the Wigner [47] nor Husimi [48] function representation of the quantum thermal state corresponds to the classical thermal phase space distribution. Additionally, the Wigner function in general can become negative while the Husimi function depends on the choice of coherent states.

To circumvent such issues, we will compare quantum and classical *energy distributions* rather than individual states. Instead of focusing on the maximum work that can be extracted from a particular initial state, we will consider the maximum work that can be extracted given a particular initial energy distribution. We begin by defining *energy equivalence classes* in Section 4.1, then in Sections 4.2 and 4.3 we compare maximum work values for corresponding quantum and classical energy equivalence classes.

4.1. Energy Equivalence Classes

We define a quantum energy equivalence class to consist of all states $\hat{\rho}$ that share a particular energy distribution, that is, a particular set of diagonal density matrix elements, with respect to $\hat{H}_0$. An example is the thermal energy equivalence class given by

$$\Pi^q = \{\hat{\rho}\, |\, \text{diag}\, \hat{\rho} = \hat{\pi}_0\} \tag{48}$$

where $\hat{\pi}_0 = \exp(-\beta \hat{H}_0)/Z^q$ is the thermal equilibrium state. In addition to the state $\hat{\pi}_0$, the set Π^q includes exotic non-equilibrium states with significant energy coherences such as the pure state $|\pi_0\rangle\langle\pi_0|$, where

$$|\pi_0\rangle = \sum_n \sqrt{\frac{e^{-\beta \epsilon_n}}{Z^q}} |n\rangle. \tag{49}$$

Examples of this state arise in quantum optics [49,50].

More generally (that is, not restricting ourselves to the thermal energy equivalence class, Equation (48)), every quantum state $\hat{\rho}$ belongs to a unique energy equivalence class Σ^q

defined by the diagonal elements of $\hat{\rho}$ in the $\hat{H}_0$ basis. Within this class, the von Neumann entropy is maximized by the state $\hat{\sigma} \equiv \text{diag}\,\hat{\rho} = \sum_n p_n |n\rangle\langle n|$:

$$\max_{\hat{\rho} \in \Sigma^q} \mathcal{S}^q(\hat{\rho}) = \mathcal{S}^q(\hat{\sigma}) = -\sum_n p_n \ln p_n \geq 0 \tag{50a}$$

where $p_n = \langle n|\hat{\rho}|n\rangle$. The von Neumann entropy is minimized within Σ^q by pure states such as $|\psi\rangle\langle\psi|$, where $|\psi\rangle = \sum_n \sqrt{p_n}|n\rangle$, and for these states the entropy vanishes:

$$\min_{\hat{\rho} \in \Sigma^q} \mathcal{S}^q(\hat{\rho}) = \mathcal{S}^q(|\psi\rangle\langle\psi|) = 0. \tag{50b}$$

A classical energy equivalence class contains all phase space distributions $\rho(\Gamma)$ with a given energy distribution $\eta(E)$. An example is the thermal energy equivalence class

$$\Pi^c = \{\rho(\Gamma) \,|\, \text{diag}\,\rho(\Gamma) = \pi_0(\Gamma)\} \tag{51}$$

where $\pi_0(\Gamma) = \exp[-\beta H_0(\Gamma)]/Z^c$. While the state $\pi_0(\Gamma)$ is homogeneous, the class Π^c contains states with substantial energy-shell inhomogeneities. For instance, if the system is a one-dimensional harmonic oscillator, the thermal equivalence class Π^c includes the state

$$\rho(E, T) = \underbrace{\left(\beta e^{-\beta E}\right)}_{\eta_{\pi_0}(E)} \underbrace{\left(\omega \frac{e^{\delta \cos(\omega T)}}{2\pi I_0(\delta)}\right)}_{\zeta(T)} \tag{52}$$

where E and T are the canonical energy and tempus (angle-like) coordinates [51] defined by $x = \sqrt{2E/m\omega^2}\cos(\omega T)$ and $p = \sqrt{2mE}\sin(\omega T)$, with $\omega T \in (-\pi, +\pi]$; δ is a non-negative parameter; and I_0 is the modified Bessel function of order zero. For this example, it is convenient to use (E, T) rather than (x, p) to identify a point in classical phase space. $\zeta(T)$ is the von Mises distribution [52], an analogue of a Gaussian distribution for an angular coordinate. In Equation (52), the mean of $\zeta(T)$ is zero and its variance is controlled by δ. For $\delta = 0$, $\rho(E, T)$ reduces to the canonical distribution, which is homogeneous over every energy shell. With increasing δ, the distribution becomes more and more concentrated on the positive x-axis of phase space (where $T = 0$) and as a result its Shannon entropy $\mathcal{S}^c[\rho]$ decreases, with no lower bound. Specifically, for large δ, we have

$$\mathcal{S}^c[\rho(E, T)] \approx -\ln\left(\hbar\beta\omega\sqrt{\frac{\delta}{2\pi}}\right) + \frac{1}{2}, \quad \delta \gg 1. \tag{53}$$

Every classical state $\rho(\Gamma)$ belongs to a unique energy equivalence class Σ^c, defined by its energy distribution $\eta(E)$ (Equation (37)). Within this class, the Shannon entropy is maximized by the diagonal state $\sigma(\Gamma) = \text{diag}\,\rho(\Gamma) = \eta(H_0)/\Omega(H_0)$, but there is no lower bound on the minimum entropy, as the phase space distribution can be concentrated to an arbitrary degree without affecting the energy distribution:

$$\max_{\rho \in \Sigma^c} \mathcal{S}^c[\rho(\Gamma)] = \mathcal{S}^c[\sigma(\Gamma)] = -\int dE\,\eta(E) \ln\left[h^N \frac{\eta(E)}{\Omega(E)}\right] \tag{54}$$

$$\min_{\rho \in \Sigma^c} \mathcal{S}^c[\rho(\Gamma)] = -\infty. \tag{55}$$

These extrema are illustrated by the values $\delta = 0$ and $\delta \to \infty$ in the example in the previous paragraph.

To take another illustrative example—which will prove useful in the next section—consider an ideal gas of n particles inside a three-dimensional cubic box of volume $V = L^3$, oriented parallel to the x-, y-, and z-axes, with one corner at the origin—see Figure 3. A point in phase space is given by $\Gamma = (\mathbf{r}_1 \cdots \mathbf{r}_n; \mathbf{p}_1 \cdots \mathbf{p}_n)$. For $0 < \alpha \leq 1$, let $\rho_\alpha(\Gamma)$ denote the distribution for which the momenta $\mathbf{p}_k$ are sampled from the Maxwellian distribution at temperature β^{-1}, and the positions $\mathbf{r}_k$ are sampled uniformly within the region defined by $0 < x, y < L$ and $0 < z < \alpha L$. This distribution belongs to the thermal energy equivalence class Π^c, and $\rho_{\alpha=1}(\Gamma)$ is exactly the (homogeneous) thermal distribution, whereas $\rho_{\alpha<1}(\Gamma)$ is an inhomogeneous, non-equilibrium distribution, in which the gas is entirely located within a fraction α of the volume of the box. For arbitrary $\alpha \in (0, 1]$, we have

$$\mathcal{S}^c[\rho_\alpha(\Gamma)] = n \ln\left(\frac{\alpha V}{\lambda_{\text{th}}^3}\right) + \frac{3n}{2} \tag{56}$$

where $\lambda_{\text{th}} = \sqrt{\beta h^2/2\pi m}$ is the thermal de Broglie wavelength. The value $\mathcal{S}^c[\rho_\alpha]$ is maximized at $\alpha = 1$, that is, for the homogeneous state, and it has no lower bound as $\alpha \to 0$.

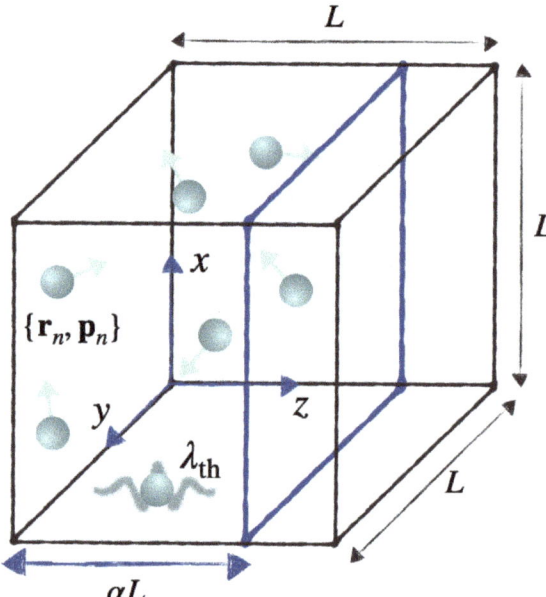

Figure 3. An ideal gas inside a box of volume L^3. The value of $\alpha \in (0, 1]$ parametrizes a family of energy equivalence classes, with $\alpha = 1$ corresponding to thermal class Π^c. See text for details.

In both of the above examples, by "squeezing" $\rho(\Gamma)$ into an arbitrarily small region of phase space ($\delta \to \infty$, $\alpha \to 0$) we obtain a distribution with arbitrarily large, negative entropy.

4.2. An Unfair Comparison

We now determine the maximum amount of work that can be extracted in a cyclic isoenergetic process where all states in the quantum equivalence class Σ^q are considered. Using Equations (21) and (50b), we have

$$\max_{\hat{\rho}_i \in \Sigma^q} \mathcal{W}^{q\star}(\hat{\rho}_i) = \beta^{-1} \max_{\hat{\rho}_i \in \Sigma^q}[\mathcal{S}^q(\text{diag}\,\hat{\rho}_i) - \mathcal{S}^q(\hat{\rho}_i)]$$

$$= \beta^{-1}\left[\mathcal{S}^q(\hat{\sigma}) - \min_{\hat{\rho}_i \in \Sigma^q}\mathcal{S}^q(\hat{\rho}_i)\right] = \beta^{-1}\mathcal{S}^q(\hat{\sigma}) \tag{57}$$

where $\hat{\sigma} = \text{diag}\,\hat{\rho}_i$ is the unique diagonal state belonging to Σ^q. The minimal value of $\mathcal{S}^q(\hat{\rho}_i)$ on the second line is achieved for any pure state $|\psi\rangle\langle\psi| \in \Sigma^q$, an example of which can always be constructed using the same argument as in Equation (50b). Hence, the maximum work is obtained by starting in a pure state, then quasistatically removing the coherences (e.g., following the protocol given by Equation (19)) so as to end in the diagonal state $\hat{\sigma}$. This result has a simple interpretation in terms of the bound $\mathcal{W}^q \leq \beta^{-1}\left(\mathcal{S}_f^q - \mathcal{S}_i^q\right)$ (see Equation (16)): we maximize the extracted work by starting in a state with the lowest entropy and ending in the state of highest entropy, within Σ^q. By Equation (50) these are, respectively, any pure state and the unique diagonal state in Σ^q. Equivalently (since $\mathcal{U}_f^q = \mathcal{U}_i^q$ by Equation (13)), the maximum extracted work is obtained when starting in the state of highest free energy and ending in the state of lowest free energy. We emphasize that, here, free energy and entropy are defined by Equations (7) and (9), which apply to generic (not necessarily equilibrium) quantum states $\hat{\rho}$.

The analogous classical calculation, using Equations (47) and (55), gives

$$\max_{\rho_i \in \Sigma^c} \mathcal{W}^{c\star}[\rho_i(\Gamma)] = \beta^{-1} \max_{\rho_i \in \Sigma^c}(\mathcal{S}^c[\operatorname{diag}\rho_i(\Gamma)] - \mathcal{S}^c[\rho_i(\Gamma)])$$

$$= \beta^{-1}\left(\mathcal{S}^c[\sigma(\Gamma)] - \min_{\rho_i \in \Sigma^c} \mathcal{S}^c[\rho_i(\Gamma)]\right) = +\infty \qquad (58)$$

where $\sigma(\Gamma) = \operatorname{diag}\rho_i(\Gamma)$. In other words, for a given classical energy distribution, there is no upper bound on the amount of work that can be extracted, as there is no lower bound on the entropy of the initial state. By "squeezing" a given phase space distribution *within* each energy shell, without altering the distribution of probability *among* energy shells, we can construct a distribution $\rho_i(\Gamma)$ that is compressed within an arbitrarily small volume of phase space, hence we can make the value of $\mathcal{S}^c[\rho_i(\Gamma)]$ arbitrarily small. This idea is illustrated by Equation (52) for the harmonic oscillator example of the previous section: as $\delta \to \infty$, the von Mises distribution $\zeta(T)$ becomes ever more concentrated around $T = 0$, and the entropy of the distribution becomes arbitrarily large and negative.

The example of the ideal gas discussed at the end of Section 4.1 provides further intuition for Equation (58). For that example, consider the thermal equivalence class Π^c, and imagine an initial inhomogeneous distribution $\rho_i(\Gamma) = \rho_\alpha(\Gamma)$ at $t = 0$, with $\alpha < 1$, that is, with all gas particles initially located in the region $0 < z < \alpha L$. To maximize the extracted work, we first suddenly insert a partition at the location $z = \alpha L$, and then quasistatically move this partition to the location $z = L$, while the system remains in contact with a thermal bath at temperature β^{-1}. The process ends with the system in the homogeneous, thermal state $\rho_f(\Gamma) = \rho_{\alpha=1}(\Gamma)$. The total work extracted during this process of removing inhomogeneities is

$$\mathcal{W}^c = n\beta^{-1} \ln \frac{1}{\alpha} > 0 \qquad (59)$$

which follows from a well-known expression for the reversible isothermal expansion of an ideal gas: $\mathcal{W} = n\beta^{-1}\ln(V_f/V_i)$. It is easy to see why there is no upper bound on the extractable work: at $t = 0^+$, just after the insertion of the partition, the gas is an equilibrium state, confined within a volume αV, with free energy $\mathcal{F}^c(t = 0^+) = -n\beta^{-1}\ln(\alpha V/\lambda_{\text{th}}^3)$. The smaller the value of α, the larger the initial free energy and therefore the greater the amount of work that can be extracted through reversible, isothermal expansion. In this idealized example, we can begin with an arbitrarily dense initial state, i.e., arbitrarily small $\alpha > 0$.

In both the quantum and classical cases, the extracted work is maximized by evolving quasistatically from the state of lowest entropy to the state of highest entropy, within the equivalence class Σ^q or Σ^c. Thus, there appears to be an inherent quantum thermodynamic *disadvantage*, since $\mathcal{S}^q$ is bounded from below by 0, while $\mathcal{S}^c$ is unbounded from below.

The comparison, however, is unfair. Quantum mechanics obeys the Heisenberg uncertainty principle, a loose semiclassical interpretation of which states that every quantum state occupies a cell of volume h^N in phase space. If we view classical mechanics as an approximate model of an underlying quantum reality, then when considering initial distributions $\rho_i(\Gamma)$ we should allow only such distributions as are consistent with the uncertainty principle. To impose this constraint, let us imagine dividing phase space into cells of volume h^N. A distribution $\rho(\Gamma)$ that is consistent with the uncertainty principle is one that is uniform within any such cell, but whose value differs from cell to cell: any finer-grained structure is offensive to the uncertainty principle. For such a distribution, we have $p_k = h^N \rho(\Gamma_k)$, where Γ_k is a representative point in cell k and $p_k = \int_{\Gamma \in \text{cell } k} d\Gamma \, \rho(\Gamma)$ is the probability to find the system in that cell. The Shannon entropy of this distribution is given by

$$\mathcal{S}^c[\rho] = -\int \rho(\Gamma) \ln[h^N \rho(\Gamma)] d\Gamma = -\sum_k p_k \ln p_k \geq 0 \tag{60}$$

where $\mathcal{S}^c = 0$ if and only if $p_k = \delta_{kl}$ for some cell l.

If we thus reject distributions with negative entropy as being incompatible with the uncertainty principle, then Equation (55) is replaced by $\min_{\rho \in \Sigma^c} \mathcal{S}^c[\rho(\Gamma)] = 0$, and Equation (58) becomes

$$\max_{\rho_i \in \Sigma^c} \mathcal{W}^{c\star}[\rho_i(\Gamma)] = \beta^{-1} \mathcal{S}^c[\sigma(\Gamma)]. \tag{61}$$

Thus, after imposing consistency with the uncertainty principle (in an admittedly heuristic fashion), we conclude that for both the quantum equivalence class Σ^q and the classical equivalence class Σ^c, the maximum extractable work is given by the entropy of the diagonal or homogeneous state, multiplied by β^{-1} (Equations (57) and (61)).

Throughout the following section, and in Section 5, we impose the constraint $\mathcal{S}^c[\rho] \geq 0$ on the initial classical phase space distribution, to exclude states that are incompatible with the uncertainty principle.

4.3. A Fair Comparison

The final step in making a fair comparison between quantum and classical work extraction is to establish a correspondence between equivalence classes Σ^q and Σ^c. That is, we want to establish a correspondence between quantum and classical energy distributions. There is no unique way to do this, as energy takes on discrete values in one case and continuous values in the other. As a reasonable way to proceed, let us choose a real function $\kappa(\cdot) \geq 0$ with the property that both $\mathcal{K}^q = \text{Tr}\,\kappa(\hat{H}_0)$ and $\mathcal{K}^c = \int d\Gamma \, \kappa(H_0(\Gamma))$ are finite. We then define the diagonal quantum and homogeneous classical states

$$\hat{\sigma}_\kappa = \frac{\kappa(\hat{H}_0)}{\mathcal{K}^q} = \sum_n \frac{\kappa(\epsilon_n)}{\mathcal{K}^q} |n\rangle\langle n| \quad , \quad \sigma_\kappa(\Gamma) = \frac{\kappa(H_0(\Gamma))}{\mathcal{K}^c} \tag{62}$$

along with the associated energy equivalence classes

$$\Sigma^q[\kappa] = \{\hat{\rho} \,|\, \text{diag}\,\hat{\rho} = \hat{\sigma}_\kappa\} \tag{63a}$$
$$\Sigma^c[\kappa] = \{\rho(\Gamma) \,|\, \text{diag}\,\rho = \sigma_\kappa, \mathcal{S}^c[\rho] \geq 0\}. \tag{63b}$$

The equivalence class $\Sigma^q[\kappa]$ contains all quantum states with diagonal density matrix elements $\rho_{nn} = \kappa(\epsilon_n)/\mathcal{K}^q$, whereas $\Sigma^c[\kappa]$ contains every classical state with energy distribution

$$\eta(E) = \frac{\kappa(E)\Omega(E)}{\mathcal{K}^c}. \tag{64}$$

Thus, a given choice of $\kappa(\cdot)$ specifies both a quantum and a classical energy distribution. As an example, for the choice $\kappa(x) = e^{-\beta x}$, the reference states are $\hat{\sigma}_\kappa = \hat{\pi}_0$ and $\sigma_\kappa(\Gamma) = \pi_0(\Gamma)$, and the energy equivalence classes are the thermal sets defined earlier: $\Sigma^q[\kappa] = \Pi^q$ and $\Sigma^c[\kappa] = \Pi^c$.

In the semiclassical limit $h \to 0$, as the level spacing between adjacent energy eigenvalues approaches zero, the normalized energy distribution associated with $\Sigma^q[\kappa]$ is conveniently written as $\zeta(E) = \kappa(E)g(E)/\mathcal{K}^q$, where $g(E) = \sum_n \delta(E - \epsilon_n)$ is the quantum density of states. In turn, $g(E)\,dE$ is approximated by the number of cells of volume h^N that fit into the classical phase space volume between E and $E + dE$, for small dE. Equivalently,

$$\lim_{h \to 0} h^N g(E) = \Omega(E) \tag{65}$$

where $\Omega(E)$ is the classical density of states, Equation (39). Hence, the quantum energy distribution is, semiclassically,

$$\zeta(E) = \frac{\kappa(E)\Omega(E)}{h^N \mathcal{K}^q}. \tag{66}$$

Since both the classical and quantum energy distributions $\eta(E)$ and $\zeta(E)$ (Equations (64) and (66)) are normalized to unity, we have

$$\lim_{h \to 0} h^N \mathcal{K}^q = \mathcal{K}^c. \tag{67}$$

From Equations (64), (66) and (67), we conclude that in the semiclassical limit $h \to 0$, the discrete energy distribution associated with the equivalence class $\Sigma^q[\kappa]$ approaches the continuous distribution associated with $\Sigma^c[\kappa]$. In this sense, we view $\Sigma^q[\kappa]$ and $\Sigma^c[\kappa]$ as having equivalent energy distributions.

Now, finally, for a given quantum reference Hamiltonian $\hat{H}_0$ and its classical counterpart $H_0(\Gamma)$, and for a given choice of the function $\kappa(\cdot)$, let

$$\mathcal{W}^{q\star}_{\max}[\kappa] = \max_{\hat{\rho}_i \in \Sigma^q[\kappa]} \mathcal{W}^{q\star}(\hat{\rho}_i) \quad \text{and} \quad \mathcal{W}^{c\star}_{\max}[\kappa] = \max_{\rho_i \in \Sigma^c[\kappa]} \mathcal{W}^{c\star}[\rho_i(\Gamma)] \tag{68}$$

denote the maximum quantum and classical work that can be extracted during a cyclic, isoenergetic (in the sense of Equations (13) and (42)) process, for initial energy distributions determined by $\kappa(\cdot)$. We assert that by comparing the values of $\mathcal{W}^{q\star}_{\max}[\kappa]$ and $\mathcal{W}^{c\star}_{\max}[\kappa]$, in the semiclassical limit $h \to 0$, we make a fair comparison between quantum work that can be extracted from coherences, and classical work that can be extracted from inhomogeneities.

From Equations (57), (61) and (63), we have

$$\mathcal{W}^{q\star}_{\max}[\kappa] = \beta^{-1} \mathcal{S}^q(\hat{\sigma}_\kappa) \quad , \quad \mathcal{W}^{c\star}_{\max}[\kappa] = \beta^{-1} \mathcal{S}^c[\sigma_\kappa(\Gamma)], \tag{69}$$

therefore, let us inspect the difference between these two values,

$$\Delta \mathcal{W}^\star = \mathcal{W}^{q\star}_{\max}[\kappa] - \mathcal{W}^{c\star}_{\max}[\kappa], \tag{70}$$

in the limit $h \to 0$. Following the semiclassical approach used above, we obtain

$$\begin{aligned}
\lim_{h \to 0} \Delta \mathcal{W}^\star &= \beta^{-1} \lim_{h \to 0} \left\{ -\sum_n \frac{\kappa(\epsilon_n)}{\mathcal{K}^q} \ln\left[\frac{\kappa(\epsilon_n)}{\mathcal{K}^q}\right] + \int \frac{\kappa(H_0)}{\mathcal{K}^c} \ln\left[h^N \frac{\kappa(H_0)}{\mathcal{K}^c}\right] d\Gamma \right\} \\
&= \beta^{-1} \lim_{h \to 0} \left\{ -\int g(E) \frac{\kappa(E)}{\mathcal{K}^q} \ln\left[\frac{\kappa(E)}{\mathcal{K}^q}\right] dE + \int \Omega(E) \frac{\kappa(E)}{\mathcal{K}^c} \ln\left[h^N \frac{\kappa(E)}{\mathcal{K}^c}\right] dE \right\} \\
&= \beta^{-1} \lim_{h \to 0} \left\{ -\int \Omega(E) \frac{\kappa(E)}{\mathcal{K}^c} \ln\left[h^N \frac{\kappa(E)}{\mathcal{K}^c}\right] dE + \int \Omega(E) \frac{\kappa(E)}{\mathcal{K}^c} \ln\left[h^N \frac{\kappa(E)}{\mathcal{K}^c}\right] dE \right\} \\
&= 0.
\end{aligned} \tag{71}$$

Here, Equation (62) has been combined with the expressions for von Neumann and Shannon entropy (Equations (9) and (31)) on the first line; the sum over energy eigenstates and the integral over phase space have been replaced by energy integrals on the second line; and Equations (65) and (67) have been used to get to the third line.

For $\kappa(x) = e^{-\beta x}$, Equation (71) can alternatively be established from the result (see Equations (4) and (26))

$$\Delta \mathcal{W}^\star = \beta^{-1}\left\{\mathcal{S}^q(\hat{\pi}_0) - \mathcal{S}^c[\pi_0(\Gamma)]\right\} = \beta \frac{\partial}{\partial \beta}(\mathcal{F}^{q,\mathrm{eq}} - \mathcal{F}^{c,\mathrm{eq}}) = \left(-\frac{1}{\beta} + \frac{\partial}{\partial \beta}\right)\log \frac{Z^c}{h^N Z^q} \quad (72)$$

where Z^q and Z^c are equilibrium partition functions. Taking the limit $h \to 0$ and using the known result [47,53–55] that (for kinetic-plus-potential Hamiltonians) $h^N Z^q$ can be expanded in a power series of h whose first term is exactly the classical partition function Z^c, the right side of Equation (72) vanishes.

From Equation (71), we conclude that in the semiclassical limit, the maximal work that can be extracted from the energy coherences of a quantum state $\hat{\rho}_i \in \Sigma^q[\kappa]$ is the same as the maximal work that can be extracted from the energy-shell inhomogeneities of a classical state $\rho_i(\Gamma) \in \Sigma^c[\kappa]$. In both situations, the work is maximized by starting in the state of least entropy within Σ^q or Σ^c, then quasistatically removing the coherences or inhomogeneities. This result leads us to conclude that, within our framework for comparing quantum and classical systems, quantum coherences offer no particular thermodynamic advantage over classical inhomogeneities.

5. Dropping the Isoenergetic Constraint

In the previous sections, we have imposed the isoenergetic constraint, namely that the initial and final energy distributions are identical (Equations (13) and (42)). Let us now drop this constraint and pose the following question. For a quantum or classical system described by an initial Hamiltonian $\hat{H}_0$ or $H_0(\Gamma)$, in the presence of a thermal bath at temperature β^{-1}, what is the maximum work that can be extracted during a cyclic process if the energy distribution of the initial state is determined by a given function $\kappa(\cdot)$?

In the quantum case, we first let $\mathcal{W}^{q\dagger}(\hat{\rho}_i)$ denote the maximum work extracted for a given initial state $\hat{\rho}_i$—this quantity is analogous to $\mathcal{W}^\star(\hat{\rho}_i)$ (Section 2) but without the constraint $\mathrm{diag}\,\hat{\rho}_f = \mathrm{diag}\,\hat{\rho}_i$. From Equations (5) and (10) and the non-negativity of the Kullback–Leibler divergence, we have

$$\begin{aligned}\mathcal{W}^{q\dagger}(\hat{\rho}_i) &\leq \mathcal{F}^q(\hat{\rho}_i, \hat{H}_0) - \mathcal{F}^q(\hat{\rho}_f, \hat{H}_0)\\ &\leq \mathcal{F}^q(\hat{\rho}_i, \hat{H}_0) - \mathcal{F}^q(\hat{\pi}_0, \hat{H}_0)\\ &= \mathcal{U}_i^q - \beta^{-1}\mathcal{S}_i^q - \mathcal{F}_0^{q,\mathrm{eq}}\end{aligned} \quad (73)$$

where the inequality on the first line is valid for any final state $\hat{\rho}_f$, and $\mathcal{F}_0^{q,\mathrm{eq}} \equiv \mathcal{F}^{q,\mathrm{eq}}(\hat{H}_0)$. As shown in Appendix A, the bound obtained in Equation (73) is saturated by the protocol

$$\hat{H}(t) = \begin{cases} \hat{H}_0 & t \leq 0 \\ -\beta^{-1}\ln\left[(1-\lambda)\hat{\rho}_i + \lambda\,e^{-\beta \hat{H}_0}\right] & 0 < t \leq \tau \\ \hat{H}_0 & \tau \leq t \end{cases} \quad (74)$$

where $\lambda \equiv t/\tau$ and the process is quasistatic: $\tau \to \infty$. (Note that there is no quench at $t = \tau$.) Since the bound can be saturated, and $\mathcal{W}^{q\dagger}(\hat{\rho}_i)$ was defined as the maximum work that can be extracted, we simply write

$$\mathcal{W}^{q\dagger}(\hat{\rho}_i) = \mathcal{U}_i^q - \beta^{-1}\mathcal{S}_i^q - \mathcal{F}_0^{q,\mathrm{eq}}. \quad (75)$$

Now, maximizing this quantity over all $\hat{\rho}_i \in \Sigma^q[\kappa]$, we have

$$\begin{aligned}
\mathcal{W}_{\max}^{q\dagger}[\kappa] &= \max_{\hat{\rho}_i \in \Sigma^q[\kappa]} \left(\mathcal{U}_i^q - \beta^{-1} \mathcal{S}_i^q - \mathcal{F}_0^{q,\mathrm{eq}} \right) \\
&= \max_{\hat{\rho}_i \in \Sigma^q[\kappa]} \left(\mathcal{U}^q[\kappa] - \beta^{-1} \mathcal{S}_i^q - \mathcal{F}_0^{q,\mathrm{eq}} \right) \\
&= \mathcal{U}^q[\kappa] - \mathcal{F}_0^{q,\mathrm{eq}}
\end{aligned} \qquad (76)$$

where $\mathcal{U}^q[\kappa] \equiv (1/\mathcal{K}^q) \sum_n \kappa(\epsilon_n) \epsilon_n$ is the average energy for every state $\hat{\rho}_i \in \Sigma^q[\kappa]$, and we have used Equation (50b) to arrive at the third line.

As a consistency check, we combine Equations (69) and (76) with Equations (7) and (10) to obtain

$$\begin{aligned}
\mathcal{W}_{\max}^{q\dagger}[\kappa] - \mathcal{W}_{\max}^{q\star}[\kappa] &= \mathcal{U}^q[\kappa] - \mathcal{F}_0^{q,\mathrm{eq}} - \beta^{-1} \mathcal{S}^q(\hat{\sigma}_\kappa) \\
&= \mathcal{F}^q(\hat{\sigma}_\kappa, \hat{H}_0) - \mathcal{F}_0^{q,\mathrm{eq}} = D(\hat{\sigma}_\kappa \| \hat{\pi}_0) \geq 0
\end{aligned} \qquad (77)$$

where $\hat{\sigma}_\kappa$ is the unique diagonal state belonging to $\Sigma^q[\kappa]$. Thus, $\mathcal{W}_{\max}^{q\dagger}[\kappa] \geq \mathcal{W}_{\max}^{q\star}[\kappa]$, which makes sense: the maximum work that we can extract without imposing the constraint $\mathrm{diag}\,\hat{\rho}_f = \mathrm{diag}\,\hat{\rho}_i$ must be no less than the maximum work we can extract with the constraint.

In the classical case, essentially identical calculations—which we do not reproduce here—lead to the result

$$\mathcal{W}_{\max}^{c\dagger}[\kappa] = \mathcal{U}^c[\kappa] - \mathcal{F}_0^{c,\mathrm{eq}} \qquad (78)$$

where $\mathcal{W}_{\max}^{c\dagger}[\kappa]$ is the maximum work that can be extracted over all initial states $\rho_i(\Gamma) \in \Sigma^c[\kappa]$, without imposing Equation (42), and $\mathcal{U}^c[\kappa] = (1/\mathcal{K}^c) \int d\Gamma\, \kappa(H_0) H_0$ is the average energy for every state in $\Sigma^c[\kappa]$. Following steps similar to those of Section 4.3, we obtain

$$\begin{aligned}
\lim_{h \to 0} \mathcal{U}^q[\kappa] &= \lim_{h \to 0} \frac{1}{\mathcal{K}^q} \sum_n \kappa(\epsilon_n) \epsilon_n \\
&= \lim_{h \to 0} \int dE\, g(E) \frac{\kappa(E)}{\mathcal{K}^q} E \\
&= \int dE\, \Omega(E) \frac{\kappa(E)}{\mathcal{K}^c} E = \frac{1}{\mathcal{K}^c} \int d\Gamma\, \kappa(H_0) H_0 = \mathcal{U}^c[\kappa]
\end{aligned} \qquad (79)$$

and

$$\lim_{h \to 0} \left(\mathcal{F}_0^{c,\mathrm{eq}} - \mathcal{F}_0^{q,\mathrm{eq}} \right) = -\beta^{-1} \lim_{h \to 0} \ln \frac{Z^c[H_0]}{h^N Z^q(\hat{H}_0)} = 0 \qquad (80)$$

using Equation (67), with $\kappa(x) = e^{-\beta x}$.

Defining $\Delta \mathcal{W}^\dagger \equiv \mathcal{W}_{\max}^{q\dagger}[\kappa] - \mathcal{W}_{\max}^{c\dagger}[\kappa]$, Equations (76) and (78)–(80) give us

$$\lim_{h \to 0} \Delta \mathcal{W}^\dagger = 0 \qquad (81)$$

which is the counterpart of Equation (71), after abandoning the constraint of equal initial and final energy distributions. We again conclude that quantum coherences provide no inherent thermodynamic advantage over classical inhomogeneities, in the semiclassical limit.

6. Conclusions

In Sections 2 and 3 of this paper, we argued that quantum energy coherences (as shown earlier [9]) and classical energy shell inhomogeneities represent thermodynamic resources, which can be leveraged to deliver work. In Sections 4 and 5, we argued that a fair comparison shows these resources to be equivalent: in the semiclassical limit, and for a given initial energy distribution, the amount of work that can be extracted from quantum coherences is the same as the amount that can be extracted from classical inhomogeneities.

Our study has focused on processes during which the system of interest is in contact with a thermal reservoir, and here (as we have seen) the free energy $\mathcal{F}$ plays an important role. Sone and Deffner [18] have recently carried out a similar investigation for isolated quantum and classical systems, in which case *ergotropy* (defined in Ref. [1] for quantum systems and in Ref. [18] for classical systems) plays a role analogous to free energy in our paper. In Ref. [18], as in our paper, energy-shell inhomogeneities are classical counterparts of quantum energy coherences.

In making our comparison in Sections 4 and 5, we invoked a quantum–classical correspondence based on canonical quantization, in which the system of interest is described by coordinates $x_1, x_2, \cdots$ and conjugate momenta $p_1, p_2, \cdots$, which are either quantum operators or classical observables. For such systems, the classical phase space is unbounded and the quantum Hilbert space is infinite-dimensional.

However, in the quantum thermodynamics literature one often encounters systems with finite-dimensional Hilbert spaces, such as the illustrative qubit example analyzed in Ref. [9]. It then seems natural to take, as the quantum system's counterpart, a discrete-state classical system of equal dimensionality. Thus, a qubit's counterpart may be taken to be a classical bit. For such discrete-state systems there is no opportunity to introduce a classical analogue of quantum coherences, as the statistical state of a classical D-state system is specified *entirely* by the probabilities $P_1, \cdots P_D$, and these are in one-to-one correspondence with the diagonal elements of the corresponding quantum system's density matrix $\hat{\rho}$. In this situation, it seems that quantum coherences really do provide a unique thermodynamic resource that is unavailable to classical counterparts.

This conclusion, however, is misleading, as an apparently discrete-state classical system is in reality a coarse-grained version of a more microscopically detailed system. For example, an effective classical bit can be obtained by coarse-graining a classical particle in a double-well potential, such that the location x of the particle in the left (right) well indicates a bit value of 0 (1). The apparent quantum thermodynamic advantage—due to coherences—arises in this case because potentially useful classical information (e.g., how the particle's potential energy depends on its location x) has been thrown out in the process of coarse-graining from the double well to the bit. Comparing a qubit—an intrinsically two-state quantum system—with an effective classical two-state system obtained by discarding microscopic information, is an apples-to-oranges comparison.

There is no generally applicable procedure for identifying a proper classical counterpart of a quantum system with a finite-dimensional Hilbert space. It is instructive, however, to consider the simplest case of a spin-1/2 particle (qubit) in a magnetic field, governed by a Hamiltonian $\hat{H} = g\mathbf{B} \cdot \hat{\mathbf{s}}$, where $\hat{\mathbf{s}} = (\hbar/2)(\hat{\sigma}_x, \hat{\sigma}_y, \hat{\sigma}_z)$. In the absence of a thermal bath, the unitary dynamics in the Heisenberg representation are given by the equations of motion

$$i\hbar \frac{d}{dt}\hat{\mathbf{s}}_\mathrm{H} = [\hat{\mathbf{s}}_\mathrm{H}, \hat{H}] \tag{82}$$

where the right side is evaluated using the commutation relations

$$[\hat{s}_j, \hat{s}_k] = i\hbar\, \varepsilon_{jkl}\, \hat{s}_l \tag{83}$$

and ε_{jkl} is the Levi-Civita symbol. Kammerlander and Anders [9] showed how work can be extracted from energy coherences in such a system, using a protocol involving quenches and the quasistatic variation of $\mathbf{B}$, along with coupling to a thermal bath.

As a possible classical counterpart, instead of a two-state bit let us consider a system whose microscopic state is described by a vector $\mathbf{S} = (S_x, S_y, S_z)$ of fixed magnitude, governed by a Hamiltonian $H = g\mathbf{B} \cdot \mathbf{S}$, evolving under the Poisson bracket formulation of Hamiltonian dynamics,

$$\frac{d}{dt}\mathbf{S} = \{\mathbf{S}, H\} \tag{84}$$

with

$$\{S_j, S_k\} = \varepsilon_{jkl} S_l. \tag{85}$$

The phase space for this classical system is bounded: it is the two-dimensional surface of a sphere of radius $|\mathbf{S}|$. An energy shell is represented by a circle on that sphere, oriented along the **B**-direction. The dynamics given by Equation (84) describe an isolated system, and would have to be supplemented by appropriate terms in order to include the effects of contact with a thermal bath. It would then be interesting to investigate classical protocols designed to extract work from an initial distribution that is inhomogeneous on the energy shells, and to compare this classical situation with the quantum case of Ref. [9].

We note that the approach described in the previous paragraphs is readily extended to a system composed of $N > 1$ spins, interacting both with external fields and among themselves, e.g., through Hamiltonian terms of the form $c_{mn}\hat{\mathbf{s}}_m \cdot \hat{\mathbf{s}}_n$ or $c_{mn}\mathbf{S}_m \cdot \mathbf{S}_n$. Thus, comparisons between quantum and classical work extraction can be extended to multi-spin systems, within this framework. For example, it has been demonstrated that quantum correlations within a many-body system can be utilized for extracting work [56–59], and it would be pertinent to study whether one can leverage classical correlations and inhomogeneities in a similar way. Such comparisons may further elucidate whether thermodynamic advantages can be identified that are unique to quantum systems.

Author Contributions: Conceptualization, A.S., K.S. and C.J.; Investigation, A.S., K.S. and C.J.; Writing—original draft, A.S. and C.J.; Writing—review & editing, K.S. All authors have read and agreed to the published version of the manuscript

Funding: This research was funded by the United States National Science Foundation under grant DMR-1506969 (AS, CJ).

Institutional Review Board Statement: Not applicable.

Informed Consent Statement: Not applicable.

Acknowledgments: We gratefully acknowledge stimulating discussions with Janet Anders, Sebastian Deffner, David Goldwasser, Wade Hodson, Paul Riechers, and Nicole Yunger Halpern.

Conflicts of Interest: The authors declare no conflict of interest.

Appendix A

Here, we show that the work bounds appearing in Equations (18), (45) and (73) are saturated by the protocols given by Equations (19), (46) and (74), when these protocols are performed quasistatically ($\tau \to \infty$). In both the quantum and classical cases, our key assumption is that in the absence of driving the system relaxes to the thermal equilibrium state. Hence, under quasistatic driving, the system tracks the instantaneous equilibrium state.

In the quantum case, we first note that for a time-dependent Hamiltonian $\hat{H}(t)$ and the corresponding equilibrium state $\hat{\pi}(t)$ and free energy $\mathcal{F}^{q,\text{eq}}(t) = -\beta^{-1} \ln Z^q(t)$, the following relation holds:

$$\frac{d}{dt}\mathcal{F}^{q,\text{eq}}(t) = \text{Tr}\left[\frac{d\hat{H}}{dt}\hat{\pi}\right] \tag{A1}$$

as can be verified directly from Equations (3) and (4). This identity is the quantum counterpart of the classical thermodynamic integration identity, Equation (A8), which underlies the thermodynamic integration technique for free energy estimation [60,61]. Equation (A1) states that the rate of change in the equilibrium free energy, with respect to time, is the equilibrium average of the rate of change in the Hamiltonian.

Now, consider a quantum system whose initial state is $\hat{\rho}_i$, which is driven according to the protocol given by Equation (19). The initial step of this protocol is an instantaneous change in the Hamiltonian from $\hat{H}(0) = \hat{H}_0$ to $\hat{H}(0^+) = -\beta^{-1} \ln \hat{\rho}_i$. The state of the system does not change during this step. The resulting work performed is

$$\begin{aligned} \mathcal{W}^q_{0 \to 0^+} &= -\int_0^{0^+} \mathrm{Tr}\left[\frac{d\hat{H}}{dt}\hat{\rho}\right] dt \\ &= \mathrm{Tr}\left[(\hat{H}(0) - \hat{H}(0^+))\hat{\rho}_i\right] \\ &= \mathrm{Tr}\left[(\hat{H}_0 + \beta^{-1} \ln \hat{\rho}_i)\hat{\rho}_i\right] \\ &= \mathcal{U}^q_i - \beta^{-1} \mathcal{S}^q_i = \mathcal{F}^q_i. \end{aligned} \quad (A2)$$

During the quasistatic stage of the protocol, the system evolves through a sequence of equilibrium states, $\hat{\rho}(t) = \hat{\pi}(t)$—see Equation (20). Applying Equation (A1), the resulting work is

$$\begin{aligned} \mathcal{W}^q_{0^+ \to \tau^-} &= -\int_{0^+}^{\tau^-} \mathrm{Tr}\left[\frac{d\hat{H}}{dt}\hat{\pi}\right] dt \\ &= -\int_{0^+}^{\tau^-} \frac{d}{dt} \mathcal{F}^{q,\mathrm{eq}}(t) \, dt \\ &= \mathcal{F}^{q,\mathrm{eq}}(\tau^-) - \mathcal{F}^{q,\mathrm{eq}}(0^+) \\ &= -\beta^{-1} \ln \mathrm{Tr}\, e^{-\beta \hat{H}(\tau^-)} + \beta^{-1} \ln \mathrm{Tr}\, e^{-\beta \hat{H}(0^+)} \\ &= -\beta^{-1} \ln \frac{\mathrm{Tr}\, \mathrm{diag}\, \hat{\rho}_i}{\mathrm{Tr}\, \hat{\rho}_i} = 0. \end{aligned} \quad (A3)$$

Proceeding as in Equation (A2), we obtain

$$\mathcal{W}^q_{\tau^- \to \tau} = -\mathcal{F}^q_f \quad (A4)$$

for the Hamiltonian quench at $t = \tau$. Thus, the total work over the entire process is

$$\mathcal{W}^q = \mathcal{F}^q_i - \mathcal{F}^q_f = \beta^{-1}[\mathcal{S}^q(\mathrm{diag}\,\hat{\rho}_i) - \mathcal{S}^q(\hat{\rho}_i)] \quad (A5)$$

(using $\mathcal{U}^q_i = \mathcal{U}^q_f$), as claimed at the end of Section 2.

Similar calculations for the protocol appearing in Equation (74) give

$$\mathcal{W}^q_{0 \to 0^+} = \mathcal{U}^q_i - \beta^{-1} \mathcal{S}^q_i \quad (A6a)$$
$$\mathcal{W}^q_{0^+ \to \tau^-} = -\mathcal{F}^{q,\mathrm{eq}}_0 \quad (A6b)$$
$$\mathcal{W}^q_{\tau^- \to \tau} = 0, \quad (A6c)$$

hence,

$$\mathcal{W}^q = \mathcal{U}^q_i - \beta^{-1} \mathcal{S}^q_i - \mathcal{F}^{q,\mathrm{eq}}_0 \quad (A7)$$

as claimed in Section 5, just after Equation (74).

In the classical case, for a Hamiltonian $H(\Gamma, t)$ we have the identity

$$\frac{d}{dt} \mathcal{F}^{c,\mathrm{eq}}(t) = \int d\Gamma \, \frac{\partial H}{\partial t}(\Gamma, t) \pi(\Gamma, t). \quad (A8)$$

For the protocol given by Equation (46), calculations essentially identical to those appearing above in Equations (A2)–(A4), but with quantum traces replaced by integrals over classical phase space, give

$$\mathcal{W}^c_{0 \to 0^+} = \mathcal{F}^c_i \quad (A9a)$$
$$\mathcal{W}^c_{0^+ \to \tau^-} = 0 \quad (A9b)$$
$$\mathcal{W}^c_{\tau_- \to \tau_+} = -\mathcal{F}^c_f, \quad (A9c)$$

hence,
$$\mathcal{W}^c = \mathcal{F}_i^c - \mathcal{F}_f^c = \beta^{-1}(\mathcal{S}^c[\text{diag}\,\rho_i] - \mathcal{S}^c[\rho_i]) \tag{A10}$$
as claimed at the end of Section 3.2.

References

1. Allahverdyan, A.; Balian, R.; Nieuwenhuizen, T. Maximal work extraction from finite quantum systems. *Europhys. Lett.* **2004**, *67*, 565–571. [CrossRef]
2. Horodecki, M.; Oppenheim, J. Fundamental limitations for quantum and nanoscale thermodynamics. *Nat. Commun.* **2013**, *4*, 1–6. [CrossRef] [PubMed]
3. Brandão, F.G.; Horodecki, M.; Oppenheim, J.; Renes, J.M.; Spekkens, R.W. Resource theory of quantum states out of thermal equilibrium. *Phys. Rev. Lett.* **2013**, *111*, 1–5. [CrossRef] [PubMed]
4. Li, H.; Zou, J.; Yu, W.L.; Xu, B.M.; Li, J.G.; Shao, B. Quantum coherence rather than quantum correlations reflect the effects of a reservoir on a system's work capability. *Phys. Rev. E* **2014**, *2014*, 052132. [CrossRef]
5. Skrzypczyk, P.; Short, A.J.; Popescu, S. Work extraction and thermodynamics for individual quantum systems. *Nat. Commun.* **2014**, *5*, 1–8.[CrossRef]
6. Baumgratz, T.; Cramer, M.; Plenio, M.B. Quantifying coherence. *Phys. Rev. Lett.* **2014**, *113*, 140401. [CrossRef] [PubMed]
7. Åberg, J. Catalytic coherence. *Phys. Rev. Lett.* **2014**, *113*, 150402. [CrossRef]
8. Korzekwa, K.; Lostaglio, M.; Oppenheim, J.; Jennings, D. The extraction of work from quantum coherence. *New J. Phys.* **2016**, *18*, 023045. [CrossRef]
9. Kammerlander, P.; Anders, J. Coherence and measurement in quantum thermodynamics. *Sci. Rep.* **2016**, *6*, 22174. doi: [CrossRef]
10. Strasberg, P.; Schaller, G.; Brandes, T.; Esposito, M. Quantum and Information Thermodynamics: A Unifying Framework Based on Repeated Interactions. *Phys. Rev. X* **2017**, *7*, 021003. [CrossRef]
11. Elouard, C.; Herrera-Martí, D.A.; Clusel, M.; Auffèves, A. The role of quantum measurement in stochastic thermodynamics. *Nat. Quantum Inf.* **2017**, *3*, 9. [CrossRef]
12. Solinas, P.; Miller, H.J.D.; Anders, J. Measurement-dependent corrections to work distributions arising from quantum coherences. *Phys. Rev. A* **2017**, *96*, 052115. [CrossRef]
13. Francica, G.; Goold, J.; Plastina, F. Role of coherence in the nonequilibrium thermodynamics of quantum systems. *Phys. Rev. E* **2019**, *99*, 042105. [CrossRef] [PubMed]
14. Pan, R.; Fei, Z.; Qui, T.; Zhang, J.N.; Quan, H. Quantum-classical correspondence of work distributions for initial states with quantum coherence. *arXiv*, **2019**, arXiv:1904.05378v1.
15. Francica, G.; Binder, F.; Guarnieri, G.; Mitchison, M.; Goold, J.; Plastina, F. Quantum Coherence and Ergotropy. *Phys. Rev. Lett.* **2020**, *125*, 180603. [CrossRef]
16. García Díaz, M.; Guarnieri, G.; Paternostro, M. Quantum Work Statistics with Initial Coherence. *Entropy* **2020**, *22*, 1223. [CrossRef]
17. Touil, A.; Çakmak, B.; Deffner, S. Ergotropy from quantum and classical correlations. *J. Phys. A Math. Theor.* **2021**, *55*, 025301. [CrossRef]
18. Sone, A.; Deffner, S. Quantum and Classical Ergotropy from Relative Entropies. *Entropy* **2021**, *23*, 1107. [CrossRef]
19. Francica, G. Class of quasiprobability distributions of work with initial quantum coherence. *Phys. Rev. E* **2022**, *105*, 014101. [CrossRef]
20. Pusz, W.; Woronowicz, S.L. Passive states and KMS states for general quantum systems. *Comm. Math. Phys.* **1978**, *58*, 273–290. [CrossRef]
21. Alicki, R. The quantum open system as a model of the heat engine. *J. Phys. A Math. Gen.* **1979**, *12*, L103–L107. [CrossRef]
22. Nielsen, M.A.; Chuang, I.L. *Quantum Computation and Quantum Information*; Cambridge University Press: Cambridge, UK, 2000.
23. Alicki, R. On the Detailed Balance Condition for Non-Hamiltonian Systems. *Rep. Math. Phys.* **1976**, *10*, 249–258. [CrossRef]
24. Callen, H.B. *Thermodynamics and an Introduction to Thermostatistics*; John Wiley and Sons: New York, NY, USA, 1985.
25. Parrondo, J.M.R.; Horowitz, J.M.; Sagawa, T. Thermodynamics of information. *Nat. Phys.* **2015**, *11*, 131–139. [CrossRef]
26. Esposito, M.; Lindenberg, K.; Van den Broeck, C. Entropy production as correlation between system and reservoir. *New J. Phys.* **2010**, *12*, 013013. [CrossRef]
27. Hasegawa, H.H.; Ishikawa, J.; Takara, K.; Driebe, D. Generalization of the second law for a nonequilibrium initial state. *Phys. Lett. A* **2010**, *374*, 1001–1004. [CrossRef]
28. Takara, K.; Hasegawa, H.H.; Driebe, D.J. Generalization of the second law for a transition between nonequilibrium states. *Phys. Lett. A* **2010**, *375*, 88–92. [CrossRef]
29. Esposito, M.; Van den Broeck, C. Second law and Landauer principle far from equilibrium. *EPL* **2011**, *95*, 40004. [CrossRef]
30. Deffner, S.; Lutz, E. Nonequilibrium Entropy Production for Open Quantum Systems. *Phys. Rev. Lett.* **2011**, *107*, 140404. [CrossRef]
31. Cover, T.M.; Thomas, J.A. *Elements of Information Theory*; John Wiley & Sons, Inc.: New York, NY, USA, 1991.
32. Vinjanampathy, S.; Anders, J. Quantum thermodynamics. *Contemp. Phys.* **2016**, *57*, 545–579. [CrossRef]
33. Solinas, P.; Gasparinetti, S. Full distribution of work done on a quantum system for arbitrary initial states. *Phys. Rev. E* **2015**, *92*, 042150. [CrossRef]

34. Seifert, U. Stochastic thermodynamics, fluctuation theorems and molecular machines. *Rep. Prog. Phys.* **2012**, *75*, 126001. [CrossRef] [PubMed]
35. Van den Broeck, C.; Esposito, M. Ensemble and trajectory thermodynamics: A brief introduction. *Phys. Stat. Mech. Appl.* **2015**, *418*, 6–16. [CrossRef]
36. Talkner, P.; Hänggi, P. Aspects of quantum work. *Phys. Rev. E* **2016**, *93*, 022131. [CrossRef] [PubMed]
37. Kurchan, J. A Quantum Fluctuation Theorem. *arXiv* **2000**, arXiv:cond-mat/0007360v2.
38. Tasaki, H. Jarzynski Relations for Quantum Systems and Some Applications. *arXiv* **2000**, arXiv:cond-mat/0009244.
39. Mukamel, S. Quantum Extension of the Jarzynski Relation: Analogy with Stochastic Dephasing. *Phys. Rev. Lett.* **2003**, *90*, 170604. [CrossRef]
40. Gour, G.; Müller, M.P.; Narasimhachar, V.; Spekkens, R.W.; Halpern, N.Y. The resource theory of informational nonequilibrium in thermodynamics. *Phys. Rep.* **2015**, *583*, 1–58. [CrossRef]
41. Lostaglio, M.; Jennings, D.; Rudolph, T. Description of quantum coherence in thermodynamic processes requires constraints beyond free energy. *Nat. Commun.* **2015**, *6*, 6383. [CrossRef]
42. Jarzynski, C. Microscopic Analysis of Clausius-Duhem Processes. *J. Stat. Phys.* **1999**, *96*, 415–427. [CrossRef]
43. Seifert, U. Entropy production along a stochastic trajectory and an integral fluctuation theorem. *Phys. Rev. Lett.* **2005**, *95*, 040602. [CrossRef]
44. Deffner, S.; Lutz, E. Information free energy for nonequilibrium states. *arXiv* **2012**, arXiv:1201.3888v1.
45. Case, W.B. Wigner functions and Weyl transforms for pedestrians. *Am. J. Phys.* **2008**, *76*, 937–946. [CrossRef]
46. Hillery, M.; O'Connell, R.; Scully, M.; Wigner, E. Distribution functions in physics: Fundamentals. *Phys. Rep.* **1984**, *106*, 121–167. [CrossRef]
47. Wigner, E. On the Quantum Correction For Thermodynamic Equilibrium. *Phys. Rev.* **1932**, *40*, 749–759. [CrossRef]
48. Husimi, K. Some Formal Properties of the Density Matrix. *Proc. Physico-Math. Soc. Jpn.* **1940**, *22*, 264–314.
49. Dodonov, V.V. 'Nonclassical' states in quantum optics: A 'squeezed' review of the first 75 years. *J. Opt. B Quantum Semiclass. Opt.* **2002**, *4*, R1–R33. [CrossRef]
50. Barnett, S.; Pegg, D. On the Hermitian Optical Phase Operator. *J. Mod. Opt.* **1989**, *36*, 7–19. [CrossRef]
51. Kobe, D.H. Canonical transformation to energy and "tempus" in classical mechanics. *Am. J. Phys.* **1993**, *61*, 1031–1037. [CrossRef]
52. Mardia, K.V.; Jupp, P.E. *Directional Statistics*; John Wiley & Sons: Chichester, UK, 2000.
53. Uhlenbeck, G.E.; Gropper, L. The Equation of State of a Non-ideal Einstein-Bose or Fermi-Dirac Gas. *Phys. Rev.* **1932**, *41*, 79–90. [CrossRef]
54. Kirkwood, J.G. Quantum Statistics of Almost Classical Assemblies. *Phys. Rev.* **1933**, *44*, 31–37. [CrossRef]
55. Landau, L.D.; Lifshitz, E.M. *Statistical Physics 3rd Ed Part 1*; Elsevier: Amsterdam, The Netherlands, 1980; Section 33.
56. Oppenheim, J.; Horodecki, M.; Horodecki, P.; Horodecki, R. Thermodynamical Approach to Quantifying Quantum Correlations. *Phys. Rev. Lett.* **2002**, *89*, 180402. [CrossRef] [PubMed]
57. Alicki, R.; Fannes, M. Entanglement boost for extractable work from ensembles of quantum batteries. *Phys. Rev. E* **2013**, *87*, 042123. [CrossRef] [PubMed]
58. Dağ, C.B.; Niedenzu, W.; Müstecaplıoğlu, Ö.E.; Kurizki, G. Multiatom Quantum Coherences in Micromasers as Fuel for Thermal and Nonthermal Machines. *Entropy* **2016**, *18*, 244. [CrossRef]
59. Francica, G.; Goold, J.; Plastina, F.; Paternostro, M. Daemonic ergotropy: Enhanced work extraction from quantum correlations. *NPJ Quantum Inf.* **2017**, *3*, 12. [CrossRef]
60. Kirkwood, J.G. Statistical Mechanics of Fluid Mixtures. *J. Chem. Phys.* **1935**, *3*, 300–313. [CrossRef]
61. Frenkel, D.; Smit, B. *Understanding Molecular Simulation: From Algorithms to Applications*; Academic Press: San Diego, CA, USA, 2002.

Article

Amplification, Inference, and the Manifestation of Objective Classical Information

Michael Zwolak

Biophysical and Biomedical Measurement Group, Microsystems and Nanotechnology Division, Physical Measurement Laboratory, National Institute of Standards and Technology, Gaithersburg, MD 20899, USA; mpz@nist.gov

Abstract: Our everyday reality is characterized by objective information—information that is selected and amplified by the environment that interacts with quantum systems. Many observers can accurately infer that information indirectly by making measurements on fragments of the environment. The correlations between the system, $\mathcal{S}$, and a fragment, $\mathcal{F}$, of the environment, $\mathcal{E}$, is often quantified by the quantum mutual information, or the Holevo quantity, which bounds the classical information about $\mathcal{S}$ transmittable by a quantum channel $\mathcal{F}$. The latter is a quantum mutual information but of a classical-quantum state where measurement has selected outcomes on $\mathcal{S}$. The measurement generically reflects the influence of the remaining environment, $\mathcal{E}/\mathcal{F}$, but can also reflect hypothetical questions to deduce the structure of $\mathcal{SF}$ correlations. Recently, Touil et al. examined a different Holevo quantity, one from a quantum-classical state (a quantum $\mathcal{S}$ to a measured $\mathcal{F}$). As shown here, this quantity upper bounds any accessible classical information about $\mathcal{S}$ in $\mathcal{F}$ and can yield a tighter bound than the typical Holevo quantity. When good decoherence is present—when the remaining environment, $\mathcal{E}/\mathcal{F}$, has effectively measured the pointer states of $\mathcal{S}$—this accessibility bound is the accessible information. For the specific model of Touil et al., the accessible information is related to the error probability for optimal detection and, thus, has the same behavior as the quantum Chernoff bound. The latter reflects amplification and provides a universal approach, as well as a single-shot framework, to quantify records of the missing, classical information about $\mathcal{S}$.

Keywords: quantum-to-classical transition; quantum Darwinism; decoherence; amplification; inference; Holevo; quantum Chernoff bound

1. Introduction

The emergence of objective, classical information from quantum systems is due to amplification: Many pieces of the environment—e.g., many photons—each interact with a quantum system and acquire an imprint of certain states, the pointer states. This is the process by which select information becomes redundant and accessible to many different observers. The framework, where the environment decoheres systems and acts as a communication channel for the resulting information, is known as quantum Darwinism [1–20]. It is the pointer states that survive the interaction with the environment and create "copies" of themselves from which observers can infer the pointer state of the system. This process has been seen experimentally in both natural [21] and engineered [22,23] settings, and both theory and practical calculations are steadily progressing [24–38].

Within this framework, one primary question concerns the information available within an environment fragment as its size increases. This allows one to quantify redundancy: If small fragments $\mathcal{F}$ of the environment $\mathcal{E}$ all contain the same information about the system $\mathcal{S}$, then that information is available to many observers. Given a global state, $\rho_{\mathcal{SE}}$, the accessible information

$$I_{\mathrm{acc}}(\Pi_{\mathcal{S}}) = \max_{\Pi_{\mathcal{F}}} I(\Pi_{\mathcal{S}} : \Pi_{\mathcal{F}}) \tag{1}$$

can quantify the amount of information an observer learns about $\Pi_\mathcal{S}$ (a positive operator-valued measure, a POVM, on $\mathcal{S}$) by making a measurement $\Pi_\mathcal{F}$ on only $\mathcal{F}$. The quantity $I(\Pi_\mathcal{S} : \Pi_\mathcal{F})$ is the classical mutual information computed from the joint probability distribution from outcomes of $\Pi_\mathcal{S}$ and $\Pi_\mathcal{F}$. The POVM $\Pi_\mathcal{S}$ has elements π_s that generate an ensemble $\{(p_s, \rho_{\mathcal{F}|s})\}$ of outcomes s with probability $p_s = \text{tr}_{\mathcal{SE}} \pi_s \rho_{\mathcal{SE}}$ and conditional states $\rho_{\mathcal{F}|s} = \text{tr}_{\mathcal{SE}/\mathcal{F}} \pi_s \rho_{\mathcal{SE}} / p_s = \text{tr}_{\mathcal{SE}/\mathcal{F}} \sqrt{\pi_s} \rho_{\mathcal{SE}} \sqrt{\pi_s} / p_s$ on $\mathcal{F}$ (i.e., assuming the POVM acts on only $\mathcal{S}$ and an auxiliary system but $\mathcal{F}$ is not directly affected). Allowing $\Pi_\mathcal{S}$ to be arbitrary, the accessible information, Equation (1), depicts a situation where some auxiliary system $\mathcal{A}$, perhaps a special observer or another part of the environment, has access directly only to $\mathcal{S}$, makes a measurement $\Pi_\mathcal{S}$, and holds a record of the outcome s, leaving a joint state (after tracing out the now irrelevant $\mathcal{S}$)

$$\sum_s p_s |s\rangle_\mathcal{A} \langle s| \otimes \rho_{\mathcal{F}|s}. \tag{2}$$

An observer $\mathcal{O}$ then wants to predict the outcome s by making measurements only on $\mathcal{F}$, e.g., correlations are generated between $\mathcal{A}$ and $\mathcal{O}$ but indirectly from separate measurements on $\mathcal{S}$ and $\mathcal{F}$, for which Equation (1) quantifies this capability. One could then maximize the accessible information over all $\Pi_\mathcal{S}$ to see what quantity the observer can learn most about. This allows one to quantify the structure of correlations between $\mathcal{S}$ and $\mathcal{F}$ induced by, e.g., a decohering interaction between them.

Within the context of physical processes that give rise to quantum Darwinism, $\Pi_\mathcal{S}$ is not arbitrary, however. For redundant information to be present, there must be at least two records of some information, which, when decoherence is the main interaction, will be the pointer information. Hence, there must be an $\mathcal{F}$ that almost, to a degree we want to quantify, makes a measurement of the pointer states. At the same time, the remaining part of the environment, $\mathcal{E}/\mathcal{F}$, has already made an effective measurement for all intents and purposes, to a degree that we can retroactively validate. This entails that the correlations are effectively of the form of Equation (2) but with $\mathcal{A} = \mathcal{E}/\mathcal{F}$ or $\mathcal{S}$ and $\Pi_\mathcal{S} = \hat{\Pi}_\mathcal{S}$ (the pointer observable),

$$\sum_{\hat{s}} p_{\hat{s}} |\hat{s}\rangle \langle \hat{s}| \otimes \rho_{\mathcal{F}|\hat{s}}, \tag{3}$$

where $\hat{s}$ labels the pointer states (see Refs. [39,40] for a discussion of pointer states). This form is a consequence of "branching" [3] and appears in the good decoherence limit of purely decohering models, which will be extensively discussed below. Here, it is sufficient to note that the state, Equation (3), is the most relevant to quantum Darwinism. It makes little difference if one treats the $\mathcal{A}$ as $\mathcal{E}/\mathcal{F}$ or as just the fully decohered, or directly measured, $\mathcal{S}$, even when $\mathcal{F}$ is extremely large in absolute terms. Only for "global" questions, where $\mathcal{F}$ is some sizable fraction of the environment, does it matter. Since the environment is huge for most problems of everyday interest, such as photon scattering, $\mathcal{F}$ can be very large—even asymptotically large—without concern for this. However, Equation (3) does drop exponentially small corrections in the size of $\mathcal{E}/\mathcal{F}$ and one can not formally take the asymptotic limit of $\mathcal{F}$ without first doing so in $\mathcal{E}$. The degree to which asymptotic approximations work thus relies on the balance sheet—how well records are kept in the environment components compared to $\mathcal{E}$'s absolute size. Ref. [14] has dealt with retaining corrections to Equation (3). Hereon, I treat the auxiliary system $\mathcal{A}$ as if it were $\mathcal{S}$.

2. Results

With states of the form in Equation (3), the mutual information between $\mathcal{A} = \mathcal{S}$ and $\mathcal{F}$ is the Holevo quantity

$$\chi(\hat{\Pi}_\mathcal{S} : \mathcal{F}) = H\left(\sum_{\hat{s}} p_{\hat{s}} \rho_{\mathcal{F}|\hat{s}}\right) - \sum_{\hat{s}} p_{\hat{s}} H\left(\rho_{\mathcal{F}|\hat{s}}\right) \equiv H_\mathcal{F} - \sum_{\hat{s}} p_{\hat{s}} H_{\mathcal{F}|\hat{s}}, \tag{4}$$

where $H(\rho) = -\mathrm{tr}\rho \log_2 \rho$ is the von Neumann entropy for the state ρ. This quantity upper bounds the capacity of $\mathcal{F}$ to transmit pointer state information (the variable $\hat{s}$ is encoded in the conditional states $\rho_{\mathcal{F}|\hat{s}}$). Moreover, for an important class of interactions—purely decohering Hamiltonians with independent environment components—the quantum Chernoff bound determines the behavior of the optimal measurement on $\mathcal{F}$ to extract $\hat{\Pi}_\mathcal{S}$ and, thus, is related to the accessible information, Equation (1) with $\Pi_\mathcal{S} = \hat{\Pi}_\mathcal{S}$. One can generalize Equation (4) by allowing one to maximize over measurements on the system,

$$\chi(\check{\mathcal{S}} : \mathcal{F}) = \max_{\Pi_\mathcal{S}} \chi(\Pi_\mathcal{S} : \mathcal{F}), \tag{5}$$

where, when good decoherence has taken place, $\Pi_\mathcal{S} = \hat{\Pi}_\mathcal{S}$ maximizes the Holevo quantity [14]. The good decoherence limit is when $\mathcal{E}/\mathcal{F}$ is sufficient to decohere the system and, thus, the $\mathcal{SF}$ state is exactly of the form in Equation (3) [10,14]. Here, I employ the notation $\check{\mathcal{A}}$ of Touil et al. [38] to indicate that the Holevo quantity is maximized over measurements on $\mathcal{A}$, see also the next equation.

Touil et al. [38] examined an alternative Holevo quantity with the measurement on the fragment side,

$$\chi(\mathcal{S} : \check{\mathcal{F}}) = \max_{\Pi_\mathcal{F}} \chi(\mathcal{S} : \Pi_\mathcal{F}) = \max_{\Pi_\mathcal{F}} \left[H_\mathcal{S} - \sum_f p_f H_{\mathcal{S}|f} \right], \tag{6}$$

where the maximization is over all POVMs $\Pi_\mathcal{F}$ and f labels the outcomes of $\Pi_\mathcal{F}$ and p_f their probabilities. In that work, they compute the quantum mutual information, the Holevo quantity in Equation (4), and the alternative Holevo quantity in Equation (6) for a "c-maybe" model of decoherence of $\mathcal{S}$ by $\mathcal{E}$, a model that falls into the class of purely decohering models (see below). They analytically found $\chi(\mathcal{S} : \check{\mathcal{F}})$ by making use of the Koashi–Winter monogamy relation [41] and showed all the mutual information quantities above that approach the missing information, $H_\mathcal{S}$, with a similar dependence on $\mathcal{F}$.

If one were to interpret this alternative Holevo quantity, Equation (6), in the typical way, then it would bound the channel capacity of $\mathcal{S}$ to transmit information about (the optimal) $\Pi_\mathcal{F}$. One important observation, however, is that, in the good decoherence limit—when the $\mathcal{SF}$ state is of the form in Equation (3)—$\chi(\mathcal{S} : \Pi_\mathcal{F})$ lower bounds $\chi(\hat{\Pi}_\mathcal{S} : \mathcal{F})$ for any $\Pi_\mathcal{F}$ by the data processing inequality since $\hat{\Pi}_\mathcal{S}$ is already measured on $\mathcal{S}$ by $\mathcal{E}/\mathcal{F}$. In this limit, $\chi(\mathcal{S} : \check{\mathcal{F}})$ is the actual accessible pointer information.

For an arbitrary $\mathcal{SF}$ state, however, there is no strict relation of $\chi(\Pi_\mathcal{S} : \mathcal{F})$ or $\chi(\check{\mathcal{S}} : \mathcal{F})$ with $\chi(\mathcal{S} : \Pi_\mathcal{F})$ or $\chi(\mathcal{S} : \check{\mathcal{F}})$. In that case, the Holevo quantities with measurements on the $\mathcal{F}$ side can not upper or lower bound quantities with $\mathcal{S}$ side measurements. For a particular state with a given inequality between $\mathcal{F}$ and $\mathcal{S}$ side measurements, one can swap $\mathcal{S}$ and $\mathcal{F}$ in the state $\rho_{\mathcal{SF}}$—it is arbitrary after all—and reverse the inequality. Instead, the inequality

$$\chi(\mathcal{S} : \check{\mathcal{F}}) \geq I_{\mathrm{acc}}(\Pi_\mathcal{S}) \tag{7}$$

holds for any $\Pi_\mathcal{S}$. The measurement on the two sides of the inequality is generically different—the measurement that maximizes $\chi(\mathcal{S} : \check{\mathcal{F}})$ is not the measurement, $\Pi_\mathcal{F}^\star$, that maximizes $I(\Pi_\mathcal{S} : \Pi_\mathcal{F})$ to get the accessible information, Equation (1). The proof of Equation (7) is straightforward,

$$\begin{aligned}
\chi(\mathcal{S} : \check{\mathcal{F}}) &= \max_{\Pi_\mathcal{F}} \chi(\mathcal{S} : \Pi_\mathcal{F}) \\
&\geq \chi(\mathcal{S} : \Pi_\mathcal{F}^\star) \\
&= \chi(\mathcal{MS} : \Pi_\mathcal{F}^\star) \\
&\geq \chi(\Pi_\mathcal{S} : \Pi_\mathcal{F}^\star) \\
&= I_{\mathrm{acc}}(\Pi_\mathcal{S}),
\end{aligned}$$

where the system $\mathcal{M}$ is adjoined in a product state with $\rho_{\mathcal{SF}}$ and a unitary on $\mathcal{MS}$ makes a measurement $\Pi_{\mathcal{S}}$. The fourth line follows from data processing.

Equation (7) is an accessibility bound. Any information about $\mathcal{S}$ (i.e., that can be extracted by a direct POVM on $\mathcal{S}$) can, at best, have $\chi(\mathcal{S}:\check{\mathcal{F}})$ amount of shared information with $\mathcal{F}$. Then, as already noted, if the good decoherence limit is reached, that bound becomes equality,

$$\overset{\text{Good Decoherence}}{\chi(\mathcal{S}:\check{\mathcal{F}}) = I_{\text{acc}}(\hat{\Pi}_{\mathcal{S}}),} \tag{8}$$

for the pointer information. This follows from the form of the state in Equation (3). To determine $\chi(\mathcal{S}:\check{\mathcal{F}})$ for this state, an apparatus makes a measurement $\Pi_{\mathcal{F}}$ and records the outcome, leaving a joint system-apparatus state $\sum_{\check{s},f} p_{\check{s}} |\check{s}\rangle\langle\check{s}| \otimes p_{f|\check{s}}|f\rangle\langle f|$. This is a classical-classical state that yields, after maximizing over $\Pi_{\mathcal{F}}$, both $\chi(\mathcal{S}:\check{\mathcal{F}})$, Equation (6), and the accessible information, Equation (1). This makes $\chi(\mathcal{S}:\check{\mathcal{F}})$ desirable in the context of quantum Darwinism: It not only is a better bound on the accessible information in the good decoherence limit—the main limit of interest for quantum Darwinism—but it is the actual accessible information.

To proceed further—to compute the accessible information and the associated redundancy—we need to specify a model or class of models that provide the global states of interest. The everyday photon environment has a particular structure where independent environment components (photons) scatter off objects, acquire an imprint of the state, and transmit that information onward, interacting little with each other in the process [11,12,16,42–44]. This structure is captured by purely decohering Hamiltonians by independent environment components. I will consider this general class here. Under this evolution, the quantum Chernoff bound (QCB) provides a universal lower bound to the accessible information and the associated redundancy. The quantum Chernoff result is also meaningful on its own as a single-shot result, quantifying how well an individual observer (with the best measurement apparatus) can learn the pointer state of $\mathcal{S}$ indirectly from $\mathcal{F}$.

Pure decoherence occurs when environments select, but do not perturb, the pointer states of $\mathcal{S}$. When the environment components do so independently, the Hamiltonian is of the form

$$\mathbf{H} = \mathbf{H}_{\mathcal{S}} + \hat{\Pi}_{\mathcal{S}} \sum_{k=1}^{\#\mathcal{E}} Y_k + \sum_{k=1}^{\#\mathcal{E}} \Omega_k \tag{9}$$

with $[\hat{\Pi}_{\mathcal{S}}, \mathbf{H}_{\mathcal{S}}] = 0$ and the initial state

$$\rho(0) = \rho_{\mathcal{S}}(0) \otimes \left[\bigotimes_{k=1}^{\#\mathcal{E}} \rho_k(0)\right]. \tag{10}$$

Here, k specifies a component of the environment $\mathcal{E}$ of size $\#\mathcal{E}$. The operators, Y_k and Ω_k, are arbitrary. This class of models contains the c-maybe model of Touil et al. [38]. That model has $\hat{\Pi}_{\mathcal{S}} = 0 \cdot |0\rangle\langle 0| + 1 \cdot |1\rangle\langle 1|$ and $\exp[\imath Y_k t] = \sin a |0\rangle\langle 0| + \cos a(|0\rangle\langle 1| + |1\rangle\langle 0|) - \sin a |1\rangle\langle 1|$ for all k, where a is the angle of rotation of the "target" environment bit after a time t. Note that all the coupling frequencies (i.e., the energy scales divided by the reduced Planck's constant) are absorbed into the definition of the operators $\mathbf{H}_{\mathcal{S}}$, Y_k, and Ω_k, while $\hat{\Pi}_{\mathcal{S}}$ is dimensionless. All other operators are 0. The collection of operators act similarly to those in the controlled NOT gate. They only swap as well, only a bit more lazily, as here a is any number, so it is called c-maybe.

Starting from the initial product state, Equation (10), and evolving for some time under the Hamiltonian, Equation (9), one can obtain the conditional states that appear in the Holevo quantity, Equation (4),

$$\rho_{\mathcal{F}|\check{s}} = \bigotimes_{k \in \mathcal{F}} \rho_{k|\check{s}}. \tag{11}$$

Due to the structure of the evolution, these are product states over the components of the environment fragment. However, they need not be identically distributed (that is, they need not be fully i.i.d.—independently and identically distributed—states).

The structure, Equation (11), is a manifestation of amplification. The pointer states $\hat{s}$ leave an imprint on the environment components, of which there are many. Observers intercepting those environment components can then make a measurement to infer the pointer state. This is the setting of quantum hypothesis testing. For instance, in the binary case with two pointer states $\hat{s} = 0$ or 1, one wants to decide whether the fragment state is $\rho_{\mathcal{F}|0}$ or $\rho_{\mathcal{F}|1}$ with a minimum average probability of error, $P_e = p_{\hat{s}=0}\text{tr}\Pi_{\mathcal{F}|1}\rho_{\mathcal{F}|0} + p_{\hat{s}=1}\text{tr}\Pi_{\mathcal{F}|0}\rho_{\mathcal{F}|1}$. This is based on a POVM measurement, $\Pi_{\mathcal{F}}$, composed of two positive operators $\Pi_{\mathcal{F}|0}$ and $\Pi_{\mathcal{F}|1}$ (with $\Pi_{\mathcal{F}|0} + \Pi_{\mathcal{F}|1} = I$) that indicate the occurrence of "0" or "1", respectively. The first contribution to this average error is when the actual state is $\rho_{\mathcal{F}|0}$, with *a priori* probability of occurring $p_{\hat{s}=0}$ (where I explicitly show $\hat{s} = 0$ to connect to Equation (3)) but the measurement yielded the incorrect outcome $\Pi_{\mathcal{F}|1}$. Similarly for the second contribution. Moreover, when amplification occurs, i.e., the conditional states are of the form in Equation (11), one is specifically interested in how the error probability behaves as the fragment size grows. This is the setting of the QCB.

To employ the QCB, one makes use of a two-sided measurement. The first is on $\mathcal{S}$, putting it into its pointer states (i.e., $\chi(\hat{\Pi}_\mathcal{S} : \mathcal{F})$ now provides the mutual information between $\mathcal{S}$ and $\mathcal{F}$). This reflects the action of $\mathcal{E}/\mathcal{F}$ and is the good decoherence limit—, i.e., $^\sharp\mathcal{E} \to \infty$ provided $\mathcal{S}$ and $\mathcal{E}$ have interacted for some finite time under the evolution given by Equations (9) and (10). This also requires that the coupling strength to the environment components do not depend on $^\sharp\mathcal{E}$. The second is on $\mathcal{F}$ to access the pointer state. By Fano's inequality [45,46],

$$\chi(\hat{\Pi}_\mathcal{S} : \mathcal{F}) \geq I_{\text{acc}}(\hat{\Pi}_\mathcal{S}) \geq H_\mathcal{S} - h(P_e) - P_e \ln[D-1], \quad (12)$$

where P_e is the error probability for extracting information about a (sub)space of pointer states (of dimension D) from a measurement on $\mathcal{F}$. One could replace the left hand side of this inequality with $\chi(\check{S} : \mathcal{F}) \geq \chi(\hat{\Pi}_\mathcal{S} : \mathcal{F})$. Here, I use the binary entropy, $h(x) = -x \log_2 x - (1-x) \log_2(1-x)$. The QCB upper bound, $P_e^\star \geq P_e$, gives a second inequality

$$I_{\text{acc}}(\hat{\Pi}_\mathcal{S}) \geq H_\mathcal{S} - h(P_e) - P_e \ln[D-1] \geq H_\mathcal{S} - h(P_e^\star) - P_e^\star \ln[D-1], \quad (13)$$

which is partway to the final QCB result [16,19].

The QCB upper bounds the error probability, $P_e^\star \geq P_e$, for both the $D = 2$ case [47–49] or the $D > 2$ cases [50]. There is no fundamental difference between these cases, it is only the closest two states that determine the asymptotic decay of P_e when $D > 2$. I will restrict to $D = 2$ from hereon to make a correspondence with Touil et al. [38]. The error probability (bound) is

$$P_e^\star = \min_{0 \leq c \leq 1} p_1^c p_2^{1-c} \prod_{k \in \mathcal{F}} \text{tr}\left[\rho_{k|1}^c \rho_{k|2}^{1-c}\right]. \quad (14)$$

For pure $\mathcal{SE}$ states in the purely decohering scenario, Equations (9) and (10), c can be any value between 0 and 1 within the generalized overlap contribution, $\text{tr}\left[\rho_{k|1}^c \rho_{k|2}^{1-c}\right]$, and it will give the exact overlap $\left|\langle \psi_{k|1} | \psi_{k|2} \rangle\right|^2 = |\gamma_k|^2$ (which is also the decoherence factor γ_k squared for this case of pure states). Touil et al. [38] consider the homogeneous case where $\gamma_k = \gamma$ for all k, which I will also consider (see Refs. [16,19] for inhomogeneous results).

For pure states, therefore, only the prefactor needs optimizing over c as the generalized overlap gives $|\gamma|^{2^\sharp\mathcal{F}}$ for all $0 \leq c \leq 1$ and with $^\sharp\mathcal{F}$ the number of components in $\mathcal{F}$. The prefactor is optimal at one of the two boundaries ($c = 0$ or $c = 1$), giving

$$P_e^\star = \min[p_1, p_2] |\gamma|^{2^\sharp\mathcal{F}}. \quad (15)$$

I use a slightly different notation here than Ref. [38] to keep the correspondence with prior work. Opposed to pure states, for mixed $\mathcal{SE}$ states within the pure decohering scenario, Equations (9) and (10), the error probability (bound) is $\sqrt{p_1 p_2} \prod_{k \in \mathcal{F}} \text{tr}\left[\rho_{k|1}^{1/2} \rho_{k|2}^{1/2}\right]$ for both spin and photon models [16,19] (i.e., $c = 1/2$ is optimal). Either prefactor, $\min[p_1, p_2]$ or $\sqrt{p_1 p_2}$, will give a bound for the pure state case. Letting the prefactor to be just some C, the QCB result for pure, homogeneous $\mathcal{SE}$ is

$$I_{\text{acc}}(\hat{\Pi}_\mathcal{S}) \geq H_\mathcal{S} - h\left(C|\gamma|^{2\sharp\mathcal{F}}\right) \equiv \mathcal{X}_{QCB}, \tag{16}$$

where I stress that this is a classical-classical information about random variable $\hat{s}$ (pointer states on $\mathcal{S}$) with measurement outcomes on $\mathcal{F}$. If we want general $\mathcal{SE}$ states, but still the pure decoherence model, Equations (9) and (10), we have exactly the same form as Equation (16) but the decoherence factor (the pure state overlap) is replaced by the generalized measure of overlap, $\text{tr}\left[\rho_{k|1}^{1/2} \rho_{k|2}^{1/2}\right]$, see Ref. [19] for these expressions in terms of generic angles (between conditional states) and lengths on the Bloch sphere for spins and Ref. [16] for photons.

The QCB is a universal result. The bound Equation (14) is true for all models of pure decoherence by independent spins or the standard photon model, all dimensions in between (qutrits, qudits, etc.), inhomogeneous models, pure and mixed $\mathcal{SE}$ states, and ones with individual self-Hamiltonians on $\mathcal{E}$. The only stipulation for Equation (14) and the lower bound $H_\mathcal{S} - H(P_e^\star)$ is that one is distinguishing within a two-dimensional subspace of $\mathcal{S}$ pointer states. For higher dimensional subspaces, the number of pointer states, D, appears in Equation (13) and the exponent in the decay of $P_e^\star$ requires a pair-wise minimization of the generalized overlap over conditional states (as well as a different prefactor outside of the exponential).

The most important aspect of the compact form, Equation (16), and its generalization to higher D, is that the right hand side reflects actual, inferable information about the pointer states that the observer can retrieve by interaction with just $\mathcal{F}$ *in a single shot*. Moreover, while the QCB is traditionally cast as an asymptotic result, we have not actually used any asymptotic limits to obtain Equation (16). Both of these aspects—single shot and finite $\mathcal{F}$—provide a natural setting for our world, where observers are "agents" within these regimes. One can then ask questions about resources of observers (for instance, global versus local measurements on $\mathcal{F}$ subcomponents [51] or the ability to perform coherent measurements [52]) that further refine the results but do not change the fundamental framework of single-shot, finite $\mathcal{F}$ inference.

Let us return to the c-maybe model and the Holevo quantities. Touil et al. [38] present results for the quantum mutual information, $\chi(\hat{\mathcal{S}} : \mathcal{F})$, and $\chi(\mathcal{S} : \hat{\mathcal{F}})$. In the good decoherence limit, the latter two are

$$\chi(\hat{\mathcal{S}} : \mathcal{F}) = -\frac{1}{2}\log_2\left[p_1 p_2\left(1 - |\gamma|^{2\sharp\mathcal{F}}\right)\right]$$
$$- \sqrt{1 - 4p_1 p_2\left(1 - |\gamma|^{2\sharp\mathcal{F}}\right)} \text{Arctanh}_2\left[\sqrt{1 - 4p_1 p_2\left(1 - |\gamma|^{2\sharp\mathcal{F}}\right)}\right] \tag{17}$$

and

$$\chi(\mathcal{S} : \hat{\mathcal{F}}) = H_\mathcal{S} + \frac{1}{2}\log_2\left[p_1 p_2 |\gamma|^{2\sharp\mathcal{F}}\right] + \sqrt{1 - 4p_1 p_2 |\gamma|^{2\sharp\mathcal{F}}} \text{Arctanh}_2\left[\sqrt{1 - 4p_1 p_2 |\gamma|^{2\sharp\mathcal{F}}}\right] \tag{18}$$

in the form as they appear in their main text but using the notation here (Equations (17) and (20) in Ref. [38]). Rewriting these in terms of binary entropy gives

$$\chi(\hat{\mathcal{S}} : \mathcal{F}) = h\left[\frac{1}{2}\left(1 + \sqrt{1 - 4p_1 p_2\left(1 - |\gamma|^{2\sharp\mathcal{F}}\right)}\right)\right], \tag{19}$$